THE EMERGENCE OF

Modern Southeast Asia

The Emergence of Modern Southeast Asia

A New History

Edited by NORMAN G. OWEN

DAVID CHANDLER

NORMAN G. OWEN

WILLIAM R. ROFF

DAVID JOEL STEINBERG

JEAN GELMAN TAYLOR

ROBERT H. TAYLOR

ALEXANDER WOODSIDE

DAVID K. WYATT

University of Hawai'i Press *Honolulu*

LIBRARY OF CONGRESS CATALOGING-IN-PUBLICATION DATA
The emergence of modern Southeast Asia : a new history /
edited by Norman G. Owen . . . [et al.].
p.   cm.
Includes bibliographical references and index.
ISBN 0-8248-2841-0 (hard cover : alk. paper)
ISBN-13: 978-0-8248-2890-5 (pbk. : alk. paper)
ISBN-10: 0-8248-2890-9 (pbk. : alk. paper)
1. Asia, Southeastern—History.   I. Owen, Norman G.
DS525.E44 2005
959—dc22
2004007660

University of Hawai'i Press books are printed on acid-free paper
and meet the guidelines for permanence and durability
of the Council on Library Resources.

Book design and composition by Diane Gleba Hall

Printed by Thomson-Shore, Inc.

For
JOHN R.W. SMAIL

whose ideas live with us
even though his voice
has fallen silent.

Contents

Maps and Tables

Maps

Tables

How to Use This Book

❋

ALTHOUGH we would like everyone to read this book from cover to cover, we realize that very few people will actually read it (or any other general history) straight through. We would therefore like to point out some features of its organization that may help readers in approaching it.

Those who do read the book from start to finish will find it oscillating between general thematic chapters, primarily on social, economic, and cultural change, and "country" chapters emphasizing developments, mostly political, within specific areas. *The Emergence of Modern Southeast Asia* is concerned as much with the processes of historical transformation as with the chronological narrative of events.

Readers interested in synoptic analyses of developments that do not fit easily into conventional chronology and are not unique to a single country may wish to focus primarily on the "general" chapters. Part 1 introduces the eighteenth-century world, when colonialism was still marginal to most of Southeast Asia, and the first chapter of part 2 ushers in imperialism. Part 3 examines change in the era of direct Western domination in the region, roughly from the middle of the nineteenth century to the middle of the twentieth. The first two chapters of part 5 are about the social and economic transformation of Southeast Asia over the last half century.

Readers primarily interested in a particular society may follow its history in the "country" chapters in parts 2, 4, and 5. (Vietnam, for example, is the topic of chapters 7, 23, and 34.) Beyond the facts and interpretations presented, readers might note that the periodization of these national histories often diverges from more conventional patterns, even those employed in the predecessor of this book. They should remember, however, that much information on these countries—particularly on social, economic, and cultural change—can also be found in the "general" chapters and located there through the index.

In "Changing Names" (below) we briefly describe how the countries and peoples of Southeast Asia came to be called what they are today—which is rarely what they were called in the past. A short list of recommended "Further Readings" appears at the end of each chapter; many of the works cited contain substantial bibliographies. The sources of most of the quotations in the text can be found in the notes at the back of the book.

Preface

❋

ON THE tiny island of Mactan in the Philippines, there is a monument erected by the Spanish in the nineteenth century to glorify God, Spain, and Ferdinand Magellan. In 1941, during the American era, a historical marker inscribed "Ferdinand Magellan's Death" was erected nearby. It stated: "On this spot Ferdinand Magellan died on April 27, 1521, wounded in an encounter with the soldiers of Lapulapu, chief of Mactan Island. One of Magellan's ships, the *Victoria,* under the command of Juan Sebastian Elcano, sailed from Cebu on May 1, 1521, and anchored at San Lucar de Barrameda on September 6, 1522, thus completing the first circumnavigation of the earth." Exactly a decade after the erection of this marker, a new one was attached to the other side of the same stone pedestal. Titled "Lapulapu," it read: "Here on 27 April 1521, Lapulapu and his men repulsed the Spanish invaders, killing their leader, Ferdinand Magellan. Thus Lapulapu became the first Filipino to have repelled the European aggression."

As the famous Japanese film *Rashomon* demonstrates, narrative truth depends on perspective, on who is telling the tale and why. All interpretations of the past are subjective, since every historian must decide where to place the emphasis, how to draw meaning from the "facts" that he or she has selected. The challenge facing anyone writing a history of Southeast Asia is compounded by its myriad peoples, each with its own past, sense of cultural and social identity, and shaping geographic reality.

This book rests on the belief that the interaction and expertise of joint authorship maximizes the possibility of achieving a more rounded account of the collective Southeast Asian experience. Its predecessor, *In Search of Southeast Asia,* was written in 1969, when five of us came together in Ann Arbor, Michigan, for a summerlong effort in communal authorship, with funding generously provided by the Ford and Rockefeller foundations. Also in that original group was the late John R. W. Smail, to whom the present volume is dedicated. In 1969 we lacked a Burma specialist—David Wyatt courageously stepped in to fill the gap—but Robert H. Taylor took that role when *In Search of Southeast Asia* was revised at Cornell in 1987 and has carried on since.

The seeming triumph of secular nationalism in Southeast Asia and the ongoing war in Vietnam had shaped the first book in ways that have become increasingly apparent in retrospect. *In Search of Southeast Asia* became dated. We therefore decided that it would be worth the effort to regroup in order to rewrite the history of the region. Norman G. Owen, who as a graduate student in Ann Arbor had compiled the index for the first edition, was welcomed in, this time as the book's editor as well as a full contributor, and John Smail was succeeded as the Indonesia specialist by his former student Jean Gelman Taylor (unrelated to Robert).

To fund the new project, David Steinberg approached the Henry Luce Foundation through its vice president, Terry Lautz, who knew well the earlier book's strengths and weaknesses. With a measure of rare faith, he urged us to add an additional year to the project by meeting first with a number of younger scholars who would critique the 1987 edition and help us identify what still worked and what needed to be changed or added. So under the auspices of the Luce Foundation, we were joined by Barbara Watson Andaya, Robert Elson, Eva-Lotta Hedman, Paul Kratoska, John Sidel, and Eric Tagliocozzo. This expanded group met on the C. W. Post campus of Long Island University during July 2001 in what proved to be vital, lively, and collegial discussions of every aspect of *In Search of Southeast Asia.*

The younger scholars advised us to break the original book completely open, take a fresh look at modern Southeast Asian history, and draft a shorter, more accessible text for the twenty-first century. We are deeply grateful to these men and women, who came from all over the world to participate, and we thank profoundly the Trustees of the Henry Luce Foundation, and, in particular, Dr. Lautz, for making their sojourn possible. We also wish to make it clear that any factual errors or conceptual shortcomings that remain are our responsibility alone.

Chagrined but enthusiastic, we set off for our homes on four continents, and over the next twelve months drafted or revised chapters based on our new outline. Thanks to the wonders of technology that did not exist in 1969, we could exchange these chapters and comment on them electronically. In the summer of 2002, we reassembled at Long Island University for a second seminar. As young scholars, each of us had focused on a specific country; we had quibbled and occasionally argued over interpretations of Southeast Asian history. Thirty-three years later the arguments occasionally still flickered, since perception depends always on perspective, and each of us has a predilection—which we try, not always successfully, to keep in check—to see regional events from the vantage point of "our" country of specialization. But in time, we think, we reached an acceptable consensus (a thoroughly Southeast Asian process), and *The Emergence of Modern Southeast Asia: A New History* is the result.

The list of people to whom we are indebted is eight times longer than would be the case if only one author had written this book. To begin with, we recognize and apologize for the inconvenience this project has caused our families. We remain grateful for their support and good cheer. We are also very grateful to Pamela Kelley and her colleagues at the University of Hawai'i Press, the 1987 publisher of *In Search of Southeast Asia*. It was Ms. Kelley who first pushed us to "think outside the box" by writing a new text. We wish to thank publicly Gail Allan and her colleagues at Long Island University for all their help, encouragement, and logistical support in bringing this motley crew together twice and in assuring that all were fed and cared for properly, and Iris Ng and her colleagues at the University of Hong Kong for assistance in preparing the manuscript. We were fortunate to get Robert Cribb to prepare the maps. Countless others will have to be unnamed, lest the acknowledgments swamp the text of the book.

Finally, the authors hope that their efforts through this book may have a sustaining impact, exciting future generations of historians and regional specialists to love this marvelous part of the world as much as we do.

Changing Names

Cambodia

"CAMBODIA" is the English-language rendering of a Sanskrit word usually transliterated as "Kambuja" and pronounced "Kampuchea" in modern Khmer. The word, which means "born of Kambu," a mythical, semidivine forebear, was part of the name Kambujadesa (Cambodia-land), which the empire of Angkor, centered in what is now northwestern Cambodia, gave itself after the tenth century C.E. The nomenclature remained in use after the abandonment of Angkor in the sixteenth century.

Under the French colonial protectorate (1863–1954) the kingdom's name came to be written "Cambodge" in French but was still written and pronounced in Khmer as "Kampuchea." The transliteration "Kampuchea" reappeared briefly in documents written in French in March 1945, when Cambodia was told to declare independence by Japanese forces occupying the region, and it renamed itself the Kingdom of Kampuchea. By November 1945, when the French returned to power, the kingdom's name in French had reverted to Cambodge (Cambodia for English speakers).

In 1970, following a coup against Norodom Sihanouk, the country named itself the Khmer Republic. When the Republican regime was defeated by local communists five years later, the Marxist-Leninist government that took power called the country Democratic Kampuchea. A Vietnamese invasion in December 1978 drove this regime from power and the newly established, pro-

Vietnamese government came to office under the name of the People's Republic of Kampuchea. When the Vietnamese withdrew their forces in 1989, the ruling party remained in power, but its leaders renounced Marxism-Leninism and renamed their country the State of Cambodia. This name lasted until 1993, when Sihanouk, who had abdicated the throne in 1955, became king for a second time, and the country restored its pre-1970 name, the Kingdom of Cambodia.

The word "Khmer" refers to the major ethnic group in Cambodia, comprising perhaps 90 percent of the population, and also to the language spoken throughout the country. The etymology of the word is obscure, but it has been in use to describe the inhabitants of the region for over a thousand years. In general the terms "Khmer" and "Cambodian" are interchangeable, and in conversation most Cambodians refer to their country as *sruk Khmer* (Khmer-land).

Indonesia

THE TERM "Indonesia" was first used in 1850 by the British anthropologist J. R. Logan to designate islands called the "Indian Archipelago" by other Western writers. For Logan, "Indonesia" did not designate a political unit but a cultural zone that included the Philippines. The forebears of today's Indonesians had no term for the region or concept of a single political unit linking communities across seas. From ancient times Java had been known by that single name, but most of Indonesia's islands derive their names from European labeling. Early European traders at the port of Samudera named the entire island Sumatra, and visitors to the sultanate of Brunei called the whole island Borneo.

The Dutch named their colonial possessions Indië (the Indies). Initially the Indies meant Java and a few ports scattered across the archipelago. Between 1850 and 1914 Dutch power engulfed over three hundred separate sultanates and communities, and welded them into a single administrative unit called the "Netherlands Indies." Subjects were called "Natives," a legal category alongside "Europeans" and "Foreign Orientals" (local Chinese and Arabs), replacing the terms "Moor," "Christian," and "Heathen" used in the seventeenth and eighteenth centuries.

Associations in the early years of the twentieth century identified themselves by geography and generation, such as "League of Sumatran Youth" and "Ambonese Youth." As ideological identities developed, parties took the colonial unit as their geographic marker but opted for Logan's "Indonesia" instead of the Dutch "Indies." The first to do so was the Communist Party of Indonesia, founded in 1921. Opponents of the Dutch understood "Indonesia" as both a political and a cultural entity; they adopted as a common language a variant of Malay spoken in Sumatra, already widely used as a lingua franca, and called it the "Indonesian language" (Bahasa Indonesia). The political unit they eventually won was the Dutch colony stretching from Sabang Island off northern

Sumatra to Merauke on the border with eastern New Guinea, but many wanted the cultural definition of "Indonesia"—Islamic and Malay-speaking—translated into a state that would include Malaya, southern Thailand, the southern Philippines, all of Borneo, and Portuguese East Timor.

Following independence Indonesian place-names were substituted for the Dutch. Batavia became Djakarta; Buitenzorg, Bogor; and Borneo, Kalimantan. Indonesian spelling was revised in 1972, making Djakarta Jakarta and Atjeh Aceh. In this book Indonesia designates the state established by Sukarno on 17 August 1945; for the period before 1945, it is used as a shorthand for the islands constituting today's republic.

Laos

THE WORD "Laos" was first used by European missionaries and cartographers in the seventeenth century to pluralize the word "Lao," the name of the country's predominant ethnolinguistic group. In the Lao language, which is closely related to Thai, there is no orthographic distinction between plural and singular nouns. In Lao, Laos is known as *pathet lao* or *muang lao,* both meaning "Lao country" or "Lao-land," along the lines of *prathet thai* (Thailand).

The French used the term "Laos" as the name for their protectorate in the colonial period. After independence in 1954, the country became known as the Kingdom of Laos. In 1975, when the communists came to power and the monarchy was abolished, it was renamed the Lao People's Democratic Republic.

Malaysia

THE NAME "Malaysia" is derived from the term "Malay," long applied by locals and foreigners to the Malay Peninsula in recognition of the predominance there of Malay-speaking peoples (whose geographic extent, however, also includes much of Sumatra and other islands of the archipelago). The peninsula became widely known from the late eighteenth century simply as "Malaya" and, in the course of the nineteenth and early twentieth century, when its individual states fell under British colonial rule, as British Malaya. British Malaya also included the three Straits Settlements on the fringe of the peninsula: the islands of Penang and Singapore and the small west coast state of Melaka (Malacca). When the Malay states (including Penang and Melaka but not at that time Singapore) became independent in 1957, they did so as the Federation of Malaya. In 1963 a larger federal unit called Malaysia was formed, bringing together the Federation of Malaya, Singapore, and the British-ruled protectorates of Sarawak and Sabah in northern Borneo. The oil-rich protectorate of Brunei, situated between British North Borneo and Sarawak, declined to join Malaysia, and Singapore was expelled in 1965.

Much of Malaysia has been the recipient during the past two centuries of immigrants of other than indigenous stock (which is held to include local Malays, the aborigines or *orang asli* ["original people"] of the peninsula, the tribal peoples of the Borneo states, and immigrants from Java, Sumatra, and elsewhere in Indonesia). The largest immigrant group was "Chinese," a term used for individuals hailing originally from many different parts of south China, often speaking distinct local languages. Those immigrants referred to as "Indian" included Muslims as well as Hindus from Tamilnadu in south India, Bengalis, and others, in addition to many from Ceylon (now Sri Lanka). One political result of the large immigrant influx has been the coining of a term that seeks to distinguish between Malaysians who are of Malay or other local descent and those who are not (no matter whether locally descended or long resident): *bumiputera* (son[s] of the soil), which confers constitutionally derived advantages of various sorts. The Malay language, now the national language of Malaysia, is known either simply as Malay or as Bahasa Melayu.

Myanmar

THE MILITARY government of what is now officially known as Myanmar Naingngan (State of Myanmar) abandoned the older and more familiar English name of the country, Burma or the Union of Burma, in 1989. As a result of the authoritarian nature of that regime, the United States and many European countries have refused to recognize the change in nomenclature, as have some of the domestic political opposition to the military government, in particular the National League for Democracy.

This controversy masks a number of more complex issues. During the colonial period (1824–1948), "Myanmar," a traditional term for the territory under the dominion of the kings of the central Ayeyarwady (Irrawaddy) valley (possibly related to the Chinese name for the area, *mian*), fell from use. Rather, in line with the European idea of a nation-state where ethnicity and territory are seen to be coterminous, "Burma" became the common name for the area governed by the monarchs reigning at Inwa (Ava), Amarapura, and Mandalay and their British successors. The name derived from the idea of the territory of the Bama or Burmans, the majority people of the area, whose language, Burmese or Myanmar, is the official language of the country. Linguistically, "Burma" and "Myanmar" can be linked by substituting a "b" sound for an "m" sound and an "r" sound for a "y" sound, common phonetic shifts.

By the late colonial period the term "Myanmar" had largely fallen from common usage. Rather, as ethnicity rose to dominate nationalist debates, and the structures of colonial society privileged ethnicity over other forms of social and economic differentiation, "Bama" or Burman/Burmese came to be more frequently used. For example, most of the leaders of the nationalist elite that eventually took power in 1948 had previously been members of the Do Bama Asiayon, or We Burmans Association. English-medium historians largely forgot the term "Myanmar," though it had been used in the 1920s as the title of the leading nationalist organization of that period, the Myanma Athin Chokkyi, usually translated as the General Council of Burmese Associations, and in the 1940s by Prime Minister Ba Maw's Myanmar Wunthanu Aphwe, or Myanmar Nationalist Organization.

The 1948 constitution of Pyihtaungsu Myanmar, or the Union of Burma (the official English name at the time), was an attempt to create a modern, plural society and federal political system out of the many ethnic divisions of the country, the most significant of which was the difference between the majority, lowland Bama and the upland minority peoples, such as the Shan, Kachin, Chin, Kayin (Karen), Kayah (Karenni), Wa, Pao, Palaung, and so on. "Myanmar" might then have become the collective name for all the ethnic groups and territories of the country, rather as "The United Kingdom of Great Britain and Northern Ireland" is the collective term for England, Scotland, Wales, and Ulster. However, because the term did not come back into usage by non-Myanmar speakers until the controversial period of the military government in 1989, it remains contested. In this book "Myanmar" will be used except for the period of British rule and the postwar "Union of Burma."

The Philippines

THE PHILIPPINES was named by Spanish conquistadors in the sixteenth century for the prince who would become King Philip II of Spain. The national language, adopted from Tagalog in the twentieth century and spoken by most inhabitants of the capital city, Manila, has been called at various times Pilipino or Filipino. All of the indigenous languages are linguistically related to Malay, although many Spanish, Chinese, and English loan words have been incorporated.

The Spanish called most of the indigenous inhabitants *indios* (Indians) using the term "Filipino" only as an adjective or to describe Caucasians born in the archipelago. These were white-skinned, not brown: creoles, of European ancestry but born in the empire rather than on the Iberian Peninsula. Since the late nineteenth century the term "Filipino" has been transformed to describe any person born in the archipelago who chose to owe allegiance to the Philippines, while the term *indio* is generally considered derogatory. "Mestizos" (literally people of "mixed" ethnic ancestry) may have Caucasian and *indio* blood, Chinese and *indio* heritage, or a combination. In sharp contradistinction to many other places throughout Southeast Asia and the world (where the comparable term "half-caste" is a pejorative), to be mestizo in the Philippines carries no negative connotation or constraint.

There are many Hispanic names in the Philippines, but after the United States took over, most Filipinos began to abandon the use of accent marks on these names. We will follow this practice and omit accent marks on the names of persons living after 1898.

The Spanish referred to the various Muslim peoples of the south, such as the Tausug and the Magindanao, as "Moros" (Moors), a term they brought with them from their long encounters with the Muslims of North Africa. This term, which was originally rejected by Filipino Muslim communities as a slur, has recently been embraced by them as a marker of their separatist dream.

Thailand

THE POLITY now known as Thailand was generally referred to as "Siam" for many centuries. Nationalists renamed it in 1939 in an attempt to be more inclusive of people, particularly in the north, northeast, and south, who had never considered themselves "Siamese" (i.e., indigenous subjects of the state centered on Ayutthaya or Bangkok) but might be persuaded to think of themselves as "Thai." After World War II "Siam" briefly was restored as the country's name in 1946, but little more than a year later "Thailand" became permanent.

The term itself is a neologism, combining the traditional ethnic identity "Thai" with "land" (*prathet* in Thai). As the word "Thai" also means "free," some people translate the country's name as "Land of the Free," but it is unlikely that that was the original meaning. Many other peoples speaking closely related languages live nearby in Myanmar, China, Laos, and Vietnam; for purposes of convenience, linguists and other scholars sometimes label all of them, along with the Thai, as "Tai" (without the "h").

There is wide variation among systems of transliteration of Thai into the Western alphabet, but in general place-names in this book follow those adopted by the Board on Geographic Names, as used on most published maps.

Vietnam

"VIETNAM" is a relatively recent name for the kingdom of the "Viet" people. ("Viet" is cognate with the Chinese "Yue," a generic term for ethnic groups in what is now southern China and beyond.) Its official use began only in the nineteenth century. From the eleventh century to 1800, Vietnamese rulers usually called their country as a whole the "Great Viet" (Dai Viet) domain.

Of the other premodern names for the country, "Annam" is probably the most familiar. This Chinese colonial term emerged in the late seventh century, when the Tang empire named its colony in northern Vietnam the "Pacified South" (Chinese: Annan) protectorate. Vietnam stopped being a Chinese colony in the tenth century, but the Chinese continued to refer to their now independent southern neighbor as "Annam" until the end of the 1800s, rather as if the British were to continue to call Zimbabwe "Rhodesia" for the next nine centuries. Many Westerners picked up on this locution and referred to the country as "Annam" (and its people as "Annamites" or "Annamese"), although Vietnamese generally did not appreciate this terminology. The nomenclature was further confused when the French, in dividing Vietnam administratively into three parts, called the middle one (centered on Hue and Danang) "Annam," as distinct from "Tonkin" to the north and "Cochinchina" to the south.

In the early 1800s the new Nguyen dynasty tried to secure international (i.e., Chinese) recognition of a new name for the country: "Nam Viet." But to the rulers of China the term (Nan Yue in Chinese) conjured up memories of an ancient state of that name, founded by a dissident Chinese general, which had existed in modern Guangdong and Guangxi between 203 and 111 B.C.E. Chinese rulers feared that their acceptance of the term "Nam Viet" might signal approval of resurrected Vietnamese claims to south China. They therefore reversed the components of the proposed new name to detoxify it politically, and thus "Viet Nam" (Vietnam) came into existence. Nineteenth-century Vietnamese rulers, not liking it, privately preferred to refer to their country as the "Great South" (Dai Nam).

THE EMERGENCE OF
Modern Southeast Asia

Introduction

Places and Peoples

A FIRST-TIME visitor to Southeast Asia will be captivated by the brilliance of the light, the profusion of exotic wildlife, the scents of tropical flowers mingling with the pungent odors of a spice market. Travel on any national airline and flight attendants will be in ethnic dress. The menu will include "native" items, and local beers on the beverage cart—Singha, Tiger, San Miguel, or "333"— may be labeled in various scripts. The newspapers routinely distributed may be written in Chinese, Indonesian, Thai, or Vietnamese as well as English. But the sanitized, denatured quality of any international airline can only hint at the hot, dynamic, dense, noisy, polluted, fascinating universe on the other side of the airport customs area.

Conjure up arriving in Malaysia and landing at Kuala Lumpur, although the experience would be similar at Jakarta, Manila, or Bangkok. Perusing the map in the back of the airline's monthly magazine, you can see that the plane is traveling between Sumatra and the Malay Peninsula, flying over the Strait of Melaka (Malacca), one of the most important maritime passages in the world, linking the Indian Ocean to the South China Sea. On one side of the strait is Sumatra, an island of the Republic of Indonesia; on the other, looking much the same, is the plane's destination, a peninsula described by Ptolemy two millennia ago as the "Golden Chersonese" for its legendary (but long since depleted) gold deposits.

Kuala Lumpur ca. 1880.

On both sides of the strait rise high mountainous ridges, volcanic in origin, seemingly blanketed by tropical rainforest, which are sliced by rivers running down to the sea. As the plane crosses over the Malaysian coastline in its initial descent, it becomes increasingly apparent that not all the land is covered by this dense foliage. Indeed parts of the mountains are barren, brown, and stripped of timber, evidence of the tin sluicing and dredging once so important in Malayan history. The plane passes through enormous cloud formations, tens of thousands of feet high, periodically producing violent thunder and rain but usually brilliantly white against an azure sky. As the plane descends in preparation for landing, it becomes possible to see that parts of the forest are planted row upon row in rubber trees, from plantations first established during the colonial era to make automobile tires. At this lower altitude it also becomes easier to see rice paddies—especially beautiful when the fields are flooded with lush green young rice shoots—and villages, clusters of bamboo huts, and tin-roofed factories. There are ribbons of roads crisscrossing this landscape, linking hamlets to cities and Malaysia to the world.

The capital, Kuala Lumpur, like most of the capitals of Southeast Asia, is not an ancient city. In the late nineteenth century it was still a tiny town at the confluence of two streams (the name means "muddy estuary"). Today the visitor sees a vast, sprawling city under a pall of gray pollution with a skyline that juxtaposes traditional wood and palm-thatched buildings, squat cement structures painted garish pastel colors, air-conditioned shopping malls, and a cluster of soaring high-rise buildings, including the Petronas Twin Towers, at the millennium the tallest buildings in the world.

Kuala Lumpur today.

How did this small outpost, created by Chinese immigrants in the late nineteenth century, become a city of 1.5 million people? Who planted those rubber trees and built those staggeringly tall buildings? Why and how were the great royal capitals of Southeast Asia—Ava, Ayutthaya, Yogyakarta, Melaka—not only replaced by modern cities but relegated to economic and political obscurity? And why are Sumatra and the Malay Peninsula, apparently similar in so many ways, now in separate countries with distinct governments, priorities, and identities? It is around questions such as these, as well as the narratives of individual country histories, that this book is organized.

It is not only the physical reality that has changed over the past several centuries. Ideas, institutions, cultural priorities, and social values have also evolved. Consider what time and space mean in the twenty-first century: scientifically anchored and universally accepted norms. In eighteenth-century Southeast Asia, as in much of the world at that time, such definitions were far more fluid; almost every country had its own calendar and its own way—or variety of ways—of calculating distance. Today the whole world is measured in kilometers or miles and every country marked the same millennium. Everyone counts the years off a European, Christian calendar. The satellite dish and the computer, along with other technological marvels, have altered fundamentally the concept of borders and boundaries, made migration and mobility easier, and identified the metropolitan city as a portal to opportunity, a seductive beacon of aspiration well within reach by bus, train, or plane.

In this process much has been lost as well as gained. Intimacy, familial obligation, piety, and cultural identity have been challenged by foreign values and modern ideas. It is easy to equate change with progress and to see the eighteenth-century world as "backward," because it lacked such modern comforts as plumbing or electricity. The benefits of modernity are seductive to people the world over, and yet the price paid for development may be far higher than either individuals or societies realize.

Change has produced some wonderful gains (life expectancy in Southeast Asia is up dramatically, education is nearly universal, standards of living have improved unevenly but significantly) but also has spread dislocation, pain, and misery. Technology means helicopter gunships and government surveillance as well as jet travel and computer games. The environment has been polluted, natural resources savaged. Ruthless exploitation, the lack of appropriate government regulation, war, colonialism, and human greed and stupidity have all played a part. Yet our aim is not to tell a morality tale but to describe and analyze the profound transformation of Southeast Asia in the modern era.

We will thus be reflecting on how the "modern"—in contradistinction to the "traditional"—came about in Southeast Asia, while understanding that "modern" and "traditional" are never absolutes, simple concepts that can be completely isolated from each other. This book attempts to chronicle the diverse stories that created the societies and nation-states of the region. It details the impact of global forces of change, including Islam and Christianity, mercantilism, colonialism, imperialism, and the industrial revolution, and traces the spread of secular ideological systems such as capitalism, communism, socialism, and nationalism. It examines local adaptations of international influences: food that looks Chinese, for example, may not be; ancient Sanskrit tales become twenty-first-century Indonesian shadow puppetry; Filipinos use cell phone "texting" to organize a popular revolution. It tries always to be comparative, both globally and regionally, as when we contrast the modern history of Siam (now called Thailand) with that of Myanmar (which some still call Burma).

We start our story in the eighteenth century, when we can discern fundamental shifts in the patterns of life of peoples living within the region. Historiographically this starting point is arbitrary, but it is defensible, even though no two "country" histories begin (in this volume) at the exact same moment. The cusp of change revealed itself unevenly, as it has done throughout human experience.

Some Geographic Realities

SOUTHEAST ASIA is that part of the world located south of China, east of India, and north of Australia. Known to the Chinese and Japanese as the "South Sea" (Nanyang or Nampo), the region was first widely described as "Southeast Asia" during World War II, when the term was assigned to the allied zone of war commanded by a British Admiral, Lord Louis Mountbatten. Initially a military shorthand, the name now is accepted as referring to a region with unique characteristics and shared customs. The total land area of Southeast Asia is slightly more than 1.5 million square miles, a little smaller than the Indian subcontinent. Just over half of the territory is a peninsula jutting from the Asian mainland, while the rest is an archipelago or series of archipelagos, unevenly divided among the contemporary states of Indonesia, the Philippines, Malaysia (whose eastern half incorporates part of the vast island of Borneo), Brunei, and East Timor (Timor Leste, Timor Loro Sa'e). (See Table 1.)

Throughout Southeast Asia, there are recurring similarities of flora and fauna, of climate, and of cultivation methods. The region is tropical, straddling the equator; one of the first impressions most Westerners have on visiting Southeast Asia is of the oppressive heat that strikes them the moment they leave the air-conditioned airport or hotel. Photographs in *National Geographic* hint at an exotic environment of fertile soil; rice paddies, coconut palms, banana plants, and the rainforest itself all reinforce this impression.

Yet except where the earth is fecund because of volcanic loam, as in Java, or by alluvial deposit, along the major river valleys, there is a precarious ecological balance in the rainforest. Plants compete to live through photosynthesis rather than soil chemistry. Often there are only a few inches of topsoil, so trees do not develop the deep taproots characteristic of richer soils and more temperate climates. Instead the great banyan trees of Angkor, in Cambodia, which must grow tall to maximize their access to rain and sun, stretch their roots out laterally, like veins in a hand, seeking nourishment from decomposing plant and animal matter on the forest floor all around. If the forest is burned or felled, the hammering of torrential rains has disastrous consequences for the now

Table 1: Population and Area of Southeast Asian States Today

Country	2003 Population (x 1,000)	Land Area sq. miles	sq. km
Brunei Darussalam	358	2,035	5,270
Kingdom of Cambodia	14,144	68,154	176,520
Democratic Republic of East Timor (Timor Leste)	833	5,794	15,007
Republic of Indonesia	219,833	741,095	1,949,440
Lao People's Democratic Republic	5,657	91,428	236,800
Malaysia	24,425	126,853	328,550
State of Myanmar	49,485	261,226	676,577
Republic of the Philippines	79,995	115,123	298,170
Republic of Singapore	4,253	264	683
Kingdom of Thailand	62,833	198,455	514,000
Socialist Republic of Vietnam	81,377	125,699	325,360
Total	539,193	1,736,126	4,526,377

Source for population data: United Nations, *World Population Prospects, 2002 Revision*

exposed thin layer of soil, which is swiftly eroded and vanishes into the rivers and out to sea. Melaka, once a great port of call for ships from all over Asia, is today some distance from the navigable coastline of Malaysia because of centuries of siltation.

The destruction of the tropical rainforest is a reality in every Southeast Asian nation. Some denudation happened through "slash-and-burn" agriculture, some from government-authorized cutting. The rest has been from illegal logging and forest fires—often set by loggers—which have on occasion cast a pall of smoky haze over much of the region. Indonesia, Vietnam, and other nations may be effectively stripped bald of timber in another decade, as much of Thailand and the Philippines already has been. (In the Philippines, 60 percent of the land was forested in 1960, but by 2000 only 10 percent was still covered by timber.) Crop loss and other physical damage far exceed the market value of this cut timber; because of indiscriminate cutting, the floods in Cambodia in 2000 were the worst in seven decades. The depletion of the fishing stock of the region is a similar sorry tale, equally serious because so many Southeast Asians get most of their protein from fish.

While the languages and architecture change from place to place, both "wet rice" farming and slash-and-burn (or swidden) agriculture exist, and have long existed, from Myanmar to Nusatenggara (the Lesser Sundas). Rice is for most Southeast Asians the staff of life, though in a few districts people live on corn or root crops like taro or cassava. In upland clearings, on the one hand, the existing vegetation is first slashed, then burned, and a passable harvest of rice and other crops can be produced with minimal labor. Wet rice cultivation, on the other hand, is more labor-intensive. It is virtually a type of hydroponics; the soil of the "paddies" in which it is grown—essentially mud basins to hold water, seed, and nutrients—rarely supplies much nourishment, which instead must come from systems of irrigation, simple or intricate, and fertilizers, natural or chemical. Some early Southeast Asian techniques for cultivating rice were so advanced that they were exported to China. Under the demographic and technological circumstances that have characterized most of human history, wet rice yields the highest caloric output per area of land of any grain.

The seasonal growing cycle of wet rice shapes the calendar throughout rural Southeast Asia. Knowing when the rain will start and end or when the river levels drop is vital for farmers, who have always been at the mercy of nature. If it rains too much or too little, if the rains arrive or depart too early or too late, a crop can be ruined, bankrupting the farmer. The growing cycle carries constant risk, especially in dry areas like east Java, Madura, and Upper Myanmar.

Virtually all of Southeast Asia experiences the monsoon, although different localities have their wet and dry seasons at different times in the calendar. The word "monsoon" itself comes from the Arabic *mawsin* (in Malay, *musim*), which means season. The existence of these wet and dry monsoons—prevailing strong southwest or northeast airflows—creates the seasons. During the summer months in the northern hemisphere, the great Asian continental landmass heats up far more than the surrounding oceans. In the winter months that landmass cools more than the sea. This heating and cooling, along with the rotation of the earth, determines prevailing wind flows that, in turn, determine whether the wind carries moisture from the sea onto the land or dry air from the land out across the sea. For any given locale a variety of factors help shape the onset of the rainy season, the timing of which is thus relatively predictable—but never guaranteed. These annual rains, which can reach above 200 inches a year, fall with ferocity. Although there is real winter in the upper Red River Valley of northern Vietnam and a temperate climate in the mountains of Myanmar and Luzon, for most Southeast Asians hot, rainy, tropical weather is the everyday reality.

The prevailing wind flows caused by the monsoons have also had a major impact on transportation, especially in the age of sail. The great maritime city of Melaka (Malacca), for example, was an essential port of call where ships could not only refit and resupply, but also wait for the prevailing winds to shift. Only then could a junk, prau, or carrack that had sailed through the Strait of Melaka or the Sunda Strait proceed onward or homeward on the next leg of its journey. It was not until the introduction of steam power in the mid–nineteenth century that most warships and cargo vessels could travel readily against these prevailing winds.

In many other ways geography and ecology have also shaped Southeast Asian history. On the mainland, the landscape is dominated by several great rivers, which begin near each other high in the Himalayas, carrying water, silt, and people from a mountainous interior down through fertile valleys to broad, swampy deltas, shaping political boundaries and cultural dynamics. The Mekong River, for example, flows from Tibet more than 4,300 kilometers (2,700 miles) through China, Myanmar, Laos, Thailand, Cambodia, and Vietnam before reaching the South China Sea. One of the world's greatest rivers, it supplies food and water to more than 100 million Southeast Asians. Long ago, Cambodia became a major empire because the Khmer people learned how to harness floodtide water during the rainy season and its reverse flow during the dry season from the Tonle Sap (the great lake) back to the lower Mekong. The canals and reservoirs built by the medieval empire of Angkor were technological triumphs. And now, in the twenty-first century, the various competing national plans for the exploitation of the waters of the Mekong may prove to be a cornerstone of new regional development—or the spark for renewed regional conflict. The Ayeyarwady (Irrawaddy) and Thanlyin (Salween) rivers in Myanmar, the Chaophraya in Thailand, and the Red River in northern Vietnam, though not

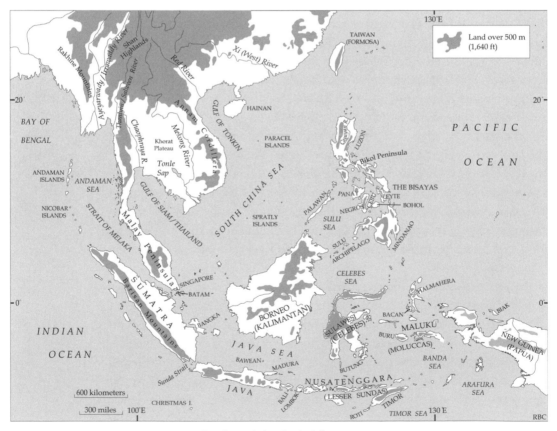

Southeast Asia: physical features

as majestic as the Mekong, have played similar pivotal roles in their countries' histories.

The mountainous ridges cascading from the Himalayas down the mainland also created distinct environmental niches within which Southeast Asians created distinctive ways of life. The peoples who lived in the valleys and plains and those who dwelled in the mountains have always had complex relationships. The flood plains, ideal sites for wet rice, could support greater population densities, while the hinterland usually could only support a limited number of mobile slash-and-burn cultivators. This geographic reality had dramatic socio-cultural and political consequences. The great mainland agrarian kingdoms in Myanmar, Siam, Vietnam, and Cambodia generated surpluses that sustained urban centers, military power, religious institutions, and an artistic and cultural elite. But these kingdoms rarely managed to establish long-term political, economic, religious, or linguistic control over the uplands that surrounded them.

Whenever a monarch attempted to impose his will on frontier tribes, tensions increased, as such efforts threatened the delicate balance of regional power. The hill peoples, often ethnically and linguistically different from those below—today these uplanders are customarily described as "ethnic minorities"—would seek protection from the next adjoining kingdom, manipulating tribute relationships to try to sustain their security. Borders were porous—in the modern sense they did not really exist—and allegiances fluid. Only the Khmer of Cambodia, among the major sedentary wet rice societies, lacked the luxury of mountainous buffer zones, and they suffered the consequences of frequent invasions and losses of territory to the neighboring kingdoms of Vietnam and Siam.

Farther downstream, the vast southern deltas of the Ayeyarwady, Chaophraya, and Mekong split into many branches before reaching the sea through a landscape of mangrove forests and shifting sandbars. They were underpopulated until the mid–nineteenth century. Wet rice can only grow in a flooded paddy, but the grain will not ripen unless the paddy can be drained. Without modern technology—especially the steam pump—to control drainage, the fertile soil of the deltas could not be cultivated effectively; the Mekong Delta, like that of the Mississippi River, was a swampy bayou. Starting in the mid–nineteenth century, the "rice bowls" of Indochina, Burma, and Siam began to feed growing populations while producing enormous surpluses exported across an interconnected world. Today they support population densities unimaginable before the modern era.

Mountain ridges not only defined mainland geography but also rippled across the ocean to form maritime Southeast Asia: the Malay Peninsula and the archipelagoes of the Philippines and Indonesia. There are approximately 7,100 islands in the Philippines and 17,500 in Indonesia. Most of them are uninhabited, since people only live where they can grow enough food. Java, extraordinarily fertile because of the nutrients spewed forth by volcanic eruptions, is one of the most densely populated areas in the world, while the far larger island of Borneo has a relatively modest population, because most of it is marginally fertile. With nearly 25,000 islands Southeast Asia has an extraordinary amount of coastline, supporting tens of thousands of fishermen and sailors. Insular fragmentation encouraged linguistic variations, and geographic isolation helped those far from political centers to minimize the domination of Java or Luzon. Even though the specific geographical causes were distinct, the historical reality, in both maritime and mainland Southeast Asia, was a dynamic tension between "center" and "periphery." Great states might form where the natural environment allowed for high population density, but though they could occasionally assemble the force necessary to conquer their smaller hill and island neighbors, they could rarely sustain effective control over them.

Nature has often been violent in Southeast Asia. Typhoons and cyclones are common, especially in the Philippines and Vietnam, and the island chains are part of the "Pacific Rim of Fire," sitting atop seismic weak spots where major tectonic plates grind against each other. The eruption of the Indonesian island of Krakatau (Krakatoa) on 26 August 1883 was the worst volcanic disaster in recorded history. Thirty-six thousand people were killed, many by huge tidal waves, the effects of which crossed the entire Indian Ocean in just twelve hours. The sound of the explosion—seven times more powerful than the atomic bomb dropped on Hiroshima—was heard nearly 3,000 miles (5,000 km) away, and the ashes circled the globe, blotting out the sun for two days in nearby Java and Sumatra, and reddening sunsets throughout the world for three years. More recently, on 9 June 1991, the Philippines' Mount Pinatubo, dormant for six hundred years, erupted with a violence that left 200,000 acres (800 sq km) covered with 9 billion tons of fine white ash and thick volcanic sludge; it killed an untold number of people, left 1.2 million homeless, and rendered much of the nearby provinces—including a major U.S. military installation, Clark Air Base—useless for agriculture. Earthquakes are also frequent in both Indonesia and the Philippines. In 1990, for example, northern Luzon was devastated by an earthquake that measured 7.7 on the Richter scale; the city of Baguio was cut off from the rest of the country for days, as bridges and roads disappeared in the devastation.

Geography also helped to determine political loyalty. Today's concept of clearly defined national boundaries, within which everyone is obliged to pay allegiance to the nation-state, did not begin to exist in most of Southeast Asia until the nineteenth century. While many wars around the world have been fought to assert or defend clearly demarcated frontiers, the Vietnamese-Lao wars of the seventeenth century were resolved wisely when the Le rulers in Vietnam and the Lao monarch agreed that every inhabitant in the upper Mekong valley who lived in a house built on stilts owed allegiance to Laos, while those whose homes had earth floors owed allegiance to Vietnam. In effect, allegiance

A violent environment: Krakatau erupts, August 1883.

was determined not by cartography but by cultural preference, an indigenous concept that has not survived into the twenty-first century. One angle from which to approach modern Southeast Asian history, in fact, is to see it as a long struggle by one elite or another to impose hegemony on all inhabitants—whatever their ethnicity, religion, or language—living within defined contemporary boundaries, even if those boundaries were originally imposed by European mapmakers.

Technological and scientific power developed in the West was applied to taming nature in Southeast Asia. Western colonialists, uncomfortable and fearful in the tropics but unwilling to abandon potential profits, sanitized, literally and figuratively, the natural environment. In the Klang area of Selangor, Malaya, British science eradicated the malarial *anopheles* mosquito primarily to enhance the productivity of the estate workers on the rubber plantations but glorified this action on humanitarian grounds, thus claiming a medical justification for colonial conquest. Rudyard Kipling, the English poet of imperialism, urged Americans to take up "the White Man's burden," because Westerners knew how to "fill full the mouth of Famine and bid the sickness cease."

Whatever the motives of colonialists, the modern science and engineering technology they introduced to Southeast Asia effectively modified the environment, permitted the introduction of new crops, fueled a population explosion, and helped to transform where power was centered and on what basis it was legitimized. New cities rapidly grew to staff an economic and geopolitical revolution. The doctor or sanitary engineer, whether foreign or native, was an agent of change. Plant species were destroyed; subsistence crops were replaced to satisfy an export market. As we shall see, there were visible winners and forgotten losers as traditional values, cultures, societies, and states were swept into the maelstrom of modernization.

The Peoples

AT THE millennium Southeast Asia was the home of some 540 million people. Millions of them were descended from families that had been living in the same immediate area for centuries (or even millennia), while the ancestors of millions more had migrated into the region, moved across it, or relocated into its cities in the last 250 years. Ethnically, there are people from many "races" and cultures, speaking an extraordinary array of different languages, some indigenous to the region, others brought in by immigrants.

Southeast Asia was until recently relatively sparsely populated, especially in contrast to its two giant neighbors, India and China. Historian Anthony Reid has noted that the population of Southeast Asia today is equal to approximately 40 percent of China's, but in 1800, when some 33 million people lived in the region, they represented only about 12 percent of China's population. Southeast Asia evidently experienced a much more dramatic demographic upheaval—falling mortality, rising fertility, and increasing immigration—than either China or India over the same time period. Such growth reshaped every Southeast Asian society, redistributed the people on the land, and challenged the cultural verities of an earlier time.

In the premodern era, the relative scarcity of labor gave individuals and their local communities greater bargaining power with their indigenous or imperial rulers. The scarcity made it possible to avoid onerous taxation or despotic control. There was still vacant land, which permitted minority groups or families in economic distress to seek a new beginning by moving a few miles away—a frontier that gradually disappeared during the modern era. As it did so, some governments, particularly in Indonesia and the Philippines, began to sponsor the migration of landless peasants to more distant and less populous islands, although this was rarely more than a stopgap solution to problems of overcrowding and rural discontent, and it often created new conflicts when the settlers clashed with the local inhabitants of the "transmigration" sites.

Central to modern nationalism is the assumption that economic development and social justice will improve the standard of living for every citizen, yet in the second half of the twentieth century, the population explosion seemingly inhibited economic progress, a conundrum plaguing most of the nations of the region. The population of Vietnam had been under 5 million two centuries ago; by the 1870s it had reached about 7 million, rising to 20 million just before World War II, over 50 million by 1979, and nearly 80 million twenty years later. Moreover, this growth was unevenly distributed; in 1995 the Red River delta in northern Vietnam had a population density of over 1,100 people per square kilometer, but the midlands and hill country nearby had a density less than 125.

Uneven growth among different ethnic, linguistic, or religious groups could even threaten to shift the balance of political power. Before the late nineteenth century the ethnic minority populations in the kingdom of Vietnam grew less rapidly than did the population of the ethnic Viet, but a hundred years later it was decidedly the reverse. In late-twentieth-century Singapore, the relatively low fertility of ethnic Chinese, compared with Malays and Indians, became a matter of concern for the government, which feared a shift in the social and political composition of the republic.

Population growth occurred because more babies survived and life expectancy increased. There was also a massive immigration of South Asians and Chinese, who came to Southeast Asia on a scale similar to the great migrations of Europeans to the United States or of Russians moving eastward across the land frontier of nineteenth-century Siberia. The dynamic force of these demographic changes cannot be overstated. Some families (and the groups they represented) triumphed, while others lost status, wealth, or land. Traditional values were buffeted and priorities upended. A few grew richer and many grew poorer. Tens of millions moved to the cities, while many millions more were forced to seek new ways of making a living, having lost control or ownership of land. Kinship patterns were challenged and family solidarity weakened as people made choices, both large and small, about what was essential to their lives and what could be jettisoned.

Consider the city-state of Singapore, at the southern tip of the Malay Peninsula. When Thomas Raffles founded this outpost as a British colony in

"Indies Types": Arab, Javanese, and Chinese in Surabaya, 1860. Merchants of unspecified ethnicity appear to the left and between Javanese and Chinese. Lithograph by Jancigny Dubois.

KITLV, Leiden, #51 D-8

1819, it was a flat, swampy, malarial island with potential military value but little else. Now it has a population of 4.3 million people; three-quarters of them are ethnic Chinese, with Indians making up an additional 6.5 percent of the population. It is one of the richest, most sophisticated, postindustrial cities in the world, a global leader in shipping and electronics. Chinese, Malay, Tamil, and English are all official languages, and among the major religious groups are Buddhists, Daoists, Muslims, Christians, and Hindus. Today, less than two centuries after its founding, Singapore's gross domestic product is in excess of $100 billion annually, and life expectancy in this shiny metropolis equals that of Western Europe and exceeds that in the United States. What an extraordinary story exists behind those facts!

And yet there remain hundreds of millions of peasants still living in hundreds of thousands of Southeast Asian villages. There are still dusty dirt roads and serene Thai temples that present a sharp contrast with the din and traffic congestion of modern Bangkok. But just as that isolated peasant farmer in his or her "timeless" routine may watch television programs off a satellite dish at night, so the Bangkok stockbroker may change from suit and tie at night to meditate in Buddhist tranquility in his home.

In sum, we believe that Southeast Asia can be understood by holding in focus its current realities while going back to explore conditions in the preceding two centuries (and more). We need to probe the past, noting what has been forgotten, what remains unaltered, and what has been transformed, striving to understand the discontinuities and new events, to understand how the different peoples of the region—now increasingly called "Southeast Asians"—

have managed to sustain their unique values, traditions, customs, and priorities while adapting to new realities, ideas, institutions and lifestyles.

Further Readings

Anderson, Benedict. *The Spectre of Comparisons: Nationalism, Southeast Asia, and the World.* London, 1998.

Christie, Clive J. *Southeast Asia in the Twentieth Century: A Reader.* London, 1998.

Dixon, Chris. *South East Asia in the World Economy.* Cambridge, U.K., 1991.

Hill, Ronald. *Southeast Asia: People, Land and Economy.* Crow's Nest, N.S.W., 2002.

Leifer, Michael. *Dictionary of Modern Politics of Southeast Asia.* London, 1995.

Lieberman, Victor. *Strange Parallels: Southeast Asia in Global Context, c. 800–1830.* Cambridge, 2003.

Pluvier, Jan M. *Historical Atlas of South-East Asia.* Leiden, 1995.

Reid, Anthony. *Southeast Asia in the Age of Commerce, 1450–1680.* 2 vols. New Haven, 1988–1993.

Reid, Anthony, and David Marr, eds. *Perceptions of the Past in Southeast Asia.* Singapore, 1979.

Rigg, Jonathan. *Southeast Asia: The Human Landscape of Modernization and Development.* 2d ed. London and New York, 2003.

Tarling, Nicholas, ed. *The Cambridge History of Southeast Asia.* 2 vols. Cambridge, U.K., 1992.

Tate, D. J. M. *The Making of Modern South-East Asia.* 2 vols. Rev. ed. Kuala Lumpur, 1977–1979.

PART I

❋

The Dynamics of the
Eighteenth Century

Chapter 1

Southeast Asian Livelihoods

Travelers to Southeast Asia in the eighteenth century found two main patterns of political and economic life. In major river valleys and plains were kingdoms whose ruling classes levied taxes from subjects in labor on public works and in agricultural produce. They promoted the clearing of forests and an expanding frontier of settlement through awarding land use rights to pioneering families. There, royal decrees ordered officials to bind farmers to villages, enumerate them, and prevent their flight from royal tax agents. Rulers in eighteenth-century Myanmar, Siam, Vietnam, and Java dominated core populations, while they launched raids against other communities to build up their populations and skill pools. Similarly, Spanish governors and archbishops were extending civil and religious bureaucracies to form the state of the Philippines.

In mountain regions and on coasts and seas, there was a second pattern. Here peoples based their economic life on mobility, collecting agricultural, forest, and sea produce to sell along land and water trading routes. Ruling groups used female and slave labor to boost cultivation, collection, and processing of produce. A great variety of ethnicities interacted with trading networks operated by Chinese, Arabs, Indians, and Europeans. Among sea workers the Dutch were dominant over much of the area. From a chain of fortified ports in the Indonesian archipelago, they controlled the ocean highways by a system of passes and naval patrols, while agents of the Dutch East Indies Company (Vereenigde Oost-Indische Compagnie, or voc) jostled with Asian competitors, who dominated northern waters, for market share. In the early 1700s the Dutch

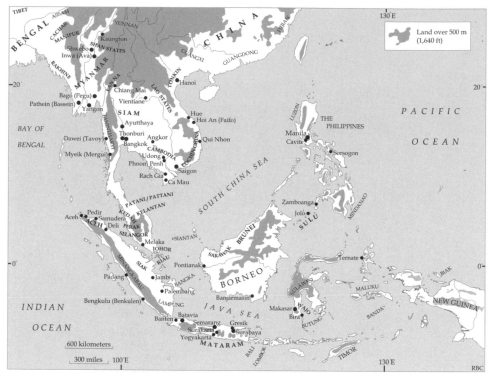

Eighteenth-century Southeast Asia

lived more at sea than on land and, like Indonesian sultans, sited their head-quarters at important harbor mouths, extracting export goods through alliances with indigenous aristocrats and land-based agents. In Indonesian waters the Dutch dominated bulk trading and relied on Asian networks to integrate smaller ports into their economic zone. During the course of the eighteenth century, the Dutch leased land in west Java and along the north coast, becoming more like the Southeast Asian rulers of mainland kingdoms and Spanish governors of the Philippines, settling populations and overseeing their export production.

While the Dutch dominated Indonesian waters, the seaborne commerce of mainland Southeast Asia was dominated by Chinese and South Asians. China's population was expanding and could only be fed by the import of rice from Vietnam and Siam, paid for by Spanish silver from Manila (and ultimately from Spanish America) and by pottery. Meanwhile, the severe fabric deficiency of Southeast Asia was supplied by imports of cotton cloth from India, usually in Indian ships.

Farmers of the Sea and Forest

VISITORS who came to Southeast Asia by sea found communities living along the extensive coastlines in bays, along waterways, and on little islands clustered at river mouths. Houses constructed of bamboo and thatch were built on poles at water's edge, with steps leading down to small boats and rafts. Fishing boats were sites of residence and workplaces for families, as well as means of transport. In Southeast Asia's history people who lived on both sea and land have played important roles as traders, pirates, slavers, naval warriors, and mercenaries. They are termed variously in the literature sea nomads, sea gypsies, and sea hunters and gatherers.

Men, women, and children were farmers of the sea. Fish offer a food supply year-round. Marine foods were reliable, because they could be preserved and stored by boiling and drying in the sun, smoking over a fire, or salting. Such methods were within the capacity of preindustrial technology, requiring simple tools and a division of labor between land and sea. Shellfish beds along shore and reefs could be harvested with hooks, rakes, or spades. Developments in boat construction and sailing techniques extended the range of catch from inshore to deep-sea fish. Visitors who recorded their travels describe a gendered division of labor in fishing communities. Men cut wood, built and sailed boats, and engaged in deep-sea fishing; they trapped turtles and dived for mother-of-pearl. Women and children worked on shore; they made and mended fishing nets, gathered shellfish and sea cucumbers from reefs, collected firewood, and processed the sea harvest. Before the nineteenth-century draining of the major river deltas of the mainland, these watery, treed landscapes did not make for easy living, and vast areas were still lightly inhabited.

A traveler who joined caravans of merchants crossing from Yunnan into Laos and Myanmar, or who journeyed upland from Sumatra's coasts, would discover that Southeast Asia's mountain chains were home to a great variety of peoples, who spoke many languages and whose customs and histories linked them loosely in extended family alliances and chains of economic exchange. Some lived in fortified villages in fertile valleys, growing rice, while others were, like the harvesters of the sea, mobile farmers. Using machetes and fire, they would clear a patch of forest of its trees and creepers, then raise vegetables, rice, fruits, and nuts on land temporarily fertilized by ash and watered by rainfall, a pattern referred to by scholars as slash-and-burn (or swidden) agriculture. The soil in such clearings was quickly exhausted, so after a year or two the farmers would move on to another part of the forest—"shifting cultivation"—leaving the jungle to recapture the first clearing and let it recover its fertility, suitable for slashing and burning again in another decade or generation.

Over centuries, farmers living among trees learned to read their landscape. From the forest surrounding their temporary clearings, they collected tree resins to coat and repair waterproof containers and seal carrying baskets. They burned dammar resin in torches for interior light and to illuminate night performances; essential oils provided incense for their religious ceremonies. Extraction of resins and barks required local knowledge, tools of stone or iron, and collecting baskets. Trees were tapped while a community farmed a site, then abandoned when it moved to clear a new plot. In areas occupied by semi-sedentary communities, resin collection changed from random tapping to regular gathering, the change in lifestyle leading to the ownership and inheritance of trees. Forest farmers also hunted birds for their bright plumage, deer for their hides, and elephants for their tusks.

Resins, barks, hides, feathers, and ivory were easy to carry and traveled well. A man walking along a jungle path could introduce his harvest of basic and luxury items into intricate networks of exchange that reached into Southeast Asia's lowlands and ports, and from there through sea networks to China, the world's largest market in the eighteenth century. Products harvested from mainland forests could also be transferred to merchants on land trade routes through China to Central Asia and farther west to the Mediterranean.

China's manufacturers used resins collected by Southeast Asian hill peoples for gluing, sealing, cleansing, preserving, and beautifying. Southeast Asian tree saps were the source of lacquers and varnishes that Chinese woodworkers applied to furniture, screens, and containers. Camphor crystals from pine trees in northwest Sumatra and west Java were used as fungicides and fumigants, and applied to wounds to stop bleeding. Deer hunted in Cambodia's forests were brought by Cham peoples to central Vietnam's ports, where traders shipped the hides to Japan for manufacture into the leather armor worn by soldiers in service to shoguns.

Farmers of the Moving Frontier

THE VISITOR who journeyed inland to the central river valley plains of Myanmar and Siam or to Java's north coast and its south central plains would find many farmers growing rice in permanent fields. The earliest evidence for rice cultivation in Southeast Asia comes from settlements along rivers. People grew rice in fields that were inundated by river waters during the rainy season. When settlements were established farther away from rivers, farmers dug canals and holding dams to channel water to their fields. They built walls of earth to retain the rains of the wet season and create a growing medium for young plants, later draining the fields to allow the rice to ripen for harvesting. Domesticated rice grown in such permanent fields was to provide the economic base for major kingdoms like Inwa (Ava) in Myanmar, Ayutthaya in Siam, Mataram in Java, and the Trinh domain in northern Vietnam.

Over the centuries, the basic technology of wet rice agriculture was adapted and improved by Southeast Asian farmers. Where water buffalo were domesticated, heavier soils could be tilled faster and deeper than by human muscle power alone. It is not known when Southeast Asian farmers domesticated them, but a panel on the ninth-century Borobudur temple in central Java

Paddy plowing with water buffaloes, Java, ca. 1925.

shows a buffalo harnessed to a plow. In the eleventh century Cham farmers of central Vietnam reversed a historic pattern of technology exchange by sending to China faster-ripening rice seeds they had developed. And although most of Southeast Asia's rice growers preferred the lowlands—paddies must be flat to retain water—when population densities began to fill up the plains, as happened in Java and Luzon, farmers developed techniques of building terraces into hillsides and mountain slopes to extend the cultivable land surface for rice as well as for fruit trees and vegetables.

Southeast Asia's farmers were always willing to try new crops. Originally they raised Asian crops, such as rice, sugar, cotton, indigo, fruits, and pepper, experimenting with seed selection and breeding to increase yields. They developed a seedless banana, gathered rambutan, durian, and breadfruit, and manufactured cloth and paper from tree bark. But they also learned quickly to incorporate into their home plots American plants introduced by Europeans in the 1500s and 1600s. Tomatoes, potatoes, sweet potatoes and yams, capsicums (peppers, including chiles), corn (maize), cassava, and peanuts became permanent ingredients of Southeast Asian cookery. In the late 1700s farmers in west Java learned how to raise coffee seedlings introduced by the Dutch from Yemen and harvested the berries for export.

Farming families adapted their animal husbandry and adjusted their diets in response to other external contacts. Over the seventeenth and eighteenth centuries pork was eliminated from cuisines in Islamized parts of Southeast Asia, ending in those areas the hunting and breeding of pigs. Farmers took up goat breeding instead, and Muslim methods of slaughtering animals for human consumption were adopted. The changes in Southeast Asian farming tech-

23

niques and the variety of crops grown, cooked, and consumed are evidence of dynamic response by men and women to new possibilities and to new markets.

Also important in the eighteenth century were spices native to Maluku (known to Europeans as the "Spice Islands") in Indonesia's eastern archipelago. These islands are volcanic peaks in a zone of very high rainfall; their mountain slopes and coastal swamps were densely covered with sago and coconut palms, clove trees, and evergreens producing nutmegs. In the hot, humid rainforests and dense shade, rice could not be grown. This environment produced another Southeast Asian adaptation: islanders raised tubers on forest floors, gathered fruits from wild trees, and harvested both the sago palm and the sea. Root crops are perishable, but sago has a long life when baked into loaves. Sago was both survival food and a form of currency with which long-distance traders could purchase other goods. The female industry of processing the palm starch into loaves was closely linked to the male industry of harvesting the sea for fish and trade goods such as mother-of-pearl.

Cloves are native to five small islands along the west coast of Halmahera, while nutmeg and mace are products of a tree native to the Banda islands. These products were desired for their fragrance, added to foods, and used as dyes and in preparations for health and beauty. Southeast Asian traders used spices as currency to acquire goods from other regions; archipelago rulers sent them as tribute to China. Since the nineteenth century spices have been superseded in most of their uses by food processing and refrigeration, chemical dyes, imported medicines, and cash. Foreigners generally gave up the spice business, but in Indonesia a new use was developed: clove cigarettes, made by cottage industry since the early nineteenth century.

Spice production required the labor of family teams or slaves, simple tools and processing techniques, and sea highways well traveled by purchasers and suppliers. It evolved during the seventeenth century from gathering the fruit of wild trees into organized agriculture in special plantations and was matched by the development of stapling centers that moved spices into other trade networks far from their original home markets. Portuguese traders moved into spice wholesaling and distribution in the 1500s, the Dutch in the 1600s. For over a century European demand for spices commanded economic life in the eastern archipelago. Ternate's sultans levied taxes in spices, tree resins, bird-of-paradise plumes, and shell bracelets, and exchanged them with Javanese, Malay, and European traders for textiles, metal goods, coins, and rice, which, in the Spice Islands, was a prestige food for the elite consumed on ceremonial occasions. They financed war fleets and expanded their empire to include seventy-two territories from eastern Sulawesi (Celebes) to the northern shores of New Guinea. But growing Dutch control of the major spice production zone forced many Asian traders to find new markets along the flexible sea routes and to relocate their businesses and families.

Few Southeast Asians in the 1700s lived a completely self-sufficient economic life. People sustained families through multiple occupations, exchange, and sales. Men who farmed might also be carpenters, cart builders or drivers, wheelwrights, boat builders, makers of tile and brick, operators of limekilns, potters, or blacksmiths. Women farmers were also spinners, weavers and decorators of cloth, or market sellers. Artisans operated from small workshops on a part-time basis. People traded their rice for metal tools, textiles, coconut and palm sugar, cooked foods, medicines, pots and utensils, mats, and baskets. When they were doing well, they bought fine porcelain, jewelry, daggers, and goods worked in leather.

Southeast Asian villages were linked by markets, where people traded their goods for items they could not themselves produce or that it was not worth their time to make. Goods were carried by peddlers to more distant markets for sale to traders who employed porters to carry larger amounts to major markets, collection centers, and ports. Between markets there was small-scale movement by locals going to sell a few coconuts, buy some medicine, or enjoy entertainment, as well as the long-distance movement of porters and peddlers. Some markets were located at river mouths that opened into sheltered bays. Small, flat-bottomed boats could sail right in to shore to disgorge cargoes to waiting porters. Larger vessels—Javanese, Chinese, and European—anchored in deeper water, sheltered among the islands, and sent representatives and cargoes ashore in rowboats. In some places locals rowed out to the big ships and traded directly in foodstuffs, fresh water, and services such as laundry and sex. In port cities like Pathein (Bassein), Manila, and Melaka harbormasters constructed warehouses to store the rising volumes of trade goods.

Evidence of women as marketers of agricultural produce comes from written records of Chinese, Arab, and European travelers. A painting titled *Spice Shop,* commissioned by the voc and executed in 1715 by Frans van Mieris de Jonge, shows a market seller using scales to weigh cloves and mace for her woman customer. Le Quy Don, the

Courtesy of R. H. Taylor

Handicrafts: woman carrying pots (probably from Kyan Kmyaung or Shegu) to her shop near Sagaing, Upper Myanmar.

25

eighteenth-century Vietnamese historian, describes female traders of central Vietnam as indispensable to the export trade; Western travelers in the Philippines rarely fail to mention women selling vegetables in every village market.

An early prerogative of kings, known from inscriptions, was to charge fees or taxes on the passage of goods in and out of an area. Tollgates, where troops were often stationed, were erected at crossroads, bridges, and entrances to markets, near shrines and religious foundations, and at rest houses along royal roads. Porters had to open their baskets, while the tollgate staff assessed the value of goods and estimated the charges to be paid.

Local Labor and Immigrant Enterprise

EIGHTEENTH-CENTURY visitors to Mataram or Inwa would see gangs of men repairing roads, building bridges, constructing palaces and monasteries, and supporting armies as animal keepers, grass cutters, porters, servants, and foot soldiers, as well as vast numbers of men and women accompanying royal processions. Most of these were farmers, drawn off their fields at intervals to pay taxes through compulsory labor, or corvée. Siamese kings extracted up to six months a year from men and women whose labor obligations were indicated by numbers tattooed on their skin, an eighteenth-century form of identity card.

Everywhere in the region there was a quest to augment labor forces. Vietnamese, Myanmar, and Siamese armed bands raided hill zones to enslave captives and resettle them at lowland work sites. Siamese and Myanmar armies regularly invaded each other's territory to bring back as prisoners of war skilled and unskilled workers from palaces, workshops, and huts. Captured populations were distributed among religious foundations to raise crops for their business enterprises, set to work in artisans' quarters in palace compounds, or assigned to military support duties. In maritime Southeast Asia pirates attacked ships for their cargoes and crews, and raided coastal villages for able-bodied men and women to sell in the region's harbor towns as dockhands, porters, construction workers, market assistants, domestic helpers, and sex workers. The visitor who sailed through the central and southern Philippines or eastern Indonesia might find coastal villages emptied because their inhabitants had fled inland behind bamboo fortifications or been scattered by slave markets across Southeast Asia. Law and custom also operated to trap labor, dictating that children born to a slave woman were themselves slaves and that women and children could be enslaved to work off debts entered into by their male relatives.

Slaving, however, could not produce a supply of labor large enough or steady enough for all of Southeast Asia's needs. Rulers of Southeast Asian states encouraged the immigration of Chinese men, both as entrepreneurs and as general laborers (generally recruited by the entrepreneurs). Chinese stonemasons built Manila's cathedral and city walls; Siamese kings hired Chinese to pilot their fleets and conduct the royal trade. Rulers might assign Chinese entrepreneurs specific shares of their import and export trade, their tax collection, the carrying trade between producers and markets, or leases of land for agriculture and mining, sometimes providing both living and working space. In the nineteenth century Vietnam's Nguyen emperors settled Chinese specialists in pepper and sugar cane cultivation in the new territories they were opening in the Mekong delta, as Chinese financiers and their networks of peddlers facilitated the moving frontier of Vietnamese colonization south and west into Khmer territory.

Royal revenues were raised from taxes on imports and exports, from the rental of market stalls, and from gifts from foreign traders. Southeast Asia's rulers did not generally use their wealth to promote local industry or local entrepreneurs. Wealth was seen as static, something to be accumulated or spent lavishly. It purchased political power, because it made possible the hiring of men as sailors and soldiers. But it was not envisaged as a dynamic agent that might be invested in the hope of multiplying revenues or fostering among local subjects the skills that foreigners possessed.

Sultans of Banten (Bantam) in northwest Java welcomed Chinese traders to their markets and rented to Chinese allotments of land to raise vegetables and fruits to feed the growing population of their port. They leased more land to Chinese men who organized the growing, processing, and export of sugar cane, and allowed skilled Chinese craftsmen to establish forges for metalworking, manufacturing arms, gunpowder, and copper cash. In the eighteenth century Chinese mined copper in northern Vietnam, tin in Bangka Island (east of Sumatra), and gold in west Borneo, and they grew pepper and gambier in Riau (south of the Malay Peninsula). Throughout the region they drew on skills developed in China and on their extensive knowledge of other countries—their location, history, products, minerals, markets—to integrate Southeast Asia's ports into regional and international networks of trade. Under their own bosses and labor recruiters they worked primarily for Chinese markets; historian Carl Trocki has characterized eighteenth-century Southeast Asia as a zone of offshore production for China.

Many Southeast Asian kings and high officials found it attractive to auction the business of tax collection—the tax "farm"—to Chinese businessmen, for it gave them a predictable cash income at minimum administrative cost. The system appealed to the Chinese, because taxes collected in produce generated goods salable in local and distant markets. They supplied advances of consumer goods to their networks of porters, shopkeepers, and peddlers, who carried these goods into villages and markets, sold them at ferry crossings and tollgates, and lugged them up jungle paths to collecting centers in hill districts or carried them by boats along canals through mazes of rice paddies. The Chinese funneled textiles, tools, salt, dried fish, and earthenware pots into Southeast Asian markets, creating desires and then transforming desires into necessities. They extracted rice, coconuts, timber, and other produce and transported them to collection points for bulking and moving on to bigger markets. Chinese would purchase the right to operate tollgates and market stalls, and to sell opium and sex to the passing traffic of porters, cart drivers, boatmen, ferry operators, and traders. They employed spies and private police forces or thugs to protect their businesses and ensure regular supplies.

Siamese kings who appointed Chinese to important posts such as harbormaster or allotted them large land leases conferred on them Siamese names and titles. In island Southeast Asia some Chinese merchant communities were Muslim; leaders converted to Islam in order to gain access to sultans and to qualify for important positions carrying indigenous titles and ranks. The Jayaningrat and Puspanagara families controlled the rice areas of Pekalongan and Batang in Java in the eighteenth century and made themselves useful to Java's royals as lenders of money. Chinese converts worshiped in their own mosques and were represented to the authorities by their own headman. In the Philippines some Chinese converted to Christianity for similar reasons.

Europeans trading in eighteenth-century Southeast Asia also ran many of their operations through Chinese networks. Dutch and English at Jambi on Sumatra's east coast acquired pepper and gold from the Chinese there. In areas under European control, such as Manila and Batavia (Jakarta), Chinese collected market taxes, managed toll booths, supplied vegetable markets, operated rice and saw mills, and poured consumer goods into rural hinterlands through their opium shops, pawnshops, and village stores. They were often the only sources of credit for local manufacturers who ran family businesses. Most indigenous entrepreneurs could not compete, because there were no alternative sources of credit until colonial governments created rural banks in the twentieth century.

Yet the position of such aliens in Southeast Asia was always precarious, dependent on the attitudes of the ruler of the day, rival elites, and the general populace. In Manila and Batavia, where Europeans headed the government, Chinese were massacred in pogroms in 1603 and 1740, respectively. Nevertheless, Chinese communities turned to Europeans for protection and jobs. The VOC saw advantages in working through the Chinese from its earliest operations in the Indonesian archipelago. In 1677 it had negotiated with King Amangkurat II of Mataram rights to protect Chinese when they traveled and worked in his territory, clauses that were continued in every subsequent treaty with Java's kings. In 1736 the company employed 1,035 Chinese in the royal territories of central Java to collect taxes, deal in opium and rice, and act as purchasing agents.

Ships and Cities

WHILE Southeast Asian kingdoms were expanding their territories in the eighteenth century by capturing and settling populations in their domains, the real engines of economic growth were the international trade networks operating in maritime Southeast Asia. Chinese, Arab, Indian, and European trading conglomerates operating in Southeast Asia's ports increased demand for regional products and provoked dynamic responses by local ruling elites, traders, and farmers.

A great variety of craft ferried people across rivers, floated them downstream to ports, and carried them across seas linking the mainland and archipelagoes. They ranged from barges and flat-bottomed boats suitable for river traffic to outrigger canoes with single sails and great multimasted oceangoing ships. In the first millennium C.E. Southeast Asian boat builders were already constructing double outrigger canoes, seacraft with rudders, support masts and fixed sails, a kind of ship that can be seen carved in reliefs on the Borobudur. Boat building arose in an environment of island clusters linked by shallow seas and strong, predictable winds; impassable terrains of swamp, jungle, and mountain generally made sea travel more attractive than land travel.

From the thirteenth century onward, Southeast Asians were building larger and faster boats with several masts and decks. By the sixteenth century there were large, oceangoing vessels with two to four masts of woven rattan, capable of carrying up to one thousand men and many tons of cargo. Ship construction sites were located where suitable stands of timber, sheltered bays, and skilled workers—woodcutters, carpenters, shipwrights, and sail makers—were to be found, places like Bago (Pegu) in Myanmar, Bira in Sulawesi, and Cavite and Sorsogon in the Philippines.

As in agriculture, Southeast Asians were open to borrowing and innovation in naval technology. From Chinese "junks" Southeast Asian shipbuilders learned the technique of building decks and compartments for holding goods. They borrowed from European ships the rigging of sails and the material from which sails were made. Indonesian archipelago sailors replaced their stone or wooden anchors with iron anchors copied from Dutch models. In the twentieth century shippers added motors and refrigerated space; the old trade in slaves was reborn in the transport of illegal migrants.

Large oceangoing ships belonging to archipelago rulers had generally disappeared by the end of the seventeenth century, although the kings of Siam continued to own them and even added steamships by the 1840s. Most local owners and financiers, however, could no longer compete with the fleets sustained by rulers and companies in China, India, and Europe, so Southeast Asian rulers licensed foreigners to conduct large-scale sea trade. This did not mean that local shipping and the skills of boat building, navigation, sailing, and trading disappeared entirely, but sea trade and vessels became the concerns of Asian men with less capital than before. They traded among a few ports, in places where it was neither physically nor economically feasible for the big ships to sail. On their trading vessels goods were stored in baskets, straw bags, and clay jars under mats secured in place by rattan ropes.

Southeast Asian boats: (above) Chinese-style *tongkang* carrying *atap* palm, off Deli, Sumatra, ca. 1910. (Facing page, top) "Flying" praus (with outriggers) off Zamboanga, Philippines, ca. 1930. (Facing page, bottom) Boatman on Perfume River, Hue, Vietnam, 1991.

In the eighteenth century ship owners who captained their own ships were generally Chinese, Javanese, Malays, or Buginese, each selecting his crew from fellow countrymen. The captain had to combine the skills of navigator, leader, diplomat, and salesman. A maritime code from Wajo (South Sulawesi), written in 1676, stated that a captain should be diligent, accurate, and pious, treat his crew as sons and teach them the techniques of sailing, have capital and knowledge of sea routes, own a good ship, and have a supply of weapons. Shippers sailed by the stars, relying on their knowledge of currents, winds, coastal landmarks, reefs, and inlets. Muslim sailors included meditation and religious ritual as part of their navigational techniques; they would visualize a whole journey before departure and set departure times to follow Islamic sunset prayer. Some sailors were fishermen who engaged themselves as crew for occasional voyages; others were seminomadic men available for hire in archipelago ports, men detached from permanent families and villages, who rented wives in the ports they visited.

Ships and crews were armed because of the likelihood of attack from sea dwellers whose economic specializations included piracy. Operating especially from bases in the Riau Archipelago, Lampung (south Sumatra), northern Borneo, and Mindanao, pirates enslaved crew and passengers on boats they captured, seized the goods on board, and stripped boats of their iron fittings. The weapons

KITLV, Leiden, #30570

Photo by N. G. Owen

carried on archipelago ships came from two main sources. Some were of local manufacture. In the eighteenth century, for instance, indigenous metal workers around Palembang, in southeast Sumatra, with the assistance of Chinese iron borers, produced muskets, while the Chinese bronze and copper casting industry at Gresik, in north Java, made cannon and muskets. The VOC imported from Europe arms and ammunition for its own needs and as sale items, and English private traders who sailed along the fringes of Dutch naval power sold artillery, handguns, and ammunition to Asian purchasers, especially in Riau, Bengkulu (west Sumatra), east Java, and Bali. From registers kept by Dutch harbormasters at ports along Java's north coast for the years 1774–1777, we can follow a ship owned by a Chinese skipper that left Gresik for Bali armed with two swivel guns and two muskets, carrying a cargo of salt, rice, and 5.5 kilograms of opium. When it returned to Gresik it brought back seventy thousand *pinang* nuts but no guns, for these had been sold along with the cargo. (The *pinang,* or areca nut, wrapped with various other seasonings in the leaf of the betel pepper, was chewed as a mild stimulant throughout almost all of Southeast Asia, one of the region's most distinctive practices.)

Meanwhile, maritime peoples such as the Buginese, Makasars, Mandarese, Bajau, Tausug, Madurese, and Butung had established colonies in many places in island Southeast Asia and the southern mainland, where they performed sea functions for settlements without a boat culture. Some of their vessels were specialized warships; individual boats had crews of up to two hundred rowers— generally slaves or corvée laborers—and large fleets were assembled to police subject territories or raid other settlements. These warships could maneuver among shoals, sandbanks, reefs, and islands, against currents and whirlpools. Against such vessels the deep-water naval superiority of Europeans, which had been reached by the 1650s, was of little relevance in many areas; only with the introduction of the flat-bottomed steam-powered gunship in the 1850s were Westerners able to assert their supremacy in Southeast Asian waters.

Sea journeys could last for months. After a year and more at sea, boats were in need of repairs, and the crew was exhausted. Sales, purchases, repairs, provisioning, and sailing times had to proceed according to a timetable dictated by monsoon winds, so Southeast Asia's ports always contained a migratory community of captains, crews, and merchants. Wealthy men often established households in their major ports of operations, installing wives to manage households and businesses, but most crewmen rented mistresses during their brief stays or used the more limited services of prostitutes. Mistresses and prostitutes were generally slave women, part of the great mass of individuals who were trafficked along trade routes to jobs in ports. By contrast, a wife was usually the daughter of some locally established family. Marriage gave the foreign trader local in-laws, who connected him to commercial networks, provided assistants and partners, and served as a source of local knowledge. Polygamy, in this context, did not mean having a harem of many women but maintaining separate households in different cities along a trader's regular route, each headed by a wife whose kin and business interests extended her mobile husband's operations. Throughout maritime Southeast Asia there was a common pattern of home-based women and children, while part-time husbands and fathers spent many months at sea and in other ports.

The port was one of the two characteristic city forms of eighteenth-century Southeast Asia, which was far more urbanized than we usually recognize. Anthony Reid, in fact, has argued that in the "Age of Commerce," beginning in the fifteenth century, Southeast Asia was one of the most urbanized regions of the world, quoting population figures comparable to those of cities in Europe and East Asia at the time. Melaka, once described by the Portuguese as a city "made for merchandise," had by the eighteenth century fallen into relative decline, but other archipelagic centers such as Batavia, Manila, Banten, Makasar, and Aceh were still of substantial size and commercial vigor. On the mainland, too, there were cities whose lifeblood was maritime trade, including Pathein (Bassein) in Myanmar, Hoi An (Faifo) in central Vietnam, Saigon-Cholon in southern Vietnam, and even Ayutthaya in Siam, which doubled as a royal capital.

Royal cities were, in fact, the other typical urban form in precolonial Southeast Asia. Besides their ceremonial and administrative functions, they also served as sites of manufacturing. Textile production, gold- and silversmithing, leather working, and furniture making employed free and slave men and women in artisans' quarters and palace compounds. Southeast Asian craftspeople were flexible. Blacksmiths made gongs for orchestras, but they also copied muskets imported by Europeans, made armor, and cast cannon. Women textile workers copied designs and colors from Indian fabrics and worked Chinese motifs into their cloth; they sewed jackets and blouses for Muslim converts, who required more modesty in their attire than before. Brewers of palm wine and salt makers operated seasonal industries. There were also construction workers, porters, grooms, and all kinds of palace workers: cooks, seamstresses, domestics, nursemaids, singers, dancers, and teachers. There were officials who wrote in Arabic, Indic, or Latin scripts, interpreters, translators, seal makers, and personal advisers to kings. In Aceh and Vietnam villages supplied eunuch boys for palace careers. In Java the innermost circle of bodyguards were women, who might also double as temporary wives. Royals employed priests, monks, and religious scholars, astrologers, poets, chroniclers, and flatterers. European-governed cities had similar complements of workers, plus operators of mechanical printing presses.

The image we have of Southeast Asia as quintessentially rural derives largely from the nineteenth century, when, as Reid points out, the "Age of Commerce" had given way to an "Age of Peasantry." Mobility had characterized workers in the earlier period, but in the nineteenth century workers became harnessed to producing crops for export on permanently cleared fields or on plantations that had been carved out of rainforests. Labor gangs laid roads and railway lines across Southeast Asia's land surfaces. Where forests were ripped out and steam-powered boats patrolled the seas, effective government extended its reach, and places of refuge from authority shrank. Newly demarcated borders on land and sea reduced the mobility of hill and sea populations, and fused diverse peoples into new administrative unions, propelling them into new relationships with the state and new ways of earning a living.

Further Readings

Andaya, Barbara Watson, ed. *Other Pasts: Women, Gender and History in Early Modern Southeast Asia.* Honolulu, 2000.

Boomgaard, Peter, Freek Colombijn, and David Henley, eds. *Paper Landscapes: Explorations in the Environmental History of Indonesia.* Leiden, 1997.

Bruijn, J. R., and F. S. Gaastra, eds. *Ships, Sailors and Spices: East India Companies and Their Shipping in the Sixteenth, Seventeenth and Eighteenth Centuries.* Leiden, 1993.

Kathirithamby-Wells, J., and John Villiers, eds. *The Southeast Asian Port and Polity: Rise and Demise.* Singapore, 1990.

Lombard, Denys. "Questions on the Contact between European Companies and Asian Societies." In Roderich Ptak and Dietmar Rothermund, eds., *Emporia, Commodities, and Entrepreneurs in Asian Maritime Trade, c. 1400–1750,* pp. 179–187. Stuttgart, 1981.

Manguin, Pierre-Yves. "The Southeast Asian Ship: An Historical Approach." *Journal of Southeast Asian Studies* 11, 2 (September 1980): 266–276.

Reid, Anthony. *Southeast Asia in the Age of Commerce, 1450–1680.* 2 vols. New Haven, 1988–1993.

Trocki, Carl A. "Chinese Pioneering in Eighteenth Century Southeast Asia." In Anthony Reid, ed., *The Last Stand of Asian Autonomies: Responses to Modernity in the Diverse States of Southeast Asia and Korea, 1750–1900,* pp. 83–101. New York, 1997.

Wicks, Robert S. *Money, Markets and Trade in Early Southeast Asia: The Development of Indigenous Monetary Systems to AD 1400.* Ithaca, 1992.

Chapter 2

Inner Life and Identity

WHO WERE the "Southeast Asians"? How were they divided up, how did they see themselves, and how did others see them? Theoretical and practical questions about the formation of social identity have become a major issue in the social sciences because of the way the sense of belonging can shape how people behave and how they relate to each other, as individuals and in communities. Is a sense of identity primarily fostered by language, by ethnicity, by religion, by loyalty to a ruler, or by a shared group history? All, in some degree, had relevance for Southeast Asians in the period up to the late eighteenth century.

The People

DESPITE the commonalities that, as we have seen, make it sensible to speak of Southeast Asia as a single region, there were significant internal differences in terms of both the physical and the social circumstances in which people lived. Terrain meant that many led their lives in small, isolated, kin-centric communities—in the upland interiors of the Malay Peninsula and the mainland countries, for example, or in the scattered riverine and coastal settlements that fringed the archipelago. Others inhabited the much more densely settled flood plains of Myanmar, central Java, or northern Vietnam, their cities, temple precincts, and surroundings. Remoteness fostered small-scale, separate identities, often fiercely resistant to absorption by outsiders. Numbers and proximity encouraged the emergence of larger corporate identities associated with the political and sacral power of kings, emperors, or sultans, as in Myanmar, Siam, Vietnam, and central Java.

Patterns of social diversity were linked to the many languages people spoke. Local languages and dialects, sometimes unintelligible to near neighbors, characterized the more remote areas and peoples (the Batak of highland Sumatra, the Kayin [Karen] of Myanmar, and the Torajans of Sulawesi, for example), while within the major language families, core languages came to dominate particular areas. Around the core languages there developed literatures and larger cultural complexes embracing religion, law and custom, sense of place, and a host of preferred ways of living and behaving that could be contrasted with those of others. Outsiders—the Chinese first and then the Europeans in the sixteenth and seventeenth centuries—used ethnicity, language, and religion to develop working terminologies for the people they came among, as did the Malays, who described the first Europeans as "White Bengalis." Learned social identities of this kind—self-creating and constructing the peoples we today so readily label simply as "Thai," "Vietnamese," "Filipino," and the like—emerged from social need and historical conjuncture, a process that continues today to provide the bedrock of "national" identities. We do not know precisely from whom the various Southeast Asian peoples descended, and perhaps we never will. Attempts to base ethnic identity on "race," though common, have no scientific basis.

One of the best examples for the eighteenth century of the indigenous creation and re-creation of social identity is provided by the history of the term "Malay." The language called "Melayu" originated in the area comprising south Sumatra and what became known as the Malay Peninsula. The cultural complex associated with the language centered from the fifteenth century on the Muslim kingdom and port city of Melaka, whose residents and ruling class appear to have been known to themselves, and increasingly to the foreign traders who came there, as *orang Melayu,* "Malay people." As Muslim trading activities expanded along the seaways of the archipelago in the sixteenth and seventeenth centuries, the Malay language became the lingua franca of commerce and contact in port towns from Aceh and Palembang in Sumatra, Banten in west Java, and Banjarmasin in Borneo to Makasar in Sulawesi and Patani in southern Siam. Their communities of widely diverse local origins increasingly spoke and wrote in Malay, adhered to Islam, dressed in generically "Malay" styles, participated in an increasingly common Malay culture, and were known, if not always to themselves then to outsiders, as Malays.

If Islam was an integral part of this culture, so other world religions too played formative and important roles in the life and beliefs of Southeast Asia's peoples. By the eighteenth century three such religious systems originating outside the area—Buddhism, Islam, and Christianity—had established themselves.

For historical reasons, each was primarily associated with particular parts of the region: Buddhism with the mainland countries from Myanmar across to Vietnam, Islam with much of the Malay archipelago, and Christianity with the Philippines.

Varieties of Buddhism

BUDDHISM is named after its founder, Gautama, prince and heir-apparent of a ruling family in Nepal around 600 B.C.E., who eventually became known as "the Buddha" (the Enlightened One). In his twenties, he embarked on a nomadic life of meditation, until he finally understood life and death. Thereafter, he wandered over northern India teaching that life is cut short by attachment to things and people, and that the goal of life should be to avoid greed, lust, and attachment, ultimately reaching not death but Nirvana, a state of being that transcended both life and death, escaping the never-ending cycle of death and rebirth. In its purest form, Buddhism reveres the Buddha not as a god but as a teacher. His sermons were collected to form the core of the Tipitaka (or Tripitaka), the "three baskets" of teaching still upheld by Buddhists today.

Mahayana Buddhism is the "northern school" of Buddhism, which spread historically from India to Nepal, Tibet, Mongolia, China, Korea, Japan, and northern Vietnam. Theravada Buddhism (sometimes called Hinayana) is the "southern school," which spread from India to Sri Lanka, Myanmar, Siam, Cambodia, and Laos. To cite some of the differences between the two schools, Mahayana insists on a broad and eclectic interpretation of the scriptures, whereas Theravada venerates only the Buddha himself as the founder of the religion and emphasizes his own teachings rather than the many sutras attributed to others found in Mahayana. Mahayana worships bodhisattvas—self-denying saints, lay or in orders, who had become Buddhas-to-be but compassionately helped others to reach Nirvana before entering it themselves; Theravada considers such worship to be idolatrous. Ideally, followers of Theravada practice religious devotion to save themselves, Mahayanists to save themselves and others. Mahayana tends to allow laymen and women a greater role in its religious community than does Theravada, which strictly separates monks from lay people. Theravada monks in such countries as Thailand and Myanmar wear saffron robes and accept alms for their food, while Mahayana monks in Vietnam wear brown robes and do not accept alms.

Theravada Buddhism from Sri Lanka spread rapidly between the eleventh and the fifteenth centuries through the countries of mainland Southeast Asia, from Myanmar to Cambodia and Laos. On its arrival it had to contend not only with well-established animism in both village and court (the oath of allegiance in all the courts included the threat of being punished by spirits if one broke the oath) but also with court and folk Brahmanism. In the first millennium C.E. many courts in Southeast Asia had adopted rituals learned from India, performed by religious specialists called "brahmins," as a means of codifying and legiti-mizing their rule. The beliefs associated with this practice, which developed in the subcontinent into what we call "Hinduism," do not appear to have spread widely among most local Southeast Asian populaces and are openly retained today only in Bali, but, like animist beliefs, they occasionally surface even among practitioners of other world religions.

The Brahmanical tradition, unlike Buddhism, offered absolute certainty in its explanations of natural and human action. As long as Buddhism was in-capable of giving equally certain answers when asked whether, for example, a military campaign should be undertaken or a marriage contracted, Brahman-ism remained of primary importance in everyday life. Over time, however, the Brahmanical element in religious life weakened with the strengthening of Buddhist scholarship, the popularization of sophisticated cosmological ideas, and eventual official and popular disapproval of Brahmanical rites and practices. The same developments worked to reduce animism to an essentially residual cate-gory for the explanation of phenomena beyond moral and scientific reason. Hindu religious sites, such as the temple of Angkor Wat in Cambodia, and Brah-manical institutions, such as the concept of the *devaraja* or god-king, fitted easily into Buddhist terminology and practice.

Throughout the Theravada areas by the eighteenth century every village had a monastery. A village was considered incomplete without one, though it might consist only of a small preaching hall *(vihara),* an *uposatha* building for ordinations and rites, and a dormitory for the monks. Around these, other buildings and towerlike monuments (pagodas, stupas, or *cetiya*) containing the relics of ancestors or exceptional men might in time be built, with nearby a sacred tree reminiscent of that under which the Buddha preached his first sermon. The typical monastery was inhabited by a small group of monks clad in saffron or yellow robes who had taken permanent or temporary vows of poverty, chastity, and devotion to a life of religious study and meditation. Their activities were governed by 227 specific disciplinary rules. Forbidden to touch money and bound to accept alms for their food, they began their day with a walk through the village accepting the food offerings of willing householders. The monks returned to eat at their monastery, where food was served to them by students or willing volunteers. Food obtained from the faithful was supple-mented by garden produce and delicacies—but never meat—offered to the monastery by people eager to gain merit.

The Buddhist monkhood in village society provided all males time and opportunity to perfect their moral being, to seek enlightenment, and to preach the Dhamma (Dharma), the teachings of Buddhism, to the community. The institution of the monkhood can be seen as an outlet for the community's desire to perform meritorious deeds. Women could best improve their moral state and

Modern Buddhist pilgrims visiting a pagoda at Ketku temple,
Southern Shan State, Myanmar.

hope for rebirth as men in their next incarnation by regularly giving food to the monks, attending preaching services, and offering their sons for ordination.

In day-to-day terms the monkhood's most important function was to offer boys and young men a rudimentary education in reading and writing and the principles of their faith. For this reason probably more than half the men of Siam, Myanmar, Laos, and Cambodia in the eighteenth century were functionally literate, at least able to read a simple piece of vernacular prose. To those who had the time or were unusually talented, monks offered advanced instruction not only in religious subjects, but also in the arts and sciences of Indian civilization, from mathematics and astronomy to poetics and medicine. Such instruction, however, was not often available. It was generally concentrated in the monasteries under royal or noble patronage in the towns, which could encompass large monastic populations, support paid teachers, and provide incentives for the best trained, offering them official positions or ecclesiastical advancement.

At every level of society, however, the monastery was the repository of whatever the population—which, after all, provided the monks—admired and needed in the way of sciences and arts. In out-of-the-way monasteries some of this learning was uncanonically connected with manipulating events, interpreting dreams, and setting astrological rules for conduct. In village society the institutions of monastery and monkhood provided a coherent model of religious action and belief that transcended local concerns and tended to draw the community together by ties wider and deeper than those provided by language and agricultural custom.

In each of the Theravada countries, the abbot and monks of the village monastery belonged to a hierarchical ecclesiastical organization, the sangha, that extended parallel with the civil hierarchy all the way to the king. The sangha was a channel for the transmission of information in both directions, up and down, and a vehicle of social advancement for those inside it. Monks frequently carried the complaints of their villages to higher authority, bypassing secular intermediaries, and the abbot was often the most respected leader in the village, sometimes more effective in his leadership than the headman, who deferred to him. Ambitious young men who found secular avenues to their advancement closed off by law and custom could, through ecclesiastical education and promotion, circumvent the restraints against social mobility and advance to positions of authority. Moreover, if they found the monastic life too encumbering, they could leave it and be "reborn" into the secular world at a point higher than the one at which they had left it.

The Buddhist hierarchy was for the most part organized territorially in each of the Theravada countries, save that the more remote forest-dwelling (Araññika) monks were organized separately. Each district and province had its own chief abbot, who was subject to the authority and discipline of the supreme patriarch *(sangharaja)* in the capital, whose decisions and injunctions were given force by civil authority. In Siam the monkhood was carefully supervised by the crown, and during some periods prince-monks held high ecclesiastical offices. Royal patronage, steadily strengthened, had reached the point by the seventeenth century where the monarchy was fully supporting religious education through the sponsorship of royal monasteries, which became virtual universities for religious and secular studies. The teachers of noble and royal sons and preceptors of monarchs found it difficult to remain free of political entanglements.

Popular literature and chronicle accounts, however, suggest that on the whole the sangha was ultimately a strong and independent influence in Theravadan Southeast Asia. Monks could, and probably did, mobilize public opinion for or against kings and officials. They had so established their moral influence by the last half of the eighteenth century in Siam that no king could rule without their approval. As if to mark the success of Theravada's rootedness and domestication in the region, monks from Sri Lanka visited Siam and Cambodia to obtain valid ordinations and copies of religious texts then lacking in Sri Lanka, the original source of Southeast Asian Theravadan Buddhism.

Vietnamese affinity with Chinese culture led to a predisposition to accept and adapt Mahayana Buddhism, because Vietnamese were more likely to read Buddhist scriptures and religious tracts written in classical Chinese than those written in Indian languages. Buddhism in Vietnam, moreover, intermingled with Daoism and with popular versions of Confucianism and existed as one element in a religious compound the Vietnamese called "the three religions" *(tam giao)*. The Chinese and Vietnamese religious worlds overlapped so much in the eighteenth and nineteenth centuries that many southern Chinese priests emigrated from Guangdong (Kwangtung) and Fujian (Fukien) to Vietnam and developed large followings there.

This harmony, although an integral part of Vietnamese Buddhist political thought, remained an unattainable ideal in the eighteenth century. At that time the Confucian court feared Buddhism not as a highly organized political rival but as an indirect ideological influence that could undermine the court's intricate bureaucratic order. The greatest writer of the period, Nguyen Du (1765–1820), under Buddhist influence, quite explicitly declared, in his "Song Summoning Back the Souls of the Dead," that in paradise "the superior and the lowly of this world are reseated in rank." In his poem he also reminded the wandering souls of former court officials that "the more prosperous you were, the more hatred you accumulated.... Carrying such a weight of hatred, do you really think you should seek a way to reincarnate yourselves?"

The court embarked on a policy of religious control, manipulating the recruitment of Buddhist monks and priests. To become a Buddhist ecclesiastic in Vietnam in the early nineteenth century, a peasant or scholar required an ordination certificate from the court. Applicants for these certificates had to travel to Hue, where they were given religious examinations. Furthermore, no Buddhist temple could be built in Vietnam at that time without the permission of the Nguyen court. The numbers of monks and acolytes at the larger temples were fixed by the laity, and village chiefs who did not report surplus monks at local temples were punished. The court itself paid the salaries of the head monks at the major temples. It endowed important temples with their land and even gave them their names. It bestowed on them tea, paper, incense, candles, and medicinal drugs, which it imported from China. At its command, Buddhist temples would celebrate a "land and water high mass" (in origin a Chinese ritual) for the souls of dead soldiers who had served the dynastic house. In addition to controlling existing temples, the court sponsored and financed the construction of new ones, usually in the vicinity of Hue, where they were easier to supervise. Hue's emergence as a center of Vietnamese Buddhism dated from this period of court patronage and control.

Considered purely as an organized institution, Mahayana Buddhism occupied a much more modest place in Vietnamese society than Theravada Buddhism did in Myanmar, Siamese, or Cambodian society. Needless to say, the heavily patronized Vietnamese sangha became little more than a political instrument of the Nguyen emperors. By itself it was poorly organized. There was no hierarchy of temples controlled by a central monkhood as well as by the court. There were no societywide Buddhist religious organizations to compete with the Confucian bureaucracy. The Vietnamese sangha of the early 1800s was small compared to those of the Theravada states.

The values of Confucian family worship and filial piety (which required the procreation of sons to continue the family and its ancestor worship) also made monasticism less popular in Vietnam than in neighboring societies. Widows and elderly women, however, commonly joined the important associations of temple nuns in every village that possessed a temple. These women did good works, participated in temple worship at least on the first and fifteenth days of every lunar month, and paid rice dues to the temple in the same way that village men contributed to village communal feasts. There were also major sources of salvation conceptualized in female terms, such as the Goddess of Mercy (Quan Am).

Village religious life tended to be more stable—and more parochial—in the north than in the south. Pilgrimages to religious shrines in the agricultural off-season were a feature of Vietnamese rural society. But such pilgrimages were especially popular in the south, in regions like Ca Mau and Rach Gia, where there were few long-established temples to cater to worshipers or where the monks did not yet have sufficient prestige.

Islam

MUSLIM Southeast Asia stretches in a 3,000-mile maritime crescent from the northern tip of Sumatra (sometimes known as *serambi Mekka,* the veranda of Mecca, where Islam had first taken root in the thirteenth century) to the islands of the southern Philippines. Though the faith had originated in desert Arabia in the early seventh century, internal developments in the intervening years and continuing expansion into other cultural areas, notably South Asia, had softened some of its austerities. New practices relating, for example, to saint veneration and mysticism found ready acceptance in much of island Southeast Asia by the eighteenth century. Spread mainly through trade and trading communities, Islam, in contrast to Buddhism, retained a close association with the maritime pathways that threaded the archipelago and with its port towns and riverine states.

Islam was organized in no sangha or church—despite the persistence of European observers in seeing "popes and priests" where there were none—but nonetheless possessed institutions, structures, and patterns of communication that knitted its adherents together and joined them to the heartland of Islam 4,000 miles away in the Middle East. Chief among these, perhaps, was simply the movement of people. Itinerant Arabs—teachers as well as traders—had been a feature of the port societies of the archipelago for centuries. Some had formed settled communities, and individuals were often found in religious advisory capacities at the courts of local rulers from Aceh to central Java or moving among the villagers as preachers or "holy men" able to offer healing and other services. Young males traveled regularly to teachers of this sort, Arab, South Asian, or indigenous, forming around them communities of scholars, known as *pondok* (after the huts they occupied) in peninsular Malaya and *pesantren* in Java. Some locations, such as Kelantan and Patani in the peninsula and Demak in north coastal Java, became particularly known for these institutions, attracting students from as far away as Cambodia and acting as dissemination points for a zealous form of the faith.

The *pondok*s were often centers, too, for another of the institutions that linked Muslims within and outside the area, the Sufi *tarekat*s, or orders of mysticism, based on direct apprehension of the divine through techniques elaborated by named teachers (*shaykh*s) of an often distant past. Sometimes to the disapproval of the scripturally rigorous, these afforded a more emotional approach to God than other more restrained forms of worship. Ubiquitous in the region, the largely male *tarekat* brotherhoods consisted mainly of followers centered on individual *shaykh*s who claimed spiritual lineages based on earlier teachers. Knowledge of belonging to a *tarekat* added to the sense of community provided by Islam.

Mosques in many styles: (above, top) Yogyakarta, Java, 1911. Typical Javanese ("Indies") style. (Above, bottom) Padang uplands, Sumatra, ca. 1890. Note the distinctive "buffalo horn" roof. (Facing page, top) Singapore, ca. 1900. Chinese style. (Facing page, bottom) Kuala Kangsar, Malaysia, ca. 1928. Modern "Saracenic" style.

1019. The Ubad Aiah Mosque, Kuala Kangsa

Yet another important form of physical movement for Islamic Southeast Asia, as sea communications strengthened during the eighteenth century, was the pilgrimage to Mecca, the hajj, one of the paramount duties of all Muslims able to undertake it. At the same time as it fulfilled profound spiritual goals, it conferred enhanced status and prestige on returning hajjis as well as exposing them to sometimes more rigorous forms of belief and practice. Some continued to live in Mecca, studying, writing, and teaching pupils from home.

Notwithstanding these generalizations, it is important to recognize that in the eighteenth century, Islam in island Southeast Asia was still in the process of gaining acceptance and was not always uncontested. Some places, Bali, for example, remained untouched by Islam and continued to adhere to earlier "Hindu–Buddhist" religious beliefs and practice or to an animism characterized by belief in ancestral spirits and spirits inhabiting the natural world. Even in Muslim areas, patterns of Islamic belief and practice varied considerably. It has become customary in Western writings about Java, and to a lesser extent elsewhere, to distinguish between two supposedly contrasting ways of "being Muslim." One is said to be characterized by the stricter observance and greater scriptural learning found among those termed *santri* (from the scholarly *pesantren* communities in Java); the other is associated with more heterogeneous forms of belief and practice, termed *abangan* in Java, mingling elements of animism, Hindu-Buddhism, and an often florid Sufi mysticism. Such sharp stereotypes should be treated with caution, for distinctions of this broad kind between the scripturally zealous and the less zealous existed in all Muslim societies, even Arabia.

Indeed it was in Arabia, in the mid–eighteenth century, that a puritanical movement arose aimed at cleansing Muslim society there of erroneous beliefs and practices, a movement that was to have repercussions in Southeast Asia. Known as Wahhabism, after its scholar-founder Muhammad Abdul Wahhab, it had filtered back to Southeast Asia late in the century principally through returning hajjis, who claimed on behalf of the *ulama* (scholars) the right to determine how an Islamic life ought properly to be lived, attacking moral backsliding and local practices held to contravene the *shari'a,* the laws based on the teachings of the Qur'an. The turbulent local conflict of this kind in west Sumatra in the early nineteenth century, termed by the Dutch the Padri War, led eventually to colonial rule when the Dutch intervened.

This kind of implicit or actual tension between the Islam of prescription and the Islam of practice was commonplace, if fluctuating, throughout the area as varying forms of Islamic authority waxed and waned. The numerous Malay states of the peninsula, Sumatra, the west Borneo coast and the smaller islands, lacking either the resources or the stimulus for central control, possessed little in the way of structured Islamic authority, though the sacral powers of their rulers did include responsibility for the defense and good governance of the faith. From time to time individual rulers and chiefs, for pious or other motives, might appoint officials such as state *mufti*s (law consultants) or attempt to control the appointment of local *kathi*s (judges) drawn from among the *ulama*.

For the most part, however, religious authority in these areas tended to dwell in those members of village society who, by their piety and some claim to learning, and perhaps through having made the pilgrimage to Mecca, were accepted as fit to exercise it—as imams and *khatib*s (prayer leaders and preachers) of mosques, officiants at weddings and funerals, religious teachers, and *guru tarekat* (spiritual teachers). The rural *ulama* thus described did not form a separate social class, though they were quite often among the wealthier members of the peasant society to which all belonged. In the absence of anything more than an attenuated religious officialdom, these states and principalities were only infrequently marked in the eighteenth century by institutionalized opposition between independent *ulama* and the state religious bureaucracy or between indigenous cultural forms, nominally Muslim, and an alien "Arab" Islam.

In Java, however, tensions between officially sanctioned Islamic strictness and local ways of being Muslim were evident at both state and popular levels. In the central Java kingdom of Yogyakarta, for example, principal inheritor in the last half of the eighteenth century of what was left of the old Mataram empire, the *kraton* (palace) establishment relied for the administration of Islam on an appointed hierarchy of officials, who functioned in effect as adjuncts of secular rule, staffing mosques, prayer houses, and religious courts—the "priesthood" of contemporary observers. Standing aloof from the *kraton* and often fiercely critical of imperfect secular governments and their dealings with the *kafir* (unbelieving) Dutch, under whose thrall Javanese rulers increasingly had fallen, the independent *ulama,* as charismatic teachers in often economically independent *pesantren* communities, formed a powerful focus for peasant discontent in times of trouble.

Throughout Islamic Southeast Asia's peasant society, the focus of village life was the village mosque or prayer house, where the men congregated for Friday prayers, met nightly during the fasting month of Ramadan (and at certain other times) to recite the Qur'an, and held the religious exercises associated with the Sufi *tarekat*s. For most youths it was usually also the sole place of education, where young boys learned by rote to recite the Qur'an and were taught the basic tenets of their faith. As in all Muslim agricultural societies, Islam colored but did not dominate the ritual cycle that marked planting and harvesting, feast and famine, birth and death. Most villages had special practitioners who employed a mix of Islamic and older skills to cure physical or spiritual ills or officiate at life's major junctures. Though educated and pious town- or court-based Muslims might frown at some of these practices, they formed an important part of the sense of belonging to a single religious community.

Christianity

From C. H. Forbes-Lindsay, *The Philippines*, Philadelphia, 1906

Confident Christianity: Manila Cathedral, 1906.
Note the carriage *(carromata)* in the foreground.

BY THE middle of the eighteenth century, both Catholic and Protestant Christianity were spreading across parts of Southeast Asia. Though in the nineteenth century the British were to forbid proselytization among the Muslims of the Malay Peninsula, they relied heavily on both Protestant and Catholic missions for the provision of education. The Dutch in the Netherlands Indies encouraged dissemination of Protestant religious institutions as part of their colonial penetration of the region. The Portuguese long before had brought Catholicism to the Spice Islands. French Catholic missionaries proselytized in northern and southern Vietnam (where by the eighteenth century they had made important conversions in some rural areas), Siam, and elsewhere, often openly challenging existing religious and political establishments and often persecuted by them.

By far the most important portal for Christianity, however, was the Philippines, where it was introduced early in the sixteenth century. The archipelago was colonized from Mexico at the end of that century in part to serve as a forward missionary station to convert China (a fantasy that was only reluctantly surrendered with the sinking of the Spanish Armada and military defeat at the hands of Protestant Holland) and in part to convert the *indios,* the natives of the archipelago. King Philip II believed passionately that to proselytize on behalf of the Roman Catholic Church was both his holy mission and the reason Spain had had such extraordinary success in colonizing the New World. Spain depended on dedicated members of religious orders—Augustinians, Dominicans, Franciscans, and Jesuits—to carry colonial control into the interior, the *bundok.* (These are all usually referred to as "friars," although technically the Jesuits are not friars, as theirs is not a mendicant order.) From the sixteenth century onward the friars preached and heard confession in the local vernaculars rather than in Spanish. Few other Spaniards came to the archipelago for more than brief tours of duty, and only these priests had a lifelong commitment to their mission abroad.

Over the centuries the famous Manila galleons carried Asian silks and other exotic commodities to the New World and brought "monks and silver"—

friars and Mexican and Peruvian pieces of eight—in the other direction. Spain's imperial impetus may have been spent, but its proselytizing zeal profoundly transformed the archipelago (with the exception of the Muslim south) into one of the most vibrant Roman Catholic communities in the world. The stone church in the village square, "earthquake baroque" in style, literally and figuratively dominated the landscape, bringing Filipino society "under the bells." The priest was the link between the indigenous population and a very small colonial establishment.

Making the archipelago "a showcase of the faith" shaped the archipelago's history. Friars owed allegiance to their ecclesiastical superiors, not Spanish colonial administrators or bishops. The friars had received from the pope the right to administer the sacraments and to occupy parishes free from any other supervision. In theory, they had come to the archipelago to establish new parishes before moving on to new mission fields, except that the Philippines was the end of the missionary line: there was no place else to go. The friars stayed; the orders became entrenched and, in some cases, rich. While the Council of Trent subsequently attempted to curb friar independence globally by ruling that any local bishop had the right of episcopal visitation in any parish, the friars in the archipelago held most of the power, since only they were willing to live and die there. Most of the parishes in the mid–eighteenth century were under the control of one or another of the orders; the threat to leave the archipelago en masse empowered them in any confrontation with the bishops, since temporal as well as religious authority would have collapsed with their departure.

This bureaucratic and administrative tension did not greatly affect the religious, ethical, and cultural significance of Catholicism for the individual or society. The *indios* developed an abiding faith in the omnipresence of God. Christianity became central to their lives, as an initially alien faith became domesticated. The *pasyon* (Passion) of Jesus has for centuries been experienced with intensity; death and redemption are a living reality to Filipinos. Flagellation and even crucifixion became for a devout few annual physical acts of remembrance. The virgin birth, Christ's crucifixion, and the resurrection suffused folk literature and traditional culture.

God was personalized and the creed internalized in ways that a peasant family could understand. Since God was the wise Father, the Virgin Mary the devoted Mother, and Christ the immediate Savior, a cosmic debt of gratitude (known in Tagalog as *utang na loob*) far exceeded any conceivable human repayment. The gap between the magnitude of Christ's crucifixion and the inadequacy of the individual's capacity to repay the Godhead prompted a continuing search for human and celestial intermediaries. Apostles, saints, martyrs, and the church itself were all brokers on life's journey.

Christianity thus supplied a life-affirming and communally embracing theology. It brought with it a code of behavior, a set of holidays, a way to relate an individual's own life to transcendent ethical values. The various religious orders established schools and universities, provided charitable organizations, and created an artistic, architectural, and cultural context for life. Elsewhere in Southeast Asia, Christianity was often seen as a threat, a challenge, a discontinuity; in the Philippine archipelago it became the way of life.

Animism and the Localization of World Religions

UNSURPRISINGLY, the world religions that enjoyed such a powerful presence in eighteenth-century Southeast Asia—Buddhism, Islam, and Christianity—found it necessary to accommodate themselves to preexisting beliefs about the natural and supernatural worlds, and to the life and culture of environments and societies very different from those of India, Arabia, and Europe, from which they had spread. Everywhere in the region a wide variety of spirit beliefs and practices had long characterized the daily and seasonal life of most communities, marked by the precariousness of climate and harvests, sickness and bereavement, personal misfortune and occasional good luck. Such complexes of folk beliefs, not confined to Southeast Asia, were first termed "animism" by mid-nineteenth-century Western social theorists, from the Latin word *anima,* meaning breath or soul. Animists, in this sense, believe that departed ancestors and everything in nature—from plants and animals to features of the landscape—are inhabited by spirits or souls through which they can influence human affairs, making them amenable to human supplication and propitiation.

Though the purpose of animistic ritual was less to adorn life than to try to control the conditions in which it was lived, it led to rich and colorful accompaniments to mundane existence in Southeast Asia, in ways that helped to unite communities as well as safeguard them from misfortune. Life-cycle rituals ensured that the passages into and out of life, birth and death, were appropriately marked, and the agricultural year was punctuated by seasonal ceremonies aimed at ensuring good harvests, placating the soul of the rice during harvesting, and acknowledging the power of sea and river spirits over the fortunes of fishermen. Illness and emotional disturbance, in societies with little in the way of elaborate medicines or understanding of the causes of disease, required the intervention of specialist healers and shamans to deal with the spirit possession of those affected. Belief in the power and presence of spirits and the need to cajole, reward, and placate them led to the development of song, poetry, invocation, and dance-drama directed toward praising the spirits and reciting the virtues of the community.

Rather than being seen as in conflict with Buddhism, Islam, or Christianity, many animist practices, and sometimes even the beliefs that underlay them, were perceived by most eighteenth-century functionaries of the established religions as at least akin to their own and capable of a measure of acceptance—

as part, indeed, of a single continuum reflecting humankind's attempts to grasp and come to terms with unfathomable and unseen powers. Theravada monks in the lowland villages of Myanmar, Siam, and Cambodia, while maintaining the primacy of Buddhism, also provided essentially the same assistance as shamans did in the uplands. Sufi Muslim teachers in central Java accommodated without difficulty elements of local mystical beliefs, uniting, for example, the medieval Arabic scholar Ibn al-Arabi's ideas about the five "grades of being" with "Javanist" pantheism. In the Philippines, peasant farmers obtained from Catholic priests the preplanting blessing of their rice seed that had once been provided by local shamans. Nor was the traffic one-way only. Malay *bomoh*s (spirit doctors) readily incorporated Qur'anic verses into their incantations and inserted them in the protective amulets they gave the sick who came to consult them (as Filipinos included tags of church Latin in their own protective *anting-anting*), while Javanese shadow puppet masters introduced Islamic emphases into their performances of the Ramayana and Mahabharata cycles of stories.

Only later, mainly toward the end of the nineteenth century, did the doctrinal and scriptural concerns of reformist movements prompt serious attempts to purge religious belief and practice of local, noncanonical elements associated with animism. The tensions generated by these attempts, especially in Islamic areas, were to provide one of the region's principal impulses to social as well as ideological change.

Further Readings

Keyes, Charles, ed. *Reshaping Local Worlds: Rural Elites and Culture Change in Southeast Asia.* New Haven, 1991.

Keyes, Charles F., and E. Valentine Daniel, eds. *Karma: An Anthropological Inquiry.* Berkeley, 1983.

Lopez, Donald S., Jr. *The Story of Buddhism: A Concise Guide to Its History and Teachings.* San Francisco, 2001.

Mendelson, E. Michael. *Sangha and State in Burma: A Study of Monastic Sectarianism and Leadership.* Ed. John P. Ferguson. Ithaca, 1975.

Riddell, Peter G. *Islam in the Malay-Indonesian World: Transmission and Responses.* London, 2001.

Rafael, Vicente. *Contracting Colonialism: Translation and Christian Conversion in Tagalog Society under Early Spanish Rule.* Durham, N.C., 1993.

Schumacher, John N. *Readings in Philippine Church History.* Quezon City, 1987.

Swearer, Donald K. *The Buddhist World of Southeast Asia.* Rev. ed. Albany, 1995.

"Symposium on Malay Identity." *Journal of Southeast Asian Studies* 32, 3 (October 2001): 295–395.

Chapter 3

✺

The Struggle for
Political Authority

IN THE ERA before the invention of the nation-state, eighteenth-century Southeast Asian monarchies were comparable to monarchies elsewhere in aspiring to be universal empires. Their symbolic and ideological self-images emphasized their connections to world religions or to global political traditions with universal claims. Sultan Iskandar Thani (1637–1641) of Aceh, an Islamic monarchy at the northern end of Sumatra, publicly said that he was "the king of the whole world, shining like the sun at midday," and descended from Alexander the Great, the world conqueror of centuries earlier, who, in the Islamic tradition, had prefigured the global establishment of divine law. Other ruling houses in the Malay world claimed descent from Alexander as well. Similarly, Myanmar court genealogists tried to show that Myanmar's kings were descended from Gautama, the founder of Buddhism. And Vietnamese rebels like the Tayson brothers in the 1770s justified their rebellion by claiming that they would lead Vietnam out of "disorder" into the condition of "great peace" over which the mythic Chinese sage-emperors had once presided, thousands of years earlier.

All this was not very different from the behavior of King Louis XIV of France, who in the early 1700s not only identified himself with the god Apollo but also took the sun as his image, because the sun produced universal life and joy. The difficulties of creating political legitimacy in the centuries before the appearance of mass citizenship and nationalism need more scholarly attention than they usually get. So do recurrences of situations in which ruling dynasties, if not dominant social classes, fail to establish their own ideas or moral credentials as unchallenged in the eyes of the people they are trying to govern. "Internationalizing" a monarchy's practices by associating them with one or more symbolic world systems outside Southeast Asia was one way of attempting to demonstrate legitimacy.

Southeast Asia's Universal Monarchies

IT IS IMPORTANT to emphasize what Southeast Asian political systems in the 1700s had in common with political life elsewhere because there has been an enduring tendency among Western writers to conceptualize them in exotic, or at least psychologically distancing, terms. Western strategies for explaining the politics of Southeast Asia continue to circulate even in Southeast Asia itself, so it is probably necessary to summarize some of them.

There was, first of all, the theory of "Oriental despotism." Its beginnings could be found in Aristotle's claim (in book 3 of his *Politics*) that "barbarians" were more servile than Greeks, Asians more servile than Europeans. This theory haunted Vincentius Sangermano, the Italian priest who lived in Myanmar from 1783 to 1806, when the monarchy there was in its prime. Sangermano's analysis of the "Burmese Empire," published in Rome in 1833, argued that the king of Myanmar was a "despot" whose subjects were his "slaves." The king was the absolute lord of their "lives, properties, and personal services"; without any process of law, he could kill anybody who happened "to incur his displeasure."

Sangermano's work demonstrated the European belief, which had matured in the writings of famous eighteenth-century thinkers like Montesquieu, that Asian political systems in general were tyrannical. Their tyranny was thought to lie in their supposed lack of checks on royal power, such as strong hereditary nobilities or clearly defined private property rights. This European notion of "Oriental despotisms," by theorizing that no private property owners had ever existed in the Orient, was obviously very useful to colonizers who wanted to seize territory in Asia. But it distorted the facts, and its conception of power as total and all-encompassing was so crude as to rob it of any capacity to explain specific political activities or institutions in the Asian countries to which it was applied.

As an antidote, more modern scholars have minimized the amount of centralized power that Southeast Asian monarchies commanded. They have proposed instead that many of Southeast Asia's monarchies were sponsors of religious salvation for their peoples, not tyrannies. They were, in one well-known formulation, theater states: spectacle and ceremony were their central concerns. Rituals were not enacted to strengthen the monarchy; on the contrary, the monarchy existed to enact rituals. Southeast Asian kings, queens, and priests were not all-grasping potentates so much as the impresarios and directors of the theatrical public effort to replicate the cosmic order on earth, in human terms.

In one metaphorical extension of this, Stanley Tambiah has suggested that Theravada Buddhist polities (including Myanmar, Siam, and Cambodia) were "galactic polities" whose rulers integrated their kingdoms by establishing favorable conditions for the Buddhist quest for enlightenment to flourish through their patronage of temples and monks.

But both the base and the sublime pictures of preindustrial Southeast Asian politics overlook the ways in which wars and trade-driven economic growth that encouraged both social and geographic mobility could disrupt authority structures in Southeast Asia, as they did elsewhere. Still other theories of Southeast Asian monarchies, more concerned with mundane economics than with ritual processes, have proposed that royal power was far from absolute and had to be shared, albeit in ways that contemporary constitutional lawyers would not formulate or admit. In Southeast Asian "contest states," as Michael Adas has called them, the monarchy might claim a monopoly of power. But such monarchs were never free of practical struggles with various elite factions, and even village leaders, over the control of manpower and revenues. In this scenario the struggle for political authority reduced itself almost to a stalemate among contending power centers, interrupted only occasionally by overachieving dynasty builders and heroic people of action.

The problem is that virtually all political systems are both theatrical and contested in varying degrees. Yet even friendly European analysts were frustrated by Southeast Asian monarchies' apparent peculiarities: their mixtures of authority principles seemed to contradict European classifications. A French book about Vietnam and Cambodia published in 1874 noted that the Vietnamese had recruited some of their government officials by civil service examinations ever since the eleventh century. It concluded in baffled terms that Vietnam was both an "academic democracy" and a land of "hereditary Caesars," an inescapably strange blend of "tyrannies" and "precious liberties."

All these theoretical representations of the old Southeast Asian monarchies—as Oriental despotisms, as theater states, as galactic polities, as contest states, or as academic democracies—have one thing in common. They agree that preindustrial Southeast Asian monarchies were not what we imagine a modern state to be. Influenced by the great German scholar Max Weber, we think of the modern state as a reason-based compulsory political association, with a sovereign legal personality, in which authority is relatively impersonal and rule-bound; is expressed in permanent administrative, military, and judicial institutions; employs a coercive apparatus that monopolizes all legitimate violence; is supreme within a precisely defined territory; and issues passports to its citizens. But it should come as no surprise that Southeast Asian polities in the 1700s diverged from such a model. No political systems of this idealized kind existed in fully realized form anywhere in the world before the late nineteenth century—if then.

People Scarcity and Modes of Defining Authority

THE REAL originality of Southeast Asian politics in the 1700s does not lie in monarchies' universal claims. It is to be found in the regional juxtaposition of so many different approaches to universal ideals. Southeast Asia was historically unique in harboring a large number of monarchies, all much more moderately sized than the Holy Roman Empire or China or Mughal India or the Ottoman empire, which shared the same material environment but differentiated themselves by their commitments to the standards of universality of one of the world's major creeds—Hinduism, Buddhism, Confucianism, Islam, or Christianity—within a relatively limited geographic compass. No other region of the world of this size had such a multiplicity of political universalisms. There was not even a common elite language to link the monarchies to each other, unlike the classical Arabic of the Middle Eastern empires or the Latin once shared by European monarchies.

Apart from the variety of the world systems to which Southeast Asian monarchies attached themselves, they had a second arresting feature that affected their politics. That was their relative shortage of people. In the eighteenth century Southeast Asia probably had roughly half the population density of Europe at that time. Certainly its population densities were well below those of China or India. This scarcity of labor may not have meant full-fledged legal freedom for Southeast Asian commoners, but it did give them informal bargaining power. Various rulers' struggles to create and keep legitimacy could not be confined to the elite groups who controlled their societies' economic surpluses. The struggles had to be extended downward to the laboring people who might otherwise flee into the plentiful forests or escape by sea.

The elite need to accommodate commoners' informal bargaining power can be found in the documents of culturally very different governments. Siamese politics in the 1700s were quite characteristic of Southeast Asia as a whole in being dominated by the court's fears that supplies of peasant labor would shrink, either through alienation or through capture by rival political forces. A Siamese royal decree of 1717 stipulated that if a town governor found peasants hiding in the forest, he was to find out who had oppressed them and then send the name of the oppressor to the capital. In 1784 the governor of Nakhon Sithammarat was even told to "persuade" rather than to compel "lazy" peasants who had run away to the forests and the hills to return to inhabited areas. He was also informed that he would be punished if he allowed working peasants to be captured and taken away by "Vietnamese, pirates, or enemies."

Other rulers, despite their different symbolic worlds, had the same anxieties. As early as the fifteenth century, Vietnamese court regulations made it clear that the administrative (in)competence of local officials would be measured by the numbers of peasants who had fled their jurisdictions. The peasants' "love" of their local officials would be quantified in this way to provide data for promoting or dismissing officials. Spanish governors of the Philippines, even farther removed from the symbolic world of Siamese and Vietnamese monarchs, were also obsessed by the need to keep villagers in place (requiring them to carry "passports" to travel or change residency) and haunted by the fear of "vagabonds" who lived outside the reach of church and state.

The favorable ratio of space to people did not just enable Southeast Asian commoners to flee or hide. It also allowed them to become part of a considerable floating population of nonconformists. Such nonconformists adopted what William Koenig calls "alternative social statuses" to those of the established order and sometimes refused to perform the established order's labor services. Commoners who were presumed to have special and politically unpredictable magical powers provided a core group for such floating populations. In Myanmar, possessors of magic included tattoo artists, entertainers, wizards, and soothsayers; in Java, they might include weaponsmiths, goldsmiths, puppeteers, or blind seers. A quite different alternative social status was that of the bandit chiefs who carved out independent existences for themselves in areas the courts could not control and then imitated the courts' own practices of levy and pillage in the territories they dominated. Javanese stories told of kings and saints who had begun their careers as bandits. Sometimes bandit leaders in Java were even converted into village headmen, in recognition of the local influence they already enjoyed.

In general the diversity of the global creeds Southeast Asian rulers used to legitimate themselves made their monarchies both expressions of local political genius and variations on the universal themes of rulership proper to world systems stretching beyond the region. But this doubleness in their histories should not suggest that the peoples they ruled were compartmentalized. Southeast Asia's numerous trading entrepôts allowed flexibility in social identity; the different peoples of the region may not have been as distinguishable from each other in 1750 as they are today. The shared political environment of people scarcity forced most major Southeast Asian authority structures to employ the same combination of methods of legitimation—moral persuasion, physical coercion, material inducements—in roughly similar proportions, despite the apparent incompatibilities in their official religions. In nearly all Southeast Asian monarchies, the monarchs had to convince their subjects that they had extraordinary powers. The rules of the political game required them to appear to perform at a high level under perpetual scrutiny, like Olympic athletes now, or lose their following. Poor rulers were even publicly derided as physically ugly. A Javanese royal chronicle said of the unfortunate Amangkurat III (1703–1708) that his face had lost its gleam and become drawn, "like a Chinaman" with a stomachache.

Contemporary societies expect the primary human need for justice based on moral impartiality to be satisfied by written constitutions and charters of rights. In preindustrial Southeast Asia, as in the universal empires elsewhere, the monarchies themselves had much of the formal responsibility for satisfying this need. Numerous literary texts therefore tried to create ideal examples for rulers in order to guide their behavior. In the Malay world such works might be worshipful accounts of the Islamic prophets. These would instruct rulers to be knowledgeable, brave, wary of unlawful innovations, and, above all, just. The sultan of Aceh had a personal religious adviser, based on a similar position in the Ottoman empire, and sometimes his soldiers even dressed like Ottoman warriors, but what the sultan was required to remember was that one day of

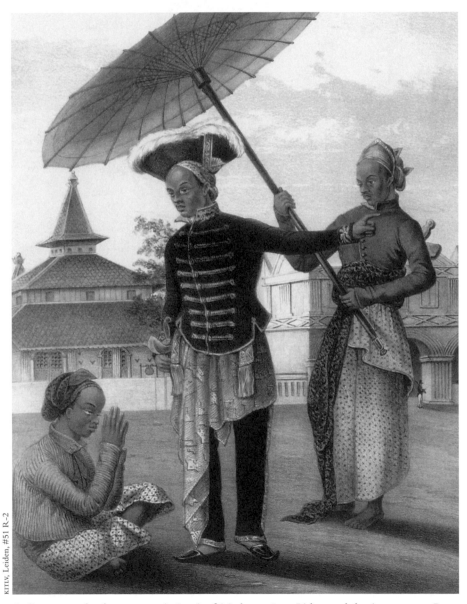

KITLV, Leiden, #51 R–2

Indigenous rule: the *pangeran* (prince) of Madura, 1850s. Lithograph by Auguste van Pers.

Courtesy of Philippine Department of Tourism

Colonial citadel: Intramuros, Manila. The image over the gate is of St. James the "Moor killer."

working justice by the ruler was equal, in God's eyes, to sixty performances of the pilgrimage to Mecca.

Similar Vietnamese essays of guidance for rulers in the 1700s, for their part, might depict the career of Confucius (Kongfuzi, 551–479 B.C.E.) as justice minister in a small north Chinese principality over two thousand years earlier. They would point out that Confucius allowed all the people to express their opinions and then, sage that he was, reconciled them. The royal function of reconciliation even furthered cosmic stability. The written form of the Sino-Vietnamese word for "king" *(vuong)* suggested the need to connect heaven, earth, and people. Its three horizontal lines represented the three elements that were to be reconciled, and its single vertical line, linking the three horizontal lines, stood for the king himself. To some extent this was a Confucian variation of the Javanese Islamic belief that the king was God's "screen" *(warana)* on earth, the screen through which people must pass to reach God and through which God must pass to reach people.

In the Theravada polities of Myanmar, Siam, and Cambodia, kings buttressed their rule by the public aspiration to be universal monarchs *(cakravartin)* who conquered the world through their righteousness. This was a Buddhist

58

adaptation of an older, more bellicose Hindu idea. The standard appellation of the king of Myanmar was "king of righteousness." Symbolizing the transcendental natural and moral law of the universe, the Buddhist monarchs also occasionally stimulated the popular belief that they were self-denying saints (bodhisattvas).

The outstanding Southeast Asian exception to this political pursuit of moral universalism in the 1700s appeared to be the Spanish-controlled Philippines. The European monarchy that had seized the Philippines in the 1500s did conform to the region's political pattern by seeing itself as universal, even if its global ambitions differed from the more modest aims of its Southeast Asian royal neighbors. The kings who annexed the Philippines at that time, after one of whom (Philip II) the country is named, were told by their advisers that they were ordained by God to be a world monarchy, obliged to destroy both Lutheranism and Islam. Spain governed the Philippines from a walled city inside present-day Manila, whose military nerve center, Fort Santiago, even had a stone carving above its main gate (still visible) of the saint whose business it was to slay Muslims.

But before the Spanish arrived, although there were "chiefs" (*datus*) with personal followings, most of the Philippines did not have an indigenous supralocal authority structure comparable to the power hierarchies elsewhere in Southeast Asia that were translating world creeds into local institutions. The Philippines had been geographically beyond the reach of major Hindu, Buddhist, or Confucian influences. The modest Islamic sultanates in the south, in Sulu and on Mindanao, had not yet incorporated the rest of the Philippines into an Islamic world system; when the Spaniards took Manila in 1570, it had only recently come under Muslim rule. Yet the Catholic Church and its friars, as the agents of a Spanish colonial order aimed at religious conversion, created a Philippine politics similar to the Southeast Asian pattern by providing an ideology of authority and a language of morality in which political obedience acquired a universalistic, rather than a purely local, flavor.

It is not easy to tell how effective the various mythologies of authority really were. Even in contemporary states, with their legions of skilled polltakers, it is virtually impossible to answer the question of the degree to which the various classes in society genuinely internalize the norms, values, and beliefs that legitimate the social order. It is fatally easy to confuse practical acceptance, in which subordinate groups comply with power because they see no realistic alternative, with normative acceptance, in which such groups internalize the moral expectations of the ruling elite and regard their own positions as proper. Southeast Asian rulers themselves often had few illusions about public commitment to their institutions. The emperor Tu-duc, in nineteenth-century Vietnam, observed that the respect the Vietnamese had given to his predecessor emperors in the 1700s had become a dispirited routine, not very different from the way irreligious people still mechanically made offerings of steamed rice cones in Buddhist temples.

Political Mobilization and the Slavery Issue

SOUTHEAST ASIA's mainland monarchies in this period were nevertheless better able to mobilize and concentrate political power over space and people than their counterparts in maritime Southeast Asia, with their longer, more vulnerable coastlines. The trend toward territorial consolidation in mainland Southeast Asia was impressive. As Victor Lieberman has shown, there were as many as twenty-two independent mainland monarchies in 1400 but only three major contending imperial systems—those of Myanmar, Siam, and Vietnam— by the end of the 1600s. In fact, the Myanmar, Siamese, and Vietnamese were all to achieve their modern unified national territories by the early 1800s at the latest, before such major European peoples as the Germans or the Italians had done so. The mainland monarchies were efficient enough to fight and win major wars with the Qing empire of China at the very moment of that empire's own triumphant annexations of Xinjiang and Tibet. In its wars with China in the 1760s, over the allegiance of Shan border princes who were vassals of both courts, Myanmar's armies outfought three invading armies from China. They trapped the last one at Kaungton and forced it to sue for peace. In Vietnam the Quang-trung emperor is said to have been able to mobilize an army of more than one hundred thousand soldiers by a rigorous system of conscription. He repeated Myanmar's feat of defeating an invasion from China at Dong Da in northern Vietnam in 1789.

The centralization of authority in the archipelago was less impressive. The island world had been the center of the global spice trade, which made it the primary target of manipulative and often predatory European trading empires, and it was easier to infiltrate, lacking the mainland monarchies' more concentrated big river valley populations. From its original base on Java, the Dutch East India Company (VOC) had put so much pressure on Javanese rulers that by 1749 the kingdom of Mataram had become a Dutch vassal, and by 1755 central Java was split into two regimes, one at Surakarta and one at Yogyakarta. But in addition to external pressures, many of maritime Southeast Asia's societies were, in Barbara Andaya's words, seminomadic. There were many places in the archipelago to which disgruntled subjects could flee from oppressive rulers or masters, to whom they were only conditionally loyal. There were even traditions of group flight, in which fleets of Buginese and Makasars fled Sulawesi for places as far west as Sumatra or the Malay Peninsula. In the Philippines, the precolonial term for coastal Tagalog communities was identical with the term for a large type of boat *(balangay),* metaphorically significant even if it does not actually confirm a pattern of frequent migrations. Their Spanish rulers tried to subdue their presumed mobility by subordinating them to a more place-bound administrative hierarchy of church-centered municipalities *(pueblos)* and provinces.

The essential point is that in both mainland and maritime Southeast Asia political authority's universal claims could both strengthen it and weaken it. Universal value systems could certainly be used to intensify acceptance of hierarchy and to reproduce relations of domination and control. But they could also be used, as Vicente Rafael points out for Christianity in the Philippines, to provide people with a language for conceptualizing the limits of political domination. They might facilitate the articulation of popular resistance as well as condition people to surrender to higher authority. Neither Islam nor Confucianism had ecclesiastical establishments of the Catholic or Buddhist kind. But all these ethical communities relied on scriptural forms of spiritual teachings, originating elsewhere, that kings, emperors, and sultans could not control.

Political critics might be relative insiders, rather than the radical outsiders, ranging from Jacobin revolutionaries to propertyless proletarians, that modern Western political theory commonly celebrates. Often their self-representation would be that of wise people whose politics had been supposedly purified of personal desire, the opposite of contemporary democratic modes of political self-promotion that feature incessant electioneering and the advocacy of specific social and economic interests. Theravada Buddhist ethics, for example, regarded aggressive competition for political power as immoral, a reflection of the vices of greed and anger; people who ruled supposedly embodied merit based on past good deeds.

Such attitudes hardly excluded political ambition and political criticism; they simply required them to be formulated in idealized ways. The Vietnamese Confucian "gentleman," as the philosopher Le Quy Don (1726–1784) described him, had to wait "calmly" for political power to pass "naturally" to him after his virtue and reputation had been successfully established in the eyes of "court and countryside" alike. In practice this might refer to a classical scholar who had withdrawn from one ruler's court in order to advise a military commander who wished to "save the age" by setting up another. Would-be Javanese usurpers, whether princes or commoners, might withdraw to the forests or to certain villages to prepare themselves to be "just kings" *(ratu adil)*. They could take advantage of the Hindu belief in a cycle of good and evil world periods and Islamic beliefs in a coming messiah who would end moral decline with a program of righteousness. More quietly, all over Southeast Asia, there were also obliquely questioning encounters between Islamic religious scholars and more worldly sultans and district chiefs, or between Buddhist monks and more worldly kings, or between Catholic priests and Spanish colonial administrators less associated with God's will, or between "uncrowned" village teachers and only nominally Confucian Vietnamese rulers.

The universalism of Southeast Asia's court creeds implied the conviction that all human beings might accede to truth and salvation. This principle prefigured the idea of freedom, but the idea remained undeveloped in pre-industrial Southeast Asia. More particularly, the relative scarcity of labor had paradoxical effects. If it gave informal bargaining power to commoners, it also created pressures for various types of compulsory labor. Indeed, as Anthony Reid has shown, transfers of captive peoples, including a regional trade in slaves, were the major form of labor mobility in Southeast Asia before 1800.

The English word "slave" hardly begins to do justice to the varied Southeast Asian terms and practices of unfree labor, hardly any of which resembled the more famous plantation slavery of the Americas in the same period. By one British estimate, up to one-third of the Siamese population in the mid-1800s were slaves. Slaves were probably a majority of the population of Dutch-ruled Batavia and Makasar in the 1700s, indeed perhaps a majority of the entire urban population of Southeast Asia once Chinese, Indians, Arabs, and Europeans were subtracted. The single island of Bali may have exported at least one hundred thousand of its people as slaves between 1620 and 1830, while raiders from Sulu captured, as slaves, over one hundred thousand Filipinos in the eighteenth and early nineteenth centuries.

There were hereditary and nonhereditary slaves as well as temporary and permanent ones. Debt bondage, highly exotic to Westerners, was a major form of enslavement. Men were legally entitled to sell themselves, their wives, or their children to other people (sometimes their own relatives) in order to repay debts or to acquire the money to pay fines, a common judicial penalty under Southeast Asian laws. Interest-bearing slaves did not necessarily have to serve their masters; provided they paid their interest to them, they could continue to live as they pleased. Hereditary slaves were usually people captured in war or special types like Myanmar's temple slaves (the descendants of people donated to temples by kings and others). Malay legal codes characteristically devoted about one-quarter of their attention to questions of slavery, viewing slaves as property. Even the legal codes of societies where slavery was waning in the 1700s, such as Vietnam, went into considerable detail about the different sources and natures of slaves. The Vietnamese law code that was in effect from the late 1400s through the end of the 1700s distinguished among "government" slaves (punished for having committed crimes), poor people who had sold themselves into bondage for economic reasons, prisoner-of-war slaves (who in Vietnam were largely Chams or Chinese), and hill country minorities, who might be "stolen" by Vietnamese landlords for purposes of conversion into unfree labor.

Unlike ancient Athens or the eighteenth-century United States, few Southeast Asian societies made absolute distinctions between slavery and freedom. Villagers who voluntarily surrendered their freedom to more powerful people often did so to gain protection and exemption from taxes, trading one form of subordination for another. Conversely, trading cities in the archipelago like Banten, Aceh, Palembang, Makasar, and Jolo grew by freeing their slaves, for which there were clear procedures in local legal codes, and then incorporating them into the dominant society.

Strong Southeast Asian monarchs tried to limit the proliferation of slaves when this threatened their tax bases. Myanmar kings were especially sensitive to the threat that crown service family members might escape from royal service by selling themselves to powerful moneylending families. The major Vietnamese law code stipulated that any Vietnamese officeholders who acquired slaves without permission from the court would be demoted or dismissed. And in the Philippines, Spanish bishops denounced slavery as a betrayal of the Spanish conscience. From the late 1500s, Spanish colonial laws rather ineffectively prohibited the buying and selling of non-Muslim slaves at least, ordering that existing ones be restored to their condition of "natural liberty."

Some Western thinkers have argued that freedom "failed" in the non-Western world, before the industrial age, because slavery there was insufficiently evil or morally degrading, compared to the two Western slave societies (Athens and America) that produced so much democratic theory. In this view Southeast Asia's slavery was too conditional to stimulate its antithesis, the progressive esteem of individual liberty. In societies where slavery was only one oppressive option in a complex social environment of many kinds of graded vertical ties and mutual obligations between high and low, or creditors and debtors, it may have been more difficult to formulate strong conceptions of personal freedom before the law. This hypothesis deserves further comparative analysis. But Reid has suggested that in at least some parts of the Malay world, including Borneo, Sulawesi, and the Philippines, if not Java, a legal concept of the free person or the nonslave did begin to emerge. It was expressed in a term *(merdeka)* derived from Sanskrit that later came to function, among Indonesian and Malay nationalists, as the term for freedom from colonial rule or independence.

Controlling People below and beyond the Court

THE HISTORY of power outside Southeast Asian courts, in the provinces and villages, raises the question of the exact weight of political authority and its effects in a different way. European colonial observers who wanted to see a ray of light in their own gloomy obsession with "Oriental despotisms" sometimes romanticized Southeast Asian village chiefs or headmen. These could be depicted by such Europeans as the potential tribunes of their fellow villagers, resisting the ravages of the monarchs above them. Here colonial observers were influenced by their pictures of European history itself, in which feudal magnates had restricted the power of bad kings. Charles Lemire, in *La Cochin-chine française et le royaume Cambodge* (1888), typically asserted that Vietnamese

KITLV, Leiden, #3617

Agents of rule: state grandees of Lombok, 1865.

village leaders "tempered" the demands of their courts, achieving the same balancing functions as had allegedly been found earlier in French feudalism. Twentieth-century Southeast Asian patriots, such as Mohammad Hatta of Indonesia, echoed this theme; Hatta said in 1956 that precolonial Indonesian rulers had been autocratic but that Indonesia's villages had preserved an "indigenous democracy" based on traditional custom.

Phan Huy Chu (1782–1840), the author of "A Classified Survey of the Institutions of Successive Courts," perhaps precolonial Vietnam's greatest single work of political theory, saw matters quite differently. In building a just and equitable society, Phan suggested, weak monarchs were the danger, not strong ones. Only the king could keep taxes and population registers impartially "balanced" and up to date. Under no circumstances were village chiefs to be allowed to distort or gerrymander them. A belief that only central authority could bring an ideal political order into existence was probably widespread, even in the villages. In the Malay system—quite different from Vietnam's—where the real power of a sultan might be little greater than that of some of his senior district chiefs, there was also a general acceptance of the ruler's office, if not necessarily of his person, as formal political head. It was to the advantage of the chiefs to maintain the sultanate as the symbol and source of legitimacy, as a basis for their position with respect to each other, as a source of reward in dynastic maneuvering, and as the embodiment of the larger political whole, with its advantages for trade and defense.

Any history of the arbitrary uses of authority in Southeast Asia is, as Phan Huy Chu hinted, incomplete if it does not look at local as well as national versions of power. In the customary Malay village, consisting of one or more groups of kinfolk linked by intermarriage, the position of primary authority fell to the headman *(penghulu)*. He was usually a member of the principal or founding family, and often had assumed the office by direct inheritance. (In the Minangkabau part of Sumatra, the headmen, although male, were the title-holding representatives of their matrilineages, whose senior women controlled the family property.)

The headmen were more frequently peasants than aristocrats. Their appointments might in effect be hereditary, but they were the explicit gifts of the ruler, sometimes accompanied by the ruler's sealed documents of authority. This imprimatur and the suggestion of external sanction it carried gave the headmen what little legitimate coercive authority they had. Apart from this, headmen relied for the most part on the mobilization of social disapproval and on the respect they earned from family status, economic success, piety, or unusual force of personality, backed up by only such force as they and their immediate followers could wield. Along with other village notables, they had to keep the peace in the villages and surrender serious wrongdoers to the district chief, provide tribute labor and sometimes produce from their villages, allocate surplus land, and function as judges. Aided and sometimes chastened by the presence of the religious teachers at the local mosque, the headmen were obliged (as the sixteenth-century Melaka code stipulated) to understand religious law, the principles of natural justice, the principles of right conduct, and customary law if they wished to be termed "men."

All this suggested restraint. But when European colonial regimes, beginning with Spain in the Philippines, began to clarify this sort of local hereditary power, they also clarified how it could be misused. The Spanish administration in the Philippines retained the local chief *(datu)*, but renamed him village headman *(cabeza de barangay)*, coopting him by increasing his privileges and guaranteeing his status. The elders of the key families in each village reshaped the system the Spanish imposed to make it accord with the high value placed on consensus, one reason why later patriots might find "democratic" traditions in village life. The headmanship, initially hereditary, came in time to be rotated among the elders who formed the village elite *(principalía)*. From them the municipal mayor, the highest indigenous official under the Spanish colonial administration and the mediator (with the priest) of relations between the foreigners above him and the villagers below him, was also selected. The mayor ruled the *pueblo,* an administrative unit composed of a church and several villages and at least five hundred adult "tribute" payers, from whom he had to squeeze tax revenues, goods, and corvée labor for his superiors, as well as his own reimbursement. By the middle of the 1700s, the village elite from which the mayors and headmen came was becoming increasingly indistinguishable from a wealthy landholding class. Their moneylending capacity and inherited titles to land gave them extraordinary power over all aspects of rural life.

Local politics everywhere were torn by one obvious tension: the need to reconcile the villagers' own desire for harmony, if not consensus, among themselves, with the demands of courts and national elites (monarchs, nobles, gentry from outside the villages) for taxes and tribute, especially labor services. Local abuses of authority, when they disrupted village life in their efforts to satisfy outside pressures, might merely reflect political pathologies higher up in the system. A complicating factor was that in large parts of eighteenth-century Southeast Asia, from Java to Myanmar to Vietnam, villages were parts of court appanage systems: that is, regions assigned to court officials as "cash cows" from which they were supposed to remunerate themselves and finance their official activities. Centralized national budgets, from which rulers paid money salaries directly to the officials who served them, belonged to a more bureaucratic future.

In Java, for instance, large villages might be divided into appanages for more than one official; each of these officials might in turn have a tax-collecting representative in the village. Village headmen in central Myanmar, who generally inherited their offices, reported not to district chiefs, as in Malaya, but to a gentry of hereditary officials *(myothugyi)* in charge of towns with rural hinterlands, who were supposed to apportion the villagers' quotas for corvée, military service, and other revenues as received from the provincial courts they served. They were also required to keep registers of all the people in their jurisdictions, including their names, ages, dates of birth, and, when relevant, their crown service groups. Countrywide censuses like the one of 1783 might try to calculate the number of households in Myanmar as a whole as well as their hereditary obligations, but it was the gentry elite who had to pass down national demands for labor service. One function of captured and enslaved prisoners of war was to soften labor service pressures from above on existing villages.

At other times, local abuses of power were genuinely local. The famous Vietnamese proverb "the village association is a small court"—as opposed to the big court in the capital city—scarcely reflected a democratic or populist consciousness. Vietnamese village chiefs were approved by the imperial court but chosen by the real village leaders, the council of notables. The notables in turn represented an even broader village elite group, the "orthodox culture" association, which was composed of males exempt from labor conscription either because of their literacy and success in Vietnam's written civil service examinations or because their wealth allowed them to purchase exemption. The notables and other corvée-exempt males used their authority to compile written village covenants, the earliest surviving texts of which date from the 1600s. The rules in the covenants buttressed the authority of the elites: they prescribed penalties, including beatings, for villagers who abandoned farmland or refused to do work on irrigation dikes, and they legitimized community ostracism as a weapon against villagers who did not comply with the notables' wishes. The evidence suggests that Vietnamese village elites resisted the desires of national rulers to equalize local landholdings or to widen entitlements to the village common lands. They could do this by invoking privileged claims to the land for elite-controlled activities (such as the support of village rituals) as laid down in their very own covenants.

Although their strengths and weaknesses in the mobilization of labor were the common element in determining their survival, there were important differences in type among Southeast Asian provincial authorities. Hereditary administrations existed in Myanmar, Siam, Cambodia, and Java; a bureaucracy based in part on written examinations rather than simple heredity, in Vietnam; a colonial bureaucracy staffed with temporarily resident foreign officials from the Iberian peninsula *(peninsulares)* or elsewhere in the Spanish empire (creoles), in the Philippines; and nonbureaucratic systems, usually localized forms of hierarchical order held together by tributary relations, in the Malay states of the peninsula, in western Indonesia, and in the Shan and Lao principalities.

Certainly the basis and emblem of authority for Malay district chiefs, the key to Malay political organization above the villages, was manpower. Much depended on the ability of a chief to gather and retain a following, both from among his own kinfolk and from the peasantry. A typical chief's household consisted of dependent kin performing the necessary tasks of administering his lands and acting as secretaries, accountants, and tax gatherers, or mercenaries and free volunteers who provided a permanent, if often idle, armed force: the "raja's bully boys" *(budak-budak raja)*. Beyond them, the household also included debt bondservants and slaves.

The chiefs in most of the Malay monarchies, stretching from Aceh and Kedah to Sulu, were members of a hereditary ruling class. They were ranked in complex orders of seniority, which served to define and determine relative position and influence. All rank and dignity were believed to be upheld by unseen forces that punished insults to lawfully constituted authority. The concept of differential status and concern for its expression were of abiding interest to the Malay elite, with a correspondingly exclusionary attitude toward those not privileged to belong to it. It was rare for people to cross the barrier from the subject class, particularly where their origins and background were known. Marriage outside one's own class also was exceptional, even if marrying children into advantageously positioned families was a well-established means within the class of chiefs itself for indulging in the constant preoccupation with rank and influence. Chiefs were virtually autonomous in their territories and jealous of their powers; they commonly held, under commission from the ruler, rights of control over specified areas of the polity, usually based on a stretch of the main river or one of its tributaries. These rights included the collection of taxes and tolls on river trade, the granting of concessions and monopolies, and the command of produce and labor from the district's inhabitants.

The kingdom of Siam offered another model of people control. The king, at the top of the hierarchy, was supported and sometimes challenged by different levels of princes and nobles who headed civil and military "regiments" or departments *(krom)*. Ordinary Siamese were divided into two types of clients *(phrai),* royal and nonroyal. As such they were registered to serve their king or their princely and noble patrons *(nai).* Control of manpower was further tightened by the appointment of senior government ministers who had authority over all the "regiments," monitoring the numbers and distribution of people inside them and otherwise attempting to protect the king's interests.

The Siamese system closely associated, if it did not merge, military and civil interests; the Thai word for government minister *(senabodi)* originally meant army general. The king might transfer some of his own clients to princes or nobles who held official positions in the royal administration; otherwise they would perform labor services for him, ranging from the construction of fortifications and temples to the defense of royal palaces. One danger was that the king could lose his clients if they became monks or debt slaves or simply escaped into the forest. Another danger was that princes or nobles who accumulated too many clients of their own might become a threat to the throne, as apparently happened in the first half of the 1700s. After the fall of Ayutthaya in 1767, the successor dynasty had to take further steps to underline the general principle that the king "owned" all the people in his kingdom.

The differences in the Siamese and Vietnamese encounters with Catholic Christianity in the 1600s and 1700s nonetheless suggest that the Siamese patron-client version of control may have been more effective than the version prevailing in Vietnam in this period. Vietnamese villagers had never been integrated into a Siamese-style chain of command based on regiments; they were supposedly governed by royally appointed bureaucrats (provincial governors, prefects, county magistrates) who served limited terms and were not lifelong patrons. Civil wars between north Vietnam (Tonkin) and central-south Vietnam (Cochinchina) for most of the 1700s had eroded this bureaucratic principle. The north reverted to a system of appanage lands for its officials; the south paid its officials by assigning them menial laborers, rather than cash salaries or lands. This was a weak echo of the Siamese and Myanmar systems but without the creation of anything like the Siamese *krom.* The absence of Siamese-style hierarchical clienteles in rural Vietnam may help to explain the success of European Catholic missionary work in Vietnamese villages in this period and the complete failure of Catholic missionaries in Siam. Siamese commoners who wished to convert would have had to challenge the patrons who were responsible for their behavior. Vietnamese Christian converts, without such patrons, simply had to create new hamlets or villages.

Women as well as men were caught up in the daily struggles of these systems of authority to create and re-create loyalty. Southeast Asian women were anything but the "artificial" figures, quarantined from reality, that the pioneering English feminist of the 1700s, Mary Wollstonecraft, famously claimed their sisters had become in England. In some Southeast Asian countries, such as Myanmar, women could on rare occasions be village chiefs. Their political importance generally reflected less severe gender inequalities in Southeast Asia than could be found at that time in Europe, the Middle East, or China. Outside observers were surprised by the recurrence of joint property ownership rights for husbands and wives in Southeast Asian laws and by the relative ease with which women in various parts of eighteenth-century Southeast Asia could initiate divorce and not suffer for it socially or economically.

But women could also be rulers. And even when they were not, they were loyalty-creating assets in political systems that repeatedly confronted loyalty deficits. The sultanates of Patani (between 1584 and 1688) and Aceh (between 1641 and 1699) each had four successive female rulers. Remarkably, Aceh's royal harem did not disappear during the reigns of its four queens, because the harem's primary function was not sexual but political. It existed to ally the monarchy to important nonroyal households. In Myanmar, polygamous kings maximized loyalty to themselves by marriages to selected gentry families and later to court functionaries' daughters. They also honored genealogically unrelated women by conferring the title of "princess" on them, creating a politically useful fictive blood tie.

Many Southeast Asian royal harems, like the Myanmar one, were divided into senior and junior ranks, similar to the male nobility and bureaucracy. The chief queen of Myanmar was supposed to be the mother of the people, as the king was their father, and possessed her own appanages and crown service units. In at least one Southeast Asian country, Vietnam, male writers treated the lives of harem women and male officials as if they were parallel. Such writers took advantage of the perceived moral interchangeability of the struggles of elite men and palace women by using the imaginary voices of the latter to reflect on their own careers. In the masterpiece of lyric poetry by Nguyen Gia Thieu (1741–1798) "The Complaints of the Royal Harem," the rejected harem women—whom Thieu depicts as accomplished artists and chess players—are surrogates for politically frustrated bureaucrats. Such literary cross-dressing was one way of probing the contingencies of political success and failure.

Power Creation and Its Discontents

VICTOR LIEBERMAN has suggested that mainland Southeast Asian political systems underwent a "synchronized" crisis in the 1700s. Growing commercialization and population changes overwhelmed existing dynasties but then led to regenerated monarchies in Myanmar, Siam, and Vietnam in the fifty years between 1752 and 1802. Certainly in much of Southeast Asia, the political struggle to control available economic surpluses became increasingly complex. This struggle in turn magnified the basic tension between the reality of multiple centers of decision making and the ideal of one universal ruler found in Southeast Asia's various state creeds. There was an intensified search for legitimacy formulas that would endow authority with both new meaning and better techniques of control. One crude expression of this search was the Siamese kingdom's insistence, beginning in 1774, that commoner clients be given tattoos that would identify them with their patrons. Another was the Quang-trung emperor's short-lived plan after 1788 to compel all Vietnamese to carry identity cards inscribed with the names of their lineages and villages.

That was control; but what about meaning? Southeast Asia's ethically demanding court religions could always stimulate discontent with elites who fell short of their own professed ideals. Yasadipura II, the famous court poet of Surakarta at the end of the 1700s, was eloquent in depicting what he thought was a decline in Javanese virtue. For him it was exemplified by socially valued people who made false claims, for example, children of religious teachers who could not recite the most basic prayers. Such a condition (Yasadipura wrote) was similar to that of being Chinese but not having a pigtail. Yasadipura set out to devise a new program of moral education that would restore the authority of the Javanese ruling class, ranging from meticulous rules for sleeping and eating to the types of batik patterns that might or might not be worn. In trying to fight the enemy within, Yasadipura was not untypical of other Southeast Asian writers of that period, even if Javanese cultural defensiveness at the end of the 1700s was unique.

Compared to Europe, Southeast Asia's greater ratio of space to people and its lack of the intense intermonarchical relations and tensions that a shared religious and cultural framework like Europe's might have fostered meant that it avoided the severe interstate warfare that encouraged Europe's ever more efficient concentration and mobilization of finance capital. But political history is broader than the history of capitalism, and there was still a consensus in much of Southeast Asia that political authority could not stand still. Universalistic legitimacy formulas might go into reverse and increase legitimacy deficits, rather than diminish them, if the people at the top did not take them seriously. Static Oriental despotisms, of the sort Sangermano imagined in Myanmar, were largely Western fantasy.

Further Readings

Adas, Michael. "From Avoidance to Confrontation: Peasant Protest in Precolonial and Colonial Southeast Asia." *Comparative Studies in Society and History* 23, 2 (April 1981): 217–247.

Andaya, Barbara. "Political Development between the Sixteenth and Eighteenth Centuries." In Nicholas Tarling, ed., *The Cambridge History of Southeast Asia,* volume 2: *From 1500 to 1800,* pp. 58–115. 1992; 4-volume edition: Cambridge, 1999.

Geertz, Clifford. *Negara: The Theatre State in Nineteenth Century Bali.* Princeton, 1980.

Koenig, William J. *The Burmese Polity, 1752–1819: Polities, Administration, and Social Organization in the Early Kon-baung Period.* Ann Arbor, 1990.

Lieberman, Victor. "An Age of Commerce in Southeast Asia? Problems of Regional Coherence—A Review Article." *Journal of Asian Studies* 54, 3 (August 1995): 796–807.

———. *Strange Parallels: Southeast Asia in Global Context, c. 800–1830.* Cambridge, 2003.

———, ed. *Beyond Binary Histories: Reimagining Eurasia to c. 1830.* Ann Arbor, 1999.

Milner, A. C. *Kerajaan: Malay Political Culture on the Eve of Colonial Rule.* Tucson, 1982.

Rafael, Vicente. *Contracting Colonialism: Translation and Christian Conversion in Tagalog Society under Early Spanish Rule.* Durham, N.C., 1993.

Reid, Anthony. *Charting the Shape of Early Modern Southeast Asia.* Chiang Mai, 1999.

———, ed. *The Last Stand of Asian Autonomies: Responses to Modernity in the Diverse States of Southeast Asia and Korea, 1750–1900.* New York, 1997.

Tambiah, S. J. *World Conqueror and World Renouncer: A Study of Buddhism and Polity in Thailand against a Historical Background.* Cambridge, 1976.

PART 2

✳

New Choices
and Constraints

Chapter 4

❀

Dynasties and Colonies, Boundaries and Frontiers

FROM THE late eighteenth century to around 1910, change and foreign intruders swept through Southeast Asia at a bewildering rate. Some of the changes came in response to the Western imperialists, ideas, and practices entering the region. Others were indigenous to Southeast Asia. Between the 1780s and 1830, for example, there were several important developments that owed little to stimulus from the West. Some of these, like the unification of Vietnam and the establishment of the Chakri dynasty in Siam, were to outlast the colonial era.

European colonists, in other words, were not the only political "winners" in Southeast Asia. Instead, in virtually every Southeast Asian society new elites and new groups of leaders emerged and did what they could to alter the balance of power. Throughout most of the region, the early nineteenth century was an era of warfare, dynastic upheaval, population displacements, and intensifying struggles for power and wealth among bureaucrats, merchants, landowners, and nobility. New states rose while others, like the Mon kingdom centered on Bago (Pegu) and the principalities of Vientiane and Champassak in Laos, disappeared. Peasants, as usual, were called away from their families to fight and later were required to feed the winners. Soldiers of the losing armies were in many cases relocated to the winners' kingdoms.

Between 1752 and 1802 three powerful new dynasties came to power on the mainland. The first of these, the Konbaung dynasty in Myanmar (1752–1885), made war on Siam and broke the power of the court at Ayutthaya, setting

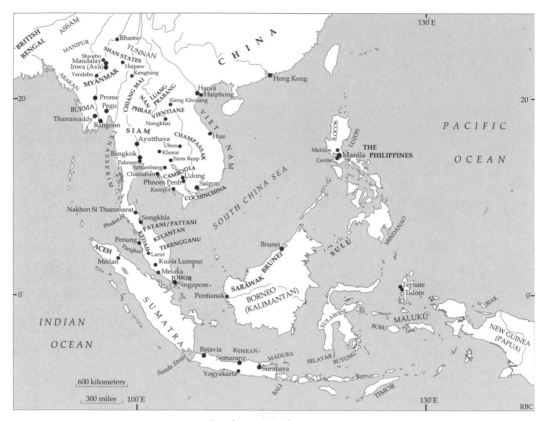

Southeast Asia about 1870

the stage for the Chakri dynasty, with its capital in Bangkok, which has ruled the country since 1782. In Vietnam the Nguyen dynasty (1802–1945) presided vigorously over a newly united country from its capital in Hue, on the south central coast.

The three dynasties started off quickly. The new rulers were concerned with legitimizing themselves, consolidating their administrations, and imposing their presence on weaker neighboring states. Institution building took more time. In Siam, Vietnam, and to a lesser extent Myanmar, the first years of the dynasties were also marked by a far-reaching cultural and political renaissance, activity caused partly by an urge on the part of the new rulers to surpass their predecessors and legitimate themselves by displaying their devotion to local tradition, partly just by the energies released as the newcomers and their followers gained power. The regimes conducted complex foreign relations among themselves, mimicking the tributary system of diplomacy taken from China but modifying and undermining it, because the three dynasties considered themselves worthy to receive tribute but not so subordinate as to send it to each other.

The faraway Napoleonic wars had important effects on the subsequent histories of maritime Southeast Asia, though most local rulers at the time were unconcerned and poorly informed about events in the West. They were unprepared for the commercial and political offensive that the Europeans, led by Great Britain, began to launch against the region in the 1820s. Before around 1850 European dominance remained the exception rather than the rule, but by 1910 most of the region was governed by European or American officials who had been put in place, often by force, to serve imperial purposes. Southeast Asia's political history in this period is often framed in terms of seemingly inexorable colonial encroachment, but the country-by-country analyses in the chapters that follow suggest that a more nuanced approach might be more fruitful.

The British intrusion into the region, largely at Dutch expense, reflected new commercial and maritime ambitions ignited by the industrial revolution. Southeast Asia's key position on the sea routes between India and China, always a feature of its history, resumed importance now. By a series of moves in the first quarter of the nineteenth century, the British sought to secure the eastern flank of their empire in India and to protect the sea routes to China. They established the city of Singapore in 1819 and gained a foothold in Myanmar (which they called Burma) in 1824, following a brief war. As the century wore on, Britain moved deeper into Burma and the Malay Peninsula, and established substantial holdings and protectorates on the northern coast of Borneo. Britain also pressed the Siamese rulers for important trade concessions. Industrial developments in Europe and improvements in international communication contributed at this time to the development of export agriculture in the Philippines and on Java and Sumatra, and opened new markets for sugar, coffee, tobacco, and rice. In the process, innovative landowning elites gained increasing wealth in much of the region and began to compete with traditional rulers.

Colonialism seems with hindsight to have been a logical, almost inevitable, process. In fact it was often, as the Duke of Wellington remarked about Waterloo, a "near run thing," and its success was contingent on many local factors as well as on differing policies and actions of the colonial powers. As kingdoms, chiefdoms, and lightly inhabited areas fell swiftly or piecemeal under various forms of European control, the governance of areas that had been colonized earlier, like Java and the Philippines, became more systematic and "rational," while previously independent rulers either compromised with the invaders and held onto some of their prestige, as in Cambodia and the Malay states, or buckled before superior military force, as in Myanmar and Vietnam. After about 1850 Siam, ironically, became more powerful and more "European" in a multifaceted response by its rulers to the imperial pressures of Great Britain and France.

The process of colonization, like other transnational ones that have affected Southeast Asia (Indianization, Islamization, and modernization come to mind), was uneven, fragmented, and contested, and its long-term effects varied in scope and intensity from place to place. Local responses varied widely. In Myanmar and Vietnam, where rulers and elites refused to cooperate with colonial powers, they were severely dealt with. In the Malay sultanates, Cambodia, and Laos, by contrast, collaboration by local rulers foreshadowed these countries' more or less peaceful departures from the colonial world almost a century later and made governance easier for the colonial powers in the meantime. The Siamese case, like that of the Philippines, was one where collaboration, resistance, and maneuvering were too entangled to permit a simplistic account of local responses.

Colonialism had many unintended effects in Southeast Asia, as it damaged, destroyed, blended with, or was absorbed by local people and traditions in a complex, interactive process. In many cases, precolonial social practices (such as patron–client and family-centered politics) persisted through the colonial era and beyond. Others, like "strong man" leadership, revived with independence, and still others, like tributary diplomacy, disappeared more or less for good. The variety of outcomes supports the argument that colonialism was less consistent and less intrusive in Southeast Asia than many have suggested.

One important effect of colonialism was that the region was broken up into units that seemed to many local people arbitrary and irrational. The Malay-speaking island of Sumatra was cut off from the Malay Peninsula as Sumatra fell under Dutch control and the British came to dominate the peninsula. Similarly, Lao states that had been closely related to the Siamese court were taken over by France and drawn into a Vietnamese administrative orbit, while parts of Borneo inhabited by similar ethnic groups were split between British and Dutch control. In the western mainland, areas that had never been subject to Myanmar's kings became parts of "Burma" as the British decided what that entity was and established its boundaries.

As colonialism gathered momentum, colonies and protectorates began to look to their so-called mother countries rather than within the region for trade, inspiration, cultural borrowings, and diplomatic relations. Southeast Asia as a whole did not share, as it had previously done (and would again later on), a community of experience linking it together. What had been a relatively coherent, interactive region in the seventeenth and much of the eighteenth century became a motley collection of dependencies, cut off from one another and developing in response to different, imposed priorities and different, imported styles of rule.

The so-called rationalization of Southeast Asia involved a range of activities that, in Benedict Anderson's apt phrase, came to "regulate, constrict, count, standardize and hierarchically subordinate" the areas and peoples of the region. Through census categories they reified "races" or ethnicities as distinct and presumably alien from each other, officially determining who was a "native" and who was not. Through regulations they officially determined who was subject to which rules, exaggerating differences between categories and obliterating differences within them. Today's boundaries between "citizen" (or "son of the soil") and "alien," or between majority and "national minority" often date from this colonial obsession with classification.

One key activity of the Europeans was mapping their possessions and defining colonial jurisdictions. The nineteenth century was the golden age of scientific mapping. For the first time, wars in Europe and elsewhere were fought over boundary issues. The notion that its frontiers rather than its inhabitants or its rulers defined a given place came into vogue in Europe and America and was exported to the colonized world. By the end of the century, Southeast Asia and Africa, two of the last parts of the world to be systematically mapped, were cartographically "defined." Almost all the present-day frontiers of both areas had been drawn by this time. Few of them had existed a hundred years before. In the nineteenth century, as Southeast Asia was divided up among European nations—as described in the chapters that follow—it was also reified, on maps, as a patchwork of different-colored "possessions."

As Siam's rulers maneuvered to avoid being taken over by Great Britain and France, they were caught up in the cartographic scramble. Eager to appear "civilized," the Chakri kings allowed Western mapmakers, accompanied by Siamese officials, to delineate what Thongchai Winichakul has called the "geo-body" of Siam. The boundaries of the kingdom were no longer determined by the extent to which the monarch could extract tribute and call on manpower but by lines drawn on the map between Siam on the one hand and French Laos, French Cambodia, British Malaya, and British Burma on the other. Boxed in by European powers, Siam was forced in the process to abandon claims to enormous swathes of territory as it assumed a European-style juridical identity.

The nineteenth-century cartographic project defined the geo-bodies of present-day Southeast Asia. Thus Indonesia occupies the same space as the former Netherlands Indies, while Malaysia contains most of the territories controlled in that part of the world by Great Britain except for Singapore and Brunei, which became separate states. Burma inherited its colonial frontiers with independence; the unwillingness of many of its inhabitants to accept Rangoon's postcolonial jurisdiction led to decades of civil war. "Laos," a French colonial invention, became a sovereign state with French-drawn frontiers; so did the older realms of Cambodia and Vietnam, while the Philippines, named after a sixteenth-century Spanish monarch, remained a diverse, multilingual archipelago whose "unity" derived primarily from its colonial experience.

The Western cartographic project prevailed not only in the realm of politics but in the imagination as well. Twenty-first-century Southeast Asian scholars write about "Indonesia in ancient times" or "The pre-Hispanic Philippines" as if these modern creations were eternal, projecting backward today's national identities on peoples who not only would not have recognized the concepts but would in many cases have denied their relationship with the neighbors to whom they are now, retrospectively, defined as kin. (There is nothing uniquely Southeast Asian about this; modern "France" and "China," for example, are similarly mythologized as eternal, although today's territories cover what once were arenas of squabbling polities and rival ethnicities. The present imposes itself on the powerless past.) In the long run, these newly created identities may be colonialism's lasting legacy to the region.

Europeans also came to Southeast Asia with firm ideas about local history, culture, and governance. By dint of their power and modernity, they felt themselves culturally superior to the peoples of Southeast Asia. They saw their forms of administration as rational improvements over the ramshackle, corrupt, and ineffective local arrangements that they encountered and took little time to understand. At the same time, by the late nineteenth century they were succumbing in some cases to an "Orientalizing" impulse, quick to recognize and eager to study Southeast Asia's distant and seemingly exotic past. French, Dutch, and British scholars gave early Southeast Asian history a chronological coherence it had lacked. In the process of delineating past greatness, they endowed some local (national) histories with a built-in, protracted "decline" that led, with apparent logic, to European "protection" and control.

Southeast Asians were considered incapable, for the time being, of self-government or modernity. To guide them slowly toward enlightenment, or merely to extend their own power, the colonists catalogued, counted, and evaluated local cultures, categorized the past, and "protected" vulnerable or even defunct institutions. In what Paul Mus (*Le destin de l'Union française,* 1955) called the "monologue of colonialism," they stifled the possibility of open-ended discussion or systematic internal change. French scholars and their Dutch counterparts deciphered thousands of ancient inscriptions, established museums, and restored medieval Hindu and Buddhist temples scattered over the landscapes of Cambodia and Java. The British performed similar work, with less fanfare, in Burma and Malaysia. American scholars in the Philippines, finding no such ancient monuments, dug for pottery shards and analyzed skull shapes to establish (or invent) a prehistory involving "waves" of settlement.

As the unruly region of Southeast Asia was being brought to order with new maps, revised chronologies, censuses, cadastral surveys, colonial police, archives, and museums, far-reaching social changes had taken place that by 1900 or so were often beyond the power of the colonial state to regulate, prevent, or control. These included the monetization of local economies, widespread population growth, the expansion of global markets, improved road and water transportation, the introduction of printing, the impact of European ideas about politics and culture, and the growth of crowded modern cities, to name a few. These changes are described in the chapters that follow, which depict the transition between earlier brands of colonialism in Java, the Spice Islands (Maluku), and the Philippines, and later, more systematic forms of exploitation.

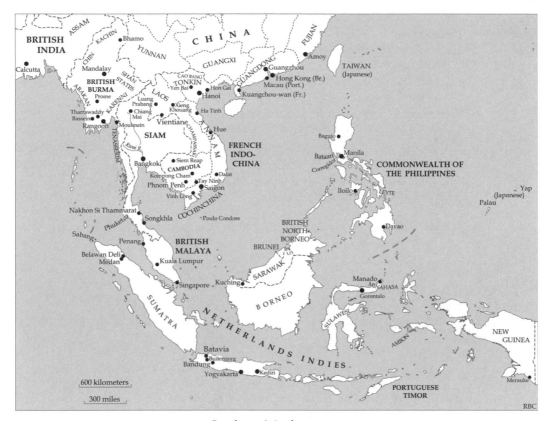

Southeast Asia about 1938

The chapters also describe how Siam and other Southeast Asian societies confronted, went along with, or sidestepped the challenges posed by the Western intruders. They remind us that before today's mega-states (by Southeast Asian standards) there were smaller polities scattered throughout the region—Sulu, Aceh, Bali, Luang Prabang, and many others—that faced eventually irresistible pressure for many years before succumbing, being absorbed into larger units, and losing their unique "histories." The era was one of new constraints and unexpected opportunities, in which the deep conservatism of rural populations came under threat, along with many of the time-honored methods of local rule. By the end of the nineteenth century, Southeast Asia had spawned a new generation of winners and losers. Once the so-called age of high colonialism emerged, the region became both more heterogeneous and, thanks to voluminous colonial archives, easier to study in a comparative, analytical fashion.

Further Readings

Anderson, Benedict R. O'G. *Imagined Communities: Reflections on the Origin and Spread of Nationalism.* Rev. ed. London, 1991.

Day, Tony. *Fluid Iron: State Formation in Southeast Asia.* Honolulu, 2002.

Etherington, Norman. *Theories of Imperialism: War, Conquest and Capital.* London, 1984.

Fieldhouse, D. K. *The Colonial Empires: A Comparative Survey from the Eighteenth Century.* 2d ed. Basingstoke, 1982.

Headrick, Daniel R. *The Tools of Empire: Technology and European Imperialism in the Nineteenth Century.* Oxford, 1981.

Lieberman, Victor. "Local Integration and Eurasian Analogies: Structuring Southeast Asian History, c. 1350–c. 1830." *Modern Asian Studies* 27, 3 (1993): 475–572.

Tarling, Nicholas. *Anglo-Dutch Rivalry in the Malay World, 1780–1824.* London, 1962.

Tate, D. J. M. *The Making of Modern South-East Asia.* 2 vols. Rev. ed. Kuala Lumpur, 1977–1979.

Thongchai Winichakul. *Siam Mapped: A History of the Geo-body of a Nation.* Honolulu, 1994.

Woodside, Alexander, and David K. Wyatt, eds. *Moral Order and the Question of Change: Essays on Southeast Asian Thought.* New Haven, 1983.

Chapter 5

Myanmar Becomes
British Burma

THE HEART of the territory that today forms the state known as Myanmar sits in the midst of a horseshoe of mountains that have provided a degree of protection and isolation, violated by only the most determined of invaders, for hundreds of years. At the same time, however, the rulers of that territory and their predominantly Bama or Burman subjects have often been in conflict with the various princes and other rulers of the various communities and peoples—Shan, Mon, Kachin, Kayin (Karen), Chin, Kayah (Karenni), Palaung, Pao, and Wa—who resided in the surrounding mountains and valleys. There has always been a great deal of human movement generated by economic, political, and military exigencies within this broad territory, resulting in a highly variegated but symbiotic multicultural polity.

The Rise of the Konbaung Dynasty

IN THE mid-1700s the then ruling dynasty, the Restored Toungoo, following a pattern typical of the decline of once strong monarchies, was increasingly incapable of generating the resources to maintain control over its former domains. Under a succession of weak kings during the first half of the eighteenth century, the dynasty fell prey to divisive forces within and enemies without. In the 1720s and 1730s raiding and plundering parties from Manipur, in what is now northeastern India, undermined the military credibility of the monarch. Rivals leading predominantly Mon forces from the south of the kingdom made a bid for restored power. Internal dissension, faltering royal leadership, and administrative weaknesses in the provinces around the capital, Inwa (Ava), further crippled the dynasty. It fell briefly to a Mon claimant to the throne in April 1752.

Alaungpaya, deputy to the lord of Shwebo, a town a few days' march north from Inwa, was a man of great charisma. Three times he repulsed stronger forces sent by the new conquerors of Inwa to exact his allegiance. Word of his power spread and his troops and reputation swelled as he moved to the offensive. By the end of 1753, he had taken the former capital and cleared the center of the empire of opposing troops. Alaungpaya shifted his headquarters from Shwebo to Inwa, assumed the usual hallmarks of a royal personage, including an appropriate genealogy, and founded Myanmar's last dynasty, the Konbaung.

The institutions of the old state were revitalized and used by Alaungpaya to defeat his Mon-led separatist opponents in the south. His initial power came from his army, a force unparalleled at the time, but his political authority grew as he developed a more complete array of means of persuasion, including religious and symbolic regalia and ethnic appeals. The momentum of his victories and the legends that swept around the new king provided him with an aura of supernatural power. By chain letters and sponsored ballads, he sowed fear among the populations ahead of his armies, thereby weakening the will of his opponents and creating massive defections. In promising release from slavery, he won over additional groups of men. During 1755 his armies moved as far south as Yangon (Rangoon) and Bago (Pegu), which fell to his forces in May 1757.

Alaungpaya's power was sufficiently great that in 1760 he sought to extend his domain over part of neighboring Siam. The excuse for war grew out of a local rebellion in Dawei (Tavoy), in which Siamese officials in neighboring Myeik (Mergui) and Tanintharyi (Tenasserim)—then under the sway of Ayutthaya—were thought to be involved. When the local authorities failed to accede to his demands, Alaungpaya concluded that an invasion of Siam was necessary to maintain central authority in the south. The Konbaung court had to make clear to potential dissidents that they could not hope for assistance from any rival monarch. For reasons of credibility and power, the subsequent war could not easily be abandoned, especially following Alaungpaya's fatal wounding before the walls of Ayutthaya in May 1760. In a mere eight years, the king had created a realm as extensive and powerful as any in Myanmar's history, and his generals and his successors were fully conscious of the extent to which their survival depended on the respect they commanded, both within and outside the kingdom.

For the next twenty years the Konbaung dynasty continually pursued its military goals, increasingly better planned and provisioned. As the power of the monarchy and its governing apparatus grew, the Konbaung armies gained a commanding strategic and political advantage. They moved through the Shan and Lao principalities and the isthmus of the Malay Peninsula before launching a final attack on Ayutthaya, which they sacked in April 1767. However, despite these strategic successes, there was increasing instability at the court. Relations were frequently strained between the crown and the highest officers. King Naungdawgyi (r. 1760–1763) executed two generals on his accession to the throne in 1760, provoking an army rebellion. Neither he nor his successor, Hsinbyushin (r. 1763–1776), ever felt completely secure.

Hsinbyushin soon found the core of his kingdom threatened from the northeast, where his armies' activities in the Shan-ruled principalities provoked a reaction from the Chinese governor of Yunnan, who launched four invasions of Myanmar territory between 1766 and 1769. The Konbaung defenses held, thanks to the overextended supply lines of the Chinese armies, and the Chinese were forced to conclude a treaty at Kaungton, the site of two of their defeats, late in 1769. The king, however, was displeased that the war had not been carried to total victory, that his generals had assumed unauthorized negotiating powers, and that therefore the prestige of the monarchy had been damaged in the eyes of his enemies. Fearful of facing Hsinbyushin's wrath, his generals marched on Manipur to place a Konbaung nominee on the throne. This victory against a minor kingdom to the northwest was not enough to salve the monarch, and the offending generals were sent into temporary exile in the Shan areas.

Hsinbyushin's treatment of the generals following the conclusion of the battles with Chinese troops was symptomatic of the nature of court politics. Any challenge or slight to the king was interpreted as a threat to his power and the status that buttressed it, and thus provoked ruthless and sometimes indiscriminate retaliation. Army units became enmeshed in political intrigues, and by the 1770s their performance in battle declined, as commanders quarreled and morale sagged. As Siam recovered under Taksin and Konbaung suzerainty over Lao princes was lost, the Konbaung empire was forced onto the defensive to its east, retaining Alaungpaya's conquests only in Tanintharyi.

During the reign of Bodawpaya (r. 1782–1819), the fifth and last of Alaungpaya's sons, the monarchy managed to restore control. The early years of his reign were marked by large military campaigns that provided evidence of both his military prowess and his administrative competence. His forces conquered the hitherto independent kingdom of Rakhine (Arakan) in 1784 and resumed warfare with Ayutthaya. Warfare was soon abated, however, and Bodawpaya turned instead to revitalizing the kingdom's administrative system, especially its means of extracting revenue and manpower from its subjects. The general revenue inquests of 1784 and 1803 were of critical importance. The country was canvassed, land and rights assessed, tax and labor service obligations and exemptions scrutinized; the population was enumerated at just two million. The inquests revealed inconsistencies and injustices in the application of the norms of taxation, which had to be corrected to ensure central control. The monarchy also revoked many of the tax exemptions granted by earlier kings to religious communities. While these were not sufficiently large to sap the strength of the administration, they did represent centers of power outside of monarchical control.

Bodawpaya's undermining of the economic independence of the Buddhist monkhood as well as his intervention in clerical disputes to favor one sect at the expense of another reflected another dimension of political conflict during his reign. Elements of the monkhood were hostile not only because of Bodawpaya's economic reassessment and his partiality to favored sects, but also because they objected to the king's religious pretenses, such as his claim to be a bodhisattva.

There were other divisions and conflicts as well. The interests of the Hlutdaw (supreme council of state), for the most part composed of elderly descendants of entrenched official families, clashed with those of the *atwin-wun,* the ministers of the royal household and court officials who enjoyed land grants, often obtained at the expense of others. Advancement was frequently tied to kinship or geographic origin. The usual jealousies within the royal family and the jockeying for preferment and position among members of the official class generated many challenges to the authority of the monarch. Thus the king had to devote much of his time to balancing the forces at court if he was to remain on the throne. His knowledge of events beyond his court was severely restricted because of his isolation as an exalted monarch.

Nevertheless, even though he was seventy-five at his death in 1819, Bodawpaya remained an effective ruler to the end. His military campaigns continued, though they were never as ambitious after 1785. Apart from occasional forays into Siam and the quelling of rebellions, as in Rakhine in 1797 and 1811, the king's imperial ambitions focused mainly on the small states to the northwest of the kingdom's heartland, especially Manipur and Assam. These principalities, which lay on the eastern frontiers of the increasingly powerful British Indian empire, were being drawn away from Inwa. From 1804 onward, Konbaung troops regularly campaigned in the region, often in support of potential vassals. The success of these armies in establishing hegemony there led to a resumed drive in the court and army to expand the empire farther west, thus challenging the new forms of power being created by the British in India.

Empires in Collision

MANY irritants in the relationship between the Konbaung dynasty and the British East India Company arose during Bodawpaya's reign. Not only were their interests antithetical, but their principles of governance and economic rationality were at odds. At the end of the eighteenth century, diplomatic contacts were established, motivated on the British side primarily by rivalry with

France, but after 1800 the principal issues involved differing concepts of sovereignty and territorial control. Anti-Konbaung rebels often sought refuge in British territory. When Konbaung troops pursued them across the river Naaf (which today forms the border between Bangladesh and Myanmar's Rakhine state), conflict resulted. The British viewed a demarcated border as giving them sole jurisdiction within it. The king's followers perceived a zone of overlapping influences. Both sides believed the other had violated their sovereignty.

The East India Company wanted to encourage local trade in order to provide capital for its operations in China. It was incensed at the treatment meted out to merchants in Yangon by the king's officials, who saw them as a threat to the monarchy's monopolistic controls. The British were also disturbed by Konbaung control of Manipur and Assam, which threatened their own influence on the eastern borders of India. In this clash of perceptions over the fundamental principles of trade and governance, each side made misjudgments as to the strength and intentions of the other. The court resented the British presumption of the company's equality with the king. Diplomatic contacts were finally severed in 1811, while conflict continued in the border area.

Bagyidaw (r. 1819–1837), who succeeded his grandfather Bodawpaya in 1819, was faced with revolts in Manipur and Assam supported by the British and appointed General Bandula as governor first of Assam and then of Rakhine. In 1823 Bandula's forces threatened the British protectorate of Cachar, in what is now northeastern India, and occupied an island in the middle of the river Naaf. When his troops crossed their assumed frontier, the British responded with force. A large naval expedition took Yangon by surprise in May 1824. Konbaung resistance against the British occupation of the lands around the port grew. In 1825, realizing that they would have to take the capital in order to gain concessions from the Myanmars, British forces advanced toward Inwa. When they reached a day's march from the capital, at Yandabo, the king's forces accepted the British demands for a resolution on highly humiliating terms. In addition to conceding Rakhine and Tanintharyi to the British and abandoning Manipur and Assam, the monarchy was required to pay a significant cash indemnity, enter into unequal diplomatic relations, and negotiate a commercial treaty.

With the army beaten and scattered, and the resources of the monarchy squandered, the Konbaung dynasty faced a difficult future. Nonetheless, the king maintained his resolve not to concede more to the British without something in return, making John Crawfurd's mission to negotiate a commercial treaty very difficult. Though a treaty was eventually reached, it proved to be ineffective. In the meantime, the court gained some concessions on the payment of the indemnity.

Only in 1830, when Major Henry Burney was appointed British Resident at Inwa, did meaningful negotiations take place. Burney, who learned to speak Myanmar and made an effort to understand the king's concerns, got on well with Bagyidaw. He agreed to the return of the Kabaw Valley, east of Manipur, while also persuading the court to pay the final installment on the indemnity in 1833. This period was the apex of relations between the Konbaung kingdom and the British. In the following months the British determined to keep the teak-bearing ranges of Tanintharyi, which not only weakened the dynasty financially and strategically vis-à-vis Bangkok, but was also a blow to the king's prestige. Rivals to his throne commenced plotting in the face of the failure of Bagyidaw's cooperative policy toward the British to yield significant concessions.

Bagyidaw became increasingly withdrawn, and power effectively passed to his queen and her brother. In 1837 Bagyidaw's own brother, the Tharrawaddy prince (r. 1837–1846), seized the throne and ordered the execution of the queen, her brother, and Bagyidaw's only son. Bagyidaw lived on in seclusion near the royal palace. In its origins, Tharrawaddy's rebellion apparently had little to do with external policy, but it came to have a decisive effect on relations with the British. Although Tharrawaddy did not denounce the treaty of Yandabo, he allowed relations with the British to deteriorate, though he still resisted those who encouraged him to attack the British. Burney, who had tried to restrain the new king from executing his opponents and offered Bagyidaw asylum in British territory, soon was forced to leave Inwa. His successors found the atmosphere at Amarapura, the new capital, and Yangon so inhospitable that attempts to maintain an official residency were abandoned in January 1840, and all diplomatic contacts ceased.

Tharrawaddy brought a number of new men into his court, having ordered the execution of many of Bagyidaw's family members and ministers. These figures survived two subsequent palace upheavals, which brought Pagan to the throne in 1846 and Mindon in 1852. Although Tharrawaddy's reign began with an overt gesture of revanchist sentiments by threatening renewed war, in the end he and Pagan after him were forced to tolerate the British occupation of peripheral areas of their empire. The loss of territory and income undermined the kingdom's power, and the king and his ministers were realistic about the obstacles that stood in the way of reconquest.

Without means of regular communications between the Konbaung court and the British, the possibility of renewed conflict was ever present. In 1852 war finally broke out again as the British attempted to protect commercial interests frustrated by royal officials. In 1850 a new governor, Maung Ok, had been appointed in Yangon. He applied heavy taxes and demanded other payments from traders by bringing indiscriminate criminal charges in order to increase revenue from court fees and from bribes to avoid prosecution. Under his administration the level of complaints by merchants rose higher than ever. In November 1851 the British Indian government sent a naval officer, Commodore Lambert, to Yangon with three ships to investigate the cases of two British shipmasters who had complained of having been imprisoned for murder by

Maung Ok and then forced to pay a significant sum of money for their release. Lambert ignored his instructions and single-handedly brought about war by seizing a ship that belonged to the king and taking it out of Yangon harbor. However, although they had not actively sought it, the British Indian government had no real objection to a war with Myanmar at that time. As the then governor-general of India, Lord Dalhousie, expressed it, "We can't afford to be shown the door anywhere in the East; there are too many doors to our residence there to admit of our submitting to that movement safely at any one of them." By July 1852 a British expedition had captured all of the major ports of Myanmar and had begun to march on the capital.

The Last Stand of Royal Myanmar

PAGAN's power and prestige was undermined as the Konbaung dynasty faced this new defeat at the hands of the British. Parts of the army and several ministers threw their support to his younger brother, Mindon, who had withdrawn to Shwebo to gather his forces and assume the mantle of Alaungpaya's true successor. On his return, Mindon was crowned king, with Pagan going peacefully into retirement. The British by then had advanced fifty miles beyond Pyi (Prome) and were planning to incorporate rich teak forests into what they would soon designate British Burma. Refusing to withdraw, the invading army demanded a treaty that recognized their conquest and defined the basis of future relations in such a way as to limit the sovereignty of the king. Mindon refused to sign any such treaty, despite the urging of his ministers. He is said to have reasoned: "It behoves me to be more cautious than anyone in an affair of this importance. I am responsible for the honour of the kingdom. If I were a Minister, or a Prince, perhaps I should give the same advice as they do."

Early in 1853 hostilities ceased. Commercial and political relations remained as before or were arranged informally between British Yangon (which they called "Rangoon") and Mandalay, to which Mindon moved his capital in 1857. The vague nature of the frontier drawn by the British was neither recognized nor challenged by Mindon. The British-dominated commerce between the two territories and the relations of the two governments with Shan and Kayin rulers to the east also constituted issues for continued conflict. The British, increasingly attracted by the idea of trade northward to China and impatient at the half conquest, frustrated those in the king's court who expected them to withdraw following the concessions Myanmar had made.

Mindon hoped to strengthen the power of the Konbaung-controlled territories sufficiently to maintain Myanmar's independence and the survival of the dynasty. He attempted to do this in at least two ways. One was to strengthen popular support for the crown by the traditional means of emphasizing its patronage of Buddhism and its institutions. Another was to enhance the administrative, military, and economic resources of the kingdom. In this endeavor he was greatly assisted by senior ministers who had served two of his predecessors and encouraged reform. It has also been argued that Mindon began to develop a sense of patriotism among his subjects, sowing the seeds for the Myanmar nationalism of the twentieth century.

The conditions under which the Konbaung principality existed in 1853 made institutional revitalization difficult, however. The king's domain was cut off from the rice-growing areas of the south on which it depended for a large proportion of its food. The dynamic markets opened by the liberal British attracted many entrepreneurial individuals to migrate from the kingdom. Many members of the royal family and nobility had lost the territories that had supported them and now turned to the king for support. The reforms Mindon undertook worked against the interests of some important sectors of the elite, but the changes became more acceptable in the face of defeat and the threatened extinction of the kingdom.

Fundamental reforms had to be implemented promptly if the kingdom was to survive, but immediate pressure from the British robbed Myanmar of the time, space, and resources to introduce reforms more gradually, as neighboring Siam was able to do. In 1861 Mindon abolished the old headman system by paying princes and officials salaries and stipends, thereby increasing their dependence on him. He further centralized the administration by instituting a provincial inspectorate. To pay for this, he introduced a new income tax assessed on households according to their relative prosperity. He abolished the military service class and required its members to pay taxes where they lived instead of to their personal master. By the 1870s the new tax was providing some two-thirds of the royal revenues, while the remainder came from traditional sources such as royal monopolies on teak, petroleum, and gems.

To strengthen his revenues further without increasing the household tax, Mindon sought money from royal sponsorship of trade and commerce, through both old monopolies and new state enterprises. He purchased and ran several river steamers in direct competition with the powerful British-owned Irrawaddy Flotilla Company and constructed factories with imported machinery to process lac, cutch, sugar, cotton, and silk as well as to manufacture armaments. He also attempted to increase food production, but with his territorial control much reduced, the resource base of the state remained insufficient for all he wished to accomplish.

Mindon also attempted to end the isolation of his kingdom. He sent some of his sons to study with an Anglican missionary, and he encouraged modern studies. He tried to establish good relations with the British without abandoning his core interests. A mission was sent to Calcutta in 1854, and Arthur Phayre, seeking a commercial treaty, was welcomed to Mandalay in 1855. In 1862 such a treaty was reached, which improved exports to the newly formed province of British Burma, consisting of Lower Burma (Lower Myanmar), Arakan (Rakhine), and Tenasserim (Tanintharyi). Extended in 1867, the treaty seemed to allow the king to import arms while encouraging British hopes of trade through Myanmar to China. However, when the British refused both to permit the import of armaments and to contemplate returning Lower Myanmar, the possibility of improved relations was lost. By then the British had adopted an extraordinarily arrogant attitude, even refusing to remove their boots in the presence of the king, which led to the cessation of all diplomatic relations.

The traditional weaknesses of dynastic politics also undermined Mindon's reforming capacity. Not only did a number of senior and experienced ministers pass from the scene in the 1860s, but jockeying for position in the court also occurred. Fearing the possible assassination of a designated heir, Mindon was unwilling to name a successor, and on his death in 1878, the succession of Thibaw (r. 1878–1885), a junior prince advanced by one of the court factions, took place. Thibaw's backers were said to have favored him over his perhaps more competent brothers because the inexperienced young prince would be compliant with their desire to establish a modern constitutional monarchy and end the absolute powers of the throne.

During the 1870s Mindon's court had conducted a rather more adventurous foreign policy than it had before. Efforts to gain support from France and Italy, however, seriously compromised the kingdom's position vis-à-vis British India, which was unwilling to contemplate the prospect of a third power gaining influence in any of the frontier areas of India. The British became particularly

By permission of The British Library, photo 15/6

Conquered capital: the royal palace at Mandalay, 1880s, surrounded by British guns.

wary of losing total control over Mandalay when Mindon sent a mission to Paris and commenced negotiating a trade treaty with the French.

The end of the Konbaung dynasty came eight years after Mindon's death, when Upper Myanmar fell to a third British assault. Young King Thibaw and his queen, Supayalat, had become the object of a massive anti-Myanmar propaganda campaign. He was accused of madness and of committing a number of heinous acts, including murdering all potential rivals to the throne. Informed public opinion in Britain and India was overwhelmingly negative toward the continued independence of the rump of what had been a hundred years before a great and expanding empire. The British, seeking a pretext to complete the annexation of Myanmar, seized on one of the last acts of sovereign power of its court. Commercial interests demanded war when a fine was imposed on a British firm for avoiding royalty payments for logs cut in the king's forest. This incident was the trigger that sent a British force up the Ayeyarwady River in 1885 to seize Mandalay and take Thibaw and his family to India and permanent exile.

Further Readings

Aung Thwin, Michael. "*Athi, Hkyun-daw and Hpayà-kyun:* Varieties of Commendation and Dependence in Pre-Colonial Burma." In Anthony Reid, ed., *Slavery, Bondage and Dependency in Southeast Asia,* pp. 64–89. New York, 1983.

Harvey, G. E. *History of Burma from the Earliest Times to 10 March 1824.* 1925; reprint London, 1967.

Huxley, Andrew. "The Village Knows Best: Social Organisation in an 18th Century Burmese Law Code." *South East Asia Research* 5 (1997): 1–32.

Koenig, William J. *The Burmese Polity, 1752–1819: Polities, Administration, and Social Organization in the Early Kon-baung Period.* Ann Arbor, 1990.

Myo Myint. "The Politics of Survival in Burma: Diplomacy and Statecraft in the Reign of King Mindon 1853–1878." Ph.D. dissertation, Cornell University, 1987.

Ni Ni Myint. *Burma's Struggle against British Imperialism: 1885–1889.* Rangoon, 1983.

Pollock, Oliver. *Empires in Collision: Anglo-Burmese Relations in the Mid-Nineteenth Century.* Westport, Conn., 1979.

Saimong Mangrai. *The Shan States and the British Annexation.* Ithaca, 1965.

Singhal, D. P. *British Diplomacy and the Annexation of Upper Burma.* 2d ed. Delhi, 1981.

Thant Myint-U. *The Making of Modern Burma.* Cambridge, 2001.

Chapter 6

Siam

From Ayutthaya to Bangkok

BEFORE 1939 Thailand was referred to as Siam, a polity originally confined to the central part of the present state, which was then the kingdom of Ayutthaya. Though Siam had existed for hundreds of years, it began to change rapidly after about 1720. That change was brought about by economic and social developments deriving particularly from growing trade with Asia, especially China. Such trade brought new prosperity to many towns as well as competition between elite groups. This distraction dulled Ayutthaya's military response to the armies that invaded it from the west in 1760.

The economic dynamism and social complexity of Siam gave it life and energy. Asian artistic influences shaped Siam's literature and Buddhist temple murals. The same contact with the outside world kept Siam alive when it was nearly starving in the warfare that began in the 1760s and went on for several decades. Many cities were leveled, and there was enormous damage (including most books and manuscripts). Hundreds of thousands died of famine and disease, and innumerable captives were led across the hills to the west. Siam was underpopulated for generations after the city of Ayutthaya was captured by armies from the west in 1767.

Rebuilding the Kingdom

THE INVADERS, having plundered and destroyed Siam's capital and kingdom, rapidly withdrew, leaving small garrisons behind. At least five Siamese moved to contest for the succession; the winner was the half-Chinese former governor of Tak, named Sin, who had fled from Ayutthaya and had begun his campaign at Chanthaburi in the southeast. This official, generally called Taksin, had the initial strategic advantages of easy water communications, a position nearer the center of the old kingdom, and a large personal following. His shrewd generalship and force of personality won him a commanding position. Taksin defeated the remaining invaders and was crowned king in December 1767. He constructed a new capital at Thonburi, across the Chaophraya River from present-day Bangkok. In the next two years he defeated his rivals and built his own administration.

Taksin's lasting achievements as king were military. In subduing his rivals and in pressing renewed campaigns to the west, he restored the influence of Ayutthaya. Campaigns in Cambodia restored Siamese influence by 1779. In the north Chiang Mai was captured in 1773, and a Siam-backed ruler, Chao Kavila (r. 1775–1816), was successfully established a few years later. Major expeditions enforced Siam's hegemony over the separate states of what was to become Laos—Vientiane, Luang Prabang, and Champassak—in 1777–1779.

King Taksin, however, was not successful as a politician. He retired from the personal command of his armies in 1775 and stayed in his palace, where he was obsessed by his own divinity. He attempted to force the Buddhist monkhood to accept him as a bodhisattva, thereby alienating them profoundly. His arbitrary rule increased the opposition of his officials. Traders found their former privileges revoked. A revolt against the excesses of some of his officers broke out in Ayutthaya in March 1782, quickly rallying the opposition forces until Thonburi was taken and the king surrendered. Chaophraya Mahakasatsuk, the chief of Taksin's generals, who had been campaigning in Cambodia at the time of the revolt, was named king by the rebels and began his reign as King Rama I on 6 April 1782.

This reign, which lasted until 1809, was critically important for Siam. Taksin had reestablished the Siamese state, but he had failed to nourish the political institutions that could help it prosper. Rama I set a new tone, establishing patterns of rule that went beyond a simple restoration of old Ayutthayan institutions in his new capital of Bangkok. He was able to gain the confidence of the nobility by granting them representation in high office and carefully consulting his officers in his decisions. He made clear his expectations for the performance of his officers, using his powers of appointment and dismissal early and well. He restored the orthodoxy and hierarchy of the Buddhist monkhood and regularly asked its advice on moral issues. His leadership was marked by open consultation and discussion, while the rule of principle reduced arbitrary authority and factionalism.

The style of Rama I's reign is evident in his religious, legal, and literary work, which exceeded what was expected of a king. He called a council of the

Buddhist monkhood in 1788 to undertake a revision of the Tipitaka to restore accurate texts. In 1805 he convened a commission to edit Siam's law and to bring it into conformity with contemporary standards of justice. The king frequently took pains to explain himself and to justify his actions. His works were suffused with self-consciousness, objectivity, and selectivity.

Rama I extended Bangkok's influence in the central portion of mainland Southeast Asia. Siam's contacts were established with the Lao and Shan states as far north as the Chinese frontier. In the south, after invading the Malay states in 1785, Siam encountered considerable disaffection among the nearer states brought into submission. Rama I's success culminated in the succession of his son as King Rama II in 1809.

The major developments of Rama II's reign were political. The king encouraged his brothers and other senior princes to take an active role in government, appointing some to act as superintendents of various ministries. His eldest son, Prince Chetsadabodin, was given superintendency over the ministry of foreign affairs and trade *(phrakhlang),* where he developed an important working relationship with a high official of that ministry, Dit Bunnag. Dit was from a prominent noble family of the Ayutthaya period and was closely related to the king's own mother. These two worked together to develop trade with China for both personal and official profit. Both gained new wealth and profitable foreign contacts. Through Dit, who in 1822 was to become a minister (Chaophraya Phrakhlang), Chinese planters introduced commercial sugar production around 1816. The crop soon became an important item in a new export trade with Western merchants, concentrated after 1819 in Singapore; in exchange, Siam was able to import arms from American traders.

The British hoped to secure recognition of their possession of Penang, restore the sultan of Kedah (who had been expelled from his state by Siam's troops in 1819 after dealings with the enemy), and increase Siam's trade with Penang and Singapore. These hopes led the governor-general of India to dispatch John Crawfurd in 1822 as an envoy to the court in Bangkok. His mission was almost totally unsuccessful, as he could offer Siam no more than abstract arguments for free trade. By the time a second mission, headed by Captain Henry Burney, reached Bangkok late in 1825, however, conditions had changed.

Prince Chetsadabodin, the son of Rama II by a concubine, had succeeded to the throne as King Rama III in 1824, primarily because of his maturity, his administrative experience, and his political backing. His younger half-brother, Prince Mongkut, born of a queen and barely twenty years of age, had recently entered the monkhood. Burney came seeking Siam's participation in the Anglo-Burmese War on the side of the British but failed to obtain it. It was not until news of the British victory reached Bangkok (in March 1826) that Siam's court reacted to the presence of a new neighbor on their western frontier by opening discussions. After protracted negotiations, the two sides reached agreement.

In return for British recognition of Siam's position on the Malay Peninsula, British merchants obtained changes in trading procedures in Bangkok. The court agreed to take an immediate cut in its revenues, hoping that in the long run an increasing volume of trade would compensate for its short-term losses. Chaophraya Phrakhlang (Dit Bunnag) played a critical role in gaining acceptance of this arrangement, even though he personally and officially stood to lose most if it did not work out as planned. Siam's foreign trade in fact increased, and the threat of Britain abated. This success stemmed from the strengths of the Bangkok monarchy: an open working relationship between the sovereign and his officials, and receptivity to the outside world through overseas trade.

Throughout the reign of Rama III (r. 1824–1851) Siam's rulers interpreted the 1826 treaty as an accommodation they could live with. The trade through Bangkok grew, especially the export of sugar to Singapore, while the *phrakhlang* and his supporters continued to strengthen their economic and political position. The new system of tax farming, under which the rights to collect internal taxes, transit dues, and commodity levies were contracted out to private individuals (frequently recent Chinese immigrants), worked well. The government regulated its own labor supply by tattooing those liable for labor service.

However, some of the old nobility, whose wealth traditionally was derived from personal control of manpower and from official position, subverted the intent of the labor regulations by amassing large forces of debt-slaves for their personal service. By the 1850s foreign observers estimated that half the population of the kingdom lived in a state of such voluntary servitude, easygoing though it may have been. In contrast, the Bunnag family, some other elements of the nobility and royal family, and Chinese immigrants based their wealth on new economic patterns of trade, tax farming, and commercial agriculture, an easy and natural response to external developments like a boom in world sugar markets and the heavy influx of Chinese immigrants available for wage labor and retail commerce.

The British annexation of Burma's coastal provinces blocked the route by which armies formerly had attacked Siam from the west. The 1826 Burney Treaty also encouraged the Lao ruler of Vientiane, Chao Anu, to believe that his suzerain in Bangkok was weak and threatened by the British. In 1826 he launched an attack from the east, across the Khorat Plateau, and was within three days' march of Bangkok before Siam responded. The counterattack escalated until it spread over most of the Lao area, from Champassak in the south to Xieng Khouang in the northeast, and included troops from the northwestern principalities of Nan and Chiang Mai. Siam moved tens of thousands of Lao from mountain valleys in eastern and southern Laos and regrouped them on the Khorat Plateau. The small kingdom of Luang Prabang, isolated in the north and long friendly to Bangkok, was left alone.

Siam's armies, busy in the south and northeast in the 1830s, gained considerable field experience. Their officer corps, under Chaophraya Bodindecha (Sing Singhaseni), became more professional. They experimented with tactics and imported American rifles. In the Cambodian crisis of the 1840s, Siam now could stand against Vietnamese forces, which had benefited from French training and arms. An 1846 agreement with Vietnam allowed Siam to maintain a resident at the Cambodia court. Siam had dealt successfully with challenges to its authority in the Lao states, in Cambodia, and in the Malay states. Its military efforts were followed by visits of commissioners to the tributary states and by the establishment of administrative control over provinces where populations had been regrouped and defenses strengthened.

The influence of the West quietly overtook Bangkok. As late as 1850, there were seldom more than a handful of merchants and a few missionaries present there. However, a few important people sought them out and learned from them. Prince Mongkut, passed over for the throne in 1824, began a personal quest for religious commitment and a satisfying intellectual system within the Buddhist monkhood. He rejected a life of meditation as well as what he felt was the laxity of traditional Buddhism and sought a return to the rigor and universalism of the original faith. In 1828 he informally established a new Buddhist sect, the Dhammayut. With time to study and travel through the countryside and later with ecclesiastical authority as the abbot of an important temple, Mongkut soon began the study of languages, science, and foreign ideas. Similarly engaged in such studies were Prince Chuthamani, several other important princes, and some sons of the *phrakhlang* (Dit Bunnag). Prince Wongsathiratsanit studied medicine, Chuang Bunnag learned navigation and shipbuilding, and Chuthamani studied military affairs. The significant legacy of these studies was close contact with the West and with each other on a regular basis. These men, who closely followed the course of the "Opium War" in China and the activities of the Western powers in the region, were less likely to underestimate the West than their fathers had been.

American and British envoys came to Bangkok in 1850–1851, demanding free trade and extraterritoriality. Neither envoy was able to conclude a treaty. They found the court divided and the progressives fearful of making concessions that might compromise their chances of manipulating the succession to the throne. Prince Mongkut and Chuang Bunnag were convinced that their country's future depended on a policy of generous accommodation with the West and privately assured the envoys that their demands would be met once Rama III had died.

The progressives prepared for the end of the reign as Rama III fell ill in January 1851. To prevent civil war, an extraordinary meeting of the highest dignitaries of the realm was held on 15 March, when Chaophraya Phrakhlang (Dit)

Mixed influences: Wat Po (Wat Phra Chetupon), Bangkok. Note the presence of Indic, Western, and Chinese elements of design.

made an impassioned plea on behalf of Mongkut—the "rightful heir," as he termed him—and declared that any who would challenge Mongkut's right would have to fight him first. He carried the day; he had too much power for others to defy him, and the case he was pleading was strong. Mongkut was approached by the *phrakhlang*'s officers and invited to ascend the throne. He agreed to do so. A guard was posted around Mongkut's temple residence and remained there until Rama III died, when Mongkut was escorted to the Royal Palace to be crowned as Rama IV. Mongkut insisted that his own full brother, Chuthamani, be elevated to rule jointly with him as his coequal and "second king." Chuang Bunnag was appointed Chaophraya Si Suriyawong, minister of war and the southern provinces *(kalahom),* and chief among the king's ministers, while his younger brother, Kham Bunnag, became minister of treasury and foreign affairs. Their father and uncle, who together had run both those ministries for more than twenty years, were given honorific royal titles and began to retire from public life.

Western demands soon were revived by Sir John Bowring, the British governor of Hong Kong and minister to China. By the time he arrived in Bangkok in March 1855, the Second Anglo-Burmese War had taken place. Mongkut's reading of the Singapore newspapers and his prior correspondence with Bowring had made clear what was expected of him. While Mongkut sat chatting with Bowring, offering him cigars and pouring wine, Suriyawong revealed his detailed knowledge of European economic theory and the principles of good government. Though they exuded self-confidence and conviction, Mongkut and Suriyawong had battles to fight at court and a thirty-day deadline, set by Bowring, against which to work. Extraterritoriality—the legal jurisdiction of consular officials over their own nationals—could be easily conceded, but Bowring's insistence on free trade at nominal duties and on the abolition of all government trading and commodity monopolies threatened the economic interests of many, at court and elsewhere. From Bowring's journal, it appears that Suriyawong's belief in the benefits of free trade—his conviction that the country could make up in trading volume what it lost on the duties paid by each ship and on each commodity—and his faith that alternative sources of income could be found to replace those lost by conforming to the treaty won the day against considerable opposition.

The Bowring Treaty, signed in April 1855, served as the model for more than twenty other such agreements. Under its terms, Siam accepted extraterritoriality, the abolition of trading monopolies and transit dues, and the establishment of low ad valorem tax rates of 3 percent on imports and 5 percent on exports. Taxes on land held by British subjects were also fixed at low rates, effectively preventing Siam's government from increasing the land taxes charged to its own citizens; earlier prohibitions on the export of rice were removed. The only concession to Siam was the stipulation that the import and sale of opium was to continue to be a government monopoly. Siam gave away a great deal for the sake of security, without any way of knowing if it could withstand the sacrifices. Its rulers did so because they believed they had to, because the threat of foreign intervention or war was real, as they recognized from following closely what had been happening in nearby countries.

Mongkut had to undertake "a total revolution in all the financial machinery of the Government." The monopolies and tax farms were replaced with new monopolies—opium, gambling, lottery, and alcohol—contracted to Chinese, which provided the major share of government revenues well into the next century. The number of ships visiting Bangkok multiplied, and Siam became one of the world's largest exporters of rice and teak. Government revenues recovered within one year; the domestic political dangers to which Mongkut and Suriyawong had exposed themselves declined.

With expanded foreign trade and contact, life in Bangkok rapidly changed. Harbor facilities, warehouses, and shops were constructed, and the king himself invested funds in new streets of shops. Following the traders came more missionaries, artisans, and professionals, and soon a few Westerners were formally employed by Siam as tutors, translators, police officers, and shipmasters, though there were just fourteen of them during Mongkut's reign. Their impact was echoed by the larger community of diplomats and missionaries. Men like Mongkut were aware that their country's fate depended on learning from the West. They borrowed and adapted Western ideas and techniques in areas where their security was at stake. Foreigners were employed to represent Siam's government abroad, later to be replaced by Siamese officials. Europeans were engaged to advise the foreign minister, Suriyawong, and the king in Bangkok. Siam hired drillmasters to train troops and imported new arms. A start was made in providing new government services—such as telegraph and mail service and paved streets—required for the conduct of international trade or for the convenience of foreigners.

Mongkut did not attempt to promulgate any fundamental reforms. The bureaucratic nobility remained semihereditary and unsalaried, and its educational preparation and recruitment were unchanged. No revisions were made in laws or in slavery. Most of the military forces were untouched, and provincial administration remained inefficient and resistant to central control. Mongkut and Suriyawong may have thought it foolish to proceed rapidly with change, particularly since the pressure for reform was still not strong as late as 1870. As in most governments, reform was less an issue than political power at court. The nobility and the royal family were divided on the issue of reform, its pace and extent, and on the issue of the balance between royal and bureaucratic-noble power. These issues at times conflicted, pulling individuals in opposite directions. The political environment suggested caution; changes could not easily be introduced without upsetting the balance of power at court. However sincere Mongkut or Suriyawong were about reform, they believed that changes had to be introduced gradually and care taken not to disturb established interests.

In the 1860s two incidents caused Siam to reconsider its relations with the West and the urgency of domestic reform. First, the shelling of Terengganu by British ships in 1862 reminded Siam of the fragility of its relationship with Britain, which had previously acknowledged Siam's suzerainty over that Malay *negeri* (polity). In 1863 came the beginning of France's elimination of Siam's power in Cambodia. King Mongkut was distressed at the severance of a long-standing paternal relationship with the king of Cambodia and frightened by the uncontrolled behavior of the French naval authorities in Cambodia. Mongkut had hoped that his charm, rationality, and good intentions would convince the West of Siam's right to survive as an independent nation. Neither incident was serious enough to force Mongkut to alter his basic policy, but both were warnings of more difficult times ahead. The era of high imperialism had not yet reached Southeast Asia, and Mongkut was able to deal successfully with the West. One of his diplomatic efforts was to invite foreign consuls and the governor of the Straits Settlements to accompany him on a visit to the village of Wa Ko to witness a total eclipse of the sun in September 1868. There he contracted the malaria that caused his death five weeks later, at the age of sixty-five.

Since the sacking of Ayutthaya in 1767, the kings of Siam had reconstructed a kingdom that was alive to the dangers and opportunities around it. The smooth relationship between king and ministers led to the formation of durable interest groups at court. These lent flexibility to the workings of government and broadened the range of economic and foreign policy alternatives. The growing immigrant Chinese community proved a source of great strength, first in operating the tax-farming system of the third reign and then in providing a rapidly expanding tax base, which kept the national treasury solvent. Perhaps most important was the self-confidence of a few of Siam's leaders—their conviction that they could concede to the West without losing much—and their faith that they could persuade their countrymen to accept the sacrifices required of them. They felt strong enough to take economic and political risks for the sake of security. Each risk successfully accepted, from the treaty of 1826 to the treaty of 1855, strengthened the party of accommodation.

Meanwhile, the kingdom of Lan Na at Chiang Mai had come under the loose suzerainty of Bangkok in 1775, after forty years of almost constant warfare. Once invaders had been expelled from the area in 1804, the state was left alone while it regrouped its population in towns and sent raids into the Shan states to capture manpower. After midcentury, as a result of European interest in Chiang Mai's teak forests, disputed forest leases, and what British Burma viewed as unacceptable restraints on its trade in the region, the Bangkok monarchy became alarmed that Chiang Mai's rulers might bring on a collision between themselves and the British. Bangkok therefore put its own candidate on the throne of Chiang Mai in 1870 and, five years later, appointed the first commissioner there to guard its interests and to prevent further conflict with the British.

The old kingdom of Nan—between Chiang Mai and Luang Prabang—was a more durable ally of Bangkok and was left alone until 1931. In the Lao states to the east, Bangkok's resettlement of the population of the middle Mekong valley on the Khorat Plateau had left as independent Lao powers only the kingdom of Luang Prabang and a few minor principalities to the east and north that were tributary to it. From 1872 onward, the whole northern region was threatened by roaming brigands of indeterminate origin (known as Ho or Haw), who reached even to Vientiane. The king of Luang Prabang appealed for aid to Bangkok, who sent repeated military expeditions northward, achieving little.

Imperialist Pressures, Siamese Responses

THE PRESSURES of Western imperialism reached Siam later than nearby countries, giving Siam extra time to cope with them. The kingdom needed the time, especially to resolve problems of domestic politics. King Chulalongkorn (Rama V; r. 1868–1910) was fifteen when he succeeded to the throne, and for five years he was powerless in the hands of his regent, Chaophraya Si Suriyawong (Chuang Bunnag). The young king traveled abroad—to the Netherlands Indies,

Singapore, British Burma, and India—and gathered about him a group of young men, some of whom had received a Western education. When he became king in his own right in 1873, he embarked with their support on a series of reforms, announcing the abolition of slavery, changing the judicial and financial systems, and establishing a council of state and privy council to advise him. The changes provoked a strong reaction. The "second king," Wichaichan, who had been named heir presumptive in 1868 by Suriyawong in the expectation that Chulalongkorn would soon die, was alarmed at the moves by the king and his supporters. He fled to the British consulate early in 1875. The British and French consuls, each exceeding his government's instructions, attempted to take the opportunity to strengthen their influence in the kingdom, but they were thwarted by their home governments, who refused to act, while the king rallied his support. Chulalongkorn survived this "front palace" crisis only by making promises; in the next ten years many of the earlier reforms were rescinded, and no new ones were launched.

In the mid-1880s, as the ministers of his father's generation died off, King Chulalongkorn resumed his reforms. Because most families of the old nobility had been reluctant to send their children to modern schools, the king's own brothers (he had twenty-seven) were the best-educated men of their generation. One by one, they were put in charge of departments and ministries. In 1885, following the urgings of his brothers and supporters, the king began the reorganization of the government into ministries structured on functional lines. The new system was inaugurated in March 1888, with the young ministers-designate, most of them brothers of the king, attending cabinet meetings even before their ministries were formally proclaimed. Over the next four years departments were rearranged, new ones were created, and men were prepared and trained for the new cabinet government, which finally went into operation in April 1892.

Among the changes accompanying the reorganization was an extension of the capital's controls over provinces and distant dependencies. Patterning their system on the model of the British in India and Burma, the Siamese grouped their provinces into circles *(monthon)*, controlled by commissioners who were often brothers of the king. Commissionerships were established at Luang Prabang, Chiang Mai, Phuket, and Battambang in the 1870s, and then at Nongkhai, Champassak, Nakhon Ratchasima (Khorat), and Ubon in the 1880s. The commissioners' powers and activities became substantial around 1890, when they began instituting reforms, building local military units, and regularizing financial and judicial administration.

The new system extended the authority of Bangkok outward, absorbing former vassals and consolidating its administrative control. But in Luang Prabang and Champassak it was too late, as the thrust of French imperial ambitions against Siam increased through the 1880s. The French regarded Siamese efforts at improving control over outlying dependencies and quelling the disturbances caused by the Ho in Laos as a new imperialism that challenged the supposed "rights" of Vietnam over the Lao principalities east of the Mekong. They manufactured claims to territory and posted agents there, provoking incidents that were blown up into a war. They sent columns of troops into the regions of the lower and middle Mekong, where they met stiff resistance. In the tense days that followed in July 1893, the shore batteries at Paknam fired on two French gunboats forcing their way up the Chaophraya River to Bangkok. Siam, lacking sufficient force to roll back the naval blockade then imposed or to resist the military forces then in preparation on the Lao frontier, had to accept a French ultimatum demanding the surrender of all Lao territories east of the Mekong and the payment of a large indemnity.

Siam's survival through the period was partly a product of Anglo-French rivalry. Each European power was anxious not to border the other or to allow the other a disproportionate advantage. Bangkok played upon the rivalry and made Siam a fulcrum for balancing the powers. The most that the French and English could agree on in 1896 was to guarantee the independence of the Chaophraya River valley, which left in doubt the fate of Siam's rule on the Malay Peninsula, in the provinces bordering Cambodia, and in what is now northeast Thailand. Bangkok retained most of this territory only through a combination of luck, modernization, and diplomacy.

Through the king's personal diplomacy with European rulers and through the diplomatic contacts that for forty years were Prince Devawongse's responsibility as foreign minister, Siam cultivated a reputation abroad for responsibility and willingness to accommodate Western demands and to reform along Western lines. The image was sustained by the prominence of foreign advisers in Siam's government. They made an impressive display and contributed much useful technological advice, but it was the basic policies of the ministries for which they worked that were decisive for the country. This was particularly true in the case of the Ministry of the Interior under Prince Damrong Rajanubhab, which extended a modern administration over the provinces. Damrong enlarged the system of "circles" and high commissioners after all the provinces were handed over to his ministry in 1894, creating an extensive system of provincial administration. The powers and prerogatives of princely families and families of provincial governors rapidly eroded as they were displaced by men from the capital and as the timber-cutting leases previously paid to the rulers of Chiang Mai, Nan, and Phrae were bought out by the central government. This was not accomplished without resistance. In 1902 three separate rebellions erupted—in the north, northeast, and south. Suppressing them with its modernized army, the central government demonstrated its strength.

Siam survived the crisis of 1893, but unresolved claims and undrawn boundaries preserved the possibility of further inroads on its territory. The

Adapting Western diplomacy and dress: adjutant to the Siamese ambassador, Batavia, 1870? Photo by Woodbury & Page.

treaties of the 1850s had restricted many of its taxing powers, and an oppressive system of extraterritoriality placed not only Europeans but thousands of Chinese, Lao, Cambodians, Shan, and Burmese with French and British registration certificates outside Siamese legal jurisdiction. The difficulties with France were resolved in a series of treaties, which, by 1907, gave Siam its current eastern border at the expense of territorial cessions in Laos and Cambodia, in return for an end to further claims and to French abuses of extraterritoriality in the kingdom. The British price for similar concessions was equally high; it was finally paid in 1909, when Siam ceded four Malay dependencies in the south—Kedah, Perlis, Kelantan, and Terengganu—to Britain. The basic principle of extraterritoriality and the treaty restrictions on taxation remained in effect for some time, but the agreements after 1900 eased the pressure on Siam's sovereignty and secured its territorial boundaries. When Anglo-French rivalry came to an end in 1904, and then when World War I broke out, Siam's fears of Western imperialism rapidly diminished.

It was in the same quarter century after 1885 that the real transformation of the internal structure of the kingdom began with the creation of a nation knit together by administrative control and countrywide institutions within defined boundaries. A system of modern government schools spread throughout the country between 1898 and 1910, as enrollments jumped from 5,000 to 84,000 pupils. The drafting of modern legal codes, the creation of modern military services and financial and tax administration, and the ending of compulsory labor service (corvée) were all accomplished within a limited time. Ultimately, the chief obstacle in the way of reform and modernization was not conservative opposition, which died out in the decade after 1885 as the necessity of change became clear, but rather the extremely limited educated leadership available to carry it out. When this leadership, composed for the most part of young men trained abroad, came to prominence at the very end of Chulalongkorn's reign, the success of the reform program was assured, though it was far from completed.

Further Readings

Akin Rabibhadana, M. R. *The Organization of Thai Society in the Early Bangkok Period 1782–1873.* 1969; reprint Bangkok, 1996.

Bowring, Sir John. *The Kingdom and People of Siam.* 1855; reprint Kuala Lumpur, 1969.

Cushman, Richard D., trans. *The Royal Chronicles of the Kingdom of Ayutthaya.* Edited by D. K. Wyatt. Bangkok, 2000.

La Loubère, Simon de. *The Kingdom of Siam.* 1691; reprint Kuala Lumpur, 1969.

Smithies, Michael, ed. *Alexander Hamilton: A Scottish Sea Captain in Southeast Asia 1689–1723.* Chiang Mai, 1997. Selections from *A New Account of the East Indies,* 1727.

Vella, Walter F. *Siam under Rama III.* Locust Valley, N.Y., 1957.

Wyatt, David K. *Reading Thai Murals.* Chiang Mai, 2004.

———. *Siam in Mind.* Chiang Mai, 2002.

———. *Thailand: A Short History.* 2d ed. New Haven, 2003.

Wyatt, David K., and Aroonrut Wichienkeeo. *The Chiang Mai Chronicle.* Chiang Mai, 1995; reprint 1998.

Chapter 7

Vietnam, 1700–1885

Disunity, Unity, and French Conquest

ONE DOMINANT FEATURE of the premodern history of Southeast Asia was the cultural and religious variety of its royal governments. Not surprisingly, the Vietnamese monarchy differed from the monarchies of Inwa and Ayutthaya. The imported political theories that Vietnamese rulers tried to apply in their country had originated in China, not India. The Vietnamese people's limited but significant sinicization had begun during the more than one thousand years that northern Vietnam had been a colony of the Chinese empire, before Vietnam became independent in the tenth century C.E. During those centuries, the ethical and political doctrines we call Confucianism, based on the teachings of the philosopher Confucius, had spread among Vietnamese scholars, some of whom—like Indians at twentieth-century Oxford or Cambridge—may have studied at schools in China.

Tensions in Vietnamese Politics

THE CONFUCIAN ideal of the monarchy, domesticated in Vietnam above all by the country's single greatest architect of government, Le Thanh-tong (r. 1460–1497), pictured the monarch as a "son of Heaven" or sage who mediated between nature and humankind. As such, he supposedly governed by means of his moral virtue, in an ideally faction-free environment that fused the two processes of "administration" and "moral indoctrination" *(chinh giao)*. But few flesh-and-blood rulers could live up to this ideal. Inevitably, divided authority was the norm in Confucian Asia. Regional warlords in China, shoguns in Japan, and *yangban* aristocrats in Korea all shared and contested their monarchies' power. In eighteenth-century Vietnam there was also a split between the ultimate embodiment of political legitimacy (the Le dynasty, 1427–1788) and actual power, vested in regional ruling families.

From 1528 to 1802, real political control in Vietnam was subdivided. The Trinh family lords *(chua)* governed the northern region of "Tonkin" (as Europeans knew it) from Thang Long, later Hanoi. The Nguyen family lords governed the southern region of "Cochinchina" (as Europeans called it) from a series of capitals that shifted eight times between 1558 and 1738 before a final one was chosen (Phu Xuan, later Hue). But the Le monarchs in the north, although relatively powerless, survived the fragmentation. The great counterweight of Confucian stress on the value of one civilizing political center, upheld by literati and reinforced by the memory of the Le emperors of the 1400s, ensured that Vietnam's political system remained dualistic until the 1700s. The north's Trinh lords merely supervised the Le imperial court's classical Six Ministries *(luc bo)* of government (civil appointments, taxes, the administration of schools and examinations, the armed forces, justice and punishments, and public works). In 1718 they created their own parallel six "duty groups" at the Trinh lord's residence. But they adapted (and degraded) the imperial bureaucratic structure imported from China in the 1400s without being able to create anything like an ideological or functional alternative to it, let alone displace the existing dynasty.

The long spell of coexistence between monarchs and regional lords was finally broken in the late 1700s only because economic growth undermined the capacity of the dualistic political system to control and tax its increasingly mobile population. The result was a new cycle of integration, in which the descendants of the south's Nguyen lords created a territorially enlarged Vietnamese polity, with themselves as emperors, at Hue in 1802.

The economic transformation between 1500 and 1800 was especially marked in the south. Before the 1700s the Nguyen lords had ruled the south through an elite of military officers, who helped them end the political life of the Hinduized Cham kingdom (in present-day Khanh Hoa and Binh Thuan provinces) by 1697. One of their more developed administrative agencies was the shipping affairs office, designed to tax overseas trade, which suggested their dependency on commerce as well as agriculture. Trade with Japan in the 1500s, based on the port of Hoi An (Faifo), had greatly expanded Vietnam's incorporation into a far-flung regional trading network. One Nguyen lord adopted a Japanese merchant as his son; another married his daughter to a Japanese trader. When the shoguns curtailed merchants' activities outside Japan in the 1600s, overseas Chinese merchants, married to Vietnamese wives who connected them to the languages and resources of the Cochinchina interior, replaced the Japanese. The Nguyen lords appear to have seen foreign traders as being essentially stateless, rather than as bearing highly charged "national" identities; they discriminated among different Chinese regions, with their taxes favoring traders from Fujian and Siam over those from Guangdong.

By the middle of the 1700s, the South China Sea trade, which linked the Nguyen domain to places as far away as Shanghai and the Philippines, had created a wealthier and more egalitarian consumer society in southern Vietnam than had ever existed in the north. Two different regional standards of living—and economic psychologies—were now in place in Vietnam. These were to be magnified later, but not initiated, by French colonial (and American neo-colonial) capitalism. Vietnamese men may have been changed less than women by the realm's economic growth. Army conscription for the Nguyen lords' civil wars with the north and the attractions of bureaucratic careers diverted many men away from commerce, so it was horseback-riding women traders who so astonished north Vietnamese observers when they came south to study the Cochinchina experience.

The problem was how to reconcile the pressures of an expanding commercial society with the ideal features of the Vietnamese political consolidation that had occurred in the 1400s, which had retained their historical persuasiveness even as Vietnamese society grew. The institutions of the Le Thanh-tong era remained the great prototypes of Vietnamese politics down to 1885. Under Le Thanh-tong, Vietnam had made a transition to a more bureaucratic, more intensely Confucian political system. Not only had the specialized Six Ministries of government, reflecting Chinese and Korean practices, become a permanent part of Vietnamese political life in 1471, but county magistrates—officials whose titles *(tri huyen)* literally suggested that they "knew their counties" through empirical investigation rather than through hereditary personal ties—had made their appearance (1460). They were an integral part of a Chinese-style provincial administration, which by 1490 had reengineered the Vietnamese landscape into provinces, prefectures, counties, and 6,851 administrative villages *(xa)*. Extending the principle of bureaucratic surveillance, Le Thanh-tong had prescribed the evaluation of all his officials for promotion or demotion every three years, striking at cryptoaristocratic officeholders who wanted to make hereditary claims to their positions. He had also insisted on the importance of recruiting his officials through public civil service examinations, which had further compromised aristocratic privileges.

Civil service examinations, modeled on China's, had been introduced into Vietnam as early as 1075 C.E., but they do not appear to have been widespread, or entirely Confucian, before the 1400s. The Le dynasty broadened the principle of holding lower civil service examinations in the provinces every three years; success in them led to higher examinations in the capital city, presided over by the ruler himself, who became in effect the country's chief examiner. Students who passed the higher examinations were given welcome home parades in their villages, had their names engraved on stone monuments that can still be read, and could usually count on good government appointments. Even passing preliminary tests could gain students exemption from the labor service tax, as in the Nguyen examination rules of 1740.

To pass the examinations, students had to write essays about Confucian philosophy and "Northern" histories (the most famous histories of China became public administration guidebooks), write poems with standardized rhyme schemes, and even prepare policy notes for their rulers. Vietnamese elites often used borrowed Chinese institutions to assert themselves against China; in 1724, the Trinh lord of Tonkin ordered examination candidates to sketch a reply to officials in China's Yunnan province defending Vietnamese claims to certain border villages. Some villages set aside "studies fields" whose harvests paid for teachers and for the education of bright but poor village youths who hoped to transform themselves from "fishes" to "dragons" (mandarins who shared the ruler's power). The cost of a mandarin's education nonetheless remained high for most peasants.

In Confucian eyes the point of bureaucratic government was to avoid disorder by guaranteeing a certain minimal level of welfare to those most vulnerable. In 1460 Le Thanh-tong had decreed that all rich people who donated surplus unhusked rice to the government for redistribution to the poor would receive official titles as a reward. Like his other legacies, this principle of giving low and relatively harmless official titles to people who contributed grain for the poor degenerated in the succeeding centuries, ultimately endangering the meritocratic standards of the examinations. In the 1700s the Trinh regime sold government offices for cash, as it struggled to squeeze more out of its limited economic surplus in order to renew its long-standing war with the Nguyens. Bureaucratic personnel evaluations themselves were switched from every three years to every nine years after Le Thanh-tong died. By the eighteenth century they were virtually a dead letter.

Two kinds of tensions therefore influenced Vietnamese politics in the 1700s. One was political dualism: the tension between the Le emperors' theoretical legitimacy and the practical power of the regional lords. The other was generated by the struggle between the feudal principle of government, based on clientelism and personal loyalties, and the bureaucratic principle of government based on educational and administrative achievement. There was a reason why the ghosts of Le Thanh-tong and his court could not be banished. The scholar-official Phan Huy Chu (1782–1840), in the prodigious administrative history of Vietnam that he wrote between 1809 and 1819, argued that what had been important about Le Thanh-tong's reign was not so much the institutions it had created as the "rules" those institutions had implied. Such rules underwrote "equitable conditions" in social life. Even monarchs had to conform to them; discoverable moral standards for tax rates and property distribution existed independently of rulers' whims, which governments could not "avoid." Phan's observation helps to explain why the government of Vietnam in the 1800s was as similar as it was to the Le dynasty model of 1497 even though society as a whole had changed and expanded. This was not "Oriental" inertia, as some Western colonial analysts supposed. The continuity reflected an effort to give politics a predictable framework with inherent notions of a public good. The long survival of Roman law, in different types of European societies over many centuries, offers a possible parallel.

Confucian ideology was the source of the "rules" of politics, although historians will always disagree about how deeply Confucian eighteenth-century Vietnamese society was. But the Vietnamese Confucian elite's relative lack of interest in the philological and metaphysical debates that so consumed their Chinese counterparts does not mean that they did not take the ideal of the Confucian "gentleman" seriously, even if few of them could fully exemplify the code of the "gentleman" as laid down by the preeminent philosopher Le Quy Don (1726–1784). Le Quy Don described the "gentleman" as someone whose serenity was strong enough to transcend poverty or loss of office, whose virtue impressed "court and countryside" alike, whose calligraphy was good enough to recapture the spiritual essence of ancient sages, and whose talents included both commanding armies and writing poetry. Even weak facsimiles of this sort of "gentleman" were stubborn enough to confound the French and American imperial proconsuls in the twentieth century who wanted their cooperation.

The basis of Confucian ethics in Vietnam was the "three bonds": the obedience of ministers to their rulers, of children to their parents, and of wives to their husbands. Society was properly a hierarchy. Daughters, wives, and younger brothers counted for less than sons, husbands, and older brothers. Rituals like ancestor worship, whose repeated performance was supposed to make people so self-conditioned to be good that they would not be tempted into wrongdoing, were crucial to maintaining Confucian ethics. Vietnamese worshiped their ancestors with incense, rice wine, betel, and prayers and obeisances on the anniversaries of their deaths and on other family occasions. The ancestral cult was designed to keep the family united as an eternal corporation. It supplied each family with a gallery of paragons from the past whose memories, kept in view by their tombs, might improve the behavior of the living.

The Le court reinforced the "three bonds" with a set of forty-seven rules for reforming and indoctrinating the people, published in 1663 and reissued in 1760. Local officials were supposed to expound them to "ignorant" villagers. Intended to be antidotes to the worst weaknesses in the Vietnamese practice of Confucian ethics, the rules significantly targeted younger brothers and wives. Younger brothers were enjoined to respect older brothers; even if they were wealthier than their older brothers, they were not to presume to claim equal status with them and thereby violate the family age hierarchy. As for wives, they were in an awkward position in a patriarchal society in which brides not only married into their husbands' families but owed their husbands' parents greater ritual obligations than they owed their own. The Le monarchs enjoined wives to be obedient, to become chaste widows when their husbands died, and to cherish the children of their husbands' secondary wives (concubines) as if they were their own.

That was a large demand. The collision it set up between official ethics and private emotions was not confined to wives and younger brothers. Recurrent civil war also undermined Confucian conditioning. One edict that a northern Trinh lord issued in 1720, demanding the improvement of Vietnamese customs, suggested the extent to which Confucian ideals had to be re-created continually in the face of antagonistic pressures; it denounced such "ordinary" Tonkinese violations of Confucian punctilios as "incestuous" marriages between first cousins as well as commanding all villagers to stand up in the presence of officials and not ridicule them.

Among the educated elite there were also critics of Confucianism. The northern poet Ho Xuan Huong, who lived at the very end of the 1700s, was one of the most lively. Twice married to elite men as a secondary spouse, and discontented with Confucian values, Ho Xuan Huong wrote about sex, freely and wittily and bawdily. Among other things, she compared the life of a woman to the situation of a jackfruit on a tree (into which farmers drove wedges to test its ripeness) or to the plight of a hedge being butted by goats (male examination system students). But if Ho Xuan Huong was a feminist who used erotica as a weapon to put men in their place, she turned more sadly serious when she attacked concubinage as an institution, complaining that secondary wives were nothing but exploited "wageless maids." Vietnamese critics could write their subversive poetry not just in classical Chinese, Vietnam's language of public administration, but in a separate vernacular writing system called *nom*. It represented the non-Chinese words in the Vietnamese vocabulary and was sufficiently unstandardized to evade control by Vietnam's rulers. Mandarins pretended to find Ho Xuan Huong's poems embarrassing, but the poems survived, suggesting that she spoke for a significant side of Vietnamese life.

Beyond such criticism, Confucianism and classical Chinese institutions in Vietnam experienced the same encounters between totalism—the determination to enforce an imported creed and its institutional necessities in as pure a manner as possible—and relativism—the acceptance that loyalty to international creeds permitted their coexistence with long-standing local customs—as could be found elsewhere in Southeast Asia, for example, in the Islamic polities of Sumatra. Relativism triumphed with the greatest of all premodern Vietnamese law codes. Begun by Le Thanh-tong in 1483 and known conventionally by one of his reign period names as the Hong Duc code, it was in effect until the end of the 1700s. Inspired by Chinese law codes, it nonetheless deviated from them by treating women more generously. The Vietnamese code allowed women to inherit their parents' property almost equally with their brothers and to own property after marriage, rather than insisting on the complete incorporation of the wife's property into the husband's estate. For a Confucian political order, these were substantial concessions. Unfortunately, the Nguyen court was to replace the Hong Duc code in 1815 with a new law code (commonly called the Gia-long code), more totalistic in its ambition to copy the latest Chinese codes, that imposed a purer form of legal patriarchalism on Vietnam.

The Rise and Fall of the Independent Nguyen Dynasty

MORE civil war in the 1700s ended Vietnam's system of multiple polities. It led to the formation of a united Vietnam in 1802—earlier than Germany or Italy was unified—which for the first time allowed one court to control both the Red River delta in the north and the Mekong River delta in the far south. The Vietnamese state of the twenty-first century is the beneficiary of this process. In the north the Le-Trinh regime committed a slow suicide by mobilizing large numbers of soldiers and then paying them by distributing village common lands to them. This policy of treating public lands as reserve sources of army finance deprived ordinary villagers of a source of poverty relief and touched off peasant rebellions. Famine and floods accompanied the north's renewed war against the south, which briefly succeeded in 1775. The agrarian misery was such that perhaps one out of every ten Tonkinese villages of the early 1700s disappeared; Tonkin's population, in so far as it is possible to calculate it, may have been slightly smaller in 1750 than it had been in 1550.

In the south the manpower shortage was so severe, despite famine-driven migrations from the north, that the Nguyen lords authorized the capture of ethnic minority children and their public sale as serfs for purposes of farm labor. A system of serfdom that had largely vanished from the north by the late 1400s thus made a belated reappearance in Cochinchina, even if ethnic Vietnamese were no longer enslaved. The Nguyen lords also lost control of their money supply, which had been based on Japanese copper until Tokugawa Japan withdrew from world trade. They turned to zinc coinage and tried to disguise its inferiority by giving it the appearance of famous Song dynasty coins from eleventh-century China. Finally, in a desperate bid to consolidate his government, Nguyen Phuc Khoat (r. 1738–1765) took the title of "king" of Cochinchina for the first time in 1744. He converted his household affairs offices into the more classically imposing Six Ministries and ordered the people of his realm to change to Chinese-style clothing (as prescribed in a sixteenth-century Chinese encyclopedia).

The Nguyen lords ultimately survived the civil wars of 1771–1802 not because of these measures but because of foreign help (from the Siamese and the French) and because they never completely lost access to the Mekong delta rice supply. Their defeat by the Trinh in the 1770s became meaningless when the Trinh lords and the Le emperors themselves were subsequently overwhelmed by a rebellion by the three "Tayson" brothers, known to us by the name of their hamlet in south-central Vietnam. Preaching the equality of rich and poor as they launched their uprising in 1771, the Tayson brothers were not—despite the myth attached to them by later nationalist historians—simple peasant rebels. They had some education, and they attracted some Confucian scholars as advisers. Nor were they purveyors of progress and freedom: they sacked such towns as Qui Nhon and Hoi An and massacred ethnic Chinese in Saigon in 1783. But Nguyen Hue, the most intelligent brother, was a brilliant army commander. He destroyed both the Le and Trinh dynastic houses, and proclaimed himself Quang-trung emperor, a "cotton clothes" commoner hero who would "help the world," in 1788. He then defeated the large army that the emperor of China, responding to all the turmoil, had sent into northern Vietnam against him. As a ruler, Quang-trung dreamed both of translating the Confucian classics into the vernacular *nom* script and of seizing the two southern Chinese provinces of Guangdong and Guangxi. But his death in 1792, when he was not yet forty years old, doomed the Taysons and allowed a great revival of Nguyen power in 1802, this time over all Vietnam.

The Nguyen dynasty (1802–1945) ruled less than six decades before it began to succumb to the piecemeal French colonial conquest of Vietnam (1859–1885). Yet its achievements were considerable. Abandoning Vietnam's old northern capital, the dynasty created at Hue, in central Vietnam, a new walled capital city complex that was a smaller, more floridly ornamented Southeast Asian copy of the Chinese capital at Beijing. It consisted of a series of palaces arranged on a north-south axis; a Beijing-like "Forbidden City" at the core for the emperor himself; and a "Meridian Gate" at which proclamations were read and prisoners of war presented. The Nguyen emperors also built Chinese-style imperial tomb complexes for themselves, outside Hue, with stone horses and elephants to guard them; through architecture, they aspired to become eternal moral paradigms for their kingdom after they died. Nor were Nguyen monuments only in stone. Lacking an archival tradition of their own comparable to that of the Le dynasty, the Nguyen court produced an enormous encyclopedic handbook to their own bureaucratic behavior, a "compendium" of Vietnamese "institutions and institutional cases" *(hoi dien su le)* that runs to fifteen volumes and almost eight thousand pages in its modern romanized reprint. For the first time in centuries, relatively greater political stability allowed Vietnam's population to grow significantly, from 5 million people at most in the early 1800s to 7 million people in the 1870s.

But hindsight tells us that the Nguyen rulers' administrative ambitions probably exceeded their resources. Their demographic base was limited; there were probably fewer people per square kilometer in the territorially enlarged Vietnam of 1820 than there had been in the smaller Le kingdom of the 1400s. Nor could the bitter spiritual legacy of three centuries of civil war be overcome quickly. The bureaucracy was riddled with tensions between southerners and northerners, reminding the emperor Minh-mang (r. 1820–1841) of the terrible administrative factionalism of Song dynasty China. The great scholar-official Nguyen Du (1765–1820) wrote a magnificent verse novel about a beautiful, melancholy heroine named Kieu who is forced to turn to prostitution to ransom her father from official thieves; Du may have seen himself as a "political Kieu," a northerner and Le dynasty loyalist compelled to serve the Nguyens in order to protect his family.

As recently as 1993, a prize-winning French novel about Vietnam, reflecting French missionary propaganda of the 1800s, characterized Minh-mang himself as a "Confucian of Chinese culture who closed the country to outside influences." This is nonsense. Minh-mang may well have been the most intelligent Vietnamese state-builder since 1497; he showed his interest in "outside influences" by sending envoys to Batavia and British India, and he hoped to use Vietnamese sugar exports to expand trade with the West. But Minh-mang

Gateway to the "Forbidden City": the Citadel, Hue.

Photo by N. G. Owen

feared the "heterodox" teachings of a globalizing Christianity, which he felt threatened Confucianism, and he executed French Catholic missionaries, whom he saw as colluding with Vietnamese rebels. The French government refused to negotiate with the diplomats he sent to Europe to discuss the missionaries' behavior.

Politically, Minh-mang was a centralizer. As he saw it, the decentralized administration of his predecessor (Gia-long, 1802–1820), in which Hue had shared power with overlords in Hanoi and Saigon, had perverted bureaucratic accountability to the point where "failures were seen as achievements and nothing was seen as something." Minh-mang restored the power of the central Six Ministries, ruled through civil and military bureaucracies divided into eighteen grades each, and tried to impose finite six-year terms of office on his officials. Civil service examinations were revived and made more resistant to intellectual subversion by examiners and students through the introduction of word limits to policy questions and answers. Minh-mang's conception of Vietnam's identity remained broadly similar to that of medieval rulers. He saw Vietnam as a "south" that opposed itself to the Chinese "north," but he also believed the Vietnamese had the right to call themselves "Han people"—proprietors of the heritage of the ancient Han empire of which they had once been part—when they pursued a Confucian civilizing mission (including the imposition of Sino-Vietnamese surnames) among Cambodians or other ethnic minorities. Yet even Minh-mang felt some need for what we would now call Southeast Asian solidarity. He urged the Siamese diplomats who came to his court in 1826 to support Myanmar in its war with the "Red Hairs" (the British).

But Vietnam's own independence eroded less than two decades after Minh-mang's death. The French navy seized the six provinces of Vietnam's far south and converted them into the colony of "Cochinchina" between 1859 and 1867. The Vietnamese court, under the far less competent leadership of the emperor Tu-duc (r. 1848–1883), was then forced to agree to the transformation of north and central Vietnam into French "protectorates," between 1873 and 1885, after appealing to China for help against the French. China, itself in decline, lost the Sino-French war (1884–1885) that resulted from Vietnam's appeal. The fiercely patriotic southern poet Nguyen Dinh Chieu (1822–1888) depicted the French invaders as barbarians "garbed in wool" who had wrecked Confucian ethics; another southern poet (Phan Van Tri, 1830–1910) saw the French takeover as an "opera" in which too many Vietnamese actors wore the white makeup of traitors.

French imperialism succeeded not just because it possessed the superior weaponry of an industrializing Europe, but because it exploited fatal social divisions in Vietnam. These were expressed both in peasant rebellions and in the conversions of hundreds of thousands of poor Vietnamese, especially in the north, to Catholic Christianity. The Nguyen court's prohibition and mistreatment of French missionaries had in fact provided the French government with its major excuse for intervention in the first place. Some members of the Vietnamese elite had also become Catholics by this time. The most noteworthy of them, Nguyen Truong To (d. 1871), was a modernizing reformer who rather quixotically tried to combine Confucian loyalty to the Nguyen court with a Catholic defense of the (anti-Catholic) Tu-duc emperor as the representative of God on earth. To this he added an admiration for nineteenth-century Europe's rule of law and its independent judiciaries. The rich contradictions in To's thought failed to save the country's independence. Nonetheless they demonstrated the unheralded flexibility of Vietnamese political theory in the 1800s and anticipated Vietnamese anticolonial thinkers' worries, in the next century, about the legitimacy deficits of established Vietnamese institutions.

Further Readings

Dutton, George Edson. "The Tayson Uprising: Society and Rebellion in Late Eighteenth-Century Vietnam, 1771–1802." Ph.D. dissertation, University of Washington, 2001.

Elman, Benjamin, et al. *Rethinking Confucianism: Past and Present in China, Japan, Korea and Vietnam*. Los Angeles, 2002.

Li Tana. *Nguyen Cochinchina: Southern Vietnam in the Seventeenth and Eighteenth Centuries*. Ithaca, 1998.

McLeod, Mark W. *The Vietnamese Response to French Intervention, 1862–1874*. New York, 1991.

Nguyen Du. *The Tale of Kieu*. Trans. Huynh Sanh Thong. New York, 1973.

Nguyen Ngoc Huy and Ta Van Tai. *The Lê Code: Law in Traditional Vietnam*. 3 vols. Athens, Ohio, 1987.

Taylor, K. W., and John Whitmore, eds. *Essays into Vietnamese Pasts*. Ithaca, 1995.

Whitmore, John K. "Literati Culture and Integration in Dai Viet, c. 1430–1840." In Victor Lieberman, ed., *Beyond Binary Histories: Reimagining Eurasia to c. 1830*, pp. 221–243. Ann Arbor, 1999.

Woodside, Alexander Barton. *Vietnam and the Chinese Model*. Cambridge, Mass., 1971; reprint 1988.

Chapter 8

Cambodia, 1796–1884

Politics in a Tributary Kingdom

BY THE END of the eighteenth century, Cambodia had fallen from its days of glory almost a millennium before, when the great monuments of Angkor were built and Khmer kings presided over a realm that included all of Cambodia and much of what is now southern Vietnam, southern Laos, and eastern Thailand. Caught between the expanding powers of Siam and Vietnam, the kingdom had been reduced to the status of a tributary state, fought over by its neighbors.

Between Siam and Vietnam

IN 1794 a young Cambodian prince named Eng traveled to Bangkok, where he was crowned by Siamese authorities and sent back to Cambodia to be king. For the next seventy years, Siam was either an active patron of the Cambodian court or was striving to regain that status, having been displaced by the recently consolidated Vietnamese empire to the east. Rivalries between the Siamese and Vietnamese royal houses, exacerbated by factional rivalries inside Cambodia itself, led to repeated invasions by Siamese forces and to a Vietnamese protectorate over the kingdom in the 1830s. In terms of its paternalism and assumed cultural superiority, this protectorate foreshadowed the later French protectorate and its "civilizing mission." For the first half of the nineteenth century, Cambodia was a battleground between its larger neighbors. In the process, it almost disappeared.

Soon after Eng's coronation, and in exchange for placing him on the throne, the Siamese court installed a pro-Siamese Cambodian official named Ben as governor of the Khmer provinces of Battambang and Mahanokor ("Great City," later known as Siem Reap, which contained the ruins of Angkor). The two provinces soon severed their connections with the Cambodian court. They remained under loose Siamese control, governed by Ben and his descendants, until they were restored to the French protectorate of Cambodia in 1907.

When Eng died in 1797, his eldest son, Chan, was only seven years old, and the Siamese continued to administer Cambodia through local officials loyal to Siam. In 1806 Chan was crowned in Bangkok, where several of his aunts and uncles were held as hostages by the court. When he returned to his own capital of Udong, north of Phnom Penh, Chan swiftly sought recognition from the recently constituted Nguyen dynasty in Vietnam. His precise rationale for doing so is unclear but was probably connected with what he thought was the disdainful attitude of the Siamese court toward him, coupled with the pro-Siamese bias of some rival members of his family. In any case, for the remainder of his reign, which lasted until 1835, Chan displayed a pro-Vietnamese, anti-Siamese bias. The Siamese, for their part, soon welcomed two of Chan's brothers, Duang and Em, to Bangkok, where they stayed more or less as hostages for the remainder of Chan's reign.

From his capital in Hue, the Vietnamese emperor Gia-long, following Sino-Vietnamese diplomatic practice, replied to Chan's request for recognition by sending him a seal of office and Chinese-style court costumes for his supposedly "barbarian" entourage. Cambodia's tribute to the Vietnamese court, sent every four years, consisted of forest products such as lac, ivory, and beeswax, resembling what Vietnam transmitted as tribute to the Chinese court, extracted in the Vietnamese case from the peoples living in the forested mountains that lay between Cambodia and Vietnam. That the Nguyen court viewed Cambodia as a "barbarian" region (just as China viewed Vietnam) must have been galling to Chan and his entourage. Faced with the realities of power and the need to seek a balance against Siamese encroachments on his kingdom, however, the Cambodian king had no alternative but to go along and offer tribute both to Bangkok and to Hue. By 1816 his court had become, in Siamese phraseology, a "two-headed bird." A Cambodian chronicle from the 1850s, allegedly quoting Gia-long, explained these relationships in familial terms: "Cambodia is a small country," the emperor said, "and we should maintain it as we would a child. We will be its mother; its father will be Siam. When a child has trouble with its father, it can relieve its suffering by embracing its mother. When a child is unhappy with its mother, it can run to its father for support."

The next fifteen years receive scanty coverage in Siamese, Cambodian, and Vietnamese chronicles, but in 1833 a large Siamese army, accompanied by Chan's two brothers, swept through the kingdom and on into the Mekong delta in Vietnam, where an antidynastic uprising was in progress. Fearing for his life, Chan fled his new capital, Phnom Penh, to seek asylum in southern Vietnam. The Vietnamese responded to the incursion by invading Cambodia themselves, routing the Siamese army and reinstating Chan, who died shortly afterward in Phnom Penh. At this point the Vietnamese sought to institutionalize their control over the kingdom, renaming it Tan Tai, or "western commandery," and administering it directly through Vietnamese officials.

Chan had no male heirs, and to maintain a semblance of continuity the Vietnamese installed his teenaged daughter Mei as queen, the first female ruler in Cambodian history. The bewildered, powerless girl stood by helplessly as Vietnamese bureaucrats remodeled Cambodian society and administration along Vietnamese lines. In contrast to the Siamese, who had always been content to work through local institutions, which resembled their own, Vietnamese concepts of government were too different and their disdain for Cambodia's culture was too great for them to temper or delay what they saw as an urgent, thoroughgoing civilizing mission. They encountered resistance to their ideas and their programs at every level of Khmer society. Their frustrations in Cambodia are encapsulated in a memorandum that a Vietnamese official posted there transmitted to the emperor Minh-mang in 1834, soon after Vietnam's victory over Siam:

> We have tried to punish and reward Cambodian officials according to their merits and demerits. We have asked the king to help us, but he has hesitated to do so. . . . Cambodian officials only know how to bribe and be bribed. Offices are sold. Nobody carries out orders. Everyone works for his own account. When we tried to recruit soldiers, the king was willing but the officials concealed great numbers of people. When we wanted to compile a list of meritorious officials, the king was unwilling, because he was jealous.

The intrusive Vietnamese programs set off a series of uprisings in the 1830s. At least one of them was led by Buddhist monks. The Khmer objected specifically to the imposition of cadastral records, submitting to a census, and paying taxes on land. Other aspects of the Vietnamese program, such as forcing high-ranking officials to wear Vietnamese costumes, dismantling traditional patronage networks, desecrating Buddhist temples, and renaming provinces *(sruk)* must also have been offensive to the Cambodian elite and to many ordinary people as well.

In 1840, fearing renewed unrest and a Siamese invasion, the Vietnamese secretly exiled the Cambodian queen to southern Vietnam. As the rumors spread that she had been killed, uncoordinated revolts broke out in many parts of Cambodia and among the Cambodian minority in Vietnam. These were put down with difficulty by Vietnamese troops. By this time a massive Siamese expeditionary force was poised in Cambodia's northwest, accompanied by

Chan's brother, Duang, and skirmishes soon broke out between Siamese troops and Vietnamese forces in the region.

Minh-mang died in 1841, and Vietnamese policies toward Cambodia lost some of their momentum. Minh-mang, after all, had been a firm believer in Vietnam's civilizing mission. His son Thieu-tri (r. 1841–1848) was less committed to this. He began his reign looking for a solution to the Cambodian problem that would be acceptable to the Vietnamese elite and to the Cambodians as well, if not necessarily to the Siamese. Distance, distrust, and the ongoing momentum of the war, however, as well as the ambiguity of Vietnamese long-term objectives in Cambodia, kept the fighting going until 1847. For several years, Siamese and Vietnamese troops, aided by rival Cambodian factions, fought each other and devastated the landscape in a ferocious pattern not to be duplicated until the civil war of the 1970s. Throughout this period, Cambodian chronicles tell us, no rice was planted in much of the country, and the population, reverting to seminomadism, survived to a large extent "by eating leaves and roots." It took the country several decades to regain its balance and momentum.

Negotiations calculated to save face for the two exhausted armies and for the rival monarchies in Hue and Bangkok lasted until 1846, when Siam and Vietnam agreed to withdraw from Cambodian territory and to accept Duang as Cambodia's king. The treaty heralded the resumption of Siamese influence at the Cambodian court and the end of Vietnam's civilizing mission. Duang was crowned in Udong in October 1848 on an astrologically auspicious day, in the presence of representatives sent from Bangkok and Hue, but the Siamese, who took Cambodia's regalia back with them to Bangkok, had clearly become the dominant force in Cambodian politics even though their army had left the country.

A "Two-Headed Bird"

DUANG was a vigorous, popular ruler, fifty-two years old. His ostensibly divided loyalty to Bangkok and Hue, combined with war weariness on the part of those larger powers, freed him to take a wide range of initiatives. Cambodian sources written at the time give the impression that he was unwilling to be anybody's puppet. Although he had spent most of his life in Siam, for example, one of his first official actions was to forbid the use of Thai administrative terminology in Cambodia. He rebuilt and rededicated Buddhist monasteries in Udong and elsewhere that had been damaged or destroyed in the fighting. To his subjects, Duang's timely return from exile, his assiduous performance of rituals, and his prompt and thorough restoration of Buddhism were thought to be proofs of his kingliness, legitimacy, and merit. Several elegant didactic poems that he composed when he was living in Siam are still included in Cambodia's school curriculum.

Duang also tried very tentatively to open up Cambodia to the outside world. In 1853, encouraged by French missionaries at Udong, he secretly communicated with the French court, transmitting a letter to Emperor Napoleon III that offered his homage in exchange for the emperor's friendship. The presents that accompanied the letter—four elephant tusks, two rhinoceros horns, and quantities of sugar and white pepper—were lost en route, and Napoleon's reply, if there ever was one, has also disappeared. Three years later a French official named Montigny came to Cambodia to negotiate a full-scale commercial treaty, but Duang backed off, because he knew that Montigny had discussed the treaty with the Siamese court, which disapproved of it. When a French missionary later urged Duang to accept France as an ally, the king replied, "What do you want me to do? I have two masters already, who always have an eye fixed on what I am doing. They are my neighbors, and France is far away."

When Duang died in 1860, his eldest son, Norodom, succeeded him. Over the next few years, the new monarch, still uncrowned, rode out a series of dynastic and religious rebellions in northern Cambodia and along both sides of the frontier with Vietnam. Two of the rebel leaders claimed spuriously to be heirs to the throne; a third was one of Norodom's younger brothers. Meanwhile, as the French consolidated their control over southern Vietnam, where they had intervened in the late 1850s, they began to take an interest in Cambodia. Travelers convinced them that Cambodia's economic potential was enormous and that the unmapped Mekong River would lead straight to central China. In the early 1860s, moreover, French interest in the region was piqued by the published report of the "discovery" by a French explorer, a few years earlier, of the ruins of Angkor, in the Thai-controlled Cambodian province of Siem Reap. The ruins, of course, were well known to local people, who guided the Frenchman to them, but the "discovery" foreshadowed more than a century of French scholarship and restoration.

King Norodom was friendless and uneasy. He welcomed the presents and attention given him by French naval officers who traveled to his court from Saigon in 1863. He soon signed an agreement with them, accepting their protection as heirs to the suzerainty exercised by the Vietnamese court. Several French officers remained in Udong to set the treaty in motion. Norodom prudently tried to neutralize his action by signing a secret protocol with Siam, pledging his loyalty to the Siamese court, which had been angered by his negotiations with the French.

Norodom needed friends in Bangkok because he wanted to be crowned. The Siamese had retained Cambodia's regalia after his father's coronation. Invited by King Mongkut to be crowned in Bangkok, Norodom set off for the coast by elephant early in 1864, only to learn that a French flag had been hoisted in Udong in his absence. Hurrying back to his capital, Norodom apologized to the French, who graciously hauled down the flag. It was the last time that they would do so for nearly a hundred years.

A few months later, following ancient custom, Norodom was finally anointed by court brahmins and crowned himself king of Cambodia. He received his crown from a French naval officer sent up from Saigon for the occasion and his regalia from a Siamese official. Technically, Cambodia was still a "two-headed bird," but the royal regalia remained in the country, and all subsequent kings received their crowns from French officials. Siamese influence at the court ceased after the Franco-Siamese treaty of 1867, in which France recognized Siam's rights to the Cambodian provinces of Battambang and Siem Reap, while Bangkok accepted the existence of the French protectorate over the remainder the country.

By 1866, the French had moved Cambodia's capital back to Phnom Penh, which was more accessible to the port of Saigon than Udong had been. Over the next twenty years, their efforts in Cambodia consisted largely of ineffectual attempts to curb Norodom's power and to tidy his fiscal practices, with a view to siphoning off some of his revenue to pay for administrative costs. Norodom balked at the reforms, and French investment languished. In 1884, after the king had refused to allow the French to collect Cambodian customs duties, the French governor of Cochinchina, Charles Thomson, arrived in Phnom Penh aboard a gunboat at night, forced his way into the palace and presented Norodom, at gunpoint, with an eleven-point ultimatum, written in French, that drastically expanded French control. The document also abolished what the French referred to as "slavery," permitted the sale of land, extended the French resident's powers, and stated that Norodom was henceforth to accept "all the administrative, judicial, financial and commercial reforms that the French government shall judge, in the future, to be useful." Norodom was signing a blank check. He probably knew that another turning point in Cambodian history had been reached. Facing the pistols of Thomson's bodyguard and knowing that his brother Sisowath was favored by the French to succeed him, Norodom had no choice.

Further Readings

Chandler, David. "Cambodia before the French: Politics in a Tributary Kingdom, 1794–1848." Ph.D. dissertation, University of Michigan, 1974.
———. *Facing the Cambodian Past: Selected Essays, 1973–1994*. Chiang Mai, 1996.
———. *A History of Cambodia*. 3d ed. Boulder, Colo., 2000.
Ebihara, May. "Societal Organization in Sixteenth and Seventeenth Century Cambodia." *Journal of Southeast Asian Studies* 15, 2 (September 1984): 280–295.
Mabbett, Ian, and David Chandler. *The Khmers*. Oxford, 1995.
Osborne, Milton E. *The French Presence in Cambodia and Cochinchina: Rule and Response (1859–1905)*. Ithaca, 1969.
Tully, John. *France on the Mekong: A History of the Protectorate in Cambodia, 1863–1953*. Lanham, Md., 2002.

Chapter 9

Realignments

The Making of the Netherlands East Indies,

1750–1914

THE YEARS 1750 to 1914 can be understood as framing a period of expanding Dutch power within the Indonesian archipelago. In 1750 Dutch East Indies Company (VOC) envoys to the kingdom of Mataram in Java brokered a truce between warring princes that divided the royal domain into two kingdoms, Surakarta and Yogyakarta. Dutch administrative zones hemmed in this dwindling royal space. During the nineteenth century Dutch power expanded across Indonesian seas to draw into one colonial state, called the "Netherlands Indies," islands and communities that formerly had maintained vassal relations with Java's kings. Through treaties signed with the British in 1824 and 1871, the Dutch defined a state that in the west cut through Muslim sultanates straddling Sumatra, Borneo, and the Malay Peninsula. Treaties with Portugal in the 1890s determined that the southeastern end of the colony would terminate in the central mountains of Timor. Treaties signed with the sultans of Ternate and Tidore brought their vassal states in western New Guinea into the Indies in 1898.

Boundaries outlined a space in which a colony could be created through conquest, negotiation, expansion of economic zones, and Christian missionary enterprise. By 1914 all of present-day Indonesia had one capital, Batavia. Each region had Dutch administrators, public schools, post offices, banks, commercial companies, factories, plantations, and transport hubs, and a circulating population of laborers, foremen, soldiers, clerks, and students for whom the colony provided a workspace and career path greater than their ethnic base and home region offered. For the Dutch, this was a period of change from trading company to colony. After 1800 Dutch outposts were no longer administered by employees of a private commercial company responsible to a board of directors in Holland. Government was transferred to men responsible to the Dutch crown—after 1848, to an elected parliament—through a minister of colonies.

The dates 1750 to 1914 can also be placed within a local framework of changing experience. They mark a journey from archipelago lives to Indonesian lives. In 1750 most archipelago residents were subjects of sultans. During this period their rulers became allies, then vassals of the Dutch, or there was an abrupt ending to rule by sultans, as the Dutch deposed hereditary kings and ruled directly through Batavia's representatives. It was a period when some archipelago residents used colonial transport and communications systems to journey to Cairo and into identities as modern Muslims. For others it was a period of withdrawal, rejection of change, and demands for the restoration of a golden age of monarchy or for release from supracommunity government, a time when mystics and prophets emerged from forest retreats and religious schools to denounce alliances of their sultans with the Dutch. The last years of the period produced men, and a few women, enamored with modernity; their Dutch-language educations and travel within the colony and in Holland propelled them into identities as "Indonesians."

Archipelago inhabitants in 1750 were people who derived their livelihood from forest clearings or from the seas; most paid taxes to sultans through labor services and produce. By 1914 many archipelago residents paid their taxes to the Dutch in cash, were wage workers for European enterprises, and purchased most of their daily needs, rather than making their own clothes and growing their own food. Foremen and managers from different ethnic groups supervised their working hours. They were mobile in new ways; by the end of the nineteenth century, small rowing craft linked into the schedules of large steam-powered ships, while marketers boarded trains or extended their selling range through the bicycle. There was a new, archipelagowide prominence of Ambonese and Batak men who had converted to the Protestant religion of the Dutch ruling class and opted for careers as soldiers, clerks, and schoolteachers. There were itinerant men in new occupations such as photographers, professional students, and politicians. By 1914 elites throughout the archipelago were crossing boundaries in terms of costume, gender roles, and identity.

Many Kingdoms and One Republic

IN 1750 most archipelago residents were ruled by Muslim kings whose genealogies traced their descent back to a time when Hindu gods walked the earth and married humans. Muhammad and Muslim saints, inserted into royal lineages, and titles such as caliph or "shadow of Allah on earth" ensured a continuing association of royalty with divinity. Genealogies also carried a history of royal marriages linking regions around the Java Sea.

Within this world was the "republic" of Batavia. It was headed by a governor-general appointed by the Amsterdam-based directors of the VOC from a group of men whose workspace was the archipelago and who were often related to each other through their locally born wives. The governor-general headed a Christian administration. Its network of agents operated within a region stretching from southern Africa to Japan. Within the Indonesian archipelago the governor-general's vassals included Dutchmen who headed outposts in Makasar, Ambon, Banda, and Semarang. In the eyes of the VOC, the governor-general was the agent of Dutch commercial power, but archipelago sultans addressed him as "elder brother" and feted him with dignities accorded to fellow royals.

Maritime states operated navies recruited from sea peoples and slaves. The VOC recruited its navy in Europe and supplemented it with sailors hired in Asia. Archipelago states raised armies by drafting farmers who provided transport and services to a core of professional soldiers, boosted by bands of hired fighters—Buginese, Balinese, or Javanese—who served under their own leaders. Dutch armies had a core of professionally trained European soldiers, augmented by levies drawn from villages surrounding their command centers in the archipelago, and they, too, employed bands of local mercenaries.

The revenues of both the sultanates and the VOC were based on the export of produce such as rice, timber, salt, and sugar. Both sultans and the Dutch encouraged immigrant Chinese to mine for gold and tin, raise and process sugar, collect taxes, operate markets, and circulate goods between coast and interior. Labor was controlled through forms of slavery or extracted through debt bondage and service duties. The VOC paid men and women employees a combination of rations (clothing, food) and cash—primarily copper coins of Chinese or local manufacture plus paper currency, which was introduced by the company in 1782.

Royal power rested on invented pasts and was regulated in manuals on kingship, translated from Arabic, which said that a ruler should be male, royal, a warrior, pious, generous, and the enforcer of Islamic law. Dutch rulers based their legitimacy on appointment by the VOC, while their local power rested on factions among senior officials. Policies were set in Holland and worked out by the Council of the Indies in Batavia. Archipelago natives and Dutch immigrants developed ways of understanding each other, inserting each other into existing thought patterns. Religious leaders elaborated the Islamic concept of *kafir* (unbeliever) into the Occidental "Other"—foreign, polluting, unbelieving—whose rule over Muslims was insulting. Dutchmen drew on Christian tradition to construct the Oriental "Other"—fanatical, superstitious, warlike, and slavish to Eastern despots.

The major languages of archipelago palaces and poets were Malay and Javanese, while Arabic and Malay were languages of religious scholarship. Devotional poetry, stories of prophets, charms, and family records were handwritten in both Indic and Arabic alphabets. Malay was the common language in ports for speakers of many different languages. In Batavia, Dutch was the language of administration, dictionaries, and scientific reports, while Malay became the language of diplomatic intercourse, trade, schools, and popular religious texts. Dutch and Malay texts were printed in the Roman alphabet for use in church and school; Malay was set in Arabic type for school primers and catechisms.

By 1750 the Dutch had been working and fighting in Indonesian settings for a century and a half. They propped up Javanese kings on their thrones, controlled ports at key hubs along archipelago shipping lines, and were involved in a web of commercial relationships with sultans for the mining of tin, the export of timber, and the production of rice. They monopolized the large-volume end of shipping and sales. Through contracts with sultans, they acquired set shares of production at fixed prices and guaranteed sultans annual payments in silver for the smooth operation of business. Bulk trade depended on a myriad of smaller Asian entrepreneurs, who filled Dutch quotas for exports and who broke down Dutch cargoes for resale in batches at smaller markets.

The Dutch presence generated movement around the archipelago. When sultans succumbed to Dutch pressure and reserved sales of sought-after export goods for the VOC, local entrepreneurs responded by moving their business headquarters elsewhere. Javanese moved to Banjarmasin; Buginese set up operations in Riau. The VOC provided opportunities for some ambitious men to escape vassalage to Java's kings. But networks need continuous connections to the home base. Dutch ties to Europe weakened in the last years of the eighteenth century, owing to the localizing tendencies of Eurasian culture in archipelago towns and the Fourth Anglo-Dutch war (1780–1784), which reduced the numbers of ships and men traveling between Batavia and Holland. At the end of 1799, the VOC collapsed in bankruptcy in Europe, although its senior employees in Asia were rich. In Europe the company had been a standardizer, a modernizing corporate power directed by an elected board. But it was not modern in Indonesian settings, where it was allied to hereditary kings, committed to preserving monarchical rule, and employed local methods of labor control and taxation in the forms of slavery and corvée obligations.

By 1800 the strongest state in the archipelago was the sultanate of Yogyakarta. Eastern Indonesia, the source of spices, was becoming a backwater, for spices were losing their importance to industrializing economies. The Aceh sultanate, which led Islamic life in the archipelago, was turning away from its focus on esoteric learning to the new orthodoxy preached by Wahhabi reformers from Arabia. Between 1796 and 1816 the Dutch lost their settlements in South Africa, Ceylon (Sri Lanka), Malaya, and the archipelago to the British.

When commissioners for Holland resumed administration in 1816, the Dutch field of action had been narrowed to the Indonesian archipelago.

Fusing Islamic Sultanates into a Colony Ruled by Christians

IN 1824 the Dutch and British drew a line down the Strait of Melaka. The narrow sea passage that had connected the territories of Muslim states now became a boundary marking off separate Dutch and British spheres of political influence and economic activity. The agreement set the framework for the creation of two new states, the Netherlands Indies and Malaya, where before there had been many states. The agreement also created two new legal identities, "Native" and "Malay," where before people had identified themselves primarily as subjects of their sultan, or by their ethnic group and home region.

The Diponegoro War (or "Java War"), fought between 1825 and 1830, was another defining action in the creation of the Dutch colonial state. This label obscures the reality of a series of wars pitting an alliance of Javanese princes against the reigning sultan of Yogyakarta and his Dutch backers. Fighting ranged over a broad territory and involved a number of mixed motives and issues. Prince Diponegoro himself, while admitting to secular grievances over taxes and titles, also invoked a spiritual dimension to the conflict, describing his mystical encounter with the "just king" of Javanese lore:

> The Ratu Adil
> was standing on the summit of the mountain
> and his radiance outrivalled that of the Majestic Sun
>
> . . . .
>
> The Ratu Adil said gently:
> "Oh Ngabdulkamit!
> The reason I have summoned you
> is that you must lead all my soldiers
> in the conquest of Java.
> If anyone should ask you
> for your mandate, it is the Koran
> let them seek there."

Forces allied with Diponegoro struck Dutch patrols from mountain hideouts and disrupted marketing links that kept Yogyakarta supplied with food and labor. Religious leaders levied workers in their farming and manufacturing businesses to fight under Islamic banners. But the Dutch alliance proved unbeatable. For the Dutch the war sorted out friend from foe. They rewarded their Javanese allies, shoring up royalty, confirming district heads in office, and guaranteeing positions to pliant successors.

Java's new masters now borrowed from its former rulers their methods of extracting agricultural produce for export. They launched the "Cultivation

KITLV, Leiden, #7836

Resplendent royalty: the Susuhunan of Surakarta (Pakubuwono IX) and his wife,
ca. 1865. Photo by Woodbury & Page.

System" (Cultuurstelsel, sometimes translated "Culture System") as a new
method for creating wealth. In flat, well-watered rice areas, farmers were
required to raise a quota of sugar or tobacco for surrender to the government's
tax agents, and they were encouraged to sell (for cash or payment in consumer
goods) any surplus raised in excess of the tax quota. Through this system, tens
of thousands of farmers working tiny plots of land raised minute quantities of
produce that together amassed high volumes for export. In hilly regions coffee

bushes had been introduced into local gardens in the last years of the voc. Coffee, tea, and rubber plantations, worked by labor gangs composed of farmers working off their taxes and men detached from landownership and tenancy, now permanently replaced rainforest.

The Cultivation System turned Javanese into producers for world markets. It made them dependent on experiments planned in Batavia and on fluctuations of world prices. For some it brought new opportunities. Expanding agriculture brought more jobs for cart drivers, carpenters, potters, and road builders as well. The system increased work hours and introduced new levels of inspection and regulation into villagers' lives. It forged an alliance between the small core of Dutchmen who oversaw it and the greater number of Javanese who implemented it. They paid themselves through percentages of crops delivered and were, mostly, beyond external controls, so that laborers found their burdens to the state increased, their exposure to corruption generally without remedy. The system also fostered the growth of mobile wage labor, for tea and coffee plantations were established in forests on mountain slopes in the habitat of shifting farmers, far from the home bases of people on the plains. It also drew on wage labor to build the network of roads, bridges, and railways servicing plantations, and caught up the mobile landless in work gangs that moved through Java harvesting crops in areas where labor demands were greater than local farmers and tenants could supply. Mobile laborers paid in cash generated demand for food, laundry, shelter, and sex in villages where they were temporarily stationed.

By the 1860s the colonial government was turning over the exploitation of Java's land and people to private enterprise and focusing on providing conditions to make private business successful. It dropped restrictions on immigration from Holland by private businessmen in 1870 and permitted foreigners (Europeans and Chinese) to take up leases on "empty" or "waste" land for ninety-nine years. They could lease land Javanese were already cultivating for three years at a time. Ten thousand new immigrants arrived in the following decade to make Java their workspace and the Javanese their labor force. To get regional rural economies going, the government licensed Chinese entrepreneurs to open pawnshops, where money was lent and goods were sold on credit, and opium outlets, where a Javanese laborer could buy a cigarette dipped in opium or a cup of coffee laced with opium drops to relieve the aches and stresses of a new proletarian lifestyle. Between 1890 and 1910 the government financed the clearing of 1.5 million hectares of forested land on Java for peasant agriculture, thereby turning scattered farmers into villagers settled under government-appointed headmen.

The Cultivation System caught up men, women, and children in its labor force. It rested on coercion, applied through each region's ruling aristocratic and religious families. The proceeds from the sale of sugar and other products financed the industrialization of Holland and the expansion of Dutch power into all corners of the archipelago. The system taught the Dutch that Javanese farmers could rapidly adjust to new ways of earning a living and could gain the skills required to raise successfully new crops under new systems of supervision. The Dutch learned they could contain local manifestations of anger at unfair work practices—expressed through arson, murder, and armed revolt—by coopting religious and local elites and isolating "fanatic" leaders. Sons of the heads of mosques were made managers of coffee warehouses, and sons of provincial leading families were appointed to posts in the colonial service.

While Java was becoming a gardened landscape, cultivation for export in eastern Indonesia was declining. In 1864 the Dutch gave up their monopoly on the cultivation and marketing of spices. Very soon, people in the centers of clove production were without incomes in a region offering few other possibilities. Men in Ambon, long converted to Protestantism, now turned to Dutch schooling. They gave up farming for employment as soldiers, clerks, foremen, and schoolteachers, expanding and maintaining Dutch colonial space. They came to view the colony as the site where they controlled Holland's Muslim subjects and furthered the interests of the Dutch and their Christian allies within the Malay world.

At the western end of the archipelago, which European treaties had designated as Dutch space, colonial power expanded when the Dutch identified local elites as partners and adapted their military tactics to the specific terrain and fighting methods of local opponents. Treaties with the British, command of armed forces on land and sea, and modern management techniques gave the Dutch an imperial perspective. This perspective produced decisions to keep out European rivals, subdue local threats, and promote economic development for Dutch business interests. Archipelago communities were not signatories to European treaties and politics, so they did not perceive the forward march of European colonialism as a threat to their very existence. Located in different thought systems, confronted with different problems, their elites responded to immediate, local challenges by seeking allies. From the array of competing forces in the archipelago, local rulers often chose the Dutch, as the histories of the Minangkabau and Acehnese illustrate.

The Minangkabau heartland was in Sumatra's Barisan mountains, where farmers raised rice, coffee, pepper, and gambier and panned for gold. Minangkabau social organization had evolved an export economy, through both east coast and west coast ports, by means of female agricultural labor and male trading. Lineages based on descent through women controlled housing, farmlands, and village government, and owed loyalty to a royal clan that claimed descent from Java's kings. The mobility of Minangkabau men connected them to Islamic trade and knowledge networks, and made them receptive to a social model that substituted Qur'anic teacher for king and male ownership for lineage control of

KITLV, Leiden, #12186

A gardened landscape: women transplanting rice, near Garut, west Java, ca. 1890.

family property. Early-nineteenth-century Anglo-Dutch rivalry was irrelevant to men who looked to Arabia and its Wahhabi reformers of Islamic folk practice.

Minangkabau called these reformers "Padri." Some scholars believe this term comes from the Portuguese for "priests," while others believe it derived from Pedir, the Sumatran port of embarkation for Mecca, underlining their connection to the Islamic world, rather than to the Dutch Indies. Reformers attacked specific male practices, such as cockfighting and opium, and Minangkabau traditions governing dowry, residence upon marriage, and income. Centers of "correct" Islamic practice formed around religious teachers in fortified villages, from which raids were launched on neighboring communities. Prescriptions in Qur'an and Hadith (collected sayings of Muhammad) were applied to taking slaves, distribution of booty, and administration of conquered villages. In 1815 Padri troops killed most members of the royal family. Surviving lineage heads turned to the Dutch. In 1821 they signed a treaty transferring sovereignty to the Dutch in exchange for the confirmation of "tradition" and their leadership roles. It took the Dutch until 1837 to defeat the Padri. The terrain of sheer mountain, forest, and narrow passes made columns of troops vulnerable to ambush; muskets and gunpowder were unreliable in humid weather; and Padri fighters were based in fortified towns and rural schools. Their fighting units finally dispersed after the Dutch captured and exiled their leader, Tuanku Imam Bonjol (1772–1864).

Aceh remained independent until 1871, when Dutch and British nego-tiators allocated it to the Dutch sphere of influence. When its sultan sought to purchase a steamship, the Dutch sent troops to incorporate Aceh into the Indies. Acehnese soldiers, mobilized by their religious leaders, used mountain and jungle as weapons against colonial troops, launching raids on them from hidden bases. As in Minangkabau, half a century earlier, rugged terrain and humidity rendered much of the Western military arsenal ineffective, so Dutch strategies changed. Cannon from ships bombarded shore defenses. Swathes of forest were cut and rails laid down to speed troops on pedal-powered vehicles. Rails were laid in a large circle around Aceh's capital, with spokes linking the perimeter to the center. Javanese Muslim soldiers, whom the Dutch considered unreliable, were replaced by Ambonese armed with swords and rifles; the Ambonese received higher pay than the Javanese and had superior living con-ditions in separate barracks, with amenities for their families, such as schools and churches. The Dutch abolished the sultanate in 1899 but offered the sultan's agents, the *uleebalang,* the right to continue to administer Aceh in return for opposition to the religious leaders and their troops. By 1903 Aceh was enfolded into the colonial state.

Sumatra's east coast was colonized by plantation companies, which nego-tiated treaties with local sultans to operate in their territories. Laborers from

Subjugating indigenous resistance: Ambonese soldiers in Aceh, ca. 1874.

KITLV, Leiden, #2744

China and Java were imported to rip out the rainforest and to plant rubber and palm oil trees and tobacco. The colonial state supported private enterprise by policing plantation laborers and licensing construction of roads and railways, post and telegraph systems. The Dutch guilder became Sumatra's official currency. Forest dwellers were pushed further back into Sumatra as their jungle habitats were destroyed. New cities, such as Medan, became second-level hubs for the colony's commerce, schooling, and administration. Their populations took in foreign minorities (Dutch, Chinese, Arabs) and an array of Sumatran peoples attracted to the jobs opening up in construction, retail, and government.

On the other side of Java, Bali had encountered the VOC through trade, exchanges of official envoys, and visits by Dutch travelers. Many Balinese also had the experience of living in Java, whether as professionals (artisans, soldiers) or as slaves. From 1848 north Bali was a vassal state of the Dutch, coming under direct rule in 1882. Between 1906 and 1912 colonial troops stormed south Bali's independent principalities. Royal families and supporters attacked Javanese soldiers of the colonial army or turned daggers on themselves in mass suicides known as *puputan*. The peasants did not rise, and the remaining royal houses negotiated a peace that preserved their privileges in slaves and landholding. Balinese now paid taxes to representatives of the colonial state; their customs were codified, and their royalty were given fixed incomes and introduced to Dutch schooling. Roads, telegraph wires, and post offices transformed their landscape, and the Royal Steamship Company connected their ports to archipelago shipping and schedules.

Dutch scholars collected manuscripts from Bali's royal libraries, produced translations, and publicized their contents through academic forums, newspaper and magazine articles, and school textbooks. They perceived Bali as a museum for the study of a culture destroyed on Java by Islam, a site of the exoticized "Other" with an alluring background of trance, human sacrifice (widow-burning), and temple culture. Bali seemed to be an isolated Hindu society and culture in a larger, hostile world dominated by local and international Islam. This vision of Bali was endorsed for political purposes by Dutch officials in the 1920s and 1930s. They made Balinese, rather than Malay, the language of village schools, created institutions for the promotion and study of Balinese culture, and confirmed the identity of Bali as unique, distinct from a hostile Javanese Islamic modernism.

Archipelago wars of 1860 to 1914 established borders to keep European rivals out and subdue the myriad of communities living inside those borders. Grids of control reached out from Batavia. Dutch reformers who wanted to stamp out headhunting, the burning of widows, and slavery supported colonial wars and the application of Dutch solutions to archipelago problems. New colonial ministries for agriculture, forestry, health, and education put Christian Batak, Manadonese, and Ambonese into Muslim territories and Muslim Javanese

KITLV, Leiden, #30505

Proud ethnicity: "captain" of the Malays of Makasar, ca. 1870.
Photo by Woodbury & Page.

into Balinese and New Guinean territories. Dutch rule brought archipelago inhabitants into regular contact with each other.

Muslim thinkers and businessmen questioned why foreign minorities dominated economic life. They linked Chinese and Dutch together, and condemned archipelago princes who cooperated with the colonial government and sent their sons to Western schools. The Dutch elaborated ideas about race and culture. They created the identity of "Native," which excluded people whose heritage lay in China. They operated pass, residence, and dress laws to regulate Chinese business and isolate Chinese from the host community. Colonial officials wrote down oral tradition and catalogued separate law codes for governing the archipelago's many ethnic groups. Archeologists' excavations of Hindu-Buddhist pasts contributed to intellectual constructs of Eastern "wisdom," "spirituality," and "passivity," contrasted with the "dynamism" of the West. Government schools transmitted Dutch ways of seeing to men and a few women from privileged layers of "Native" society. Graduates of academic schools and of technical training programs for auto mechanics, typesetters, and agricultural extension agents began to think of the colony as a single space for the pursuit of their ambitions. As products of secular, coeducational schooling, they veered away from traditional Islamic schooling, which was chiefly religious in content and for men only.

Between 1860 and 1914 people in all parts of the archipelago became colonial subjects and objects. For example, in the 1880s residents of Selayar Island, south of Sulawesi, became integrated into Europe's oils and fats industry as producers of copra. Thousands of Javanese men and women tried their luck in Sumatra as plantation employees. People in Roti Island, southwest of Timor —the southernmost outreach of Dutch power—converted to Christianity; church and school made them literate in Malay and propelled them into new careers in colonial space. As a consequence of colonial conquest, the Indies, which had once meant just Java to the Dutch, came to mean the entire archipelago by 1900. Natives whose careers circulated them through the Indies began to adopt Dutch conceptions. Sukarno's nationalist slogan "from Sabang to Merauke" was lifted from the classroom map that showed pupils the stretch of Dutch-administered territories from the tip of Aceh to the border with eastern New Guinea.

The idea of Indonesia challenged the Dutch, but it also challenged others. It challenged those who promoted the idea of an Islamic universal community and archipelago sultans who presented colonial rule as a fraternal exercise with Holland's royals. Sultans and colonial officials together selected items of local craftsmanship to represent the colony at European exhibitions. Dutch engineers created the "Native" house from an amalgamation of Balinese, Javanese, and Sumatran building styles, and placed live Indonesians among the exhibits. Inside the colony Dutch government funds financed new mosques designed by European architects in "Indo-Saracenic" style, which they claimed was more authentically Muslim than local mosque architecture, with its multiple roofs and split gates.

By 1914 all the territories of today's Republic of Indonesia were secured within the Netherlands Indies. Inside it the Dutch elaborated the myth of colonial "law and tranquility," while their colonial subjects were turning into nationalists, Islamic revivalists, or potential Dutch citizens, such as the Christian residents of Manado who proclaimed their territory the "twelfth province of Holland."

The era can be thought of as a period of Dutch expansion and predominance acquired through the superiority of Western organization, management techniques, science, and weaponry. Or it can be thought of as a period when individuals began taking journeys on steamships, trains, and trams through Dutch-administered territories, viewing a multitude of linked landscapes and gaining a conception of a place greater than their home region and community of birth. By 1914 some princes and graduates of Western schools were wearing European-style business suits and shoes and keeping their hair short and uncovered. Such a look stood for modernity, espousal of enlightened principles, and a desire to push the Dutch aside. Suits and European hairstyles also challenged the turbans and veils advocated by Muslim religious reformers and the costly costumes of aristocrats, which denoted inherited status and privilege.

The Dutch broadcast a rhetoric of "Netherlands Peace" and the "Ethical Policy," claiming that Dutch-imposed solutions to archipelago warring had made possible orderly economic development and the moral improvement of "Native" peoples. Proponents of "uplift" supported military expansion because it would create a colonial space in which to introduce schools, health clinics, and irrigation, and permit the elimination of practices they abhorred, such as headhunting and human sacrifice. The rhetoric of peace and ethics overlaid a reality of endemic violence. Colonial wars, revolts led by prophets, and the coercive reach of the state through government departments and regulations brought turmoil where apologists claimed only to seek "order."

The year 1914 saw the finalization of the Dutch colonial state. It also inaugurated new discourses—the nation versus imperial rule, the discovery of ancient pasts through archeology and the invention of history—as well as new dreamings and a search for new forms of cultural, religious, and political life that might recover the Malay world.

Further Readings

Boomgaard, Peter. *Children of the Colonial State: Population Growth and Economic Development in Java, 1775–1880.* Amsterdam, 1989.

Booth, Anne, ed. *Indonesian Economic History in the Dutch Colonial Era.* New Haven, 1990.

Breman, Jan. *Taming the Coolie Beast: Plantation Society and the Colonial Order in Southeast Asia.* Delhi, 1989.

Coté, Joost, ed. and trans. *On Feminism and Nationalism: Kartini's Letters to Stella Zeehandelaar, 1899–1903.* Clayton, Victoria, Australia, 1995.

Cribb, Robert B. *Historical Atlas of Indonesia.* Richmond, U.K., 1999.

Elson, Robert E. *Village Java under the Cultivation System, 1830–1870.* Sydney, 1994.

Ricklefs, M. C. *War, Culture and Economy in Java, 1677–1726.* Sydney, 1992.

Schutte, G. J., ed. *State and Trade in the Indonesian Archipelago.* Leiden, 1994.

Taylor, Jean Gelman. *Indonesia: Peoples and Histories.* New Haven, 2003.

Wachlin, Steven. *Woodbury & Page, Photographers Java.* Leiden, 1994.

Chapter 10

The Malay *Negeri* of the Peninsula and Borneo, 1775–1900

FOR THE maritime Malay *negeri* (polities) of the peninsula, the last quarter of the eighteenth century was a tumultuous and confused period of changing alliances and fortunes. The century as a whole is sometimes called the Buginese (Bugis) century because of the political ascendancy achieved by those war-like and highly mobile traders from Makasar. The Buginese had established themselves as the paramount power in Malay waters as far back as 1722, when they gained effective control over Melaka's successor *negeri*, Johore, at the southern end of the peninsula. From the Johore capital of Riau (on the island of Pulau Penyengat), they extended their control over the tin-producing *negeri* of Kedah and Perak against the rival ambitions of the Minangkabau ruler of Siak in eastern Sumatra. In 1742 a Buginese was installed as first sultan of a new *negeri,* Selangor, carved out of the western coast of the peninsula.

Trade, War, and Alliance

MALAYS and Dutch alike were disconcerted at the rise of Buginese power, which undermined established political relationships and threatened the tin trade, and they made alliances with other local powers to try to control their common foe. The Buginese responded by attacking Dutch Melaka in 1756 but were defeated as a result of Malay aid to the Dutch. Buginese fortunes fell to a low ebb, but by the 1760s they had recovered, owing to the military prowess of the great warrior of the time, Raja Haji. Under his influence Johore-Buginese authority was reimposed on the principal Malay *negeri* flanking the Strait of Melaka. These included Jambi and Indragiri on Sumatra, and Kedah and Perak on the peninsula. Riau, with a population, it was claimed, of more than 90,000 (50,000 Malays, 40,000 Buginese, and a mixture of others), prospered. By the late 1770s, with Raja Haji as underking to the Malay sultan, its harbor was regularly frequented by hundreds of Buginese, Javanese, Siamese, and Chinese vessels, trading in fine goods and staples ranging from European chintz, Javanese batik, and silk-weave from the nearby island of Siantan to the best shellac and top quality Siam rice. The best and most vivid Malay-language history of the time (the *Tuhfat al-Nafis,* written by a grandson of Raja Haji) adds that Riau was also a great religious and cultural center, and a stopping place for itinerant Arabs from the Hejaz and Yemen.

Riau's greatness did not last long undisturbed, for in 1782 the Dutch and the Buginese again fell out. After an unsuccessful siege of Melaka (during which Raja Haji lost his life), the Dutch in 1784 expelled the Buginese from both Selangor and Riau. At Riau they extracted from Johore's Sultan Mahmud a treaty permitting the establishment of a Dutch garrison and official resident on Pulau Penyengat, but this arrangement had scarcely become effective when Ilanun sea raiders from Mindanao, summoned by the sultan, expelled the Dutch in turn—though Mahmud and the Malays also left, fearing Dutch revenge. The Buginese remained for the moment in Selangor (which they had regained) and in their possessions in Borneo.

In the meantime, in 1786, the British had established themselves at Penang by means of an agreement with the sultan of Kedah negotiated by East India Company official Francis Light. The agreement rapidly proved unsatisfactory to the sultan, who was under strong pressure from an aggressive Siam, which included Malay Muslim areas among its southern realms. The two rival European powers—the Dutch to the south of the Straits, the English to the north—now became the target of an unstable Malay coalition, led by Sultan Mahmud, which set out to drive the aliens from the Malay world. The coalition was ineffectual and the hope vain, though the Dutch were to be effectively removed from the scene for a time as a result of war in Europe.

Ironically, however, the attack by revolutionary and expansionist France on the Netherlands in 1794 led to a temporary cessation of the rivalry between Britain and Holland. William of Orange, having fled to London, instructed all Dutch governors and commanders overseas not to oppose the entry of British troops into Dutch possessions, to forestall the French. In return, the British undertook to make restitution of all colonies placed under their protection when peace in Europe was restored and the Dutch state reconstituted. Not all the Dutch possessions in Southeast Asia obeyed Prince William's injunction, but in the course of the twenty years following 1795, most fell to the British by one means or another, though some for only brief periods of time. So began the uneasy alliance between the two great European maritime powers in Southeast Asia, which was to result, before the next century was out, in the extinction or subjugation of virtually all indigenous political authority throughout the Malay world and a permanent redrawing of the map. Already the empire of Johore had all but disappeared as a political force, for, even after the restoration of Sultan Mahmud at Riau by the English in 1795, persistent argument and feuding between Malays and Buginese concerning the succession to Riau and to the mainland dependencies of Johore and Pahang was tearing it apart. The sultan's death in 1812 merely intensified the conflict, and a new era of British and Dutch cooperation was embarked on, with the Malay powers in disarray in the south and under attack from Siam in the north. The outcome could scarcely be in doubt.

From being an Indian power interested primarily, where Southeast Asia was concerned, in the free passage of trade through the Strait of Melaka and beyond to China, the East India Company suddenly found itself the possessor not merely of a proposed naval station on the island of Penang but of numerous other territorial dominions and responsibilities. Nor were the company's servants at all reluctant to assume these responsibilities and indeed, in some cases, to extend them. Chief among the visionaries and expansionists was Stamford Raffles. When Java, which he coveted for England, was given back to the Dutch in 1816 (by a company anxious to return to a situation in which it was concerned not with territorial governance but with the through trade to the Far East), he urged upon his superiors the acquisition of the small fishermen's island of Singapore at the foot of the Malay Peninsula.

The Rise of Singapore

WHAT Raffles sought, aside from his desire to continue to thwart the Dutch, was a base for "communication with the native princes; for a general knowledge of what is going on at sea, and on the shore, throughout the Archipelago; for the resort of the independent trade, and the trade with our allies; for the protection of our commerce and all our interests; and more especially for an *entrepôt* for our merchandise." These arguments were of much the same force and nature as those that had characterized European maneuvers for commercial power in the archipelago throughout the eighteenth century. Indeed, one can as easily imagine their use by a "native prince" as by an English trader or company servant. The 1819 acquisition by treaty of Singapore—by the time-honored means of playing off one claimant, Riau, against another, Johore—was, however, marked by one particularly important departure from the patterns of the past: it was set up as a "free port," living not by taxation on trade but on trade itself. Its tax-free status was to turn the island within a few decades into the most flourishing exchange port Southeast Asia had ever seen, the center of a vigorous and politically demanding mercantile community.

During the first few years of Singapore's existence, the British sought to reduce systematically the potential for disturbance, and hence for expensive political or military involvement, in the area in which they were then interested. They wanted to reach an understanding with the Netherlands in the archipelago compatible with a foreign policy of supporting the Dutch in Europe (as part of the balance of power against France). In the interests of untroubled continuance of the trade between India and China, they also wanted to secure peace in the environs of Singapore and, more especially, Penang, where Siam-Kedah tensions were proving disruptive. Underlying all this was a firm determination not to become involved in any major way in the internal affairs of the Malay *negeri* of the peninsula or to engage in any form of territorial aggrandizement.

The attempts to reach understandings with the Dutch and the Siamese were, on the whole, successful, though less so for a time in the latter case. Under the Anglo-Dutch Treaty of 1824, Singapore was retained by the British and Melaka was turned over to them, in exchange for the British surrender to the Dutch of their settlement at Benkulen in western Sumatra and their recognition that Dutch interests were paramount in Sumatra and the islands south of Singapore. In return for British willingness to abstain from all political interference in Sumatra, the Dutch gave a similar promise to stay out of the Malay Peninsula, a division of interests that fifty years later was to lead to the final separation of the political destinies of those two parts of the Malay world, breaking centuries-old patterns of interdependence as well as conflict.

Two years after the signing of the Anglo-Dutch Treaty, Henry Burney, a British envoy to the Siamese court, was successful in 1826 in concluding another treaty, which, while limited, did offer some real satisfaction to British interests in the Malay area. Under it, the Siamese agreed to accept the southern boundary of Kedah (whose sultan, in exile in Penang, the British undertook to restrain) as the farthest extent of direct Siamese control on the west coast and to recognize effective Perak and Selangor independence, putting an end to the harassments that had marked the preceding decade.

Despite some years of uncertainty over the implementation and effectiveness of the 1824 and 1826 treaties, the result by midcentury was to establish the East India Company as the paramount power in the Malay Peninsula. The interests of the company and relative peace in the neighborhood of its settlements had been secured. They were based, however, on notions of international law deriving from Western practice that were not fully accepted by all the participants and on political considerations that did not take sufficient account of the changing nature of trade or the changing interests of traders.

In the years following its establishment, Singapore rapidly achieved paramountcy in the maritime commerce of Southeast Asia, a position earned partly by its strategic location but most importantly by its jealously protected free-port status. Before long it surpassed Penang in importance (also a free port, but less well situated for trade), and in 1826 it became the governmental center for what were known henceforth as the "Straits Settlements" of Singapore, Penang, and Melaka. Demographically, it grew from a fishing village to a flourishing port town, which, by the time of the first census, taken in 1840, had a total population of more than 35,000. Variegated though this population was—and mid-nineteenth-century accounts of Singapore seldom fail to describe the concourse of Tamils, Arabs, Javanese, Buginese, Minangkabau, Terengganu and Kelantan Malays, Bengalis, and countless others who thronged the streets and markets—by far the largest part, at least half, was Chinese.

Though the first Chinese immigrants to Singapore were from the neighboring settlement of Melaka, they came increasingly from south China itself after the arrival of the first junk from Amoy in February 1821. One observer listed the Chinese as engaged in 110 separate occupations. They were concentrated primarily in trade and merchandising of all kinds, in agriculture (from vegetable gardening for Singapore's growing population to pepper and gambier cultivation on the north side of the island), and in labor of every description. The Chinese brought with them distinctive forms of social organization, which continued to characterize their life in Nanyang (the "Southern Ocean"). None has occasioned more comment (and often misunderstanding) than the *hui,* or "secret society," which, in its various manifestations, formed the principal base of social solidarity among the Chinese and the means whereby recruitment to the community, absorption of newcomers, maintenance of social order, and the organization of new economic enterprises could be undertaken.

British Involvement in Borneo

BRITISH involvement in northern Borneo was a by-product of the growing weakness and fragmentation of the Malay sultanate of Brunei toward the middle of the nineteenth century. Brunei, historically powerful, had long exercised a fluctuating control over the northern coastal regions of the huge island (often referred to, incorrectly, as the world's largest). This control was shared or contested in its northeastern corner with the nearby sultanate of Sulu in what is now the southern Philippines. The situation at the western end of Brunei was even more complicated. Here, in the area bordering on the nominally Dutch-controlled region of Pontianak, warlike Iban slash-and-burn cultivators had come into conflict with Malay and Arab coastal chiefs subordinate to the sultan of Brunei. Unable to quell the unrest, the sultan turned for help to a British merchant-adventurer, James Brooke, who was recompensed in 1841 with land concessions based on the Sarawak River. Over the next twenty-five years Raja Brooke, as he styled himself, was able to expand his domains at the expense of Brunei, to eliminate Malay sea power on the coast, and to establish administrative control over the Iban peoples of the interior.

In the northeastern part of the island, successive Western commercial interests obtained land concessions from the Brunei and Sulu sultanates in the 1860s and 1870s from which they attempted to turn a profit. (A century later the Philippines used Sulu's treaties at this time as a basis for claims against Malaysia to northeastern Borneo.) In 1881 a British financier, Alfred Dent, formed a trading concern that was granted a royal charter as the British North Borneo Chartered Company. The company built a railroad to link the interior and its tribal peoples with the coast, encouraged the immigration of Chinese settlers to work the land, and established the rudiments of a unifying administration. Though neither Sarawak nor the Chartered Company was a British colonial possession, their external relations, though not their internal affairs, were regulated from 1888 by their recognition as British "protectorates." The sultanate of Brunei itself, shorn of its territories to north and south and in the interior, and threatened with further depredations from both the Chartered Company and Brooke's Sarawak, similarly accepted protectorate status in 1888, while retaining a nominal independence that has continued to the present day.

Developments in the Peninsula

WITH THE access of settled trading conditions on the periphery of the Malay Peninsula, sheltered under British power and free trade practice, and with the expansion of population and trade that resulted, Straits merchants and financiers grew increasingly interested in the Malay *negeri* of the interior as a field of investment. The rulers and chiefs of the *negeri* began in turn to look to the Straits Settlements as a source of both money and manpower. Already in the 1830s the ruler of Johore, long independent of the old polity at Riau, had encouraged Chinese agriculturalists to plant pepper and gambier in the interior of the state, and there were few major rivers on which Chinese shopkeepers and peddlers were not to be found in increasing numbers.

The real economic prize, however, was tin, or the opportunity to mine it, in the west coast *negeri*. European and Chinese merchants in Melaka, the natural outlet for Negri Sembilan (and later Selangor) tin, appear to have been the first to engage in large-scale investment in the mines, followed before long by Penang interests operating in Perak. Though loans were sometimes made to Malay chiefs, who used the money to make speculative advances to Chinese miners, the more usual pattern in the long run was for Chinese traders in the Straits Settlements to make advances direct to Chinese miners and mine managers in the fields, while the Malay chiefs tapped the resulting production by levying tribute and other taxes. As a result of this process of expansion, which was accompanied by Chinese innovation in the actual techniques of mining, production greatly increased, and in the 1850s and 1860s there was a "tin rush" marked by large-scale Chinese immigration into the west coast states. As one example, Larut, in northwestern Perak, which had few Chinese residents in 1848, when tin was first found there, had an estimated population in 1872 of between 20,000 and 25,000.

Changes of this magnitude placed severe stress on the Malay political system. The traditional balance of power within the *negeri*—both between ruler and chiefs and among the territorial chiefs themselves—was based on relatively small differences in wealth. Access to greatly increased revenues, open to those chiefs fortunate enough to be in control of the richer tin-bearing areas, introduced into the system radical elements of imbalance and desperate rivalries over the possession of the important fields. Rivalries among Malay chiefs were paralleled by those among different groups of Chinese miners, the latter usually organized by competing secret societies, which in turn were backed with men, money, and arms by wealthy Chinese merchants in the Straits Settlements. The interaction of these factors, complicated by Malay succession disputes and by piracy bred of the breakdown of traditional patterns of trade and the increasing climate of lawlessness, led to a situation on the west coast of the peninsula that, by the late 1860s, seemed to many observers in the Straits Settlements (most of whom, it must be said, had never set foot on the peninsula) to be degenerating into anarchy.

Affected by adverse trade conditions east of Singapore at midcentury, Straits merchants unable to pursue sustained economic exploitation of the western states (or to develop markets there for the increasing flow of cheap industrial goods from Europe) began to press the Straits Settlements government to intervene. They were encouraged in this by two independent developments: the gradual extension of Dutch authority up the east coast of Sumatra after 1850 and the transfer of authority over the Straits Settlements from the English East India Company to the India Office and then, as a crown colony, to the more amenable—or so the merchants hoped—Colonial Office in 1867.

British Intervention in the Malay Negeri

THROUGHOUT this period, the East India Company and then the Indian government had remained adamantly opposed to involvement in the internal affairs of the Malay *negeri* of the peninsula. Despite official policies, however, actual commitments in the area had tended to grow, though certainly not fast enough to satisfy the Straits merchants. Governors on the spot were prone to take action first and to explain it later. In this way, for example, Melaka found itself embarked on a "war" in 1831 with the tiny neighboring *negeri* of Naning over disputed tax collection. And in the early 1860s, in the course of succession strife in Pahang, Governor Cavenagh took decisive action in Pahang and Terengganu to forestall Siamese intervention. At all times, the officials in Singapore and Penang found themselves under pressure from commercial interests to safeguard British subjects, British trade, or British protected persons in the peninsular states. Partly to relieve such pressures and assuage mercantile anxieties over the downturn in trade and partly from motives that had nothing to do with Southeast Asia, the British government in 1871 concluded another treaty with the Dutch. In return for a promise of equal treatment for British traders in Sumatra, the Dutch were given freedom to extend their sovereignty over the whole of that island. This agreement was a death warrant for Aceh as an independent polity, although execution had to await the conclusion of a thirty-year war of resistance.

Though these imperial maneuvers may have improved, for the moment, the position of British commerce, they did little to lessen the demands for similar aggressive action in the Malay states. Three years later, in 1874, in an about-face of policy that has been discussed by historians ever since, the Colonial Office gave approval to limited intervention in the confused affairs of Perak. The British "forward movement" was about to begin, and, as an appropriately realistic Malay proverb acknowledged, "Once the needle is in, the thread is sure to follow."

In January of that year three small groups of men convened on the island of Pangkor, off the Perak coast, to discuss the disputed succession to the throne. Only one of several Malay contenders was present, Raja Abdullah, who had appealed to the governor of the Straits Settlements, Sir Andrew Clarke, to call the meeting. Along with Abdullah and Clarke and their officials were the Chinese leaders of two of the secret societies whose fighting over the rich tin fields at Larut had become caught up in Malay rivalries over the succession. Clarke had not long before arrived from London with instructions to inquire into the Perak and other west coast disturbances, and to consider whether it was desirable to appoint a British officer to reside in any of the west coast *negeri*. The meeting resulted in the signing of what became known as the Pangkor Engagement. This accomplished three things: settlement of the Perak succession in favor of Abdullah, an end to the fighting among the Chinese miners, and acceptance by Abdullah and his court of a British officer to be styled Resident, "whose advice must be asked and acted upon on all questions other than those touching Malay Religion and Custom," with the further proviso that collection and control of all revenues and the general administration of the *negeri* be regulated under the advice of the Resident.

The enabling fictions embodied in these arrangements and in the circumstances in which they were signed (the new sultan Abdullah owed his throne to the British and henceforth advised the Resident, while the Resident effectively ruled) were to provide a rationale during the next four decades for the extension by treaty of British rule into each of the Malay *negeri* of the peninsula in turn. Perak was followed by Selangor, Negri Sembilan, and eventually Pahang, brought together administratively in 1896 as the Federated Malay States (FMS); and by the northern and eastern *negeri* of Kedah, Kelantan, and Terengganu early in the new century, and finally by Johore in the south in 1914, collectively coming to be known as the Unfederated Malay States (UMS). Underlying all the protectorate treaties was the claim, in the rhetoric of the time, that the "inability of the Malays to govern themselves" could only be remedied by "protectorate" rule by the British. But the key to understanding the agreements reached at Pangkor and elsewhere between the two principal groups, Malay and British, is supplied by the silent presence of the third, the Chinese entrepreneurs, representing the forces of capitalist economic development. It was sometimes said subsequently that "the British held the cow while the Chinese milked it," but before long direct British participation in the extractive economy was to overtake that of the Chinese.

Though the extension of British influence in the peninsula *negeri* was based on earlier patterns of suzerain or vassal relationship and was seen by some of the Malay rulers as a means of obtaining powerful and knowledgeable assistance in profitable governance of their territories, it rapidly came to entail different and more far-reaching subordinate relationships. Despite attempts by some disgruntled district chiefs deprived of traditional tax and toll revenues to rebel against British control, the Malay ruling class accepted the steady advancement of colonial authority for reasons that ranged from the elaborate palaces and substantial incomes provided for the sultans to political pensions for dispossessed district chiefs, membership of new state councils, and salaried posts at the lower levels of local administration.

But to say that the sultans and their establishments, while retaining titular status, lost all substantial powers of decision and control is to take something of a Western view. Within Malay society itself they not only remained paramount but had their position considerably strengthened by the reduction of previously competitive territorial chiefs to the status of titled courtiers or government-paid officials and by the strengthening of their authority over all things Islamic. Treaty clauses exempting from Residential advice matters touching on "Malay religion and custom" encouraged both a turning to the ceremonial trappings of Malay life and, more important, the eventual creation in most states of elaborate and powerful administrative and judicial establishments for the governance of Islamic matters, which became major repositories of conservative authority.

The maintenance of the traditional Malay elite was paralleled by a marked absence of Malay peasant involvement in the mushrooming economy. The

British sought actively to shield Malay peasant society from the disruptive effects of the new economic order, partly in the interests of the "protectorate" relationship and a sentimental view of the idylls of *kampung* (village) life, partly as a means of ensuring continued food production for a rice-eating immigrant labor force. The demands of expanding export industries and burgeoning government services were met by the wholesale importation of immigrant workers from south China, British India, and Sri Lanka, and to a much smaller extent from Java and elsewhere in the Netherlands Indies. By 1891, less than two decades after Pangkor, Malays in the FMS (including immigrants of Malay stock) could muster only 53 percent of the total population of 218,000. Rapid urban growth, the construction of road, railway, and telegraph networks, and the creation of an elaborate colonial administrative system knitting the whole together were to redraw completely the social, economic, and political map of "British Malaya," though it would still bear some relationship to the "Melayu" past.

Further Readings

Ali Haji Ahmad, Raja. *The Precious Gift (Tuhfat al-Nafis)*. Translated and annotated by Virginia Matheson Hooker and Barbara Watson Andaya. Kuala Lumpur, 1982.

Andaya, Barbara Watson, and Leonard Andaya. *A History of Malaysia*. 2d ed. Basingstoke, 2001.

Cowan, C. D. *Nineteenth-Century Malaya: The Origins of British Political Control*. London, 1961.

Turnbull, C. M. *A History of Singapore, 1819–1988*. Singapore, 1989.

Wright, L. R. *The Origins of British Borneo*. Hong Kong, 1970.

Chapter 11

The Spanish Philippines

ALTHOUGH it had long been involved in Asian circuits of trade, the Philippines was not "discovered" by Europeans until Magellan arrived there in 1521. The conquest of the islands and the conversion of most of their inhabitants to Catholicism began with Legazpi's expedition in 1565 and was largely complete within a century, except in the south—Mindanao and the Sulu archipelago—where Islam had already become entrenched. Administered from Mexico, which also subsidized its government, the Philippines remained the farthest outpost of Spain's empire, as grandiose ambitions to conquer the Muslim south, or even China and Japan, dwindled away.

The Bourbon Reforms

OBSERVED from Acapulco or Seville, the mid-eighteenth-century Philippines seemed a static place. Galleons sailed, galleons returned. Occasionally panic and economic havoc struck the Spanish community when a galleon was sunk or intercepted by some foreign power, but a year or two later the vital trans-Pacific trade was always restored. In the walled city of Manila, the Spanish "governor and captain general" often feuded with the Spanish archbishop, while the Spanish *audiencia* (court/council) intrigued against both. Since the threatened invasion by the Chinese outlaw "Koxinga" (Zheng Chenggong) in 1662, nothing else of obvious significance had happened. The priorities of a distant Mexico

City and an even more distant Madrid were barely relevant to the archipelago. Yet simultaneously several unrelated forces were stirring that would unleash a century and a half of dramatic change.

The Tagalog revolts on the friar estates in the 1750s demonstrated a violent anger at the loss of control over land and suggested the emergence of a complex, multiethnic, multilinguistic society. It also exposed the friars to more scrutiny than before; although they suppressed the revolts and won the court cases, it was harder for them to maintain the fiction that their interests were identical with those of the people of the Philippines. Their struggle to hold on to their power—political and economic as well as religious—would become a major theme of the remaining years of Spanish rule.

There were also problems arising from the Muslim south, which Spain had long claimed but had never been able to control. When Spain had first come to the Philippines, it discovered that Islam had arrived there more than a century earlier. The friars demanded that the government "pacify" the south so that they could complete their missionary work there. But Spain did not succeed there as it had in Luzon, except for a few missions precariously perched in northern Mindanao. Islam had already become domesticated into the life of the south, and the Spanish lacked the technological superiority to defeat the sultanates there. Indeed, the renewed Muslim raids after 1750—spurred in part by Sulu's rising trade with China, which created a demand for more slave labor— raised fears within the Christian community, seriously disrupted the economy, and threatened the stability of the colony well into the nineteenth century.

Meanwhile, directed by the reformist Bourbon dynasty in Spain, the Philippine government began to shake off its lethargy. Up to then, most governors-general had accepted the status quo. Each saw his tenure as brief, his goal to stay alive in the tropics, and his reward to return to Spain wealthy. The new governors, however, saw as their mission transforming a dysfunctional economy and theocratic colony; they had been sent out by modern, secular kings, mercantilist reformers of an archaic colonial structure, with a new dream for the Philippines.

First they moved to reduce the economic power of the Chinese, forcing some into a new ghetto (Parian) and expelling others. Chinese mestizos, Christian and culturally integrated, filled the gap. The government maintained that unless new trade routes could be opened and new exports developed, the archipelago was doomed economically. It sought to expand iron mining and to encourage the production of indigo, tobacco, and cinnamon for overseas markets.

These efforts at reform, however, were overwhelmed by a half century of intermittent global war, beginning with the Seven Years War. When Britain occupied Manila in 1762, a direct consequence of Spain's alliance with France, it found a colony isolated and unprepared. Manila was easily conquered, although one high-ranking Spanish official escaped, repudiated the surrender, and organized an effective resistance that limited British power to the Manila Bay area. A year and a half later, again as part of a global settlement, Britain restored the archipelago to Spain.

The interregnum had substantial domestic consequences. The interruption of trade created economic dislocation. Local Chinese, still angered by the expulsion order, openly supported the British, further exacerbating a tension between Spanish authorities and this powerful but exposed minority. Civil unrest caused by the guerrilla conflict with the British fueled a spate of native uprisings, of which the Ilocano revolt led by Diego Silang was the most significant. Operating on the premise that his enemy's enemy was his friend, Silang (ably supported by his wife Gabriela) allied himself with the British, achieving some temporary success before his ultimate crushing defeat.

After the occupation, the bankrupt colonial government recognized the need for developmental measures. A series of governors-general, especially José Basco y Vargas (served 1778–1787), tried to foster plantations, establish trading companies that could carry goods directly from the Philippines to Spain, encourage new Spanish immigration, reform the army and the bureaucracy, and create a viable tax structure. In 1781 Basco established an "economic society" to promote agricultural and mining production, print texts on techniques of cultivation, and publicize agronomy. He imported mulberry trees to grow silk in the Bikol region. Entrepreneurs were offered incentives to mine copper and iron or to grow indigo; others tried to grow cinnamon, pepper, or cotton. The longest-lasting success, in fiscal terms, was the establishment in Luzon of a tobacco monopoly, which controlled prices and volume by demanding forced delivery of tobacco in certain districts, while banning its growth anywhere else.

The Royal Philippine Company, established in 1785, was modeled on the British and Dutch trading companies. It was authorized to sail around the world in either direction and was specifically mandated to invest 4 percent of its profits in economic development schemes in the archipelago. Manila was also opened to foreign ships, provided they carried Asian rather than European goods. The galleon merchants and the friar-owned fiscal foundations underwriting them found themselves in competition with the company and with "country traders" from British India. They fought many of these reforms, and Basco noted that "the first task must be to level the massive mountain of prejudice that stands in the way of the enlightened purposes of central government."

But decades of war in Europe weakened Spain, diverting attention and resources from colonial development projects. The Napoleonic era produced civil war in the peninsula and a British invasion, along with a blockade of the entire continent that disrupted burgeoning international trade. The subsequent revolutions that raged across Central and South America overturned the last remnants of the old order. The Royal Philippine Company only funded sixteen direct voyages to Manila between 1785 and 1820, and finally folded in 1834.

With the independence of Mexico and the consequent abandonment of the galleon trade, Manila also lost its annual subvention, a long-term cash infusion from the New World to the Philippines. Over the centuries the galleons had carried perhaps 400 million silver pesos from Latin America to Manila (most winding up in China), one of the great premodern bullion transfers in world history. Not surprisingly, its termination represented near economic chaos to the Spanish community of Manila. A new way of managing the Philippines—the largest jewel left in the battered crown of Spain's empire—would have to be found.

The Struggle for Clerical Equality

THE GOVERNOR-GENERAL was in theory an enormously powerful figure with authority to do virtually anything he wished, but he had only marginal control over the friars. Over the generations, some of these religious orders had become major landlords, dominating the colony and imposing Spanish and canonical law onto pre-Hispanic peasant life. The pope had granted them autonomy in exchange for their missionary work around the world; instead of reporting to a local bishop, friars reported to a "provincial," one of their own, who reported in turn to the order's own hierarchy in Rome. Thus though the Philippines was divided into bishoprics, with an archbishopric in Manila, friar priests enjoyed an independent structure of accountability.

Embracing Enlightenment ideas, the Bourbon reformers challenged this virtual autonomy of the religious orders, seeing in it a threat to the authority of the state. They insisted on "episcopal visitation" and threatened to expel the friars if they ignored the king's command. In 1767 the Jesuits were in fact expelled from the entire Spanish empire. The Dominicans, witnessing this, reluctantly acknowledged that the archbishop of Manila did have the right to "visit" and to enforce his will on their parishes; other orders followed suit. The Bourbons also tried to exclude the friars from worldly affairs, urging that they sell their estates, which were inconsistent with their ministry.

Centuries before, the pope had granted the Spanish kings extraordinary powers as royal patrons of the church, so governors-general were delegated the authority to appoint parish priests. In the late eighteenth century they attempted to replace friars with "secular" (nonfriar) diocesan priests. All of the Jesuit parishes fell vacant with the expulsion; others opened when friar priests fell ill or died. In the absence of Spanish clerics willing to serve in this distant outpost of empire, the Bourbons decided to appoint indigenous *(indio)* and mestizo priests to these vacant parishes and established new seminaries to train them, although the friars, openly hostile to this effort, viewed these new priests as a joke or sacrilege.

Eventually the friars won the struggle, since the government regarded them as indispensable agents of political control in the archipelago, fearing that local priests might display subversive tendencies. The tide began to turn in 1803, when the friars successfully extracted the governor-general's support to retain three parishes, including an important one near Manila. In 1826, after much of Latin America had won its independence from Spain, most Philippine parishes were returned to friar control. *Indio* priests, savaged by Spanish clerical hostility, were demoted to curates; pro-friar advocates argued that the moral fiber of the colony had deteriorated because native clergy had been ordained. Moreover, some Latin American priests sought political and clerical refuge in the archipelago, easing the pressure to ordain locals. What began as a struggle over ecclesiastical authority evolved into a racial one, as the newly ordained *indio* or mestizo priests were held up to derision by Spanish clerics, who saw them as inadequately trained and innately incapable of learning. One Spanish publicist called the native priest "a caricature of the *Indio,* a caricature of a Spaniard, a caricature of the mestizo, a caricature of everybody. He is a patchwork of many things and is nothing. I put it badly; he is something after all; more than something . . . he is an enemy of Spain." The native aspiration for clerical equality became the first major issue for nineteenth-century Philippine nationalism.

Displaced empire loyalists, including mestizos from the New World, fled to the Philippines defeated, angry, and determined that Spanish authority there would never be compromised by indigenous nationalism. The Iberian-born, known as *peninsulares,* distrusted everyone, even the creoles of the Philippines, known as "Filipinos," who were Caucasian by race but local by birth. In 1824 a revolt within the King's Own Regiment, led by a Mexican mestizo captain, Andres Novales, was quickly and brutally suppressed but seemed to confirm the worst fears of the *peninsulares,* who saw in it a revolutionary threat. From then until 1898, there was a growing polarization between those who were Iberian-born and everyone else.

A pinched, suspicious, and oppressive racism doomed Spanish sovereignty and shaped Philippine history. Spanish control rested on repression and seclusion. One midcentury official observed that restrictions on foreigners were "suspicious and unenlightened but still useful *for preserving the colony.*" Later liberalization was undercut by Spain's own ineptitude. Between 1835 and 1898 there were fifty governors-general appointed to the Philippines, as Spain itself stumbled to find a new national coherence. Whether liberal or conservative, pro-church or antichurch, pro- or antimonarchy, Spain became a backwater, incapable of sustaining any policy that could win consensus, while its economy fell further and further behind the flourishing industrial centers of Europe.

The Emergence of a National Elite

IT WAS amid this nineteenth-century turmoil that the current Philippine oligarchy emerged. Village headmen *(cabezas de barangay)*, presumably descended from pre-Hispanic chiefs *(datus)*, were drawn from a pool of leading families, which became known as the *principalía*. This local elite made colonial government function, under the guidance of the local friar. The wealthiest and most powerful of them, sometimes referred to by the Caribbean term "caciques," came to own land directly or to manage the vast estates of religious orders.

Many Chinese married into *principalía* families. Such marriages made economic sense: the Chinese husband had access to capital and a commercial network, the *india* wife's family had land and local power. The mestizos descended from such unions were far more numerous than the "Spanish mestizos," though over the course of the nineteenth century, ethnic diversity increased as wealthy families from differing backgrounds intermarried. Mestizos, whatever their ancestry, transformed the colony—and benefited mightily in the process.

Mercantilist exclusion, no longer seen as a viable economic policy by Spain, was succeeded during the course of the nineteenth century by relative freedom of trade and foreign commercial investment. By 1879 the Philippines could be described as "an Anglo-Chinese colony with a Spanish flag." It had become an export economy based on agriculture, much of it on small landholdings. Even large friar estates were rarely run as plantations, like those elsewhere in Southeast Asia, but as clusters of tenant farms. Foreign merchants, especially British and Americans, linked the Philippines to world markets. Local entrepreneurs, often mestizos, developed the infrastructure to produce these commodities. Modern banks and trading companies conducted foreign business in dollars or pounds, not pesos.

Sugar was one of the crops that transformed the Philippines. It was first exported in the eighteenth century, using old-fashioned milling techniques. In 1856 the sparsely populated island of Negros produced just 280 tons of sugar. Within twenty years Negros had become a major new center of wealth and power, with 274 steam-operated sugar mills supporting a population that had grown tenfold. Foreign corporations, individual families, or Chinese owned the sugar mills; mestizos dominated the new planter class. The growth of the abaca (Manila hemp) industry, mostly in the eastern half of the archipelago, was more gradual and less dramatic, being a smallholder rather than an estate crop, but abaca rivaled sugar among Philippine exports for most of the century, with tobacco, under the government monopoly, a distant third.

As Manila and other ports opened to international commerce, British merchants dominated the import market of textiles, machinery, and other finished goods. For a few decades before 1870, the archipelago had in good years exported rice, primarily to China, but as land was shifted into sugar, copra, hemp, or tobacco, the Philippines became a chronic importer of rice. Land became more valuable; taxes were assessed in money, not crops. Many peasants were pushed into tenantry, driven to migrate, or forced to change their traditional ways of life as the country entered the global economy.

On the socioeconomic margins, some expressed their discontent. Much of their resistance was framed in religious terminology, but their revolts were not "aberrations," to use Reynaldo Ileto's phrase, "but occasions in which hidden or inarticulate features of society reveal[ed] themselves." Ileto argues that "the mass experience of Holy Week fundamentally shaped the style of peasant brotherhoods and uprisings." The crucifixion of Jesus, the *pasyon,* was a metaphor to express the suffering and longing within peasant society. One major uprising began in 1841 because Apolinario de la Cruz, a devout provincial Catholic, discovered that he could not enter a monastic order. He then established his own native religious brotherhood, the Confraternity of San José, which spread rapidly in Tayabas (now Quezon) province. De la Cruz launched this movement because of clerical exclusion, but his supporters apparently responded to a broad range of rural grievances. The Spanish military was hard-pressed to suppress the rebellion, and "Brother Pule," when finally captured, was hacked into pieces and displayed around the province as a grisly expression of increasing colonial repression.

There were also winners. Over the course of the century—especially after the Suez Canal shortened the trip substantially—there was a steady increase in Iberian immigrants (for the first time including a noticeable number of women), some of whom now settled outside Manila. More significant, the opening of markets encouraged a new wave of immigration from China. In 1839 the Chinese were given "complete liberty to choose the occupation that best suited them" and, subsequently, to live anywhere they wished. In 1844 Chinese gained the legal right to enter local trade; in 1857 the government permitted them to collect taxes. These Chinese brought capital and an entrepreneurial spirit into the hinterland, helping link local producers to foreign markets.

Chinese immigration pressured the mestizos to define themselves culturally. Unlike the immigrants, they did not use chopsticks or speak Chinese at home. They now ate with spoon and fork, were Roman Catholic, and socio-culturally resembled their *india* mothers, speaking local languages and moving across the society in ways that recent arrivals could never achieve. Threatened commercially by new Chinese energy and capital, they became sugar planters, developers of indigo for export, and lessees *(inquilinos)* of rice land from the friars, intermediaries between tiller and landlord. Sometimes they cleared open land, subletting it to peasant cultivators *(kasamahan)* for a percentage—often outrageously high—of the crop yield. Sometimes they evaded restrictions on moneylending by nominally "buying" land from local peasants while granting them an option to repurchase it later; in the event, they frequently ended up keeping title permanently. Well before the export economy was fully developed, one friar had warned that "if no remedy is found within a short time, the lords of the entire archipelago will be the Chinese mestizos."

This new prosperity did not resolve the question of identity, however. Mestizos were not *indios,* or creoles, or Chinese; over time their culture became more Spanish in style, more Catholic in observance, more clearly identified with the land. They eventually appropriated for themselves the term "Filipino," transforming it to mean anyone born in the archipelago, irrespective of ethnicity, and thus they came to define the parameters of nascent Philippine nationalism. Within "Filipino" society, elite status was not determined by caste or lineage, but by wealth, of which landownership was the tangible symbol. To climb higher would require access to modern education and equality in the pulpit, which became the wedge issues this emerging elite demanded. One Spaniard, noting that "the work-hand, the goatherd, does not read social contracts," warned in 1843 that the colleges in Manila should be closed, "because in a colony, liberal and rebel are synonyms."

Filipino Nationalism and Spanish Repression

DESPITE such reactionary sentiments, educational opportunity increased, especially after the Jesuits were readmitted to the archipelago in 1859. Ateneo de Manila, the Jesuit high school, accepted *indios,* mestizos, and creoles without distinction. The ancient University of Santo Tomás, founded in 1611, also opened its doors to males of all ethnicities, although ordination of *indios* and mestizos remained rare. In 1871 only 181 of 792 parishes were administered by non-Spanish priests. Starting in the 1860s, the government mandated the opening of public schools for both boys and girls in every municipality throughout the archipelago, though the implementation of this order left much to be desired.

One mestizo priest, José Burgos, wrote a manifesto calling for clerical equality in 1864, when the Madrid government was relatively liberal and anticlerical. Burgos wanted any newly arrived Spanish priest to learn the local dialect before receiving a parish assignment. When there was a sudden shift to the right in Madrid, the new governor, Rafael de Izquierdo, announced he would rule "holding in one hand a cross and in the other a sword." In 1872 he used the suppression of a mutiny of the garrison at the Cavite Arsenal as an excuse to arrest, try, and execute the clerical advocates of Filipino religious nationalism, including Burgos and fathers Mariano Gómez and Jacinto Zamora.

The archbishop of Manila refused to excommunicate these three priests, despite Izquierdo's strong pressure, rejecting those allegations. Forty thousand came to witness the execution, hearing Burgos cry out: "But what crime have I committed? Shall I die in this manner? Is there no justice on earth?" The governor's crackdown led to many arrests and deportations; others fled to Europe or to Hong Kong. These moves in turn helped radicalize a younger generation of nationalists, including Marcelo del Pilar and José Rizal.

Del Pilar, the son of a town mayor, turned nationalist when his oldest brother, a priest, was exiled to Guam in 1872. Rizal, the most famous of these new Filipinos, was a relatively wealthy fifth-generation Chinese mestizo, whose family was also among those persecuted. Trained as a medical doctor, Rizal was a skilled linguist, speaking many languages, and a man of culture and letters, best known for two scathing satirical novels that were attacked as heretical, scandalous, and subversive. He later wrote that had it not been for 1872, he would have become a Jesuit, and instead of writing the *Noli me tángere* (his first novel), he would have written the opposite. He dedicated his second novel, *El filibusterismo,* to the memory of the three martyred priests, and by 1896, when the national struggle was secularized, the password for the rebels was the initial syllables of their surnames: "Gom-Bur-Za."

Exiled or at home, these new upwardly mobile Filipinos became known as *ilustrados* (educated ones). They advocated a meliorist, evolutionary approach to political reform, including equality for all Filipinos, representation in the Spanish parliament, freedom of speech and assembly, nonrepressive taxation, and clerical equality. Some of the young men who had managed to get to Spain to further their education launched a "Propaganda Movement," emphasizing cultural nationalism, including Tagalog literature and the arts. Romantic and moralistic, these *ilustrados* fused their own aspirations for status with a newly articulated nationalism. Few acknowledged that their own families had grown rich within a socioeconomic system deeply implicated with Spanish colonialism. They raged against a transforming order that had created them.

By the early 1890s the exiled Propagandists, disillusioned that their criticism from abroad had achieved little, drifted home. Del Pilar, long the editor of the overseas newspaper *La Solidaridad,* surrendered all hope of peaceful reform and by his death in 1896 was actively contemplating revolution. In 1892 Rizal organized "La Liga Filipina" to promote peaceful economic and educational advancement, but jittery Spanish officials had him arrested and deported to Mindanao.

Others, from lower socioeconomic strata, also sought independence. Andrés Bonifacio, a clerk in the Manila port area, founded the Katipunan, a Tagalog abbreviation for the "Highest and Most Respectable Association of the Sons of the People." The Katipunan, secretive and neo-Masonic, descended from a long tradition of popular unrest. Bonifacio's language was suffused with the religious images of the *pasyon*. The camaraderie of a secret brotherhood resonated with many Filipinos. It fused a secular Western concept of political independence with a Christian promise of redemption. The Tagalog word for independence, *kalayaan,* suggests both salvation and redemption.

Bonifacio sought unsuccessfully to attract *ilustrados,* including Apolinario Mabini, Antonio Luna, and, most important, Rizal himself, to his Katipunan. He then decided to implicate them through forgery, hoping that Spanish repression would achieve his goals. He succeeded. A friar, discovering the revolutionary plot—supposedly during confessional, though this seems unlikely—reported it to Spanish authorities, who moved to arrest the conspirators. As the police swept across the city searching for Katipunan members, Bonifacio and his supporters fled to a Manila suburb where he issued a call to open rebellion, known today as the "cry of Balintawak," and they tore up their hated *cédulas* (identity papers).

Spanish heavy-handedness accomplished Bonifacio's goal. Rizal was brought back to Manila and tried for treason, because the Spanish believed he was "the principal organizer and the very soul of the Philippine insurrection." Rizal, who considered the Katipunan plan "disastrous," was convicted after a sham trial and publicly executed. Many years earlier, Rizal had written, "The day on which the Spanish inflict martyrdom on our innocent families for our fault, farewell, pro-friar government, and perhaps, farewell, Spanish Government." Rizal's execution forged an alliance, albeit fragile, between the *ilustrados* and Bonifacio's rebels. Hatred of the Spanish unified many Filipinos of every social class. Some years before Rizal had noted: "A numerous, educated class, both in the archipelago and outside it, must now be reckoned with.... It is in continuous contact with the rest of the population. And if it is no more today than the brains of the nation, it will become in a few years its whole nervous system. Then we shall see what it will do."

In his prison cell Rizal wrote a "Manifesto to Certain Filipinos," reiterating that the education of the people was a prerequisite to liberty. Noting that without education and "civic virtues," Filipinos would not find "redemption," he stressed that reforms, if they were to bear fruit, would have to "come from *above,*" because reforms from below would be "violent and transitory." In spite of this cautionary note and his professions of loyalty to a Spain that he still hoped might govern justly, he was shot on 30 December 1896, ensuring the very revolution he had hoped to avoid.

Further Readings

Bankoff, Gregory. *Crime, Society, and the State in the Nineteenth-Century Philippines.* Quezon City, 1996.

Cushner, Nicholas. *Spain in the Philippines.* Quezon City, 1971.

De la Costa, Horacio. *Readings in Philippine History.* Manila, 1965.

Ileto, Reynaldo C. *Filipinos and Their Revolution: Event, Discourse, and Historiography.* Quezon City, 1998.

———. *Pasyon and Revolution: Popular Movements in the Philippines, 1840–1910.* Quezon City, 1979.

McCoy, Alfred W., and Ed. C. de Jesus, eds. *Philippine Social History: Global Trade and Local Transformations.* Honolulu, 1982.

Rizal, José. *Noli me tángere.* Translated and with an introduction by Jovita Ventura Castro. Quezon City, 1989.

Schumacher, John N. *The Making of a Nation: Essays on Nineteenth-Century Filipino Nationalism.* Quezon City, 1991.

———. *The Propaganda Movement, 1880–1895: The Creation of a Filipino Consciousness, the Making of the Revolution.* Rev. ed. Manila, 1997.

Wickberg, Edgar. *The Chinese in Philippine Life: 1850–1898.* New Haven, 1965.

PART 3

❋

Economic, Political, and Social Transformations

Chapter 12

❊

Globalization and Economic Change

FROM at least the time of Marco Polo, Westerners have tried to comprehend Asia's economy, but for centuries most saw it as unique, for better or worse, rather than trying to situate it within a global context. The interconnectedness between East and West only became obvious in the age of imperialism. Even then many colonial officials and their supporters at home simply and happily insisted that contact with the West meant progress, and therefore ultimate benefit, for the natives of "traditional" societies, regardless of the immediate flow of wealth toward Europe. Karl Marx himself, in his nineteenth-century newspaper articles about British India, took a similar line: by destroying "feudalism" in India, however brutally, the British were actually forcing it on the road to capitalism and thus to future socialism and liberation.

Eventually critics such as J. A. Hobson (*Imperialism,* 1902) and V. I. Lenin (*Imperialism: The Highest Form of Capitalism,* 1917) tried to analyze the structural imbalances created by the forcible incorporation of Asia and other areas into Europe's economic orbit. Yet Hobson and Lenin concentrated more on what the wealth extracted from colonies did for Europe than on what its loss meant to Asia; it remained to Asians like Romesh Chunder Dutt (*The Economic History of British India,* 1902) to spell out the local consequences of exploitation, such as the "colonial drain."

In the postcolonial era, scholars of Latin America began to articulate theories to explain what they saw as the structural link between Western progress and non-Western poverty. The latter they saw not as a result of primeval backwardness but as a direct consequence of the former, what Andre Gunder Frank called "The Development of Underdevelopment" (*Monthly Review,* 1966). Africanist Immanuel Wallerstein came up with perhaps the most influential formulation of the relationship in his study *The Modern World-System* (1974). Although he acknowledged the existence of earlier and smaller "world systems" —"world" in this sense does not mean "global" but refers to a broad sphere of economic interconnection—he dated the origins of the modern system to the rise of capitalism in sixteenth-century Europe, which, he suggested, led eventually to the incorporation of the entire globe. Like all its predecessors, the modern world system was divided into a "core," which controlled the political economy and dictated the terms of production and distribution, and a "periphery," from which resources flowed toward the center; thus areas newly incorporated were almost inevitably subordinated from the start.

Asia in the Global Economy

THIS VIEW of a modernizing, expansionist Europe beginning in the sixteenth century to move ahead of—and cast its net over—the rest of the world has had considerable appeal. From the perspective of Asia, however, there are serious questions about the chronology as well as the causality implied in these interpretations. Recent studies suggest that Europe's supposed superiority over Asia was by no means so early or inevitable as it once appeared. The ongoing debate is a useful reminder, in the face of a historiographical tradition still permeated with residual Eurocentrism, of questions originally raised by J. C. van Leur (*Indonesian Trade and Society,* 1955) about the automatic assumption that Europeans became the epicenter of Asian development as soon as the first Portuguese vessel rounded the Cape of Good Hope.

Southeast Asia itself was never the dominant center of a global, or even Asian, world system. From the earliest historical times, the region exported such luxury goods as pearls, resins, and gold to China and India. Over the centuries its reputation eventually attracted Europeans, who came to find the "Spice Islands." Since their adventures, and the rivalries among them, are dramatic and well documented, it is easy to assume that they controlled trade in the region from the time they first arrived in the early 1500s. But at the dawn of the modern era, it was still the China-centered world system that dominated Southeast Asia's external economic relations. Although by the eighteenth century the Dutch effectively monopolized cloves and nutmeg from Maluku, for most of the region the great external markets were China and India. It was to other Asians that Southeast Asians sold pepper and camphor from Sumatra (though the ultimate consumer might be European), edible birds' nests and pearls from the eastern archipelago, resins and rare woods from the mainland, and a host of other exotic commodities as well as staples such as rice.

In return Southeast Asia imported Indian textiles and Chinese ceramics as well as coinage, which circulated widely in areas where official local currency was rare or nonexistent. Except for the two Manila galleons a year that brought "monks and silver" from Mexico to the Philippines, Western traders were, like the Arabs before them, largely interlopers in an Asian mercantile system. They might pay for spices with cotton goods or opium from India or rice from Java, or obtain in Southeast Asia a cargo of teak or maritime products (such as sea cucumbers, tortoise shell, and mother-of-pearl) to exchange for tea or silk in China, where their own manufactures, such as woolen goods, had little value.

How significant was international trade before the middle of the nineteenth century? If we tried to estimate how many Southeast Asians produced export goods or how much they consumed in the way of imports, the figures would not be high. But the profits could be an important source of state revenue, especially in the islands, where polities such as Melaka, Makasar, and the ministates of the north coast of Java depended on trade to finance their rule. The uplands of mainland Southeast Asia, too, relied on overland trade, especially with China, as part of their ordinary circuits of exchange. Moreover, although Southeast Asians made their own pots and textiles for everyday use, Asian imports enjoyed considerable prestige as "objects of desire." Fancy Indian fabrics were worn on ceremonial occasions, and valuable Chinese ceramics often showed up deep in the jungle, miles from the coastal ports where they had entered the territory. Objects of foreign manufacture were rendered comprehensible in local contexts. Cannon, for instance, were given honorific names and titles, such as Kiai Setomo, their destructive power presented as venerable and holy.

Global Markets in the Capitalist World System

BY THE END of the nineteenth century, however, Southeast Asia's long involvement in this Chinese world system was overwhelmed by the rise of Western industrial capitalism. A great expansion of global trade, centered on Europe, swept the world, impelled by demographic growth (which began to accelerate in the eighteenth century), expansionist capitalism, and the industrial revolution. World per capita income grew more than 800 percent from 1820 to the end of the twentieth century, as opposed to only about 50 percent over the previous two millennia. This increase in wealth was built on and fostered even greater increases in world trade.

Throughout the world, industry demanded raw materials, including tin (for canning), cordage fiber (for ships' ropes and binder twine), oil (for lighting and internal combustion engines), and rubber (for transmission belts and bicycle and automobile tires), all of which Southeast Asia could supply, as well as cotton, coal, and iron from North America, wool from Australia and New Zealand, and copper and nitrates from Chile. Beyond the needs of industry itself were the needs of those who worked in factories or benefited from the wealth they created. Workers might be fed on wheat and meat from areas as distant as Australia, Argentina, and the American midwest, while the consumption of the proletarian hunger killers sugar, coffee, tea, and tobacco—all of which could be grown in Southeast Asia—increased exponentially in Europe. Sugar intake in England alone rose sixfold during the course of the nineteenth century, to 90 pounds (41 kg) per person per year. The Asians who grew commercial crops instead of their own food also had to be fed, leading to a boom in rice exports from the mainland states to maritime Southeast Asia as well as to China and British India. In return the West found ready markets in Southeast Asia for inexpensive machine-made cotton goods, kerosene, scissors, nails, and matches, though one of the most profitable imports, well into the 1930s, continued to be Asian opium, sold primarily to the immigrant Chinese in the region.

Connection to this world system transformed Southeast Asia's economy almost beyond recognition. It was said extravagantly of Java under the Cultivation System that the island was one vast government plantation (though such plantations actually covered only 5 percent of Java's terrain), and there has been a widespread impression that in the high colonial period the whole of Southeast Asia's economy was given over to export production. In fact peasant subsistence farming, especially of rice, remained the largest single sector of the regional economy, while commercial agriculture for domestic consumption and small-scale domestic industry also grew steadily. Nevertheless, the burgeoning export industries were the key to the transformation that took place between 1850 and 1940.

The global market did not automatically benefit all who participated in it, of course. High prices did not always stay high, and those who chose to start production in good times were often stuck with their choice when the market turned against them. Price trends favored primary products over industrial manufactures throughout the latter half of the nineteenth century, but the international terms of trade reversed early in the twentieth century, as economies all over the tropics competed to sell the same commodities on the world market, catching many Southeast Asian export industries just as they were starting to mature. Per capita incomes declined throughout most of Asia, in fact, between 1913 and 1950.

Within these broad secular trends, there was variation by both time and commodity. Cyclical downturns were caused by business crises in the West, which over the century before World War II occurred with alarming regularity, affecting even the most remote producers. In the Bikol provinces of the Philippines, which specialized in growing Manila hemp, for example, we can trace the impact of rising and falling New York and London fiber markets from the 1850s onward on such local indicators as wages, land prices, cockfight revenues, and even the marriage rate. Stock market slumps in the West almost inevitably sent down the prices of Southeast Asian exports. This culminated in the great depression of the 1930s, during which there was significant unemployment in the region, as smallholders reverted to subsistence farming, and plantations and mines struggled in collapsing markets or were forced to close, leaving the laborers to scrape a living from the jungle or find their way home.

Linkage to the markets and technology of the West was a two-edged sword, which could benefit or ruin Southeast Asian producers almost indiscriminately. The most important date in Malayan history, someone once quipped, was the day they invented the internal combustion engine, since the need for automobile tires created an insatiable demand for rubber, the backbone of the Malayan economy during the first half of the twentieth century. Similarly, coconuts became a profitable export crop in maritime Southeast Asia once chemists started to discover all the uses that could be made of coconut oil, including margarine, soap, and nitroglycerine.

At the same time, however, science effectively ruined the indigo industry of the Philippines when the dye from that plant, once the finest blue coloring in the world, was supplanted in the nineteenth century by aniline dyes made from petroleum byproducts. Southeast Asian cane sugar producers suffered from the political decision of several Western governments to subsidize the growing of sugar beets in the late nineteenth century, while the cigar tobacco of Sumatra and the Cagayan Valley of the Philippines declined in importance when consumers developed a preference for cigarettes after World War I. One way or another, the fate of much of the Southeast Asian economy came to depend in large part on factors outside local control—though the example of more remote parts of the region, such as Laos and Nusatenggara (the Lesser Sundas), does not suggest that isolation from the world system was any more beneficial in the long run.

The Transportation Revolution

THE GLOBAL demand for raw materials and the need of manufacturers for ever-expanding consumer markets did not produce an automatic response in the non-Western world. For the demand to be effective, barriers to trade needed to be knocked down—essentially the task of nineteenth-century imperialism—and Southeast Asia needed to improve its connections to the industrial West, develop new monetary and commercial institutions, and find both entrepreneurs to organize production and workers to undertake the actual labor. It is in the coming together of all these elements that the drama of regional economic history in the modern era unfolds.

Steamship and port city: Singapore's Bund, ca. 1900.

Transportation had to improve greatly, since before the nineteenth century almost nothing except luxury goods of high value for bulk (such as silk, spices, tea, or silver) was worth carrying any distance. Historians commemorate the opening of the Suez Canal (1869) and the introduction of the steamship and the railroad as milestones in the transportation revolution, but even before these took full effect, the average passenger journey between Europe and Asia had fallen from ten months to four, and improvements in the efficiency of sailing ships had lowered oceanic freight rates substantially.

British steamships serving Southeast Asia—at first mainly in passing, on the way to the China coast—began to appear in the 1860s, as coaling stations were established all along the route from Europe. Other European, American, and Japanese lines, along with privately owned tramp steamers, soon joined them. This international shipping, steadily increasing in tonnage, frequency, and scope of service, provided the most fundamental link between Southeast Asia and the world economy. By 1900 oceanic shipping rates had fallen to just a quarter of what they had been a century earlier. Steamships brought into Southeast Asia textiles, canned goods, and heavy machinery, as well as most of its Western, Chinese, and South Asian immigrants, and carried out most of the millions of tons of sugar and rubber exported as well as Southeast Asian Muslims making the hajj to Mecca—fifty thousand a year by the 1920s.

When improved roads, expanded canals, and railroads were also introduced into Southeast Asia by colonialism (or by local states emulating colonial development strategies), transportation costs fell even further, making it possible to ship bulk commodities like rice or rubber halfway around the world at a profit. Inland transport had traditionally been slow, expensive, and difficult: it took three months to go upriver from Yangon (Rangoon) to Mandalay, a month and a half by ox cart from Nongkhai on the Mekong to Bangkok, several weeks from Semarang to Surakarta in Java. Movement along the coasts, particularly throughout island Southeast Asia, was much easier, but vessels such as praus *(perahu),* junks, and European square-rigged ships had only a limited capacity for bulk shipments.

To this situation government authorities in Southeast Asia brought new determination and new machinery. Road improvement depended mostly on the will to mobilize resources, since there were no significant advances in road-building technology, except for a few steel-girdered bridges over major rivers. New rulers did what their predecessors had done: got masses of men with machetes and shovels to cut down forests and level a path by hand. The Nguyen emperors constructed the Mandarin Road from Hanoi to Saigon, though they used it mainly for political communications; most goods, even rice sent as tax to the court at Hue, still went by sea. The French were somewhat more successful with roads, opening up several new passages into the mountainous spine of Indochina and along the Mekong. But it was colonial Java, mobilizing vast amounts of compulsory labor, that developed the most significant road networks in the region.

Rivers were the major inland waterways, and perhaps the most important of these was the Ayeyarwady River, navigable from Bhamo to the sea. In the age of steam the British-owned Irrawaddy Flotilla Company, with its large fleet, dockyards, warehouses, rice mills, and sawmills, came to dominate the traffic. It carried migrant laborers between central Myanmar and the delta rice frontier and hundreds of thousands of tons of paddy to the mills at Rangoon and Bassein (Pathein), and permitted British troops to steam upriver in a few days in order to overthrow Thibaw's kingdom in 1885. Steam launches and barges also plied other rivers, such as the Chaophraya, the lower Mekong, and the Solo, in east Java.

Canals, actually more efficient than roads for moving goods over comparatively flat terrain, had long been important in Southeast Asia. Mostly still dug by hand—though a few steam dredges were employed—they were extended in the colonial era throughout the delta areas of the mainland, particularly the Trans-Bassac (far western) districts of southern Vietnam. Wherever canals were constructed, settlers followed, suggesting that they created an attractive economic environment. Even today, in some Southeast Asian villages houses are oriented toward the canal rather than the nearest road, which may be some distance away; each house has its own rickety pier from which children embark to school and parents to work or the market.

Where canals were not feasible, the railroad led the transport revolution. The first of Siam's three major lines, begun in 1892, ran northeast to Khorat (Nakhon Ratchasima) to help counter the French advance through Laos, and later extended toward the Mekong. The second line ran north, pushing through to Chiang Mai in 1921. The third line was begun in 1909—with a British loan rewarding the final Siamese cession of claims over northern Malay states—and connected Bangkok to Penang by 1922. The economic results were impressive; the northern and northeastern lines permitted major rice exports from those areas for the first time, while the southward line encouraged tin mining, though it also reinforced southern Siam's economic orientation toward Penang. The political effects were even greater. By 1930, a national system of 1,875 miles (3,000 km), centered on Bangkok, enhanced the primacy of that city and the government located there, helping to bind modern Thailand together. After the railroad reached Chiang Mai, the baht replaced the rupee as the basic currency throughout the north, and Bangkok began in earnest to collect taxes there. Much the same was true in the northeast, where the line also reinforced a long-standing tendency of the Mekong Lao to orient themselves toward Siam.

Similarly, the Rangoon-Prome line in British Burma opened up large areas to export rice cultivation after 1877. By the 1920s, the colony possessed a 2,000-mile (3,300 km) railway network, with no outside connections, defining in its way a distinct economic as well as political domain. In contrast, the grandiose French railway system in Indochina was of limited economic significance. The major line, completed just before World War II, ran along the coastal route of the Mandarin Road and, like it, had limited impact on the local economy, though it may have helped reunify Vietnam politically and psychologically. Two other lines led off into China, reflecting old dreams of tapping the "China market"; they are more significant in the history of southern China than that of Southeast Asia.

Even in island Southeast Asia well-situated railroads could have considerable impact, as the populace responded positively to new opportunities. In Luzon the line from Manila north across the central plain opened up rich lands for rice and sugar production. Luis Taruc, the future guerrilla leader, who as a teenager worked as a baggage handler, was fascinated: "If I could ride those trains I might even be able to reach places where there were no poor people." In central Java there were fifty thousand passengers in 1869, when there were only 21 miles (35 km) of track. By 1876, when the line connected Semarang, Surakarta, and Yogyakarta, nearly one million Javanese bought third-class tickets —mostly one-way, suggesting that the railroad may have represented an escape

Triumphant technology: train on Gote Hteik Viaduct, Shan State, Myanmar.

KITLV, Leiden, #31924

Coastal trade: steamship and praus off Gorontalo, North Sulawesi, ca. 1925.

from the village to new destinations and occupations. The railroad also provided employment to local labor in these colonies—photographs show Javanese men digging the railway beds, while women and children carried away the soil— whereas in British Burma and Malaya, immigrant Indians built most of the system, and Siam employed Chinese laborers.

Steamships represented a less dramatic break with traditional intraregional transportation than railroads but had similar effects. Militarily, they were an important weapon in the piracy suppression campaigns that eventually made the region safe for other kinds of economic exploitation and political intrusion, and were eagerly sought by local rulers, such as Emperor Minh-mang of Vietnam and the sultan of Aceh. Economically, they were not at first much more efficient than sailing vessels, which predominated in coastal traffic until about the 1890s and continued to play an important role through the twentieth century. Eventually steamship lines prevailed in the carrying trade in maritime Southeast Asia, helping to create closer and more regular ties among the islands and peoples of the Netherlands Indies (dominated by a single far-flung shipping enterprise, the Royal Steamship Company) and the Philippines. Well into the twentieth century, however, the general trade of much of the Indies was still centered on Singapore rather than the "national" market.

Forging Financial Links

ECONOMIC machinery of many other sorts was no less important for being less visible than steamships or locomotives. One precondition for a more efficient economy was a standardized monetary system. In Siam in 1850, to take an extreme case, the largest unit of traditional currency was the *chang,* equal to 20 *tamlung,* or 80 baht, or 320 *salung,* or 640 *fuang,* or 1,280 *sik,* or 2,560 *siao,* or 5,120 *at,* or 10,240 *solot,* or 512,000 cowrie shells. In addition, Indian rupees circulated in the teak areas around Chiang Mai, and Mexican and other silver dollars circulated elsewhere, especially in the south. Minted coins, which circulated early in Mongkut's reign, simplified matters somewhat, but it was not until foreign coins were made legal tender in 1857 that foreign commerce and exchange were rendered manageable.

Elsewhere, the comparatively well-developed Vietnamese currency system was not modified but replaced, starting in Cochinchina, by a French colonial system using the piaster as its basic unit. British Burma did not even get its own currency until 1937; instead it got the rupee and was thus annexed financially as well as politically and administratively to the Indian empire. In island Southeast Asia, which for centuries had done most of its business through a whole family of different silver dollars, the political partition among colonial powers had its counterpart in the field of currency. In the Philippines the silver peso carried on, tied two to one to the U.S. dollar after 1903; the guilder spread rapidly over the Netherlands Indies after 1900; and the British sphere got its first Straits dollar notes, pegged to sterling, in 1906.

The introduction and spread of new currency systems helped draw together the different regions of Siam and the colonies, as economic activities within each "national" unit were increasingly expressed in terms of a single medium of exchange. They also linked Southeast Asia to the economies of the various metropolitan powers and to the world system in general. New tariff systems had more limited effects, except where colonial policy dictated tight links with the metropolitan country. This was particularly true of Indochina and the Philippines. France surrounded Indochina with its own highly protectionist tariffs, thus forcefully cutting Vietnam's close economic association with China, just as it had cut Vietnam's ancient but loose political subservience to China. Vietnamese were thereby forced to buy higher-priced French textiles and other goods, while large quantities of Cochinchinese rice went to France (though the bulk of exports still went to Asian markets), spurred by a program of popularization that brought rice, for the first time, into everyday French cuisine.

In the Philippines the impact was far more profound. Spanish restrictive tariffs had little effect on Anglo-Chinese domination of Philippine foreign trade, except briefly in the 1890s. But when virtual free trade within the United States tariff walls was established in 1913, the Philippine economy was shaped to conform to the needs and opportunities of the lucrative American market and eventually would conduct more than 80 percent of its overseas trade with the United States. This comfortable dependence, while providing fortunes for Filipino sugar barons, among others, reinforced inefficient production methods, which priced many Philippine products out of the world market and left the country economically subordinate even after political independence was attained in 1946.

Meanwhile, the telegraph and the submarine cable—coated with Malayan gutta-percha—were introduced into the region in the late nineteenth century. Such improvements in communications enabled commercial information to travel around the world almost instantaneously, allowing brokers to buy and sell intelligently in markets all over the globe. All-purpose service institutions, such as the agency houses of the Straits Settlements (which dominated the export-import business, managed plantations, sold insurance, and much more), also helped integrate the emerging export economies of Southeast Asia into the

By permission of The British Library, photo 578/2

International finance: the staff of the Chartered Bank of India, Australia and China in Batavia, ca. 1900.

world market. For their part, European, Chinese, and Indian chambers of commerce, though representing export-oriented interests, tended to serve business communities whose primary frame of reference was the economy in which they operated.

Concentrated in the major city of each country, modern commercial banks stood at the center of ever more complex financial and credit systems, alongside less formal Asian networks. The official Bank of Indochina dominated the economy of that colony, but in general central banks, such as the Java Bank, developed rather slowly, and private banks with global connections were predominant in most of Southeast Asia. British banks, notably the Chartered Bank of India, Australia and China, and the Hong Kong and Shanghai Bank, came first, establishing major branches in most Southeast Asian countries. Dutch, American, French, Japanese, and Nationalist Chinese banks followed them. At the same time some Europeans (including agents of the Catholic Church in the Philippines), a few overseas Chinese and Indians, and even fewer Southeast Asians also founded banks that operated locally. Like all of these other institutions, their net effect was to facilitate the commercialization of Southeast Asian life and link it to the capitalist world system.

Immigrant Talent

NEW PEOPLE, as well as new institutions and market forces, were vital to modern economic change in Southeast Asia. Immigrants, who by the late nineteenth century seemed to be everywhere, greatly facilitated export production in the region. The most prominent and best documented were the Westerners, but Chinese and South Asians were far more numerous, and the Japanese became important in the early twentieth century. Each of these groups brought with them values, connections, and technology that helped shape the regional economy, though we must be careful not to let their colorful careers overshadow the Southeast Asians themselves, who did most of the actual work.

The story of the migration of Westerners, who poured across the world in this period, is a familiar one. In the age of high imperialism, they came to Southeast Asia as government officials and military men, traders, mining engineers, plantation managers, missionaries, and teachers; some brought their families with them. Those who survived the tropical heat and unfamiliar germs lived lives of more luxury and power than they would have enjoyed back home. Even those who were genuinely dedicated to the welfare of the "natives" generally prospered, "doing well by doing good."

They were relatively few in number but enjoyed disproportionate economic influence because of their political privileges, their freedom of action, and their superior access both to the capital and markets of the West and to modern technology and scientific expertise. The advantages of the latter should

From C. H. Forbes-Lindsay, *The Philippines*, Philadelphia, 1906

Bamboo rafts and workers in Binondo, the Chinese district of Manila, 1906.

not be overemphasized; one Western device after another failed to strip Manila hemp efficiently (though the Japanese finally built one that worked), and British tin-mining machinery was unable for many years to compete with Chinese labor gangs using more "primitive" means. In spite of their pride in hydraulic engineering, Europeans did not actually introduce dams and water channels to Southeast Asia, but rather coordinated the large-scale centralized planning and financing of irrigation, including techniques developed in British India for recruiting, provisioning, and supervising labor. It was new forms of organization like this (and the modern plantation) and new crops like rubber and oil palm, as much as steam-powered rice mills, sugar mills, locomotives and dredges, that constituted the Western contribution to the Southeast Asian economy.

When it came to hard physical labor, however, Westerners were not interested in doing it themselves and in many cases could not find Southeast Asians willing to work for the pay and under the conditions they offered. Tapping rubber, mining tin, laying railroad track, and pulling rickshaws under the tropical sun were arduous compared with village life and offered little more material reward. Few Southeast Asians had any interest in this kind of work at all, and some even opposed it on principle. "People in Perak once thought it a disgrace to work for wages," said the future Sultan Idris in 1880, though he added, "but the feeling is rapidly dying out." So planters, miners, and government authorities looked for more desperate societies, where near-starving peasants were less choosy, and found large and readily available supplies of labor in China and South Asia.

Most of the immigrants came as simple laborers, packed in the steerage of "coolie" ships, owing passage money to those for whom they first worked. They came to work on the plantations of Malaya and Sumatra's East Coast Residency, to build railways in British Burma and Siam, to mine tin in Malaya and silver in Burma, and to labor on the docks, hand sawmills, rice mills, and building sites of port cities throughout Southeast Asia. Almost all intended to stay in the region only a few years, sending cash home to their impoverished villages and returning later with some savings. At the very least, "an immigrant, if he could afford it, would return to China every few years," said one such sojourner. "He would keep his eyes open for a desirable burial-plot," for "while alive we did not mind being men of *Nanyang* (Southern Ocean), but . . . dying, we would hate to be ghosts of *Nanyang*." The great majority did return, but some stayed on—whether too successful to leave or too broke to return home in shame— and local communities of resident aliens grew up, creating what J. S. Furnivall called "plural societies" in many parts of Southeast Asia.

The Chinese in Southeast Asia came almost exclusively from the coastal areas of the southeastern provinces of Guangdong and Fujian. They belonged to many speech groups whose spoken languages—Cantonese (Guangfuhua), Hokkien (Fujianhua), Teochiu (Chaozhouhua), Hakka (Kejiahua), and Hailam (Hainanhua)—were often mutually unintelligible, whose customs and economic specializations were often different, and who were frequently hostile to each other. But all had long experience of a complex economy marked by general use of money and credit, considerable manufacturing, and substantial long-distance trade, especially with Southeast Asia.

During the nineteenth century, their numbers steadily increased in Southeast Asia. After 1870, the influx became a flood, rising each decade to 1930; tens of millions moved back and forth, and at least four million ended up staying in the region. Their migration was pushed by rapid population growth in eighteenth-century China and the widespread disruption of the Taiping Rebellion in the nineteenth century, as well as pulled by the open frontier of opportunity in Southeast Asia. In a few places, such as the lower Rejang River in Sarawak and the northeastern corner of Vietnam, they settled down as peasants; others became market gardeners near booming cities like Bangkok or Batavia. Some came to Southeast Asia as merchants from the beginning, moving outward from China coast cities along commercial channels. But many who ended up as shopkeepers and intermediaries in the export trades were originally laborers, changing professions when they could and settling down and marrying in what became their new home.

Some parts of Southeast Asia saw a much greater influx of Chinese than others. The outstanding example was peninsular Malaya, which, with a total population in 1850 of perhaps 500,000, mainly Malays, saw no fewer than 19 million Chinese arrive between the early nineteenth century and World War II. Most stayed only for a few years, but the residue—1.7 million—accounted for almost 40 percent of the total population in 1931. In the western coastal states, where they were most strongly concentrated, they far outnumbered the Malays. The next greatest concentration was in Siam, where at a conservative estimate, some 12 percent of the population in the 1930s was ethnically Chinese. Elsewhere the figures were lower, ranging from about 3 percent in the Netherlands Indies through 1.5 percent in French Indochina and British Burma to under 1 percent in the Philippines.

All of these statistics, however, should be treated with great caution, because all depend on assumptions about who was "Chinese." Except for those "fresh off the boat," the answer to this question was far from self-evident. Early immigrants from China, in the port settlement days, often married local women. In some societies, such as Siam, the resulting offspring were regarded as indigenous as much as Chinese, since most Chinese were at least nominally Buddhist and thus could be incorporated into local society more readily than in places where exclusivist Islam or Christianity reigned. Elsewhere, the mixed communities—mestizos in the Philippines, *baba* Chinese in Melaka, *peranakan* in Java—acquired distinct identities of their own, although highly acculturated to the local society.

With the greatly increased immigration of the late nineteenth century, this began to change. Large, almost entirely male, Chinese communities arose, unassimilable by local societies. As circumstances improved in the early twentieth century, women were brought from China to join the men, sex ratios began to stabilize, and the resulting enlarged communities became biologically as well as culturally more distinct from their neighbors. At the most basic level, new immigrants mostly spoke their own Chinese languages, learning only the rudiments of the local vernaculars, whereas the earlier mixed communities were fluent in local languages and in some cases had almost forgotten how to speak Chinese.

Chineseness, however, lay in the eye of those who beheld them as well as in the individuals themselves. In many mainland states, where past assimilation had proceeded more rapidly (even if there were occasional anti-Chinese outbursts, some violent), it was often not easy to determine who was "Chinese" and who was not. But governmental policies were also important, and where colonial regimes insisted on categorizing all their subjects by "race" and then treating these "races" differently—as in the Netherlands Indies then or Malaysia today—this tended to make "racial" distinctions more real. And when such definitions affected wealth and livelihood—when people could pay higher or lower taxes, or be granted access to or excluded from certain professions and privileges according to their "race"—it is no wonder that the census categories are not to be relied upon.

The economic role of the Chinese in Southeast Asia was far greater than their numbers, however calculated, would suggest. Except for major enterprises, where Westerners had a bigger share, by the early twentieth century the Chinese enjoyed a general ascendancy in business and commerce, from rice milling and marketing to urban-based wholesale trade and rural retailing, penetrating right into the heart of the countryside. At the local level, their involvement in shopkeeping and procuring export produce drew them into moneylending as well, and when governments "farmed" taxes to the highest bidder, the Chinese were often the most conspicuous tax farmers. "The Chinese," said one Javanese, "have no more idea of polite manners than an ape climbing a branch. When they lease the right to tax a village, they strip it of all its crops, even down to the coconut lands, even before the tax is due. They go to any length to claim their rights, and are equally insistent in demanding payment of tolls." Like the white heron, they are "very quick and adroit in chasing any small advantage."

Not surprisingly, when times were bad, Southeast Asians, like people everywhere, tended to lash out at aliens generally and particularly at tax collectors and others to whom they owed money. The economic predominance of the Chinese was not built on malicious cunning, as detractors implied, but neither was it built simply on hard work and thrift, as the protagonist of the novel *Letters from Thailand* suggests: "If the Thai work 50 per cent and spend 110 per cent, we Chinese work 100 per cent and spend 10 per cent." Essential ingredients in Chinese success were their trading experience and connections, family and lineage networks that transcended state boundaries, and specifically Chinese institutions like loan associations. It was an almost unbeatable combination. One result was the virtual exclusion from large-scale commercial or trading activity of indigenous Southeast Asians and the corresponding absence of an economic "bourgeoisie" based on those activities. Thus the indigenous middle class in most Southeast Asian societies, when it began to emerge in the twentieth century, was largely composed of government servants and the sons of rural gentry.

Like the Chinese, the South Asians came from overcrowded lands with a long history of manufacturing, extensive and sophisticated commerce, and monetized economies. Their late-nineteenth-century migration, however, did not unfold as naturally from historical precedents. Merchants from many parts of South Asia had been trading throughout Southeast Asia, mostly selling cotton goods, as long as the Chinese, and their textile shops remain a characteristic feature of many Southeast Asian cities even today. But new groups formed the bulk of the immigrants in the high colonial age, and they went almost entirely to British Burma and Malaya, following the lines of the new imperial connection rather than older maritime expansion. The most important came from southern India: the Chettyars, a moneylending caste who played a decisive role in Burma's rice export industry, and Telugus and Tamils, who went to Burma and Malaya as laborers but (unlike their Chinese counterparts) seldom became shopkeepers. Substantial numbers of South Asians also migrated as clerks, professionals, and civil servants already familiar with British ways and with the English language, a white-collar movement quite without a Chinese equivalent.

The Japanese were the last major group of "outsiders" to enter Southeast Asia during this period, and they have left the least visible trace, since their role in World War II has cast a shadow back over their earlier presence. They first immigrated, like Chinese and Indians, at the bottom end of the labor market, providing the "coolies" who built the Baguio road in the Philippines and

Photo by N. G. Owen

South Asian heritage: Sikhs in Kuala Lumpur, 1990.

prostitutes for the brothels of Singapore. But as Japan itself industrialized and prospered, its role in the regional economy shifted. Japan turned from an exporter of cheap labor to an importer (abandoning the prostitutes working outside their own empire, who had become an embarrassment) and was increasingly represented in Southeast Asia by merchants and investors, much like the West. Except for a few Manila hemp plantations and timber concessions in Davao (Mindanao), Japanese direct involvement in Southeast Asian economic production was rare. Instead they sold their own textiles and other manufactured goods—which by the 1920s had become the cheapest in the world—and bought local raw materials. In linking the Southeast Asian economy to that of industrializing East Asia, they foreshadowed both the failed "Greater East Asia Co-Prosperity Sphere" of World War II and more positive postwar developments in the region.

Thus in the nineteenth and early twentieth centuries Southeast Asia came to be connected to the world economy in a complex variety of ways. It was opened to a flood of industrial manufactures from the West (and then Japan) and heard a clamoring demand for primary products in return. Improvements in transportation linked the region to the markets of Europe and the Americas as well as its traditional markets in Asia. New machinery and new economic institutions facilitated increased production and improved exchange, while millions of new migrants brought a variety of skills and technologies. What remained was for Southeast Asians to "localize" these connections and transform their modes of production.

Further Readings

Booth, Anne. *The Indonesian Economy in the Nineteenth and Twentieth Centuries: A History of Missed Opportunities.* Basingstoke, 1997.

Brown, Ian. *The Élite and the Economy in Siam c. 1890–1920.* Singapore, 1988.

Cushman, Jennifer W. *Family and State: The Formation of a Sino-Thai Tin-Mining Dynasty 1797–1932;* ed. Craig J. Reynolds. Singapore, 1991.

Hong Lysa. *Thailand in the Nineteenth Century: Evolution of the Economy and Society.* Singapore, 1984.

Hyde, Francis E. *Far Eastern Trade, 1860–1914.* London, 1973.

Legarda, Benito J., Jr. *After the Galleons: Foreign Trade, Economic Change and Entrepreneurship in the Nineteenth-Century Philippines.* Madison, Wisc., 1999.

Lewis, W. Arthur, ed. *Tropical Development, 1880–1913: Studies in Economic Progress.* London, 1970.

Maddison, Angus. *The World Economy: Millennium Edition.* Paris, 2001.

Murray, Martin J. *The Development of Capitalism in Colonial Indochina (1870–1940).* Berkeley, 1980.

Purcell, Victor. *The Chinese in Southeast Asia.* Rev. ed. Oxford, 1965.

Reynolds, Lloyd G. *Economic Growth in the Third World, 1850–1980.* New Haven, 1985.

Sandhu, Kernial Singh. *Indians in Malaya: Some Aspects of Their Immigration and Settlement (1786–1957).* Cambridge, 1969.

Chapter 13

Modes of Production, Old and New

THE EXPORT industries that developed in Southeast Asia were based on many kinds of soil, climate, crops, and land rights; they used widely varying amounts of capital and machinery; and they involved many ethnicities. Yet the great variety of ways in which those commodities were produced and marketed can be reduced to three basic types: coercion, capitalism, and peasant-intermediary industries.

Coercion

COERCIVE modes of production were dominant in the early export industries, as they had been in the traditional political economy of much of Southeast Asia. State power or outright slavery had been used to compel people to build the great monuments of Angkor, to crew warships, and to cultivate fields for monasteries. Now compulsion was used to force ordinary Southeast Asians to dive for pearls in Sulu and grow rice on the crown lands of Siam. Corvée was used everywhere for building or repairing roads and bridges, transporting rice to royal warehouses, and providing domestic service. In times of war, men were drafted as foot soldiers, porters, and animal keepers.

European powers, even when they formally deplored "slavery," were willing to use the power of the state not just to draft corvée labor, but also to force peasants to grow crops for local consumption or export. Early examples of this use of state power were the attempts of the Dutch to enforce a monopoly on cloves and nutmeg in Maluku and the Spanish tobacco monopoly in the Philippines, which helped balance the colonial budget in the half century after its founding in 1781 but had become a fiscal drain before it was abandoned in 1880.

The most celebrated use of governmental coercion in agricultural production occurred on Java. At the end of the Diponegoro War in 1830, when the Netherlands Indies were in grave financial trouble, the new Dutch governor-general introduced the Cultivation System, clothing traditional means of extraction in new bureaucratic and commercial forms. Under the system, peasants throughout most of Java were required to provide specified quantities of export crops—or the land and labor necessary to produce them, which amounted to the same thing—as their principal obligation to the government. The government no longer exported the products itself, as the VOC (the Dutch East Indies Company) had done; that became the task of the Netherlands Trading Company (Nederlandsche Handels Maatschappje, or NHM). But despite ostensibly capitalist forms, this was essentially the old "tribute" system in new guise. The government of Java was once again a machine for collecting export goods; in return it recognized Javanese inheritance, land, and labor rights, thus reinforcing the position and authority of the nobility *(priyayi)*.

During the four decades it lasted, the Cultivation System produced an enormous surplus of goods—particularly sugar and coffee (though much of the latter was not technically under the system)—which revived Dutch shipping and the wealth of Amsterdam and paid off Holland's public debt. The *priyayi* were seemingly content, and the Javanese were described as "the most docile folk on earth"; in 1861 an admiring Englishman called J. B. Money wrote a book titled *Java, or How to Manage a Colony.*

Sugar had been an export crop since the seventeenth century, managed by Chinese entrepreneurs licensed by the VOC. The Dutch government now required villages in many areas to devote sections of their land on a rotating basis to sugar cane cultivation, which has the same agronomic needs as wet rice. Both Dutch officials and Javanese overlords were paid a percentage of the returns from the crop. Meanwhile the government contracted with Dutch and Chinese entrepreneurs to process the cane, lending them money for expensive milling machinery and requiring them to deliver the sugar to the NHM for shipment on government account. Thus farmers, local Javanese officials, and Dutch and Chinese businessmen became deeply enmeshed with each other and with the colonial government.

After about twenty years the system came under attack by Dutch liberals, especially Eduard Douwes Dekker ("Multatuli")—in his searing novel *Max Havelaar; or, The Coffee Auctions of the Dutch Trading Company* (1859)—who charged that it exploited the peasants unjustly. Meanwhile these peasants, who still owed corvée labor to the state, were constructing a physical infrastructure

Construction labor: railroad building near Bandung, Java, 1879.
Photo by Woodbury & Page.

that made the prospect of investment in Java much more inviting for European businessmen. The convergence of these forces resulted in the piecemeal abolition of the Cultivation System—effectively the privatization of a government monopoly—customarily dated to about 1870 (though it began earlier, and elements of the system lasted much longer). Thereafter the Javanese were no longer compelled to work by the state, but in practice most of them kept growing the same crops under very similar conditions.

By the late nineteenth century the use of direct coercion in export production was generally disappearing in Southeast Asia, less because it violated principles of human rights and dignity than because it was inefficient. Legal "slavery" was phased out in Siam at the end of the century—it was already prohibited almost everywhere else—as the system of direct property rights in humans was dismantled throughout the region in favor of indirect control through wages and prices. At about the same time, corvée was generally abolished, reduced, or made redeemable for cash, so the state could employ full-time laborers with developed skills rather than rely on perpetually underskilled part-timers. Corvée continued in some colonies well into the twentieth century, however—until 1974 in Portuguese Timor—and even though slavery is no longer legal, there are still many "unfree" laborers, particularly among sex workers and female factory workers, in the region today.

Capitalism

CAPITALIST ventures—in which entrepreneurs brought together land, labor, and capital—took various forms in Southeast Asia. Western mines and plantations, characterized by large units under unitary management employing modern technology and wage labor, were the most visible. But there was also considerable production by Chinese capitalists and a few Southeast Asians and Chinese mestizos, who managed to thrive despite operating on a smaller scale and with less modern technology and political privilege.

By the early twentieth century practically all of the substantial mineral exports of Southeast Asia were being produced by Western firms: oil from Burma, Sumatra, and Borneo; coal from the Hong Gai mines in northern Vietnam; gold from Luzon; and tungsten and other minerals from Mawchi and Bawdwin in Burma. Though many of these deposits had been worked on a smaller scale before, the modern, large-scale production of the minerals was dominated by European firms, which had access to the heavy equipment and advanced technology needed for optimal extraction. The major exception was tin in Malaya and Siam, where alongside Western mines were Chinese ones, still able to compete by efficient deployment of cheap labor.

The same technological imperatives did not generally apply in agriculture, but capitalism nevertheless made its mark. Except for sugar (always a special case), plantations were generally established where land was abundant and cheap. Thus entrepreneurs located most of their plantations in areas of sparse population, such as Malaya, Sumatra, Mindanao, and the hilly interior of Vietnam and Cambodia. (Some plantation crops, such as coffee and tea, also benefited from being grown on slopes or at altitude.) Generally the locals had no need or desire for wage labor—their eventual response to the rubber boom, for example, was smallholding rather than working on the estates—so plantation managers imported immigrant labor to work the fields. As frontier institutions, set down in "empty" places where at first no other methods were possible, plantations were inherently transitional. Over time many immigrant workers settled in, local peasants began to change their economic outlook and accept wage labor, and some Chinese and Southeast Asians began taking over the management of enterprises, so plantations began to lose their unique historical character.

Though smallholdings produced an increasing proportion of total rubber production over time, plantations dominated the early industry in Southeast Asia, the most spectacular economic success of its day. Virtually no rubber was grown in 1900, but by the 1930s it had become the most important export from both British Malaya and the Netherlands Indies. Between 1905 and 1929 rubber growing in Malaya increased from 50,000 to 3 million acres (20,000 to 1.2 million hectares, about three times as much area as rice, the next largest crop),

KITLV, Leiden, #8044

Plantation labor: (above) Rubber tapping, southwest Borneo, 1946. (Facing page, top) Coffee picking on European plantation, Deli, Sumatra, ca. 1905. (Facing page, bottom) Chopping and sorting sugar cane for planting, Java, 1912.

and exports rose from 6,000 tons in 1910 to 446,000 tons in 1929. Around 1914 rubber passed tin as Malaya's largest export, and it produced 60 percent of the colony's exports by 1929. Over the first four decades of the twentieth century, Southeast Asia consistently supplied 90 percent or more of world rubber, with Malaya and the Netherlands Indies alone accounting for over 75 percent; Vietnam and Thailand supplied most of the rest. The industry was immensely profitable; dividends to fortunate investors averaged over 70 percent in 1911–1912, with some syndicates reaching over 250 percent.

At the same time conditions were terrible on rubber plantations, with long hours, poor food, inadequate medicine, and strict discipline leading to high desertion and mortality rates. Tran Tu Binh described the Michelin rubber plantation at Phu Rieng, Cochinchina, where he worked in the late 1920s, as "Hell on Earth," where the owners applied "a policy of brutal whippings," and the life of the workers was desperate:

> At the end of the day a person really had no enthusiasm left, but wanted nothing more than to slip into the barracks and fall asleep so that the next day, when the overseer's siren sounded again, he could get up, eat, and begin another day of backbreaking work. One's strength today was never what it had been the day before. Every day one was worn down a bit more, cheeks sunken, teeth gone crooked, eyes hollow with dark circles around them, clothes hanging from collarbones. Everyone appeared almost dead, and in fact in the end about all did die.

A classic plantation system grew up in what became the East Coast Residency of Sumatra, a rectangle about 150 miles (250 km) long and 50 miles (83 km) deep. In 1863, when an errant Dutch tobacco planter, Jacobus Nienhuys, arrived there—summoned by the sultan of Deli, apparently—it resembled its coastal neighbors on both sides of the Strait of Melaka. It was an area of small riverine sultanates and chiefdoms set over a sparse, Malay-speaking population cultivating dry rice as a staple and exporting small quantities of pepper and other forest products, including tobacco, which the local Batak had integrated into their slash-and-burn repertory. But the soil was unusually good, and the local sultans were happy, in exchange for large annual payments, to sign over

great stretches of land to Nienhuys and the planters who followed him. The plantations, prospering from the sale of unusually fine cigar tobacco, spread out around the new town of Medan. Before industrial fertilizers came into use, they dealt with soil depletion by raising tobacco for one season, then turning the land back to the Batak to plant their mixed crops; after eight to ten years, when the soil quality was restored, the plantations would resume the fields for another season of tobacco.

In the 1890s and after, new crops were added—coffee, tea, palm oil, and, above all, rubber—and the half-empty land gradually filled up with new plantations. Medan became a city and through its port, Belawan Deli, passed a quarter or more of all Netherlands Indies exports in the decades before World War II. In the residency, everything but the soil and the complaisant sultans was imported: the planters (Dutch, English, American, and Belgian), their capital (U.S.$250 million invested by 1929), their scientific technique, and, above all, their labor and most of their food. The original inhabitants numbered only some tens of thousands and in any case were not interested in wage labor for the pay and under the conditions offered. The planters therefore imported their work force, first Chinese and, after about 1890, as the Chinese began to move into shopkeeping and other urban occupations, Javanese. By 1930 the population of the residency had risen to 1.8 million—half the size of Cambodia—of whom 645,000 were Javanese (225,000 then working on the plantations) and 195,000 were Chinese (just 11,000 on plantations).

The plantations, averaging 8,000 acres (3,400 ha) in size, were almost complete societies in themselves. They had their own barracks, staff doctors, processing plants, and, in effect, their own law and government. Under the "penal sanction" breaking a labor contract was a criminal offense, and local Batak hunted down runaways and returned them to the companies for a bounty. Indonesian communist Tan Malaka called Deli "a land of gold, a haven for the capitalist class, but also a land of sweat, tears, and death, a hell for the proletariat. . . . What the Dutch had called 'the gentlest people on earth' changed its character after suffering so much torment and cruelty, and . . . became 'like a buffalo charging and trampling its enemies.' When I was there [1919–1921], between one and two hundred Dutch people were killed and wounded in attacks by [Indonesian] coolies every year."

A few capitalist enterprises in Southeast Asia employed local labor rather than immigrants housed on the premises. One example was the teak industry of Burma and northern Siam, the second or third largest export earner in those countries. On the management side, it was fully capitalist, dominated by a handful of European-run firms with the funds necessary to pay for elephants and withstand the long waiting period between the first girdling of a teak tree and its sale as board feet in India or Europe six or more years later. Labor arrangements, however, were vastly different from the company housed, doctored, and schooled battalions of Tamil workers on a Malayan rubber plantation. Using largely local labor—a gaudy mixture of Myanmars, Shan, Lao, Kayin and hill tribesmen—and traditional technology, the teak industry had an impact that was more ecological than social.

The sugar industries of the Netherlands Indies and the Philippines were by far the largest and most important of the enterprises using local labor. Sugar production has traditionally been dominated by large-scale operations, since the value of the crop depends so heavily on efficient and rapid milling, ideally within twenty-four hours of cane cutting. To a greater extent than almost any other agricultural commodity, therefore, it has significant economies of scale; a large plantation or company that can coordinate its harvests and link them efficiently to up-to-date processing equipment will almost always outproduce smallholder rivals. With advances in technology, moreover, this advantage increased, owing to the greater costs of milling equipment; a modern Philippine centrifugal "central" (mill) cost about U.S.$1 million in 1920. In labor relations, however, sugar in Southeast Asia was unique. Elsewhere—the Caribbean being the classic example—sugar cane had generally been grown by imported (often slave) labor living on huge plantations. In Southeast Asia, however, most of the labor consisted of local peasants or seasonal migrants.

Between 1870 and 1930 the Java sugar industry grew enormously, shipping 100,000 tons in 1865, 750,000 in 1900, and 3 million in 1930. By the latter date some 500,000 acres (200,000 ha) of land were in cane, with the industry employing 90,000 permanent workers and a million more who worked the six-month season of harvesting and processing. Mills were built in populated areas, where irrigated rice land highly suitable for sugar was already available. Men prepared the land for planting, women and children weeded, and everyone harvested. After harvest, men cleared the ground of cane stumps by burning, and the cycle began again. Meanwhile, labor was needed to build rail tracks, load cars with cane, and roll them to the nearby mills, also staffed with local workmen. Even when mills modernized, they still needed local labor, some of it skilled: machine operators, laboratory technicians, labor supervisors, pay clerks, and managers. Thus sugar in twentieth-century Java remained fully integrated with—or parasitic upon—Javanese rural society.

Similarly, Philippine sugar relied on local rather than imported labor. In central Luzon, where the industry began, cane was grown on terrain already occupied by tenant farmers on estates whose landlords effectively controlled their labor. The mills did not need their own fields and full-time work force but simply contracted for cane with the estates and shared profits with the landlords, who in turn passed a fraction down to the tenants who actually grew the cane. Economically this arrangement was a success, but socially it worsened relations between landlords and tenants, contributing to radical political movements there from the 1930s onward.

Farther south, a new "sugarland" began to develop on lightly populated Negros Island after 1855, when the nearby port of Iloilo was opened to world trade. Encouraged by British export-import firms, Chinese mestizos from Iloilo crossed to Negros and set up mills, while workers migrated, seasonally or permanently, from Panay and other nearby islands. Most of the estates were characterized by familiar landlord-tenant relationships, as in Luzon, rather than the "industrial agriculture" practiced on plantations elsewhere in Southeast Asia. In social and political terms Negros, dominated by wealthy "sugar barons," was calmer than central Luzon in the early twentieth century, but the consequent failure to address the issues created by the extraordinary gulf between rich and poor made it a hotbed of insurrection in the second half of the century.

Chinese tended to engage in commodity production, rather than trade or wage labor, mainly in areas where the original population was very sparse. In such places small frontier societies sometimes arose, organized on lineage lines and based economically on their own export industries. Many of the early enterprises—pepper and gambier plantations in Kampot (Cambodia) and Singapore, gold mines in western Borneo, and sugar plantations in southeastern Siam—declined over the course of time. But tin mining in the belt of deposits running from Phuket in southern Siam to Negri Sembilan in Malaya continued vigorously through the export boom, with many small partnerships and companies using labor-intensive technology based on large supplies of cheap immigrant labor.

Chinese miners did make a few changes—most adopted the more effective European steam pump at the end of the nineteenth century—but only those that were compatible with their established ways of doing business. When heavily capitalized European firms built large modern smelters in Penang and Singapore, they drove small-scale Chinese smelters in southern Siam out of business, forcing all Siamese tin to be shipped south. The Chinese also failed to take up the tin dredge, introduced by English and Australian companies around 1900; it appears that the Chinese were not yet ready to switch to an unfamiliar capital-intensive mode of production or the kind of limited-liability company needed to raise the funds needed for such enormous and expensive machines. In both Siam and Malaya, although Chinese tin production remained well above nineteenth-century levels, the output from European dredges surpassed it between the mid-1920s and the mid-1930s, jumping from about one-third to about two-thirds of total production.

Peasants and Intermediaries

COLONIAL rule and the domination by alien Asians of much of the economy of Southeast Asia were sometimes justified on the grounds that the "natives" were lazy or lacking in the rationality that characterizes "economic man."

When prices went up, it was alleged, the "natives" worked less instead of more, only enough to feed themselves for the day. Some scholars, particularly Dutch economists, developed a whole academic industry explicating the so-called backward-sloping supply curve of Indonesians.

This myth, promoted by Westerners who themselves spent little time laboring under the tropical sun, was, of course, nonsense. Even William Cameron Forbes, the American governor-general of the Philippines, recognized it: "To some of the employers of labor who complained that the Filipino would not work, it was suggested that they add 'unless paid.'" An even more telling refutation, however, comes from the export production undertaken by Southeast Asians in response to rising prices for crops that they could grow without entirely abandoning their traditional way of life.

Within Southeast Asia these prices rose originally in the port cities and were transmitted out into the countryside by a chain of intermediaries. Overseas traders arriving at the ports would seek goods from local merchants—Western, Chinese, South Asian, or Southeast Asian—who in turn would obtain the commodities upcountry from a whole network of dealers and agents, extending out to the local shopkeepers or "jungle brokers" who dealt with the peasants growing the crop. The commodities in turn would come downstream through the same network. Some of these linkages were kept within a single group—the Chinese in particular were well known for dealing with other Chinese whenever possible—but others were gloriously multiethnic. In the Bikol region, for example, Manila hemp might be grown by a Bikolano, who sold it in the village to a mestizo or Tagalog "little agent," who passed it on to a Spanish agent in the provincial capital, who was working for an American merchant house in Manila, who actually exported it to London or New York.

The intermediaries did not simply provide prices and transportation, however. They also provided credit, without which the whole system would have collapsed. At every level each participant in this process demanded from those above an "advance" on the crop long before it was delivered—or, in some cases, even planted. "A Javanese without an advance," one Dutchman complained, "fades away and dies an early death." Whether this credit was necessary for bringing new crops into production or whether it was an expensive option, either offered to lure producers into a debt relationship they could not escape or (conversely) extorted by producers from merchants and brokers who had no choice but to pay, was a question disputed then and now. In any case a constant supply of credit was the lubricant without which the whole machine would seize up and stop.

Peasant production, provoked and facilitated by such credit, was responsible for a number of Southeast Asia's major exports in this period, including Manila hemp, coconuts—widely exported from the Philippines and eastern Indonesia as copra (dried coconut meat)—and pepper. (Some foreign plantations also grew these crops, but as there were no particular economies of scale, they could not dominate the market.) But of all the commodities peasants produced, the most profitable was rubber, and the most widespread was rice.

When the rubber boom began early in the twentieth century, word of the fabulous prices spread rapidly. Smallholders, beginning large-scale planting about a decade after the plantations, caught up with them in total production by the 1930s, by which time one million smallholders in Sumatra, Malaya, and Borneo were growing more than four million acres (1.6 million ha) of mature trees, capable of supplying most of world demand at prices that few plantations could meet. Only gross discrimination under colonial commodity control programs prevented them from dominating global production in the 1930s.

Rubber was an ideal crop for peasants in many ways. Ecologically, the rubber tree, native to tropical Brazil, was well adapted to the poor soils and fierce botanical competition of Southeast Asian forests. It took little effort to plant rubber seedlings within the slash-and-burn cycle or on permanently cultivated land. Once planted, the trees grew quickly and required little tending. Tapping techniques were easily learned by men and women alike. (In traditional Southeast Asia both genders worked in the fields, and this remained true after the shift to export production, although in a few cases men wound up specializing in new products, leaving women to cultivate the subsistence crops.)

Rubber was also ideal in economic terms. While waiting for their seedlings to mature or in bad times when rubber prices were low, peasants could live as before on their subsistence crops. In good times a small stand of trees, tapped by the family themselves, provided cash for buying a year's worth of rice—more than a one-family rice farm would yield (even with much harder work)—as well as for taxes and imported goods. At assembly points in the rubber districts, dealers set up the inexpensive equipment necessary to prepare rubber for shipment, and from there the smoked rubber sheets moved down to the larger ports, such as Singapore.

Finally, rubber was ideal in social terms for subsistence peasants venturing into a cash economy. Though some peasants hired share-tappers to help them at peak periods, and a few had large enough stands to require regular assistance, most smallholders of the 1930s owned only as many trees as they and their relatives could tap themselves. Cultivating plots near the village while continuing to grow rice or other subsistence crops, peasants could enjoy the advantages of a cash income without leaving village society or risking great losses.

Rice, the other major smallholder export crop of Southeast Asia, was generally less profitable for cultivators and less spectacular in terms of impact on the global economy. Although Southeast Asia produced 70 percent or more of world rice exports in the first half of the twentieth century, this represented only a small fraction of total world production, most of which went to domestic Asian markets. The long-term significance of rice in the economic history

Photos by N. G. Owen

Lifting water onto rice paddies, North Vietnam, 1991, using a centuries-old technique. (Top) The basket is dropped into a nearby water source as workers lean in. (Bottom) They then pull back, tossing water from the basket into the paddy field.

of Southeast Asia, however, was greater than that of rubber, for it involved many more people, women as well as men. (Customarily men plowed, women transplanted, and both sexes harvested, but local circumstances could alter these roles.) Rice was also the export that introduced Burma, Siam, Vietnam, and Cambodia to the modern world system, and it remained their leading export earner up to World War II.

The large-scale rice export industries that grew up in mainland Southeast Asia had much in common. They were made possible in the first place by the fact that the deltas of the Ayeyarwady, Mekong, and Chaophraya rivers, soggy alluvial plains, had never been heavily settled before. The flat, undifferentiated landscape, with no nearby hills or forests to provide dietary diversity or useful household products, was unattractive for most Southeast Asians before rice became a cash crop. Unlike Vietnam's Red River delta and Java, which also produced large quantities of rice but had substantial populations to feed and therefore did not yield an export surplus, those three deltas were able to grow huge rice crops for export without any major change in farming practices. When worldwide demand increased in the mid–nineteenth century, peasants in or near the deltas responded readily.

The social implications of this frontier settlement depended on how far (and from where) the migrants had come, how much capital was invested, the nature of the credit relationships established, and the speed of the whole process, as well as strictly agricultural considerations. Growth was most rapid in Burma, which also had the most capital investment and the largest number of alien immigrants, laborers as well as merchants and moneylenders. Not surprisingly, perhaps, it both enjoyed the greatest prosperity in the good years and suffered the greatest social friction in the depression.

In 1855, when the British seized the Myanmar delta, there was an estimated total of one million acres (400,000 ha) under rice in the delta. By 1873 a second million had been added, and thereafter the amount of land under rice increased by one million acres every seven years, reaching ten million (4 million ha) in 1930, at which point the frontier was effectively closed. In the same period, the population of the area increased from about 1.5 million to about 8 million, more than twice as fast as the population of central Burma but only half as fast as the rice acreage. Though the British, famous for their engineering skills, employed local and South Asian labor to build embankments and drains throughout the delta, and would claim credit for much of this growth, the peoples of Burma themselves were largely responsible for it.

The complex social history of the rice export industry from 1870 to 1941 can be divided into three phases: 1870–1900, the open frontier; 1900–1929, maturity and internal change; 1930–1941, depression and social collapse. Independent smallholders dominated the first phase. Steadily rising cash prices for rice drew pioneers from settled areas of the delta and from central Burma to clear and plant holdings much larger than traditional peasant subsistence plots, requiring sizable amounts of seasonal labor not only for harvesting but also for forest clearing and plowing. Meanwhile, the connection with British India facilitated the immigration of South Asians, at first mostly as urban laborers and moneylenders.

In the second phase, rice acreage, production, exports, and immigration all continued to rise, though the rates of increase tended to flatten out over time. The peasant pioneers of the earlier phase now faced new difficulties, however. Having committed themselves to commercial agriculture, they encountered the inevitable risks of this system. A downturn in the price of rice, the death of a costly plow animal, or an impulsive extravagance could suddenly turn a precariously balanced load of credit into an unpayable debt—and since there was no longer a nearby frontier where they could easily start over, insolvent peasants slid swiftly into tenancy or landlessness.

Tenancy had begun earlier—cash tenants operated 25 percent of the land in the main rice-producing districts of the delta in the early twentieth century —but rents were low and conditions still comparatively good then. By 1928, however, the figure had risen to 42 percent; rents were much higher, tenants were more liable to eviction, and increasingly land was rented annually to the highest bidder. Some of the land that smallholders lost passed into the hands of Chettyars and Chinese shopkeepers, but the bulk of it went to other Myanmars—former smallholders, moneylenders, government officials, and rice millers —who formed a new landlord class. At the same time, more and more field labor was done by organized Indian work gangs who circulated through the rice districts. Indians, too, provided a steadily increasing proportion of tenants in these districts, where their competition helped drive up rents.

This curious and unpleasant social machine continued to operate, producing huge exports and profits, until the Great Depression. Then, suddenly, it broke down. The symptoms of social collapse were many. Labor gangs and annual renting of land to the highest bidder grew more common. The amount of land owned by landlords in the main rice-producing districts rose sharply, to 58 percent in 1935, and many of the remaining smallholders were by that time little more than debt-bondsmen on their own land.

One very clear sign of crisis was the rapid increase in foreclosures by Chettyars. As late as 1930, they owned only 500,000 acres (200,000 ha)—6 percent of all farmland—in these districts. By 1935 they had acquired 1.5 million acres (600,000 ha) more, although they disliked landownership and were forced into foreclosure only by the catastrophic insolvency of their debtors. Other symptoms of collapse were the anti-Indian and anti-Chinese riots between 1930 and 1932, and the anti-Indian riots of 1938. Partly as a result of this hostility and partly because of the general stagnation of the economy, almost the same number of South Asians left Burma each year as entered, so that the South Asian minority, which had almost doubled to one million (7 percent of the total population) between 1901 and 1931, stayed level over the next decade. Home-rule governments made some serious efforts to solve the delta problem, but World War II proved more efficient, driving several hundred thousand refugees home to India and making exports impossible. It was left to the independent nationalist governments after the war to pick up the pieces and try to construct a new economic order, in part by discrimination against South Asians.

Elsewhere in mainland Southeast Asia, developments were similar, if less dramatic. The Mekong delta, like the Ayeyarwady, was still sparsely populated in the mid–nineteenth century, with comparatively small Vietnamese settlements mainly confined to the eastern region around Saigon. The French conquered that area between 1858 and 1867, and over the next two or three decades a peasant rice frontier began moving southwest, deeper into the delta. Beginning in the late nineteenth century, vast colonial canal and drainage projects further accelerated the expansion of the industry, and by the mid-1930s the population of Cochinchina had increased three times (to 4.5 million), its rice area four times (to 5.5 million acres [2.2 million ha]), and rice exports about five times (to 1.2 million tons).

Around Saigon the longer-established peasant society drifted into a familiar Vietnamese pattern of medium-sized landlord holdings, built up mostly by local moneylending. Farther west, especially in the area beyond the Bassac (the westernmost branch of the Mekong), much larger properties predominated, as the colonial government sold off great blocks of land cheaply to Frenchmen, the Catholic Church, and wealthy Vietnamese. These holdings were called "plantations" but operated like Philippine estates, with the land parceled out among tenants and heavy use of seasonal labor by landless laborers living nearby or migrating from elsewhere in Vietnam. Since the rice itself passed through Chinese channels, the profits to the absentee landlords came from rent and moneylending to tenants. The social friction this inequitable system created would become apparent, especially after 1945.

The Siamese rice industry, by contrast, had a generally steady and serene history, at the cost of falling behind Burma and Indochina in total production and exports. One reason is that Siam was opened to world commerce not by conquest but by the relatively conservative formula of the 1855 Bowring treaty, which entrenched the authority of pragmatic and cautious indigenous modernizers. The regime moved slowly to abolish corvée and slavery, and refused, for fiscal reasons, to invest more than small sums in irrigation and drainage, which retarded the pace of expansion and tended to keep rice land in peasant hands. More generally, much less outside capital—from government investment or alien moneylenders—seems to have gone into growing rice there than in Burma and Cochinchina; the most important irrigation scheme (in Rangsit, near Bangkok) was financed by wealthy Siamese. Thus the rice industry in the Chaophraya delta, from which virtually all exports came until the 1920s, grew more slowly and was always less commercial than that of its colonial neighbors. As Siamese peasants moved into the open lands of the delta, they cleared smaller farms than Myanmars or Vietnamese, used less seasonal labor, and largely financed the expansion by themselves; they remained independent subsistence farmers who also grew rice as a cash crop.

In all three societies (and Cambodia) intermediaries supplied credit and imports, and assembled the rice for eventual milling and export. In Burma big mills in Rangoon and Bassein gave cash advances to the larger rice brokers, who in turn gave advances to smaller brokers. At the heart of the credit system stood a tightly knit caste of Chettyars who asked relatively low interest rates, confining themselves mainly to well-secured loans. They specialized in rural banking— making mortgage loans to cultivators needing capital to pay for clearing and plow animals—and played virtually no part in commerce. Chinese shopkeepers also made short-term loans to cultivators to pay for migrant labor or marriage ceremonies. But perhaps the most remarkable feature, in comparative perspective, was the vigorous thrust of Myanmars themselves into intermediary functions. Myanmar shopkeepers and moneylenders undertook much of the brokerage by which a few dozen baskets of rice here, a hundred there were assembled into the hundreds of thousands of tons that flowed into the mills in the ports; they worked not just as "jungle brokers," acquiring the rice directly from the cultivators, but farther up the network as well.

In French Indochina and Siam, by contrast, the Chinese dominated rice marketing and processing. French citizens who owned a handful of mills in Saigon did much of the shipping, but otherwise the Vietnamese and Cambodian rice business was almost entirely in Chinese hands, while European-owned mills in Bangkok gave way to Chinese competition after the 1890s. Chinese were everywhere in the trade, from the big millers (employing Chinese labor) and exporters in Saigon and Bangkok, through the large rice dealers and their agents in rural market towns, down to the thousands of shopkeepers and small-boat traders who sold goods on credit to the actual producers: dealing with a familiar clientele, bringing news, selling imported goods, advancing supplies, loaning money, and taking out the surplus rice at harvest time. By the 1930s the Siamese elite in Bangkok—not yet extensively intermarried with wealthy Chinese—was unhappy with Chinese commercial dominance, but the peasants found the Chinese indispensable and easy to deal with.

Local Trade and Manufacturing

IN FOCUSING on the major export industries that produced primary products for the international markets, we risk overlooking all the other economic activities that characterized Southeast Asia in this period. Not only did subsistence agriculture continue to occupy and sustain the majority of the population, but peasant producers and intermediaries also served a variety of regional markets. There had always been a certain amount of local trade, particularly in essential foodstuffs like fish and salt, but with rapidly rising population, improving

Domestic labor: women pounding rice. Watercolor by Gancan, Bali, 1920s.

transportation, increasing economic specialization, and the growth of cities and towns, the volume of this trade increased enormously. In the early twentieth century, various parts of central Burma sent almost 100,000 draft animals a year to the rice areas of the delta; the Chinese fishing villages at Bagan Si-Api-Api in east Sumatra shipped 80,000 tons of fish a year to markets in Malaya and Sumatra; and the Hindu-Buddhist Balinese sent shiploads of pigs stacked noisily in wicker baskets to feed the Chinese and Europeans in most of Islamic Indonesia and Malaya. Rice for the growing population of Manila came not just by cart and barge from nearby provinces in Luzon, but by coastal vessels down from Ilocos and up from the Bisayas as well as by steamers across the South China Sea from Saigon.

Most of the agricultural and sea products, baskets, hats, pots, knives, and the like involved in local trade were produced by peasant smallholders, often as a cash sideline to subsistence farming. In many areas even rice ceased to be something most farm families grew, stored, and prepared themselves. As urban demand increased, smaller local mills spread through the countryside, and villagers developed a taste for the white milled product; women may also have appreciated their release from the arduous daily chore of pounding unmilled rice to remove the husk before cooking. Except for short-distance trading of foodstuffs to markets, which peasants—especially women—often conducted themselves, and some of the wider activities of *santri* traders (trained in the Islamic scriptures in *pesantren* schools) in the Indonesian archipelago, the Chinese tended to dominate internal trade. Because of their near monopoly of the regional rice traffic, the Chinese had great economic leverage in such rice-deficit areas as northern and central Vietnam, Java, and the Philippines.

Some Southeast Asians also became involved in manufacturing during this period. From the earliest days of courts and ports, a few artisans had specialized in making fancy pots, textiles, and metalware—including gamelan instruments—but rarely for more than a local market. As the economy became monetized, cottage industries evolved, much as they had in Europe, producing such goods as textiles (including batik), clothing, pottery, basketry, cutlery (knives and machetes), cigars, and cigarettes. The organizer and financier of cottage industry was often a landowner who employed others on the family fields; he or she would supply a series of households with materials for partial processing and set the timetable and piecework price. Some of the workers were tenant farmers or landless laborers during the agricultural high season and worked in the house compound of the organizer.

Employment at home was particularly suited to women, whose other responsibilities typically included the care of children, domestic chores, and part-time farm work. It required less capital than factory production, and its raw materials—often fibers, foodstuffs, and bamboo or rattan products—were cheap and easy to obtain. As most artisan households employed fewer than a dozen workers, they were not governed by labor legislation, and the workers were beyond the reach of the labor unions that began to form in the early twentieth century.

In the eighteenth century most Southeast Asians still wore textiles woven by local women, either members of the household or small-scale artisans. Imported cotton goods (from India, then Europe, finally Japan) started to displace this production whenever cash cropping developed—as early as the seventeenth century in some areas—culminating in the saturation of local markets by the late nineteenth or early twentieth century. This released women not into idleness, which few could afford, but into other kinds of economic labor, particularly farming and marketing. It ought to have represented a net economic gain to the household, since the imported goods presumably represented better value for the effort invested, but at some expense to women's prestige and pride in their unique craft. "Little by little they feel that their life is no longer of such value," said a Javanese noblewoman early in the twentieth century. "The majority of them are considered by men only as ornaments, all the more so as they are no longer contributing to the household coffers . . . the work of women is become insignificant [and] they always feel that men esteem them less and less."

As global and regional markets for modern manufactures developed, however, Southeast Asians were not well situated to take full advantage of most of them. There might have been a potential for modern industries processing the raw materials the region already produced—making gasoline out of crude oil, cans out of tin, furniture out of teak, jam and candy out of sugar, or tires out of rubber—but very little actually developed, mostly because the technology, capital, and entrepreneurship were not available. The colonial powers had reasons of their own for failing to encourage industrialization, which might have posed competition to factories at home, but little took place even in independent Siam.

The colonial era, especially the 1920s and 1930s, was an epoch of global protectionism, when manufactures in general had great difficulty gaining access to markets to which they were not politically connected, as Japan learned to its cost. Even when there were imperial linkages, however, metropolitan tariffs tended to block the development of Southeast Asian infant industries. The United States, usually generous toward imports from its Philippine colony, tended to draw the line at processed goods, so it let in copra more cheaply than coconut oil, hemp rather than cordage.

One of the rare exceptions of export-oriented manufacturing under colonialism was the cigar industry that arose in the Spanish Philippines. When the tobacco monopoly was established in the late eighteenth century, the colonial government decided to include not just the growing and sale of tobacco, but the processing of leaves into cigars, both for local consumption and for remittance back to Spain. The factories established for this purpose were among the first Southeast Asian enterprises to centralize manufacturing labor under a single roof rather than rely on goods produced by workers at home. The prime reason for this arrangement was to secure the monopoly—body searches took place at the end of every morning and afternoon shift to ensure workers were not smuggling tobacco out—but it also facilitated the division of labor among those who hand-rolled the cigars, those who cut or twisted the ends, and those who checked the weight or packed and boxed them, as well as managers, accountants, and supervisors at every level. Thus, even though machinery played little part in production, these factories can be regarded as early examples of modern industry in Southeast Asia. Visitors to nineteenth-century Manila were frequently taken on tours, and the cigars enjoyed a decent reputation in Europe, though never as high as those of another Spanish colony, Cuba.

By the second half of the nineteenth century, there were four factories in Manila and another in nearby Cavite, employing around twenty thousand workers, making the monopoly by far the largest employer in the city. More than 90 percent of the workers were females; these were "same-sex" factories, with four employing only women as *cigarerras,* one only men. A visitor described the Binondo factory in the 1860s:

> You walk down the middle of these galleries, where at long low
> tables on each side the women work, seated upon mats placed on the
> ground. The noise is very deafening, for each female is provided with
> a stone, about the size of a large lemon, with which she beats the
> leaves continually, reminding one of cooks beating beefsteaks. When
> the "coat" is thus prepared, they put a quantity of small chopped-up
> tobacco in the center, a little gum on one edge, and then roll it very
> adroitly till it assumes the desired form, after which the small end is
> neatly tapered off.

Women were hired—as they had been in the Seville of *Carmen* and would be
by electronic firms throughout Southeast Asia a century later—because they
were believed to be honest, nimble-fingered, and docile workers, unlikely to
cause trouble. Perhaps surprisingly for the time, they were paid as much as men
in equivalent positions, making them among the better-off members of the
urban work force, though over time their wages did not keep up with the rising
cost of living.

In 1816 the cigar workers went on strike not against the usury and extortion practiced by some of their (female) supervisors, but against other abuses
by (male) guards and foremen. Although they succeeded in forcing some
reforms, this did not lead to the creation of a union, and it would be many years
before there was a strong labor movement in the Philippines. The factories
themselves continued to operate to the end of the monopoly and carried on
in private hands after its abolition; *cigarerra* ranked first among all the occupations of women in Manila in 1887. But when the cigar industry faltered in the
twentieth century—as global, and even Filipino, tastes turned to cigarettes
instead—the pioneering role of these factories faded and was all but forgotten.

Colonial governments were generally willing to tolerate, or even to foster,
import-substitution industries so long as these did not harm the trade of the
metropole: cement plants, shoe factories, breweries (such as the Philippines' pioneering San Miguel), cigarette factories, and other enterprises that produced
cheap goods for local consumption. In the critical textile sector, governments
were torn between the desire to protect exports from their home countries and
the need to make inexpensive cloth available to the Southeast Asians on whose
behalf they claimed to be ruling. The Philippines actually established some
modern textile mills in the late colonial period, while batik—which the
Netherlands itself did not produce (although it did make cloth in "Javanese
colors" and designs)—flourished in twentieth-century Indonesia and even
benefited from the tariffs introduced by the Dutch to keep out Japanese competition. Overall, however, manufacturing remained underdeveloped in Southeast
Asia in this period; its significance lay chiefly in whatever preparation and
precedent it set for postwar developments.

Further Readings

Adas, Michael. *The Burma Delta: Economic Development and Social Change on an Asian Rice Frontier, 1852–1941.* Madison, Wisc., 1974.

Cheng Siok-hwa. *The Rice Industry of Burma, 1852–1940.* Kuala Lumpur, 1968.

Drabble, J. H. *Rubber in Malaya, 1876–1922: The Genesis of the Industry.* Kuala Lumpur, 1973.

De Jesus, Ed. C. *The Tobacco Monopoly in the Philippines: Bureaucratic Enterprise and Social Change, 1766–1880.* Quezon City, 1980.

Elson, R. E. *Javanese Peasants and the Colonial Sugar Industry: Impact and Change in an East Java Residency, 1830–1940.* Singapore, 1984.

———. *Village Java under the Cultivation System, 1830–1870.* Sydney, 1994.

Feeney, David. *The Political Economy of Productivity: Thai Agricultural Development, 1880–1975.* Vancouver, 1982.

Ingram, James C. *Economic Change in Thailand: 1850–1970.* Kuala Lumpur, 1971.

Larkin, John A. *Sugar and the Origins of Modern Philippine Society.* Berkeley, 1993.

Lim Teck Ghee. *Peasants and Their Agricultural Economy in Colonial Malaya, 1894–1941.* Kuala Lumpur, 1977.

Owen, Norman G. *Prosperity without Progress: Manila Hemp and Material Life in the Colonial Philippines.* Berkeley, 1984.

Wong Lin Ken. *The Malayan Tin Industry to 1914: With Special Reference to the States of Perak, Selangor, Negri, Sembilan and Pahang.* Tucson, 1965.

Chapter 14

Consolidation of Colonial Power and Centralization of State Authority

THE GLOBALIZING PROCESSES introduced by the industrial revolution in Europe at the end of the eighteenth century changed the nature of Western interests in Southeast Asia and eventually the relationship of the West with the rest of the world. As they did, a revolution in government, the consequences of which are still apparent throughout Southeast Asia, took place. Not only were the processes and institutions of formal political authority transformed by imperialism, but the ideas that had justified and explained political power were first challenged, then significantly undermined. In retrospect this seems inevitable and even necessary, but it did not seem so to those caught up in the process. The hubris of the makers of the new colonial states blinded them to the fact that by changing the nature of rule in the societies they controlled, they were creating the popular forces that would eventually remove their successors.

Maps on the Page and in the Mind

No longer content to trade with Southeast Asia through a few entrepôts, the increasingly powerful major trading nations of Europe and the United States ended up taking effective control of the entire region. As is often noted, colonialism drew the map of Southeast Asia, and to a large extent it is true that the borders of contemporary Southeast Asian states were effectively drawn by the beginning of the twentieth century. But that simple phrase hides more significant intellectual and political processes that were generated by these changes. People were forced to rethink the very nature of authority in their communities. Indigenous political power, which had been sanctioned and justified by religious authority and sacred obligation, was soon to be challenged by power derived from remote, seemingly arbitrary, and secular sources. Government came to be judged not so much by whether it bestowed respect and status to individuals, but by whether it was efficiently and economically rational. It was increasingly seen as a set of institutions that created the conditions for economic growth and world trade, not one that in informal, ad hoc ways adjusted itself to prevailing conditions. In time the colonized came to perceive the world in much the same terms as the colonizers did. Though the creation of political and social order, backed up by force, lay at the root of both pre-colonial and colonial governments in the region, the end of the nineteenth century witnessed a watershed in the role of government in controlling people's lives.

For the individuals caught up in this revolutionary process, coming to terms with such new forces was not easy to reconcile with earlier formed and still cherished ways of thought and action. There was often a lag between changed structures and changed ideas. People were forced to accept new institutions before they could justify them to themselves. This made colonial rule seem more arbitrary and even capricious than would have been the case had this process been conducted more gradually, by a government perceived as legitimate. Even when colonial rulers kept in place remnants of the displaced old orders, such as the emperor in Hue or the sultans in Malaya, and even when personalized patron-client ties still informed day-to-day dealing with official-dom, this merely obscured the new order with a veneer of tradition.

This point is underscored by the one exception to the colonization of Southeast Asia, Siam. Though it came increasingly into the British sphere of influence, its monarchy was able to maintain its independence and authority within the shrinking sphere that became internationally recognized as the Kingdom of Siam. Within that territory, the modernizing kings Mongkut and Chulalongkorn carried out a transformation in government almost as revolutionary as that imposed by the British, French, and Dutch in their respective colonies. But because indigenous rulers—culturally aware and sensitive to the ideas and interests of their subjects—led this movement, it was achieved without generating the resistance that created so much organized opposition to foreign rule elsewhere in the region. Whereas Siam was transformed through internal reforms, British Burma, French Vietnam, and the Netherlands Indies had modernity thrust on them, or in some cases kept from them. As we shall see, Malaysia, Singapore, Cambodia, Laos, Brunei, and the Philippines stood some-where in the middle of this scale of trauma, as the shock of the new was trans-lated into modern political institutions at the end of the nineteenth century.

It might seem surprising, in view of the relatively brief period of time that colonial governments existed in much of Southeast Asia, that at independence there were no concerted moves to restore the old monarchies to their thrones and resurrect the indigenous instruments of government that the colonial rulers had destroyed. Rather, the colonial administrations were merely transformed into new independent states. Similarly, the often quite arbitrary boundaries imposed on the political map of the area by about 1910 are virtually identical with those of today. It is ironic, given the intensity of anticolonial feelings at the time of independence, that great old capitals such as Mandalay, Hue, Surakarta, and Yogyakarta have remained the secondary towns they became in the colonial period, while the capitals of independent Myanmar, Indonesia, and Malaysia are the upstart colonial cities Yangon (Rangoon), Jakarta, and Kuala Lumpur.

Such details show how deep a reorganization took place within the minds of the colonized as well as in the institutions of rule that colonialism created. What began as conquered territories ended up as viable entities that created enduring legacies in the minds of their subjects, turning them in the end into citizens. The redrawing of the map of Southeast Asia undertaken by the Japanese during World War II was quickly reversed in 1945. The failure of the one sustained attempt to redraw the map of Southeast Asia after independence, when Indonesia absorbed East Timor, reveals the tenacity of the colonial legacy

The majesty of bureaucracy: Sultan Abdul Samad Building, Kuala Lumpur.
Originally colonial government offices, built 1897.

for the entire region. Similarly, despite myriad postcolonial separatist movements, Rangoon remained the capital of Burma, because during the high colonial period it had become the seat of a modern administrative network, a new judicial system, and an internationally recognized government, as well as the hub of a modern sea, rail, and river transport network and the focal point of a ramifying tax, banking, and credit system. The Union of Burma retained essentially the same boundaries as British Burma because these interlocking bureaucratic and economic structures had created a new interdependence for all who lived within those boundaries and, by the same token, increasingly separated them from all who lived beyond.

As the economic and political networks that the colonial states created gave meaning to the lines on the maps the conquerors drew, this was represented visibly to their new subjects in the art and architecture of the new administrations. Whereas, for example, Buddhist kings had always lived in timber structures that symbolized the impermanence of the temporal world, reserving brick and stone for the permanent edifices of the sacred (temples and stupas), the new states built for clerks and ministers offices of durable materials, many still in use more than a hundred years later. Efficiency and speed became the hallmarks of good government, supplementing the pomp and ceremony designed to impress the onlooker with their suggestion of privileged access to the supernatural.

"Rationalizing" Governance

THE GROWING bureaucratic and economic frameworks both built on and helped create the pervasive economic transformations of the period. Rapid economic growth made ever larger bureaucratic structures possible; these same structures facilitated further growth. Export taxes on Siamese rice and Malayan tin financed the railway systems, which in turn facilitated further rapid increases in exports by linking the hinterland to the coastal ports and dramatically reducing the cost and time involved in shipping goods. Rising receipts from taxes on the peasants helped to pay for irrigation works in Java and Cochinchina, while the newly irrigated areas accommodated hundreds of thousands of peasants who faced ever more efficient methods of tax collection. In these ways, conquest, new frameworks, and sweeping economic changes reinforced each other in a cycle of revolutionary transformation that some resisted but all eventually were forced to accept.

One can describe the bureaucratization of Southeast Asian systems of governance as the rationalization of administration. A rationalized bureaucracy is characterized by its hierarchical and linear nature; stretching uniformly across the state's domains, a "machinery" of government was envisaged that could regularize and homogenize power and authority into individual departments and functions. This utilitarian system replaced the more elaborate and ramshackle

The political milieu: local chief and retinue, Simeulue Island (off Aceh), ca. 1894.

mosaic of patron–client relationships that characterized monarchical rule, except in precolonial Vietnam, where the Confucian mandarinate had many of the characteristics of a rationalized bureaucracy. But while the Confucian scholar-official was examined for literary skills, the skills demanded by the new forms of bureaucracy introduced by colonialism often demanded new forms of education.

The personalized nature of the old order was replaced by a depersonalized bureaucracy in which interchangeable officials held temporary power on behalf of an abstract order. The magic and majesty of kingly rule were, in the minds of imperial planners, to be replaced by requirements of law and order. And many of the givens of the old order—such as that wealth, power, and the right to rule were synonymous—eventually gave way, at least in theory, to the principles of modern government in a capitalist economy and the idea that power is in trust to the people and held only temporarily.

To understand the origins of modern bureaucratic government in late-nineteenth-century Southeast Asia, we should begin not with charts of the offices of power but with the political milieu in which new experiments in organization were first carried out. Acehnese chiefs posed proudly and rather menacingly for photographers in front of a thatched hut; we can also see Siamese court ladies in the crew-cut hairstyle of the time, Chinese with pigtails, Vietnamese mandarins in their long robes, and alongside them beefy Westerners in field boots or covered with sashes and medals. We can get glimpses of this milieu by reading the reports of such European visitors as John Crawfurd, Auguste Pavie, and the governess Anna Leonowens or the autobiographies of Achmad Djajadiningrat and Munshi Abdullah—all in their ways explorers in strange lands—or by reflecting on the last section of Joseph Conrad's novel in which an English drifter comes to Patusan and there finds his vocation, bringing peace and order to the small valley and becoming its "Lord Jim."

Gunboats and uniformed troops established physical power—not new to Southeast Asians—but did not dictate how and why it was to be exercised afterward. The building of modern administrations was a great human achievement, first in the minds of the aliens holding the new power, who envisioned a net of knowledge and control cast over these diverse lands, and eventually (and more significantly) in the minds of Southeast Asians themselves.

The Men on Top

THIS PROCESS began with and within the colonial administrative elites who held power in 1870 or acquired it soon after and the modernizing Siamese elite grouped around Chulalongkorn and his brothers. These were tiny minorities —all male, of course—who commanded disproportionate material power compared to their predecessors. Fundamental to their situation was the degree to which they differed intellectually from their subjects. Most were Christians attempting to govern Buddhists, Muslims, and Confucians, speaking foreign languages and wearing trousers instead of the various sarongs and robes most Southeast Asian men wore. More important yet—for Chulalongkorn was Siamese and the Spanish were Catholics like the Filipinos—they were separated from those they ruled by their modern education. Most believed in "progress" and the new certainties that the scientific and industrial revolution had spawned as it had remade Europe during their lifetimes. Most saw power as a way to create a world they understood out of the Southeast Asian reality they perceived hazily and often disparagingly. Living in the midst of an alien culture, they tended to share the prejudices of their fellow countrymen and often created a distorted and unfocused but idealized image of the home country they had left behind.

At the beginning of the high colonial period, their goals were still only sketches of a possible future. The new administrations, even where they were not newly inaugurated or politically precarious, still did not reach very far outward or downward. Communications were difficult and slow, and both colonial governors and their subordinates in the field operated very much on their own initiative. Field officers lived far apart in their separate districts and, at a time when few European women came to the colonies, often took Southeast Asian mistresses or wives. In such conditions, accommodation to local practice—in way of life and style of rule—was almost universal.

In the areas under European rule longest, like the Christian Philippines and Java, such accommodation had become systematized and acquired the inertia of tradition. In new colonial areas, the same circumstances led to wide variations in practice and highly personal systems of government. Conrad's Lord Jim had dozens of counterparts in real life, such as the well-known late-nineteenth-century Malayan district officer Humphrey Berkeley, the "King of Grik." But the apparently inevitable force of bureaucratic regularity was never far behind these pioneers, as Mr. Blundell, the commissioner of Tenasserim, learned when the long arm of the Honourable Judges and the Board of Revenue in Calcutta demanded in the 1830s that he conform to their new standards, not those that his subjects approved. Blundell was forced to ensure that juries in his jurisdiction did not apply the punishments favored in Myanmar traditions, such as parading miscreants in public to humiliate them in front of their peers, but sent the guilty to prison instead.

The colonial rulers believed that change was a justification of their rule. Only progress could uplift not only their subjects but also the prosperity of their own country and the larger world. Berkeley's "kingdom," like the loose supervision exercised by the first of Chulalongkorn's royal commissioners over principalities like Chiang Mai in the 1870s and 1880s, was a frontier institution within an expanding bureaucratic system. That system grew to incorporate almost the entire region, except for the more remote and isolated frontier areas, especially along the new borders between China and mainland Southeast Asia.

In the last decades of the nineteenth century, as administrations gained greater revenues, better communications, and more staff, older accommodations began to give way. A new generation of colonial officials, the first wave of those trained as civil servants, often had a stronger sense of mission and of superiority than their more amateurish but less presumptuous predecessors had. The new men were often earnest and idealistic. Many had been trained in public administration and public health. Unlike their predecessors, who came with a well-founded skepticism about the degree of change they could accomplish, they were convinced of the malleability of humans and nature to their designs. As a group they lacked the personal charm of so many of the older generation, spoke local languages less fluently or not at all, and often misunderstood the societies they thought they were improving. By about 1900, almost everywhere in Southeast Asia, they had become bureaucrats in fully routinized general administrative services, which governed the countries of the area with an increasingly efficient but insensitive hand.

In a series of circulars issued in the years after 1900, the Netherlands Indies government discouraged its officials from using the ceremonial appurtenances by which they symbolized their Javanese-style rule. Colonial officials more often married European wives, creating tensions reflected in Somerset Maugham's Malayan short stories, which return obsessively to the theme of wives, native mistresses, and Eurasian children. French fiction from Indochina treats these subjects more tolerantly but just as obsessively. The implicit ideas of cultural superiority that Westerners had initially carried to Southeast Asia had been transformed into a form of racism that went beyond snobbery to the heart of government. Sex and power became interwoven in a way that helped to fuel the growth of nationalism and sometimes a counterracism amongst observant (and often Western-educated) Southeast Asians.

In noncolonial Siam the new elite around Chulalongkorn was Siamese to begin with and thus retained many of the values of traditional culture. But in the 1880s, the members of "Young Siam" were very different from the conservative bureaucratic nobility they were replacing and sometimes appeared to be foreigners in their own land. They consciously followed European administrative organization and behavior, kept regular office hours, dressed in modified European fashion, drank Scotch, and began to conduct business in a pattern of paperwork quite unlike the personalized administration of their elders.

Indirect and Direct Rule

SUCH CHANGES in lifestyle reflected the growing self-confidence and broadening vision of change among the upper echelons of the new administrations. In the last decades of the nineteenth century, while the colonial and Siamese elites were being transformed, other changes were taking place in the relationship between them and the subordinate Southeast Asian elites with whom they dealt. From their first arrival, the tiny European ruling elites had found it prudent, convenient, and necessary to leave direct governance of the overwhelming majority of the population to whatever indigenous Southeast Asian leaders and classes would cooperate with them. Such groups varied enormously in the nature of their ties to particular European regimes and in the changes in these ties over time, but there were three main patterns in the period.

The numerous small principalities and communities of the Shan-Lao and Malayo-Muslim zones were in general the last to be brought under some form of European or Siamese control, mostly in the years around 1900. In those areas, the colonial powers began with some form of indirect rule, recognizing (or in some cases creating) kings, sultans, chiefs, and other leaders with whom they entered into treaties or agreements. These agreements allowed the subsequent posting of political agents to supervise and instruct the local rulers to the satisfaction of their new overlords. Throughout these areas, with a few exceptions, comparatively loose and informal administrative arrangements continued in effect until the end of colonial rule. Before 1900 much the same was true, for quite different reasons, of the overseas Chinese communities, which largely governed themselves through "secret societies" and other institutions of their own, dealing with the ruling powers through leaders generally called—at least in the Malay world—"Kapitan China."

A much swifter and more far-reaching pattern of change characterized a second group of societies, including the west coast Malay states, Sumatra's East Coast Residency, Java, Siam, northern and central Vietnam, and, to some extent, Cambodia. All were originally governed under formulas of indirect rule, but in the course of the nineteenth century, the growing power of the colonial and Siamese governments overtook that form of minimally intrusive rule. Moreover, rapid economic change or the large populations of these areas called for increasingly complex methods of administration. The central elites who extended and manned these systems, eager to run things their own way and increasingly confident of their ability to do so, became less tolerant of the formalities of indirect rule.

The indigenous rulers, for their part, often ill-equipped to govern in the new style and generally unsympathetic to what it stood for, became increasingly irrelevant. In most cases they were bought off with substantial emoluments and encapsulated in ceremonial roles, rather like European monarchs, while colonial officials bypassed them to deal directly with indigenous officials at lower levels. Javanese regents continued to be treated with great deference, although increasingly Dutch residents gave the orders and young Dutch *controleurs* supervised Javanese district and subdistrict officers in the field. The Nguyen court was infiltrated with French officials in key positions, while mandarins throughout northern and central Vietnam came under the control of French *résidents supérieurs*. The west coast Malay sultanates were federated in 1895, and a unified British Malayan civil service under a resident general dropped all but the pretence of "advising" sultans, while British district officers, operating at an unusually low level of administration, dealt directly with Malay *penghulu* (headmen), themselves well on the way to becoming British-style functionaries. By 1910 the old Siamese bureaucratic nobility in the center and subordinate rulers and regional elites in the outer reaches of the kingdom were being pensioned off, so that from Bangkok to the district level, Siam was coming to be governed by a single national administrative elite.

The third and most thoroughgoing pattern of change was found in Cochinchina and central and southern Burma. It was similar to what occurred in the Philippines in the sixteenth and seventeenth centuries, when the Spanish effectively eliminated the titles and traditional power base of local chiefs, choosing to rule directly down to the provincial level. The French severed Cochinchina from the remainder of Vietnam. Similarly, the British first annexed to India sections of the Konbaung dynasty's territories and then, after the final war in 1885, abolished the monarchy entirely. In these two areas, therefore, the Westerners dealt from the beginning with lower-level chiefs and headmen and even, as in Cochinchina for a time, experimented with direct local rule themselves.

In both cases, moreover, a new indigenous administrative class emerged before 1900. Members of this class often came from ethnic minorities or others who had enjoyed no social status under the monarchical order. Known as the "interpreters" in Cochinchina or the "lords of government" *(asoyatmin)* in Burma, they soon became essential collaborators with the colonial rulers. In Burma they were recruited through an examination system testing knowledge of English, surveying, and administrative procedures before entrance into the Burma Civil Service. Beginning at the bottom, they were able to rise through the ranks of the modern administrative hierarchy. The first indigenous deputy commissioner, a quite high post, was appointed in 1908. While these new classes of indigenous administrators soon made themselves indispensable to the colonialists, they came increasingly to be perceived by much of the population as part of the machinery of oppression. Among the most anticolonial Burmese nationalists, to be a bureaucrat was to become a bloodsucker *(thweisutthu)*.

The Rise of the Civil Service

THE EARLY YEARS of the twentieth century were a watershed in the history of Southeast Asia. The last corners of the region were being incorporated into six large units—British Burma, Siam, French Indochina, British Malaya and associated protectorates, Netherlands Indies, and the Philippines—and the basic administrative grids covering the six polities had been laid down. The Western and Siamese central administrative services were in full running order, with graded hierarchies, regular recruitment and promotion procedures, and paperwork recording every individual and the taxes on thousands of transactions. They kept careful oversight of the indirectly ruled outlying regions and closely supervised the general affairs of the major concentrations of population.

By then the administrative order had reached below the preexisting ruling elites in most areas to work directly through Southeast Asian chiefs and leaders at regional and local levels. There was thus an interface in the administrative systems where the lower Western or Bangkok Siamese officials dealt with local elites across a cultural and historical chasm beyond which lay the overwhelming majority of the population, who rarely dealt with a Western or Bangkok official on any kind of business. It was at this interface, symbolized by the need for bilingualism or interpreters, and in relations between the modern bureaucracy and the peasantry that the governmental developments of the decades before World War II were most striking.

The gap between the educational experiences of the Westerners and the Southeast Asians in government service had appreciably widened in the earlier stages of colonial expansion. That gap was largely closed by 1930 or so, as thousands of Southeast Asian civil servants acquired modern education. Whereas in 1900 most Southeast Asians in government service—apart from the Bangkok Siamese—were educated in premodern modes and held office because of their social status, by 1940 virtually all had a modern education, and many had achieved their positions on that basis, rather than through inherited status.

The primary cause of this development was not a general faith in the transformative power of education but the specific needs of modern governance. In the twentieth century, with more ambitious goals and a greater confidence in the efficacy of state intervention in people's lives, governments felt justified in interfering in what had previously been perceived as private affairs. Especially with the rise of welfare liberalism in Western political thought, the growth of the state became inexorable. Administrations grew enormously, as whole new specialist services—state schools, agricultural research stations, archeological departments, public health departments—were created to join the older and more basic general administrative services.

To keep costs low as well as to be true to ideals of tutelage, colonial governments attempted to fill many of the new positions with Southeast Asians. To do so, they needed men and women educated in modern ways not only for specialist services such as veterinary medicine and hydrology, but for general administration as well. By this time village headmen were beginning to be required to keep written records and accounts. The colonial and Siamese governments therefore opened an increasingly wide range of modern educational opportunities. The general European-language or Siamese-language government schools, which burgeoned in the early twentieth century, produced a large proportion of the Southeast Asian civil servants of the period. It was characteristic that governments from the beginning provided modern schooling specifically intended for such jobs. Early examples can be seen in the small schools founded in late-nineteenth-century Java for training vaccinators, teachers, and future administrators. Such education spread rapidly in the early years of the twentieth century—for example, in the schools for training district officers, police, agricultural officers, and other specialists in virtually every Bangkok ministry and government department.

Some Southeast Asians found the new schools and the bureaucratic jobs that they led to increasingly attractive. Many came from old elite families that had been bypassed in the late nineteenth century. The regent class on Java was restored to relevance by the 1920s on a new basis, wearing neckties, speaking Dutch, and merging fully into the modern administration. The sons of Chiang Mai and Lao princes loosened their connections to their home areas as they were coopted into the national Siamese elite. Other new recruits were sons of lesser officials or provincial or local elite families. For them a civil service position obtained on the basis of training and merit rather than birth represented a step toward higher status, which had been largely closed to them under the previous order.

Many who entered government service in Burma came out of still more humble families, often from previously illiterate ethnic minorities that had benefited from missionary education in English. It was not unusual for individuals from peasant families to join the civil service in the Philippines in the American period as a result of the new colonial education system. This was also possible elsewhere, particularly among the Minangkabau of west Sumatra, where the higher-status families tended to look down on modern education and civil service jobs, while large numbers of poorer boys got their start in this way. Throughout much of the region in the early decades of the twentieth century, jobs in the expanding civil services were the single most important avenue of social mobility. Families sacrificed immediate pleasures in order to finance the education that could make a son into a forest officer or a postal clerk, let alone a judge or a commissioner.

It would be an oversimplification, however, to see the phenomenon simply in terms of financial or social ambition. Government training schools and civil service positions were becoming available, but nothing compelled Southeast Asians to enter them. Many Southeast Asians resisted such careers. What is striking, however, is the adaptability of many other Southeast Asians in the early twentieth century who were willing to trust their fates to the requirements of the modern civil service and accept the premises of modern bureaucratic government. In time, nationalists were to criticize colonial civil servants as collaborators, but they too rejected the precolonial political structures in favor of the power and efficacy of the newer institutions.

Three broader consequences of the process require attention. First, almost everywhere in Southeast Asia in the twentieth century, a civil service career became the dominant ambition of the new "middle class." Often lacking the capital or skills to enter into trade and commerce, like those members of immigrant minority communities who were excluded from government service, Southeast Asians could rationalize entrance into government service as a route to status and dignity. Only the growth of market economies from the 1970s onward eventually undermined the attractiveness of secure, if sometimes poorly paid, employment in government service.

The second consequence had more immediate political significance. By 1940 the vast disparities in educational expectations and expertise among the members of the governing elite had significantly lessened. Now, from the governor-general to just above the village level, most of Southeast Asia was ruled by bureaucratic elites, Western or indigenous, that shared most of the same operating assumptions about government and, within each political unit, one sole language of administration. Nevertheless—in sharp contrast—the bureaucratic interface retained its racial aspect: Westerners on top, Southeast Asians below. Awareness of this contrast did much to stimulate nationalist movements.

The third consequence was very significant for the future development of government and politics in Southeast Asia. The process described above tended inevitably to pull modern-educated Southeast Asian civil servants away from the life of the peasant. A new divide in education and expectations appeared between the great majority of the population and the bureaucrats who governed them. The formation of these new cosmopolitan elites, with tastes in food and lifestyle remarkably different from their peasant and worker compatriots, created a social fissure that was to have significant implications in the second half of the twentieth century.

Regent in a necktie:
Raden Djajadinangrat, Batavia, 1920.

The State and the Populace

MEANWHILE the burgeoning colonial administrations were also reaching deeper and deeper into the affairs of the rural populations of Southeast Asia, leading to what historian Harry Benda called "the revolution of rising irritations." The general administrative services that arose in the late nineteenth century had confined themselves mainly to the bare fundamentals of government—maintaining order, administering the law, and collecting the taxes to pay for the other two. In this—though they differed markedly in other respects—they resembled their predecessor governments and thus could incorporate indigenous local elites more or less unchanged, appearing to the peasantry less as alien rulers than as new dynasties.

The rapid expansion of government activities after 1900, however, implied quite new relations between the state and its subjects. This was especially true of the specialist services. With few exceptions, they were established precisely to perform functions that had no precedents. Unlike the earlier general administrative services, they rarely incorporated existing leaders into their ranks. From the beginning they were staffed almost exclusively with modern educated men—Westerners, local Southeast Asians, and a characteristically high proportion of South Asians, Chinese, and nonlocal Southeast Asians. George Orwell's novel *Burmese Days* (1934) nicely captures the racial divisions of labor in government service and the jealousies and misunderstandings that they generated. Born out of the needs of economic interests, but also out of some genuine desire to improve the health and well-being of the public in general, the specialist services were dedicated by their very nature to change.

The same came to be increasingly true of the general administrative services. While they continued in the twentieth century to perform the basic functions of government, they also became much more deeply involved in programs of change, if only in coordinating activities of the specialist services at the local level and in enforcing their policies. The capacity to effect change, moreover, was greatly increased by the replacement of older Southeast Asian local officials by a new generation of modern educated men who cherished many of the same ideas of progress as the Westerners.

While some of these new government programs had nothing to do with the majority of the population (e.g., geological services) or affected them only indirectly (e.g., postal, telegraph, and telephone services, railroads, censuses), many were directed specifically at changing village life: a wide variety of public health programs, forest reserves, village schools, rural credit services, cooperatives, agricultural extension services, and the reorganization of local units of government. The list was praiseworthy, or so it seemed to the European district officers or Southeast Asian schoolteachers who introduced or imposed the measures on the villages. But peasants seldom understood or shared the assumptions and goals of these agents of modernity and judged the new programs by their own standards. A few of the programs, such as public health nurses and village schools in some areas, gained wide approval. Others, such as rural credit services and agricultural extension, were well received by at least the minority who made use of them. But many of the impositions aroused discontent or passive resistance, in some cases contributing to the rise of rebel movements. Governments often forced the villages to pay for these changes or undertake forced labor for their construction; when these were not wanted in the first place, it added insult to injury.

Forest reserves (established to check erosion) were universally disliked because they hampered the collection of firewood and other forest products. The slaughter of cattle to prevent the spread of rinderpest could bring ruin to those whose animals were killed. The rearrangement or amalgamation of hamlets and villages, mainly for administrative convenience, broke up communities or submerged them in arbitrary groupings. New rules for the appointment or choice of village headmen—such as the 1921 village reform laws in northern Vietnam, which caused most of the notables to withdraw from public life— often generated dissatisfaction. Everywhere new duties and closer supervision tended to draw headmen apart from village life, making them appear the lowest agents of the government rather than leaders of their own communities.

Well-intended welfare programs represented an unprecedented assault on village ways by imposing restrictions on aspects of everyday life. Previous indigenous rulers had extracted all the taxes and forced labor they could, but except in time of war they had not been able, nor had they wanted, to intrude directly upon village affairs. Indeed the welfare of the people was of little importance to them. Twentieth-century colonial and Siamese governments were both able and eager to intrude, and thus drew the peasants, despite their obvious reluctance to accept the new methods (with their often foreign purposes), into new frameworks of administration and control.

The introduction of new forms and institutions of taxation and law in the course of nineteenth-century colonization had dramatic consequences for nearly everyone in Southeast Asia. Though one cannot generalize across the entire region, many people in the more developed economies encountered conceptions of ownership, usufruct, and obligation greatly different from those that had prevailed in the precolonial order. The effect was to redefine established relationships, some as fundamental as the nature of the family and the obligations of the ruler and the ruled to each other. Much of the hostility toward colonialism had its origins in new fiscal and legal systems imposed on societies that lacked the intellectual or institutional infrastructure required to understand or manage them. Systems that had evolved in different conditions over long periods of time were thrust upon Southeast Asians without prior thought as to their social and political consequences.

The colonial and Siamese tax systems during this time changed very rapidly. Within less than three generations, informal, locally managed systems for the collection of surpluses were replaced by highly impersonal and intrusive forms of taxation. This change not only speeded monetization of local economies, but may also have fueled economic growth in the region, as people were forced to produce and sell more in order to meet their new masters' tax demands (sometimes, but not always, getting richer themselves in the process). The growing administrative machines demanded ever-increasing revenues in order to fund their growing salaried bureaucracies. As J. S. Furnivall argued in the case of Burma, a vicious circle was created of ever-increasing taxation to pay for an ever more intrusive and demanding government, which the taxed had little or no opportunity to influence or escape.

Not only did salaried employees manage the new administrations, but they were required to implement uniform and regular taxes that were auditable. Whereas older systems of taxation were flexible, capable of taking account of prevailing economic conditions (if the ruler wished), the more powerful new governments insisted on regular fixed returns in order to meet their annual budget requirements for both recurrent expenditures and new capital projects. These included building roads and irrigation systems and, in some cases, making annual payments to the metropolitan treasury back in Europe. Such remittances—the "colonial drain"—were nominally for expensive services provided, such as the defense and diplomatic representation of the colony as well as for the large salaries (and eventual pensions) of the Westerners employed in the colonial administration.

Even independent Siam was forced to adopt new forms of tax collection, as the sources of income available for central administration became squeezed and eventually inadequate. One of the methods by which kings had been able to raise revenues for themselves was denied them and their successors by the European (particularly British) insistence on free trade. Forced to abandon his role as the country's largest monopoly trader, King Mongkut, for example, turned to revenue farming as an interim measure in the evolution of new income generation methods. Revenue farming, whereby a political authority sells the right to collect taxes in a particular area or on the consumption of a particular good, had existed for many years in Southeast Asia but became much more widely used in the nineteenth century. (The Dutch in the Indies and a number of Malay rulers also ran tax farms in this way until near the end of the century.) The more dynamic economies that were developing provided greater opportunities for tax farming, particularly among new immigrant communities. "Farms" on opium, gambling, and alcohol, all popular with Chinese laborers in Southeast Asia's mines, plantations, and cities, soon became major earners for governments throughout the region, sometimes generating as much as 50 to 70 percent of all revenue.

The tax farmers who managed the collection of these revenues for the ruler became very wealthy and increasingly powerful themselves. Fearful of the independence of these wealthy tax farmers and increasingly confident of their own ability to collect revenues directly from their subjects, by the turn of the twentieth century, governments had abolished most of the tax farms. Abandoning the free market, they replaced the tax farmers by state-run monopolies on opium and other key commodities. As late as 1938 opium accounted for 15 percent of the total revenues of French Indochina, with alcohol, tobacco, and salt making up another 24 percent. Nor was this merely a colonial connection: opium accounted for 26 percent of Thai revenues in 1917, falling to just 9 percent in 1938, but then rising once more to 21 percent during the war.

Corvée had been a standard method by which individuals were required to provide their labor to the king and his projects in the premonetized economies of Southeast Asia and was continued by some colonial regimes, though it was generally scaled back and greatly diminished during the twentieth century. Nonetheless, in some places, such as Burma, the power of local officials to commandeer the labor of citizens under their authority remained enshrined in the Village Act and other legislation—some of which continued on the books in independent Burma/Myanmar until 1997.

Among the new forms of taxation, one of the most unpopular was the tax on land. Southeast Asians were long familiar with head taxes, but land taxes imposed a new burden on agriculture. Initially, as in the Burma delta, land taxes were acceptable, because if peasants paid the "revenue" on their fields for twelve years, they gained legal title to them. Whereas land had previously been seen as a free gift of nature, it was now turned into a commodity that could be bought, sold, and mortgaged. The creation of real property in this way allowed for new forms of economic activities to evolve. But land taxes tended to be fixed at standard, uniform rates, taking little account of variable agricultural conditions, and came to be seen as a cause of grievance against the new colonial rulers.

The Imposition of "Law and Order"

ONE OF the justifications that Westerners advanced for establishing colonial rule was that the majority of the population would welcome them for ending the "arbitrary" power of indigenous rulers. But the new rulers failed to understand the nature of elaborate and interlocking institutions of these societies, ignoring or overriding indigenous concepts of justice and order, especially when these did not fit with recently adopted Western notions of government and economy. Elaborate systems of hierarchy and custom that had traditionally provided the social cement for the societies they were attempting to rule were abandoned in favor of Western laws or, as in the Netherlands Indies, turned to Western ends. In the Malay and Indonesian world the system of customary laws was known as *adat,* a term taken from Arabic. Meaning simply "custom," *adat* prescribed the rules for right and proper conduct for all aspects of life, large and small. It was often local in character, and minor individual variations were a matter of pride and distinction to the communities concerned. Although codifications of *adat* are sometimes recorded, it resided mainly in the memories of the elders of communities, and one of its hallmarks was its flexibility over time. On this basis the Dutch constructed and codified an elaborate system of *adatrecht* (*adat* law) alongside but subordinate to colonial law. Among other things this system had the effect both of calcifying what had once been flexible and responsive, and of dividing "law communities" one from another in the interests of easier governmental control.

Whereas the Westerners believed that they were granting "rights" to people who up to then had had none, their enforcement of colonial law and order generated occasional outright defiance as well as extensive passive resistance. The imposition of colonial law did much to undermine the social solidarity of Southeast Asian communities. Not only did Western law emphasize the rights of the individual and his or her property against the rights of the community, but the colonial practice of applying different laws to different ethnic groups, indigenous and immigrant, and privileging some legal traditions over others—which would have been considered discriminatory if applied at home in Europe—tended to create barriers within society, compartmentalizing rather than unifying the populace. (Whether this was a conscious policy of "divide and rule" or the inadvertent outcome of well-intentioned efforts to respect local customs, the result was the same.) In the Netherlands Indies, for example, Europeans, "foreign orientals," indigenous civil servants, and the peasantry each had separate law codes that applied to them. In the case of conflicts in law between members of these different categories, the laws of the Westerners over-ruled everyone else's. *Adat* continued to be applied to indigenous Muslims according to the interpretations applicable to their particular area.

Whereas the adoption of European-style legal systems was imposed on colonized Southeast Asia, in Siam changes to the legal order were brought about by the king in order to free his country from the insultingly unequal treaties that it had been forced to accept in the nineteenth century. These were based on the premise that Siamese courts were inferior in nature and practice to European and American legal proceedings, so the subjects of Western powers, including Asians from their colonies, could only be tried in Western courts, the practice known as extraterritoriality. To meet the objections of the imperialists, the Siamese reformed their judicial system by introducing a variation on the Napoleonic code, under the advice of French and Belgian jurists.

Unlike in Indonesia, where *adat* continued to be applied to the relevant population category, and in Siam, where reforms were introduced gradually by the Siamese themselves, in British Burma the precolonial order was largely ignored, and British Indian legal codes were introduced overnight. Administered by colonial judges, often British or Indians with little or no knowledge of Burmese notions of justice, the new courts became widely despised but frequently used. The law became one of the avenues of social mobility, and many budding Burmese politicians made their public mark by trying to manipulate the judicial process in a popular manner. Bribery and corruption tended to win in the end, bringing the whole process, which had been crafted to protect the rights of trade and commerce, into disrepute. Justice, which under the Buddhist law tales (the guides to judicial decisions under the kings) was sought through a search for a virtuous decision fair to all sides, now became a contest or competition designed to condemn the guilty and provide rewards for the victor. The first substantial public building the British built in Burma was a jail.

The Filipinos were of all Southeast Asians the most familiar with at least the rudiments of Western law, which had been introduced by Spain in the sixteenth century, and over time they had become skilled in manipulating it. Even in the provinces, Spanish officials were complaining of "caviling little lawyers and pettifoggers" by the early nineteenth century. The United States expanded and claimed to reform a legal system that seemed to them rife with injustice, though they stopped short of introducing trial by jury, regarding it as hopelessly vulnerable to corruption. It is perhaps not surprising that so many Philippine presidents—seven of eight who served between 1936 and 1986—were trained as lawyers or that the Philippines has by far the highest number of attorneys of any country in Southeast Asia today.

Like all states, the colonial governments had behind them a variety of coercive instruments with which they enforced their authority, such as the introduction of armed and unarmed police forces in the towns and cities, or the granting of formal police powers to village headmen or local notables in rural areas. Many urban policemen, especially at the officer level, were aliens who had little or no sympathy with the political aspirations or social grievances of their wards. As Orwell wrote of his experiences as a subdivisional police officer in the mid-1920s, "In Moulmein, in Lower Burma, I was hated by large numbers of people—the only time in my life that I have been important enough for this to happen to me."

The formation of armies posed a potential problem for colonial governments: how is it possible to ensure the loyalty and reliability of an armed force composed of members of a subject population? The necessity of employing "natives" in the armed forces was dictated by cost. Like governments everywhere, colonial rulers wanted to keep costs down, which meant employing as

From C. H. Forbes-Lindsay, *The Philippines*, Philadelphia, 1906

Colonial justice: a Filipino justice of the peace, constables, and prisoner, 1906.

few expensive Westerners as were necessary to maintain their authority. The calculus of cost versus reliability was to pose a constant problem for all the colonial governments until it was resolved by the Japanese invasion of the region in 1941. Before that time, colonial armies, like the Siamese army, were effectively deployed to keep internal order rather than for external defense.

The Philippine Scouts, an auxiliary infantry force organized by the Americans to fight in the 1899–1902 war, became useful adjuncts to the American army in what was seen by the U.S. military as an imperial backwater and remained a significant presence in the archipelago afterward, along with the Philippine Constabulary, a paramilitary national police force; both were used to suppress dissidents throughout the American period and after independence. Colonial wars fought by the Dutch around the archipelago between 1890 and 1914 were not won by Dutch soldiers or by the latest Western weapons technology developed for European and American wars fought on plains. They were fought in densely forested mountainous areas by Asian troops, trained in Western drill but often equipped with swords as well as rifles. The colonial army was invincible against local armies because the latter were held together primarily by personal loyalty to a ruler or cause rather than by regular training supported by technology that could build and maintain seemingly limitless supplies of arms and ammunition. Modern colonial armies—and the Siamese army, modeled on European forces—confronted part-time soldiers conscripted by sultans or lured to martyrdom in the holy war of a charismatic leader. The Dutch never represented more than 0.4 percent of Indonesia's population; it was the hierarchical organization of society, alliance with local elites, and the military arts (technology, training, and logistics) that kept the Dutch in power.

The fear that local troops might be swayed by indigenous religious or political figures to turn against their officers was not unfounded. During the colonial period there were a number of instances where this happened. In 1924 there was an attempted mutiny by some Philippine Scouts in a bid for equal treatment with their American counterparts. On 10 February 1930 Vietnamese troops at Yen Bai mutinied against their French commanders at the instigation of the Vietnamese Nationalist Party, the Vietnam Quoc Dan Dang (VNQDD). Had it not been for miscommunication among other elements of the indigenous forces, this isolated revolt might have spread through the French security apparatus, posing a major threat to colonial authority throughout Indochina, as, in a pattern common across the region, the French used Vietnamese troops to control Cambodia and Laos. Nor was Siam immune from the threat of mutiny even though its troops, like its rulers, were indigenous; apparent attempts at coups against the monarchy were thwarted in 1912 and 1917.

The British pursued a slightly different strategy from the other colonial powers in the region. The vast reserves of relatively inexpensive military manpower available in their empire were vital to the security of the Southeast Asian

colonies. At the outbreak of World War II, by which time the British had reinforced their troops in Singapore and the rest of Malaya, nearly half of all troops
in these possessions were Indian, the remainder being Australian and British,
with fewer than 5,000 from the indigenous-recruited Malay Regiment. A
similar pattern existed in British Burma, where the British feared that the
recruitment of Burmans (Bamas) would generate insubordination if not worse.
There members of the so-called hill tribes were recruited in preference to the
majority population, creating ethnic animosities that persisted after independence. On the eve of World War II, of the nearly 28,000 armed men in the
colony, 17,500 were Indian; and of the remainder, fewer than 4,000 were Bama,
while 5,000 were recruited from the 30 percent of the population considered
to be minorities.

While globalization created the conditions for the consolidation of colonial power and the centralization of political and administrative authority, the
colonial powers learned, as the Siamese kings already knew, that to carry out
the enterprise of government successfully, rulers must adapt their purposes to
local needs and requirements. This the colonial rulers did to varying degrees,
with significant implications for the postcolonial states that succeeded them.

Further Readings

Adas, Michael. "From Avoidance to Confrontation: Peasant Protest in Precolonial and
  Colonial Southeast Asia." *Comparative Studies in Society and History* 23 (1981):
  217–247.

Benda, Harry J. *Continuity and Change in Southeast Asia: Collected Journal Articles of Harry
  J. Benda.* New Haven, 1972.

Butcher, John, and Howard Dick, eds. *Rise and Fall of Revenue Farming: Business Elites
  and the Emergence of the Modern State in Southeast Asia.* London, 1993.

Emerson, Rupert. *Malaya: A Study in Direct and Indirect Rule.* New York, 1937.

Furnivall, J. S. *Colonial Policy and Practice: A Comparative Study of Burma and Netherlands
  India.* Cambridge, U.K., 1948.

———. "The Fashioning of Leviathan." *Journal of the Burma Research Society* 29, 3
  (1939): 1–138.

Owen, Norman G., ed. *Compadre Colonialism: Studies on the Philippines under American
  Rule.* Ann Arbor, 1971.

Skinner, G. William. *Chinese Society in Thailand: An Analytical History.* Ithaca, N.Y., 1957.

Sutherland, Heather. *The Making of a Bureaucratic Elite: The Colonial Transformation of the
  Javanese Priyayi.* Singapore, 1979.

Trocki, Carl. *Prince of Pirates: The Temenggongs and the Development of Johor and Singapore,
  1784–1885.* Singapore, 1979.

Wyatt, David K. *The Politics of Reform in Thailand: Education in the Reign of King Chulalongkorn.* New Haven, 1969.

Chapter 15

Living in a Time
of Transition

THE NINETEENTH and early twentieth centuries forced remarkable changes on the peoples of Southeast Asia. There were few individuals, even among residents of remote hills or marginal coastlands, who remained unaffected by a century or more of Western military and economic penetration of the region; by World War II most Southeast Asians lived in a social landscape their grandparents would not have recognized. Modern scientific thought and new technologies, which were transforming Europe and North America at the same time, drew the world together in ever more integrated networks, which both greatly increased commerce and created stark cultural juxtapositions.

Even the working poor were bound together globally. Myanmar farmers raised rice for Malay households; South Vietnamese grew rice for North Vietnamese. Western workers rode to factories on bicycles whose tires were fashioned from rubber tapped by Southeast Asian or immigrant laborers. They drank tea or coffee with sugar and smoked tobacco, their few moments of leisure resting on the toil of plantation workers halfway around the world. In factories they produced the goods that Southeast Asians purchased with their plantation wages, such as matches, sewing needles, canned food, and mass-produced clothes.

Southeast Asians, who had always proved themselves open to innovations in agriculture, added tea, coffee, and sugar to their own minimal diets once colonial production systems made them cheap and readily available. In the Philippines almost every household grew its own tobacco (originally brought in by Spaniards) before the establishment of the government monopoly; in northeastern Sumatra Batak farmers raised tobacco in forest clearings along with corn (maize)—also a New World crop—rice, pepper, and gambier vines. Agriculture also benefited from advances in science. Botanical gardens were established in Asia, where naturalists raised Western varieties of grains, vegetables, herbs, and flowers, and experimented with imported plants as well as trying to improve local crops like rice and sugar. Southeast Asian laborers who tended coffee bushes from Arabia and rubber from Brazil were in effect part of a global scientific enterprise.

Winners and Losers

PARTICIPATION in colonial economies differed according to age, gender, class, ethnicity, religion, and location. Women were hired as pickers on tea plantations, because they were regarded as nimble-fingered and meticulous. Aristocrats who leased land to foreigners built houses in Western style, went to the races, and made tours of Europe. Javanese men were hired to replace Chinese on Sumatra's plantations, because they were regarded as less aggressive. Whole ethnic groups and classes, such as rural Malays, the Khmer elite, and the Balinese, were protected from the revolutionary effects of new ideas and international capitalism, made into virtual museum pieces to preserve colonial notions of innocent rural ways and exotic ritual.

All these developments depended on new conceptions of time and space. Until the twentieth century, most Southeast Asians calculated travel in terms of walking or sailing time. Nineteenth-century Western technology refined the significance of distance and divorced communications from transport, enabling messages to travel faster than people could. Few Southeast Asians owned automobiles before the 1950s, but the bicycle came within the reach of the more prosperous. For many Southeast Asians the most important use of rubber tires was for the pedicab (trishaw), which reached Singapore in 1914. As cheaper means of transport opened to them, ordinary people could shift goods more easily between home and market, raise the volumes they traded, and expand their range of customers.

Some Southeast Asians clearly welcomed these new developments and saw in them opportunities for more material rewards, greater freedom, and the chance to carve out new social identities. Although Javanese noblewoman Raden Ajeng Kartini complained that "only too frequently have we been made to feel that we Javanese are not really human beings," she went on to say: "We are very fond of the Hollanders & are grateful to them for all the good things which they have taught us.... We owe [them] the awakening of our intellects and the nurturing of our spirit." Others, however, were drawn unwittingly into a vast political and economic machine that they did not fully understand and felt impoverished, materially and culturally, by forces beyond their control. The peasants of Vietnam "accept their wretched fate because they do not understand the cause of their misery," said Truong Chinh and Vo Nguyen Giap in 1938. "However, when they cannot bear it any longer they suddenly wake up and see reality. . . . They leap into battle, determined to wage a decisive struggle against their exploiters to satisfy their anger." And on the margins, some Southeast Asians still remained unconscious of and scarcely affected by these changes. Any generalization as to regional welfare over this period must founder on such fundamental differences of experience. We can, nevertheless, gather some sense of how these historical changes affected the lives of Southeast Asians and find evidence of their reactions in what they did as well as in what they said.

The Paradox of Population Growth

THE PARADOX of population growth in Southeast Asia can be simply expressed. Until the nineteenth century the region was sparsely populated except for the rice-rich enclaves of northern Vietnam (the Red River delta) and central Java. Average annual population growth over the previous millennium was at most probably 0.2 percent a year. Then, starting around 1800—earlier in some areas, later in others—growth accelerated to an average of about 1 percent a year (1.5 percent in the Philippines and Java), then on to nearly 2 percent in the first half of the twentieth century. This increase occurred not only before most significant advances in modern medicine—only around World War II were antibiotics developed that could cure many of the diseases that killed Asians—but also without an industrial revolution like that which accompanied the early "demographic transition" in the West. (See Table 2.)

Historical demographers agree on these basic facts, though they continue to quibble over just when population growth accelerated in different areas within the region. Where they chiefly disagree, however, is over the demographic and social variables that explain it. Why was Southeast Asia sparsely populated, compared to its neighbors in South and East Asia, for so long? When it started to grow rapidly, was this because mortality finally fell or because fertility started rising? What social, economic, political, or even cultural factors triggered this change—earlier than received demographic wisdom, based on the European experience, would have predicted?

(Migration was not a major element in the rapid population growth of Southeast Asia as a whole. Indigenous mobility was far greater than stereotypes suggest, but in regional terms it simply reshuffled local populations. Millions of Chinese and South Asian immigrants entered Southeast Asia, but they would only have accounted for about 7 percent of total regional growth during the nineteenth century.)

Table 2: Population Growth, 1800–2000 (in millions, based on modern borders)

Country/Countries	1800	1900	1950	2000
Myanmar (Burma)	3.5	10.0	17.8	47.5
Thailand (Siam)	3.5	7.5	19.6	60.9
Laos	0.2	0.5	1.8	5.3
Cambodia	0.4	1.1	4.3	13.1
Vietnam	5.0	13.5	27.4	78.1
Malaysia/Singapore/Brunei	0.4	2.0	7.2	27.3
Indonesia/Timor	13.0	40.0	79.5	212.4
(Java)	(6.0)	(30.0)	(51.5)	(125.0)
Philippines	2.0	7.5	20.0	75.7
Total	28.0	82.1	177.6	520.3

Sources: 1800–1900, based on estimates derived from a variety of historical data and scholarly calculations; 1950–2000, taken from United Nations, *World Population Prospects, 2002 Revision*.

From the sketchy evidence available on premodern Southeast Asia, it appears that fertility, though high by today's standards, was constrained by a variety of factors. Women did not generally marry at puberty but in their late teens or even early twenties, and although marriage was nearly universal, divorce was also common, so that at any given time a fair proportion of fertile females were not married. Within marriage, fertility was probably limited by prolonged breast-feeding, of up to two years, and by regular spousal separation (in many communities men were absent for three to six months every year fighting, trading, or undertaking compulsory labor), as well as by conscious attempts to restrict family size. Almost every Southeast Asian society knew of contraceptive herbs or potions—though their efficacy was dubious—and many also practiced abortion and infanticide from time to time.

Mortality, too, was less high than it might have been, despite the dangers of epidemic disease as well as wild animals, floods, earthquakes, volcanic eruptions, and human violence. We know that many Southeast Asians died in epidemics of smallpox and unspecified "fevers," perhaps malaria or typhoid. The majority, however, probably died either in infancy (one baby in four did not live a year) or of diseases scarcely noted in the historical records, such as tuberculosis, diarrhea, dysentery, and endemic malaria.

Death from these diseases is often associated with malnutrition, but some evidence suggests that in the early modern period food supplies were generally adequate, and Southeast Asians were as tall and as healthy as Europeans at the time. Outside of densely populated northern Vietnam, famines mostly appear in the annals in conjunction with warfare or epidemics, except during the seventeenth century, when the "little ice age" affected crop production all over the world. Warfare itself, though chronic, probably did not kill many Southeast Asians directly, since its usual aim was the capture of slaves rather than territory, but by disrupting agriculture and spreading disease, it contributed significantly to mortality. In the absence of war, however, Southeast Asia seems to have had the potential for real demographic growth.

The acceleration of this growth in the nineteenth century coincides with the expansion of Western imperialism in Southeast Asia, and many have speculated as to the relationship between these two developments. Colonialists themselves had no doubt that they had simply made life better for the "natives" and boasted of how rapidly population had grown under their benevolent rule. Yet Western medicine—which before the twentieth century probably killed as many people as it cured—was not the primary explanation for demographic increase, though smallpox vaccination, introduced in the early nineteenth century to Dutch Java, the Spanish Philippines, and Siam, seems to have been effective where it was administered properly. The region continued to be swept by major epidemics, including cholera, which first arrived with terrifying force in the early nineteenth century, and the great influenza pandemic of 1918–1919, but they do not seem to have been as devastating as earlier epidemics; at any rate, they did not reverse the long-term pattern of population growth.

Sanitation, especially the provision of clean water for drinking and cooking, had been proven to be a significant factor in public health in nineteenth-century Europe, but its implementation in Southeast Asia was generally late and underfunded, though where serious efforts were made, as in the Dutch quarters of Batavia, they too helped reduce mortality. The efficacy of governmental measures depended as well on the efforts of Southeast Asians themselves. Mothers brought their children to be vaccinated, and most villagers were happy enough to ensure a clean water supply by digging latrines and wells when the necessity was explained and equipment was provided.

To the extent that mortality did decline, however, it was probably attributable primarily to improved food supplies. It does not appear that general nutrition improved in colonial Southeast Asia, and there is even some evidence suggesting that it worsened, as farmers turned from subsistence to cash crops and governments collected taxes more efficiently. Peter Boomgaard has calculated that food consumption per capita fell in Java between 1815 and 1840, and though it recovered by 1880, the quality had declined and the average workload had increased. Studies of indigenous "welfare" conducted by colonial governments in both Java and Vietnam—where population pressure was greatest— seem to indicate that in the early twentieth century the food available per capita was actually declining.

At the same time, however, the incidence of famine may have fallen. This was attributable in part to improved transportation and famine relief efforts, in part to the ongoing spread of New World crops such as corn, cassava, and sweet

Colonial sanitation: horse-drawn chemical fire engines disinfecting Manila, ca. 1914.
From D. C. Worcester, *The Philippines,* New York, 1914

potatoes. The former, which meant that food supplies could usually get to the hungriest areas, is better documented, since it involved official action; the social and political breakdown of this system led to terrible famines in Vietnam and British Bengal during World War II. Probably more important in the long run, however, was the choice of ordinary Southeast Asians to adopt and adapt new staple crops that, even though less palatable than rice, could be rapidly grown on almost any terrain.

Another possible, if highly controversial, factor in population growth was the "imperial peace" established by the West after it conquered most of the region. Colonialism was founded in violence and based on coercion, but under it strong centralized governments were able to impose order on many of the rival kingdoms, bandits, pirates, slave raiders, petty chiefs, and local warlords whose unending fighting had been so disruptive before. This enforced order may have reduced the net level of armed conflict in the region and so allowed food production to keep pace with population growth. The earliest and fastest demographic takeoff apparently occurred in two of the parts of Southeast Asia that had been longest and deepest under colonial rule—the Spanish Philippines and Dutch Java—which supports this conjecture.

Rising fertility may also have been a factor in accelerating population growth. There is some evidence for a decline in the average age at marriage in the nineteenth century, presumably as a result of an expanding cash economy, since weddings and the establishment of new households cost money, now easier to earn. There may also have been some decline in spousal separation within marriage, as corvée obligations were reduced or abolished. Both of these developments would have tended to increase the average number of children per family.

Much more speculative is the hypothesis that Southeast Asian values shifted—whether in response to new economic opportunities and pressures (the "labor demand" theory) or to the spread of world religions—leading couples to decide that they wanted more children than before and thus to abandon previous practices of contraception, abortion, or infanticide. Unfortunately, there is virtually no evidence supporting this theory or the possibility that the period of breast-feeding, and therefore the average interval between births, was shortened in response to unknown factors.

Clearly the beginnings of accelerated population growth in nineteenth-century Southeast Asia cannot be attributed primarily to colonial action. Most key decisions were made by the Southeast Asians themselves on a household, not a national, basis: what food crops to grow, when to get married, whether to try to limit family size. The challenge that arose in the latter part of the twentieth century, when mortality fell faster (as medicine finally became effective) and rising populations threatened to eat up economic growth, was how to alter this domestic calculus so that it became rational for families—not just countries —to try to limit their size.

Finally, it should be noted that through the nineteenth century most governments still saw population as an asset and were delighted to see it grow as rapidly as possible. In 1855 Siamese minister Sisuriyawong, after comparing his country to "a small house with few servants," observed that "a soil without a people is but a wilderness." Eventually, however, some rulers began to look on demographic growth as a potential drain on the economy or even a threat to survival. Early in the twentieth century the Dutch, making dire predictions about Java (whose population had grown from about 6 million to 30 million over the previous hundred years), commissioned investigations into declining welfare and made plans to transport landless, impoverished Javanese families to the "empty" spaces of their expanding colony. It was not until the 1950s, however, that the "population problem" would begin to be generally perceived as such in Southeast Asia and governments would contemplate taking action to control it. Yet three decades later Mahathir Muhammad was still actively pursuing pro-natalist policies, claiming that Malaysia, which then had about 15 million inhabitants, could support 70 million.

The Changing Village (1):
Land and Labor

WHATEVER its causes, accelerated population growth in Southeast Asia had profound consequences, though many of them were imperceptible in the colonial era. At the household and village level, there were simply more people than before, people who had the choice of whether to stay and make the best of more crowded situations—the average village *(desa)* in large parts of Java more than tripled in size during the nineteenth century—or go elsewhere. Those who stayed were forced to intensify their farming efforts ingeniously on the limited lands available, in what anthropologist Clifford Geertz has called "agricultural involution," or to supplement their farm income with artisanry or wage labor, already features of the rural economy in much of Java.

At the same time, laws imposed by central governments were superseding customs and local rules governing access to land. Traditional landholding was often based on ideas of usufruct rather than absolute title. The "owners" of land were constrained to some extent in how they could use it (or how long they could leave it fallow), and in some places it could not be alienated outside the village. Land might be acquired simply by clearing and planting it, with no mapping or written record required. Now new systems of land registration, in the service of a rationalizing state creating a basis for taxation, lent themselves to abuse. This was especially true in the initial stages of implementation, when opportunistic officials or others adept at the new legalism could get away with registering claims to land already worked by less savvy peasants.

Even when such land-grabbing or usurpation did not occur, the new titles acquired by owners could generally be mortgaged or sold without restraint, a development that had the potential for shattering customary rural relationships. It was all too easy to go into debt—to a local landlord or an alien money-lender—and wind up losing the family farm completely, thus falling into the ranks of the landless. Over time, village land tended to be concentrated in fewer hands than before, especially in Lower Burma, where the British allowed the laws of the market to operate with the least restraint. In Java colonial surveys in the early twentieth century revealed growing signs of differential wealth in rural areas, marked by houses built of brick, purchase of buffaloes and jewelry, and pilgrimages.

For those who did not own land, systems of tenantry and dependency, which had long existed in Southeast Asia, became more cumbersome and onerous. Customary rental arrangements, including the division of inputs (supply of seed, responsibility for field preparation, and so forth) as well as the sharing of the crop, were constantly renegotiated. Although the balance of power between landlords and tenants could shift back and forth, the long-run tendency ran in favor of the former, who provided fewer inputs and took more of the crop. The owners themselves had become more sophisticated and market-oriented; many moved to nearby cities and as absentee landlords felt less bound by local customs and values. Potential tenants multiplied in number with the growth of population (including immigrants, in some districts). Although there were some attempts to invoke class solidarity to resist the whittling away of customary "rights," these were rarely strong enough to reverse the economic and demographic trend toward greater competition for scarce resources. Thus even before the troubled 1930s, there was a growing gap between rich and poor within many Southeast Asian villages, resulting in tensions between those who had enough land to feed themselves and those who had to work others' land in order to survive.

Other labor arrangements were also subject to renegotiation in this period. In many parts of Southeast Asia, families had long paid their taxes by contributing work to their superiors for specified periods of time: building or repairing roads and bridges, transporting rice to royal warehouses, or performing domestic or military service. By the late nineteenth century, however, colonial governments and private enterprise preferred wage laborers, because corvée could not provide a steady stream of sufficiently skilled labor. In Siam, for example, the government first reduced and then abolished corvée, while importing labor from China, going so far as to put its own recruiting agents into Amoy and to set up a biweekly steamship service.

Where rice growing was closely integrated with cash cropping of sugar, as in Java, almost every aspect of village life was altered. Sugar mills were located near cane fields, creating a close connection between rural life and factory labor. When the Cultivation System (which as a government institution was able to deploy corvée labor) gave way to commercial companies, agents recruited laborers by offering potential workers cash advances, often to pay off debts. Many seasonal workers in the sugar industry became wage laborers the entire year, moving among a variety of paid jobs; they were no longer a semiproletarianized peasantry but a workforce detached from the land, completely enmeshed in a capitalist economy. Some semimigrants moved between town and village, rural factory and farm, sending remittances home and introducing the products of Western factories, such as sewing machines, into their villages

Meanwhile, landlords who rented their land to sugar companies received lump sums in cash, allowing some to expand their holdings or to take on the additional role of village moneylender. As the industry grew, land that might have been cleared for rice cultivation was turned over to sugar. As a result, more rice had to be grown on each plot than before, when there had been ample forest to be cleared for new fields, and farmers needed extra cash to purchase fertilizer and hire weeders. Families in sugar areas tended to blame sugar for all social problems, and at times locals protested by burning cane fields.

The Changing Village (2): Cash and Credit

ONE OF the major changes in Southeast Asia in this period was the increasing monetization of the rural economy. Although long familiar with money, most

Southeast Asians in the precolonial era had little need for it much of the time. They grew most of their food, made most of their own clothes, built their own houses, and bartered for what they still lacked. Even their obligations to the state had been largely payable either in corvée labor or in kind, some specified local product that the government demanded. Now not only were taxes payable in money, but the Southeast Asians involved in commercial agriculture, rather than subsistence, needed cash to buy most of their food and, increasingly, other commodities like imported textiles.

Where was this money to come from? Some came from the direct sale of the "cash crops" now grown; some, as noted, came from wage labor. Another solution, especially in Siam, was debt bondage. A borrower deposited the labor of junior siblings or of his wife and children with a lender. They entered household service or worked in the lender's business. Men who could not repay their debts with cash put up their labor and that of their families in order to pay the interest accumulating. In most cases such families continued in permanent debt status to their patrons, not free to search elsewhere for employment.

Some Southeast Asians also obtained cash through cottage industries. Households were traditionally sites of limited domestic production. For example, a woman might use a handloom to make clothing for the family, or a man might make a yoke for his buffalo. As wage labor took up the householders' time and replaced it with cash, workers could purchase goods manufactured by specialist households and distributed through local markets, often by underemployed farm labor.

The precarious state of the economy meant, however, that many Southeast Asians still lacked cash, especially when taxes were due or some local crisis or celebration created an unexpected demand for money. Western-style banks and credit unions were introduced in the last decades of colonial rule, but long before then Asian systems of credit had already permeated Southeast Asian countrysides. Chinese and Indian moneylenders, often preceded by indigenous lenders with more limited resources, financed small farmers who aimed to expand or intensify their holdings and entrepreneurs who set up village shops, organized cottage industries, and opened factories.

Shops appeared in response to the monetization of the rural economy. Whether a shop was a movable stall or a fixed structure, its operator handled cash and was linked to a network of suppliers and purchasers. When purchasers shopped on credit, the shopkeeper also filled the function of a moneylender, buying surplus crops from local farmers for cash or with goods such as salt and cloth. Shops on plantations or at mines also sold alcohol, sex, and opium, and ran gambling outlets. Small-town shops distributed consumer goods such as metal pans and cheap clothing to village markets, while local traders bought such merchandise and carried it to sell in villages without shops, bartering these goods for local products such as peanuts, cotton, and palm oil.

Another potential source of cash was the pawnshop, which advanced small amounts to people who deposited personal possessions with the owner as security for the loan. Borrowers not able to repay their loans lost their property, which the pawnshop owner then sold to recoup the loss. The pawnshop therefore became a secondhand store as well as a source of short-term loans. Its staff typically included an owner or manager, his porters, agents, and guards. While indigenous women were busy in the markets as open-air vendors, they do not seem to have been workers in pawnshops.

Borrowers from pawnshops, moneylenders, shopkeepers, or local landlords needed cash for a variety of reasons: to improve their farms, to tide them over a bad harvest, to pay taxes or gambling debts, or to celebrate in style the wedding of a daughter or the circumcision, baptism, or ordination of a son. Rural lenders thus served a range of social classes and needs, keeping the poor afloat as well as financing ostentatious display by prominent families and fostering their desires for consumer goods.

When colonial governments finally established rural credit-lending institutions, they rarely benefited small farmers. Most of the agricultural lending of the Philippine National Bank, for example, was specifically designated for sugar, an industry dominated by large plantations. Even where small loans could be obtained at low, fixed rates of interest, few small farmers had the confidence to approach the official lenders. In Vietnam, for instance, landlords borrowed

Retail trade: Chinese *toko* (shop), Batavia, 1892.

money at government rates and then reloaned it to tenants and dependents at higher rates.

Most shopkeepers and moneylenders in Southeast Asian communities were Chinese or Indians. Many of the "Chinese" were in fact the children of immigrants and local women, with ties of family across Southeast Asia and to China itself. As mobile groups involved in commerce, Indians and Chinese were often seen by indigenous Southeast Asians as making money from the very poor and regarded as props of the government, favored by colonial policy. Shopkeepers, pawnshop managers, and tax farmers were easy targets of hostility, which ranged in its expression from derision and enmity to attacks on person and property. As one nineteenth-century Thai poet put it:

> At the tax farmer's shed with its loud gong
> > The important figure sits illuminated by candlelight.
> He's wearing his queue and displaying his fair-skinned young wife,
> > A Chinese from somewhere else, another province.
> He has no schooling and no learning, striving only to make
> > > himself influential
> Knowledgeable only in [the trade in] big hog-legs.
> > Thinking about this, we Thai grow angry.
> We do not operate the gambling fees. We starve.
> How do we overcome this fate?

Recently historians Robert Elson and Peter Boomgaard, among others, have turned away from conventional analyses that contrast "conservative" peasants with "dynamic" foreigners. They argue that Western capital and science created opportunities to which some Southeast Asians responded actively. When plantation crops needed to be transported to market, Southeast Asians became cart builders and drivers; when factories and railroads or bus companies hired large numbers of wage laborers, other Southeast Asians became specialists in raising food crops and making and selling snacks. Such scholarship recognizes the injustices that laborers endured and explores how they were exposed to movements in world markets. It locates the changes brought to the lives of working men and women in the freeing of ties to aristocrats, increased mobility, the expansion of job opportunities, and the new availability of mass-produced goods. It casts peasants not as passive victims of colonialism but as active agents in the modern transformation of Southeast Asia.

The Moving Frontier—and Beyond

FOR MANY Southeast Asians pioneering was an attractive alternative to village life, even if it involved braving the untamed jungle, full of imagined spirits and the very real dangers of disease, bandits, and wild animals. Forests were still the habitat of tigers and wild boar; well into the twentieth century annual reports of plantation companies recorded numbers of workers who were victims of tiger attacks. Despite the myth of a timeless peasantry, cultivating the same fields that their ancestors always had, Southeast Asian history is full of the stories of new settlements, particularly in the nineteenth century, characterized by John Larkin as the "century of the frontier" in the Philippines. The opening up of the rice deltas of Burma, Siam, and Cochinchina has already been described, but there were also major migrations of Ilocanos south into the Central Luzon plain and across the mountains into the Cagayan valley, of Bisayans into northern Mindanao, of Javanese into Sumatra, of Thai and Lao into the Khorat Plateau, of Minangkabau into Malaya, and of lowlanders into the foothills everywhere.

Unlike frontier societies in the American west and elsewhere, which tended to be heavily masculine, characterized by both more violence and more freedom than the societies from which they sprang, in Southeast Asia most rural migrants were not single men but families, who sought to reproduce their traditional social patterns. There were, nevertheless, inescapable differences in their new environment. With labor in short supply, agriculture tended to be extensive, rather than intensive, bringing more land under cultivation rather than trying to grow larger crops on existing landholdings. On the open frontier, this often involved reversion to shifting cultivation or "broadcasting" rice onto rain-fed fields rather than transplanting it carefully into irrigated paddies. Instead of houses clustered closely around a village center that included a meetinghouse, a shrine, or communal lands, the huts of the settlers might sprawl over a wide area or stretch out along the road or canal that linked them to the world. It is likely that, in the absence of local customs and constraints applicable to immigrants, there was also less social complexity at first, though over time these new settlements would develop their own traditions.

Such migration had profound consequences not just for the settlers themselves, but for the environments they entered. Deforestation, which had begun as far back as the origins of agriculture, accelerated as pioneer farmers slashed and burned clearings in the jungle to plant their crops—though they often worked around larger trees, less out of respect for nature than from an inability to remove them easily. Capitalist enterprises made more systematic inroads into the forests, hiring labor gangs to fell trees and pull stumps to clear large expanses for plantations. The commercial demand for timber was also enormous. Not only was teak exported in large quantities, but timber was also needed to build warehouses and factories; railroads used it for sleepers (which had to be replaced every three to four years) and trestles; and it served as firewood for boiling sugar cane, roasting coffee beans, and smelting tin. In the short run such forest clearance created more room for settlers; in the longer run it was a step toward the ecological crisis that afflicts the region today.

The transformation of Southeast Asia's land from forest to open fields also had political consequences. The forest had been the place for flight, a sanctuary

Timber industry: elephant lifting logs, Rangoon, ca. 1900.

from conscription into army or work force; it offered escape from taxes and epidemics; it was a haven for losers in political fights, for religious thinkers with views or visions opposed by orthodox authorities, for runaways and dissidents. The ability of governments to regulate the people more closely grew with increases in population, plantation agriculture, and irrigated fields. Communities were no longer separated by tracts of swamp and jungle; the landscape was no longer a patchwork of independent enclaves but one vast, cleared site potentially available for control by a centralized government.

Frontier expansion also displaced those already living in the wilderness, which was never truly "uninhabited." There were hill and forest dwellers of different ancestry from the settlers (Negritos in the Philippines, *orang asli* in Malaya), others of the same ancestry but different culture (Igorots in the Philippines, Kachin in the Shan states), and the advance party of lowland society: renegades, hermits, and drifters. Many of the hill peoples practiced hunting and gathering or shifting cultivation, which require a considerable expanse of territory to sustain a small population. When new arrivals intruded, the earlier inhabitants, even if they were not killed or enslaved—as they often were—were generally forced by ecological pressure into invidious choices. They could abandon their way of life—from diet and agricultural practices to costume and religion—and become settled farmers, tied to one area, subject to tax collectors and other government

authorities, and linked to services such as schools, clinics, and railway stations;
or they could try to maintain their traditional livelihood and customs by moving
farther away, up the mountains or deeper into the diminishing jungle, where
they inevitably impinged on other groups even more remote. Thus the farthest
corners of Southeast Asia were affected by global demographic and economic
changes, even if those concerned were often unaware of these larger forces.

Plantation and City Life

SOME Southeast Asians who left the village moved in other directions, toward
wage labor in the plantations and mines or toward the colonial cities. Not many
made these choices, however; in terms of regional demography, their numbers
are almost inconsequential. The reason most Southeast Asians avoided plantation and mine labor is simple: no one would do it who knew what it was like
and had any choice in the matter. Only where population pressure was greatest, in Java and northern Vietnam, were peasants willing to go any distance—
to Sumatra and Cochinchina, respectively—to work on plantations, and even
then most of them had to be recruited by trickery and retained by force. "The
rubber plantations are heaven on earth," sang the recruiters to Vietnamese
peasants. "The world of rubber is the world of money / To live in the rubber

Chinese coolies in Borneo, 1890.

world is to live in a fairyland scene / And when the contracts are expired, nobody will want to return to his native place."

This was, of course, a cruel fantasy, and to find labor willing to work under brutal conditions for the paltry pay they actually offered, capitalists generally had to go farther afield, to East and South Asia, in search of hungrier workers. Plantations reduced Vietnamese, Indians, Chinese, and Javanese laborers to cogs of industry. The experience demonstrated the alliance between Western commercial power and indigenous political power, as workers remained chained to their workplaces by their contracts and the police powers of the colonial state.

The term "coolie" makes its appearance in colonial reports and studies of plantation labor from the late nineteenth century. It meant a person, often assumed to be inferior or degenerate, contracted to perform menial labor for wages. In Southeast Asia coolies were often men and women detached from the ownership of or tenant rights to farmland: unemployed service workers, artisans, and day laborers. Labor recruiters found them on the main roads, at river crossings and tollgates, at markets, ports, and pilgrimage sites, searching for a day's pay. They were mobile workers, who became immobile once they signed a contract to work for three or five years on a European plantation. Coolies might have had previous field experience, but the regime of work on the plantation was new to them, for it entailed fixed hours (sunup to sundown), supervision by a foreman from another ethnic group, and ultimate subordination to a white manager. Poor food, overwork, overcrowding, verbal abuse, and blows were the lot of most coolies.

They were hired as individuals, cut off from the moral order that revolved around domestic and village life. Because they were coolies, their employers regarded them as amoral and condoned gambling, prostitution, and even drug use as inescapable concessions to their natural depravity. Some coolies provided personal services for Europeans: males as household staff and messengers, females as housekeepers and sex partners. The number of men far outstripped the number of women hired, and competition for women among workers and between workers and bosses was the cause of most murders on plantations. Women were paid less than men, their lower wages justified on the grounds that they would make extra money by selling sex and domestic services to men in the barracks. Few chose to bear children in such an inhospitable environment, which rarely included family housing units, schools, or hospitals. Plantations did not need (or want) a reproducing work force, as it was cheaper to rely on a constant supply of new workers; labor recruiters rarely had problems filling their quotas, overseas if not locally.

Cities were hardly as unpleasant as plantations, but Southeast Asians in general were not much more enthusiastic about migrating there. To the extent that we can measure it, in fact, the growth of the indigenous population of most Southeast Asian cities during the colonial era barely kept pace with the growth of the population as a whole, suggesting that urbanization, in the sense of permanent rural-urban migration, was negligible. In Java, in fact, the proportion of the population living in towns actually fell by almost half between 1850 and 1900, at which date more than 90 percent of Javanese lived in settlements of fewer than five thousand inhabitants. However, hundreds of thousands of other Southeast Asians visited or worked in the cities as seasonal or temporary labor, returning to their home villages for the harvest season or special occasions in a pattern of "circular migration."

Southeast Asia had no preexisting system for the recruitment of urban labor. Most nineteenth-century Southeast Asians lived in rural villages or in small towns around royal residences, so workers could not be found by advertising on notice boards or in city presses (which most of them would not in any event have been able to read). Managers of urban enterprises relied on the services of agents who recruited laborers from the countryside or overseas, found them accommodations, and enforced their regular attendance at the worksite. For these services they received both a fee from the business for every worker recruited and a kickback from each new recruit's wages. Labor bosses—whose ranks included union organizers, paid cadres of political parties, and police informants—sometimes expanded their operations, employing a staff of assistants and enforcers. Connected both to foremen and managers and to men of power in the countryside, they could move between two worlds. Some became the urban equivalents of brigand chiefs, involved in extortion, control of prostitution, and general thuggery.

The cities of Southeast Asia in the colonial era suffered from all of the disadvantages that cities everywhere do. They were crowded, dirty, crime-filled, expensive, and unhealthy. Colonial cities were administrative centers, but the higher offices were all reserved for Westerners, who generally filled the middle ranks of the bureaucracy as well or else imported other aliens (Indians in British Burma, Vietnamese in French Cambodia and Laos) to fill them. Colonial governments did not generally make a great effort to demonstrate their spiritual power by public rituals, or do much to sponsor traditional religion, arts, or learning. The spiritual symbolism or cultural value that might once have attracted Southeast Asians to royal capitals at Mandalay or Yogyakarta or Hue was largely absent from British Rangoon, Dutch Batavia, and French Hanoi.

Bangkok, was, again, an exception to these tendencies and remained a vibrant center of Siamese politics and culture throughout the colonial era, but in terms of economic opportunity, it resembled most other new cities of Southeast Asia. They were commercial centers in which most trade was dominated by Westerners or alien Asians. They employed unskilled labor in construction, stevedoring, and transportation, but few who did not have to would have worked on the pitiful wages of a day laborer or rickshaw coolie, competing with

KITLV, Leiden, #29182

City life: Singapore street scene, 1895.

hungry Chinese or Indian immigrants. What was left for prospective migrants from the countryside was petty commerce (where the competition of alien Asians grew daily), some factory work (where they would be bound by rules and schedules, their routines controlled by foremen and Western managers), artisanry, domestic service, and other service industries, none of them enormously appealing to most Southeast Asians.

Nevertheless, those Southeast Asians who made their way to the cities found or created there many of the most characteristic institutions of the modern era: education, journalism, literary societies, mutual help and other voluntary associations, labor unions, and nationalism. José Rizal and other Philippine "Propagandists" first met as students in Manila's schools; Vietnamese radicals plotted in the cafes of Saigon; dock workers went on strike in Surabaya and Iloilo; Burmese intellectuals and Buddhist monks redefined the meaning of politics in Rangoon newspaper offices. Not many Southeast Asians, pushed by population pressure or attracted by bright lights, moved into the cities of the colonial era, but those who did became the prime shapers of modern Southeast Asia.

Making Themselves Heard

NO DOUBT most Southeast Asians, when they considered how their lives were changing, expressed their thoughts in mundane, nondurable ways, virtually inaudible to the historian: private conversations and everyday behavior, praising or seizing the opportunities that appealed to them, quietly resisting forces they could not openly oppose. Only occasionally was their collective behavior so visible that it attracted the attention of colonial authorities (and historians). If we interpret migration as "voting with the feet," for example, the movement from Upper Myanmar into British Lower Burma in the decades before 1885 implies that something (economic opportunity, no doubt) made the new colonial state more attractive than the beleaguered Konbaung realm. In contrast, the great difficulty capitalist enterprises had in persuading most Southeast Asians to work on plantations and mines suggests how little appeal such wage labor had, while the influx of immigrants from China and South Asia is an indicator of just how desperate they were.

In terms of Western cultural influence, Southeast Asians often petitioned for more schools and eagerly filled up such educational slots as were open to them. They also responded positively to movies and the radio, when these became available, and even to certain Western foods and popular music, though by no means all. In contrast, they generally displayed little or no interest in the religion of the colonizers. Conversion to Christianity was generally negligible where other world religions were previously implanted; in Burma and Indonesia most of the converts were from minority groups, not the majority population, which remained steadfastly Buddhist and Muslim, respectively. The one significant exception, Vietnam, where a sizable proportion—up to 10 percent—of the majority population became Roman Catholics, raises complex interpretive issues about personal faith, communal identity, state ideology, and economics (whether the despair of the poor or the opportunism of the would-be rich).

During the colonial era there also arose new forms of written expression that provide deeper insights into the experience of modernization, at least as perceived by the literate minority. Journalism began in the late nineteenth century and flourished in the early twentieth century, as the spread of education expanded its potential audience. Southeast Asian newspapers did not emphasize local "news," as we conceive of that today; rather they were compendia of essays, literature, observations on happenings elsewhere in the world, commentary on political or religious issues, and whatever else occurred to their editors. Few of them were viable for long in a commercial sense, and we cannot tell how extensive their readership was or how seriously their ideas were taken, but they clearly articulated at least some of the concerns of Southeast Asians at the time.

Prompted originally by Westerners, or by Western examples, a few Southeast Asians also wrote autobiographies, of which the best known is the *Hikayat Abdullah* of Abdullah bin Abdul Kadir. In the twentieth century memoirists ranged from national leaders like Manuel Quezon (*The Good Fight,* 1946) to "ordinary" people like Kumut Chandruang (*My Boyhood in Siam,* 1940). The letters of Kartini to her Dutch friends were probably not intended for eventual publication, but they indicate a similar desire to explain a personal life—and the society that gave birth to it—to a wider audience.

In the twentieth century some urban intellectuals also attempted to gather systematic information about conditions in the countryside. In a few cases they were able to do so as part of governmental surveys, especially in Siam and in the Philippines, where the civil service had been largely localized by the 1920s. More often they challenged the official line on welfare as part of the nationalist struggle. Hsaya San was investigating rural conditions in British Burma for the General Council of Burmese Associations before he rebelled, while Truong Chinh and Vo Nguyen Giap studied the peasant question in Vietnam for the Indochina Communist Party. Their findings could be as biased and politicized as those of the colonial regimes they challenged, but in the very nature of the issues they raised and the charges they levied, we can see Southeast Asian reactions to certain aspects of the "modernizing" process.

Sometimes the most insightful commentaries on and telling indictments of change were found in fiction. Filipino nationalist José Rizal was also a medical doctor, essayist, and historian, but his bitter satirical novels directed against Spanish colonial rule—and the complicity of some Filipinos in that rule—constituted his lasting legacy. In Vietnam literary magazines that rose up between the two world wars gave authors the opportunity to lash out at landlords, collaborators, tax collectors, and unfeeling government officials in a way that the French censors would never have allowed in essays or reportage. Throughout the twentieth century, in fact, much of Southeast Asian literature had a strongly social and political cast; the idea of "art for art's sake" had few exponents (e.g., the expatriate Filipino poet Jose Garcia Villa). Hearing these Southeast Asian voices almost invariably problematizes any simplistic "progressive" interpretation of the changes wrought by colonialism and capitalism.

The great limitation of these sources is that they all represent the views of Southeast Asian elites. Even today, with the possibility of doing systematic surveys of public opinion, we are hard put to know just what ordinary Southeast Asians think of what is going on around them. How did Filipinos regard the declaration of martial law in 1972? Did most Indonesians ever regard Suharto as a "just king"? Just what do Thai or Myanmars mean when they invoke "democracy"? Does the movement of Southeast Asians into modern cities reflect more the attraction of bright lights or the depressing lack of alternatives in the countryside? The answers that we—not just Western scholars but urbanized Southeast Asian elites as well—provide for such questions too often are anecdotal, based on what we were told by our taxi driver or hairdresser, or, worse, are projections of what we ourselves believe. The voices of ordinary Southeast Asians can hardly be heard today: how can we hope to hear them through the echoes of history?

Further Readings

Adas, Michael. *State, Market, and Peasant in Colonial South and Southeast Asia.* Brookfield, Vt., 1998.

Boomgaard, Peter. *Children of the Colonial State: Population Growth and Economic Development in Java, 1795–1880.* Amsterdam, 1989.

De Bevoise, Ken. *Agents of Apocalypse: Epidemic Disease in the Colonial Philippines.* Princeton, 1995.

Doeppers, Daniel F. *Manila, 1900–1941: Social Change in a Late Colonial Metropolis.* New Haven, 1984.

Doeppers, Daniel F., and Peter Xenos, eds. *Population and History: The Demographic Origins of the Modern Philippines.* Madison, Wisc., 1998.

Elson, Robert E. *The End of the Peasantry in Southeast Asia: A Social and Economic History of Peasant Livelihood, 1800–1990s.* Basingstoke, 1997.

Larkin, John A. "Philippine History Reconsidered: A Socioeconomic Perspective." *American Historical Review* 87, 3 (June 1982): 595–628.

McVey, Ruth T., ed. *Southeast Asian Transitions: Approaches through Social History.* New Haven, 1978.

Owen, Norman G., ed. *Death and Disease in Southeast Asia: Explorations in Social, Medical and Demographic History.* Singapore, 1987.

Scott, James C. *The Moral Economy of the Peasant: Rebellion and Subsistence in Southeast Asia.* New Haven, 1976.

Stoler, Ann Laura. *Capitalism and Confrontation in Sumatra's Plantation Belt, 1870–1979.* New Haven, 1985.

Talib, Shaharil. *After Its Own Image: The Trengganu Experience, 1881–1941.* Singapore, 1984.

Chapter 16

✳

Perceptions of Race, Gender, and Class in the Colonial Era

WESTERN COLONIALISM in Southeast Asia raises the question of how so few colonizers could rule such large colonized populations for so long in conditions of relative tranquility. The easy Japanese conquest of the West's Southeast Asian colonies in 1942 was to expose the superficiality of this tranquility, but it still requires assessment. In 1930 the "European" population of the Netherlands Indies—and here "European" meant white or Eurasian Dutch citizens, other Westerners, and even the small group of Indonesians, Filipinos, Chinese, Thais, Egyptians, and Japanese who had become "legalized" Europeans—was only about 250,000 people. They were badly outmatched but hardly seriously threatened by a population of 60 million non-European "natives." In 1931 there were only about 11,000 French civilians in French Indochina, backed up by a very modest colonial military establishment. They lived a relatively serene life among over 20 million non-European subjects, even if there were diffuse, poorly organized anticolonial sentiments everywhere about them that they did not yet fully appreciate. Many Southeast Asians appeared to be wearing a colonial "straitjacket by choice" rather than having it daily forced upon them, as Renato Constantino so aptly put it in speaking of his fellow Filipinos' submission to the Americans.

Western Power and Southeast Asian Self-Consciousness

THE SHORT explanation of the West's ability to control Southeast Asia without big armies and to win cooperation from at least some elite figures is to be found

Racial caricature: Dutch sheriff, Acehnese prisoner, Indonesian policeman. Aquarelle by Heldring, 1880s.

in the West's monopoly of the culture of the industrial revolution until well into the twentieth century and the hint of limitless power it suggested. This was not just a matter of guns. Such a monopoly allowed Western colonial regimes to create an impression of efficiency, even of infallibility, that Southeast Asians found difficult to challenge. In the last decades of the 1800s, when Western colonial administrations were consolidating or renewing themselves or changing hands (as in the Philippines), Western industrialism enjoyed some of its most remarkable triumphs. The internal combustion engine, the automobile, the telephone, wireless telegraphy, electric lights, bicycles, typewriters, and cheap mass-circulation newsprint all emerged in the West between 1870 and 1914. When the French naval officer and colonial official Eliacin Luro, in *Le pays d'Annam* (1878), told the Vietnamese elite that their own knowledge, on the contrary, was no better than that of the retarded scholasticism of the European "middle ages," they had few rejoinders. Western industrial culture and its consumer tastes threatened to annex and trivialize some of Southeast Asia's most prized landmarks. The French not only constructed multiple copies of Angkor temples at their colonial expositions in Marseilles and Paris in 1922 and 1931 but used images of Angkor to advertise refrigerators and wristwatches. Western factories, military academies, medical institutes, forest services, and quantification-obsessed surveys all seemed to embody forms of organized power that Southeast Asians could not match.

One obvious response by Southeast Asians was to identify themselves with their rulers, through the appropriation of their resources and behavior. Long before the industrial revolution, at the outset of Spanish rule in the Philippines, the Tagalog printer Tomás Pinpin had promoted this strategy. Pinpin had urged his people to learn Spanish as a "cure" for their weaknesses; he had even supplied them with a Tagalog primer in "Castilian" as a means of enabling them to do so. By the 1890s the wish to imitate had turned into retrospective fact. The question-and-answer initiation rites of the Katipunan, the lower-class nationalist movement, compelled prospective Katipunan members to describe the condition of the Filipinos at the time of the Spanish conquest as one in which they already possessed artillery and silk dresses, and thus a useful proximity to modern culture.

The ways in which superior organizational skills seemed to accompany Western industrial culture made a deep impression on Southeast Asian elites. This was true even in Thailand, psychologically if not politically a colony. Phibun Songkhram, the Thai military dictator during World War II, even tried to create a more regimented Thai national solidarity by a Westernizing behavioral revolution. Thais were ordered to wear Western clothing, to sit on chairs rather than on the ground, to use forks and spoons, to join clubs, and to applaud at shows; the regime expressed its surprise that the Thai people had been able to survive for so long without following a Western diet. When the country changed its name (1939), one local journal, defending the spelling of "Thai" with an "h," explained that "Thai with an H is like a sophisticated girl with her hair set, her lips touched with lipstick, and her brow arched with eyebrow pencil, while Thai without the H is like a girl who is naturally attractive but without any added beautification."

Other Southeast Asians responded to Western industrial and colonial hegemony very differently. Far from identifying themselves with the West, they accepted the differences between civilizations as permanent, in effect "Orientalizing" themselves. Western colonizers, Edward Said has famously argued, created a tendentious body of knowledge about Asia, "Orientalism," which they used to control their colonies better. "Orientalism" meant the highly subjective study of non-Western cultures by privileged Westerners, in which such cultures were simplified and managed by a series of reductive, essentializing categories of analysis, such as "the Arab mind" or "the Burmese soul." Such categories were typically static as well as reductive. They enabled their users to contrast a dynamic West with a timeless Asia apparently devoid of any autonomous capacity for historical change.

An early British colonial official in Burma, James George Scott, published books in the 1880s whose contents and titles (*The Burman: His Life and Notions* and *Burma As It Was, As It Is, And As It Will Be*) might have been expressly designed to confirm Said's accusations. But what Said overlooked was that Asians might entertain equally static images of Westerners. Moreover, Asians as well as Westerners participated in the rhetorical construction of an imaginary

"Orient" that was separate and different from the West. In 1920 Soeriokoesomo, a member of a Javanese princely house, showed how "self-Orientalization" might work by arguing (in Dutch) that there was an unbridgeable moral difference between wisdom-seeking, hierarchy-accepting Javanese and money-loving, quarrelsomely egalitarian Westerners.

"Self-Orientalization" in the face of Western power satisfied fewer and fewer Southeast Asians, however. One reason was that Western colonialism inevitably marginalized and in some instances publicly degraded the precolonial ruling classes who were most supposed to embody "traditional" values. This was particularly true in Soeriokoesomo's Java. Power corrupts, but so does powerlessness. Pramoedya Ananta Toer's long historical novel about the decolonization of the Indies, *The Buru Quartet,* composed on Buru prison island in the 1970s, looks back at the decay and frustrations of the colonial Javanese nobility, as in the scenes in which the nobleman father of the hero drags his son away from his Dutch school to make him cringe and walk on his knees before him and then derides him for becoming an insolent "brown Dutchman" who has forgotten Javanese ways. The attractions of the industrial culture the colonizers had brought with them were so strong that another descendant of the Javanese nobility, Kartini, the famous social reformer, could tell a Dutch friend in 1899, "I completely share the feelings of my progressive white sisters in the far-off West" about the "excitement" of the "new era," which she did not expect to experience in her Indies homeland. But if so many Southeast Asians before the 1930s appeared to wear their colonial straitjacket by choice, why should George Orwell, a former British police officer in Burma, have argued in his novel *Burmese Days* (1934) that for Westerners in their own colonies free speech was unthinkable and the life of the colonizers a life of lies?

The Instability of Inclusion and Exclusion

AMONG the Western colonizers, the colonial project required forms of self-indoctrination or self-mystification about the rightness of their rule that could never quite transcend the obtrusive effects of their own internal divisions. These included class divisions, gender divisions, and disagreements over both the legitimacy of Western rule and the methods by which it was to be sustained. The colonial project itself was riddled by its own contradictions. Its ideals (expressed in the language of humanitarianism and the desire to incorporate Southeast Asians into the free and equal civilization of the Western Enlightenment) were hardly consistent with its practices (racial discrimination and political exclusion). Moreover, the colonial project depended on the maintenance of clear racial and cultural boundaries between colonizers and colonized, between Westerners and Southeast Asians, if it was to preserve its mission and coherence. These boundaries were surprisingly difficult to defend. The divisions, contradictions, and threats to internal boundary maintenance all led to a world in which, as Orwell suggested, the words and the thoughts of the colonizers themselves had to be censored.

Prescriptions about gender and gender interactions became crucial to the preservation of the racial hierarchies at the center of the colonial enterprise. Any effort to inflate the prestige of the white rulers of Southeast Asian colonies soon encountered a predictable obstacle: sex. That topic dominated colonial literature. Until the second half of the nineteenth century, the VOC (Dutch East Indies Company) and the Dutch government in the Indies had accepted and even encouraged interracial marriages and relationships, in part by restricting the emigration of European women to their colony. After 1870 racial sensitivities hardened. Asian wives or partners became perceived as a threat to colonial power. Eurasian children complicated colonial regimes' more and more comprehensive efforts to decide who was "white" and who was Asian, who was the ruler and who was the ruled. Ann Stoler has argued in detail that the increased rationalization of Western colonial administrations in Southeast Asia after 1918 coincided with their increased interest in bourgeois respectability and an increased stress on the custodial power of European women to protect their men against moral and racial subversion.

In order to continue to believe in their own mission, it was important to the colonizers to be able to defend their prestige in their own eyes. For this reason

KITLV, Leiden, #42660

Colonial complications: European and Eurasian girls, Batavia, ca. 1910.

Western colonialists often tried to convince themselves that their passion for Asian women was different, inherently less noble, than their love of white women. Hugh Clifford, a British official in Malaya who also wrote *Studies in Brown Humanity: Being Scrawls and Smudges in Sepia, White, and Yellow* (1898), published a novel (*Since the Beginning: A Tale of an Eastern Land,* 1898) in which he described the feelings his English hero, a government officer, had for his Asian mistress as entirely physical, not to be dignified with the name of love. These feelings were then pointedly contrasted with the purer emotions the hero supposedly felt for the English bride he later brought back with him to Malaya. Such literary exercises in self-mystification nonetheless fell a bit flat. So in 1909 the British Colonial Office issued a circular (inevitably known as the "Concubine Circular") formally denouncing officials who had Asian mistresses for "lowering" themselves in the eyes of the "natives."

Colonial medical authority was mobilized to certify the objectivity of racial exclusiveness and to cope with the threat of blurred distinctions. A 1928 decree in French Indochina stipulated that locally born people whose ancestry was unknown but possibly half French could seek legal recognition of their "French quality." But "medico-legal experts" would have to evaluate their physical features before recognition was actually granted. Vietnamese newspaper satirists greatly enjoyed poking fun at aspiring "Vietnamese Frenchmen" who appealed the decisions of court-appointed doctors about the authenticity of their claims to have "French flesh and skin." One such satirist wrote that he thought that "French skin, especially French skin that is under colonial skies, has a special characteristic that makes it superior to our skin: whoever lays a finger on it is imprisoned. On the other hand, our skin is thick, you can thrash it with oxhide, or slap it with fingers that are as large as bananas, and in court these things are still . . . 'acquitted as usual.' "

The boundaries between rulers and ruled were also threatened by the specter of reverse assimilation, of colonial whites who "went native." A prominent Dutch lawyer in the Indies warned that Europeans, particularly children who encountered native servants at home and native influences at school, would have to struggle hard to remain "truly European": European birth and kinship were no longer enough. Hill stations such as Dalat (Vietnam), Baguio (the Philippines), Buitenzorg (Bogor, Java), and the Cameron Highlands (Malaya) were supposed to have a morally and physically reinvigorating function. Sojourns in these isolated, high-altitude environments could rescue white colonials from degeneracy and allow them to recapture their consciousness of their civilizing virtues.

As Stoler has shown, colonial women occupied the front line in the struggle against reverse assimilation. They were considered less vulnerable to it than their men, but they had an ambiguous dual position in colonial society as important agents of Western rule who were nonetheless themselves subordinates in the gender hierarchy. Should they then be allowed to marry native men? The Indies Mixed Marriage Law of 1898 tried to discourage this by its patriarchal insistence that the legal status of wives must reflect that of their husbands. But bullying Western women with the weapon of downward mobility was hardly a solution. It implied the probability that such women who did marry native men would be publicly degraded by their subjection to the native penal code, and white prestige would again be shaken.

In this murky labyrinth of political and sexual transactions, however, the need to preserve a moral and cultural distance between one's own community and that of racial "others" as a key to self-esteem worked both ways. Sexual mingling was a threat both to the colonial regimes and to the communities that had been colonized, especially in the Islamic part of Southeast Asia. Malay-language novels about native mistresses to white rulers were widely read in the Dutch Indies. Ironically, they were often written by Eurasian authors. These stories made it clear that women who lived with white men would be ostracized by their racial community *(bangsa)*. In one such story, published about 1900, a Javanese father tries to escape prosecution for stealing by forcing his daughter to cohabit with a Dutch official. She escapes shame by infecting herself with smallpox, which kills her Western lover; but she avoids death herself and successfully reenters Javanese life, marrying a Javanese as a reward for her communally correct behavior.

What George Orwell called the "taboos" of inclusion and exclusion in colonial societies were thought to be endangered by mismanaged class relations as well as by mismanaged sexuality. The presence of too many visibly lower-class Europeans in the colonies undermined the colonizers' fictive prestige as natural rulers and as the bearers of progress; "poor whites" were therefore a political menace. Lower-class Britons who migrated to the Malay states to drive the colonial trains were deliberately discouraged and eventually involuntarily replaced by Asian and Eurasian train drivers. Grants to migrate to Australia were quickly supplied to Europeans in Malaya who had lost their jobs in their business firms or rubber colonies; white men were not allowed to shine shoes in the Orient. English nurses in Malaya preserved their status as white colonizers by only washing white bodies in the hospitals, letting Malay orderlies wash Malays and Chinese; they were still excluded from the colony's English clubs. Western soldiers and prison guards in the colonies, being both enforcers of colonial power and underlings in Western class structures, were another ambiguous group. Dutch sailors stationed at Surabaya, resentful of low wages and of Dutch civilians' disdain, organized pro-Bolshevik "Red Guards" in Java in 1917–1918 in support of the Russian revolution; Corsican jailers on French Indochina's prison island of Poulo Condore allowed themselves to be befriended by their Vietnamese communist prisoners, who astutely performed plays about the life of Napoleon for them.

Of the various kinds of lower-class natives, domestic servants were probably the most problematic category because of their intimate involvement with the Westerners they served. Indies colonial manuals recommended at least seven servants per Dutch household, partly as a means of preserving the rulers' prestige by dissociating whites from manual labor; about 2 percent of the total Indies working population in 1930 were classified as domestics. But Western women were warned never to lose their tempers with their native servants, because rage in public would destroy their dignity; they were also told to keep their children away from the servants' quarters to prevent them from assimilating improper native ideas about sexuality.

Colonialism's vulnerable psychological underbelly may help to explain why George Orwell could picture the colonial project in Southeast Asia as a treacherous and entangling mind game that Westerners living at home could never imagine, one in which Westerners living in the colonies themselves had to surrender much of their own freedom of thought. The conflict between the colonizers' racial determinism, on the one hand, and their evolutionary, progressive civilizing mission, on the other hand, encouraged many Southeast Asians to take a somewhat schizoid view of the West itself. The metropolitan West was thought to be liberal, the colonial West oppressive. Kartini anticipated the distinction perfectly. She told her Dutch friend in 1899 that the European women who were in the Indies were part of Java's general "slumber," cut off from the exciting social reform ideas their sisters were supposedly elaborating back in the Netherlands.

To some extent, Southeast Asian intellectuals' actual journeys to the West confirmed this schizoid view. Their travels enabled them to discover that the colonizers were doing things in their colonies that they would not have done at home. Nhat Linh, the budding Vietnamese novelist, writing about his first visit to France in 1927, told his readers just how bizarre and mutable the hypocritical double standards of French colonial behavior really were:

> The farther my ship got from Vietnam, and the closer it got to France, the more decently the French people aboard the ship treated me. When we reached the Gulf of Siam, they were looking at me with scornful apprehension, the way they would regard a mosquito carrying malaria germs to Europe. When we entered the Indian Ocean, their eyes began to become infected with expressions of gentleness and compassion. And when we crossed the Mediterranean, suddenly they began to entertain ideas of respecting me. I was very elated. But I still worried about the time when I was going to return home!

Yet the frustratingly conditional forms of admission to life in the colonial metropolises that Southeast Asians experienced when they got there may have caused the worst traumas of all. The reason for this was that Western colonialism did not socialize Southeast Asians to think of themselves as Vietnamese or Burmese or Filipinos, but as Westerners of a junior or incomplete kind. The incompleteness rankled. Burmese statesman Ba U, in his memoirs (*My Burma,* 1958), recalls the Burman law student at Cambridge University who killed himself and explained in his suicide note that he was very unhappy, because he could never in this life "reach the woolsack" (become British lord chancellor, presiding over the House of Lords). Carlos Bulosan, a Filipino peasant boy who migrated to the United States, recounts (in *America Is in the Heart,* 1943) the painful experiences of such immigrants when they got there: indentured serfdom in Alaska fish canneries, labor as underpaid tubercular farmhands in California, racial laws that prevented Filipinos from marrying whites. Yet the contradiction between the daily face-to-face humiliations many Southeast Asians suffered and the universal ideals and identities that the colonial civilizing mission cultivated in them could remain unresolved for a surprisingly long time. Bulosan ended his book by referring to Filipinos' continuing desire to "know America" and to contribute toward the final fulfillment of the American dream. The transformation of the contradiction into a conscious sense of betrayal required the development of a new type of Southeast Asian agency: the one imagined in anticolonial nationalism.

Further Readings

Butcher, John G. *The British in Malaya, 1880–1941: The Social History of a European Community in Colonial South-East Asia.* Kuala Lumpur, 1979.

Fane, Brenda. "Transgressing the Boundaries of *Bangsa:* An Examination of *Soesa* in Malay Language *Njai* Stories." *Review of Malaysian and Indonesian Affairs* 31, 2 (December 1997): 47–61.

Locher-Scholten, Elsbeth. "Orientalism and the Rhetoric of the Family: Javanese Servants in European Household Manuals and Children's Fiction." *Indonesia,* no. 58 (October 1994), 19–39.

Rafael, Vicente. *White Love and Other Events in Filipino History.* Durham, N.C., 2000.

Said, Edward W. *Orientalism.* New York, 1978.

Stoler, Ann L. "Making Empire Respectable: The Politics of Race and Sexual Morality in Twentieth-Century Colonial Cultures." *American Ethnologist* 16, 4 (November 1989): 634–660.

———. *Race and the Education of Desire: Foucault's History of Sexuality and the Colonial Order of Things.* Durham, N.C., 1995.

———. "Sexual Affronts and Racial Frontiers: European Identities and the Cultural Politics of Exclusion in Colonial Southeast Asia." *Comparative Studies in Society and History* 34, 3 (July 1992): 514–551.

Taylor, Jean Gelman. *The Social World of Batavia: European and Eurasian in Dutch Asia.* Madison, Wisc., 1983.

Woodside, Alexander. *Community and Revolution in Modern Vietnam.* Boston, 1976.

Zinoman, Peter. *The Colonial Bastille: A History of Imprisonment in Vietnam, 1862–1940.* Berkeley, 2001.

Chapter 17

Channels of Change

NATIONALISM and its imperatives have been a potent force in the history of modern Southeast Asia. The driver and repository of anticolonial freedom movements, nationalist ideas have also been a means of determining who is within and who without what political scientist Benedict Anderson has called the "imagined communities" of modern nation-states and anthropologist Shamsul A. B., their "nations-of-intent." Holding out the promise not only of political and cultural equality with the Western nations whose domination was being contested, but of control over the economic forces that underlay colonialism, collective nationalist visions acted as powerful agents of social mobilization.

The Making of New Identities

THE IDEOLOGICAL foundations of Southeast Asia's nationalisms have been various and in many ways locally specific, but most sprang ultimately from the circumstances fostering social identity formation discussed in earlier chapters. The close-knit, small-scale identities of relatively isolated upland and riverine peoples, fiercely resistant to outside absorption, can be contrasted with the larger and more complex corporate identities associated with high-population-density areas; the political and sacral power of kings, emperors, and sultans; and the core languages, religions, and customs they drew upon. Over time ideologies developed centering on the monarch as the epitome and validator of the body politic, defined in terms less of territory (effective political power was seldom exercised at the margins) than of a universe of moral discourse that, through shared religion, language, law, and custom, exercised authority over all who came within its reach. This process is evident, for example, in the Malay *negeri,* where the body politic was known as the *kerajaan*—the condition of possessing a raja, or ritually consecrated ruler, and thereby a distinct and nameable corporate identity, such as Kerajaan Melaka or Kerajaan Jambi. The peoples of those parts knew themselves and were known by others as *orang Melaka* or *orang Jambi* (Melaka or Jambi people), and though this identity might in certain circumstances be subsumed under the wider rubrics *orang Melayu* or *orang Islam*— Malays or Muslims—it provided an important bedrock of being. Much the same kind of process is evident too among the indigenous peoples of the core regions of Burma, Siam, Vietnam, Java, and elsewhere. Central to all such identities were the components of language, religion, knowledge of a shared past representable in song and story, and not least a perceived common ethnicity expressed in cultural terms—indeed, one contemporary scholar uses the concept "ethnie" to refer to such groupings.

The wholesale extension of Western political and administrative control over most Southeast Asian societies from the last half of the nineteenth century ushered in a period of radical changes in the ways life was experienced and understood by their inhabitants. It was from this turmoil of change and the loss of control over their own lives and futures that went with it that there emerged new nationalist identities and the political movements that gave expression to them.

The Beginnings of Nationalism

FULL-BLOWN nationalism, however, was frequently preceded by episodes of what has sometimes been seen as pre- or proto-nationalism, episodes of mainly peasant unrest or rebellion against the cultural alienness of colonial rule and the irksomeness of colonial regulation. Movements of this sort were characterized by protest against changing times, rather than by forward-looking programs of social, let alone national, reconstruction, but they frequently drew on a repertoire of cultural particularities related to religion, custom, and language not dissimilar to that of later nationalists. Though directed at colonial authority, peasant movements seldom had far-reaching aims beyond the improvement of the immediate situation of the peasantry. The leaders of such revolts came less often from the rank and file of the peasantry than from what is sometimes called the rural elite—the better-off landholders, religious leaders, or minor government functionaries at the village level. In general, leadership was characterized by an emphasis on the traditional rather than the modern and offered a return to previously known (or imagined) patterns of stability. Many revolts had strong religious overtones or were explicitly religious, and some sought through puritanism and reform to create the conditions for a millenarian return to or quest for the perfect state.

Two examples, of differing types and at different times, may serve to illustrate the variety of prenationalist peasant protest: the Samin movement in Java early in the twentieth century and the Hsaya San rising in Burma in 1930. Surontiko Samin was a fairly well-off but unlettered villager in the Blora district of central Java who, from about 1890, began to attract followers from his own and surrounding villages. Though Samin's initial ideas and beliefs are unclear, they came to be associated in the new century with resistance to Dutch administrative interference in village organization and rural taxation systems. From about 1905 the Saminists became known for their explicit withdrawal from the existing social and bureaucratic order by refusing to contribute to village rice banks and other communal agricultural institutions and by their insistence that taxes, if paid, were to be regarded as donations, not obligations.

Even at the peak of Saminism in 1907, the movement was credited with only some three thousand members. Nevertheless the Dutch, always on the lookout for "fanaticism" and rebellion, and despite the movement's careful nonviolence, feared a more general rising and banished Samin and his followers to the outer islands. Though it is possible that some peasant farmers saw in Samin the messianic *ratu adil,* or "just king," of Javanese tradition, who would lead his people out of tribulation, there is little actual evidence of this. But the movement continued sporadically in the district until the 1920s and beyond as an expression of protest at colonial rule and is said to have had some revival during the much later Suharto era.

Hsaya San, leader of the 1930 peasant revolt in southern Burma, was not himself a peasant but a former Buddhist monk who in the late 1920s conducted a survey of peasant grievances for a branch of the General Council of Burmese Associations. Retreating, symbolically, from the town, Hsaya San, as self-proclaimed heir to the Buddhist-Burmese kings—complete with the regalia of royalty and a forest "capital"—gave reality to the peasantry's desire not merely to rid itself of the ills of the present (born in part of the Great Depression) but to create an ideal past. Attacks on police stations, forestry headquarters, and the homes of village functionaries associated with the colonial administration began a revolt that took the British more than a year and a half to stamp out.

Peasant movements of a variety of kinds were in the long run to lend substance to—if not always to find common cause with—the rising nationalisms of the region. It was chiefly in the new cities, however, that political organizations with programs directed at independent nationhood and the substitution of indigenous for alien rulers had their origin and being. Many of the traditional elites of Southeast Asian societies had been pushed aside under the impact of intensive Western rule in the nineteenth century and thereafter, leaving a vacuum that was now to be filled either by elements of the old elite made over or by new urban classes, whose aims and ideas owed much to the West itself and to its organizational forms. The new elites were influenced not only by the phenomena of urbanization and Western education, but also by the presence in almost all Southeast Asian societies of powerful alien mercantile communities, principally the Chinese. Along with this went the presence in the air, as it were, of a range of new ideas, some alien in origin, others less so, which did much to determine some of the patterns that nationalist movements assumed.

It has been a persistent feature of the history and society of Southeast Asian polities that many of their commercial and trading functions have been in the hands of foreigners, particularly Chinese, resident in long-standing settled (if to some extent seasonal) communities. Though many incomers were employed in mining and agricultural areas, a majority of Chinese lived in—often in effect created—the new towns of the colonial era, so a great many urban communities in Southeast Asia were substantially Chinese. It was in the towns, therefore, that modern Chinese political and cultural activity found its most lively expression.

During the first three decades of the twentieth century, Chinese national-ism on the mainland—and its eventual polarization between the Guomindang (GMD) and the Chinese Communist Party (CCP)—generated strong responses in overseas Chinese communities. Sun Yat-sen, who visited the area many times, was largely financed by overseas Chinese capital, and the Chinese Revo-lution of 1911 was accompanied in Singapore, Bangkok, Manila, and elsewhere by growing enthusiasm for modern education (in schools staffed mainly by teachers brought from China), study and reading clubs with political overtones, and a flourishing popular press. Such activities, strengthened again by the politi-cization that followed the GMD-CCP split in 1927, greatly fostered internal Chinese cohesion and awareness of distinctness, and helped to retard further assimilation in the host societies—a process reinforced by suspicion and some-times hostility on the other side. More than that, however, the material success of the overseas Chinese, their ability to organize, educate, and otherwise improve themselves, and the fervid nationalism and anti-imperialism of main-land Chinese politics (as reflected in Southeast Asia) acted as irritants, stimu-lants, and sometimes models, providing an important part of the environment in which Southeast Asian nationalism grew.

It is important to note that indigenous Southeast Asian nationalisms, though necessary agents of social mobilization against colonial rule and Western domi-nance, were not in all respects benign. Like all nationalisms they encouraged exclusivism and even racism, and were often divisive of the larger community. In Siam, for example, King Vajiravudh published in 1914 a pamphlet describing the Chinese as "the Jews of the East," promoting anti-Chinese sentiment even though many of the Thai elite, including the royal family, were of Chinese descent. In peninsular Malaya, Malays in the early 1930s found it necessary to distinguish between "pure Malays" *(Melayu jati)* and those of Arab or "Keling" descent—the latter term itself a derogatory one for Indians. Other examples are not hard to find, and in some quarters such perceptions and attitudes have continued into recent times.

Urbanization

ONE OF the most obvious things that colonialism and European domination did was to invert older patterns of urban life so that at the heart of the new towns lay not the monarchy but money—the counting houses of the Chinese and other traders, the shophouses full of consumer goods from Manchester, Marseilles, Bombay, and Hong Kong. The citadel was forced to give way to the market, as mammon became king; economic gain was both the raison d'être of the new towns themselves and the motive of most of those who came to them, peasant or profiteer. Southeast Asia's royal cities had been situated by divination and dominated by palaces, temples, or mosques, with architectural designs and

Cathedral of commerce: the Hong Kong and Shanghai Bank, Singapore, 1900.

layout evolved on cosmic principles from models in Sanskrit manuals. By contrast, colonial capitals were constructed at important points of commerce, their public architecture derived from classical Greece and Gothic Europe. The palace gave way in importance to the governor-general's official residence, while cathedrals and churches joined temples and mosques as places of public worship, with Christianity potentially supplanting Buddhism and Islam as the ritual focus of the state, insofar as it still possessed one.

Most of the new towns, then, were the focus for new or intensified economic energies and new or changing social groups. Some were frontier towns associated with rapidly developing extractive industries. In Siam, for example, as in Malaya, a number of new towns sprang up with the opening of the tin mines, such as Phuket, probably the first town in Siam to have paved roads and automobiles, around 1910. Like Taiping and Seremban in the Malay states, it was substantially a Chinese town, with its lines of communication running mainly to Singapore and Penang. In northern Siam, where the major extractive industry was teak logging, towns such as Paknampho arose for the collection and milling of timber. Kuala Lumpur, which began in 1858 as a huddle of Chinese huts at the confluence of two small rivers, was built from tin revenues. By 1896 it was the capital not only of Selangor but of the Federated Malay States as a whole. It had a population of more than 32,000, of whom 23,000 were Chinese and only 3,700 Malays. Rangoon by 1900 had substantially more South Asians than Myanmars in its population.

Virtually all these towns produced for export, not for local consumption. To facilitate their trade, great seaports arose, funneling tin, rubber, rice, and other primary products into world markets. Some of the ports, like Manila and Batavia, were old towns transformed; others, like Haiphong and Rangoon, were essentially creations of the nineteenth century. But the archetype, perhaps, was Singapore. Founded in 1819 to participate in older patterns of archipelago trade, it became in the course of the nineteenth century a vast export entrepôt for the produce of its immediate region as well as a transshipment port of the old kind. At the close of the century, it was perhaps the most polyglot city in Asia. With nearly three-quarters of its 228,000 inhabitants Chinese, it can in one sense be described as a Chinese city run by the British for the benefit of both. But it was also a meeting place for 23,000 Malays from the peninsular states, more than 12,000 assorted Javanese, Sumatrans, Buginese, Filipinos, and other Southeast Asians, numerous Muslim and non-Muslim Indians, and at least a thousand Arabs.

Singapore exemplified in this way something that was true of all the new cities of Southeast Asia—they brought together large numbers of people from many different social backgrounds and varieties of experience to share a common, or at least contiguous, life. Bangkok offers another example, as this 1894 description by a British merchant shows:

The Chinese do all the heavy coolie work and cargo boat work. The Siamese do the boating work, rafting and light manual work. The tradesmen, carpenters, sawyers, tinsmiths and blacksmiths are Chinese; the Malays work the machinery in the steam mills and take a share in paddy cultivation and cattle-dealing, and do a good deal of fishing; the Javanese are the gardeners. The market gardening is a large Chinese industry. The Annamites [Vietnamese] are fishermen and boat builders; the Bombay men are merchants; the Tamils are cattle men and shopkeepers; the Burmese are sapphire and ruby dealers and country pedlars; the Singhalese [Sri Lankans] are the goldsmiths and jewellers; and the Bengalis are the tailors.

The main function of the cities and towns was to serve the ends of foreign trade and commerce by draining out primary products and pumping in consumer goods. As an adjunct to that, most urban areas developed as important communications and administrative centers for the surrounding countryside. Towns like Kuala Lumpur in Malaya, Saigon in Cochinchina, and Medan in Sumatra became junctions for networks of road, rail, and other communications, which transported not merely rubber, tin, and powdered milk but people and ideas. At the same time, improved communications were integral to the increasingly elaborate administrative systems (ranging from land survey and police to schools and traveling dispensaries) that were regarded by colonial governments as necessary aids to economic development and proper government in rural areas. Though the interactions between town, communication and administrative systems, and countryside were complex, they can for simplicity be represented as a two-way flow. From the town moved carriers of metropolitan values and urban culture, performing integrative and dissemination functions similar to, but much more intense than, those performed by the town in the precolonial past. In the other direction, large numbers of people from village and rural society poured into the town, carrying with them not merely the mixture of hope and fear that approach to the city arouses in all travelers, but their own values, ideas, and habits to throw into the urban crucible. Each side of the transaction fed and reinforced the other, making the city one of the most important single agents of change in modern times.

In most of the new cities, as in their older counterparts, people of one ethnic or territorial origin or one language group tended to live together in the same part of town. Though sometimes the initial "quartering" of towns was the result of administrative decision, the residents themselves tended to prefer it, for it assured them neighbors whose speech, religion, and habits of life they shared and understood, helping to perpetuate a sense of community. Sometimes, as in Manila before the late nineteenth century, ethnic groups even had their own form of governing council, there known as the *gremio* (guild). Localized patterns of residence were often found in association with specialization of occupation; the two practices together assisted newcomers to find both a place to live and work to do. Singapore, although too variegated to be altogether typical, nevertheless offers many examples of situations in some degree found everywhere. In the principal "Malay quarter" of downtown Singapore, Bugis Street was the merchandizing center for Buginese maritime traders from the eastern archipelago, Kampung Jawa contained many of the quarter's eating houses, coffee shops, and flower stalls kept by Javanese women, and Kampung Glam housed mainly Malay incomers from the peninsula, huddled round the Jamiah Mosque.

As cities grew bigger, by natural population increase and by continued immigration, and as rising land values and house rents combined with the decay of older areas to encourage commercial preemption and urban renewal, original patterns of residence and occupation became diversified and confused. Transitional institutions, such as the urban *kampung* (village), which had eased peasant movement onto the labor markets of Batavia, Kuala Lumpur, and Rangoon, were pushed farther out of town or became overcrowded and unsanitary urban slums. Traditional forms of social organization or replicas of them (the joint houses of migrants to Singapore from the island of Bawean, off Java, for example, which re-created their villages of origin) became more vulnerable to the disintegrative effects of urban individualism. More important, they became less relevant to the new quest for status and prestige in the totality of the urban social structure.

Though there were many casualties along the way, the process was by no means a wholly negative one. While it is true that urban life tended to weaken traditional societies and loosen the hold of traditional beliefs and values, it also offered much that was positive: new opportunities for specialization and skills, new relationships with others of differing social background and experience, new points of contact and common interest, and, in the most general way, new and enlarged liberty of thought and action. For many, particularly the young, urban life offered not the breakdown of the known, the familiar, and the secure that is so often described, but an opportunity to rid themselves of parental and other authoritarian constraints and to make life anew.

One product of the evolution of traditional institutions in the city—and specifically of the need to seek new forms of social security, the discovery of new interest groups, and the desire for self-improvement in a competitive environment—was the emergence of "voluntary associations." Individuals joined or helped to form such clubs and societies out of choice, rather than belonging ascriptively, by accident of birth. Associations blossomed throughout Southeast Asian urban societies in the late nineteenth and early twentieth centuries. Their enormous variety reflects the complexity of city life itself, but it is possible to distinguish a few general categories. Many of the first clubs were purely recreational, especially football clubs, which in Singapore, for example, were taken to task by the more serious sections of the Malay press as time-wasting frivolities. Another early and very common form of voluntary association was the burial society, established to ensure that, by common subscription, members and the immediate families of members would be assured of a properly conducted funeral. One of the largest and, to the social historian, most interesting categories was what might be called "cultural welfare and progress" societies—debating clubs, literary circles, study groups, religious reform societies, language improvement associations. Whether led by Western-educated government servants, vernacular or religious schoolteachers, or occasional members of the traditional elite, all were endowed with private visions, each setting out to create a new and better version of its own society.

Such associations could scarcely fail to find themselves at odds with the assumptions on which colonial rule was based. The fact of their existence, let alone the content of the largely ephemeral newspapers and journals by means of which they propounded their ideas, brought them under the surveillance of the colonial authorities, and on occasion they were suppressed—most often, perhaps, in French-controlled Vietnam. The relevance of the first associations, however, lay less in what they accomplished by means of political confrontation than in the training ground they afforded for wrestling with new problems and shaping a new generation of leaders and followers—experience in organizing clubs, running meetings, keeping accounts, operating elective institutions, handling information from outside, and transmitting it within. Most of the cities of Southeast Asia were essentially foreign bodies within the societies in which they were embedded, but the importance of the city lay outside the realm of numbers or proportion. It lay in its ability to give birth to new elites.

Education, Language, and the Printed Word

A NINETEENTH-CENTURY Malay writer once observed that the founding of Singapore had made "dragons out of worms and worms out of dragons." Nothing contributed more to the metamorphosis, which was a general phenomenon in Southeast Asia, than the education systems of the colonial powers. But "the knowledge that is given to people under foreign influence," argued another Malay in 1927, "has no purpose other than to impoverish the intellect and teach them to lick the soles of their masters' boots." Between those two remarks, the first sociological and descriptive, the second political and heated, both pointing to change, lie the problems and complexities of understanding the incidence, the impact, and the intent of the process often termed by the colonial powers "public instruction."

Alien systems of colonial rule were imposed on Southeast Asian societies with varying degrees of intensity, but most had one common purpose: the organization of the state in such a way as to maximize its potential as a producer of raw materials and foodstuffs for export to the West and as a market for Western manufactures. The type of control and the extent of direct interference in the administration of the state necessary to accomplish that purpose varied with the society's economic importance and promise, on the one hand, and, on the other, with the extent to which indigenous elites and systems of administration could be adapted to Western organizational purpose. In the so-called indirectly ruled, economic low-pressure states—like those on the east coast of the Malay Peninsula, Cambodia, or the outer edges of the Netherlands Indies—traditional elites continued in some measure to play an active part in the administration, even as it was reshaped to meet Western needs. In many other states, however, in spite of initial efforts to work through indigenous administrative institutions, the urgency of Western demands prompted the growth of complex bureaucracies that set a high premium on efficiency and technical competence of a kind either not available or not forthcoming from within the traditional social order. The main need of the colonial authorities, as economic development gathered speed, was for what one might call an administrative labor force: overseers, deputy supervisors, clerks, accountants, and technical subordinates. This provided the first and most obvious motive for Western-style training of segments of the population of Southeast Asian colonies—and an adequate explanation of why it was often called "instruction" rather than "education," the latter usually understood to have a nobler purpose than mere equipment to earn a living on someone else's behalf.

But other motives were at work, too, some of them clear and some confused or contradictory. None of the Western powers assumed territorial responsibilities in nineteenth-century Southeast Asia without at the same time taking upon themselves in some degree the tasks of the *mission civilisatrice,* or civilizing mission. Many Europeans (and Americans) really did see themselves as waiting "in heavy harness, on fluttered folk and wild—[their] new-caught sullen peoples, half devil and half child." Intoxicated not only by their own power and inventiveness but by then fashionable theories of evolution, Westerners readily accepted justifications of colonial rule based on tutelage.

In parts of the region some attempt was made to sustain or adapt indigenous educational institutions. Simple literacy was already more widespread in the Buddhist countries of mainland Southeast Asia in the mid–nineteenth century than it was in Europe. For a time from the 1860s, the British in Lower Burma left education in the hands of the monastery schools, giving them, however, additional books on Western subjects such as arithmetic and land measurement to enlarge their curricula. In Vietnam early French policies regarding education, together with the decision of the Nguyen emperor to withdraw educational as well as other officials from the directly controlled French areas in the south, spelled the end of the Confucian examination system in Cochinchina in the 1860s. In need of greater linguistic access to the society, the French then attempted, by means of interpreters' schools (which trained teachers as well as interpreters), to spread at least limited Franco-vernacular education, adopting at the same time the *quoc ngu* romanization of the Vietnamese language, which eventually became the mode of instruction in the peasant village schools. In Java, Dutch attitudes toward education in the nineteenth century were inconsistent but mainly ungenerous, and by the 1860s the government had clearly embarked on educational policies directed solely toward the production of a suitable range of officials and subordinates. It was partly against this wholly self-interested approach to education that the Ethical Policy was to react at the beginning of the new century.

As the twentieth century opened, several distinct features of colonial education had emerged that were to do much to determine the shape of the new societies that were taking form. At the base was the vernacular education offered to some proportion of the rural peasantry. Though in a few places, such as Burma and Cambodia, vernacular education was still largely supplied by traditional institutions, the colonial powers accepted at least some responsibility for financial aid or direct, government-run schemes. Answering probable critics of the small amount spent on vernacular education in the Malay states, an official remarked in 1908 that "the Government has never desired to give the children a smattering, or even a larger quantity, of knowledge which will not help them to more useful and happy lives than they now lead. To the Malay, the principal value of school attendance is to teach him habits of order, punctuality, and obedience." Similar arguments were employed elsewhere; vernacular education was intended merely to make the peasants better peasants, to reconcile them to their lot. The important thing was to avoid what was often called "overeducation," by which was meant taking people off the land and disturbing the even tenor of village life, or producing people who, unsatisfied with the dignity conferred upon them by manual labor, acquired aspirations that could not be satisfied under colonial rule.

If this was so of colonial mass education in the vernacular, it was held to be even more true of education in Western languages. Too rapid an extension of English education, Malayan administrators were wont to say, would bring about "economic dislocation and social unrest." The only colonial power to dissent seriously was the United States in the Philippines, where it was held, to the contrary, that a greater risk of social unrest lay in "a vast mass of ignorant people easily and blindly led by the comparatively few." Between 1901 and 1902 more than a thousand American teachers were recruited to teach in Philippine schools, and by 1920 there were nearly one million children receiving English-language education at all levels, from primary schools to colleges and universities.

In most of Southeast Asia, it was the restricted nature of vernacular education (invariably limited to little more than the rudiments of drilling in the three R's), rather than the relatively small proportion of the peasantry granted it, that led to serious dissatisfaction among its recipients at their exclusion from the more rewarding paths of Western education. Above the level of vernacular education, colonial administrations and Western economic enterprises alike were increasingly demanding trained subordinates. Pressures from both quarters fused with policies based on ethical recognition of past injustices and on a new desire for cultural association (as in the Netherlands Indies), on the transmission to a select few of an allegedly superior culture (as in French Indochina), or on slightly apologetic fulfillment of promises to introduce democratic institutions (as in the American Philippines) to make available increasing amounts of Western-language education.

In some areas the principal beneficiaries were the existing traditional elites. Everywhere, to some degree, the already socially and economically advantaged were in the best position to obtain the Western education through which, it seemed clear, all future advantage lay. But gradually, in response to two factors in particular—the leveling effect of impartially applied academic standards and the virtually exclusive location of Western educational opportunity in the multicultural towns—the range of those affected became diversified. The new elites who emerged from the system did so as a heterogeneous group, drawn from no one social class, and they found their identity in a common interest in the future rather than a common relationship with the past. In the event, many identified progress and modernization exclusively with Western learning. "In our country," said Indonesian intellectual Syahrir, "there has been no spiritual or cultural life and no intellectual progress for centuries. There are the much-praised Eastern art forms but what are these but bare rudiments from a feudal culture that cannot possibly provide a dynamic fulcrum for people of the twentieth century?"

As systems of Western education became thoroughly established, they grew in complexity and in internal stratification, which they imposed on those who passed through the various meshes of the sieve. One of the more complex examples of this was found in Vietnam, where, by the end of World War I (and after the final destruction of the Confucian examination system), entry into the civil service required not merely completion of "horizontal plane" vernacular education (a graphic image) in the village, but ten years of "vertical plane" education through the three formal stages of French education. Following that, a handful of students might go on to French education overseas or to the university in Hanoi, where specialized schools gave additional training for the public service to students drawn from all of Indochina. Talented or fortunate Javanese followed a similar pattern, ending up in the engineering, law, or medical schools formed between 1919 and 1926. At each stage of the process, many fell by the wayside, and it must be recalled in any case that the total numbers affected were small. Around 1937 Indochina, with a population of some 23 million, had only about 500,000 children being educated, nearly all of them in the first two grades of elementary school; it had only about 600 university students. In the Netherlands Indies, with a population of 68 million, only 93,000 Indonesian children were receiving Dutch-language education, the vast majority in elementary schools, and there were a mere 496 students at university level.

Though the Indonesian proportions were probably the smallest in Southeast Asia, the picture was much the same throughout, save for the two important exceptions of the Philippines and Siam. In the Philippines, where mass education in English had been embarked upon early in the century, there were, by 1938, more than 2 million pupils attending school at all levels and more than 7,000 at local universities. In Siam, vernacular education was not affected by colonially imposed limitations, and in the mid-1930s there were some 45,000 students at Thai secondary schools, out of a population of 14 million, and 800 or so more at universities in the country. Both the Philippines and Siam also had considerable numbers of students studying at universities overseas.

Education outside the colonial society, though intended as merely an extension rung on the instructional ladder, was actually, for most of the handful of people who achieved it, an experience qualitatively so different as to set it quite apart. Probably the first thing that metropolitan education did was to cut the colonial powers, and Westerners in general, down to size. Many Indonesians have recorded their astonishment and incredulity at discovering Holland to be so small geographically, for the colonial metropole had always loomed so large to them, appearing in schoolbooks in enormous-scale maps on which they could study every rock and rill. In addition, it was a liberating experience to be treated as a human being and not as a member, however "evolved," of an inherently inferior people. It was instructive, even when it was only a matter of having one's luggage carried by an English porter, to learn at first hand that Western societies themselves were highly stratified. And finally, many of the students met Westerners who were not merely critics of the existing social order in their own societies but who also argued fiercely against colonial subjugation and held theories of economic exploitation that both explained imperialism and forecast its eventual termination. Overseas students returned to Southeast Asia not only to take up senior positions in the indigenous levels of the public service, but also to provide leadership in nationalist struggles for independence.

In the Muslim societies of Southeast Asia, as elsewhere (except Siam), the channels opened by strictly vernacular education meant that the most a student could hope for was a poorly paid teaching post in the same system or a precarious life as a journalist. But there was for some an alternative similar to that afforded to a few of the Westernized elite. Following the great improvements in communications with the Middle East—which, it is sometimes forgotten, is also "West" for Southeast Asia—at the end of the nineteenth century, greater numbers of people from the Netherlands Indies and Malaya were able to make the hajj. Though the majority spent only a few weeks in Mecca, rising cash

From D. C. Worcester, *The Philippines*, New York, 1914

Colonial education: lowland Filipina teaching English to upland minorities, ca. 1910.

incomes from the export economy made it possible for increasing numbers to stay on there or in Cairo for some years, primarily to study religion. The advantage of Cairo, one young man remarked, was that there one could study politics as well. Amid the intellectual and political ferment that possessed the Arab world at the time—engaged both in the renovation of Islam and in nationalist struggles for freedom from the West—students from Indonesia and Malaya acquired new language and new ideas with which to combat the colonial rule that possessed their own society and determined their disadvantaged position within it.

The urban intelligentsias of the mid-1920s had as vessels for their strivings and instruments of their discontent a wide range of voluntary associations, culminating in the actively nationalist political parties of Burma, the Netherlands Indies, and Vietnam, and nascent movements of a similar kind elsewhere. They also had the printed word, and though some had made an extremely thorough job of assimilating Western language and culture, it was to their own in the last resort that both they and the vernacular-educated turned. Language has a peculiarly intimate relationship with cultural identity, both as the most expressive vehicle for a society's beliefs, values, and sentiments—for its innermost spirit—and as a means of self-recognition. The travails of colonial domination crystallized, for many, first and foremost around concern for the language of the people, or, where there was no single language, around the need to adopt one as a symbol and expression of unity in the face of cultural as well as political imperialism.

In Vietnam, the language issue tended to center on the schools, where French cultural aggressiveness punished even the informal use of Vietnamese in institutions of higher education. In the Netherlands Indies, the Dutch had, since the nineteenth century, used Malay as the language of "native administration" and, in contradistinction to the French, discouraged or forbade the use of Dutch by indigenous civil servants. The almost universal use of Malay in the press and organizational life of the early-twentieth-century Indies helped modernize and entrench the language—already for centuries the lingua franca of the archipelago—and led eventually to its adoption in the 1920s as the national language, thereafter called Indonesian. In the Philippines, where the mass education policies of the American administration were doing so much to spread a knowledge of English, the desire of nationalists to have an indigenous national language finally led in 1936 to the establishment of an Institute of National Language and to the eventual adoption of Pilipino (Filipino), based on Tagalog, a Manila-dominated compromise among the possible alternatives. Even in Siam fears were expressed about the purity of the language, and a special commission, which later became the Thai Royal Academy, was set up to nurture it.

Much of the force given to national language growth was expressed through the vernacular press, which everywhere in Southeast Asia played an increasingly prominent role in cultural and political life. The files of old newspapers and journals constitute an invaluable repository of the inner history of the times. Throughout the area, the first newspapers in the vernacular tended to be wholly or partly translations from the foreign language press. By the 1890s, however, and certainly in the twentieth century, most of the principal cities had at least one vernacular newspaper appearing with fair regularity and usually a host of smaller and more ephemeral weeklies and monthlies, often the product of the new voluntary associations. With basic literacy slowly increasing, the press became a vitally important influence in the dissemination and discussion of new ideas and in shaping the intelligentsia, training its leaders, and extending their influence. Few coffee shops or tea houses, even in the village, did not possess a newspaper from time to time, which could be read to the illiterate and argued over by budding politicians. In 1906 one of the most important of the early Malay journals listed

The power of the press: men reading wall newspapers, Yogyakarta, 1948.

KITLV, Leiden, #31624

no fewer than twenty-six different virtues of newspapers, among them that they were "the light of the mind, the talisman of the thoughts, the mirror of events, the servant of the wise, the prompter of the forgetful, a guide to those who stray, a prop to the weak, the guardian of the community, and the forum for all discussion." In the hands of the new elites, that was scarcely an exaggeration.

Further Readings

Adas, Michael. *Prophets of Rebellion: Millenarian Protest Movements against the European Colonial Order.* Chapel Hill, N.C., 1979.

Anderson, Benedict R. O'G. *Imagined Communities: Reflections on the Origin and Spread of Nationalism.* Rev. ed. London, 1991.

Benda, Harry J. *Continuity and Change in Southeast Asia: Collected Journal Articles.* New Haven, 1972.

Ingleson, John. *In Search of Justice: Workers and Unions in Colonial Java, 1908–1926.* Singapore, 1986.

Kartodirdjo, Sartono. *Protest Movements in Rural Java: A Study of Agrarian Unrest in the Nineteenth and Early Twentieth Centuries.* Singapore, 1973.

Lai Ah Leng. *Peasants, Proletarians and Prostitutes: A Preliminary Investigation into the Work of Chinese Women in Colonial Malaya.* Singapore, 1986.

Leung, Y. M., and C. P. Lo, eds. *Changing South-east Asian Cities: Readings in Urbanization.* Singapore, 1976.

McGee, T. G. *The South East Asian City: A Social Geography of the Primate Cities of South East Asia.* London, 1967.

Milner, A. C. *Kerajaan: Malay Political Culture on the Eve of Colonial Rule.* Tucson, 1982.

Shamsul A. B. "Nations-of-Intent in Malaysia." In Stein Tonesson and Hans Antlov, eds., *Asian Forms of the Nation,* pp. 323–347. London, 1996.

Smith, Anthony D. *Nationalism: Theory, Ideology, History.* Malden, Mass., 2001.

Warren, James Francis. *Rickshaw Coolie: A People's History of Singapore (1880–1940).* Singapore, 1986.

Chapter 18

Depression and War

THE PROCESSES of economic, social, and political change in Southeast Asia generally appeared linear and rising, at least to imperial eyes, from the nineteenth century through the first two decades of the twentieth. There was more of almost everything material, and in social and political institutions, there was clear development along lines that we might describe as "modernization." Global terms of trade favored Southeast Asian producers; population growth accelerated; education expanded; bridges and roads spread everywhere. Almost every index of development seemed to show a steady upward trend—though of course such indices do not measure psychological stress or cultural anomie. Even Southeast Asian participation in colonial systems of politics and administration increased, though generally at too slow a pace to satisfy local aspirations. It was not difficult to believe in a myth of perpetual "progress," though Southeast Asians were beginning to clamor—with good reason—that they were not getting their share of it.

And then the wheels began to come off. There were some unexpected economic downturns in the 1920s, as global commerce was impeded by rising tariff walls and surplus production of export commodities began to turn the terms of trade against primary producers, but most officials and observers saw this as only a minor bump on the path of progress. In the 1930s, however, the Great Depression struck, and before Southeast Asia could recover from it, the region was pulled into World War II and the orbit of imperial Japan. The tumultuous years from 1929 to 1945 put severe and unprecedented strain on all of the processes and institutions that had developed over the previous century and led to, or accelerated, the passage of Southeast Asia out of colonialism into an unknown future. During the war even those areas that the British were to continue to control into the mid-1950s became aware that political independence was imminent, though most people in Portuguese East Timor still might not have contemplated the prospect. This period thus provides a final opportunity to assess the impact of imperial rule, in particular the human consequences of linking Southeast Asia to a capitalist world system susceptible to periodic depressions and the threat of total war.

The Great Depression

HOW SEVERE was the Great Depression for the peoples of Southeast Asia? There were some obvious local repercussions. The prices and wages peasants and workers received for their crops and labor fell as the demand abroad for their products declined. Perhaps the most dramatic example of this was the collapse in the price of rubber from the plantations of Malaya, Sumatra, and Cochinchina as the sales of automobiles dropped off. But the market for other commodities such as tobacco, abaca, and tin also fell, though differentially. On Java the price of sugar fell almost 60 percent between 1929 and 1934, and the sum of sugar land rents and wages fell 92 percent between 1929 and 1936, as peasants abandoned the profitless industry and intensified their rice cultivation.

Starting in the 1920s, the colonial powers established international cartels—forerunners of OPEC (the Organization of Petroleum Exporting Countries)—to restrict production and thus maintain prices of commodities like tin and rubber, but all failed to stop the saturation and weakening of global markets. For a few commodities, growing demand from Japan compensated in part for the loss of Western markets, but by and large almost every export industry in Southeast Asia was in decline during the interwar years. The fall of export prices reverberated in the countryside, where we can trace, for example, parallel drops in cockfight revenues, wages, land prices, payment of head tax and excise taxes, retail sales, the profits of bus companies, and even the sale of Bible "portions" by missionaries.

The depression was more than a period of falling export volumes and values. It was also a period of restricted credit; whereas Southeast Asia had been a capital-importing region for most of the imperialist era, now finance became very tight, even for peasant producers tied into the capitalist world economy. Capital began to flow out of the region, with devastating consequences for small-scale farmers. This was demonstrated most graphically in the delta region of British Burma. The Chettyars, who provided credit for most agriculturalists there (either directly or indirectly via loans to Myanmar moneylenders), obtained their capital from banks in India, which were ultimately dependent on banks in Britain. In the depression of the late 1920s and early 1930s, as British banks began to call in their loans, Indian banks had no choice but to demand repayment from the Chettyars, who in turn were forced to try to recoup their outlays to Myanmar peasants, generating the combustible social and economic conditions that underlay the Hsaya San rebellion. Thus, largely unrecognized by both of them, the dispossessed Myanmar peasantry and the unemployed of industrial Britain suffered the effects of the same global crisis of capitalism.

The depression affected different classes and categories of people in different ways. For the most remote communities, largely untouched by the previous century of change, it probably passed by unnoticed. A few Southeast Asians, such as government employees, actually did relatively well during these years. Though some had their wages reduced, they were protected by their otherwise secure salaries, while a decline in consumer prices—often much larger than their pay cuts—significantly reduced the urban cost of living. The growing desire for government jobs, once attributed by historians to cultural phenomena, can be seen as a rational response to economic dislocation. The depression did, however, contribute to the end of the absolute monarchy in Siam, as educated commoners who had expected employment opportunities in the civil and military service found their chances limited by a combination of royal favoritism and government budget cuts. King Prajadhipok himself admitted his helplessness in the face of global economic forces: "The financial war is a very hard one indeed. Even experts contradict each other until they become hoarse. Each offers a different suggestion. I myself do not profess to know much about the matter and all I can do is listen to the opinions of others and choose the best. I have never experienced such hardship; therefore if I have made a mistake I really deserve to be excused by the officials and people of Siam."

Although at first concentrating only on balancing their budgets, governments eventually were forced to respond to the wider consequences of the depression so as to maintain social order. Often, however, they did too little too late to alleviate the greatest distress. Because the currency of the Netherlands Indies was tied to the Dutch guilder, which was not devalued until the latter half of 1936, Indies exports were particularly overpriced in world markets, so the effects of the depression in the outer islands were more severe than they might have been had Holland allowed its colonies control over their own currencies. As a consequence, the value of outer island exports declined by more than two-thirds between 1925 and 1935. The government of Siam, too, stuck to the gold standard for essentially political reasons—to prove to the community of Western nations that it was "responsible"—well past the point where it made economic sense.

Taxes were sometimes lowered to compensate for reduced farm incomes. In the Philippines, for example, the government sometimes waived earlier tax bills if farmers were willing to pay during the current year. (Where the government seemed unbending in its claims, as in French Indochina, rural tensions increased.) Similarly, landlords were often forced to lower rents or risk losing all income from bankrupt, absconding, or rebellious tenants. Farmers could use violence or the threat of violence to demand reductions in their rents or extensions to their loans. The application for licenses for hand guns by Chettyars and their agents always increased in the months before annual rent collections as they sought to protect themselves from angry tenants.

Sometimes class and race became synonymous in the eyes of those facing distress and dislocation. The poorest elements in society were willing to work for less, and if they were identified with one ethnic group, the result could be bloody. In rural Burma, for example, landless Indian farmers were often willing to pay higher rents than Myanmars, resulting in a mass of landless peasants who expressed their rage not at the landlords, but at those who had taken their places on the land. Meanwhile, in British Rangoon, when Myanmar workers were willing to work on the docks for less than the Indian laborers who had held those jobs for years, the result was heightened racial tension, which led to intermittent rioting during the 1930s. Elsewhere in the region governments tried to solve the worsening "Chinese problem" by restrictive legislation or encouraging the repatriation of immigrants.

But to emphasize these problems is to exaggerate the impact of the depression on Southeast Asia as a whole. The greatest shock was felt by Western plantation owners, miners, and traders, Chinese and South Asian immigrants, and the urban sector in general. The conditions of Southeast Asian peasants, unlike those of urban factory workers in industrialized nations, could often be ameliorated by means other than government intervention. Peasants, for example, could increase their output by putting in even longer hours in the fields, thus maintaining their real incomes in the face of declining market prices. Those who produced nonedible crops like rubber, tobacco, or abaca could sometimes switch to food crops instead. For all but the very poorest, the decline in food prices meant that impoverishment did not normally result in actual starvation; if preferred items such as meat, fish, and rice were out of reach, cheaper staples such as roots and tubers were usually available. The demographic record shows that although there was hunger, it never reached the point of famine; Southeast Asia's population continued to grow steadily through the 1930s. For many Southeast Asians, the depression years were not much worse than what had gone before. Certainly they were not nearly as bad as World War II, which would lead to widespread distress for millions of Southeast Asians over the next decade.

Southeast Asia in the Pacific War

WORLD WAR II was a major historical turning point throughout Southeast Asia. The conquest of the region by imperial Japan shattered irrevocably a white, colonial domination of Southeast Asia and helped to end the imperial system globally. For seventy-five years a rapidly modernizing militarizing Japanese state attempted to achieve parity as an imperial nation, one accorded the equivalent of contemporary superpower status. World War II ended the arrogance of colonialism, unleashing national responses that have shaped Southeast Asia ever since. Just as World War I permanently altered the continent of Europe, establishing national rights to self-determination, the chaotic violence of World War II permitted indigenous national movements to smash colonial structures in Asia. The peoples of Southeast Asia were given a unique chance, one not necessarily preordained.

In many ways World War II touched virtually every Southeast Asian's life and livelihood, destabilizing decades of colonial accommodation with favored indigenous elites. Beginning in Southeast Asia when Japan moved troops into northern Vietnam in 1940, it did not end in the region until some months after the Japanese government had formally surrendered to the Allied Forces on the battleship *Missouri* on 2 September 1945, since in many areas stranded Japanese garrisons continued to play an important role in determining who gained power. Holland, France, and Great Britain all tried to reassert administrative and political hegemony, even while various indigenous movements were jockeying for political advantage in a chaotic, often lawless, period.

This was the first moment in history that the same dynamic of military and political forces affected all Southeast Asia, even though the outcome differed from one place to another. In some places the conquering Japanese armies were welcomed as liberators, because they overthrew oppressive colonial regimes. In others the Japanese were viewed as marauding barbarians, unwelcome and hated; the resultant civil unrest, partially shaped by ideology and partially by competing elites jockeying for advantage, divided those former colonies. In yet other places, responses were ambivalent, as people saw political and economic opportunity in the invasion but were repelled by Japanese racism and imperialism. Sometimes families split and regional, linguistic, religious, and sociocultural tensions were aggravated. People in urban areas experienced the war very differently than those in the countryside. Social classes might turn against each other in new and violent manifestations. The war became a crucible in many Southeast Asian societies, raising questions of loyalty, national identity, and patriotism: What did allegiance signify in a Southeast Asian colonial context? And to whom was such allegiance due? Was the queen of Holland, herself a political refugee in Great Britain, still deserving of fealty and loyalty by the inhabitants of what she claimed as her Dutch East Indian empire? And, if not, what new, transcendent, secular symbols could provide the various ethnic and geographic groups in the Indies common identity? What was treason? And if it was committed, against whom?

The Japanese had arrived proclaiming "Asia for the Asiatics." Proposing a restructured economic order they called the "Greater East Asia Co-Prosperity

Sphere," they insisted that Japan would become the financial, industrial, military, and commercial center of Asia. Yet few in Southeast Asia believed the new imperial order would last. Even as the warfare raged, it became clear that postwar arrangements had to be considered and contested.

The war brought a whirlwind of death and destruction in Burma and the Philippines. Malaya and Timor were fought over savagely. Other parts of the region, Java, for example, saw virtually no fighting. Communal violence erupted primarily when Japan took over and at the war's end. Old grudges and struggles for local hegemony often shaped responses. The military struggle continued episodically across the region from 1940 to 1946. While some places were spared, many were scarred. The city of Manila, for example, was the second most damaged city of World War II, just behind Warsaw, Poland. In the Philippines, starvation, economic dislocation, monetary chaos, destruction of infrastructure, and loss of income were widely felt. It was an era of hardship, cataclysmic change, and political turmoil, which transformed the Japanese dream of "a new dawn for Asia" into a Southeast Asian nightmare.

In Singapore, the vaunted guns of British imperialism all pointed out to the sea. The Japanese conquered this bastion in part by bicycling an army down the Malay Peninsula to attack it from the rear as well as by establishing air supremacy; General Yamashita Tomoyuki was given the sobriquet "The Tiger of Malaya" for this campaign. This humbling of European military power and political legitimacy broke the mystique of invincibility that had been so carefully cultivated by colonial administrators, who were themselves astounded by Japanese prowess.

All over the region Europeans and Americans, who had lived in colonial Southeast Asia as if they were nobility, were suddenly thrown into concentration camps by the Japanese. Western languages were replaced with native vernaculars. Street names were changed, statues toppled. Indigenous institutions were celebrated by a Japanese military intent on shattering the symbolic and psychological hold of the West. Petty humiliations and ruthless brutality were employed to destroy colonial complacency, and like Humpty Dumpty, the smug prewar colonial universe fell shattered to the ground. Dislocation encouraged indigenous nationalist leaders to seize this unique opportunity to alter forever the future destiny of their nations. The war years were thus both brutal and exhilarating, destructive and empowering.

Invasion and Occupation

WITH THE fall of France and the Netherlands to Germany in June 1940 and the prospect of the imminent victory of Germany over England, some Japanese leaders, especially in the navy, pressed for a decisive move into Southeast Asia. This, they thought, would both thwart Germany from assuming sovereignty over the British, French, and Dutch empires in the region and, more important, gain control over the indigenous resources required by Japan to prosecute its own war in China, which had begun in 1937. Malayan rubber and tin, Sumatran oil and bauxite, and Indochinese and Burmese rice were seductive attractions for Japanese planners.

When France surrendered to Hitler, Japan demanded from the now isolated colonial regime in Indochina strategic access to northern Vietnam in order to interdict a supply route up the Red River used by the anti-Japanese Nationalist (GMD) Chinese government. This move eventually led to the construction of the "Burma Road," across which the Jiang Jieshi (Chiang Kai-shek) government continued to receive food and arms, trucked from Rangoon to Yunnan. The incursion into northern Vietnam also prompted Franklin Roosevelt to warn Japan not to push any farther into Southeast Asia.

And thus, when Japan subsequently demanded from the Vichy government its military bases in southern Vietnam, the United States froze Japanese assets, cut off the sale of oil and scrap metal to Japan, and set the stage for war in the Pacific. America saw south Vietnam as the place where it was vital to halt Japanese expansion, an action that was to presage events a quarter of a century later. The struggle between these two Pacific powers would ultimately determine the future of Southeast Asia.

On 8 December 1941 (dawn on 7 December 1941 east of the international date line), Japanese forces attacked the U.S. fleet at Pearl Harbor (Honolulu); all other American military installations in the western Pacific, the Aleutians, and the Philippines; and the British garrisons in Hong Kong, Singapore, and the northern coasts of Malaya. Japan also attacked Thailand at seven points on the Gulf of Siam and across the border from Cambodia, striking at the main Thai airbase north of Bangkok. Thailand immediately capitulated, allying itself with Japan within hours of the initial attack. The British, American, and Dutch forces resisted, but within four months Japan had conquered the region. Manila was occupied on 2 January 1942, Kuala Lumpur on 11 January, Singapore on 15 February, Rangoon on 7 March, and the last parts of the Dutch East Indies on 9 March. The American fortress of Corregidor, at the mouth of Manila Bay, held out until 6 May 1942. Only the Vichy government, in French Indochina, was allowed to sustain the fiction of continuing European control. The war, which rapidly expanded throughout the Pacific, also encouraged Hitler to declare war on the United States, expanding the fighting globally, fusing European and Asian conflicts.

In the Philippines the war actively engaged the anti-Japanese passions of the Filipinos. It was their war, not simply America's; for every American soldier forced to endure the Bataan Death March, there were ten Filipinos. Elsewhere, local resistance rallied to British-organized forces coordinated (from India) by Lord Mountbatten. Virtually everywhere in the region, the Japanese encouraged the formation of indigenous military and paramilitary forces to offset the groups that remained loyal to the Allies. Many of the national armies of independent Southeast Asia evolved from these contending wartime militias, often fighting against each other in postwar struggles as they had during the war.

To achieve its economic objectives, Japan also resorted to forced labor, demanding that thousands of peasants join "sweat armies of conscripts," build the infamous Burma-Thailand railway—dramatized in the 1957 film *The Bridge on the River Kwai*—transport military supplies, and produce (at below subsistence level) whatever was necessary for the Japanese war machine. The export-driven economies of Southeast Asia shriveled, since traditional markets were now closed. The export of raw materials and the import of manufactured items suddenly stopped, producing massive dislocation. The Japanese hope of diverting Southeast Asian commodities to northeast Asia was thwarted by Allied submarines, which increasingly sank their merchant ships. Tokyo's economic blueprint could not be achieved.

Respect for and the maintenance of law and order collapsed, with profound long-term consequences. Anti-Japanese guerrilla movements sprung up, supported by Allied forces—some motivated by ideology, some by local politics, some by greed, self-interest, or the simple attempt to survive. These guerrilla forces altered the local balance of power. Malayan Chinese, anti-Japanese because of the Sino-Japanese war, were the core of a guerrilla resistance that was tied to the ethnic politics of the peninsula. Throughout the region guerrillas sabotaged tin mines and oil fields; bombed roads, bridges, and railway lines; and pinned Japanese forces down.

Whatever their motivation, guerrillas, along with many noncombatants, rejected the authority and the legitimacy of the Japanese-sponsored governments. Patriotism became clouded. Resistance was defined by some as heroic, by others as treasonous. Individuals and groups often played one side against the other or proffered allegiances based on short-term tactical decisions or the ebb and flow of geopolitics.

Some leaders, established or new, chose to collaborate; others became guerrillas. Each claimed the regalia of national identity. There was economic corruption on a massive scale, as people bought and sold contraband everywhere; some purchased (with Japanese-sponsored currency) tangible assets such as land, so the ownership of property also became clouded. All, whatever they actually did, claimed to be motivated by a national dream. People settled family grudges in the name of patriotism; ethical values were a casualty in the struggle to survive.

In the Philippines the wartime governor of Leyte Island, Bernardo Torres, argued, "I am a Filipino agent working to the best of my ability to serve my unfortunate country in an unfortunate time in her history." He asked rhetorically: "Who will say I am a traitor to my country because I happen to have been called to make government—peace, order, security—function in our provinces?

I was not privileged to fight in the battlefield and to make a military choice. I was fated by circumstance to be the governor of our province before and during this war."

The countervailing argument was made by guerrilla leader Tomas Confesor, who said that "this struggle is a total war in which . . . the question at stake in respect to the Philippines is . . . what system of social organization and code of morals should govern our existence." Confesor argued that "something more precious than life itself: the principles of democracy and justice, the honor and destiny of our people" was the basis on which personal behavior had to be judged. The prewar chief justice of the Philippine Supreme Court, Jose Abad Santos, was one of the very few early in the war who refused to cooperate with the Japanese—and he was executed. His sacrifice has remained an ambivalent legacy ever since, since most of his colleagues chose to collaborate.

The Riptide

JAPAN HAD invaded Southeast Asia anticipating that the war in Europe would end in 1942, but by mid-1943 Hitler's attack against Russia had failed, and the Allies had fought from North Africa to Italy. The failure of Japan's invasion of India from Burma and its losses in the Pacific, starting with the battle of Midway in June 1942, suggested that it could not prevail. To rally indigenous support in Southeast Asia, the Japanese military increasingly made political concessions to cooperative local nationalists, establishing quasi-independent regimes in the Philippines and Burma, and transferring parts of British Burma, northern Malaya, Laos, and Cambodia to its ally, Thailand.

As the military reconquest of Southeast Asia by the Allied forces came ever closer, Japanese policy evolved into doing anything that might impede their advance. By 1944 British troops were moving across Burma, and the Americans under Douglas MacArthur were returning (as he had promised) to the Philippines. Allied bombing of Japan's naval routes obliterated both its merchant marine and its naval squadrons. Guerrilla movements were increasing in strength and coordination across the region. The Japanese needed Southeast Asian allies and found them in some newly empowered indigenous nationalist leaders. Imperialism was transformed into support of radical nationalism.

Many of these indigenous leaders had been in and out of jail for decades before the war, while others were in exile. Some had surrendered their dreams and were living quiet, ordinary lives in their communities. Before the war their prospects had seemed dim and their visions of their various nations' futures unlikely fantasies. In every colony there were already native elites who held key jobs and who believed that they were by education and position entitled to lead their nation forward. Their colonial collaboration with the Europeans had offered status, influence, and the likelihood of an evolutionary access to greater power in the years ahead. (In noncolonized Thailand the Japanese also intervened dramatically in the political balance, especially in the power structure of the army.)

During the last stages of the war, no one knew what would happen next: how soon the European colonial powers could return and whether they would try (and still have the power and will) to restore the status quo. The Japanese formally took direct control over Vietnam and planned to secure parts of Thailand. No one imagined that the Pacific War would end abruptly once atomic bombs were dropped on Hiroshima and Nagasaki on 6 and 9 August 1945.

With the exception of the United States, which in 1934 had negotiated its postcolonial relationship with the Philippines, none of the colonial regimes had articulated a coherent postwar policy or developed a clear consensus about what to do once the war ended. Lacking a political crystal ball, the various and often competing elites of Southeast Asia had to gamble on the outcome. Was it best

War and mobilization: Indonesian youths march before Japanese reviewers, Jakarta, ca. 1944. Note Sukarno (in white) standing at the top of the steps. KITLV, Leiden, #25252

to jump to a previously banned nationalist movement, cooperate with the returning European power, splinter from a movement for personal ambition, or build bridges to those geographically, linguistically, or ethnically different? Ideological issues, especially the radical fusion of communism and anti-imperialism, which excited many searching for a rational validation of the nationalist goal, further polarized both elite groups and mass movements. Every choice was dangerous, no decision guaranteed.

Ultimately secular political nationalism in Southeast Asia proved victorious, and the historical outcome, in hindsight, seems obvious. But it was not obvious at the time. If the British Labour Party under Clement Attlee had not defeated the Conservatives of Prime Minister Winston Churchill in the 1945 elections, would the history of Burma have been different? Would different leaders have achieved power? Would its nationalism have been more evolutionary? World War II and the Japanese occupation of Southeast Asia unequivocally represented one of those historical moments when what came after was dramatically different from what came before. Yet one can accept that Southeast Asia could not return to a colonial framework demolished by war without having to concede that the outcome of the historical story was preordained.

The war years made possible what otherwise might never have happened: the birth of modern, independent Southeast Asian nation-states based almost exactly on the colonial geography that had existed in 1940. New nations were born into a maelstrom of conflicting values; ideological consensus was lost. Violence may always be the midwife of wars of national liberation, but what happened in Southeast Asia was particularly brutal, unleashing an era of communal tension, death, loss of cohesion, and physical destruction.

Further Readings

Anderson, Benedict R. O'G. *Java in a Time of Revolution: Occupation and Resistance, 1944–1946*. Ithaca, 1972.

Baker, Christopher. "Economic Reorganization and the Slump in South and Southeast Asia." *Comparative Studies in Society and History* 23 (1981): 325–349.

Boomgaard, Peter, and Brown, Ian, eds. *Weathering the Storm: The Economies of Southeast Asia in the 1930s Depression*. Leiden, 2000.

Friend, Theodore. *The Blue-Eyed Enemy: Japan against the West in Java and Luzon, 1942–1945*. Princeton, 1988.

Goodman, Grant K., ed. *Japanese Cultural Policies in Southeast Asia during World War*. London, 1991.

Ikehata Setsuho and Ricardo Trota Jose, eds. *The Philippines under Japan: Occupation Policy and Reaction*. Quezon City, 1999.

Lebra, Joyce C. *Japanese-Trained Armies in Southeast Asia: Independence and Volunteer Forces in World War II*. New York, 1977.

McCoy, Alfred W., ed. *Southeast Asia under Japanese Occupation*. New Haven, 1980.

Post, Peter, and Elly Touwen-Bouwsma, eds. *Japan, Indonesia and the War: Myths and Realities*. Leiden, 1996.

Reynolds, E. Bruce. *Thailand and Japan's Southern Advance, 1940–1945*. Basingstoke, 1994.

Steinberg, David Joel. *Philippine Collaboration in World War II*. Ann Arbor, 1967.

Tarling, Nicholas. *A Sudden Rampage: The Japanese Occupation of Southeast Asia, 1941–1945*. London, 2001.

PART 4

✳

Passages Out of
the Colonial Era

Chapter 19

The Philippines, 1896–1972

From Revolution to Martial Law

Periodization in history is never easy. In the Philippines, as elsewhere in Southeast Asia, the Great Depression and World War II were clearly turning points in history, viewed from one perspective. These calamitous events brought an end to a lengthy period of apparent progress, and they helped precipitate (and complicate) the demise of the region's dominant political institution, colonialism, by shattering the assumptions of political stability and inevitability that had loaned colonial authority such power. Suddenly new individuals, groups, and movements were given the opportunity to challenge existing verities and hierarchies of authority and to offer alternate scenarios, increasingly nationalistic, to define the future.

In most countries of Southeast Asia, the depression and the war opened opportunities and empowered individuals in ways that would have been impossible a decade earlier. In the Philippines, which had the oldest and most mature secular national movement in the region, they created different kinds of stress. Class tensions, a highly distorted distribution of wealth, and the maintenance of political dominance by a self-arrogating elite generated spasms of violence and raised profound questions about the core promise of a nationalist dream.

Philippine history is normally divided so that a new period begins at the end of the colonial era, with formal independence in 1946. But throughout the twentieth century, the mostly-mestizo elite continued to dominate the socioeconomic, political, and cultural environment (as friar priests had earlier), a

historical truth perhaps even more important than the transfer of legal authority from Spain to the United States in 1898 or from the United States to the
Republic of the Philippines in 1946.

Imperial Transition

IN 1896 Andrés Bonifacio, an urban nationalist but no general, hoped that the
Cuban revolution a half a globe away would deplete Spanish resources, allowing
the Katipunan to triumph. Yet it was only in nearby Cavite, where the friars held
half of all rice land, that Emilio Aguinaldo, a young mayor of Chinese mestizo
stock, defeated Spanish troops. Aguinaldo challenged Bonifacio for leadership,
arresting and ultimately executing him for "treason," a spurious allegation that
stained Aguinaldo's memory, split the Katipunan, and alienated *ilustrado* support.
The Katipuneros had to retreat and negotiate a cease-fire with the governor-
general. Aguinaldo sought much but only got amnesty, safe passage to exile, and
a pledge of 800,000 pesos in three installments (the last was never paid). He
went to Hong Kong; the Spanish celebrated a *Te Deum* at the Manila cathedral.

The sinking of the U.S. battleship *Maine* in Havana on 15 February 1898
altered the revolutions in both Cuba and the Philippines. President William
McKinley claimed not to know where the Philippines was, but America understood imperial opportunity. Whether it was the voice of God intoning Manifest
Destiny or, in Richard Hofstadter's graphic phrase, "the carnal larynx of
Theodore Roosevelt," the Americans took up the "White Man's burden."
Roosevelt, then acting secretary of the navy, ordered the Asian squadron to sail
to Manila to destroy an aging, rusted Spanish fleet lest it cross the Pacific to
attack California. On 1 May 1898 Commodore George Dewey sank the Spanish
fleet so easily that he was able to interrupt his attack to serve breakfast. Lacking
further orders, he anchored in Manila Bay and decided to bring Aguinaldo back,
over the opposition of the State Department.

From then through the election of 1900, there was a passionate debate
within the United States between pro-imperialists, mainly Republicans, who
saw great opportunity in Asia, and anti-imperialists, who saw no lasting American interest in the Philippines. One satirist irreverently told the president, "Tis
not more thin two months since ye larned whether they were islands or canned
goods." But McKinley, intrigued with imperial opportunities, concluded that
he had no choice but "to educate the Filipinos, and uplift and civilize and Christianize them and by God's grace do the very best we could by them." To
achieve that, he strengthened Dewey's flotilla by sending more than ten thousand ground troops across the Pacific.

Spain still controlled Manila. Aguinaldo, whose insurgent forces controlled
most of the archipelago, established himself in the provincial city of Malolos,
declaring Philippine independence on 21 June 1898. A cabinet controlled by a

brilliant *ilustrado,* Apolinario Mabini, pushed Aguinaldo into a titular role. A constitutional convention was summoned, a parliamentary system chosen. Of the 136 delegates, 45 were lawyers and 35 others were trained as other modern professionals. The Malolos constitution guaranteed private property, limiting suffrage to men of high character, social position, and honorable conduct. The government of the Philippine Republic, inaugurated on 21 January 1899, was conservative. Mabini, who had sought a more authoritarian structure and radical agenda, lost.

This dispute became moot, because the United States decided to colonize the archipelago. The Spanish garrison had surrendered Manila to American forces after a sham battle in August 1898, from which Aguinaldo's troops were excluded. On 4 February 1899, under disputed circumstances, fighting erupted between Americans and Filipinos. During the war that followed, Aguinaldo, repeating his folly toward Bonifacio, arranged the ambush of an *ilustrado* officer, Antonio Luna, who had eclipsed him militarily. Mabini lambasted Aguinaldo for his "immeasurable ambition of power," subsequently writing that "with the loss of Luna . . . the Revolution fell, and the ignominy of the fall, weighing entirely on Aguinaldo, caused his moral death, a thousand times bitterer than the physical."

For the United States the conflict, which lasted officially until 1901, unofficially even longer, proved more costly and prolonged than the fight against Spain. For the Philippines it was a vicious, violently destructive encounter, the first war of national liberation in Southeast Asia, a struggle that left a half million noncombatants dead or maimed and produced severe economic dislocation. Thousands of Americans and tens of thousands of Filipino soldiers died of disease or in combat. The American military, to its shame, resorted to collective punishment (including the "reconcentration" of civilian populations) and torture in its effort to suppress what they referred to as the "Philippine Insurrection" and Filipinos, more appropriately, named the Philippine-American War. General Arthur MacArthur noted in 1900 that "this unique system of [guerrilla] war depends upon almost complete unity of action of the entire native population." The brutality of its suppression was acutely embarrassing to the Republicans; America's imperialist binge left a wicked hangover.

Compadre Colonialism

MEANWHILE, the United States sent several fact-finding commissions to the islands. The first was led by the president of Cornell and the second by William Howard Taft, who rapidly understood the need to establish a "policy of attraction" for the *ilustrados* if America wanted to transform hostility into friendship. America promised a government designed "for the happiness, peace and prosperity of the people of the Philippine Islands. . . . The measures adopted should be made to conform to their customs, their habits and even their prejudices." It was in effect a self-liquidating form of colonialism, with an evolutionary nationalism to be given the opportunity to take over gradually. Taft (who went on to be governor-general, then secretary of the army, and finally president) made colonial politics an extension of imperial war by other means. As early as 1900, he invited a group of *ilustrado* leaders to form a political party. Led by T. H. Pardo de Tavera, this Federal Party, misunderstanding McKinley's vague promise of "benevolent assimilation," actually sought statehood within the United States—something closely akin to what Rizal had sought from Spain.

Taft's policy of attraction, said one of his successors, "charmed the rifle out of the hands of the insurgents and made the one-time rebel chief the pacific president of a municipality or the staid governor of a province." *Ilustrados* accepted this tacit deal to collaborate with the United States. The Philippine-American War ended more with a whimper than with a bang. Aguinaldo was captured by subterfuge and lived on for decades, honored but largely irrelevant; all but a few "irreconcilables" gained positions of power. Imperialism was re-packaged as altruism. An American vision of capitalism, electoral democracy, and mass education seduced the newly empowered *ilustrado* elite. Other political

A modern politician: the speaker of the Philippine Assembly, Sergio Osmeña, Manila, ca. 1910.

From D. C. Worcester, *The Philippines*, New York, 1914

parties soon emerged. Local and provincial elections were held in 1903, a national assembly elected in 1907.

The United States, long committed to separation of church and state, sought to remove the church from temporal affairs. Since the friar charitable foundations still functioned as banks, the government started chartering commercial banks, while negotiating with the Vatican to sell off friar lands. Rome replaced Spanish friars with English-speaking priests, primarily Irish Americans, while seminaries hastened to train an adequate number of Filipino clerics. This response was accelerated by the emergence of a national Philippine church seeking to replace Rome's authority. A Filipino priest, Gregorio Aglipay, the chaplain general of Aguinaldo's forces (for which he was excommunicated by the Spanish hierarchy) became "supreme bishop" of the Iglesia Filipina Independiente (Philippine Independent Church) in 1902. Under its lay organizer, Isabelo de los Reyes, it seized possession of many rural parishes previously staffed by friars.

But Taft blocked the forcible dispossession of Roman priests, and in 1906 a conservative Philippine Supreme Court, including both American and mestizo jurists, ruled that all Catholic property taken by the Aglipayan church had to be returned. Some peasants followed Aglipayan priests into makeshift chapels, but many continued to worship where they had always prayed, in the massive baroque structures that dominated town plazas. Gaining support from the American Episcopal Church, Aglipayanism retained a presence in the archipelago, but its growth ceased, so it remained strong only in northwest Luzon, where it originated. Instead, a native Catholic clergy, substantially mestizo, now ministers to most Filipinos; Jaime Cardinal Sin, the long-serving archbishop of Manila, carried the Chinese surname of his paternal ancestors. Other Philippine-based churches, most notably the Iglesia ni Kristo (Church of Christ), minister to those seeking evangelical alternatives.

By 1908 Taft was fretting that American colonial policy was to "await the organization of a Philippine oligarchy or aristocracy competent to administer and turn the islands over to it." American policy postulated that mass education, if properly extended, would eventually break "the feudal relationship of dependence which so many of the common people feel toward their wealthy or educated leaders." But by granting *ilustrados* enormous landownership opportunities and validating their near monopoly of influence, the United States abdicated its chance to rework the Philippine polity in more equitable, democratic ways. When the friar lands were sold, after negotiations in Rome, *ilustrado* families gained ownership of most of that land, even though the ostensible policy had been to encourage homesteading tenants. (Colonial official Dean C. Worcester also acquired sizable holdings, to the irritation of Filipino nationalists.) American colonial policy, though proclaiming its intent to establish a "showcase of democracy," in fact conformed to the customs, habits, and even prejudices of *ilustrados*. Pardo de Tavera sadly predicted in 1907 that the "government would not be democratic but autocratic, and the people would be oppressed by those who would be in power."

Peace, trade, and American investment stimulated the economy. Manila grew rapidly; its population quadrupled under the Americans. Public health measures helped tame tropical and poverty-born diseases. English spread across the archipelago. Young American recruits, known as "Thomasites" for the first ship that brought them to the archipelago, fanned out across the country to teach in English. In 1901 functional literacy was about 20 percent; by 1941 it was over 50 percent. Newspapers, radio, then ultimately television connected the countryside to Manila. Road construction, interisland shipping, and eventually air service did the same.

The Timing of Independence

AFTER 1907 the key political debate in both Manila and Washington was over the timing of independence. The Nacionalista Party, first led by a Chinese mestizo, Sergio Osmeña, and later by a Spanish mestizo, Manuel Quezon, demanded immediate independence, even though privately neither leader saw it as feasible. The opposition party, led by Juan Sumulong, wanted something more gradual, believing that premature independence would further entrench the oligarchy.

In the United States Republicans argued for a gradual process, while the Democrats, harking back to 1900, sought early independence. Woodrow Wilson's election in 1912 led to rapid Filipinization of the colonial government. Governor-General Francis B. Harrison increased the proportion of Filipinos in the bureaucracy to 96 percent. In 1916 the Democrats passed the Jones Act, promising independence "as soon as a stable government can be established"; a proposed Senate amendment, defining that time limit as two to four years, was barely defeated in the House of Representatives. Independence seemed imminent, especially after Wilson articulated self-determination as a worldwide goal at the end of World War I. In 1919 a Philippine independence mission came to the United States to negotiate that transition, but Wilson's stroke, the Republican electoral victory in 1920, and America's decision to reject the League of Nations delayed an early transition, which would have had a palpable impact throughout Southeast Asia. Instead the Republicans appointed a former "Rough Rider," General Leonard Wood, as governor-general. Wood sought to put the nationalist genie back into the colonial bottle, but Quezon, manipulating Wood's rigidity, thwarted him and soon replaced Osmeña as the leading Filipino politician.

The 1932 election of Franklin Roosevelt as U.S. president, with overwhelming Democratic congressional majorities, again accelerated the likelihood of early independence. Japanese militarism, depression-stimulated hostility by

American labor to Filipino immigrants, and protectionism by American farm interests trying to exclude cheap Philippine produce were also important factors. The Tydings-McDuffie Act (1934) established a ten-year transitional Philippine Commonwealth. In 1935 Quezon was elected president of that commonwealth, with Osmeña as his vice president. Sumulong lamented that "any reunion of the followers of Quezon and Osmeña—call it fusion, coalition, cooperation or conjunction—would mean the restoration, inexcusable from all angles, of the feared and detested oligarchy." But despite his jeremiad, most Filipinos optimistically anticipated independence under Quezon.

Geographic, linguistic, and ethnic distinctions softened as national norms emerged. Most Filipinos, whatever their economic class or social status, identified with Philippine nationalism and its symbols: the flag, the anthem, and the glorification of Rizal as the great symbol of national identity. They saw themselves as a bridge for the rest of Asia, prompting one to exclaim that they were "an oriental people standing at the portals of Asia, in deep sympathy with its kindred neighbors, yet with hands outstretched to the cultures of Spain and America." "Compadre colonialism," that tacit collaboration between American colonial authorities and the *ilustrados,* transferred political power and created economic wealth for those best able to profit. Young Filipinos were regularly sent for modern career training in the United States. Known originally as *pensionados* (scholarship holders), they were educated in law, medicine, and liberal arts and sciences as well as mining, agronomy, forestry, accounting, and all types of engineering.

One of the anomalies of American colonialism was the disconnect between rapid devolution of political power and a seemingly immutable economic framework that sheltered Philippine exports within an American tariff zone. Sugar, copra, and other coconut products prospered even during the depression by having access to the protected U.S. market. Philippine sugar production expanded, while the Indonesian sugar industry was decimated. There was little economic planning for independence, minimal effort to diversify the economy, and hardly any fiscal and monetary planning to parallel the self-liquidating colonialism of the political sphere.

War and Liberation

THE AMERICAN MILITARY had realized early that the conquest of the Philippines left the United States exposed in any future Pacific war. Despite having a superb harbor at Subic Bay, the Philippines was too far from the United States and too close to Japan, so Pearl Harbor (Honolulu), became America's forward naval base. As early as 1907 Theodore Roosevelt had recognized that the Philippines "form our heel of Achilles." From the earliest contingency plans, "War Plan Orange" became the code name for a future struggle against Japan. It postulated that any attack on the Philippines by Japan would be answered by the arrival of the battle fleet from Pearl Harbor. Since the Philippines was obviously in harm's way, early independence became increasingly attractive to the American military, especially after 1931, when the Japanese seized Manchuria.

The cataclysm of World War II swept over the Philippines at the end of 1941. With independence almost achieved, most Filipinos, in stark contrast to much of the rest of Southeast Asia, felt that the American colonial interregnum had been beneficial and that the Japanese invasion violated their own defined sense of nationhood. But inadequate Filipino-American military resistance, organized by Douglas MacArthur (Arthur's son), merely delayed the Japanese conquest. Quezon and Osmeña were evacuated with MacArthur to Corregidor and then taken to Washington via submarine. Other government leaders, bankers, landowners, and jurists were left behind, as one colonial regime was swept away by another.

Collaboration by the elite opened profound fissures in the body politic. Most Filipinos were anti-Japanese, but virtually all of the prewar elite chose to cooperate with the occupiers. America, meanwhile, encouraged widespread guerrilla activity. Factionalism played a role. Many individuals or families who were political losers during the commonwealth became guerrillas, especially since their archrivals were usually collaborating. And many who were poor, rural, or trapped in a socioeconomic hierarchy used the war to challenge the establishment. Some peasants in central Luzon joined the Hukbalahap, a guerrilla force with a pro-communist, anti-Japanese ideology. Recalling earlier peasant movements, the Huks rebelled against an inequitable class structure, fusing anti-Japanese nationalism with a long-simmering peasant rage at an economic system in which absentee landlords collected very high rents and extracted usurious interest.

Savage fighting produced monumental destruction, social upheaval, and vast personal and property loss. The modern sector, disproportionately located in Manila, was literally and figuratively pulverized, especially during the "Liberation" in 1944–1945. Hospitals, universities, radio stations, transportation hubs, government infrastructure, and private homes were in rubble by the end of the war. Political consensus was equally shattered. Quezon had died of tuberculosis in exile, while Osmeña returned to the Philippines without experiencing the trauma of war. The monolithic Nacionalista Party split. In 1946 MacArthur's prewar friend Manuel Roxas, accused of collaboration, ran for president against Osmeña and won.

During the war both the Japanese and the guerrillas had manipulated the flag and anthem. Jose Laurel, the Japanese-sponsored wartime president, tried to implement authoritarian reforms to enhance national cohesion; he hoped to emulate Japanese discipline, patriotism, and self-sacrifice. Instead, economic corruption became rampant; the black market flourished, and some profiteers attempted to get rid of Japanese-sponsored pesos (which they called "Mickey Mouse money") by buying land. Respect for law and order collapsed. People ignored civil and criminal codes in the pursuit of family survival or even personal aggrandizement, claiming a wartime right to define for themselves what was legitimate. Everyone claimed to be a hero.

The war years also shifted the archipelago culturally closer to the rest of Southeast Asia, transforming Filipino perceptions about America. In 1935 Pio Duran, a prewar apologist for Japan, had been labeled as a right-wing extremist for advocating that the Philippines was "inextricably linked with" Asia. But in the postwar era his theme would become mainstream; leading political figures like Claro Recto, Ferdinand Marcos, Carlos P. Romulo, and Benigno Aquino each tried to reposition the Philippines within the region. During the war the Japanese had promoted Tagalog, emphasizing indigenous institutions and culture. General Homma Masaharu told the Filipinos that "as the leopard cannot change its spots, you cannot alter the fact that you are Orientals." It took a while, but eventually Filipinos, who often joked that they spent three hundred years in a convent and fifty in Hollywood, saw themselves as Southeast Asian.

The "Old Order": Political Independence, Neocolonialism, and Anticommunism

FROM ROXAS' inauguration on 4 July 1946 until Marcos declared martial law in 1972, the country struggled to grow economically, while resolving socio-political "anomalies." Gone were white-suited colonial bureaucrats, replaced by *ilustrados* wearing *barong tagalog*s (embroidered shirts) as emblems of their national pride. Interlocking family dynasties, rich in landownership and in commercial, industrial, and banking interests, sent their children to be educated in the United States and flaunted conspicuous wealth with Cadillacs, country clubs, and mansions. Money conferred social status. Some businesses prospered honestly, but price controls, import-export licenses, American foreign aid, Japanese restitution funds, a black market for luxury items, contract kickbacks, traditional "greasing," and imaginative entrepreneurial schemes all created extralegal opportunities by which individuals could achieve familial goals, often at the expense of inchoate national priorities. Fancy lawyers bought judges. Some super-rich maintained private armies to intimidate and enforce.

Yet this "old order" was also an era when many more people became educated, found opportunity for upward mobility in Manila and elsewhere, and entered the middle class. The first twenty-five years of independence revealed a rough and tumble, expanding capitalist environment. Those who made a fortune gained mythic status; few questioned how their fortunes were made. At every level people accepted as the norm that a driver's license or a visa to America could be acquired using "fixers." Cops could be bought off for a few pesos. Daily life was lived at substantial variance from what legal codes prescribed.

At the same time, the need to restructure the postcolonial relationship with America was seen as a sustaining priority for many Filipinos. The United States, instead of providing generous rehabilitation assistance in reciprocity for Filipino loyalty during the war, had been niggardly in its postwar aid, providing far more money to rebuild Japan. Aid was also tied to neocolonial concessions, including a rigid currency link of peso to dollar and special privileges for American corporations and individuals. For forty years thereafter, Filipinos struggled to end these unequal concessions. The United States also insisted on retaining its giant military bases for ninety-nine years, including the fleet harbor at Subic Bay and Clark Air Base. These bases became central bastions in the Cold War, fiefdoms of *pax Americana*. Philippine law did not apply to American troops; a crime committed by an American serviceman, on base or off, would be tried before a U.S. military tribunal rather than a Philippine court.

Many Filipino leaders, most prominently Recto, raged against these facilities as threats to national sovereignty, inviting future attacks and compromising Philippine integrity. Olongapo (next to Subic) and Angeles City (by Clark) became fleshpots, sin cities of bars and brothels, massage parlors, and gambling dens. The dollars thus transferred into the local economy helped support tens of thousands of Filipinos, ironically also helping to fund the Huks, who, after the war ended, had continued their armed struggle when they realized they had been liberated from the Japanese but not from their landlords. Now, in Mafia style, they skimmed the take from Angeles City to finance their insurgency.

As the Cold War erupted, U.S. president Harry Truman had become anxious about the spread of communism in Asia. Whereas it had been Roosevelt's policy to banish all collaborators from political office, Truman's administration saw these conservative oligarchs as a vital bulwark against communism, thus continuing long-term U.S. support for the *ilustrado* oligarchy under a new rationale. It became an issue in the 1946 election, since Osmeña had accepted Huk leaders into his political coalition. Later, as communists moved toward victory in China and Vietnam, Washington obsessed further about their possible victory in the Philippines. Long-existing socioeconomic tension was filtered through a Cold War prism in Washington; the Huk uprising was seen more as a part of the global "Red" conspiracy than as an indigenous reaction to tenancy, landlessness, and grinding poverty. And while some American strategists argued for effective land reform, they were not prepared to recommend funding it from Washington or to demand a significant redistribution of wealth from the Filipino elite.

Manuel Roxas suffered a fatal heart attack, ironically while visiting Clark Air Base, in 1948. Neither he nor his vice presidential successor, Elpidio

Quirino, could crush the Huks, led by a charismatic, if unsophisticated, peasant, Luis Taruc. Governmental corruption, low morale, inadequately trained troops, rampant inflation, and inadequate foreign funding all doomed governmental efforts. Because both Clark and Subic were within Huk-controlled zones, the American military closely observed the struggle. Its solution was to provide the Philippine army with increasing amounts of surplus equipment, but Filipino troops sold or lost much to the Huks, so the United States effectively outfitted both sides in the guerrilla war.

In 1949 the wartime president, Jose Laurel, ran against Quirino for president. It was a particularly corrupt and venal exercise in democracy. Most historians accept that Laurel was elected, but he refused to challenge Quirino's declared victory with force. The nation seemed trapped in interlocking economic, moral, political, and security crises. While the Huks remained circumscribed regionally, primarily in central Luzon, they appeared more likely to triumph than the government in Manila, which had to borrow from abroad just to meet its payroll.

The political rise of Ramon Magsaysay seemingly broke the sterile cycle of political corruption and economic drift. Magsaysay had been born relatively poor, or at least not of super-rich *ilustrado* stock. During the war he had become a prominent anticommunist guerrilla leader, emerging—at CIA insistence—as secretary of defense in the Quirino government. He accomplished three vital goals in defeating the Hukbalahap: he brought a new esprit de corps to a demoralized Philippine military; with the active help of the CIA, he penetrated and arrested the Philippine Communist Party's politburo, seizing lists of both sympathizers and financial supporters; and he mobilized the army to ensure that the 1951 congressional elections were free of the fraud that had so tainted the 1949 elections.

Magsaysay equally captured the imagination of the common Filipino and of Washington. In 1953 he was easily elected president, with the scarcely concealed help of American officials and funds. Rising prosperity (boosted by U.S. spending in the Korean War), Japanese reparations for wartime destruction, and a visible land reform policy that resettled landless peasants in central Luzon on the Mindanao "frontier" helped boost the economy and rekindle confidence in the political process. An uncomplicated anticommunist ideology satisfied many Filipinos while pleasing neocolonial America. The image, however manipulated, of a *tao* (peasant) elected to the presidential palace helped to transform despair into hope. Thus Magsaysay's premature, tragic death in a 1955 plane crash left a jagged scar on the psyche of the nation. Carlos Garcia, his vice president, was a pedestrian politician from the island of Bohol. Elected for a full term in 1957, he was succeeded in 1961 by Diosdado Macapagal, an attractive but ineffectual president, who was unable to stem endemic violence, jumpstart the economy, or create a transcendent political vision.

Ferdinand E. Marcos

THE LEADERSHIP vacuum was filled in 1965, when Ferdinand Marcos, an ambitious young senator from northern Luzon, defeated Macapagal's bid for reelection. Marcos and his beautiful, equally ambitious wife, Imelda, seemed to be Southeast Asian equivalents of John and Jackie Kennedy. At his inauguration Marcos claimed that "the Filipino, it seems, has lost his soul, his dignity, and his courage. Our people have come to a point of despair. We have ceased to value order." Noting that the "government is gripping the iron hand of venality, its treasury is barren, its resources are wasted, its civil service is slothful and indifferent, its armed forces demoralized, and its councils sterile," Marcos presented himself as his nation's savior.

But even in those heady first months of his new presidency, Marcos was brilliantly corrupt, far greedier than his predecessors. His avariciousness and deceit still stagger the imagination. There was a vast gulf between his rhetoric and his actions. He used the power of the presidency to reward friends, allowing them to wax very rich. Marcos manipulated a rising economy created by a Vietnam War boom. Lyndon Johnson and his successors, needing Southeast Asian allies, turned a blind eye to his personal greed, chronic dishonesty, and self-aggrandizing political agenda. Marcos was as skilled in manipulating America as in fleecing his own people.

Darlings on the world stage, Ferdinand and Imelda started a series of vast show projects in Manila and talked of land reform, "miracle rice," and rising prosperity. In 1969, running for reelection on the slogan of "rice and roads," Marcos was the first Filipino ever to win a second full term as president, with 74 percent of the vote. During that campaign, he spent liberally, contributing to a growing problem of inflation in the economy. Cemeteries have voted in the Philippines since elections were first held, but there was a new level of professionalism in the electoral corruption of 1969 that boded ill. Of the 8 senatorial seats contested, Marcos' Nacionalista slate won 7. All but 24 of the 120 House seats also went to candidates favorable to the president.

Marcos' new, overwhelming political power encouraged his corruption and, simultaneously, the likelihood that disenfranchised ethnic and geographic minorities and the economically disadvantaged, including a rising number of university students, would turn toward violence. Soon after the election, a group of students marched on the presidential palace, clashing with police at Mendiola Bridge across the Pasig River. Four student "martyrs" died. Those deaths and police brutality not only alienated student activists—this was a global age for such activism—but also encouraged peasants, migrant rural workers, and the Muslims in Mindanao to rebel.

Marcos dominated his society, controlled its politics, and manipulated both the domestic and the world media. But by 1971 he had also become a lame duck president, constitutionally obliged to surrender power after two full terms. A convention called to revise the commonwealth constitution of 1935, was, therefore, both challenge and opportunity, as Marcos plotted to extend his rule. He spoke of the need for "a new society," arguing that "constitutional authoritarianism" was necessary to give discipline to the nation, manage its growth, and help the Philippines find its way toward a secular utopia of economic progress and social well-being.

Political violence, much of it organized by Marcos himself, escalated rapidly. At an electoral rally in Manila in 1971, a bomb exploded on stage, wounding eight of the opposition Liberal Party senatorial candidates. Lawlessness, long a handmaiden of Philippine politics, encouraged politicians to organize militias, even as the president was using the military and the national police for his own political objectives. The Muslims had begun a war of national liberation. Communists and radical students had created a New People's Army, as the United States failures in Vietnam seemed to change profoundly the geopolitics of the region.

Benigno (Ninoy) Aquino was Marcos' putative successor; the son of a ranking prewar and wartime politician, he was expected to be the next elected president of the republic. In the 1971 elections, six of the eight Senate seats contested had swung to the Liberal Party and Aquino. But on 22 September 1972 Aquino and many others were arrested, as Marcos ended an era, declaring martial law in order to protect the Republic of the Philippines and its "democracy."

Further Readings

Cullather, Nick. *Illusions of Influence: The Political Economy of United States–Philippines Relations, 1942–1960.* Stanford, 1994.

Friend, Theodore. *Between Two Empires: The Ordeal of the Philippines, 1929–1946.* New Haven, 1965.

Gowing, Peter G. *Muslim Filipinos: Heritage and Horizon.* Quezon City, 1979.

Karnow, Stanley. *In Our Image: America's Empire in the Philippines.* New York, 1989.

Kerkvliet, Benedict J. *The Huk Rebellion: A Study of Peasant Revolt in the Philippines.* Berkeley, 1977.

Majul, C. A. *Apolinario Mabini, Revolutionary.* Manila, 1964.

Paredes, Ruby R., ed. *Philippine Colonial Democracy.* New Haven, 1988.

Salamanca, Bonifacio S. *The Filipino Reaction to American Rule, 1901–1913.* Hamsden, Ct., 1968; reprint Quezon City, 1984.

Stanley, Peter W. *A Nation in the Making: The Philippines and the United States, 1899–1921.* Cambridge, Mass., 1974.

———, ed. *Reappraising an Empire: New Perspectives on Philippine-American History.* Cambridge, Mass., 1984.

Chapter 20

❋

Becoming Indonesia,
1900–1959

THE YEARS 1900 to 1959 represent the first period when it is meaningful to talk of "Indonesia." The name was coined as a geographic term in 1850, but in the 1920s it took on a political meaning. Those renaming the Netherlands Indies "Indonesia" and its subjects "Indonesians" were graduates of schools the Dutch had established to supply the colony with a work force of professionals and technicians trained in the Dutch and Malay languages, who might be posted anywhere in the archipelago. The period opens with the entry of Javanese boys (and a few girls) into the colony's Dutch-language schools and closes with the expulsion of Dutch citizens from the Republic of Indonesia.

The Idea of Indonesia

ORGANIZATIONS formed in the years from 1900 to 1959 seem to signal an evolution in peoples' perspectives from local, regional, and religious to national. In 1908 Budi Utomo (Glorious Endeavor) was founded by Javanese privileged by wealth and connections to the colony's Dutch and indigenous elites. Social and intellectual contacts with Dutch theosophists rekindled their pride in Java's Hindu-Buddhist cultural heritage and inclined some to perceive Islam as a foreign intrusion that had weakened the ability of Java's kings to resist the West. The Studerenden Vereeniging Minahassa (Minahasa Study Union) and Jong Ambon (Ambonese Youth), both formed in 1918, stressed Christian identity and fluency

KITLV, Leiden, #8094

Stirrings of nationalism: Sarekat Islam leaders, Kediri, Java, 1914.

in Dutch, and this separated them from their Muslim compatriots. Those joining the Jong Sumatranen Bond (League of Sumatran Youth) chose region, rather
than ethnic identity, as the basis for their organization. This conception was quite
new in 1917, for no kin group or sultanate had ever ruled all of Sumatra.

Sarekat Islam (Islamic Union), founded in 1911, took Malay (rather than
Javanese or Dutch) to form its name, and identified Islam as the common bond
distinguishing "Natives" from colonial rulers and from groups perceived as
allies of the Dutch: the colony's Chinese and Christian communities. Sarekat

Islam's immediate goals were social and economic. Urban and rural poor were promised stone houses; local branches opposed taxes and organized boycotts of Chinese businesses.

The first associations taking the entire colony as their organizational frame were the National Indies Party, founded in 1912 by Javanese, Eurasian, and Dutch men demanding leadership of the colony by "those who make their home here," and the Indies Social Democratic Union, founded by Dutch socialists in 1914. The first to use the marker "Indonesia" were communists. Just four years after the Bolshevik revolution, the Partai Komunis Indonesia was formed to install a universalist ideology within colonial space. In 1927 one segment of the Chinese community came out for Indonesia in the Perserikatan Tionghoa Indonesia (Union of Chinese of Indonesia), and in 1929 Sukarno founded the Partai Nasional Indonesia, which is usually translated as the Nationalist (rather than National) Party of Indonesia. These parties chose the Malay language over Dutch, and, following the Youth Oath of 1928—in which a conference of men's and women's groups in Batavia adopted three goals: one nation, one homeland, and one language—they called this language "Indonesian" (Bahasa Indonesia).

In the 1930s like-minded parties allied in federations such as Gapi (Federation of Indonesian Political Parties). The nationalist movement included several women's organizations, though only women's historians tend to mention them in the narrative of nationalism. Women's parties such as Independent Daughters, Alert Wives, Mothers' Union, and Aisyah (named for an exemplary wife of Muhammad) characterized themselves by their members' relationships to men. They focused on civil rights rather than colonial rule, advocating formal schooling for girls and improved health standards and home life. But by 1928 a federation of women's organizations calling itself the Congress of Indonesian Women had placed anticolonialism first on its agenda, its members signaling with its title their conviction that citizenship should belong to women as well as to men.

This narrative of organizations suggests a unilinear march from the particular to the nation, culminating in the birth of Indonesia as successor to the Indies, with a parliamentary government that allowed both women and men to vote and run for public office. But alongside these organizations were others that continued to campaign for ethnic, religious, and regional goals. Sukarno's Nationalist Party and its successors were dwarfed by parties such as the Association of the Subjects of Yogyakarta, which championed Javanese monarchical interests, and religious organizations such as Muhammadiyah (Way of Muhammad), which demanded a state governed by Islamic rather than Western laws. Organizations taking local, national, and global perspectives existed alongside each other.

The idea of Indonesia was rooted in a concept of blood ties more than a common homeland, for the "indigenous" *(pribumi)* were defined as not Dutch, not Eurasian, nor of Chinese or Arab ancestry. The leader of independent Indonesia was implicitly expected to be male, but there was no general agreement, before 1945, as to who that leader should be. Possible candidates were the Holland-educated Sumatran politician Mohammad Hatta, Sultan Pakubuwono of the "independent principality" of Surakarta on Java, and religious leaders whose claim to rule was based on their mastery of Islamic knowledge. All were agreed that Indonesia should be modern, meaning that it would keep Dutch imports such as electricity and railways while rejecting Dutch rule, but there was no widespread agreement on the shape of the new Indonesia or what the rights and obligations of its citizens should be.

The Last Years of Colonial Rule

THE CREATION of the colonial state and the promotion of Malay as the colony's vernacular represent the Dutch contribution to the idea of Indonesia. The administrative grid that overlay the archipelago concentrated government and decision-making in Batavia (today's Jakarta), while generating common schooling and career paths as well as a geographic mobility that made individuals acquainted with a whole larger than their birthplace. From the beginning, the Dutch had used Malay as the language in which they conducted discussions with kings, taught school, preached in church, and issued commands. In 1908 the colonial government founded Balai Pustaka (Hall of Learning) to broaden literacy in Malay, commissioning and publishing grammars, school texts, and fiction.

Dutch promotion of a single language for the archipelago was paralleled by a contrary colonial policy, however: the preservation of regional languages. Dutch printers invented metallic type for Javanese and Sundanese scripts, and the government published school primers in local languages. Dutch linguists and missionaries turned spoken languages such as Roti and Gorontalo into written forms. Balai Pustaka did not publish books in the Arabic script, even though more Indonesian men could read Arabic letters than Roman. Regional and ethnic identities were stimulated and fueled political movements for narrowly ethnic concerns alongside organizations promoting a single nation-state.

The colonial government also contributed to the idea of Indonesia through tourism. In 1912 it established a tourist bureau to attract Europe's traveling class. Guidebooks, pamphlets, and postcards advertised a modern colony of hotels, mechanized transport, and factories, and presented Indonesians as "types" in regional costumes. "Our Indies" showed the archipelago's inhabitants to themselves as colonial subjects and objects, subjugated descendants of a glorious Indic past, Muslims represented to the world by Hindu Bali and Buddhist Borobudur.

Many who called themselves Indonesians were graduates of Muslim schools. Like graduates of Dutch schools, they saw the archipelago's rajas and

Promoting tourism: "Fly to Java," 1938. Poster for KNILM
(Royal Netherlands Indies Airways) by Jan Lavies.

sultans as feudal despots, propped up by colonial rule, their rivals for leadership of the common people. The Dutch saw themselves as progressive, "uplifting" the "Natives" by eradicating practices such as headhunting and widow burning; they equated monogamy with modernity. Indonesian graduates had to make choices such as whether to join the colonial work force and take a seat in the (all-male) People's Council, founded by the colonial government in 1916 as an advisory body, or to join the ranks of the "noncooperators." Families straddled the divide. Hatta, for example, refused to work for the Dutch, while his sister accepted a position in the colonial post office.

The new elites were comfortable giving orders to the folk. They simplified their critique of colonialism for villagers and chose as branch leaders *ulama* (scholars), village headmen, landowners, and small-time aristocrats who had local followings. Such men took messages of "Islamic communism" to village fishpond owners and landholders who resented paying taxes to the Dutch. They promised the return of Java's "just king" to men who had burned down a plantation's sugar cane or menaced a colonial administrator with sharpened bamboo stakes.

Some idealists turned to schooling as the way to invent Indonesians. In 1921 Ki Hadjar Dewantoro created Taman Siswa (Garden of Learning), a school system that offered subjects from the Dutch curriculum in the Javanese language, taught Java's history instead of Holland's, and insisted on pupils and staff wearing Javanese costume rather than the Western clothing that elite Javanese were adopting. Private schools that the Dutch termed "wild" (unregulated) multiplied throughout the archipelago, adapting the Taman Siswa model to regional cultures or substituting Islamic for European history and introducing Arabic alongside Dutch in the curriculum.

The last years of colonial rule brought more Dutch people into Indonesian space, including more women immigrants. By 1940 Europeans totaled 0.4 percent of the Indies population. They concentrated in cities, patronized opera, cinema, and "Europeans only" clubs; they fortified themselves against "sinking into Native ways" by furloughs in Europe and sending children to Holland for school. The colony afforded immigrants the good life of well-paid jobs, fine suburbs, and trips to mountain resorts by car. The colony to them was more a tropical Netherlands than a place where they went "Native" like former generations of Dutch men who had married local women and adjusted their lifestyle to Indonesian ways. There was a colonial patina of apartheid: practiced habits of contempt for "Natives" and separate laws for separate "races." Underneath was the reality of mixed marriage and children of mixed descent. Elite institutions such as the People's Council, European schools, freemasons' lodges, theosophy clubs, and the Movement for Women's Suffrage had multiracial clienteles.

The last years of colonial rule also saw Indonesians increase in number from perhaps 40 million in 1900 to around 70 million by 1940. Rice fields, vegetable gardens, and plantation crops covered Java's plains and crept up mountain slopes. The Dutch, worried that Java was overcrowded, moved farming families into the "empty spaces" of the archipelago, that is, into forested habitats that different ethnic groups farmed intermittently. Javanese farmers became the tool of colonial government; they advanced the frontier of permanent agriculture and spread settled rural life, which could be supervised by government. Perceived by the Dutch as the "mildest folk on earth," Javanese were seen as suitable candidates for planting among other "Natives" deemed "wild" or "fanatic." The origins of today's Javanese rural communities in Aceh lie in policies originally designed to consolidate colonial power.

New jobs, miserable living conditions, and union movements brought workers onto the streets in rallies and strikes in the 1920s. For most Indonesian men and women, the world depression of the 1930s brought great hardship through loss of jobs or reduction in wages. The same decade brought benefits to local elites: more Dutch-language schools for "Natives," Chinese, and Arabs, and "emancipation" for archipelago princes who administered territories for Dutch bosses. Western-educated men came to see their compatriots through Dutch eyes as dirty, backward, and in thrall to superstition and hereditary rulers. The Dutch-educated schoolboy A. A. M. Djelantik tells a story of seeing his father, Prince I Gusti Bagus Djelantik, lift his sarong to urinate on the wheel of his limousine before the averted gaze of a Dutch colonial official and his wife.

The 1920s and 1930s were years of new visions, new desires, and conflicting values. Automobiles owned by the Dutch sped by buffalo carts driven by a subject people. Chinese and Indonesians wrote novels deploring the loss of traditional values by the Western-educated. They singled out for disapproval young women who went to Western dances at high school and at hotels. Muslim women argued among themselves whether to accept the colonial government's offer of registered monogamous marriage or to fight polygamy through reinterpreting Islamic ideals of equality. Throughout the first two hundred years of interaction, Dutch people had been shocked by Javanese costume that bared women's shoulders and men's upper torsos. By the time most Javanese were covering the whole body, in response to colonial and Islamic pressures, Dutch women were baring their shoulders and joining men in public swimming pools, presenting models of behavior offensive to the ideals of sex segregation and modesty promoted by Muhammadiyah and Aisyah. At the same time, young men who had attended the colony's schools wanted the freedom to date young women and choose their own marriage partners. They expressed frustrations with their elders in novels of disappointed love and thwarted ambition. While some saw their relatives as backward, others, such as the Minangkabau Abu Hanifah, a medical doctor and later a nationalist leader and parliamentarian, experienced the awkwardness of not fitting in and a sense of betrayal of his own people. He recalls a moment when as a young doctor he looked down from the deck of a Dutch ship as European officers threw coins overboard and sneered at the "Natives" swimming after them. Where and with whom did he belong?

In the last years of colonial rule, there was a push for an Indies parliament that would have legislative powers. Half the members of the People's Council were appointees of the governor-general, chosen from prominent men to represent Dutch, "Natives," Chinese, and Arabs. The other half were chosen by indirect election. Men who were taxpayers, adult, and literate in Dutch voted for a slate of electors who then chose delegates to the council. Councillors of all ethnic groups voted against the colonial government's proposal in 1933 to extend the vote to adult women literate in Dutch. At the time many nationalist organizations advocated the segregation of women and men in public life, and did not permit women to attend their conventions. There was outrage among all groups when the governor-general appointed a Eurasian woman to the council in 1935 to represent social welfare organizations. Mrs. Razoux-Schultz was perceived as one of the enemy, despite her Javanese ancestry. Council members were united, too, in demanding an Indies defense force, as they perceived the power of Japan expanding and a new era of foreign rule possible.

Nationalism and Rule by Japan

INDONESIAN followers of world news read racial messages into Japan's defeat of Czarist Russia's army and navy in 1905. The idea that Asians could defeat Western armed forces encouraged admiration of Japan. In the 1930s Japan was mobilizing its population for war, suppressing dissent, and expanding its colonial rule in Asia, but it represented to visitors to Japan like Hatta an Asian path toward modernity and an Asian power expanding at the expense of Western economic interests. Nationalist politicians explained Japan's invasion in 1942 to rural clienteles as the working out of a prophecy attributed to east Java's King Jayabaya (r. 1130–1157) that rule by a white race would be followed by a short period of rule by yellow men before an age of prosperous independence. In Malaya, Singapore, Burma, and the Philippines, white power vanished. Indonesian politicians were apparently untroubled that Japanese military force preserved French power in Indochina until March 1945. People waved Japanese flags distributed by troops landing in Sumatra and Java in the early weeks of 1942 and, with the exception of Europeans, Eurasians, Chinese, Christians, and a few anti-Fascist Indonesian politicians, such as Syahrir (Soetan Sjahrir), welcomed the new era.

Indonesia was incorporated into Japan's empire during the period of its most rapid expansion. Japan had been preparing invasion for at least a decade, but its plans to administer its vast new territories were underdeveloped. The Greater East Asia Co-Prosperity Sphere was announced in 1940, but its membership was not publicly clarified until 1942. Economic policy was then broadly outlined: member states should sell their raw materials to Japan and purchase its manufactured goods. The economic program imitated those of prewar European colonial powers, and Japanese rule, like European rule, was based on notions of race hierarchy and uplift, with Japan, instead of the West, as best race and Asian states ranked in terms of their "cultural development." Japanese planners placed Indonesia in the bottom tier of Asian cultures; they excluded Indonesians from the Co-Prosperity Sphere's meeting in Tokyo in 1943 and denied them the right to administer their internal affairs when they granted these powers to Burma and the Philippines.

In December 1941 Japan had dramatically expanded its war front by attacking the United States. It offered the Dutch in the Indies the same deal it had offered Vietnam's French administration in 1940: to remain in place administering the colony but gear its economy to Japan and open its sea, air, and land routes to Japanese forces. The Dutch rejected this option, so the Japanese had to divert armed forces to administer the vast archipelago. Japan's solution was to distribute islands among army and navy commands and redraw the colonial borders. On mainland Southeast Asia Japan brought major changes, shrinking the former European colonies of Cambodia and Malaya, and expanding the friendly Kingdom of Thailand. Sumatra was joined to the truncated Malay Peninsula to form the new state of Syonan, with its capital in Singapore. Java was administered as a single state under the Sixteenth Army, headquartered in Batavia (named Djakarta in 1942), while the "Great East" (Borneo, Sulawesi, and the eastern archipelago) was placed under the navy, with its capital in Makasar. The Syonan plan was modified in 1943, but Sumatra remained separate from Java under command of the Twenty-Fifth Army. Two years of Japanese rule therefore saw the single colonial state that Dutch military power had created broken into three by Japanese military power.

For Indonesians this was a reversal of the unifying processes of the last decades of colonial rule that had planted the idea of Batavia as center of the entire archipelago. The grids of colonial administration, transport, commerce, education, and politics that had linked villages in one system and one thought-world were suddenly broken. Interisland travel and flow of trade goods halted, as each region was sealed off and oriented toward its Japanese headquarters: Singapore for Sumatra, Saigon for Java, Tokyo for the navy-administered zone. All independent communication with the world was cut. Radio contact with Europe was forbidden on pain of death. The Dutch language was banned, Dutch books were withdrawn from bookstores, Dutch newspapers shut down, and Dutch schools closed. The silence was filled by Japanese radio, cinema, books, and magazines. Indonesians became consumers of Japanese-controlled news, rhetoric of Asian victories, and vilification of Westerners and Western culture. Japanese language, culture, and accomplishments were promoted. Shielded from knowledge of Japanese defeats at sea and in the air, Indonesian leaders had a novel context in which to think and act.

In 1942 most leaders of archipelago-wide organizations were in Java. Return to their home bases or communication with deputies was impossible, because the Japanese controlled the post office, telegraph, shipping, railways, and tramlines. Political life in the form of parties, rallies, leafleting, and strikes ended throughout most of the former Indies. Only on Java did it revive, and then in the quite different form of mass organizations created by Japanese military officers, who appointed the leaders and set the agendas. Sukarno, Hatta, and Muhammadiyah leaders were marshaled to lead Putera (Center of the People's Power) and Hokokai, the Java branch of the Japanese organization civilians over fourteen were required to join in support of the emperor and his war. Women's parties were replaced by Fujinkai, a branch of the organization that mobilized women to send their men to war and make sacrifices for Japan. Most history texts support Sukarno's claim that he slipped nationalist messages into speeches and pressured Japanese officers to grant independence, but it is unclear how widely he traveled in Java or how often he was allowed to use the microphone or radio. Sukarno's major trips were to centers of Japanese power: Tokyo and Saigon.

Men determined to create strong ethnic cores within an independent Indonesia were cut off from Java and the nationalists throughout Japan's rule. Significant for the country's future was the concentration on Java of men committed to the idea of Indonesia. They seized power in 1945, following Japan's defeat by the Allies, so that Indonesia emerged as successor to the single colonial state, rather than three countries succeeding three separate Japanese administrations.

War on many fronts meant that Japan could not spare personnel to administer Indonesian territories directly. Officials collecting taxes, supervising the flow of agricultural produce to collection points, and recruiting labor for the Japanese were Indonesians. Japanese replaced Dutchmen as bureau heads; Indonesians filled lower-level jobs formerly reserved for Eurasians. Dutch male civilians were kept at their posts until Japanese control of the islands was complete; then they were imprisoned and sent to work on roads, wharves, and mines in Sumatra, mainland Southeast Asia, and Japan. Within four months of occupation, Dutch women and children were concentrated in prison camps in Indonesia's major cities. Military decisions to extract labor from prisoners and allocate them few rations and medical supplies caused high death rates and forced the former elite to the bottom of the social pyramid. Those who had been used to command were now the commanded.

Japanese specialists on the Indies advised their military superiors that goods and labor could be obtained from Java's rural communities if the orders were issued by village heads and district officials responding to demands from the

Labor Bureau, headed by Hatta in Jakarta. They further advised that rural populations would remain quiet if their religious leaders believed Japan supported Islamic causes. Japanese officers who were Muslim accompanied the invasion forces. They brought prominent Islamic leaders under surveillance by organizing them into Masyumi (Consultative Council of Indonesian Muslims) in 1943 and conducted training courses in Jakarta for *ulama*. Many *ulama* found the anti-Christian, anti-Western rhetoric attractive, but Japan's Muslim policy was less successful in its attempts to Asianize Islam. Many Indonesians resisted bowing in mosques in the direction of Tokyo instead of Mecca and were opposed to the teaching of Japanese instead of Arabic in religious schools.

Within six weeks of the Japanese takeover, nationalist symbols such as the red and white flag (proclaimed by the Youth Oath of 1928) were banned. But Allied defeats of Japanese forces in the Pacific in 1943 prompted Japanese officers on Java to recruit indigenous men into militias to take the first assaults expected from the Allies. Men chosen for militia leadership were not selected from the colony's professional fighters, the former Royal Dutch Indies Army, but from rural Islamic schools or the ranks of urban labor and crime bosses. Their job was to translate into local idiom the Japanese military creed of the warrior, while Japanese officers trained recruits in martial arts, assigned them to night watch and prison camp duties, and taught them that the military were the natural rulers of society.

Allied troops fought in Kalimantan (Borneo) and eastern Indonesia, but most Indonesians did not witness the defeat of the Japanese. Indonesian leaders did not derive racial lessons from Western defeat of Asians (as they had in the reverse case of Japanese defeating Russian forces). Instead, the weeks following Japan's surrender on 15 August 1945 saw a scramble for power across the archipelago.

The Struggle for Independence

ANTICIPATING defeat, Tokyo's military planners promised independence for Indonesia in March 1945 and established a committee to discuss formats for the independent government the Allies should encounter when the war was over. This sixty-four-member committee was similar to the colonial People's Council in that it was mainly male and represented the archipelago's major ethnic groups and the Chinese. It was different in that there were no representatives of the Dutch, and no members were elected. Delegates were selected from men (and two women) prominent on Java because of their connections to the Japanese.

Sukarno's group dominated the committee. They were able to impose their view that independent Indonesia should be a secular republic, rather than a monarchy or a theocracy. The committee hailed the five principles (Panca Sila) formulated by Sukarno and Muhammad Yamin in June 1945 as the basis for organizing the new country. These were national identity, a place in the international community, people's sovereignty, social justice, and belief in one God. The majority made concessions to the committee's minority who argued for a Muslim Indonesia by attaching the Jakarta Charter to the constitution. The charter stipulated that the head of state must be Muslim and that the state should compel Muslims to follow Islamic laws. The dominant group, operating in a thought-world created by the Japanese, did not propose democratic institutions and rejected a bill of rights advocated by Maria Ulfah Santoso, a Holland-trained lawyer. They persevered in the view that an independent country should regroup the territories of the former Dutch colony. None championed ethnic and regional interests.

Wherever Japan's defeat became known, fighting broke out. There was retribution to be exacted on village heads who had sent young men and women off to factories and military brothels, and on landlords and mill owners who had been profiteering, filling Japanese rice quotas while people went hungry. There were girls to humiliate because they had borne babies to Japanese officers. Some groups were targeted for vengeance because they had profited from relationships with the Dutch and the Japanese. In Aceh, for example, killing bands led by *ulama* murdered the *uleebalang* (administrative class), while along the east coast of Sumatra, sultans and their families were murdered by mobs. In many places people attacked businesses owned by Chinese; in Ambon Christians took revenge on Muslim Ambonese who had prospered under the Japanese. Gangs staged raids on Japanese posts to capture weapons and turf.

Sukarno and Hatta were pressured by youth groups in Jakarta to declare independence in the name of the Indonesian people instead of accepting independence as the gift of the Japanese. Indonesia's independence was proclaimed on 17 August, and on 18 August the constitution (minus the Jakarta Charter) was launched by the acclamation of people identifying themselves as representative of Indonesia's many ethnic and religious communities. They chose Sukarno as president and Hatta as vice president. Indonesians staffing the Japanese administration were declared to be simultaneously employees of the new republican government. Public space became the arena for slogans and symbols of the new country.

At first politicians established a security force rather than a national army and favored the Japanese model of channeling political life through a single mass organization. But the Japanese were no longer the power that had to be flattered. The victors were American and British, and it was their attitudes that mattered. Accordingly Syahrir, who had refused to work for the Japanese, was made prime minister. He was empowered to open negotiations and to convince the victors of Indonesia's credentials for democratic self-government by replacing the single mass party with many parties and modifying the constitution to reduce the powers of the president. Prime minister and cabinet were made answerable to an interim parliament until delegates could be elected through universal suffrage. Throughout Indonesia's struggle for independence this body, known as the National Committee of Indonesia, appointed members to cabinets that included three of the world's first women ministers.

Most prewar parties had not endorsed a Western multiparty democracy or separation of religion from politics. Most Indonesians neither understood nor admired the political system of their former colonial ruler. The National Committee largely represented the 6 percent of the population literate in the Roman alphabet. Many of the men joining militias opposed negotiating with the Dutch; *ulama* saw in the vacuum of power the chance to establish a community ruled by Islamic law, guided by themselves, freed from the oversight of sultans, governors-general, Japanese commanders, and secular politicians.

Civilian politicians lost popular respect during the revolution because their policy of winning independence through negotiation resulted in the return of Dutch administrators and troops, reconstitution of the colonial army, rapid Dutch reoccupation of eastern Indonesia, and the seizure of Sumatra's oil, rubber, and tin zones. Dutch forces pushed territory under republican administration back to central Java. The consequence of all the negotiation and bloodshed was that Sukarno's government, which had laid claim to all of Indonesia, was eliminated in December 1948, when the Dutch captured the republican capital, Yogyakarta, and transported the entire government, including Sukarno and Hatta, to Sumatran prisons.

From the beginning many Indonesian men had rejected rule by civilians. Those joining army units refused to recognize the politicians' choice for commander in favor of Sudirman, a product of the Islamic school system. Everywhere local heroes formed militias and pursued their own goals, with little recognition of any central authority. In occupied territories, the Dutch developed provincial administrations and appointed those nationalists who had favored a federal Indonesia to run them. East Indonesia was the most developed, with an elected regional parliament. On Java, where Dutch power was weakest, the different visions for an independent Indonesia took dramatic form. In 1948 in west Java the House of Islam (Darul Islam) declared itself in opposition both to the Dutch and to Sukarno's republic, while in east Java soldiers loyal to the republic fought men who had joined communist militias.

The United States pressured Holland to cede independence after Sukarno's troops had killed communist Indonesians at Madiun in 1948. In July 1949 the Dutch released the captured republican leadership; in December they transferred sovereignty to the Republic of the United States of Indonesia (RUSI). This federal republic was made up of the fifteen states created by the Dutch and Sukarno's republic but without West New Guinea (Irian), which "temporarily" remained under Dutch administration. Regional elites feared a single state would mean domination by Java and Javanese. Christian Indonesians feared rule by Muslims. Men who wanted an Islamic state opposed Sukarno's allies because they included Christians and advocated belief in one God (rather than Islamic principles) and the adjustment of Qur'anic prescriptions to twentieth-century Indonesia rather than a strict application of Islamic laws under the guidance of *ulama*. The Darul Islam movement continued to fight against the new state until the army caught and executed its leader in 1962. But at the time, despite local tensions, there was also great pride that Indonesia's independence had been recognized by the United Nations.

Sukarno devoted his presidency to nurturing the idea of Indonesia and of being Indonesian. He packaged the past as unceasing resistance to foreign rule and consciousness of national unity. He was also tenacious in achieving his goal of a single Indonesia. The state governments set up by the Dutch dissolved themselves in the first months of independence, folding RUSI into the Republic of Indonesia again. When people in eastern Indonesia declared a Republic of South Maluku in April 1950, Sukarno sent in the army and navy. He also used the armed forces to quell rebellions in the name of Islam and provincial rights in Sumatra and Sulawesi in the 1950s.

Sukarno found the Western model of parliamentary government an obstacle to building a strong Indonesia. In the first years of independence, cabinets fell every four to six months, preventing continuity of policy. The multiplication of political parties with irreconcilable agendas hampered economic recovery from the years of warfare. National elections were held in 1955. Ninety-one percent of eligible voters—men and women over eighteen years—had their say and produced an elected parliament of eighty-three parties. Only four parties attracted 16 percent or more of the vote. They were the Nationalist Party of Indonesia (22.3 percent), Masyumi (20.9 percent), Nahdlatul Ulama (18.4 percent), and the Communist Party of Indonesia (16.4 percent). Only Masyumi won votes across the archipelago; the other three drew almost all their votes from Javanese electors. Indonesia's people were deeply divided along religious, class, and ethnic lines.

Almost immediately Sukarno launched a "bury the parties" campaign to alter the political system of Indonesia. He argued that Western politics did not fit Indonesian mentalities. He said that the true Indonesian was Marhaen ("the little guy"), the inhabitant of villages where equality was the norm and decisions were arrived at through mutual consensus, rather than voting, which Sukarno considered divisive. Sukarno appealed to Muslims by using Arabic terms to describe Indonesian traditions of discussion and consensus. He appealed to the growing numbers of impoverished by denouncing continuing Dutch control of businesses, plantations, and transport systems, and the continuing presence of Dutch citizens. He also argued that Dutch control of West New Guinea was corrupting national life.

Between 1956 and 1959 Sukarno, with the backing of the national army and many Javanese, eliminated many of the problems he had identified. He banned political parties from operating in villages and closed down the elected parliament. He expropriated Dutch-owned businesses, expelled Dutch citizens, and began to build sentiment for wresting West New Guinea from the Dutch. He appointed a parliament of members chosen to represent Indonesians as constituents of groups, rather than as individuals, and brought in martial law, which meant an end to civil courts and a curtailing of liberties. Sukarno turned over the nationalized businesses to management by army officers and ruled through presidential decree. He established himself in Cold War politics as a leader of those "nonaligned" Asian and African nations that refused to be clients of the United States or the Soviet Union, culminating in his hosting of the historic Asian-African Conference at Bandung in 1955. By 1959, with Dutch businesses expropriated, Dutch people expelled, and the Dutch parliamentary system dismantled, Sukarno could believe Indonesia was truly independent.

People became Indonesian in a context of excitement, chaos, and danger. There was tremendous optimism in 1950 that a new country would deliver a society just and prosperous for all. But millions more Indonesians were born in the first decade of independence, so the new citizens struggled to find jobs. Sukarno urged people to break loose from old bonds of feudalism and imperialism, drop aristocratic titles, and produce a modern national culture. Street names that honored Dutch heroes were replaced with Indonesian ones, and every town erected its monument to revolutionary struggle. Sukarno took the image of a free Indonesia abroad on official visits. At the side of Marshal Tito in Yugoslavia in 1956, he likened their two countries because of their diverse communities, and he urged Indonesians to set aside what divided them and focus on unities or face the danger of breakup. He produced evidence of Western assistance to rebels in Sumatra. He limited newspapers to four pages and banned those that pursued their own line of interpretation. He restricted the areas where Chinese could do business and urged them to cut their cultural ties with China by taking Indonesian names and adopting the Roman alphabet. By 1960 he had closed down two parties associated with the revolution, Masyumi and the Socialist Party of Indonesia, and confined their leaders to house arrest.

Reflecting on the first years of Indonesia, political scientist Herbert Feith (*The Decline of Constitutional Democracy in Indonesia,* 1962) divided Jakarta's leaders between administrators and solidarity makers. In his analysis administrators had failed to control prices or provide food, jobs, and a satisfying vision for ordinary people. Solidarity makers, epitomized by Sukarno, caused constitutional democracy to fail by suppressing difference, overriding legal process, and focusing on grand rhetoric while neglecting the economy. Historian Harry Benda countered that under Sukarno Indonesian life had simply flowed back into its usual channels. There had been no protection of individual rights under past sultans or colonial rulers, so that the nine years of parliamentary government represented a temporary aberration in the histories of Indonesian societies rather than a unique failure.

Western historians in the 1950s and 1960s were committed to the reality of the nation-states that emerged from Japanese rule and colonial wars. Through academic programs in Western universities, they endorsed the idea of Southeast Asia as consisting of distinct and authentic nations. Soon after, young historians in Southeast Asia began writing histories that would explain the birth of their own countries. Indonesian historians took the boundaries of the colonial state as the space in which to tell their story. They placed the Dutch at the center, reversing the moral judgments but not the angle of vision that had produced histories of the Indies. Individual histories of Islamic states and ethnic communities were situated within a single narrative leading to the modern republic proclaimed in 1945.

Further Readings

Abu Talib Ahmad and Tan Liok Ee, eds. *New Terrains in Southeast Asian History.* Athens, Ohio, 2003.

Ahmat b. Adam. *The Vernacular Press and the Emergence of Modern Indonesian Consciousness (1855–1913).* Ithaca, 1995.

Cribb, Robert, ed. *The Late Colonial State in Indonesia: Political and Economic Foundations of the Netherlands Indies, 1880–1942.* Leiden, 1994.

Djelantik, A. A. M. *The Birthmark: Memoirs of a Balinese Prince.* Hong Kong, 1997.

Foulcher, Keith. "*Sumpah Pemuda:* The Making and Meaning of a Symbol of Indonesian Nationhood." *Asian Studies Review* 24, 3 (September 2000): 377–410.

Hillen, Ernest. *The Way of a Boy: A Memoir of Java.* Toronto, 1993.

Kano, Hiroyoshi, Frans Husken, and Djoko Suryo, eds. *Beneath the Smoke of the Sugar-Mill: Javanese Coastal Communities during the Twentieth Century.* Yogyakarta, 2001.

Locher-Scholten, Elspeth. *Women and the Colonial State: Essays on Gender and Modernity in the Netherlands Indies, 1900–1942.* Amsterdam, 2000.

Said, Salim. *Genesis of Power: General Sudirman and the Indonesian Military in Politics, 1945–1949.* Singapore, 1991.

Schulte Nordholt, Henk, ed. *Outward Appearances: Dressing State and Society in Indonesia.* Leiden, 1997.

Shiraishi, Takashi. *An Age in Motion: Popular Radicalism in Java, 1912–1926.* Ithaca, 1990.

Vreede–De Stuers, Cora. *The Indonesian Woman: Struggles and Achievements.* The Hague, 1960.

Chapter 21

British Malaya

THE ECONOMIC and social changes in the peninsula, particularly the west coast states, between 1874 and the 1930s were truly enormous, centered on large-scale development of European and Chinese entrepreneurial and extractive activity made possible by a startling growth in alien immigration. Between 1891 and 1931 the FMS (Federated Malay States) population grew from 218,000 to 1.7 million. Of these only 35 percent were peninsular Malays or of Malay stock, for Chinese had risen to account for 42 percent of those enumerated, and South Asians (Indian and Sri Lankan) had risen to 22 percent. Though the census taker in 1931 argued that most Chinese remained transient, there were already substantial numbers who regarded the peninsula as their permanent home as well as many thousands who had been born there. Even in the UMS (Unfederated Malay States), Johore, the state most developed for export agriculture, was by 1931 very similar in ethnic composition to the FMS, and Kedah, too, had a large immigrant component. Only in the undeveloped east coast states of Kelantan and Terengganu did large Malay populations live in relative isolation. Down the whole of the west coast, with Penang and Singapore as the northern and southern nodal points, and Kuala Lumpur as the federal capital in the middle (all three demographically Chinese cities), stretched a complex system of roads, railways, telephones, and telegraphs, which provided the bones and sinews for an export economy whose earnings rose from 10 million Straits dollars in the late 1880s to more than 300 million dollars just before the depression of 1930.

Despite their revolutionary and lasting character, many of these changes, as we have seen, did not immediately or directly affect the Malays. Manifestly, much happened to shift the peasant view of the world, but the changes that occurred did not coincide with or take their direction solely from the effects of British rule, and they coexisted with a remarkable persistence of traditional patterns of social organization. The relative sparseness of the Malay population and its involvement in a traditional social order based on the *kampung* meant that few Malays were available or willing to sign up for the wage labor needed for the development of export industry. British policy was implicitly based on a mutually profitable alliance in which, in return for the right to develop a modern extractive economy within the *negeri* with an immigrant labor force, the British undertook to maintain the social position of the Malay ruling class and to refrain from catapulting the peasant population into the modern world. Relative abundance of unoccupied land made it possible to allot large tracts to European and Chinese plantation enterprises without trespassing seriously on Malay holdings. Land policies were changed to give Malays individual title to their land, keep peasants in possession of their patrimony, and encourage their continuing cultivation of traditional crops, particularly wet rice. Such measures were reinforced by a system of elementary vernacular education (in Malay, and effectively for Malays only) that, though reasonably widespread, at least in the FMS, had as its principal objective the creation of "a vigorous and self-respecting

Colonial splendor: the Raffles Hotel, Singapore.

Courtesy of Raffles Hotel

313

agricultural peasantry" conscious of the dignity that attaches to hewing wood and drawing water. Only a tiny minority of Malay boys had access to English education, provided either by the few government schools or by Christian mission schools serving primarily the urban Chinese and Indian population.

Because the introduction of individual land title tended to encourage both the sale and the mortgaging of peasant lands, the government tried to curtail transactions in certain types of land by the creation of "Malay reservations" within which land could be disposed of only to other Malays. One effect of this policy was to hold down the price of such land and to encourage Malay rather than non-Malay landlordism, developments of doubtful value to the peasant. The only substantial participation by Malays in the export economy—the adoption by large numbers of peasants in the FMS of rubber smallholding as a means of earning cash income—led to more intensive monetization of the peasant sector of the economy. But after some years, the government, in the interests of food production and later of plantation-biased rubber restriction schemes, introduced legislation that drastically limited new Malay rubber planting. In addition, the ubiquitous presence of profit-taking non-Malay middlemen in control of preparation and marketing seriously reduced the stimulant effect that rubber growing might otherwise have had on Malay economic life. Nevertheless, rubber incomes (until the slump in the late 1920s) did enable some Malays from the first generation of smallholders to purchase for their sons a better education than was possible in the village and thus a chance to enter the upwardly mobile ranks of the government civil service.

One of the principal results of the wholesale retention of the Malay peasant within the matrix of traditional agricultural society was the small part played by Malays in the urban life of the developed western states and the Straits Settlements, and their consequent isolation from social change arising within the urban environment. In numerical terms Malays constituted in 1921 only some 10 percent of the urban population of the peninsula, a figure corresponding to perhaps 4 or 5 percent of the total Malay population. Those proportions rose only very slowly over the next two decades, despite the eventual introduction of policies designed to lessen non-Malay predominance in the urban-centered subordinate ranks of government employment. Though the small Malay component of urban society was to be of great significance for eventual nationalist movements, the great majority of Malays continued to find the town alien and strange, if indeed they had any acquaintance with it at all.

The Emergence of Early Malay Nationalism

THE SLOW PACE and limited extent of social change among the peninsular Malays, in comparison with peoples more rudely embroiled in colonial economic development elsewhere in Southeast Asia, hindered the emergence of any strong focus critical of colonial rule. Nonetheless, the first four decades of the twentieth century witnessed the appearance of a nascent Malay nationalism, appealing at first to loyalties to religion, ethnic group, and language. Loyalties of this kind transcended traditional state boundaries and sought a specifically political community that would safeguard Malay interests against the culturally alien myriads who now claimed residence in the peninsula. In the course of this process of growing self-recognition, it is possible to discern the emergence of three new elite groups in Malay society, each associated with a particular educational environment and each in turn offering its own vision of what Malay society must become to survive and prosper in the modern world. The first of the groups was grounded in the religious renewal movement of the Islamic-educated; the second was the largely Malay-educated radical intelligentsia; and the third was the English-educated bureaucracy, its upper echelons drawn from within the traditional elite.

The religious renewal movement had its ideological origins in the Islamic renaissance that took place in the Middle East around the end of the nineteenth century. Malaya-born Muslims, sometimes of Arab or Sumatran descent, returning from sojourns in Cairo or the Hejaz, brought with them a burning desire to renovate Islam in their own society and to make it a fit instrument with which to respond to the challenges posed by economic marginalization and alien domination. In propagating doctrines of the essential unity of the Islamic community without regard to potentates and powers, of the need to cleanse local Islam of accretions of custom standing in the way of progress, and of the essential equality of all Muslims before God, they came into immediate conflict with the state rulers and their religious establishments, newly developed under British rule. Though the strength of the movement lay in the urban centers, particularly Singapore and Penang (where its individualistic ethic proved attractive to those engaged in modern economic competition), it found adherents also among religious teachers and others in *kampung* society. The contest between the renewalists and the traditional establishment was essentially unequal, but its many-sided and protracted argument acted as an important modernizing force within Malay society.

In the long run, the religious group failed to create or to lead a mass movement among the Malays, primarily because of opposition from the traditional establishment (both religious and secular), which still held the loyalty of the great majority of the people. Another reason for its lack of success was that to a considerable extent the issues on which it fought were being overtaken—or taken over—by a secular nationalism more concerned with pragmatics than piety. Already in the mid-1920s a number of young Malays who had had their introduction to anticolonial ideas in Egyptian Islamic modernist circles were voicing overtly political, pan-Indonesian nationalist sentiments with little religious content in two journals published in Cairo. On their return to Malaya, they joined forces with the more numerous, secular, Malay-educated intelligentsia, which formed the second of the three new elite groups in Malay society. In large part teachers and journalists, the radical Malay intelligentsia was strongly influenced by the left wing of the Indonesian nationalist movement and looked to the creation of a Greater Malaysia or Greater Indonesia that would embrace both the British and the Dutch colonial territories. With few exceptions, the radical intelligentsia was drawn from the peasant class. Though its ideology was in many ways confused, it criticized the traditional elite and the new English-educated middle class (whose privileges it often envied) as well as British colonialism, mainly in the flourishing urban-based vernacular press. It attracted to its cause some English-educated journalists and public servants, but its program was unformed, and it never really achieved organizational coherence.

The leadership of the third new elite group sprang for the most part from within the traditional ruling class, among the English-educated administrators and public servants. Essentially, this group was reacting against increasingly vociferous claims in the 1930s from the local-born elements within the Chinese and South Asian communities (31 and 21 percent, respectively, in 1931), who were often English-educated, for a larger share in government and administration, and in the public life of a unitarily conceived British Malaya. The economic depression of the early 1930s, coming on the heels of revised policies aimed at increasing the Malay share of government employment, placed great strain on the neat plural society formulas by which Malaya had lived up to then. Many Chinese and Indian mine and estate workers, thrown out of employment, sought to settle on the land as agriculturalists, previously an entirely Malay preserve. Aspiring Malays in the towns, in receipt of slightly increased measures of English education, vied with local-born South Asians and Chinese for government clerical and technical posts at a time of general retrenchment of staff. The leaders of both the Straits Chinese and the local-born South Asian communities argued strongly that, in the new Malaya, non-Malay residents must be afforded equal rights with Malays, at least in proportion to their contribution to the economy. A frequent Malay response went something like this: "If you get someone in to build your house, you don't ask him to live with you afterward." Simultaneously, other Chinese, looking more obviously to metropolitan China for political satisfaction, were engaged in Guomindang politics in the peninsula (despite the proscription of the GMD there in 1930), or in the founding of the Malayan Communist Party (MCP, 1930), an almost wholly Chinese organization with links nevertheless to the Netherlands Indies and Vietnam.

From the late 1920s onward, the traditional Malay ruling class—both those who, like the sultans and their immediate establishments, were still part of the old structure and those who had become absorbed in the new colonial bureaucracy—expressed concern at the disadvantaged position of the Malay in the modern world. Periodic gatherings of rulers (durbars) were begun in 1927 as part of a token devolution of federal authority to the states. These became the occasion, especially toward the end of the 1930s, for proposals by the rulers to limit Chinese immigration and to encourage Javanese instead, to strengthen Malay rights to the soil, and similar measures. In the federal and state councils, the Malay members—all of high status within the traditional establishment—argued civilly for more jobs in the administrative apparatus for English-educated Malays or for more Malay reservations for the peasants. They were hampered in expressing (or perhaps even holding) views directly critical of government policies, however, because most were also in the upper ranks of the bureaucracy. To provide alternative forums for Malay opinion and to organize "constituency support" for council representatives, elements of the English-educated elite began in 1938 to form avowedly political Malay associations on a state basis. Conservative in bias, loyal to the rulers (who in most states had given their blessing to the enterprise), and displaying an almost equal enthusiasm for British colonial rule—bulwark for the time being against the clamorous demands of Malaya-born and domiciled aliens—the political Malay associations movement, linked as it was with the traditional leadership to which the bulk of the Malays still gave their loyalty, was the only prewar movement that showed real signs of gaining anything like mass support. Though little success attended efforts at national conferences in 1939 and 1940 to unite the associations in a single organization, and though state loyalties remained powerful, the growth of a genuine Malay nationalism after the Pacific War owed much in both ideology and structure to the Malay associations movement and its leadership.

War and Postwar Politics

ON THE morning of 8 December 1941, a substantial Japanese military force landed on the coast of the northern Malay state of Kelantan and began an assault on British colonial power that was to culminate less than ten weeks later in the fall of Singapore on 15 February 1942. This devastating campaign heralded three years and eight months of Japanese occupation of the peninsula, which, aside from its immediate traumatic effects and the privations that resulted, radically reshaped Malaya's future. Breaking many of the psychological bonds that had permitted the continuance of Western domination, it also exacerbated socioeconomic and political tensions between communities that had been little more than latent in the 1930s. Toward the Malays the Japanese administration were somewhat conciliatory, giving lip service to nascent Malay nationalism while pursuing, as the British had done, policies directed toward food production and the economic exploitation of the peninsula's natural resources. Toward the Chinese the invaders were initially brutal, in memory of Nanyang assistance to China during the Sino-Japanese war, and subsequently mistrustful and harassing. The Chinese, in turn, provided most of the active guerrilla resistance to Japanese rule, organized through the Malayan Peoples Anti-Japanese Army (MPAJA), the nucleus of which was the prewar MCP. Some Indians became caught up in the enthusiasms of the Indian National Army, organized by Japan to assist in their planned invasion of India, but thousands of others were carried off to work, and die, on the Burma railway. Many Malays, at least for a time, filled positions in the civil administration to which they had not been permitted to aspire under the British. Those from all communities who "collaborated" with the new rulers found themselves targets of MPAJA hostility, and the eventual Japanese surrender was followed by a settling of scores on both sides. Throughout much of the occupation, the only common experience was of hunger, sickness, misery, and demoralization, with a marked decrease in standards of social trust and an increase in corruption.

When the British returned to Malaya in September 1945, some of its inhabitants looked forward to early release from colonial rule, while others thought such aspirations premature. Malaya's gradual achievement of independence during the decade that followed, though often seen as "nonrevolutionary," was the product of new and hard-won understandings between the then-accepted leaders of the communities of Malaya. During the war years, while Malays and Chinese had been coming to a new appreciation of the complexities of their continued relationship, the British had been planning a reorganized version of the Malayan polity. Unveiled in London in a White Paper in January 1946, the intention was to create a unified Malayan state (excluding only Singapore, which was to remain a separate colony) by cession of all separate jurisdiction from the sultanates to the British crown and by conferring citizenship on all born there or resident for ten out of (effectively) the preceding nineteen years.

Malay opinion was grievously affronted by this Malayan Union plan because of the loss of Malay sovereignty it involved and the extension of full participatory rights in the state to hundreds of thousands regarded as sojourners with external loyalties—though in fact out of the 2.5 million Chinese in Malaya at the time (comprising 38 percent of the population), some 64 percent were locally born and presumably intended to stay. Publication of the plan elicited from the Malays a remarkable political response, far exceeding any demonstration of national feeling manifested before the occupation. Resurrecting and building on prewar Malay associations and similar organizations, Malay leaders—preeminent among them Onn b. Jaafar of Johore—brought into being within a few weeks a mass Malay movement, the United Malays National Organization (UMNO), to fight the union scheme.

Within eighteen months the scheme had been abandoned and a federal system of government restored, based on continuance of the traditional state structure, greatly restricted citizenship, and the introduction of a nonelective legislative council in which government officials and the Malay rulers together outnumbered unofficial members. The new Federation of Malaya was inaugurated on 1 February 1948, with Singapore remaining a separate colony under direct British rule.

The Japanese occupation had been disastrous for the British-protected states in Borneo, especially British North Borneo and Sarawak. The agricultural economies of both suffered heavily during the war, towns were severely damaged by the Allied bombing that preceded the retaking of the territories, and infrastructures were left shattered. With the chartered company unable to afford to rehabilitate the territory, North Borneo (shortly to be known as Sabah) became a British crown colony in 1946, directly administered by the colonial service. Sarawak returned briefly to Brooke rule, but the third raja, Vyner Brooke, unable to face the costs of rebuilding the territory, ceded it to the British crown in 1946, a decision bitterly contested from within the family and among local supporters. Brunei, too, suffered during the war, but revenues from its major oil reserves (first discovered in 1929) made possible an easier resumption of colonial protectorate rule and the continuance of the sultanate.

In Malaya itself, the postwar settlement faced somewhat more serious obstacles. When, at the end of the war, the MPAJA had laid down its arms and disbanded, it appeared that the Malayan Communist Party was, at least for the moment, prepared to pursue by constitutional means its opposition to the restoration of colonial rule. In this it was joined by a rather unstable coalition of broadly left-wing groups led by the multiracial Malayan Democratic Union and the pan-Indonesianist Malay Nationalist Party. Postwar economic dislocation and social unrest, especially in Singapore, encouraged the MCP to turn its attention to the industrial labor unions, and during 1946 and early 1947 it established a convincing hold over the labor movement there and in the peninsula. Most industrial labor remained Chinese, and as before the war the MCP became primarily identified with the Chinese community. Strict British regulation of union practice combined with an upturn in the economy and factional disarray within the party led the MCP to abandon constitutionalism for armed struggle in mid-1948.

The resulting "Emergency," as the British called it, lasted for twelve years, though the back of the revolt was broken by the mid-1950s. The initial aim of the MCP, and of the Malayan Races Liberation Army (MRLA) it shortly set up, was to subvert the economy by disrupting the rubber plantations and tin mines that provided most of Malaya's wealth, to destroy authority by attacking and defeating government security forces, and to win mass support from the populace. Though some early successes were recorded in assassinating European and Chinese rubber planters and tin miners and in isolated acts of sabotage, the MRLA by 1949 was forced to retire to the jungle, where it engaged in a sporadic guerrilla war. Protracted though this struggle became, it early proved an unequal one.

While numbers of Chinese, through a combination of disaffection and fear of reprisals if they did not, were prepared to give aid and encouragement to the MRLA, most Malays saw the war as preeminently a Chinese attempt to gain control of the state, and not only remained loyal to the colonial power but fought actively against the MRLA. Government successes in the field, coupled with evidence of intention and ability to protect most of the populace most of the time, encouraged Chinese resistance to MCP demands, and the so-called Briggs Plan of forcible regrouping of vulnerable Chinese peasant squatting communities from the jungle fringes into "new villages" did much to restrict support for the Communists. Between 1950 and 1952 no fewer than half a million Chinese were resettled, in more than four hundred areas. During the same period, nearly ten thousand Chinese were deported to mainland China.

Toward Merdeka (Independence)

BUT THE struggle was above all a political one, and it became increasingly clear to Malays, noncommunist Chinese, and British alike that the only real way to repudiate the MRLA's claim to be a liberation army was by moving toward self-government and independence. The British, however, refused to consider this until the Malay and Chinese communities had achieved greater unity of purpose. The stringent detention and other security measures prompted by the Emergency (leading, among other things, to the virtual extinction of the democratic socialist parties, Malay and multiracial alike) stifled most overt political activity. Leading Chinese became increasingly concerned that the Chinese community lacked a politically acceptable organization comparable to UMNO to speak for it. In February 1949 a number of wealthy, Western-educated Chinese (led by the millionaires Tan Cheng Lock and H. S. Lee) were successful in forming a Malayan Chinese Association (MCA). While the MCA's constitution described its first aim as "the promotion and maintenance of interracial harmony in Malaya," Tan Cheng Lock, in an inaugural address in Melaka, said that its chief task would be to work to secure justice for the Chinese community. Though the two objectives were not necessarily incompatible, simultaneous pursuit created considerable problems of accommodation.

Paradoxically, the existence of two strong communal groupings was greatly to assist the process of compromise. Already, early in 1949, shortly before the formation of the MCA, a British-sponsored Communities Liaison Committee had taken the first steps toward a reconciliation of interests, formulating somewhat more liberal citizenship proposals for the Chinese in return for promises of special economic assistance for the Malays. In 1952, with the first democratic elections under the federation constitution approaching—for the municipality of Kuala Lumpur—the Selangor state branches of UMNO and MCA formed what proved to be a highly successful electoral pact, with the two parties taking all but two of the contested seats. This arrangement proved similarly successful in subsequent state elections, and in August 1953 a national Alliance was formally constituted, joined a year later by the Malayan Indian Congress (MIC). In the first full-scale federal elections, held in July 1955, the Alliance, campaigning on a platform demanding immediate self-government and early independence, won 51 out of 52 elective seats in a newly organized, 98-member Legislative Council, with 81 percent of the vote. Thirty-four of the Alliance seats went to UMNO Malays, 15 to MCA Chinese, and 2 to MIC Indians. Tengku Abdul Rahman (the title Tengku indicated that he was of royal birth), leader of UMNO and of the Alliance, was appointed chief minister and formed a cabinet. The way was now open for *merdeka* (independence).

The character and interest of the leaders of the Alliance—moderate, administration-minded Malays and well-to-do Chinese and Indian business-men—seemed to the British to offer future political and economic stability and a reasonable insurance for their own investments. During the long series of British-sponsored constitutional talks that ensued, there was considerable differ-ence of opinion among the communities on certain crucial issues relating to citizenship, language, the status of the Malays, and other questions. UMNO and the MCA, recognizing that neither community could successfully go it alone, finally presented to the British a joint set of Alliance proposals embodying compromises made by both sides. With little further demur, the British accepted them, and on 31 August 1957 the independent Federation of Malaya came into being.

Further Readings

Cheah Boon Kheng. *Malaysia: The Making of a Nation*. Singapore, 2002.

Harper, T. N. *The End of Empire and the Making of Malaya*. Cambridge, 1999.

Kaur, Amarjit. *Economic Change in East Malaysia: Sabah and Sarawak since 1850*. New York, 1998.

Khon Kim Hoong. *Merdeka! British Rule and the Struggle for Independence in Malaya, 1945–1957*. Petaling Jaya, 1984.

Kratoska, Paul H. *The Japanese Occupation of Malaya*. Honolulu, 1997.

Roff, William R. *The Origins of Malay Nationalism*. 2d ed. Kuala Lumpur, 1994.

Stubbs, Richard. *Hearts and Minds in Guerilla Warfare: The Malayan Emergency, 1948–1960*. Singapore, 1989.

Chapter 22

British Burma and Beyond

THOUGH Britain ruled parts of the country for twice as long, the heartland of Myanmar was a colony for less than sixty years. Abandoning the policy of working with indigenous elites in creating a colonial administration, which was followed in much of the empire, the British largely ignored the personnel and institutions of the Myanmar kings except in the upland areas populated by Shan, Kachin, Kayah, and other minority communities. In so doing, they emasculated every institution above the village level other than the Buddhist monkhood, and even that was allowed to become highly fractured. Rather, being profoundly ignorant of the actual nature of the highly hierarchical social order of Myanmar, the British assumed erroneously that the country they were attempting to rule had no indigenous principles of organization worthy of intellectual respect. The revolutionary consequences of this and of tying Myanmar economically to the global economy and politically to India were little recognized in 1886. However, by the 1930s the effect was the creation of an irresistible demand for regaining the fractured country's independence in the name of the people. World War II, which broke the grip of the British Indian army on what was now Burma, allowed young Burmese nationalists to organize themselves in an army and a mass left-wing nationalist movement to ensure that the future of the country would be in indigenous hands. Their efforts, which ultimately led to independence in 1948, failed, however, to establish a viable political system capable of restoring the country's prosperity and creating a new social order.

"The Pacification of Burma"

WHEN THE British attempted to impose their will after deposing King Thibaw, the established leadership groups in the old society—court officials, provincial governors, military commanders, and Buddhist monks—organized a strong resistance. The enfeeblement of the king's administration had enabled semi-anarchic conditions to emerge across the country, allowing localized resistance to the British to persist for nearly a decade after 1886. The authority of indigenous political leaders was highly contested and eventually undermined by the administrative reforms introduced when all of Burma was annexed to British India. In their place, Buddhist monks now arose to take a political as well as spiritual role as leaders of their communities. Freed from the discipline of the king's monastic order, the monks began to assume a secular role in opposition to the British, whom they viewed as the enemies of Buddhism.

Vagabondage and brigandage, actions that allowed individuals and groups to avoid monarchical control, had been well-established practices in Myanmar, occurring in response to official abuses or the absence of clear authority. Such activities continued under British rule, especially where, as in the Ayeyarwady delta, new villages had been founded by immigrants from the north, and political authority was defined artificially by administrative fiat. Vagabonds and brigands meant something else to the British, who were concerned with land and money rather than the control of manpower. The new utilitarian state was interested in expanding the agricultural base and increasing tax revenues rather than in performing the religious and ceremonial functions of the monarchical order.

Another source of resistance to the British came from the leaders of ethnolinguistic minorities—the Shan, Kachin, Chin, Wa, and other peripheral groups—who with great tenacity had carved out varying degrees of autonomy within the old tributary framework. As Mindon and Thibaw attempted to strengthen their control over the peripheral rulers, they provoked a resistance to central control that the British were forced to end by military means.

The resistance that swept the country after 1886 was unquestionably political in motivation. Whether those involved were "nationalists" is in dispute, but it would be a mistake to dismiss this massive uprising, as the British often did, as merely xenophobia or banditry. The fight was to maintain indigenous political authority. As the Sawbwa of Kengtung wrote to his fellow Shan ruler at Hsipaw in late 1886, rallying support for the Limbin Prince's effort to reestablish the throne, "If there be a suzerain [i.e., a king of Myanmar], the interest of the country, of the religion, of all of us, will be protected." Those who had wielded authority under the kings wanted to preserve their prerogatives against the demands of an unknown foreign overlord while defending the values of a society they cherished. But the leaders were unable to generate a coherent and unified force, as a number of pretenders to the throne were thrown up in the chaotic circumstances of the times. The discipline and might of the British Indian army, which imposed military rule on the entirety of Burma for ten years before establishing a civilian administration, had too many external sources of power to be resisted for long.

The changes that resulted from colonial rule led to the creation of social formations markedly different from those that had existed under the kings. Rather than trying to limit and control personal ambitions and economic incentives, as the kings of Myanmar had done, the colonial authorities sought to encourage individualism among the majority of the population as a means of fostering economic growth. Trade and profit replaced the sumptuary laws of the kings, and education useful for working as a lawyer or clerk replaced religiously grounded learning in village monasteries.

Education was integral to colonial rule in Burma. It was geared to providing the government and business with English-speaking clerks and functionaries possessing the skills necessary for a modern bureaucracy. The cities of Burma became centers of such learning. The British trained a bureaucracy that was not hereditary; nor did it come from the old elite. Residents in the southern zones of the country, which came under British rule first, had an advantage in gaining access to the educational institutions of the new order; this head start in acculturation to the new order permitted them to dominate the indigenous civil service.

Buddhism and Self-Government in the Empire

THE FIRST manifestation of the growing self-awareness of the new educated class came in 1906 with the formation of the Young Men's Buddhist Association (YMBA). The YMBA, which brought together a number of preexisting groups, initially sought to modernize Buddhist beliefs and practices while bridging the gap between its urban-educated members and the peasant majority. This attempt to assert a modern identity separate from that imposed by the British soon led to the growth of organized Burmese nationalism. The political implications of the formation of the YMBA were not lost on the British, who forbade government employees to join it. Subsequently, however, that ban was lifted, and for a brief time the association came to be led by members of a new indigenous elite, many of whom worked for the government.

World War I and associated events in British India rapidly widened the horizons of the urban elite and led to a split between pro-British reformers and individuals more inclined to political activism. In 1916 the YMBA raised with the government the ostensibly cultural and religious issue of the wearing of shoes and boots by Europeans when they entered the precincts of pagodas. It was not merely about the scuffing by foreigners of floors polished by countless bare feet; to wear shoes in these circumstances was an act of the highest vulgarity—even sacrilege. At issue was the implicit European assumption of cultural superiority and defiant disdain for Buddhist culture. The 1916 "footwear controversy" was a challenge to Britain's right to rule in a manner defined only by itself. After all fifty YMBA branches had mounted agitation across Burma, the government ruled in 1918 that abbots had the right to determine the appropriate dress in their monasteries. The importance of this victory can be gauged from the self-assurance with which the YMBA tackled issues more explicitly political the following year.

In 1918 the British government announced its intention of moving toward a measure of self-government in India. The YMBA responded by requesting Burma's separation from India. The unrestricted immigration of Indians, the inappropriateness of imported Indian legislation and administration, the use of Burma's revenue surpluses to support the Indian government, and the prospect that the government of Burma would pass to Indian politicians were among the grievances the YMBA leaders advanced in supporting separation. Following the decision of the British that Burma should be dealt with separately from India, the governor of Burma proposed only limited reforms and no real power for the Burmese.

Now alarmed that separation from India might mean missing out on the greater measure of self-rule to be granted to Indian provinces, elements of the YMBA and others attacked the proposed reforms. In 1919 and 1920 they sent delegates to London, who gained limited concessions. Although Burma would remain a province of India, constitutional "dyarchy" would be established, under which some limited government functions would be transferred to two Burmese ministers responsible to a partially representative legislative council. While the Burmese delegation was negotiating in London, however, their compatriots back home were demanding an even greater degree of self-government than the British were then willing to contemplate.

The agitation centered first on the proposed rules for the new Rangoon University. In 1920 the YMBA split between its younger majority and the conservative leadership, with the younger group taking the name of Myanma Athin Chokkyi, or the General Council of Burmese Associations (GCBA). The GCBA lent its support to a student-organized strike at the university. The strike soon spread to embrace all government and some missionary schools. At issue was whether the new university would be exclusive or whether a larger number of students, with lower educational qualifications, would be able to attend. The strike, although it did not change the government's policy, resulted in the formation of a larger number of national schools run by Burmese. Though these eventually accepted some government supervision in order to receive funding, they established a degree of independence from the British system.

The political activity that began with the university boycott in 1921 and continued throughout the decade increasingly involved the public, both urban and rural. The GCBA encouraged the organization of village-level nationalist associations called *wunthanu athin* (own race society). These mobilized peasants to boycott government officials, including village headmen, and the more radical leaders supported peasants who were seeking relief from economic hardships by refusing to pay taxes and rent. Both within these groups and outside them, younger Buddhist monks took an increasingly prominent role in political agitation, creating in 1922 their own national political leadership in a general council for the monkhood to direct such work. The activist monks of the 1920s were in some respects similar to those who had resisted the British in the 1880s and earlier. Theirs was a defensive position that rested upon the values of the monarchical order, but their organization, tactics, and issues were new. Significantly, unlike most of the urban political elite in the GCBA and its many factions, the political monks remained in close contact with the peasantry through the *wunthanu athin*.

The introduction of a new constitution in 1923 strained the alliance of the urban elite and rural leaders, whether religious or secular. Under the new arrangements, a 103-member legislative council was created, with 80 elected members. Of the 80, 15 were elected from communal constituencies (8 Indians, 5 Kayin [Karen], 1 Anglo-Indian, and 1 British), thus reifying Burma's ethnic diversity and making it a constitutional issue. Two of the four members of the governor's council were nominated by the legislative council and put in charge of agriculture, excise, health, public works, forestry, and education. Still reserved to the governor was control over the central administration, the courts, police, land revenue, labor, and finance, as well as the "excluded areas" (Kayah, the Shan States, and the Kachin and Chin hill areas), while the central government of India controlled defense, foreign relations, communications, immigration, and income tax.

The first election to the Legislative Council in 1922 split Burma's elite over the issue of participation or collaboration in what most regarded as an unacceptable constitution. A majority of the GCBA boycotted the election, while a minority formed the "Twenty-One Party" to enter the constitutional fold, winning just under half of the noncommunal seats. Less than 7 percent of the electorate voted. The split in the GCBA was reflected in the organization's branches and the *wunthanu athin*. The result was political fragmentation, in which opportunism, generational differences, educational background, economic concerns, differences in tactics, and other forces figured, dividing both the urban elite and village society. All agreed on the necessity for change, but many differed on its likelihood and eventual nature. The vast majority saw the formal political process as irrelevant to their concerns. In each of the other two elections held during the decade, less than 18 percent of the electorate voted.

The ideas and interests that motivated the nationalist movement in Burma before 1942 reflected the dissimilar interests of the urban political elite and the village-based leadership. The issues that moved the elite were primarily defined in terms of the political structures created by the British. Their goal was to replace the British and take over the administration. For the village leaders, nationalism meant ridding the country not only of foreign rule, but also of the bureaucratic and economic institutions that the British had introduced. Peasant unrest continued to grow during the 1920s, but there was little the urban elite could do to address their grievances, and a gulf of distrust grew between the two groups.

During the 1920s the tiny elite repeatedly split into a multiplicity of parties and factions. In the Legislative Council the increasing representation of nationalist parties at successive elections encouraged the ethnic minority representatives to support a government that the majority of Burmese disliked, thus heightening differences between the minorities and the majority population. As a result, legislation introduced to ameliorate the conditions of the peasant majority had no chance of being passed. Meanwhile, rural political activity increased substantially as a result of the large number of parties and the agitation of monks and *wunthanu athin* members. Violence against government officials, including headmen, increased, and the government had to rely increasingly on the armed and mounted military or "punitive" police to maintain control.

Rebellion and Reaction in the 1930s

POLITICAL ACTIVITY was further inflamed by the local effects of the world depression. As a result of the halving of the rice price, with no commensurate reduction in rent and taxes, peasants argued that they could not repay their loans, and more than two million acres (800,000 ha) of land—20 percent of the delta —passed into the hands of Indian moneylenders between 1929 and 1934. As Burmese sought jobs held by alien laborers, urban tensions also arose, exploding in anti-Indian riots, which began in Rangoon in May 1930 and moved out into the countryside a year later, creating openly anticolonial disorder.

The most serious was a peasant rebellion that broke out in Tharrawaddy District in December 1930. Its leader, Hsaya San, a former monk, was an indigenous medicine practitioner and an organizer for the most radical faction of the GCBA. Under its auspices, he had undertaken in 1927–1928 an extensive survey of agrarian conditions and peasant grievances. His background suggests, as does the way in which his rebellion was organized, that by the late 1920s the village organizations of the GCBA and the *wunthanu athin* were seen as the only hope for ending the economic and political plight of the peasantry. Taxation, crime, rice prices, land alienation, Indian immigration, and unemployment, as well as the denigration of Buddhism were all seen as direct products of colonialism.

Hsaya San surrounded himself with the trappings and symbolism of royalty, such as many-tiered parasols and multiple wives. However, while outwardly manifesting many of the beliefs of precolonial Myanmar, the rebellion was very much a revolt organized by modern means and directed at contemporary grievances. Hsaya San had spent the previous two years touring villages and encouraging the peasants to take action on their own behalf, but the rebellion apparently broke out spontaneously and spread rapidly. It began with attacks on police posts, the forestry service, village headmen, and any Indians and Chinese the rebels came across. The rebellion reached such proportions that additional forces had to be brought in from India, so that eventually there were 12,000 troops in the field to suppress it. With the capture of the leaders toward the end of 1931, the rebellion began to wane, and it was broken by mid-1932.

The failure of the rebellion demonstrated the futility of peasant revolt in the circumstances. Weapons were hard to get, and government troops were vastly superior in firepower and mobility. The rebels suffered 3,000 casualties, the government just 138. It was not, however, a total failure, for it awakened public opinion, setting an example of sacrifice and anticolonial zeal that few could ignore and many romanticized. Government prestige was shaken, as the seriousness of the grievances emphasized the administration's apparent indifference.

As the British began to reexamine the Indian constitution in 1929, the issue of separation of Burma from India was again revived. When an official commission recommended separation, many Burmese distrusted British intentions; they believed that India would be granted greater autonomy than Burma and were suspicious of the fact that British business also favored separation. However, the majority also viewed Burma's continued attachment to India with distrust, knowing that the only way that Burma could stop unfettered Indian immigration was by separation. The issue was tested in the general election of 1932, in which the "antiseparationists" won on the basis of GCBA, *wunthanu athin,* and monastic support. At that time representatives of Indian businesses with sizable investments in Burma contributed heavily to their cause to ensure the safety of their assets. But when it met, the Legislative Council was unwilling to indicate clearly that it favored remaining in India, and when the British decided on separation, this was accepted.

In 1935 the British gave Burma a partially democratic constitution, which came into effect when the colony was finally separated from India on 1 April 1937. This provided for a cabinet responsible to an elected 143-member House of Representatives, against which was balanced a Senate of 36 members, of whom half were to be elected from among men of substantial property. Ethnically designated electoral rolls continued to be used. Reserved to the governor were control over the "excluded areas," defense, foreign relations, and monetary policy. Political activity approaching the 1935 elections, which were to inaugurate the new order, seemed muted. The gap between the political games of the urban politicians and the grievances of the peasant majority continued to grow.

Courtesy of R. H. Taylor.

Politicians with private armies: U Saw and his followers, 1940.

Increasingly the established politicians were challenged by younger men. A movement centered initially in the Rangoon University student union and influenced by the ideas of Irish nationalism, Fabianism (democratic socialism), and Marxism-Leninism took shape in the latter half of the decade when a group of young men took control of the Dobama Asi-ayone (We Burmans Association). Founded in 1932 in the aftermath of anti-Indian riots and peasant rebellion, the Dobama Asi-ayone now became a focus of the most strongly nationalist youth. The leaders called themselves *thakin,* or "masters," implying that they, not the British, were the rightful rulers of Burma. Many of the younger leaders gained their first political experience leading a strike in 1936 over university governance. Led by Aung San, Nu, and many others who became prominent in politics and government in the 1940s and 1950s, the strike was a gesture of defiance against the colonial education system. It was called off only when the university and the legislature agreed to investigate student demands. After leaving the university, the young nationalists then devoted their energies to writing leftist political tracts and organizing peasant and labor protests. Aung San was a founder of the first Communist Party of Burma but left Rangoon in 1939 and eventually met with Japanese agents, who convinced him of their willingness to assist the Burmese in liberating their country from colonial rule.

The parties that participated with the British in government were dogged by the same strategic issue that had dominated the previous decade: the degree to which they should cooperate with the British in exchange for some degree of reform. Dr. Ba Maw—who had defended Hsaya San at his treason trial, led antiseparatist campaigning in 1932, and been education minister during the 1936 student strike—formed a coalition of minor parties, ethnic minority leaders, and defectors from other parties to lead the first government of separated Burma. For the next five years, the politics of Burma was dominated by contests for office and power among established politicians such as Ba Maw and others, especially U Saw. Three cabinets were formed during the period, and over time a new constitutional order took shape. The governor, though keeping his veto in reserve, increasingly allowed the Burmese ministers to decide what should be done to alleviate the country's social and economic ills. Agrarian issues, including land reform, taxation, and agricultural credit, as well as immigration and "Burmanization" of government and commercial positions, were all subjects of legislation. Little had changed, however, before the Japanese invasion.

War and Another Alien Ruler

THE BRITISH Indian army was too weak to put up more than a token resistance when the Japanese invasion began in January 1942. As it retreated toward India in March, several hundred thousand Indians and Britons fled. The Japanese were accompanied by a small group of young Burmans, the "Thirty Comrades," led by Thakin Aung San (and including Thakin Shu Maung, later to be known as General Ne Win), who had been trained by the Japanese to form the nucleus of a new Burma army. The new force, known initially as the Burma Independence Army (BIA), grew as it passed through Lower Burma to number about 23,000 untrained but politically inspired youth. The BIA's power was enhanced when the young officers and their *thakin* colleagues assumed the conduct of local administration. By July 1942, however, the BIA was largely demobilized at Japanese insistence, renamed the Burma Defence Army (BDA), and reduced to 5,000 men.

The Japanese sought to establish an indigenous administration that would not interfere with their military operations but would keep the population under control. With Japanese support, Ba Maw and other politicians formed an administration in collaboration with leading *thakin*. Aung San was made defense minister; Thakin Nu (the future prime minister), foreign minister; and Thakin Than Tun (the future leader of the Communist Party), agriculture minister. The Japanese granted this government a measure of administrative authority and in August 1943 nominal independence. The limited nature of this self-government was soon apparent; this inadequacy, along with the hardships of the wartime economy and Japanese demands, made the government and its Japanese sponsors increasingly unpopular.

The left wing of the *thakin* movement had refused to countenance collaboration with the "fascist" Japanese, and at the commencement of the war they began organizing an underground resistance movement, led by Thakin Soe's communists. The communist leaders met with Aung San and other military and noncommunist leaders to form the Anti-Fascist Organisation (AFO) in August 1944. Their intention was to drive out the Japanese in cooperation with the Allies and then to regain Burma's independence under a leftist government. They were aided in this by contacts made in India with the British army and a secret intelligence organization, Force 136.

Thus, when British troops reconquered Burma in the first months of 1945, they were joined by armed Burmese under Aung San's command and received assistance from resistance cells organized by the communists. Both groups were operating under the authority of the AFO, which was renamed the Anti-Fascist People's Freedom League (AFPFL). Recognizing the popularity of the AFPFL, the British tried to find a means of ensuring that the league did not turn its forces against them before the Japanese had been defeated. Though the British refused to accept that the AFPFL had established a provisional government, the league cooperated because of the "peaceful development" policy of the communists and the conciliatory pose struck by the British supreme commander, Admiral Lord Louis Mountbatten.

The military administration was withdrawn in October 1945, and the prewar governor returned. Despite the popularity of the AFPFL, the British refused to allow them a majority in the governor's advisory council, arguing that the league's demands for a prompt grant of independence should be postponed until "more settled conditions" had been achieved. The government then set about restoring the old order, importing Indian labor, and reinstating Indian and British companies. When the AFPFL organized opposition to these plans, the Labour government in London was forced to rethink its policy toward Burma, particularly as the nationalist movement was moving increasingly leftward and threatening armed rebellion.

Independence and Civil War

IN THE middle of 1946 a new governor was appointed with a mandate to offer the noncommunist leaders of the AFPFL a majority of seats on his council and Aung San the vice presidency. However, the acceptance of office by some of the league's leaders led to a split in the national front. The communist members received no seats (except briefly), and relations between them and the rest deteriorated. Toward the end of 1946, an increasing number of conservatives had joined the league, and the communists were eased out of their former leadership posts. After the expulsion of the communists, the league negotiated with the British government, and it was agreed in January 1947 that following elections for a constituent assembly that would draft a constitution, independence would be granted within one year. In April the AFPFL won 171 of the 182 seats up for election and dominated the drafting of the country's first constitution.

An important issue that faced the drafters was the status of the "excluded areas," where a variety of ethnolinguistic communities, administered indirectly under their own leaders, had remained remote from colonial Burma's nationalist politics and modern economy. With some difficulty, the assembly drew up a constitution that provided for a semifederal "union" of Burma. Nominal states with limited administrative autonomy were granted for the Shan, Kachin, and Kayah, as well as the other minorities who lived in these territories, such as the Wa. A Chin "special division" was also created. The Shan and Kayah states were given the option to secede from the union after ten years.

The situation of the Christian Kayin, many of whom lived intermingled with other Burmese, was different. Their leaders were apprehensive about the loss of minority privileges under an indigenously controlled popular state and sought to maintain the special position they had achieved under the colonial administration, some demanding a separate government of their own. But because most of them did not live in a distinct regional ethnic enclave, a separate administration proved impossible to grant, so their hopes were thwarted; within a year of independence the Karen National Union (KNU) took up arms against the government, commencing an insurgency that lasted into the next century.

On 19 July 1947 an event occurred that shattered hopes that an independent government of Burma might be able to control the various conflicting forces in Burmese society. The assassination that day of Aung San, along with seven associates, at the apparent behest of U Saw, removed from the scene the one figure thought capable of holding the nation together. The vice president of the AFPFL, Nu, who was appointed to succeed, had neither the support of the army nor the trust of the communists that Aung San had.

Within three months of Burma's independence on 4 January 1948, the new indigenous rulers and their one-time communist allies became locked in a civil war that was to last for more than forty years. Insurrections had begun as early as 1946, when the British declared the "Red Flag" communists illegal. In March 1948 the larger "White Flag" Communist Party, led by Aung San's former colleague Than Tun, took the offensive after the government home secretary ordered their arrest. They were joined in July by the largest faction of Aung San's veterans' organization, the "White Flag" People's Volunteer Organisation (PVO), as well as by about half of the troops in the government army.

Scarcely had there been time to begin to develop plans to cope with their leftist opponents when the government had to face Kayin rebels under the leadership of the Karen National Union, including some defecting government troops who took up arms late in 1948. In 1949 the government was in control of only a few urban centers. Gradually the government's armed forces, under General Ne Win, began to regain the ascendancy, although the intrusion into the Shan hills of defeated Guomindang troops at the end of China's civil war complicated and prolonged the conflict. Not until 1951 was security sufficiently established to permit the holding of elections. Even so, the army continued to function as a parallel government in parts of the country, and power in some areas was held by local bosses and their armed gangs rather than the civilian administration.

The government survived the civil war but was greatly weakened by the turmoil and conflict that the country had experienced. It was able to regain control for several reasons: the creation of a strong national army; modest aid from Britain, India, and a few other states; and the support of anticommunist elements in the bureaucracy, the commercial classes, and the monkhood. Helpful to the government also was the fact that the insurgents fought each other as much as they fought the army. By the early 1950s the government's legitimacy had also become heavily dependent on the charisma of the devoutly Buddhist prime minister Nu, known to the world, using the Burmese honorific for senior males (literally "Uncle"), as U Nu.

Elections in 1951 and 1956 demonstrated the growing skepticism of the public as to the ability of the government to achieve the reforms that it had promised. Corruption became widespread, and when it and factionalism in the

Courtesy of R. H. Taylor

State-sponsored Buddhism: U Nu's Kaba Aye (World Peace) Pagoda, Rangoon.

AFPFL became rampant, Nu resigned as prime minister in order to impose discipline on the party. When he returned to office in 1958, factionalism in the league once more threatened political order, and in what amounted to a coup in all but name, the army under Ne Win took over the government for a period of six months, which was eventually extended to a total of eighteen. This "Caretaker Government" then held general elections.

U Nu's new Union Party won, and he was returned to power. However, the concessions he had made during the campaign again endangered national unity. Nu antagonized religious minorities by passing a constitutional amendment establishing Buddhism as the state religion and then antagonized Buddhists by passing another guaranteeing freedom of religion. When Nu announced his intention to resign by 1964, his supporters began to fight over the succession. Shan insurgency also broke out in the east of the country, and there were rumors of secessionist plans. To the army it appeared that Burma was heading back to the conflicts of 1958. Despite the harshness of its previous rule, the army government had had some successes, and Ne Win and his colleagues were confident that they could rule more effectively than Nu. The army carried out a coup on 2 March 1962, imprisoned many civilian politicians, suspended the constitution, and set about reconstructing both state and society under the auspices of an army-led Revolutionary Council. Burma's first experiment with multiparty democracy, which had begun in 1921, was over.

Further Readings

Cady, John F. *A History of Modern Burma.* Ithaca, 1958.

Donnison, F. S.V. *Public Administration in Burma: A Study of Development during the British Connexion.* London, 1953.

Furnivall, J. S. *Colonial Policy and Practice: A Comparative Study of Burma and Netherlands India.* Cambridge, 1948.

Guyot, James. "Bureaucratic Transformation in Burma." In Ralph Braibanti, ed., *Asian Bureaucratic Systems Emergent from the British Imperial Tradition,* pp. 354–443. Durham, N.C., 1966.

Maung Maung. *From Sangha to Laity: Nationalist Movements of Burma, 1920–1940.* New Delhi, 1980.

Mendelson, E. M. *Sangha and State in Burma.* Edited by John Ferguson. Ithaca, 1975.

Nash, Manning. *The Golden Road to Modernity: Village Life in Central Burma.* New York, 1965.

Smith, Donald E. *Religion and Politics in Burma.* Princeton, 1965.

Taylor, Robert H. *The State in Burma.* London, 1987.

Tinker, Hugh. *The Union of Burma.* 4th ed. London, 1967.

Chapter 23

❉

Vietnam, 1885–1975

Colonialism, Communism, and Wars

FRENCH COLONIALISM divided Vietnam into three parts: Cochinchina (the far south), Annam (the central region), and Tonkin (the north). Cochinchina was a formal colony, ruled by a French governor at Saigon and by French laws. It was also the principal base of French capitalism in Vietnam. Annam and Tonkin were called "protectorates," separated from each other in 1898. They were governed by parallel administrations of French civil servants, who governed Europeans and the tiny number of Vietnamese who had become French citizens, and old-fashioned turbaned Vietnamese mandarins, who governed most Vietnamese.

But this political wonderland, bristling with administrative distinctions, was less complex than it looked. The north and center were really colonies too. A single French overlord, the governor-general of "French Indochina," dominated all three parts of conquered Vietnam, along with Cambodia and Laos, from his Hanoi palace. Under the most aggressive of them, Paul Doumer (1897–1902), a single general Indochina budget was established as well as the beginnings of a new universe of higher education that included an Indochinese school of medicine (1902), a school of arts and crafts (1902), and the French School of the Far East (École française d'Extrême-Orient, 1901), so important a pioneering venture in the study of Vietnamese culture that it was invited back to Hanoi after colonialism had ended.

French Colonial Strategies and the Modernization
of Vietnamese Patriotisms

THE SIMPLE FACT was that French colonizers could not rule Vietnam without
Vietnamese help. There were too few French to fill all the colony's administrative positions; at the time Doumer left office in 1902, there were a mere 3,778
European officials in Indochina. The colonizers therefore preserved the old
Confucian mandarinate in the north and the center; the French even maintained the precolonial Confucian examinations, through which Vietnamese
mandarins were recruited, until 1919, long after the equivalent Confucian
examinations in China had been abolished as hopelessly opposed to modern
thought (1905). The French also bet heavily on the preservation of the ancient
Vietnamese monarchy in the Hue Forbidden City. As the author of a doctoral
thesis about "Annamite Civilization and the French Protectorate," written for
the Bordeaux University Faculty of Law in 1919, put it, the continued presence
of a Vietnamese emperor was necessary to maintain among the natives "that sort
of fear of superiors, that terror of one's master, which is in Annam the basis of
public order." A series of youthful emperors served as French puppets until 1945,
looking increasingly anachronistic and out of place in a rapidly changing Asia.

In effect, this was a strategy of Confucian colonialism. Outside Cochinchina
the French tried to make the old Confucian reflexes of loyalty to the king,
obedience to one's parents, and wifely submission to husbands work to support
their superimposed authority, while they were simultaneously encouraging a
brave new world of post-Confucian global capitalism to flourish in Saigon. This
was a contradiction, but for a time it seemed that they might get away with it.
Few Confucian intellectuals could imagine abolishing the principle of loyalty
to a monarch; in 1900 the notion of a socialist dictatorship, such as was to be
the basis of government all over Vietnam by 1975, seemed scarcely more intel-
ligible than life on Mars. During the French conquest Confucian patriots who
had hated the French had been able to invoke the Confucian principle that "the
loyal minister does not serve two princes." In the 1880s such a principle had
rallied them to the cause of a boy emperor, Ham-nghi, whose advisers had
called for a general insurrection against the French invaders. Even after the
French had captured Ham-nghi in 1888 and exiled him to Algeria, the "aid the
king" *(can vuong)* resistance movement had continued in the countryside, drawing its supporters from village leaders and examination system students. But the
introverted mixture of Confucian loyalism and xenophobia that the royalist
resistance exhibited, as it made war on both Vietnamese Catholic villagers and
French soldiers, could not embrace any modern conception of Vietnam as a
nation-state in competition with other nation-states. Its spirit was one of
change-resisting ethnocentrism more than change-accepting nationalism.

What wrecked Confucian colonialism, or the "association" of French colonial authority with Vietnam's Confucian monarchy and bureaucracy, was that the French could never get full control of the shifting concerns of the Confucian world. Confucianism was an international ideology, flourishing in China and Japan as well as in Vietnam. Just as influences from Cairo might stimulate colonialism-subverting renewals of Islamic thought in maritime Southeast Asia, influences from Beijing (the site of the 1898 Chinese reform movement, which tried to combine Confucian monarchism with constitutional government and a parliament) and Tokyo (where China's 1898 reformers fled after their efforts failed) excited Vietnamese intellectuals and inspired thoughts about how to revitalize Vietnam. Japan's victory over Czarist Russia in the 1904–1905 Russo-Japanese War, the first modern defeat of a Western power by an Asian one, only increased Japan's prestige. Vietnamese saw that a country with Confucian traditions could nonetheless achieve equality with the imperialist West if it modernized itself.

About 1905, therefore, anticolonial Vietnamese students began to travel to Japan to study in Japanese schools and acquire modern political and military training of the sort denied them in French Indochina. Such students might not speak Chinese or Japanese, but as products of a Confucian education based on classical Chinese texts, they could conduct silent "writing brush conversations" with mentors who shared the same classical written language. Such conversations cast a long shadow over Vietnam's future, because the Japanese elite at the time were busy inventing a systematic new vocabulary, based on classical inspirations, for talking about modern ideas. The Vietnamese pilgrims to Japan absorbed this vocabulary: the modern Vietnamese term for "society" *(xa hoi)*, for example, is derived from an early twentieth-century Japanese coinage adapted in turn from medieval Confucian philosophy. New concepts like this helped reformers to think of their compatriots as symbolically interacting with each other beyond kinship networks.

Phan Boi Chau (1867–1940) was probably the most important Vietnamese nationalist before 1930. Born into a Confucian scholar family, Phan embodied the transition from the old to the new. He had organized a royalist militia in 1885 and passed the old civil service examinations in 1900, but he then rejected French rule and came under the spell of the 1898 Chinese reformers; he moved to Japan to study with one of them, Liang Qichao (Liang Ch'i-ch'ao). Apart from new vocabulary, what Phan got from Liang and the other Chinese and Japanese thinkers he met was an interest in Social Darwinism, with its belief that the master principle of the universe was not harmony (as many Confucian thinkers hoped) but rather endless competitive struggle, in which the chief competitors were nation-states. Applying Social Darwinism to Southeast Asia, Phan wrote in "Letter Inscribed in Blood from Abroad" (1907) that Vietnam was now as uncompetitive as the Cham kingdom that Vietnam had once conquered; it would disappear like Champa if it did not learn how to struggle against French control more effectively. In a 1908 polemical history of Vietnam, Phan further asserted that human history was a process of linear evolution, from being "animals" to being "civilized"; Vietnam was merely in the intermediate stage of beginning to civilize itself.

Japan's contribution to this moment of upheaval in the Vietnamese elite worldview weakened after 1907. The Japanese government, a colonial power in Taiwan (after 1895) and Korea (by 1910), began to see itself more as an imperialist colleague of the West than as the patron of colonized Asians like the Vietnamese. Vietnamese students were expelled from Japan or forced to hide by acquiring false Chinese identities. But by this time the writings of Phan Boi Chau had been smuggled back to Vietnam, where secret organizations of Phan's "Restoration" *(duy tan)* Society had been formed in the guise of hotels or business organizations.

This early phase of Vietnamese nationalism climaxed in Hanoi in 1907, with the opening there, sponsored by patriotic elite families, of the Dong Kinh (Tonkin) Free School, on the model of Tokyo's Keio School (later Keio University), founded in 1868 by the Japanese liberal reformer Fukuzawa Yukichi. The Hanoi imitation lasted less than a year before French authorities suppressed it. But in its brief life the Free School proposed a cultural revolution: the adoption of Western clothing, the abolition of the Confucian civil service examinations, the use of romanized Vietnamese words *(quoc ngu)* rather than cumbersome Chinese writing as an aid to greater mass literacy, and the study of the latest Western theories of nationalism and of the social contract. The school's geography teacher shocked his students by showing them the first modern map of Vietnam, with "the rivers and mountains of the ancestors" drawn on it, that they had ever seen.

But the Dong Kinh Free School had little impact on Vietnamese villagers. The major achievement of the first generation of Vietnamese nationalists was to discredit the old Confucian institutions, such as the monarchy and the examinations, that the French had been manipulating to maintain their rule. Another giant of early Vietnamese nationalism, Phan Chu Trinh (1871–1926), now advocated a republican presidency and a Western-style written constitution for Vietnam, in which (as he put it in a famous Saigon speech in 1925) the same laws would govern everybody "from presidents to peasants," rule of law would be the "brick road" that would lead to freedom, and the people would no longer be the passive "herd of goats" they had been under the emperors. Phan Chu Trinh's 1926 Saigon funeral provoked some of the earliest mass demonstrations of Vietnamese student nationalism.

The French began, grudgingly, to replace Vietnam's Confucian education, at least in the towns, with a more modern school system, in which French cultural influences were brought to bear upon Vietnamese youth. But this was a dangerous option. Much French culture, to its credit, was unhelpful to the purposes of French colonialism. Voltaire's hostility to tyranny, Rousseau's defense of popular sovereignty, and Victor Hugo's espousal of liberty and Paris workers' insurrections could all work instead to encourage the appearance in Vietnam of that curious creature the Francophile anticolonialist. Vo Nguyen Giap, the Hanoi schoolteacher who became, in the 1940s, the military brain of the communist revolution, was just one example.

Modern nationalism has been said by Benedict Anderson to be the joint product of the erosion of more religiously imagined communities and the rise of printed vernacular newspapers; the ceremony of newspaper reading allegedly replaces that of prayers, and print capitalism standardizes both popular speech and people's images of the solidarity they share with other members of their political unit. Applied to Vietnam, this theory underestimates colonialism's obstacles and also the difficulty of subtracting religious instincts from self-sacrificial faith in the "ancestral" nation. Vietnam's first *quoc ngu* newspaper appeared in the south in 1865; by the 1930s Hanoi and Hue, as well as Saigon, had newspapers with circulations of up to 15,000 copies. But French authorities controlled newspapers through subsidies, and censored and suppressed anti-colonial messages. Of the roughly 10,000 *quoc ngu* books and pamphlets published in Vietnam between 1923 and 1944, very few treated politics or history, even if Vietnamese writers did become skilled at evading censors by slipping their revolutionary pleadings into women's cookbooks or school mathematics texts. The worst obstacle of all was rural illiteracy, which anticolonial politicians could not begin to cure before the 1940s.

Then there was the fact that some modernizations of Vietnamese patriotism, rather than substituting for religion, could take religious forms themselves. For many Vietnamese, the challenge of Western colonial rule called for a religious response, not one based on Rousseau or Marx; millenarian sects' conceptions of anticolonial resistance, based on hope for messiahs, could actually block the spread of revolutionary political parties' ambitions to expel the French by more painstakingly secular means. The two most important religious sects in the Vietnamese south in the 1920s and 1930s, where the French succeeded in confining them, were the Cao Dai and the Hoa Hao Buddhism movements. Like Sarekat Islam in Java a few years earlier, both sects publicly claimed to want to rehabilitate traditional religious practices, a goal to which colonial rulers could hardly object.

The Cao Dai sect emerged in the 1920s as a coalition of spirit worship groups that engaged in fortune-telling seances. Cao Dai created its own miscellaneous pantheon of deities, which included the Chinese medieval poet Li Bo and Victor Hugo, as part of an effort to present itself as a new universal religion; its success in quickly attracting thousands of adherents allowed it to acquire a territorial base in Tay Ninh province. There it proceeded to reproduce, in defiantly nativist terms, some of the structure and imagery of the Catholic Christianity associated with Vietnam's French invaders; a symbol (a heavenly eye) was adopted to compete with the Christian cross, and a hierarchy of cardinals and bishops emerged to compete with the Catholic clergy. Services at the Cao Dai cathedral in Tay Ninh were visually stunning. Cao Dai clergy wore tunics of three different colors to suggest the restored prestige and the unity within the sect of Vietnam's three precolonial creeds of Confucianism, Buddhism, and Daoism. Along with followers of Hoa Hao Buddhism, founded in 1939 by a charismatic faith healer, Huynh Phu So (1919–1947), Cao Dai sect members had an anticolonial bias. But they were too culturally conservative to ally themselves with communists, whose worldview—emphasizing secular struggle rather than cosmic harmony—was so different from their own.

Political Parties and the Communists' Triumph

WITH HIS wispy beard and rubber sandals, Ho Chi Minh (1890–1969)—to use the most famous of his estimated seventy-six pseudonyms—is one of modern Southeast Asia's most remarkable political figures. Even if he did receive great help from his enemies, his political achievement was amazing. In 1925, as an impoverished exile living in the humid back streets of Guangzhou (Canton), Ho created a Vietnamese Communist Party of all of nine people; four decades later, he was the leader of a communist government in Hanoi that had evicted the French from Vietnam and was preparing to defeat the United States.

Ho, like numerous other Vietnamese communists, was descended from the Confucian schoolteaching intelligentsia of northern Vietnamese villages. He learned about Marxism and Leninism in France. An obscure Paris photo shop worker, Ho made his debut in world politics in 1919 by petitioning the Allied powers at the Versailles peace conference to grant Vietnam autonomy. They ignored him. This left him open to the 1920 appeal of Lenin, the leader of the newly created Soviet Union, for an alliance between the European "communist proletariat" and the Asian "revolutionary peasant movement" directed against the established Western powers. Ho converted to communism and became an international communist missionary, working as an agent of the "Comintern" (Third Communist International), the global organization sponsored by Moscow that was supposed to subvert capitalism and spread revolution.

One great advantage of this Comintern-sponsored international community of revolutionary exiles, to which Ho now belonged, was that it allowed the separation of politics from kinship ties more rapidly than would have been possible in Vietnam itself. This facilitated the growth of new loyalties to causes that went beyond family and regional interests. Creating a Vietnamese "revolutionary youth" association in Guangzhou in 1925, Ho even urged all its members to adopt the same surname (Ly) as a symbol of the new, extrafamilial solidarity they needed to make a revolution. The failure of the Chinese communists' Guangzhou commune in 1927 drove Ho out of that city. Regrouping his forces in the British colony of Hong Kong, Ho formed the Indochina Communist Party (ICP) there in 1930. Ho himself carefully remained outside French Indochina, and the clutches of the French colonial police, from 1911 to 1941.

A communist revolution in Vietnam was still hardly inevitable. Other political parties challenged the communists. One was the Vietnamese Nationalist Party (VNQDD), named after the Chinese Nationalist Party (Guomindang) and founded in Hanoi in December 1927, shortly after its namesake had seized power in China. The VNQDD's leaders saw themselves as the Vietnamese disciples of the Chinese revolutionary Sun Yat-sen. They wanted to preach in Vietnam what Sun had called his

Photo by N. G. Owen

New religions: the Cao Dai Great Temple, Tay Ninh.

"three people's principles": nationalism, democracy, and a modest socialism that limited rural landlordism. They also hoped for aid from the new Chinese Nationalist government in the struggle they planned against the French.

Unfortunately for them, the Chinese Nationalists were too preoccupied with Japanese pressures and Chinese warlords to give their young Vietnamese allies support. Nor was the Guomindang necessarily a suitable model for Vietnamese nationalists in a colony that lacked any real native equivalent of the treaty port merchant class who helped to finance the Chinese party. Hoping that theatrical acts of bravery would arouse the political consciousness of the Vietnamese, in February 1930 the VNQDD heroically fomented an armed uprising against French rule in the northern town of Yen Bai. The uprising was hopeless. In the repression that followed, the French guillotined many VNQDD leaders, including the party's head, Nguyen Thai Hoc (1901–1930).

If this repression bought French colonialism more time in Vietnam, it also helped to ensure that Vietnamese anticolonial politics would have a different future from that of anticolonialism in the Netherlands Indies. In the Indies the communists had launched a premature uprising (1926–1927) the failure of which led to their temporary eclipse; noncommunist nationalists like Sukarno took advantage of this to replace them. In Vietnam it was the other way around: Ho Chi Minh was the beneficiary of the noncommunist revolutionaries' rashness.

Nor was the VNQDD defeat at Yen Bai Ho's only asset. The international communist movement's support was indispensable to the Vietnamese communists in providing their cadres with training in sanctuaries outside Vietnam (Moscow, south China, even northeast Siam), beyond the reach of the French police. The Comintern also provided its Vietnamese disciples with a useful two-stages revolutionary strategy in which full communism, for which there was little support in Vietnam, was postponed to the second stage and a more popular patriotic mobilization for independence became the focus of the first stage. The organizational techniques the Comintern taught, featuring secrecy and a cellular party structure, worked even inside Indochina's prisons, which were full of opportunities for collusive fraternization between prisoners and guards, or between Comintern-trained Marxist teachers and more "direction-less" common criminals. Then and later, prison friendships bound communist leaders to each other.

Finally, there was the communists' success in exploiting the Vietnamese rural crisis. With China and Korea, Vietnam shared a long tradition of political theory that assumed that landownership was a moral principle, not just an economic fact; the good ruler, as custodian of the land, supposedly ensured that everyone enjoyed its yields. Such expectations also became embedded in the popular culture, if less so in the south. Vietnam's oldest regions were a maze of collectively owned welfare lands, including temple lands, lands for sustaining orphans and the familyless, lands for the support of teachers and poor students, and even lands "for feasting elders." Vietnam's most ambitious rulers, such as Ho Quy Ly in 1397 and Minh-mang in 1839, had sponsored major land reforms to limit private landholding. Under French colonialism, population growth, helped by the effect of vaccinations and inoculations on the mortality rate, worsened class exploitation of the kind emperors had feared. Landlords could easily replace their tenant farmers, from whom they demanded very high yearly rents, with the growing numbers of landless peasants who still needed fields to work; they had little incentive to behave well.

As early as 1927, in a tract about the "revolutionary road" printed in China, Ho Chi Minh had condemned the colonial economy in the south for exporting rice at a time when population growth and landlessness threatened many Vietnamese with famine. During the global depression, the ICP made its first violent bid for power (1930–1931): the creation of rural "soviets" (self-governing councils) in the north-central provinces of Nghe An and Ha Tinh. The uprising was crushed, but thousands of villagers, despite their puzzlement at the soviets' campaign to commemorate European communist martyrs like Rosa Luxemburg, eagerly joined party-organized peasant associations and engaged in "rice struggles" to confiscate landlords' estates.

Ho nonetheless told the Comintern in 1935 that few ICP members understood what a "bourgeois democratic revolution" was; their literacy was so inadequate that written indoctrination had to be kept simple. The ICP were not a serious threat to French colonialism in Vietnam before World War II. The war and the Japanese army's occupation of Vietnam (1941–1945) changed everything. In addition to undermining the reputation of French military power in Vietnamese eyes, the invasion gave the communists a matchless opportunity to blend their complex doctrines with the more easily understood patriotic cause of resisting both the French and the Japanese.

Ho returned to Vietnam in 1941, making his headquarters in Cao Bang, a northern border province. In May 1941 the ICP central committee, under Ho's guidance, founded the Vietnamese Independence Solidarity League, better known as the Viet Minh. The Viet Minh was a "front" organization, designed to accommodate anticolonial Vietnamese who had no real interest in the smaller ICP's belief in class warfare. The front also hoped to attract assistance for fighting Japan from the British, the Americans, the Chinese Nationalists, and even European communists serving in the French Foreign Legion in Indochina. In this they succeeded, up to a point: the U.S. Office of Strategic Services (OSS), forerunner of the CIA, wanted Ho's cooperation in rescuing American pilots shot down over northern Vietnam. To get it, the Americans aided the Viet Minh, trained its technicians, and tried to help Ho frame a U.S.-style declaration of independence for Vietnam. Ho seemed "an awfully sweet guy," one of his American advisers ruefully recalled later.

On 9 March 1945 the Japanese armed forces in Indochina, who had tolerated the existence of an increasingly feeble French administration since 1941, suddenly overthrew French colonialism. The last emperor at Hue, Bao-dai, signed a proclamation, under Japanese guidance, that reclaimed Vietnam's independence but accepted Vietnamese participation in Japan's Greater East Asian empire. But the Viet Minh, which had created its own tiny "Liberation Army" in the hill country in December 1944, led by Vo Nguyen Giap, was the real beneficiary of the Japanese destruction of French power.

The terrifying famine that ravaged northern Vietnam from the end of 1944 also transformed Vietnamese politics. Perhaps as many as one million Vietnamese starved to death; Tonkinese rivers were full of corpses. Giap's new army now entered northern villages, seized the granaries that were storing rice for landlords or for the Japanese army, and distributed their rice to hungry villagers. The Viet Minh combined the slogans "national independence" and "destroy the granaries and resolve the famine," under the inspiration of the 1917 Russian Bolshevik slogan "peace, bread, and land." The famine thus enabled them to overcome conservative village notables who had previously opposed them. Village chiefs were compelled to destroy their own official seals; Viet Minh "people's committees" replaced them. By the time Japan surrendered to the Allied powers in August 1945, the Viet Minh were able to mobilize thousands of peasants, armed with sticks, knives, and a few rifles, to invade the major Vietnamese cities and towns.

Bao-dai, the religious sects, and the other political parties lacked enough military resources of their own to resist the Viet Minh takeover. ICP propagandists hailed it as the "August Revolution." Bao-dai abdicated his throne when the Viet Minh demanded it, seemingly accepting their legitimacy as Vietnam's rulers. Ho announced the birth of a communist-run Democratic Republic of Vietnam (DRV) in Hanoi in September 1945, with himself as president, citing the U.S. Declaration of Independence and the French Revolution's Declaration of the Rights of Man as he did so. But a Chinese invasion of the north in the fall of 1945, theoretically to exercise Nationalist China's mandate as an allied power to receive Japan's surrender, endangered the DRV. Ho pretended to dissolve the ICP; the communist party went underground for six years, publicly reemerging under a different name in 1951.

The French and American Wars, 1946–1975

AIDED BY the British, the French army had reentered southern Vietnam in late 1945 but lacked the power to reconquer the south's countryside, to which the communists withdrew. To remove Chinese invaders from the north, Ho daringly invited French soldiers to return there as well. In March 1946 France recognized the DRV as a free state and negotiated the withdrawal of the Chinese army, surrendering French colonial concessions in China itself to obtain this; in return Ho's government accepted membership in a proposed French Union (a diluted version of the old French empire). But the French now dreamed of using the south as the basis of a French-controlled Indochinese Federation that would preserve their presence except in the north. Ho tried to flatter the French into peaceful decolonization. As president of the DRV, he visited France in 1946 to explain that Cochinchina was as much a part of Vietnam as Brittany was a part of France. But the militarists in charge of the French colonial regime resisted setting a timetable for their departure. They thus won the opportunity to perish in a revolutionary war that they would never really understand. The war between the Viet Minh and the French broke out at the end of 1946 and lasted until 1954.

As explained by Giap, the Vietnamese communists' military thought included such principles as the value of continuous attack (because attacking deepened people's political consciousness, and stationary defense did not); learning how to use small resources, cleverly deployed, to defeat larger resources

not so wisely managed; the importance of surprise; the flexible use of differ-ent force types, ranging from a main army equipped with modern weapons to less well-armed guerrillas; and, most important of all, the total involvement of the population, old and young, male and female, in fighting the enemy. The most proudly professional French (and later American) generals, unaccustomed to a world in which military actions were planned for political ends or in which sol-diers and civilians were not differentiated, found Giap's approach baffling. To recruit popular support, the Viet Minh redistributed the lands of French owners and "Vietnamese traitors" to landless peasants and launched a mass literacy cam-paign. Giap's army grew from several thousand soldiers in 1945 to more than 200,000 by 1950, in addition to many more local guerrillas and armed civilians; communist party membership itself grew from 20,000 in 1946 to 700,000 by 1954.

This popular mobilization was a real revolution, more so than its shallower 1945 namesake. Combined with the victory of Mao Zedong's communists in China in 1949, which gave the Viet Minh a powerful ally, it spelled the doom of French colonialism. Giap's military humiliation of the French in 1954 at the battle of Dienbienphu, on Vietnam's northwest frontier—the worst defeat any Western colonial power suffered at the hands of an Asian people it had once ruled—nonetheless astonished world opinion. A Geneva peace conference, opening the day after the fall of Dienbienphu, required a final French with-drawal from Indochina. But the 1954 Geneva Agreement also required the Vietnamese communist regime at Hanoi to coexist for two years with an anti-communist government, based in Saigon, which the French had fabricated in the last years of the war. This Saigon regime (and its overseas supporters) con-trolled the half of the country south of the seventeenth parallel. Nationwide reunification elections, which the communists anticipated winning, were sup-posed to be held in 1956. But the new "Republic of Vietnam," now under American patronage, refused to sign the Geneva Agreement. The elections were never held.

The reasons for the disastrous American intervention in Vietnam, which led to another two decades of slaughter, belong more to U.S. history than to Viet-nam's. Briefly put, American governments during the global Cold War were ani-mated by a rigid anticommunism that took the form, in 1954, of a deep fear of Mao's China, whose huge armies had recently confronted the United States and its allies in the Korean War (1950–1953). Washington regarded the Vietnamese communists as submissive underlings of the Chinese ones; South Vietnam was a "domino"—in the words of President Eisenhower (served 1953–1961)—whose fall to communism would lead to the collapse of Southeast Asia's other domino-like noncommunist governments. The paradox that China had been Vietnam's chief enemy over the centuries, even while it supplied the Vietnam-ese with cultural and political inspirations, was not appreciated by Washington policy-makers, who had little knowledge of Vietnamese history and even less interest in the Vietnamese as people.

Ironically, China restrained the Hanoi communists between 1954 and 1959. They did not resume what they regarded as their anticolonial war in the south until the decade's end. In 1960 the southern branch of the Viet Minh was resurrected, in the form of a patriotic coalition called the National Liberation Front (NLF), known to its enemies as the Viet Cong (an abbreviation of the terms for Vietnamese Communists), fighting a skillful guerrilla war and pursuing in the countryside tax and property distribution policies that favored the poor. By 1962 the NLF controlled or influenced—by U.S. estimates at the time—two-thirds of the south's villages. President Lyndon Johnson responded by increasing the number of American military advisers in Vietnam, then contriving, in 1964, to get Congress to pass the Tonkin Gulf Resolution, which authorized him to use "all necessary measures" in Indochina. The United States began to bomb the north systematically in 1965. Combat units were also sent to South Vietnam, the beginnings of an overt military intervention that became, by 1969, an American conscript army of 540,000 men there.

More U.S. bombing in the south, combined with ground warfare, drove much of the south's rural population into the cities as refugees, succeeding by sheer firepower in damaging the political connection between the NLF and the peasantry. In response, Giap's northern army began to come south, eventually overwhelming the previously largely southern NLF membership. In 1968 the communists launched a surprise attack—known as the Tet (lunar new year) Offensive—on the south's cities. The initial success of the offensive, gruesomely televised in millions of American living rooms, showed that there was little "light at the end of the tunnel" for this supposedly "limited" American war in Asia. But the offensive also disappointed Hanoi by failing to trigger procommunist uprisings or mass desertions by the south's army comparable to Nationalist army desertions during the Chinese civil war. Both sides therefore agreed to peace talks in Paris, which were to last for five years (1968–1973). These eventually led to a truce and to the withdrawal of American forces from Vietnam. Left to do its own fighting, in 1975 South Vietnam disintegrated during a new communist offensive and was then reunited with the north as one communist republic.

Tragically, this had also been a civil war, as the large exodus of refugees from the south after the communist victory in 1975 showed. What happened off the battlefields during the war was as important as what happened on them. Noncommunist South Vietnam's disappearance in 1975 did not just mark the end of Western colonialism; it also marked the end of a project to create a multiparty democracy in Vietnam. In 1956 the U.S. National Security Council had declared that American policy in the south must be to assist "Free Vietnam" to establish a constitutional democracy strong enough to be an attractive contrast to the communist north. In 1966, at a meeting with South Vietnam's leaders in Honolulu, President Johnson imperiously demanded that they be able to answer the questions "How have you built democracy in the rural areas? How much have you built, when and where? Give us dates, times, numbers." Johnson warned them to distinguish between promises and results or, in his language, between "high-sounding words" and "coonskins on the wall." To some degree Washington saw itself as operating in a historically virgin environment. One eminent American political scientist who was involved in this "political development" effort complained in 1968 that the main trouble with South Vietnam was that it had no organized political system at all.

The south did have a political system, but it was one in which religious sectarianism overshadowed political behavior. The Saigon rulers whom the Americans bankrolled and managed between 1954 and 1975, such as presidents Ngo Dinh Diem (1954–1963) and Nguyen Van Thieu (1967–1975), were either devoutly and ostentatiously Catholic themselves, like Diem, or depended heavily, like General Thieu (himself a Catholic convert) on the support of northern Catholics who had fled south. This was far too narrow a political base for anything like a democratic government, because most Vietnamese were still, at least residually, Buddhists.

One famous group of South Vietnamese Buddhists, linked to the An Quang temple in Saigon, responded by calling the war a battle between the "advance patrols" of "red imperialism" (Hanoi) and "white imperialism" (the Americans); Buddhists should shun both imperialisms, neither of which had mass support. Buddhist publishers issued books, like Thich Thanh Tu's 1966 treatise *Buddhism in the Life Pulse of the National People,* asserting that Vietnamese civilization itself had been created, back in the eleventh century, by great Buddhist monks like Van Hanh. The implication was that Catholic Christianity, supported by French and now American colonialists, was inorganic and antinational. Not only had French colonialism been responsible for encouraging this religious sectarianism; it had also been responsible, by its police terrorism, for generating habits of secretiveness even among noncommunist Vietnamese political parties. It was thus difficult for them to mobilize publicly large numbers of activists, even if they could rise above religious feuding. The result was fragmentation. In the early 1970s, shortly before they were repressed, South Vietnam had twenty-four political parties.

Diem hardly even paid lip service to the American hope for "constitutional democracy" in Saigon. He abolished village councils, tried to relocate grumbling peasants into large fortified villages ("strategic hamlets"), and arbitrarily arrested thousands of political prisoners, many of whom were not even communists. Diem's brother, a Catholic archbishop, publicly prophesied the end of Vietnamese Buddhism as a living religion; Diem's inept police raids on Buddhist temples in 1963, which led to monks burning themselves to death in the streets

in protest, tried to further the prophecy and ended the Americans' romance with him.

Rebellious army officers, with tacit approval from American officials, then overthrew Diem and murdered him in November 1963. For a time between 1964 and 1972, the south held real elections for National Assembly seats, in which members of the urban middle class (doctors, engineers, lawyers, professors, pharmacists) participated and experimented with coalition-building skills. The coalitions took the form of slates of allied candidates with their own pictorial symbols: lotuses, rice flowers, roosters, incense burners. Unfortunately the "khaki party" *(dang Ka Ki),* as the army came to be known, grew faster than they did, usurping civil functions and—with its careers for young men and its easy access to surplus American military hardware—making all other prospective sources of political power look irrelevant.

Finally, in 1973, President Thieu circumscribed the other political parties and switched to the model of his northern communist enemies. He created his own "Democratic Party" in which civil servants were forced to enroll; it had a Leninist-style party central committee and cadre training schools (at Vung Tau and elsewhere) for specialists in building "new life hamlets" named after medieval Vietnamese heroes. The problem with Thieu's imitative authoritarianism was that it lacked the mass support its northern adversaries in Hanoi commanded. Its hollowness meant that it had to be sustained by corruption, including the outright sale of government positions as province or district chiefs. This house of cards collapsed in 1975, yet it is understandable that since then Vietnamese refugee communities around the world have preserved a mournful remembrance of the old struggle for political freedom in the south in the late 1960s and early 1970s, or at least a sense that a historic opportunity had been missed. Equally important was their justifiable nostalgia for a South Vietnam that was also the home of a remarkably free literary culture, many of whose members fled abroad in 1975. Three women won its top literary prizes in 1970 alone, indicating something of the energies of self-emancipation that were stirring there before northern tanks rolled into Saigon.

The communist north had begun the war with the Americans as a "nervous society," the nervousness being generated by revolutionary strategies borrowed from Mao's China. The keystone of Mao's thought was the belief that purified human willpower could create a communist revolution even where the orthodox Marxist requirements for one—capitalism and an industrial working class—did not exist. But this willpower could only be purified, Mao and pro-Mao Vietnamese leaders like Truong Chinh claimed, through bullying thought reform campaigns directed against dissident intellectuals and party cadres, and a more general populist disparagement of experts and bureaucrats. In the 1950s the DRV's land reform campaign, based on Maoist stereotypes of village social classes, led to violence and to Ho Chi Minh's public denunciation of "barbaric" cadre behavior. In the early 1960s northern peasants lost their lands, being forced into agricultural cooperatives in which most land was publicly owned. Income depended on the work points party cadres awarded to each farmer, and inefficient "small producer" mentalities were supposedly eliminated.

In the end the north won the war only by abandoning Maoism and relaxing control of the land. Between 1964 and 1973 collectivized farmland actually shrank; in 1975 most cooperatives remained smaller than traditional villages, unlike the huge communes in Mao's China. The north also fought the war by means of aid from the USSR and China, which included redirected Canadian and Australian wheat imports; by the theft and domestication of the "miracle rice" crops the Americans had introduced in the south; and by a traditionalistic mass patriotism (unlike Maoist attacks on tradition in China), which American bombing only intensified. In 1967 Hanoi even approved the continued dual use of the modern solar and the premodern lunar calendar, because the latter defined traditional festivals and ritual remembrances of ancient Vietnamese heroes who had fought foreign (Chinese) invaders. Magazines celebrated the existence of an eternal Vietnamese "soul" that knew how to reconcile the use of the "sword" of struggle with the "guitar" of poetic feeling. But even here thoughtful Vietnamese Marxists had misgivings. The veteran writer and government minister Tran Huy Lieu warned on his deathbed (1969) that Hanoi's wartime promotion of Vietnamese national heroism must not degenerate into racialism or a "conservative" worship of village communitarianism. Even as the American bombs fell, the tradition of the insider critic remained intact.

Further Readings

Bradley, Mark P. *Imagining Vietnam and America: The Making of Postcolonial Vietnam, 1919–1950.* Chapel Hill, N.C., 2000.

Duiker, William. *Ho Chi Minh: A Life.* New York, 2000.

Goscha, Christopher. *Thailand and the Southeast Asian Networks of the Vietnamese Revolution, 1885–1954.* Richmond, U.K., 1998.

Huynh Kim Kanh. *Vietnamese Communism, 1925–1945.* Ithaca, 1982.

Marr, David G. *Vietnamese Tradition on Trial, 1920–1945.* Berkeley, 1981.

———. *Vietnam 1945: The Quest for Power.* Berkeley, 1995.

Ninh, Kim N. B. *A World Transformed: The Politics of Culture in Revolutionary Vietnam, 1945–1965.* Ann Arbor, 2002.

Tai, Hue-Tam Ho. *Millenarianism and Peasant Politics in Vietnam.* Cambridge, Mass., 1983.

Tonnesson, Stein. *The Vietnamese Revolution of 1945: Roosevelt, Ho Chi Minh and de Gaulle in a World at War.* London, 1991.

Turley, William S. *The Second Indochina War: A Short Political and Military History, 1954–1975.* New York, 1986.

Woodside, Alexander. *Community and Revolution in Modern Vietnam.* Boston, 1976.

Chapter 24

Siam Becomes Thailand, 1910–1973

IN GENERATIONAL terms, Siam's leaders changed much in the nineteenth and early twentieth centuries. Mongkut's generation had been one of modest change. Chulalongkorn's was one of cautious modernization. They created a third generation that began confidently to make a new nation, one that would continue to evolve over the course of the twentieth century.

New Generation, New Nation

THIS NEW GENERATION of rulers tried to remake Siam in their own image. They wore European suits, lived amidst grand pianos and printed books in houses with indoor plumbing, drank iced beverages and ate with European silver, worked with modern law, and invested in banks and businesses. Meanwhile, peasants still lived much as they had a century earlier. Some in the middle could see both sides of the modern-traditional division, especially those trained abroad. They felt they deserved a greater share of power than the existing order granted them. They expressed their commitment to modernity, to keeping up with the rest of the world, against which they constantly measured Siam and found it wanting. They wanted a unified nation enclosed within frontiers and peopled by those speaking a single language (Thai) and pledging their loyalty to a single monarch and state. Negatively, they thought their power should be directed against divisions remaining within the nation and against the injustice they felt their country had suffered and continued to suffer at the hands of the imperialist West.

The ideas of the "new men" of the 1910s were shaped by the acceptance of the West that Chulalongkorn had forced upon them, and they saw more clearly than either their royal patrons or the peasantry the problems of unfinished business and incomplete change that still faced their nation. Politically, they felt Siam's most serious problem to be the distribution of political power and specifically the relationship of the absolute monarchy to political interests in the bureaucracy. Economically, Siam's Chinese minority, which occupied a commanding position in the economic life of the country by 1910, was increasingly seen as an alien presence. The power of the Chinese was demonstrated in a strike in 1910 against paying the same tax rate as the Siamese. The local reaction against such Chinese "materialism" and un-Siamese behavior was negative.

Buddhism helped to hold society together. The Dhammayut sect was an intellectual movement within Buddhism based on rationalism, universalism, and study of the Buddhist scriptures. It created a tradition that reflected, its followers believed, the essential values of Buddhism rather than inherited local patterns. Within this framework, believers could accommodate modern science and a broader world. The sect soon expanded into the provinces, Laos, and Cambodia. Though it remained a minority movement within Siamese Buddhism, it was active and influential from the 1880s onward. Under the leadership of Prince Wachirayan Warorot, it was an important force for modernization, as it organized provincial schools and created a national ecclesiastical hierarchy in the decade following 1898. A Dhammayut monk was the only public opponent of Siamese entry into World War I. Others, in sermons and writings, were influential in giving Siamese Buddhism an intellectual strength that weathered the general acceptance of modern science and Western ideas.

Siamese secular culture, however, remained threatened by the widespread influence of European ideas. It was some decades before the elite was sure that its language would remain strong against foreign words, coining new words from Sanskrit roots for this purpose, or that Siamese literature could hold its rightful place in the minds of the people. It was only in the reign of Vajiravudh, Chulalongkorn's son, that such problems and fears were tackled head-on.

King Vajiravudh (r. 1910–1925) was educated at Oxford University and committed to ideas similar to those of others of his generation. A prolific writer, he promoted those ideas on the stage and in the public press through voluminous writings, numbering well over two hundred pieces, which ranged from translations of Shakespeare and Molière to political essays directed against the Chinese ("The Jews of the East") and Germany during World War I ("Freedom of the Seas"). Through several organizations he founded and headed, the Wild Tiger Corps (an adult paramilitary movement), the Boy Scouts, the Royal

Navy League, and his dramatic and literary groups, the king was a vocal advocate of cultural nationalism and its most effective propagandist.

Vajiravudh, however, was a poor politician. Anxious to escape the domination of his father's generation, he had forced all but one of Chulalongkorn's ministers from office by 1915 and surrounded himself with a government made up of his personal favorites, most of them from nonroyal families and many of them younger men educated abroad. Personal alliances and favoritism shaped many of his choices, and his lack of interest in administration left them beyond his direct control. He thereby alienated many. The Wild Tiger Corps in particular was the king's private army, and it sorely antagonized the regular army.

An early reaction against Vajiravudh came in 1912, when a group of junior military officers planned a coup against the king. They were reacting against the incomplete modernization of the administration, its inattention to the countryside, the degree to which personal relationships still governed administrative acts, and the low moral caliber of many around them. Their ideas had been shaped partly by the Russo-Japanese War of 1905 and the Chinese Revolution of 1911, from which they gained both a sense of their own national identity and a sense of shame in comparing their country with more advanced Asian and Western nations. Quietly subverting military posts in the Bangkok area and upcountry, they planned to carry out a revolution at the annual oath of allegiance ceremony in April 1912. Their activities were, however, uncovered in February, and ninety-one men were arrested and given prison sentences ranging from twelve years to life.

It is possible that another military coup was forestalled in mid-1917, when there was a wave of arrests in the army at the time Siam entered World War I on the side of the Allies, but it is more likely that those events simply reflected internal army politics. In any case, by participating in World War I, the kingdom gained a voice at Versailles and sufficient diplomatic momentum to end, by 1925–1926, extraterritoriality and all but a few clauses of the unequal treaties.

When Vajiravudh died without male heir in 1925, he was succeeded by a younger brother, King Prajadhipok (r. 1925–1935), who had never expected to become king and was unprepared for his new tasks. While he had strong liberal-democratic sentiments, he had neither the personal nor the political power to put them into action. His government was one in which Chulalongkorn's generation enjoyed a return to power at the expense of the younger nonroyal men Vajiravudh had favored. Unlike his elder brother, Prajadhipok made regular use of advisory councils composed of princes and high officials, and he seriously considered turning them gradually into a parliament. He was dissuaded by his uncles, the more easily because popular demand for representative government was not strong.

Demand for political change existed, however, even without popular channels for its expression. The kingdom long had been building a new elite of civil administrators, professionals, and soldiers. Their upward movement in society and government had been constant and satisfying, but it was reversed during Prajadhipok's reign, when many princes were returned to high office and when promotions and salary increases were held back at a time of retrenchment in the late 1920s. The world depression helped to reawaken sentiments expressed in the unsuccessful rebellion of 1912. A few radicals had been organizing for some years, beginning when they were studying in Europe. The royalist tone of Prajadhipok's reign made many more receptive to the idea of revolution against the absolute monarchy: young military officers deprived of promotions, students returned from training abroad to find jobs not up to their expectations, and older men no longer so certain about the dignity and generosity of the monarchy. Younger radicals and older moderates joined together to plan and execute a bloodless revolution on 24 June 1932, while the king was out of Bangkok.

After the government had been taken over by the "People's Party," they asserted their Western political ideas in a letter to the king asking that he submit to a constitution and in another letter to the general public explaining their actions. The early republicanism of some civilian members of the group was soon muted so that the group's leaders might bring in senior civil officials from the old regime favorable to their cause. The balance of power remained unmistakably in the hands of the People's Party when a constitution was inaugurated in December 1932. The radical wing of the party, led by Luang Pradit Manutham (Pridi Phanomyong), a university law lecturer, made a brief attempt to carry out the early ideals of the coup in an economic plan of March 1933, but the king and some conservative nobles moved against them, forcing Pridi from office and muting the voice of the radicals. A few months later, in June, the military staged another coup to install their own man, Phraya Phahon (Phot Phahonyothin), as prime minister. When a royalist countercoup led by Prince Boworadet failed bloodily in October, the military group was left firmly in control, having defeated all its rivals, left and right—Pridi's civilian radicals, the conservative civilians, and the royalists. Their success was confirmed with the abdication of King Prajadhipok in 1935 and with the accession of a boy-king, Ananda, then still at school in Switzerland.

The increasing prominence of the military stemmed primarily from the advantages of military organization, which helped the army to maintain strong hierarchical and personal (patron-client) relationships while promoting cohesive and modern values. Military men were much better organized than their competitors, had been less exposed to the West, and were somewhat more conservative and formalistic in their approach. The civilians, who were unable to unite and lacked physical force, were more willing to see radical change. Their numbers were small, and they were distributed in small pockets through the society of the capital, while the military was neatly organized in a single hierarchy. Together, the two elements constituted the young elite of the society. Peasants and townspeople expected them to act as "big men"—government was their business, not the public's. When these men began to talk directly to the peasant in the language of equality, on new radios and through the press, it took time for some people to realize that the game of politics had really changed— that it was now about "us" and not simply "them."

In the new constitutional regime, power was concentrated in the hands of the members of the People's Party, who maintained their primacy through an appointive monopoly in the assembly and the cabinet. Indirect elections in 1933 and 1937 gave the assembly a half-elected membership, keeping the pressure on the government to fulfill its liberal program and to maintain its democratic ideals. The government made progress in social welfare, in education and public health, and in economic affairs. Universal compulsory primary education was extended throughout the kingdom. The government was particularly sensitive to the impact of its taxation policies on the village, making efforts to reduce taxes when economic conditions were poor. In return, they got the support of the elected members for military budgets, which the army justified first in terms of internal threats and later by external ambitions and fears. From mid-1933 to the end of 1938, Phraya Phahon steered the government along a course that was moderate and progressive. His government finally fell in December 1938, when the elected members of the assembly carried out a vote of no confidence. Luang Phibun Songkhram, a colonel popular in the army for his strong championing of its cause and more widely for his role in breaking the royalist forces in 1933, came to power. He was a vigorous exponent of Thai—not just Siamese—nationalism, and the choice of the ruling group.

Phibun's first government (1938–1944) has to be seen in terms of the global political environment. The prestige of the Western democracies was low, and the capacity of Western ideas and values to solve grave economic crises and to survive international strife seemed spent, so assertive and militarized states such as Japan were attractive to the people of Siam. Thus politics took a turn to the right, with glorification of the army, assertion of national values, and strong attacks on Western culture, Western imperialism, the Chinese position in the Siamese economy, and the regime's own critics. Siam carefully cultivated relations with Japan, establishing strong economic and political ties with it. Once France had fallen to German armies in June 1940, Phibun stepped up pressure on French Indochina with territorial claims (associated with a pan-Thai movement best expressed in the 1939 change of the name of the kingdom to "Thailand"). This led to full-scale war with France in 1940–1941. The war was popular in Thailand but ended with Japanese mediation and with the cession to Thailand of western Cambodia and some Lao territories. Phibun's government was undoubtedly strengthened by the outcome of the war, but he found himself more heavily dependent on Japan's aid than he had anticipated. The limits of

Thai military power were now as clear as the real predominance of Japan in Southeast Asia.

World War and Cold War

WHEN ON 8 December 1941 Japanese forces suddenly disembarked at six points along the coast of peninsular Thailand, crossed into the country from Cambodia, and landed at the airfield near Bangkok, they met with the strong resistance of local Thai garrisons. Nevertheless, Phibun could only capitulate and join Japan. There were, after all, some national goals that could be served in the process. Although Phibun agreed to declare war on the American and British governments, it was not Thailand's affair: the war was between Japan and the West. With two such ponderous elephants fighting, the ant of Thailand scurried to avoid being crushed.

Thailand's wartime collaboration with the Japanese was useful only while Japan's power was paramount. It spared Thailand extensive damage and left the power of its government unimpaired. When the war turned against Japan, however, Thai policy had to change. In August 1944 the National Assembly forced Phibun's government to resign and installed a government led by a civilian politician, Khuang Aphaiwong, and covertly directed by Pridi Phanomyong. Since early in the war, Pridi had acted as regent for the absent boy-king Ananda Mahidol, organizing from his office an underground resistance against the Japanese, the Free Thai Movement, which was supported by Britain and America. Those connections were used to gain the good graces of the Allies, especially when some Thai offered to mount an uprising against the Japanese in May 1945, an offer then rejected.

When the war ended in August, the gravity of Thailand's international position was exposed by the victorious Allies. Thailand then held Lao and Cambodian territories annexed after the Indochina War of 1940–1941 as well as four states of northern Malaya and two Shan states of Burma granted them by the Japanese in 1943. Britain attempted to impose what amounted to a protectorate over Thailand by advancing a long list of demands, which would have established controls over the Thai economy, government, and army, and required that Thailand furnish the Allies 1.5 million tons of free rice "as a special measure of reconcilement and aid by Thailand toward those who had suffered because of Thai denial of rice exports during the war years." With strong American diplomatic pressure mobilized by the new prime minister, Seni Pramoj (the wartime ambassador to the United States, who had personally decided not to inform the American government officially of Thailand's declaration of war), the most extreme demands were moderated, but Thailand still had to agree to furnish the Allies rice at low fixed prices. French demands for the retrocession of Lao and Cambodian territories were even more strongly resisted, but it was the minimum price the French charged for allowing Thailand admission to the United Nations. After signing treaties with Britain and France, Thailand joined the United Nations in December 1946, early expressing a pro-Western foreign policy.

Postwar politics were influenced by external affairs. The army was at least temporarily discredited by its association with Japan (although it had never fought the Allies after the 1940–1941 Indochina War). Allied willingness to settle claims on terms favorable to Thailand was aided by a resurgence of parliamentary democracy. A constitution introducing an elective legislature began in 1946, when Pridi became prime minister. Economic dislocation and the problems of inflation and corruption were more than he could manage. Pridi was forced from office in the aftermath of the unexplained sudden death by gunshot of King Ananda on 9 June 1946, an event for which public opinion held him accountable. Thawan Thamrongnawasawat, who succeeded him, lacked the following that would have made effective government possible. An army conspiracy seized power in 1947 and established a nominally independent civil government under Khuang. The army was reluctant to show its full presence as long as Western disapproval threatened, but Western distrust of military rule began to lessen in mid-1948, when other countries of the region were beset by communist insurrection. At that point, Field Marshal Phibun again became prime minister.

At first, parliamentary government remained. The civilian politicians, however, were divided. Pridi's radicals were in disrepute as the investigation of Ananda's death dragged on, while the Democrat Party, led by Khuang, resented its exclusion from real power. The army itself was divided, and younger officers were still distrustful of Phibun. The government needed foreign support but was anxious not to incur American disapproval by establishing direct military rule. Phibun gradually won a substantial measure of American support when he committed Thai troops in Korea and kept Thailand relatively stable. Four abortive military coups between 1948 and 1951 reduced Phibun's rivals to two men: General Phao Siyanon, director general of the paramilitary police, and General Sarit Thanarat, who commanded the First Army in Bangkok. Caught between his two rivals as well as between them and the parliament, Phibun saw his grip on power begin to fail in the early 1950s.

Viet Minh successes in Indochina in 1953–1954 and the possibility of communist regimes in Cambodia and Laos made the government receptive to the efforts of the American secretary of state, John Foster Dulles, to bolster the region's military security by organizing the Southeast Asia Treaty Organization (SEATO) in 1954. General Phao's arbitrary acts of imprisonment of government opponents, together with rampant official corruption, brought the government under increasing attack. Phibun visited Europe and America in 1955 and returned enthusiastic about the possibilities of democratization. He legalized political parties and lifted press censorship in preparation for general elections early in 1957. A massive government party pledged to Phibun conducted an intense campaign managed by Phao, while the major opposition came from the weak Democrat Party and smaller leftist parties in the northeast, the most desperately poor region in Thailand. Despite electoral corruption, the government could win only a bare majority of the seats in the election. Sarit, who ostentatiously avoided full participation in the campaign and election, and criticized its outcome, became the focal point of agitation against the conduct of the elections, and on 16 September 1957 he led a bloodless coup d'état, which ended the long political career of Phibun.

The government inaugurated after elections in December 1957 had only a short life. The parliament reflected the divisions stemming from personal feuds, disparate ideological and economic interests, and the clash of traditional and modern political styles and outlooks within Thailand's urban elite. When the new government proved in the army's eyes incapable of acting decisively on the many domestic and international policy problems facing it, Sarit returned from medical treatment abroad to reimpose military rule in October 1958. Sarit commanded political support on a national base much broader than that of his predecessors. He was respected throughout the armed forces as well as by conservatives in the civil service and business, and he raised many professional civil servants to prominent positions in the government. He moved firmly against the radical opposition, especially the Communist Party of Thailand. At the same time he attempted to minimize its appeal by embarking on policies of economic development, welfare, and education. Not so antimonarchical as members of the generation that had ended the absolute monarchy in 1932, he encouraged King Bhumibol Adulyadej to play a stronger role in public life. Promulgating an authoritarian interim constitution based on those of Gaullist France and Nasser's United Arab Republic, he appointed a Constituent Assembly to draft a permanent constitution.

By the time of Sarit's premature death at the end of 1963, the era of the Vietnam War was beginning, and the forces set in motion by that conflict worked to change Thailand. Since the end of World War II, Thailand's security concerns had focused on the states of former French Indochina. The resurgence of Vietnam awakened Thai fears for Thailand's eastern frontiers, especially as the Viet Minh and its successor in Hanoi were seen to be strategically interested in the whole of Indochina, not just Vietnam. Naturally, the Thai army, which had been the main proponent of pan-Thai nationalism in the Indochina War of 1940–1941, was acutely aware of the dangers of Vietnamese encroachments on the sovereignty and territory of Laos and Cambodia, particularly as Thailand's natural defense perimeter (as opposed to its borders) is not the Mekong River, which is a highway, but rather the chain of mountains that divides Vietnam from the rest of the Southeast Asia mainland. Thus the Thai government was anxious about the "neutralism" of Cambodia in Sihanouk's time and took a strong interest in events in Laos, where it early supported rightist military factions. Thai disquiet over the inability of SEATO to act in the Laos crisis of 1960–1962 and over the outcome of the Geneva Conference of 1962, which established a neutralist government in Laos, led to secret agreements with the Americans providing for a U.S. commitment to Thailand's defense. Thailand became deeply involved in the Vietnam conflict, to the point of providing air bases from which Indochina could be bombed and sending troops to fight in South Vietnam and Laos.

The impact of the Vietnam War on Thailand was much more than military: it was also economic and social, and ultimately its effects were political as well. American spending in Thailand was enormous, amounting to several hundred million dollars. Forty thousand U.S. military personnel stationed in Thailand spent lavishly; and servicemen on "rest and recreation" (R & R) leaves from Vietnam spawned a thriving service sector (hotels, prostitution, bars, and nightclubs) in the Thai economy. High-rise hotels and office buildings interrupted the Bangkok skyline, dwarfing the spires of Buddhist monasteries, and the population of the city mushroomed from 1.7 million in 1960 to almost 3 million by 1975.

Furthermore, the countryside shared in the city's prosperity. Upcountry air bases stimulated the growth of nearby towns like Udon Thani, Nakhon Ratchasima (Khorat), and Phitsanulok. Rail service extended to serve provincial military needs, and roads improved to open military access to border areas could also carry farmers' produce to market. The result was impressive economic growth, which by the late 1960s was running at an annual rate in excess of 7 percent.

The triumphs of Sarit and his successor, Thanom Kittikachorn, were not accompanied by the political stability at which they had aimed. A generation earlier, in the 1940s and early 1950s, Phibun had worried about Thailand's Chinese minority, numbering in excess of two million, particularly when Pridi took up exile in communist China and became the leader of a "Thai Patriotic Front" and when the membership of the Communist Party of Thailand was composed mostly of ethnic Chinese. By the 1960s, however, most Thai Chinese were well along the road to assimilation, and the military rulers of the kingdom now feared political discontent and rural revolution like that which they could see occurring in Indochina. In particular, the impoverished northeast, with an ethnic minority akin to the Lao numbering more than ten million, was of major concern to the government. Sarit—himself a northeasterner—began a program of economic development in the northeast, promoting agricultural production; the building of roads, wells, and irrigation systems; and the expansion of educational opportunities. The government's approach to ruling was to buy political acquiescence with social and economic improvements. They could point to statistics and congratulate themselves—and yet the challenges to their domi-nance steadily mounted. By the late 1960s, they faced rural insurgency in the northeast, north, and south, led by a Communist Party that was now predomi-nantly ethnic Thai in its composition (though its leadership remained Chinese).

To repair its political support in the cities, where economic growth and educational opportunities had enlarged the middle class, the government promulgated a new constitution in 1968, providing for an elected lower house of parliament. Elections held early in 1969 initiated a brief period of demo-cratic relaxation before Thanom again stepped in to reinstitute military rule in late 1971, motivated perhaps by a deteriorating situation in Indochina and the beginnings of an American withdrawal from the region that would leave Thai-land to face heightened dangers alone. In this situation the dashing of demo-cratic hopes worked against the military. Student unrest, building in Thailand as elsewhere in the world through the late 1960s, grew until hundreds of thou-sands demonstrated in the streets of Bangkok in October 1973, erupting into violence. Leading figures within the military and police refused to send troops against crowds of youthful demonstrators that included their own sons and daughters, and Thanom and his close associates were forced to flee the country, yielding power to a civilian government. Here, perhaps, was the closest thing Thailand had ever had to a "revolution," for it was mass power mobilized on a far greater scale than any Thai had seen before.

Its immediate objective—the end to authoritarian military rule—was far easier to achieve than the students' long-term goal, the institution of that democratic government that had been talked about, but seldom seen, in Thai-land since 1932. Over the next few years, Thailand experienced democracy of the most thoroughgoing sort, with a frenetic anarchy of political parties, demonstrations, strikes, debates, activism, and turmoil. All shades of political commitment were expressed, from communism to monarchism. Students organized to study the economic plight of rice farmers or to assist striking fac-tory workers, and youth everywhere challenged the privileged, the established, the taken-for-granted. The political Left came out into the open, and the Right, increasingly alarmed, counterattacked. Tempers and violence escalated as a society that a few years earlier had been thought placid was now shown to be riven with cleavages between rich and poor, city and countryside, management and labor, monarchist and anarchist, revolutionary and conservative.

Further Readings

Batson, Benjamin A. *The End of the Absolute Monarchy in Siam*. Singapore, 1984.

Fineman, Daniel. *A Special Relationship: The United States and Military Government in Thai-land, 1947–1958*. Honolulu, 1997.

Greene, Stephen L. W. *Absolute Dreams: Thai Government under Rama VI, 1910–1925.* Bangkok, 1999.

Kamala Tiyavanich. *Forest Recollections: Wandering Monks in Twentieth-Century Thailand.* Honolulu, 1997.

Kobkua Suwannathat-Pian. *Thailand's Durable Premier: Phibun through Three Decades, 1932–1957.* Kuala Lumpur, 1995.

Muscat, Robert J. *The Fifth Tiger: A Study of Thai Development Policy.* Helsinki, 1994.

Pasuk Phongpaichit and Chris Baker. *Thailand: Economy and Politics.* Kuala Lumpur, 1995.

Suchit Bunbongkarn. *The Military in Thai Politics 1981–86.* Singapore, 1987.

Wyatt, David K. *Siam in Mind.* Chiang Mai, 2002.

———. *Thailand: A Short History.* 2d ed. New Haven, 2003.

Chapter 25

Cambodia, 1884–1975

ALTHOUGH the colonial era in Cambodia was relatively peaceful, when compared to Burma, Vietnam, and parts of Indonesia, the French encountered serious resistance to their rule in early 1885, when a nationwide rebellion broke out in response to the harsh treaty imposed on King Norodom in the preceding year. In terms of motivation, leadership, and momentum, the revolt resembled the one that broke out in Burma against the British two years later. For a year and a half, the rebellion tied down over four thousand French and Vietnamese troops at a time when France was stretched thin elsewhere in Indochina.

With some justice, the French suspected King Norodom of supporting the rebellion. To rally local support, they called on Norodom's younger brother, Sisowath, who displayed an almost fawning loyalty to France in putting down the revolt. Sisowath probably expected to be awarded the throne for his collaboration, but as the rebellion wore on, the French had to turn back to Norodom to pacify the rebels. In June 1886 the king proclaimed that if the insurgents laid down their arms, France would continue to respect Cambodian "laws and customs"— especially those affecting the patronage networks established by powerful officials, sometimes referred to as "slavery" by the French. Faced with the possibility of a drawn-out war, the French stepped back from the more intrusive of their reforms, which did not come fully into effect until Norodom was dead.

Colonialism and Nationalism

THE REBELLION taught the French to be cautious, but their "civilizing mission" in Cambodia remained the same. Like the Vietnamese in the 1830s and 1840s, they still sought to rationalize Cambodian government, to lessen the king's privileges and power, to instill their own values among the elite, and to gain sufficient revenue from taxes and customs duties to pay for their administration. To accomplish these objectives, they surrounded the increasingly powerless king with pro-French advisers drawn in large part from the small corps of interpreters they had trained in the 1870s.

In the 1890s French control of Cambodia increased inexorably, without significantly altering the patterns of Cambodian elite culture or affecting rural life. In 1892 the French began collecting taxes directly from the population. Two years later, French *résidents* were installed in all Cambodian provinces. Despite the intensification of French control, the countryside, where nine out of ten Cambodians lived, remained a mystery to all but the handful of Frenchmen who ventured outside the towns and were fluent in Khmer.

Many important, poorly documented changes were taking place. By the end of the century, for example, Cambodian farmers, like their counterparts in southern Vietnam, Burma, and Siam, had found overseas markets for their rice. Chinese immigrants played a key role in purchasing and exporting the Cambodian crop surplus. Cities and towns sprang up in response to these markets and to French administrative demands. With a prolonged period of peace, the population rose rapidly. Perched atop the society, the French froze what they called "Cambodge"—the king, the elite, and the rural poor—in place, protecting them not only from their neighbors but also from the perils of modernization, politics, or independence. Day-to-day administration and commerce fell to immigrants from Vietnam and China.

After the 1884–1886 rebellion, France's relatively benign rule met almost no resistance. Nonetheless, until the 1920s most French officials had no idea how many people lived in Cambodia or who had title to land. More important, they had no clear idea of what was going on in people's heads. As a French *résident* noted in the 1920s, "It is permissible to ask if the unvarying calm that the [Cambodian] people continue to display is not merely an external appearance, covering up vague, unexpressed feelings . . . whose exact nature we cannot perceive." French officials could argue, for their part, that they were paid to administer, not to understand, the country.

Beneath the surface, conditions for most Cambodians were grim. Although "slavery" had been officially abolished, servitude for debts, amounting to the same thing, was widespread and often lasted a lifetime. Health care and secular education were almost nonexistent. Most Cambodians were illiterate and died young. Bandits who preyed on rural populations were seldom caught. What French romantic writers sometimes depicted as a premodern paradise was in fact a poor, sad, and dangerous place for most of the people who lived in it.

After Norodom died in 1904, the piecemeal modernization of his kingdom proceeded under the new monarch, who seemed amenable to change as long as his own interests were taken care of. Sisowath came to the throne at the age of sixty-four. For roughly half his life he had feuded with Norodom and worked to please the French, who repaid him with lavish gifts, including a new palace, a steam yacht, and an allowance of 113 kilograms (249 pounds) of top-grade opium per year.

In 1906 Sisowath made a state visit to France, accompanied by the palace dance troupe and members of his entourage. He was cheered wherever he went and seemed to enjoy his stay, which coincided with Franco-Siamese negotiations that culminated, after his return, in the return of the provinces of Battambang and Siem Reap. Over the next half century, Battambang became Cambodia's leading producer of rice. Siem Reap, housing the ruins of Angkor, became associated with a backward-looking Khmer national identity—a phenomenon some have called "ethnostalgia"—that coincided with French ideas about the country and caused no trouble for the administration.

Two events in Sisowath's reign, however, suggested that violence could break out if the French overstepped the boundaries they had so carefully constructed between themselves and the population. In 1916 massive demonstrations were staged in eastern Cambodia in response to heavy new taxes imposed by France to help defray the costs of World War I. In the process several Cambodian tax collectors were killed. The demonstrations only broke up after Sisowath toured the dissident areas by automobile and promised that the new taxes would be reduced. Nine years later, Khmer villagers in Kompong Chhnang beat a French *résident,* Félix Bardez, to death when he broke into a village New Year's celebration to demand that the villagers remit back taxes. The Bardez affair was soon forgotten, although the French writer André Malraux, who attended the trial of the villagers in Phnom Penh, used the occasion to lampoon colonialism in Indochina; only in the 1970s did the Cambodian scholar Dik Kean reclaim it as a precursor of Cambodian nationalism.

Two years later, Sisowath died at eighty-seven. In his lifetime, he had seen Cambodia "protected" by a succession of foreign powers. The popular old man, who was active in supporting Buddhist constructions throughout the kingdom, had also seen Cambodian culture and identity remain remarkably intact. The king died in the midst of an economic boom that affected all of Indochina. In Cambodia the greatest beneficiaries were the firms engaged in the export of rice and the newly opened French rubber plantations in Kompong Cham. Funds generated by a widening tax base were diverted into public works that included the beautification of Phnom Penh, the electrification of provincial towns, extensive road construction, and the establishment of a railway linking Phnom Penh with the Siamese border.

Under Sisowath's son, Sisowath Monivong (r. 1927–1941), who had served briefly in the French army, the pace of modernization accelerated and the stirrings of Cambodian nationalism began to be felt. In Phnom Penh the French-sponsored Buddhist Institute, founded in 1930, and the Lycée Sisowath, founded six years later, were gathering places for young Khmer interested in modernization and reform. A mildly nationalistic Cambodian language weekly, *Nagara Vatta* (Angkor Wat), began publication in 1936 and opened a peaceable conversation between the French and their allegedly "dormant" clientele as well as among the Cambodian elite. The paper also gave thousands of Cambodians a chance for the first time to read about events in the outside world in their own language.

In the late 1930s French administrators referred to Cambodia's economic advances and the increased participation by Khmer in the colonial administration as an "awakening." Until the outbreak of World War II, however, Cambodia's elite, small compared to most of its counterparts elsewhere in Southeast Asia, was relatively docile. Nothing that has survived in print (except, perhaps, an underlying anti-Vietnamese bias) seems to foreshadow the wars and chaos of the 1970s.

The period between June 1940 and October 1945, however, must be seen as a watershed in Cambodian history. French policies in the kingdom sprang from weakness. Cambodian responses to them differed sharply from what had gone before. By the end of 1945, Cambodian independence, impracticable and almost unthought of before 1939, had become just a matter of time.

During World War II Indochina differed from the rest of Southeast Asia in that France was the only colonial power in the region to retain control of its possessions for the greater part of the period. French autonomy was restricted after August 1941, when Japan stationed tens of thousands of troops in Indochina, with French acquiescence. Elsewhere in Southeast Asia, the Japanese jailed colonial officials and encouraged local nationalists, in some cases released from prison, to establish quasi-independent regimes. In Cambodia, in contrast, as throughout Indochina, the French sought to defuse nationalist activity by increasing police surveillance, opening the upper ranks of the administration to local people, and liberalizing some of their policies. Through this mixture of harshness and compromise, France hoped to endure the war and reemerge, regardless of who won, with some of its identity and its colonial empire intact.

In late 1940, after a brief, indecisive war with Thailand (as Siam had been recently renamed), France was forced to cede most of Battambang and parts of Siem Reap to the Thai. (Under intense international pressure, the provinces were to revert to Cambodia in 1946.) This humiliation seems to have hastened the death of King Monivong in April 1941. For the last few weeks of his reign, the king refused to meet with French officials or to converse with anyone in French.

Faced with an unexpected dynastic crisis, the governor-general of French Indochina, Admiral Jean Decoux, sidestepped Monivong's eldest son, the most likely candidate for the throne, and selected the former king's grandson, Norodom Sihanouk (1922–), then a *lycée* student in Saigon, for the honor. Decoux counted on this timid and studious eighteen-year-old to be a pliable instrument of French policies, which proved to be the case for several years. He never suspected that his choice would dominate Cambodian political life for the rest of the twentieth century.

The (First) Rise and Fall of Norodom Sihanouk

FRENCH POLICIES throughout Indochina became a dead letter on 9 March 1945, when the Japanese interned French officials throughout the colony and told local rulers, including King Sihanouk, that their "countries" were now independent. The Japanese move was intended to forestall French armed resistance to the Japanese and also fit into Japanese plans to form and equip local forces to resist Allied landings in the region. In the seven-months' interregnum between March and October 1945, when the French returned in force, Cambodian leaders toyed with notions of independence, and hundreds of young men joined a green-shirted, Japanese-sponsored militia. Some Khmer nationalists were tempted to ally themselves with the anti-French forces, dominated by the Indochina Communist Party, that had sprung to life in neighboring Vietnam. Others were encouraged by anticolonial factions in the Thai political elite, who financed a Cambodian independence movement calling itself the Free Khmer, or Khmer Issarak.

In early 1946 the French signed an agreement with Cambodian officials, led by Sihanouk's maternal uncle, Prince Sisowath Monireth. The document permitted the Khmer to draw up a constitution and form political parties but was vague about independence. Two important parties almost immediately took shape, both headed by minor members of the royal family. The larger one, the Democrats, drew support from the middle ranks of the bureaucracy, educated young people, and the Buddhist monastic order. Many of its followers had been drawn into politics by the events of 1945. The Liberal Party, secretly financed by the French, was predictably less independence-minded.

The Democrats captured two-thirds of the seats in the consultative assembly that was elected to draft a constitution in 1946. The document, modeled on its counterpart in France, called for a strong legislature and envisaged the king, like the president of France, as playing a ceremonial role. In elections for a National Assembly in 1947, the Democrats again won two-thirds of the seats.

A third election in 1951 returned the Democrats to office with a reduced majority. Ironically these three referenda, monitored by colonial police, were arguably the only free, fair, and pluralistic elections to be held in Cambodia before 1993.

In early 1951 the Vietnamese communists, seeking Khmer support for their fighting in southern Vietnam, secretly formed a Cambodian Communist Party in the eastern part of the country, led by Vietnamese-speaking Khmer. Some young men drawn into the movement, including Chea Sim and Heng Samrin, were to reemerge as senior figures in the pro-Vietnamese government that took power in Cambodia in 1979.

Between 1947 and 1952, meanwhile, the Democrats presided over a series of governments that were powerless to act against the French, who controlled Cambodia's purse strings, defense, and foreign relations. Democrat leaders often quarreled with the king, who resented their popularity and was encouraged by the French to harbor political ambitions of his own. In 1952 Sihanouk dissolved the National Assembly and began to govern by decree. His peremptory move angered many Cambodians then studying in France, and a few of them, including Saloth Sar (later known by his revolutionary pseudonym, Pol Pot), joined the French Communist Party before returning home.

Buoyed up by his popularity and self-confidence, and dissatisfied with the pace of French concessions, Sihanouk embarked on what he called a royal crusade for independence. Calling attention to France's foot-dragging tactics, the king made provocative speeches while traveling abroad in 1953 and threatened to arm the Cambodian population. He was aided in his efforts by the deteriorating military situation in Cambodia. By mid-1953 almost half of Cambodia was controlled by communist-led insurgents operating under Vietnamese supervision. In November the French caved in and granted Cambodia its independence, though with the king's permission they continued to fight insurgents on Cambodian territory.

At the Geneva Conference in 1954, Cambodia resisted pressure from China and the Vietnamese to allow communist-led guerrillas to regroup in Cambodian territory. Agreements reached at the conference required Cambodia to conduct national elections before the end of 1955, coinciding with the three-year time limit Sihanouk had placed on his crusade. Fearful of the Democrats and inspired by what he saw as his "mandate" to run the country, Sihanouk set in motion a shrewd three-act scenario that by the end of 1955 had placed him fully in command of his kingdom.

First, he staged a referendum on his crusade for independence. One ballot, colored white, bore his picture and the word for "yes." The other was black with "no" inscribed on it. Balloting was open, and nearly a million citizens handed white ballots to the government officials who staffed the voting tables. Fewer than two thousand had the temerity to oppose the king.

After toying with the idea of altering the constitution so as to increase his powers, Sihanouk suddenly abdicated the throne and became a "private citizen," while retaining princely rank. Later Sihanouk called this action his "atomic bomb." He allowed the monarchy to survive by placing his father, Prince Norodom Suramarit, an affable bureaucrat, on the throne. Suramarit reigned until his death in 1960. The monarchy fell into abeyance at that point only to be revived thirty-two years later, when Sihanouk, who had single-handedly destroyed the institution, resumed the throne.

Sihanouk's final move was to assume the leadership of a recently formed national political movement, the Sangkum Reastr Niyum, usually translated as People's Socialist Community, which was designed to obliterate and overshadow existing political parties. The statutes of the party were optimistic, claiming that the Sangkum would "attain the aspirations of the Little People, the real people of the Kingdom, whom we love." In the October 1955 elections, marked by widespread violence and fraud, Sangkum candidates, all handpicked by the prince, captured over 80 percent of the roughly one million votes cast and all the seats in the National Assembly. Official statistics gave the Democrats 12 percent of the vote and the pro-communist People's Group another 4 percent.

The 1955 elections ended pluralist politics in Cambodia for the duration of the so-called Sihanouk era, which extended to 1970. The resentment of the Democrats and of pro-communist candidates and voters who had been brutalized by Sihanouk's police strengthened radical and often clandestine opposition to the prince. This opposition, in turn, contributed to Sihanouk's eventual fall from power and foreshadowed the rough and tumble electoral politics of Cambodia in the 1990s.

For the time being, however, Sihanouk basked in overwhelming popular support. For the next fifteen years, he stifled political opposition, controlled the media, quarreled with the leaders of Thailand and Vietnam, scorned the United States, and expanded Cambodia's educational facilities. In his speeches and writings, Sihanouk stressed Cambodia's past greatness, its high status in the developing world, and his own indispensability. He saw himself as a world statesman and identified himself with Cambodia. He also identified himself, as no previous ruler had done, with Cambodia's rural poor, whom he called his children and his "little people." His neutralist foreign policy, which was both risky and courageous, aimed to preserve Cambodia's freedom of maneuver in the smothering context of the Cold War. The policy earned him the enmity of the pro-American regimes in Bangkok and Saigon, whose plots to overthrow him in 1958 and 1959 were unsuccessful.

Sihanouk's popularity, his generally pro-communist foreign policy, and his police hamstrung Cambodia's clandestine communist movement, led by Saloth Sar, who had returned from France in 1953. Sar was driven into exile in Vietnam in 1963, returning three years later to establish secret bases in Cambodia's forested northeast. For the next nine years, he and a handful of associates perfected radical plans for uprooting most Cambodian institutions and empowering the rural poor. These ideas took effect almost immediately after the communists came to power in 1975.

Sihanouk's popularity seems to have peaked around 1962, before the effects of his haphazard economic policies, the ineptitude of his entourage, and his indifference to advice—to name only three factors—became fully known. Sangkum electoral victories in 1958 and 1962, with slates of candidates selected by the prince, suggested that "Prince Papa," as Sihanouk styled himself, was totally in command, but serious pressures against his rule were building up. An expanding, better-educated population began to press on Cambodia's fragile institutions in search of employment. Because of its isolation from its neighbors, Cambodia failed to benefit from the economic boom that accompanied the Vietnam War. Moreover, by 1965 tens of thousands of Vietnamese communist troops were stationed, with Sihanouk's approval, on Cambodian soil. They paid high prices for Cambodian crops, reducing government revenue normally earned from export taxes.

In 1966 Sihanouk opened up the National Assembly elections to allow Sangkum candidates to compete against each other in electorates. The result was a more representative assembly that owed little allegiance to the prince. By then, hundreds of radical students, teachers, disaffected young men and women, and discontented farmers were becoming susceptible to communist ideas. Many Sino-Khmer, dazzled by revolutionary developments in China, where the Cultural Revolution was in full swing, joined the clandestine communist movement in Cambodia, labeled dismissively by Sihanouk, speaking French, as the "Khmer Rouge," or "Red Khmer." The prince opposed them to the "Blue Khmer" who favored the United States and to his neutralist faction, the "White Khmer." The latter two nicknames never caught hold, but the label "Khmer Rouge" stuck to the Communist Party of Kampuchea, for foreigners at least, until the movement collapsed in the 1990s. In early 1968 they opened up armed struggle against Sihanouk's regime. Following the Tet Offensive in Vietnam, which had been launched to large extent from Cambodia, Vietnamese pressure on Cambodian resources intensified, and the country's export economy began to falter.

During the late 1960s, the prince became increasingly depressed. He spent his time producing sentimental feature films, making speeches, and entertaining foreign guests. He also reversed course and renewed diplomatic relations with the United States, probably expecting military assistance, which was not forthcoming. Cambodia, which he still identified with his own person, had become impossible to manage. In January 1970 Sihanouk embarked on an open-ended foreign tour, leaving ministers he knew to oppose him in charge of the country. He seems to have expected the situation to deteriorate and hoped to be asked back as a savior.

In March 1970, while he was in the Soviet Union, the Cambodian National Assembly voted to remove him as chief of state. Sihanouk traveled to Beijing, where he was quickly persuaded by Prime Minister Zhou Enlai, an old friend, to form a military alliance with the Vietnamese and Cambodian communists in order to return to power. Sihanouk agreed to lead a government in exile and took up residence in Beijing. In Cambodia, thousands of young men and women, including future prime minister Hun Sen, rallied to Sihanouk by joining the Khmer Rouge, led from the shadows by Saloth Sar. In October 1970 the pro-American regime in Phnom Penh named itself the Khmer Republic, with General Lon Nol, an inept and mystical patriot, as its prime minister. The regime received massive doses of aid from the United States, and as military equipment poured in, its bloated, courageous, and poorly organized forces suffered a series of ignominious defeats at the hands of Vietnamese communist forces and auxiliary troops provided by the Khmer Rouge.

For the next five years Cambodia was subjected to brutal American bombardment from the air (which stopped in 1973 at the insistence of the U.S. Congress), a ruinous civil war, and armed incursions, in the course of which hundreds of thousands of Cambodians, many of them civilians, lost their lives. By 1973 the Phnom Penh regime controlled less than a quarter of the country. Corruption was rampant. Hundreds of thousands of refugees, fleeing combat and the bombing, flooded into Phnom Penh and Battambang, as local administration more or less collapsed. In the meantime, U.S. combat forces had begun withdrawing from Vietnam, leaving Cambodia as what one American general called "the only war in town."

Following the cease-fire negotiated between the United States and the Vietnamese communists at the end of 1972, Vietnam withdrew most of its forces from Cambodia, leaving the Khmer to fight each other, unaided, for two more years. In a war to the death, prisoners taken on both sides were routinely killed, and civilians who resisted military units were shot. After three years of combat, the Khmer Rouge army, trained and equipped by the Vietnamese, had become skillful and dedicated fighters. The American bombing campaign of 1973, which created a firewall around Phnom Penh and killed thousands of Cambodian civilians as well as Khmer Rouge soldiers, probably forestalled a communist victory, but the collapse of the Khmer Republic was already only a matter of time.

In August 1973 the U.S. ambassador to Cambodia, Emory Swank, ended his tour and gave his first press conference, noting succinctly that the war was "losing more and more of its point and [had] less and less meaning for any of the parties concerned." It was to last for another year and a half.

Further Readings

Chandler, David. *A History of Cambodia.* 3d ed. Boulder, 2000.

———. *The Tragedy of Cambodian History: Politics, War and Revolution since 1945.* New Haven, 1991.

Edwards, Penny. *The Cultivation of "Cambodge."* Honolulu, 2004.

Jeldres, Julio A. *The Royal Family of Cambodia.* Phnom Penh, 2003.

Kiernan, Ben, and Chanthou Boua, eds. *Peasants and Politics in Kampuchea, 1942–1981.* London, 1982.

Martin, Marie Alexandrine. *Cambodia: A Shattered Society.* Translated by Mark W. McLeod. Berkeley, 1994.

Osborne, Milton. *Sihanouk: Prince of Light, Prince of Darkness.* Honolulu, 1994.

Shawcross, William. *Sideshow: Nixon, Kissinger, and the Destruction of Cambodia.* New York, 1979.

Chapter 26

Laos to 1975

IN 1904 the political geo-body we call Laos was confined for the first time in its history almost entirely to the eastern bank of the Mekong River, united for the first time since 1693, and had three of its four principalities ruled (without princes) by the French. The concoction formed a new entity in Southeast Asia by virtue of the lines that France, with Siam's reluctant approval, had drawn around it.

French Rule

UNTIL the end of World War II, Laos was, for the French, a congenial back-water governed under relatively casual ad hoc arrangements. In the north was the principality of Luang Prabang, where a single monarch, Sisavangvong, reigned over several provinces, under French protection, from 1905 until his death in 1959. The French ruled the three other Lao principalities—Xieng Khouang, Vientiane, and Champassak—more directly. A French *résident* in Vientiane monitored both forms of governance and Laos as a whole.

The burden of French colonialism in Laos was lightened by the coopera-tion of traditional leaders, the mildness of French economic involvement, the country's isolation, and the compliance of the Lao population. French novels about Laos, unashamedly Orientalist in tone, alternate between rapture and tor-por, and fail to suggest the administrative affairs that occupied much of a typical colonialist's day. Financially the French ran its operations in Laos at a deficit, balanced by the profits from their taxes in Cambodia and Vietnam.

Laos remained overwhelmingly rural. In 1943 fewer than fifty thousand of the population, estimated very roughly at one million, inhabited provincial towns, including the capital, and three-fifths of these urbanites were immigrants from Vietnam, who dominated the commercial sector. As in Cambodia, the French arrived just in time to remove the Lao from the mixed blessings of Siamese patronage and protection. By drawing lines on the map, freezing the Luang Prabang dynasty in place, and securing the loyalty of the Lao regional elite, the French bought time for the Lao and for themselves, time in which to proceed slowly with what they perceived as their "civilizing mission" there and elsewhere in Indochina. For Laos, as for Vietnam and Cambodia, the idea of independence did not enter the collective mentality of the French until after World War II.

In the 1930s, however, French administrators in Laos, as in Cambodia, hinted that the kingdom was approaching an unspecified kind of renaissance. To speed the process, the French concentrated their resources on extending all-weather roads and on cultural projects pleasing to French savants and the Lao elite. The generation of leaders that matured in the 1930s and 1940s worked comfortably with the French. Because the largely rural population was politically passive and geographically dispersed, these leaders were unchallenged, while the rudimentary condition of the French-controlled educational system (Laos had no high school until 1947) delayed the appearance of a qualified non-royal elite.

In any formal sense, Laos was swamped within the larger unit of French Indochina. It contained only 7 percent of the federation's people, generated only 1 percent of its foreign trade, and in the 1930s employed fewer than five hundred French administrators. The commercial and administrative work, such as it was, fell largely to Vietnamese immigrants. However, the French political and emotional commitment to Laos seems to have been stronger than these quantitative indices suggest. The commitment was based on the sense of helplessness that beset the Lao elite at the end of the nineteenth century and perhaps on a feeling among the French that they owed more to the Lao than they could deliver, given their limited colonial budget and limited power.

By saving and in a sense inventing Laos—a process that they had followed earlier in Cambodia—the French froze Lao politics in place. Their attitude toward Lao culture was ambivalent. The Lao elite naturally resorted to Thai newspapers, books, and radio, all in a language that they could understand, and many Lao monks sought higher education in Siam. At the same time, no members of the Lao elite, it seems, supported the idea that the Siamese state should absorb Laos. To counter Siamese influence in the sangha, the French encouraged

Lao monks to attend the Buddhist Institute in Phnom Penh or a similar body established in 1937 in Vientiane.

When France fell to Germany in 1940, the French and Lao were defenseless against the pan-Thai ambitions and irredentist claims of the pro-Japanese Phibun regime in Bangkok. After a brief war, aimed primarily to regain provinces in northwestern Cambodia ceded to France in 1907, Thailand (as Siam had renamed itself in 1939) took over those parts of Laos that lay on the west bank of the Mekong. Stung by the loss and seeking to ride out the war, the French sought to strengthen the prestige of the Lao monarch in Luang Prabang by adding to the territory under his alleged dominion and formalizing French control. In 1941 a treaty establishing a full-blown protectorate was signed, replacing the informal agreements reached by the French diplomat Auguste Pavie and the Lao monarch in the 1890s. At about this time, a handful of Lao intellectuals, encouraged by the French, launched the Movement for National Renovation, designed to counter pan-Thai pressures emanating from Bangkok. The group published a weekly newspaper and sponsored radio broadcasts in Lao. Fearful of Thai pressure, France constructed more schools in Laos during World War II than they had built since the 1890s. French sponsorship of a nationally focused Lao identity was easily absorbed by those few Lao, led by Prince Phetsarat, who envisaged a Lao nation independent from France. They benefited from several months of quasi-independence in 1945–1946, between the Japanese seizure of power and the French return to control.

A Lao Nation

THE POLITICAL history of Laos since March 1945, when the Japanese interned French officials throughout Indochina, has been dominated by the efforts of Lao and foreign groups to construct a nation-state named "Laos" where none had existed before. In 1946 the French administration named Sisavangvong the ruler of the "kingdom of Laos," which now encompassed all the French-controlled area. Until 1975, when a communist regime came to power in Vientiane, these would-be nation-builders were thwarted in their efforts to unify the country by embedded habits of regionalism and family rivalries among the Lao elite, by poor communications throughout the country, and, most important, by the pressures and devastation of the fighting that swept across all of Indochina between 1946 and 1954 and again between 1960 and 1975.

Like Cambodia and parts of Vietnam, Laos was drawn into the First Indochina War (1946–1954) at a time when few of its people gave strong support to either the French or their communist-dominated opposition. In Laos the few who did were to be found either in the ranks of the Indochina Communist Party (ICP) and its successor parties or in a less well organized nationalist movement known as the Free Lao, or Lao Issara. This was created in the mid-1940s by the quasi-independent Phetsarat regime, with the support of the recently installed anticolonial Pridi government in Bangkok.

What differentiated the Lao communists, supported by the Vietnamese, from their less doctrinaire domestic rivals was that they were optimistic about gaining and holding power throughout the country. For thirty years, their optimism seldom wavered, though in the 1940s the communist victory of 1975 would have been almost impossible for dispassionate observers to predict. French negotiations with noncommunist Lao in the late 1940s weakened the Lao Issara. Several of its leaders, including Prince Souvanna Phouma, returned from Thailand to Laos. Prince Souphanuvong, a member of the ICP, remained in the maquis, allied to the communist resistance known as the Pathet Lao (Lao Nation), all of whose leaders had close connections with Vietnam.

In late 1953 France granted Laos conditional independence, but under the terms of the Geneva accords in 1954, Pathet Lao forces were allowed to "regroup temporarily" in two northern provinces, which soon became communist strongholds. The regrouped forces probably numbered fewer than two thousand men, but the disarray of the Lao government, the collapse of French military power, and the Vietnamese insistence on the regroupment areas meant that the Lao communists benefited far more than their counterparts in southern Vietnam or Cambodia did.

For the remainder of the 1950s, the United States sought persistently but with little success to assemble and shore up regimes in Vientiane that would be capable of preventing a communist takeover of the country. Some of these regimes were more pro-American than others, but none captured more than fleeting loyalty from the predominantly rural population. None of the regimes had the time or inclination to concentrate on rural issues. The benefits and cash that flowed from U.S. economic and military aid—roughly U.S.$300 million in 1972 alone, considerably more than the official GNP of Laos—never got very far from Vientiane. By the mid-1960s, corruption permeated official Lao society, while the Cold War itself, of consuming interest to American bureaucrats, seemed far away from the lives of most Lao men and women.

In 1960, perhaps with French connivance, a Lao army captain named Kong Le staged a neutralist coup d'état that attracted widespread popular support and made both the Americans and the Pathet Lao nervous about the possibility of their ever "winning" Laos. Communist offenses following the coup caught U.S.-financed Lao forces off guard. To salvage what it could, the United States agreed in 1961 to attend a second international conference at Geneva the following year, convened ostensibly to declare the neutralization of Laos but in fact to buy time for the patrons of the warring factions. Kong Le by this time had faded from the scene. Although neither the United States nor the Soviet Union was willing to go to war over Laos, U.S. policy after 1962, like that of the communists, was to undermine the viability of any neutralist regime while seeking to place its own allies in power. Because of bad faith on both sides, the agreements reached at Geneva came apart, and by 1963 Laos was engulfed in the Second Indochina War, alongside neighboring Vietnam.

Increased Vietnamese support for the Pathet Lao and their use of Laos to funnel men and equipment into southern Vietnam (along the so-called Ho Chi Minh trail) led to a prolonged and ruinous U.S. bombing campaign. By 1970 an estimated seventy thousand Vietnamese troops were stationed or in transit through Laos. Nearly a million men, women, and children, particularly from the contested highland provinces and the largely anticommunist Hmong minority, flocked into refugee camps, while thousands of Hmong soldiers, funded by the CIA, continued to fight the communists even after their victory in 1975. (In the late 1970s and 1980s, many of these combatants and their families were to emigrate to the United States, following the example of their leader, General Vang Pao.) Morale throughout the country reached a low ebb. By the early 1970s Laos was only nominally a nation-state.

The U.S.-Vietnamese agreements of 1973 led to a cease-fire in Laos and the establishment of a coalition government in which Pathet Lao delegates had a veto over all decisions. The next two years were relatively free of full-scale fighting, as they were in Vietnam (though not in Cambodia). Neutralist Prince Souvanna Phouma, Lao prime minister throughout most of the 1960s and 1970s, had struggled courageously since the early 1960s to preserve Lao independence, but in 1975 he was outmaneuvered and cast aside. The period also saw the gradual eclipse of the six-hundred-year-old Lao monarchies.

In the months following the communist victory in southern Vietnam and the Khmer Rouge victory in Cambodia, Lao communists in the coalition government increased pressure on their colleagues until the coalition collapsed, more or less peacefully, and the monarchy was abolished. Throughout 1975 tens of thousands of Hmong and middle-class Lao fled to Thailand. Scholars have drawn parallels between what happened at that point and events in Czechoslovakia in 1948; in both cases the communists came to power without violence but not without threatening to use it. In the Lao case, they received widespread support at first because of a reservoir of disillusionment, bitterness, and fatigue that affected all strata of society.

Further Readings

Evans, Grant. *A Short History of Laos.* Crow's Nest, N.S.W., 2002.

Ngaosrivathana, Mayoury, and Kennon Breazeale, eds. *Breaking New Ground in Lao History: Essays on the Seventh to Twentieth Centuries.* Chiang Mai, 2002.

Stevenson, Charles A. *The End of Nowhere: American Policy toward Laos since 1954.* New York, 1972.

Stuart-Fox, Martin. *A History of Laos.* Cambridge, 1997.

PART 5

❀

Coping with Independence
and Interdependence

Chapter 27

Industrialization and
Its Implications

AFTER the Pacific War was over, economic modernization seemed to many Southeast Asian leaders the next logical step in their project to recover power and self-respect. Imagining the "new Vietnam" back in 1907, the Vietnamese revolutionary Phan Boi Chau had typically predicted a blessed future in which automobiles and trains would no longer be uniquely Western, and Vietnamese trade goods would be the world's finest. Such ambitions only gained ground after 1940, as the anticolonial cause triumphed. But in an era when economists were becoming kings, Western economics textbooks outdid themselves in listing the many "requirements" for successful industrialization. These included legal systems guaranteeing individual rights and full protection for property; increased farming productivity, brought about by the reform of preindustrial and colonial class structures; an abundance of skilled labor; entrepreneurs willing to take risks and innovate; adequate quantities of capital for industrial investment; and large and effectively organized domestic markets.

The Challenge of Postwar Development

ALMOST NOBODY outside Southeast Asia believed the region could ever meet such requirements. J. H. Boeke, an influential professor of "Eastern economics" at Leiden, went so far as to suggest in 1953 that Southeast Asian societies like Indonesia were incurably "dual." Alien forms of economic life, like Western capitalism, could never completely "oust" their precapitalist village cultures, which had "few wants" but would have to coexist with them indefinitely, jeopardizing all prospects of an industrial revolution. In the two decades after Boeke wrote, what modernity Southeast Asia did have appeared to be under siege. There were either large peasant insurrections going on, whose tribunes were explicitly challenging middle class urban values, as in Vietnam, Burma, and Cambodia, or at least large organized rural constituencies, as in Indonesia before 1965, with the potential for explosive rebellion.

Boeke's reservations were not unreasonable at the time and were shared by other Western scholars, such as Nobel Laureate Gunnar Myrdal, in his *Asian Drama: An Inquiry into the Poverty of Nations* (1968). In the quarter century after World War II, the global economy grew an average of nearly 5 percent a year, much faster than it had ever grown before—and around 50 percent faster than it has grown since then. Despite the Cold War—which turned hot in Korea and Vietnam—and dozens of "insurgencies" in colonies struggling to be free as well as civil wars in newly liberated states, no conflict grew so large as to impede world trade seriously. Meanwhile the United States and other industrial powers, drawing lessons on the dangers of trade war from their experience of the Great Depression, led a global effort to reduce tariffs everywhere through the forerunners of what eventually became the World Trade Organization.

Much of Southeast Asia, recovering from the devastation of the war, profited from this trade boom, insofar as it involved increased demand and higher prices for primary products like rubber, tin, vegetable oils, and petroleum. Malaya and the Philippines in particular were helped by Korean War stockpiling of strategic materials. But this prosperity, such as it was, offered only limited prospects for long-term growth. The prewar years had amply demonstrated that commodity booms do not last forever. Southeast Asia, still consolidating political independence, seemed ill prepared to change from a primary producer to an industrial power and to alter the terms on which it engaged a capitalist world system now dominated by the United States.

Its potential for development also seemed constrained by its rapidly growing population and the overwhelming problems of rural inefficiency and injustice inherited from the colonial era. Drastic reductions in mortality—symbolized by, but not limited to, the use of DDT to eradicate malaria-carrying mosquitoes—led to unprecedented levels of demographic growth, accelerating to as high as 3.5 percent in countries like Thailand and the Philippines. At this rate the population would double in size in a mere twenty years, literally eating up most of the potential growth of the economy.

The vast majority of the people, moreover, still resided in the countryside and lived by farming. The rapid growth of cities appeared an irrelevance to peasants concerned with uncertain harvests, high rents and taxes, and abusive landlords, who seemed to have increased their strength since independence.

There were cries for "land reform" everywhere, whether this simply meant rent reduction and curbs on the arbitrary power of landlords or their outright expropriation. Agricultural productivity was also a major concern; while countries such as Malaya and the Philippines still had to import rice just to survive, some Western scholars were wondering aloud whether the whole world might starve unless the "population bomb" were somehow defused.

Manufacture in this period was mostly limited to "import-substitution" industrialization (ISI), as recommended by the World Bank and most economists of the time. Assuming that no "Third World" country could possibly compete with the industrial efficiency of the West (or Japan), they believed that relatively simple manufactures targeted for domestic markets—bicycles, flashlights, rubber-soled shoes—could be profitable, especially if these industries were protected by tariffs that the newly independent governments were now in a position to erect. ISI was moderately successful, especially in the Philippines, in the early postwar period; as late as 1960 the Philippines was more industrialized than Singapore and had a higher per capita income than Taiwan or South Korea. But before long, ISI began to encounter inevitable problems, particularly the limited size of the domestic market, although it took longer to reach these limits in populous economies like China, India, and Indonesia. ISI also tended to entrench inefficiency, as protected "infant industries," now grown into adolescence, continued to lobby for legislation that would limit competition from foreign producers.

There were other difficulties, as well as advantages, of being industrial latecomers. The countries that had already successfully industrialized had either commanded large national territories (e.g., the United States and the Soviet Union) or had annexed colonies (the European and Japanese empires). Such conditions had helped them to separate their consumers from some of the real costs of industrial production, such as the disposal of wastes and the depletion of natural resources. Southeast Asia's industrialization would inevitably have to be more geographically and socially compressed. Nor were Southeast Asia's natural resources as important as they might once have been. A global technological and economic revolution after 1950—driven first by electrical goods, sophisticated internal-combustion engines, and chemical fertilizers, and later by developments such as microprocessors, computers, and genetic engineering— meant that science and technology, not older and cruder forms of production, became increasingly critical forces in the growth of wealth. Southeast Asia would continue into the twenty-first century ripping down its forests for timber and ripping up its soil for minerals, but the profits from these industries, though handsome enough for the companies involved (and the officials they bought off), were far from enough to transform, or even sustain, national economies.

These problems threatened Southeast Asian leaders with forms of global inequality that an Aung San or a Sukarno could scarcely have imagined. In a world in which information processing, knowledge production, and symbol manipulation were crucial to the generation of riches and power and the distribution of capital, Southeast Asia's strong points in 1960—unskilled labor and raw materials—dwindled in significance. (At the end of the twentieth century, over 80 percent of the Web pages on the Internet were in English, and ninety-four of the Internet's one hundred most visited Web sites were located in the United States.) Economic marginality, a new nightmare, joined old fears of being a colonial dependency.

Yet against what seemed to be enormous odds, a number of Southeast Asian countries did make remarkable industrial progress after 1965. The next decade was a watershed in regional economic history, though this was by no means self-evident at the time. A number of essentially coincidental developments created a "new international economic order," giving some Southeast Asian societies the opportunity to rewrite their role in the capitalist world system. One of these developments was the relative decline of the United States from the position of uncontested economic dominance it had enjoyed in the immediate postwar era. In part this was simply because other countries, particularly Japan and Germany, became more competitive once they had rebuilt after the war. In part it was because of America's expenditures on the Vietnam War coupled with a simultaneous attempt to build a "Great Society" without raising taxes. In part it resulted from the first "oil shock" of 1973, when the Organization of Petroleum Exporting Countries (OPEC) successfully doubled the world price of oil. Refusing to believe that what *Time* magazine had called "the American Century" was ending, the United States was slow to abandon inefficient management practices and gas-guzzling cars, yet withdrew from many of its Asian commitments as the Vietnam War wound down, leaving it to resurgent Japan to become the chief external linkage of and model for Southeast Asian economies.

At the same time, research on agriculture, some dating back to the colonial period, began to pay off. It had already revitalized Malaysia's rubber and oil palm industries, but its regional effects were multiplied by the development of "miracle rice" at the International Rice Research Institute in Los Baños (near Manila), one of the great developmental successes of the last fifty years. The goals of IRRI were to develop a vast seed bank and use modern science to increase yields. In 1966 scientists crossed dwarf Chinese and Indonesian strains of rice to create IRRI-8, which had a shorter stem that prevented it from falling over when new fertilizers created a bigger seed head. In 1982 IRRI-36 was developed, a hybrid evolved from thirteen different strains of rice that was more resistant to different field pests. Moreover, the growth cycle was shortened from approximately 180 days to 110, and the seeds could ripen with less sunlight, though additional fertilizer was needed. Such high-yielding varieties (HYVs) enabled Southeast Asian farmers to double the amount of rice they could grow in any given area. In recent years IRRI scientists have used genetics to alter rice; a new "golden rice," which has three transplanted genes that add beta-carotene, can help reduce blindness in children, while current research is aimed at fighting anemia, perhaps the world's worst nutritional disorder, by adding iron.

This "Green Revolution" had its own problems, including the fact that it simply would not work without costly inputs (fertilizer, pesticides, and effective water control), which disadvantaged poor peasants, and even poor countries, throughout the 1970s and 1980s. Like other new agricultural technology, such as simple tractors, water pumps, and harvesting machines, it tended to worsen rural disparities of wealth. Yet although the Green Revolution did not really solve the "peasant problem" in Southeast Asia, it did remove the specter of famine. Meanwhile, the population increase started to slow, whether because of deliberate government-sponsored birth control programs (especially in Singapore and, later, Thailand), or as the natural concomitant of urbanization and economic growth. There was still injustice and unrest in the countryside but no longer the general fear that Southeast Asia simply could not feed itself.

The most important development in Southeast Asia's economy began, however, as the unintended byproduct of politics. Its abrupt departure from Malaysia in 1965 forced Singapore to rethink rapidly its industrial strategy, which until then had been ISI aimed at the Malaysian market. Now reduced to a tiny domestic market of two million, its only hope was to attempt export-oriented industrialization (EOI) instead, trying to develop industries that could compete globally on their own merits—quality and price—without the benefit of any tariff preference. This strategy turned out to be wildly successful there and in Hong Kong, Taiwan, and South Korea (the other "Little Dragons") as well. Within a decade the World Bank and most economists had concluded that EOI was far superior to ISI as a development strategy, but this wisdom in hindsight should not blind us to just how big a gamble Singapore had taken in the mid-1960s.

Thus Singapore, which had seemed in the 1950s to have a devout communist lurking behind every palm tree, dazzled orthodox economists, if not human rights activists (rarely the same people), by creating an economy with remarkable growth rates and, at one point, the highest savings rate in the world. Mangrove swamps were turned into industrial estates; Orchard Road became a celebrated and sumptuous shopping street. By the mid-1990s Singapore was a major contributor to global technology, producing nearly half of the world output of disk drives. Thailand by the late 1980s ranked fourth in Asia (after Japan, Taiwan, and South Korea) as an exporter of textiles and was earning more from clothing exports than from its traditional exports of rice; it even began exporting cars (Mitsubishi Lancer compacts, assembled in Thailand and renamed Dodge and Plymouth Colts to circumvent import controls) to Canada in 1988. The Philippines developed an export economy based on manufacturing (garments, computer chips, electronic goods) in the 1970s and 1980s, rendering declines in the prices of its farm crops somewhat less threatening than they might have been.

Malaysia in the 1990s possessed perhaps the most interesting industrial landscape of them all, featuring the tallest skyscraper in the world. The sights of the single federal highway between Port Kelang and Kuala Lumpur, in the west of the Malay Peninsula, would have astonished any elderly British colonial official who returned for a visit three or four decades after independence. Electrolux, Daihatsu, and Motorola factories, along with plants for food processing and making paper envelopes, cars, and plumbing fittings, now dominated the mosques and the few surviving groves of oil palms. By the end of the twentieth century electronics and electrical goods accounted for over half of the exports of Malaysia, which had become the world's largest exporter of air conditioners and videocassette recorders.

Education and technology: Malay Chinese students building a radio, Kuala Lumpur, 1960.

Myanmar, Vietnam, Cambodia, and Laos lagged behind these success stories. In regional terms, Southeast Asia's various industrial revolutions contributed to widening and unprecedented developmental differences among Southeast Asian societies. At the beginning of the twenty-first century, the total value of Singapore's exports was more than double that of Indonesia's and triple that of the Philippines. The money value of Thailand's yearly exports was almost five times that of Vietnam's. Average life expectancy in Malaysia (seventy-three years) was far longer than that in Cambodia (fifty-four years). In 1970 the productivity and living standards of Southeast Asian countries had resembled each other much more closely.

Models, East and West

How DID these industrial revolutions happen? And how, in some interesting cases, did they fail to happen? For a long time, Southeast Asian elites' impatience to achieve an empowering industrial modernity was far greater than their actual accomplishments. In 1957 Indonesian economist Mohammad Sadli had rebuked Boeke for his theory of social dualism, arguing that the theory justified the perpetuation of Western colonialism and that there was no reason whatsoever why Indonesia could not industrialize. In 1965, just before the end of his presidency, Sukarno went even further. He told Indonesians that Western economics textbooks of all kinds were not divine laws and that a national revolution such as the Indonesian one could not be measured by the standards of textbooks, "even ones written by bald-headed professors from Oxford or Cornell University."

To many impatient Southeast Asians of the 1950s and 1960s, the giant centralized command economy of the Soviet Union and its flamboyant elaborations in communist-ruled China seemed reasonable alternative inspirations to the depression-prone capitalist economies of their former colonial masters. The Soviet Union encouraged postcolonial Southeast Asians to believe that private enterprise and free markets were largely irrelevant to national well-being, all the more so as unloved minorities like the Chinese and Indians dominated commerce in the region. Enthusiasm for the state socialist model varied from country to country. The Indonesian intelligentsia produced by Dutch colonialism tended to be the children of administrators or of Islamic religious teachers, and their sympathy for economic managerialism and disdain for "alien" (or "sinful") capitalism were consistent with their family backgrounds. Elite Filipinos, whose families were more tied to agrarian business interests, were far less interested in state socialism.

Only one Southeast Asian country—the communist state in Vietnam—surrendered itself completely to the Soviet economic dream. In so doing, it absented itself for a long time from the more successful industrial revolutions elsewhere in Southeast Asia. For Vietnamese communist leaders between 1954 and 1986, "socialism" meant large-scale state-owned heavy industries. These took the form of projects like the Thai Nguyen iron and steel complex, begun in 1960, which had few discernible connections to ordinary Vietnamese life but cost the equivalent of one entire year's harvest to build. In fact it exceeded Vietnam's capacities; it was paid for by Russian and Chinese foreign aid. Misled by Stalinist visions of self-sufficiency and increasingly (and paradoxically) dependent on aid infusions from other communist countries, Hanoi bureaucrats showed relatively little interest in international trade or in the expansion of exports, despite the country's continued need to pay for imported capital goods. Meanwhile, Vietnamese novelists served the Soviet dream by publishing a host of "proletarian" novels with titles like *Mine Workers* (by Vo Huy Tam) or *Cement* (by Huy Phuong) in order to celebrate the "new people" that Vietnam was supposed to be producing. This was a remarkable effort to force Southeast Asian economic realities to resemble idealized pictures of workers' lives in Eastern Europe.

But the realities remained unbudgingly cruel. In 1980 Vietnam had an average per capita income that was reputedly no more than one-tenth of the average per capita income of Bulgaria or Rumania in 1960. Even if savage wars with the French and the Americans had much to do with this, it was also clear that Vietnam's state ideology had estranged it from its own history and from the rest of Southeast Asia. By the 1980s Vietnam was reduced to selling its surplus unemployed labor to its Soviet bloc patrons, shipping hundreds of thousands of workers to Eastern European mines or Soviet automobile factories. By this time Vietnamese leaders had become only too well aware of which of their neighboring superpowers, years before, had bet more successfully on the future. At the very moment (1957) when Mao Zedong's China, using the old Stalinist touchstone of economic modernity, had pledged itself to overtake British steel production in fifteen years, Japan had introduced a special law for the urgent development of a national electronics industry. In 1991, the year the Soviet Union collapsed, Hanoi was belatedly ready to welcome Japanese advice, including Mitsubishi's plan for the creation of a Vietnamese car industry.

The postcolonial Southeast Asian industrial revolutions that succeeded, unlike the one in Vietnam that failed, are unimaginable without Japan. Southeast Asians' sense that Japanese strength might also empower them had begun in the late 1890s with Filipino revolutionaries requesting Japanese help in their struggles against Spain and the United States. It had only increased with the Japanese victory over Russia in 1905. Japan's aggressive behavior in Asia between 1931 and 1945 had created hostile and fearful reactions from many Southeast Asians. But even from this period there was an enduring legacy in economic theory—the economist Akamatsu Kaname's proposal that Asian societies' collective crusade to modernize be imagined as a single flight of geese. Japan, the ostensible leader of the flying geese, would industrialize first and pull the entire V-formation of other Asian countries along behind it, passing back to them technologies it had mastered and outdated industries in which it no longer had a comparative advantage.

To Southeast Asians Japan's magnetism was grounded in the perception, starting in the 1960s, that it had found a model of economic development to supersede both unruly American free market individualism and the Soviet Union's rigid and unresponsive system of government economic controls, a model that combined sensitive state planning with an insistence on at least limited market competition. Politically, it was democratic in form but oligarchic in substance: one political party ruled Japan for decades after 1955. Economically, it featured the adoption and improvement of European and American advanced technology. Computers were invented in the West, but it was Japanese thinkers who marketed them best and formulated the concept of the "information society."

In the long run Southeast Asians could not reproduce the Japanese economic system, or what they imagined it to be, but that does not alter the fact that they recognized Japan as the great Asian success story. In 1974 strategist Daud Jusuf proposed the formation of an "Indonesia Incorporated" that would work out its economic future on the basis of large-scale national business units shaped by close cooperation among politicians, bureaucrats, technocrats, and entrepreneurs; the Japanese inspiration behind this proposal was obvious. In 1982 Prime Minister Mahathir Muhammad of Malaysia launched a "Look East" program—reminiscent of Vietnamese nationalists' "Eastern Travel" movement to study Japan in 1905—claiming that Japanese values were similar to the ethic that Malaysians had "or would like to acquire." Idealized pictures of Japanese communitarian values, especially strong teamwork, cohesive networks, and group loyalty, loomed large in Southeast Asian postcolonial yearnings. In 1994 the Malaysian-based Commission for a New Asia described the family as a "sacred sanctuary" that was being undermined by Western individualism. Singapore diplomat Tommy Koh suggested that the time had come for the "West" to learn from "Eastern" respect for authority and consensus in decision making.

The optimistic celebration of the transformative possibilities of such "Asian values" foundered on the uniqueness of the Japanese historical experience: low population growth, a powerful and autonomous civil service, a high domestic savings rate, and American protection during the Cold War, which had allowed Japan to concentrate its resources on economic growth rather than military spending. Even before Japan's economy plateaued in the 1990s, some Southeast Asians had become aware of this. A. R. Soehoed, an Indonesian industry minister, complained in 1988 that Indonesia could never catch up with the Japanese lead goose by following its flight patterns. It was not just that Indonesia did not have the personnel to operate an omnicompetent Japanese-style government trade ministry, but that Indonesia's whole history as a multiethnic country with long coastlines, open to the influences of many civilizations, denied it Japan's more formidable control over its relations with outsiders. Filipino intellectuals, for their part, feared that too much respect for authority, Japanese style, would simply legitimize corrupt dictatorships of the Ferdinand Marcos type. And in Southeast Asia's one historically Confucian country, Vietnamese experts who wrote about "the invigoration of the Japanese people" in the mid-1990s pointed out that even Japanese Confucianism was unique, sanctioning more extreme and mystical definitions of loyalty than Confucianisms elsewhere.

The other side of Japan's indispensability to Southeast Asia's industrial revolutions was its development assistance and investment. According to one calculation, Japanese aid equaled 15 to 20 percent of the budget expenditures of almost every country in Southeast Asia in the late 1980s. Throughout most of the 1980s and 1990s, Japan was also Southeast Asia's leading foreign investor. Japanese investment characteristically took the form of joint ventures with local Southeast Asian interests, in which the partners chosen were members of pre-existing economic elites. The Filipino partners in some seventy-seven Japanese-Filipino joint ventures at the end of the 1970s came from forty-six of the Philippines' most eminent families, by one estimate, but the local partners of Japanese multinationals could also be Southeast Asian governments themselves. Mitsubishi supplied many of the components and much of the design for Malaysia's successful government-sponsored national car, the Proton Saga. As Japanese critics themselves pointed out, Japanese manufacturers were investing in Southeast Asia in order to create a stratified regional economy in which the traditional dual structure of wages in Japanese industry itself—with good wages paid to organized workers in big industries and poor wages paid to the less organized workers in numerous small subcontracting industries—was extended south, with Southeast Asia cast as Japan's subcontractor underclass. If Southeast Asians allowed themselves to be no more than subcontractors, the flying geese would take a long time to gain any ground on the leader of the flock.

Yet their proximity to Japan still hardly explains why Southeast Asian countries, after decolonization, were able to do something that Africa and the Middle East could not: learn how to manufacture cars and computer chips and sell them to the West. Western colonialism left behind in Southeast Asia, when it departed, small but significant elites, which compared well in creativity with their African, Latin American, and Middle Eastern counterparts, for reasons that remain to be fully explored. For all their anticolonialism, they also felt personally threatened by communist insurrections: a bigger potential danger in Southeast Asia than in Africa or even Latin America. Anxious to resist the threat of other Southeast Asian politicians, such as the Khmer Rouge, who attacked modern institutions like banks and currency, such elites staked their futures on mixed economies, including export promotion and private enterprise. The fact that the American superpower shared their anxieties did not hurt their cause as they searched for export markets and investment funds. But the leaders of these suddenly emancipated "colonial bourgeoisies," as a Marxist might have called them, were highly significant political actors in their own right. They ranged from famous politicians like Lee Kuan Yew (prime minister of Singapore from 1959 to 1990) and Mahathir Muhammad (Malaysian prime minister from 1981 to 2003) to the Indonesian economists who came to be known, jokingly, as the "Berkeley Mafia" because of their ties to the University of California.

A famous debate at the University of Indonesia in 1955, early in the postcolonial era, established the terms of the struggle. The debaters aptly represented the two different Southeast Asias that were trying to emerge. Wilopo, a former Indonesian prime minister, condemned Western economic liberalism for legitimizing exploitation and large differences in the distribution of wealth. He argued that liberalism's malignant effects had been even more damaging in colonized Asia than in Western countries. Widjojo Nitisastro, the son of a family of Javanese teachers and himself a student army fighter against the British and Dutch before Indonesian independence, rebuked Wilopo for ignoring the necessity of wealth creation as well as wealth redistribution. Widjojo reminded Wilopo that "free enterprise" included small peasant landowners as well as the Royal Dutch Shell oil company, and he raised the possibility of a progressive "antiliberal" economic system in which price mechanisms could coexist with a socially concerned managerial state.

The successful de-Westernization of capitalist economics in Japan and South Korea and the chaos and famines that Mao Zedong's autarkic communism inflicted on China in the 1960s ultimately helped the Widjojos of Southeast Asia to find a receptive audience. Even Southeast Asian policy-makers like the Thai military dictators of the 1960s and 1970s modified previous government policies and began to welcome foreign industrial investment. They allowed it such privileges as majority stockholding, tax holidays for corporate profits during an initial period of development, tax exemptions on the import of foreign manufacturing plants, and the relatively free entry of foreign technicians.

The Contribution of Southeast Asian Chinese

APART FROM their small but able and politically determined elites, the Southeast Asian countries that successfully industrialized in the postcolonial era had another asset: an economically creative ethnic minority. The history of economic growth shows over and over again the importance of creative minorities who deviate from, or are marginalized by, the dominant practices of their societies. The Jewish financiers of medieval Europe, engaging in moneylending in nominally Christian societies that demonized usury and excluded ambitious Jews from elite political or military activities, are probably the most famous example, compelled to develop trust-based personal networks among themselves as a means of dealing with the majority societies that used and abused them. In Southeast Asia this role was filled by the ethnic Chinese, including most of the prominent domestic capitalists who emerged in the postcolonial period. (*Forbes* magazine calculated in 1994 that people with some degree of Chinese ethnicity accounted for 86 percent of Southeast Asia's billionaires.) No small part of Vietnam's economic disaster before 1986 was caused, conversely, by its forced eviction of a large number of its overseas Chinese business people during the last years of Stalinist-style collectivism between 1975 and 1980.

There were many reasons for the commanding position of ethnic Chinese in Southeast Asia's economic transformation. Strong collective achievement motives were one. The Chinese immigrants from Fujian and Guangdong who sought better lives in Southeast Asia in the nineteenth and early twentieth centuries were hardly typical Chinese peasants. They might have been poor, but their ambition to migrate and their entrepreneurial skills marked them off from the neighbors they were leaving behind. In the 1980s the owner of Thailand's biggest agribusiness holding company (Dhanin Chiaravanont, head of the C. P. Group) could look back to a Teochiu (Chaozhou) immigrant father who had opened a small store in the 1920s to import Chinese seeds and export Thai eggs.

Confucianism, the ancient value system that legitimized hierarchical authority and stressed the ethical importance of kinship relationships, also undoubtedly helped Chinese businesses gain a comparative advantage. It facilitated low-cost teamwork transactions and strong family-style leaderships, "families" in this instance being understood as flexible networks of people based on geographic and fictive kinship ties as well as blood. Singapore even flirted with the government promotion of Confucian ethics in its schools in 1982, but this campaign encountered apathy and significant criticism, and waned within a decade. Non-Chinese Singaporeans regarded the campaign as a subterfuge to impose Chinese values on them, while English-educated Singapore Chinese condemned Confucianism for being antidemocratic and excessively patriarchal.

In the last analysis neither Confucianism nor the achievement motives of ambitious south Chinese really explained the success of Southeast Asia's ethnic Chinese businesses. Both factors had existed in China itself for centuries, but China had never produced capitalists as formidable as those of postcolonial Southeast Asia. A unique historical environment in Southeast Asia—which both by discrimination against the Chinese and patronage of them deflected their energies almost entirely into commerce—accounts for their particular inspiration.

Precolonial and colonial Southeast Asian societies, with few exceptions, did not allow ethnic Chinese to become political or military leaders, denying them the conventional hopes of upward mobility. Discrimination against the Chinese often worsened in the early postcolonial period. Phibun Songkhram's governments in Thailand, between 1938 and 1957, banned Chinese language schools and forced Chinese businesses to acquire Thai politicians or military officials as front men; Chinese were excluded from Thai military academies. The Philippines' Retail Trade Nationalization Act of 1957 attempted to squeeze out ethnic Chinese retailers, just as rice traders had been previously targeted. Malaysia's 1970 "New Economic Policy," intended to benefit the *bumiputera* (sons of the soil), was seen by many as being anti-Chinese in effect. And in Indonesia not only was there anti-Chinese legislation in the 1950s, but the massacres in the aftermath of the 1965 coup included Chinese, along with suspected communists, among the principal victims—and were echoed a generation later (in milder form) by attacks on the persons and property of Chinese during the economic crisis of the late 1990s.

But all the discrimination coexisted, paradoxically, with an old Southeast Asian tradition, going back to the precolonial period, of ethnic Chinese business people serving Southeast Asian kings or sultans by operating trading or mining or tax-collecting monopolies on their behalf, while enriching themselves in the process. The postcolonial Southeast Asian rulers who conferred special economic favors (like import monopolies) upon Chinese business "cronies" were in effect modernizing the practices of the old Southeast Asian courts, which had employed Chinese royal merchants as politically privileged tax farmers or overseas traders.

The Kuok Group, Malaysia's biggest Chinese-owned multinational corporation at the end of the twentieth century, shows how the old and the new could be combined in an especially effective fashion. Robert Kuok was the son of a poor immigrant to British Malaya from Fujian at the end of the 1800s. He himself was educated at the English College of Johor Baru (whose alumni included a founder of the United Malays National Organization) and at Raffles College in Singapore (whose alumni included both Mahathir and Lee Kuan Yew). With help from the social skills and ties he developed as a young man, Kuok was able to convert the sugar wholesaling and retailing business he had inherited from his father into an international empire that included insurance services, supermarkets, television networks, and the Shangri-La hotel chain. Influential Malays, including members of the Perlis and Johore royal families, were involved from the outset as his patrons and partners. Such an arrangement was jokingly known as the "Ali Baba" system, though it could be found elsewhere in Southeast Asia as well, under different names. In return for giving "Baba" (the Chinese businessman) access to government licenses and state assistance, "Ali" (the Malay director or shareholder) profited from his success.

An economic transformation apparently driven by elite "cronyism" did not win unanimous praise, either inside Southeast Asia or outside it. One particularly severe Japanese critic, Yoshihara Kunio, denounced the rise of "ersatz capitalism" in Southeast Asia. In his view Southeast Asian capitalism was not the real thing, as it remained technologically dependent on its foreign industrial partners in Japan and elsewhere, and its ethnic Chinese capitalists were supposedly "rent seekers," consumed by parasitic inclinations to seek government subsidies, licenses, and monopoly rights. There was some justice in the first criticism. Southeast Asian educational systems showed a dangerous inability to create sufficient numbers of homegrown scientists and industrial technologists. The second criticism, implying that, by contrast, Western and Japanese capitalists were paragons of economic self-sufficiency who would never dream of seeking government protection from foreign competition, was obviously less persuasive. It utterly disregarded the unending history of capitalists everywhere demanding government bailouts for failing business enterprises.

All the same, there was plenty of "crony capitalism" in Southeast Asia for those who wanted to look for it. Far from all of it was ethnically Chinese. The Indonesian national car project, which lasted for about one year (1996–1997), provided one extreme example. Indonesia's President Suharto gave pioneer "national" car-making status to a holding company created and owned by his own son, Hutomo (Tommy) Suharto. With no experience in making cars, Tommy nonetheless gained the right to monopolize a joint venture with Kia Motors of South Korea that would manufacture copies of Kia sedans, called Timors, at a new industrial complex to be built near Jakarta. Loans from state-owned banks, ordered by his father, were to pay for it. After the Suharto dictatorship crumbled in 1998, Indonesians who had purchased Timors competed with each other to rip the brand name from their cars.

But if it was non-Chinese Southeast Asian leaders who created the conditions in which ethnic Chinese capitalism was born and flourished, they did so in response to a specific international environment. Foreign critics often overlooked this environment. Southeast Asia's family-type business organizations, at the beginning of the postcolonial era, were too small to compete with existing multinational corporations. As late as 1993 one survey showed that forty-seven of the fifty biggest Asian business firms were Japanese and South Korean, with the biggest Southeast Asian contender (Pertamina, the Indonesian state oil company) placing a mere thirty-ninth. To compete with multinational capitalism, Southeast Asians at first had to find business realms that were protected, even while depending on foreign ties for technology and markets. But Southeast Asian capitalism was not frozen into one form for all eternity. By the 1990s some ethnic Chinese businesses were evolving from family firms into larger, more Western-style or Japanese-style corporations. They were also losing much of their specifically Chinese culture and identity. Here they were following a trend that had begun in the Philippines in the 1800s, the process by which the Chinese mestizos had transformed themselves into an assimilated middle class that no longer thought of itself as "Chinese."

The Price of an Industrial Revolution

THE UGLY UNDERSIDE of Southeast Asia's postcolonial economic success stories was not so much cronyism as industrial sweatshops and the repression of independent labor unions. Here Southeast Asia reproduced many of the evils of the industrial revolution in the West but amid higher expectations than nineteenth-century English factory workers ever had. President Ferdinand Marcos, in a speech to bankers in 1974, boasted that the Philippines had one of the lowest average wage levels in Asia; he said that he was determined not to jeopardize his program of exports by allowing wages to increase much. Other Southeast Asian rulers shared this ambition, despite the obvious fact that underpaid workers' weak purchasing power only increased Southeast Asia's precarious dependency on the foreign buyers of its products.

In the colonial period, as J. S. Furnivall had argued in *Netherlands India* (1944), a greater power imbalance between capital and labor existed within the West's Southeast Asian colonies than in the West itself. Such colonies were structured like factories, organized for production, not like states, organized for the good life of their members, and the lack of a coherent "common will" among the various colonized peoples of these ethnically plural societies had freed capitalism from the restraints that were being imposed on it in the West.

Postcolonial Southeast Asian leaders, for their own reasons, modernized their factory-like societies without greatly reforming them. Post–World War II developments in communications and computing, by facilitating a huge increase in the speed and volume of global trading in currencies and other financial assets, heightened the advantages of employers and investors over labor everywhere. Capital became extraordinarily mobile, labor less so. Even the West's own labor unions lost bargaining power in dealing with capital managers who could play one labor market against another. In Southeast Asia the effects were much worse, as Furnivall might have predicted. By one calculation, in 1992 Nike, which made most of its shoes in Indonesia, paid more in promotional fees to Michael Jordan than the entire Indonesian shoe industry work force of 25,000 people received in wages for the year.

During the Cold War the control or repression of organized labor varied by degree from one Southeast Asian country to another. In Thailand union organization was not legally permitted until 1972. After that date state enterprise unions (almost one-quarter of all unions) were still forbidden to strike, and those unions that were allowed to strike were subject to interference, both by the Thai armed forces and by anticommunist foreign organizations such as the U.S.-based Asian-American Free Labor Institute or the European World Congress of Labor (which secretly funded competing Thai unions in a game of divide and rule). In Singapore the governing People's Action Party controlled the National Trades Union Congress and promoted the notion that employers and workers should cooperate with each other to preserve the industrial peace; a national wages council set wages guidelines. In Malaysia, where less than 10 percent of the work force was unionized in the mid-1980s, workers in free trade zones, specifically set up to attract foreign capital, were forbidden to join unions at all. The government-sponsored Trade Union Congress of the Philippines imitated those elsewhere in trying to control labor militancy but was less effective; by the 1980s it had to contend with a more independent workers' organization, the First of May Movement (Kilusang Mayo Uno).

As for Suharto's Indonesia, it offered strong proof that the heavier the costs of government corruption—the bribes business firms had to pay to bureaucrats and soldiers—the more necessary it was to keep wage costs low in compensation. In that respect sweatshops and extreme forms of cronyism were related. No strikes could legally occur without the approval of the Ministry of Manpower; the only legal organizations allowed in factories employing a female work force were Muslim prayer groups. But by the early 1990s independent labor unions, allied to the influential Batak Protestant Church, were able to organize thousands of garment factory workers in wildcat strikes in the city of Medan, Sumatra. Indonesian soldiers' apparent abduction, rape, and murder of Marsinah, a young Javanese woman activist who had tried to organize her fellow workers at a watch factory in 1993, showed the desperation of the troubled dictatorship. Public opinion forced the regime to recognize her posthumously as a worker hero.

Such developments had little to do with the original dreams of the Southeast Asian leaders who had married their countries to export-driven capitalism in the first place, after the only real alternatives to it, socialist bureaucratic economies in Burma, Vietnam, Cambodia, and Laos, had lost their appeal. Their motives had not been those of Western liberal economics professors, bald-headed or not—the desirability of free trade and economic growth as ends in themselves—but were much more political, the postcolonial recovery of their own self-respect as independent international actors. The Cold War had obscured the potential contradiction between these aims and those of multinational capitalism. The question that haunted Southeast Asian history at the beginning of the twenty-first century was whether the large foreign business corporations on which regional economic growth relied really wanted strong postcolonial states. Perhaps they preferred weak states that could maintain police forces and collect the garbage, without being powerful enough to slow down or restrict the freedom of movement of capital.

The Economic Crisis of 1997 and Its Aftermath

A SOUTHEAST ASIAN economic crisis in 1997 temporarily curtailed visions of what Anwar Ibrahim, later deputy prime minister of Malaysia, had saluted as the "Asian renaissance" in 1994. The crisis might have been expressly designed to confirm the fear that transnational corporations and their supporters did not really want strong Southeast Asian states. In mid-1997 the Thai central bank freed, and therefore devalued, the baht, which had been tied to the American dollar since 1984. This raised the question of how business enterprises would repay their heavy debts to other countries given Thailand's trade deficit and small holdings of foreign currency reserves.

Other Southeast Asian countries shared Thailand's trade deficits and thus shared the economic disaster. Although there is a debate about the relative importance of the various factors involved, the general context of Southeast Asia's deficits included a cyclical decline in the global demand for the electronic goods on which local manufacturers had concentrated; a sudden rise in competition with Chinese exports, as post-Mao China also belatedly switched to export-led growth policies; and a decline in Japanese investment, compounded by the refusal of Japan, the richest country in Asia, to absorb more Southeast Asian imports. (According to one calculation, the United States was buying 70 percent of the non-Western world's manufacturing exports at the end of the 1980s; Japan, with an economy at least two-thirds the size of the American one, bought just 8 percent.) Coupled with unwise, opaque, and often corrupt lending practices by many of the leading financial institutions in the region, this was a disaster waiting to happen.

The worst panic was in Indonesia, whose currency lost three-quarters of its value in mid-1997. This led to factory closings and massive unemployment. As the cost of imported goods soared, the number of Indonesians who were living in poverty multiplied catastrophically. The International Monetary Fund (IMF), created under American leadership in the 1940s to promote economic liberalization, offered Indonesia assistance in 1998 at the cost of an end to government monopolies and protectionism in agriculture. This sudden forced liberalization only accelerated the immediate economic collapse. As President Suharto, months before his political demise, signed the agreement in January 1998, the director of the IMF, Michel Camdessus, was photographed standing over him, arms smugly crossed, like an Indies colonial governor returned from the dead.

Until this disaster Southeast Asian elites had shown signs of taking the continuation of their high economic growth rates for granted, ignoring the recurrent collapses and mood swings that were so much a part of the general history of capitalism, ranging from the catastrophic Dutch tulip investment mania of the 1600s to the American stock market crash of 1929. In 1994 Mahathir Muhammad of Malaysia had even cowritten a book with a pugnacious Japanese nationalist about an "Asia that can say 'No!' "—to the West—in which he had predicted that American prosperity, not Southeast Asian growth, was a thing of the past. Southeast Asia's 1997 crisis, linked as it was to Japanese economic

IMF oversight: Camdessus watching Suharto, 1998.

troubles, was therefore a huge surprise not only to most Asians, but to many outsiders of (and investors in) Asia. The immediate problem was how to build stronger states, with better regulated financial institutions and fairer domestic taxes, that would not be so heavily addicted to foreign capital infusions by investors who pursued high yields and quick turnaround times in real estate rather than in domestic industries.

The ASEAN Success Story

BUT WERE stronger Southeast Asian states, and the unprecedented forms of regional interstate cooperation Southeast Asians had begun to pursue in the 1960s, compatible with the liberal capitalism that flourished so unobstructedly in the post–Cold War world? In 1967 five nonsocialist Southeast Asian countries—Thailand, Indonesia, the Philippines, Singapore, and Malaysia—had created ASEAN (the Association of Southeast Asian Nations). ASEAN was designed to be, in the words of the Indonesian foreign minister at the time, a regional alliance that could resist both "yellow" (Chinese) and "white" (Western) imperialisms as well as curb ethnocentric nationalisms in Southeast Asia itself through greater regional economic cooperation.

ASEAN was a precarious construction from the outset. It embraced both tiny, rich countries like Singapore (and Brunei, which joined in 1984), which had little to fear from freer regional trade, and gigantic poorer countries like Indonesia, whose capacities for national political and economic cohesion remained uncertain. Yet ASEAN became a greater success than outsiders bothered to notice. It not only ended a 1960s "confrontation" between Malaysia and Indonesia (one of its original purposes) but helped to reconcile ancient enemies like Thailand and Vietnam (which joined it in 1995) and to lessen tensions among Malaysia, Indonesia, and the Philippines over Borneo. In 2003 it even seemed to be addressing the controversial issue of human rights in Myanmar, which had joined it in 1997. By its thirtieth anniversary, ASEAN had become the most successful regional organization in the non-Western world. It embraced half a billion people. It was the world's fourth largest trading bloc. And it included every Southeast Asian country except Cambodia, whose eventual adherence (in 1999) as its tenth member the organization's symbol of ten rice stalks anticipated.

For a part of the world that was not only poorer than the European Union but lacked such European advantages as a shared religious culture and a common legal heritage, these were no mean achievements. Southeast Asians were

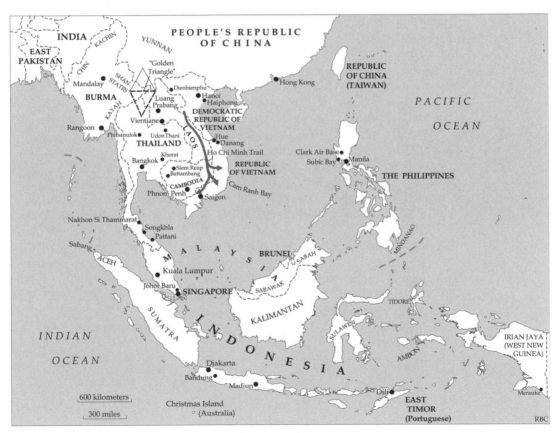

Southeast Asia about 1968

uncomfortably aware of the price of these achievements. In 1995, when Flor Contemplacion, a Filipino domestic servant, was hanged for murder in Singapore, the huge public funeral she received in the Philippines, broadcast over national television, suggested a mass sympathy for the hard life she and other Filipino migrant workers had had to lead, emotionally comparable to the sympathetic public funerals the martyred Luddites—machinery-breaking unemployed workers—had received in England in the early stages of the industrial revolution.

Among the elite the Sumatran journalist Mochtar Lubis, in his best-selling book *The Indonesian Dilemma* (1983), complained that modernization was simply a new Indonesian superstition, full of mantras and incantations such as only a people who were "expert symbol makers" could create. But the difference between this view and Boeke's old belief that Indonesia could never modernize at all, because of its traditional want-free culture, was the measure of how far Indonesia, and much of Southeast Asia, had traveled since independence.

Further Readings

Bauer, Joanne, and Daniel Bell, eds. *The East Asian Challenge for Human Rights.* Cambridge, 1999.

Bello, Walden, and Stephanie Rosenfeld. *Dragons in Distress: Asia's Miracle Economies in Crisis.* San Francisco, 1990.

Brook, Timothy, and Hy Van Luong, eds. *Culture and Capitalism: The Shaping of Capitalism in Eastern Asia.* Ann Arbor, 1999.

Cushman, Jennifer, and Wang Gungwu, eds. *Changing Identities of the Southeast Asian Chinese since World War Two.* Hong Kong, 1988.

Doner, Richard. "Approaches to the Politics of Economic Growth in Southeast Asia." *Journal of Asian Studies* 50, 4 (November 1991): 818–849.

Godemont, Francois. *The Downsizing of Asia.* New York, 1999.

Gosling, Peter, and Linda Lim, eds. *The Chinese in Southeast Asia.* Ann Arbor, 1987.

Greider, William. *One World, Ready or Not: The Manic Logic of Global Capitalism.* New York, 1998.

Hale, Christopher. "Indonesia's National Car Project Revisited: The History of Kia-Timor Motors and Its Aftermath." *Asian Survey* 41, 4 (July–August 2001): 629–645.

McVey, Ruth, ed. *Southeast Asian Capitalists.* Ithaca, 1992.

Ong, Aihwa, and Donald Nonini, eds. *Ungrounded Empires: The Cultural Politics of Modern Chinese Transnationalism.* New York, 1997.

Yoshihara Kunio. *The Rise of Ersatz Capitalism in Southeast Asia.* Singapore, 1988.

Chapter 28

❋

Human Consequences of the Economic "Miracle"

DESPITE its unevenness, all the contradictions and countercurrents that it created, Southeast Asia's belated industrial revolution allowed per capita income, in
real as well as nominal terms, to rise across the region. People lived longer and
grew taller. More goods were available everywhere, not just in the high-rise
office buildings and walled and guarded residential enclaves of the rich. Hundreds of millions of Southeast Asians had more to eat and could afford tennis
shoes, baseball caps, and Coca-Cola. Tens of millions enjoyed access to television
and the Internet. Any history that does not acknowledge this rising regional
prosperity is fundamentally flawed. Equally flawed, however, would be a history
implying that such prosperity was equitably shared, whether by country, district,
ethnicity, gender, or class. In order to assess the Southeast Asian "miracle,"
therefore, we must take it apart.

On the Bright Side

SINGAPORE was the great success story of the modern era in material terms,
with a per capita income (nearly U.S.$23,000 in 2000) more than five times as
high as any other state in the region except oil-rich Brunei—and still two and
a half times as high when adjusted for purchasing power parity. By the turn of
the millennium, life expectancy at birth was around eighty years (women, as
they do almost everywhere, lived about five years longer than men), and the

infant mortality rate had fallen to around three deaths per thousand births, figures comparable to the best in the world. Adult literacy was well over 90 percent, and an ambitious public housing program had virtually ended slums and homelessness. The city was strikingly clean, owing to such regulations as the much-mocked ban on chewing gum. Downtown traffic flowed smoothly, thanks in part to electronic sensing devices that taxed (and thus discouraged) vehicles entering the central business district, in part to an efficient bus and subway system. Its students consistently won prizes in international competitions, and the country seemed well on its way to a postindustrial "knowledge economy." To critics, the authoritarian nature of the regime counted against it; some called it, in William Gibson's memorable phrase, "Disneyland with the death penalty." Most Singaporeans, however, appeared to be willing to tolerate an intrusive government in return for the benefits they received.

As a city Singapore resembled the other great cities of Southeast Asia, which came to look more like each other than like the differing countrysides from which they had sprung. Factories and universities, malls full of retail shops and fast-food joints, tall office and apartment blocks, entertainment ranging from opera and classical dance to strip clubs and sporting events, bright lights, billboards, and—except for Singapore—filthy squatter slums and excruciating traffic jams were the visible signs of this trend. Kuala Lumpur was a smaller Jakarta overshadowed by mighty twin towers; Ho Chi Minh City (Saigon) in the 1990s aped Bangkok of the 1970s. Migrants were drawn not just by economic opportunity but by urbanism itself. As one Myanmar poet put it:

> . . . this is the thrill of living in the city,
> where else can you cross a busy thoroughfare
> and not get to the other side,
> no not even in the jungleside village
> where the guns bark at night,
> is life so cheap,
> that is why as an adventurous young man,
> when I find myself in the city,
> Rangoon, I like it here.

The proportion of Southeast Asians living in cities rose from 15 percent to 24 percent between 1950 and 1980, then shot up to 37.5 percent by 2000. By the 1990s regional population growth had slowed to around 1 percent a year, but cities were growing at three times that rate. Jakarta, Metro Manila, Bangkok, and Ho Chi Minh City had become mega-cities, with populations well over 5 million by 2000 (Greater Jakarta had nearly 17 million), but even some provincial cities, developing as subregional nodes, took off, as did a few specially designated industrial parks or export-processing zones. Chiang Mai, with fewer than 100,000 inhabitants as late as 1970 and just 350,000 in 1990, had 1.5 million by 2000. The malls of Cebu City, in the central Philippines, were equipped with showers and lockers for the convenience of day-trippers who came from as far as Bohol and Leyte on high-speed interisland ferries.

One of the most visible signs of regional prosperity, in fact, was the rise of a larger and more diverse group of wealthy Southeast Asians than ever before. Alongside the civil servants who had always formed the core of local bourgeoisies were now entrepreneurs, military officers, professionals, entertainers, and white-collar workers, most of whom were more visible as consumers—of Starbucks and Hondas, luxury apartments and Adidas shoes, Japanese *anime* and overseas vacations—than as producers. Within this elite there remained gross differences in actual wealth, and those who thought in sociostructural terms sometimes divided it into two classes: a "new rich" of owners and investors, and a "middle class" of employees and small shopkeepers.

A majority of the elite were educated at least through secondary school, and there were so many university graduates in the region by the 1990s that the Thai Constitution of 1997 could require that new members of the National Assembly possess "a Bachelor's degree or its equivalent," a measure Singapore had adopted earlier. The explosion of higher education had its critics, as some of the new colleges were far from the standards of the best regional universities. Yet despite often hopelessly inadequate circumstances, millions of young Southeast Asians learned something, even if only how to invent computer viruses (such as the 2000 "Love Bug," created by students at a Manila technical college). Many Southeast Asians also learned at least one foreign language— English, Japanese, and Chinese were the most significant—in conjunction with their work, if not their schooling.

Another characteristic of this elite was the more active public role of women. Economically the situation of most women in cities and white-collar industries improved, though they continued to fall short of men in income and status. Expanded educational opportunities meant that far more women were employed in the professions, teaching, and the growing services sector. Many elite women were no longer content, if they ever had been, to keep house and adorn their husbands' careers as "cooking-spoon wives." Expanded education was also demographically significant: the longer girls and young women were in school, the fewer children they were likely to have, both because they were postponing marriage and because they became more aware of alternative lifestyles and family planning options. As women gained decision-making power in society and within the family, they demonstrated that the birth rate would indeed slow down if women had access to education, jobs, and adequate health care.

Prosperity also encouraged a flowering of Southeast Asian arts. There was enough leisure and money for thousands of aspiring artists to sell their paintings, poetry, and short stories; to compose everything from classical *khon* (Thai songs) to pop songs; to put on *wayang kulit* (shadow puppet) performances and

Courtesy of Philippine Department of Tourism

Popular culture: a Philippine jeepney.

modern melodramas; and to produce multitudes of movies and radio and television shows. As usual, there were those who complained of declining standards, claiming that rap and rock were displacing traditional folk songs and that no one knew how to write properly any more, but others rejoiced in new forms of creativity. Thai, Vietnamese, and Filipino films often won international prizes, while ASEAN and other multinational organizations sponsored literary and musical exchanges that introduced many Southeast Asians to their neighbors' cultures for the first time.

The Dark Side of Development

UNDERNEATH this surface prosperity there was persistent poverty throughout much of the region, with continued, or even increasing, economic exploitation. In almost every country the income gap between the highest and lowest strata of society widened significantly in the postwar era. There is no doubt that the rich got richer, but whether the poor actually got poorer or simply fell farther behind the rich is still a matter of dispute. Data on the distribution of income—as opposed to the mechanical averaging implied in "per capita income"—are far from reliable, but they suggest that in many Southeast Asian countries the lowest quintile (the bottom 20 percent) often got poorer even in periods when the situation of those above them was rapidly improving. In almost every country there were urban slums of abject squalor and rural villages where most of the children were severely undernourished. Aprodicio Laquian distinguished "slums of hope" from "slums of despair," but over time the former could turn into the latter if hope was perpetually denied.

Who was responsible for this "dark side"? Outsiders bore the brunt of rhetorical blame, often justly. When independence was first achieved, it was easy to point the finger at the legacy of imperialism, and when governments like that of the Philippines continued to remain close to their former masters, ongoing "neocolonialism" was often accused of impeding development. (Over time this argument, though plausible at first, became less compelling; the Philippine economy actually did better, in comparative terms, in the immediate postwar period, when American ties were closest, than in subsequent decades, when they were looser.) Where direct ties to old colonialists were weaker, the World Bank and the IMF might be held responsible, since as a condition of aid they generally imposed austerity packages that included freezing or depressing wages. Attacks by foreign invaders on Vietnam, Laos, and Cambodia were immensely destructive; Myanmar, Indonesia, and the Philippines suffered from rebellions by disruptive minorities backed by outsiders.

Sooner or later, however, Southeast Asians asked whether their own rulers and their policies were also responsible for persistent poverty. "Since our plural society has succeeded in freeing itself from the grip of our colonial masters, we can no longer blame them for our problems," said Mahathir Muhammad in 1989. "We can only blame them for the economic, political and social imbalances they left behind, but after 31 years of independence if we fail to sort out these problems ourselves, we no longer have the right to blame others." Certainly most regimes were solicitous for the interests of local elites (as well as foreign investors) in trying to keep wages down by weakening or suppressing unions. Southeast Asian economists tended to agree with their international counterparts that "rapid restructuring of the economy to meet the challenges of the future may sometimes require the exercise of a certain degree of pain and force, however undesirable they may be"—and to assume that the poor, rather than the rich, should suffer most of the "pain and force." Similarly, governments were reluctant to tax their own wealthy citizens (or foreign investors, once it became clear that they would leave if profits fell), rendering many improvement projects underfunded.

Even when national governments actually appropriated money for health care or rural development, these funds, in order to reach their provincial targets, had to pass through political or bureaucratic channels controlled by other members of the elite on whom the regime depended (generals, governors, regional administrators), so they were vulnerable to diversion to private ends. There were endless demands for reform, but when the biggest rogues were eventually overthrown—Thanom in Thailand, Marcos and Estrada in the

Philippines, Suharto in Indonesia—most of the reformers who replaced them came from similar backgrounds, so there was little change in the overall trajectory of government policy.

Although persistent poverty was the biggest problem faced by developing Southeast Asia, it was not always the ugliest one. The region also suffered from many of the same problems that affected modern societies everywhere. Corruption was widespread, particularly on the interface between business and government. Almost everyone spoke out against it—every new Philippine president between 1946 and 1986 was elected on a platform pledging to clean up after the previous incumbent—but only in Singapore was it really curtailed. Corruption also underlay some of the most vicious violence in the region, committed not by antigovernment terrorists or by criminal gangs (though both existed) but by police, government troops, or private armies with official collusion. In much of Southeast Asia, logging companies, sugar plantations, and industrial developers could call on armed men in uniform to fend off, terrorize, or even kill those who stood in their way, while the government stood by and did little or nothing.

Corruption also protected illegal gambling, prostitution, and the drug trade. Traditionally, the drugs of choice in Southeast Asia had been relatively mild: betel, alcohol, tobacco (since the sixteenth century), and opium. In the post-

Popular violence: a Bangkok gunshop, 1992.

Photo by N. G. Owen

war period, however, more potent substances became available. Abetted by local officials and the CIA, the drug traffickers of the "Golden Triangle" (actually a quadrilateral crossing mountainous regions of China, Myanmar, Laos, and Thailand) began in the 1960s to refine opium into heroin locally, thus not only saving on transportation costs and risks, but making it available to Asian markets. Marijuana production and consumption spread in part through the example of American soldiers and other visitors to the region, some of whom also introduced methamphetamines (known locally as "ice" or "shabu"), now among the most abused substances in the region. The responses of Southeast Asian governments, like those everywhere else, were uncertain. Some, like Singapore and Malaysia, banned drugs with draconian legislation, including the death penalty. Others, like Myanmar, Thailand, and Cambodia, secretly condoned and profited from the traffic for many years even though nominally fighting it.

Commercial sex—accompanied by disease, drugs, and virtual slavery—was also important in the economy of several countries. Although prostitution has a long history in Siam, the modern sex industry of Thailand took off in the 1960s, when thousands of American servicemen were stationed there or visited on "rest and recreation" (R & R) from the Vietnam War. Long after the war the massage parlors and bars of Patpong and Pattaya were still filled with young women (and a few young men) newly recruited from the provinces or even sold to brothels by their parents. They appealed to tourists from both the West and Asia as well as to a growing domestic clientele. The government, although embarrassed by the public image of the sex trade, was mindful of its importance to the booming tourist industry so never took any serious measures to restrain it. However, the authorities were acutely aware of the danger the AIDS epidemic that hit in the early 1990s posed not just to tourism but to Thai society as a whole, which some feared might actually suffer a demographic collapse. A concerted program of sex education and condom distribution brought the epidemic largely under control by the end of the decade in Thailand but not in poorer countries like Cambodia, which moved into the low (cheap) end of this regional labor market.

Also on the gender front, the boom in light industries, such as textiles and electronics, created a demand for female workers, believed to be more dexterous and docile as well as cheaper than men. Like women in the early industrial revolution in the West, the female factory workers of Southeast Asia can be seen both as the exploited pawns of capitalism—forced to work inhumanly long hours under claustrophobic and uncomfortable conditions, vulnerable to sexual exploitation by bosses—and as canny optimizers. For the most underprivileged women, the daughters of poor farming families, industrial growth offered opportunities; factory wages, however low, enabled them to become more socially independent yet supply their village-bound parents with money and new consumer goods. A 1987 study of female workers in Malaysia by Aihwa

Ong shows them resisting oppressive factory discipline by such premodern techniques as fainting, mass hysteria, and seeing ghosts. In the countryside, where the economic squeeze was hardest, the position of the poorest women actually deteriorated under agrarian modernization. When machine harvesting replaced traditional hand harvesting of rice in peninsular Malaysia and Java, for example, poor women, who had traditionally survived by working for a share of the harvest, lost out. And as legalism penetrated the village economy, with issues of landownership, credit, and access to water increasingly governed by politics and regulation—rather than custom—those who had the least education and access to power, particularly women, were most disadvantaged.

For some Southeast Asians, the greatest threat of the modern era was more subtle and profound than corruption, drugs, prostitution, or even poverty. It was the loss of cultural identity under the flood of globalized productions pouring out of Hollywood and Madison Avenue, CNN and MTV. One critic of American influence in Europe labeled this "Coca-colonization," though in Southeast Asia the threat was not represented by the United States alone. The British pop sounds of the Spice Girls, Nintendo Game Boys from Japan, and kung fu movies from Hong Kong similarly threatened to displace local art forms and traditions. Even national cuisines seemed in danger from fast-food franchises like Kentucky Fried Chicken, though the international hamburger was successfully localized in the Philippines, where Jollibee, whose "unique flavor" appealed to the Filipino sweet tooth, outsold McDonald's. Sometimes the cultural threat could be closer to home: Laotians felt swamped by Thai music, movies, merchandise, and even language. Although consumer choice ratified all these invasions and a few self-consciously cosmopolitan Southeast Asians welcomed the breaking down of national barriers, many others regretted the potential loss of something unique and precious: language, custom, art, food, or traditional family values.

Significant regional diasporas complicated the situation. Hundreds of thousands of Southeast Asians had left their countries in the postwar period, particularly from the 1970s onward, as political refugees, economic migrants, or students. Some went only a few miles over the border—Cambodians and minorities from Myanmar and Laos escaping into Thailand, Malaysians and Indonesians working in Singapore—but many left Southeast Asia entirely, as overseas contract workers in the Middle East, Eastern Europe, and East Asia or as immigrants and students in North America, Europe, or Australasia. By the end of the millennium, many were returning, or at least sending remittances back, to their homelands. In the Philippines overseas remittances became the largest single source of foreign exchange in the 1990s, outdoing both old and new export industries. Elsewhere the figures were less dramatic, but both the remittances and the returnees were potentially dynamic.

Ecological Devastation

THE LITERAL dark side of Southeast Asia's industrialization and urbanization was the choking smog that often forced inhabitants of Bangkok, Manila, and Jakarta to wear face masks when walking the city streets and the corrupted waters that killed life in rivers, lakes, and seaside lagoons. But these were only the most visible manifestations of an ecological disaster that included the loss of around 80 percent of Southeast Asia's forest cover and coral reefs, and showed little sign of slowing as the twenty-first century rolled in. To some extent this devastation was the natural concomitant of economic and demographic growth: more wealth meant more cars, which meant more smog; more people meant more farmers, which meant more forest cutting. Some of the problems, such as the great forest fires that ravaged Indonesia and Malaysia in the summers of 1994 and 1997, sending clouds of ash as far north as Hong Kong, might even be blamed in part on El Niño.

But those who advanced such arguments were also apologists, wittingly or otherwise, for the unbridled greed that was responsible for many of the problems. The prime culprit in the deforestation of the region was not slash-and-burn farming but rapacious commercial forestry, whether legally sanctioned by governments or illegally taking advantage of weak or compliant officials. The Thai military, for example, was not only involved in the destruction of Thailand's own first-growth forests, but was also a prime contributor to deforestation in Myanmar, Laos, and Cambodia, which, when they finally opened their borders, chopped down their trees even more rapidly than Thailand itself had. In Indonesia, too, the military was a major sponsor of deforestation, whereas timber companies in the Philippines tended to use private armies. In so doing, these countries not only sold off their patrimony for a pittance, but actually weakened their national economies, since the loss of forest cover was a major factor in the periodic devastating floods that destroyed so many crops and took so many lives.

Southeast Asian governments also were unable or unwilling to curb the pollution of their waters by mining corporations or industrial plants, fearing that this might slow economic growth or create political enemies. In one extreme case, Kawasaki actually transferred a steel sintering plant from Japan, where it had provoked mass protests by environmentalists, to the Philippines, which thus became an importer of pollution. Rivers and lakes were also polluted by the overuse of chemical fertilizer to promote larger rice crops. The oceans were turned into a marine desert by giant Japanese fishing trawlers that swept up everything for miles and, closer inshore, by desperate local fishermen who used dynamite or poison to catch their share of the diminishing fish population, regardless of their effects on other marine life, including coral reefs. Huge dams

Deforestation: barren hillsides after opium fields were destroyed,
Shan State, Myanmar, 2002.

Courtesy of Kyaw Win

built for hydroelectric power drowned out the homes and culture of many indigenous minorities, as well as everything else that lived in that habitat, and as often as not contributed to siltation and pollution downstream, reducing agricultural yields there.

Many nongovernmental organizations (NGOs) arose to protest these attacks on the environment—as well as on cultural minorities and workers in general—and by the end of the twentieth century most governments paid lip service to the ideals of "sustainable development." But there was little effective action, and it remains possible that the century after 1950 will come to be seen less as the era of political independence and the "economic miracle" than as the time when the natural environment was destroyed.

Coping with Modernity: Attitudes and Analyses

SOUTHEAST ASIANS spoke out about the various problems they faced, in whatever form the political climate permitted. They did not need outsiders to point out the evils of drugs and corruption or the virtues of democracy and family planning. There is little we can say about such issues that has not already been said by Southeast Asian intellectuals with greater fervor and, in many cases, greater eloquence.

Through education, work, travel, and expanded communications, many Southeast Asians, especially the new elite, became increasingly aware of what was happening throughout the world and resented attempts to restrict information. Censorship was everywhere, ranging from businesses simply denying advertising to newspapers that annoyed them to the outright banning of offending books and movies or even the imprisonment of supposedly subversive writers. (There was also an alarming pattern of murders of investigative journalists.) But the emerging elite believed that it had a right to know what was going on and was empowered by developments in communications technology. Alternate interpretations of the assassination of Ninoy Aquino in 1982 were seen by millions of Filipinos in Betamax videotapes of foreign broadcasts, countering the official version on Philippine television, while the second "People Power" revolution, in 2001, was coordinated in part by middle-class Filipinos "texting" the location of Manila rallies to each other on their mobile phones. The Internet, often accessed through cyber-cafes, made the flow of information almost impossible to control, though some regimes, particularly in Vietnam and Singapore, did what they could to restrict access or channel it through approved outlets.

Not only did more Southeast Asians have a wider knowledge of the world than ever before, but they felt that they should have a voice in how to run it. Although the middle class was at the center of "democracy movements" in the Philippines, Thailand, and elsewhere, it would be misleading to see all members of that class as incipient democrats, much less revolutionaries. Many of them enjoyed quite comfortable lifestyles under conservative regimes and saw no reason to rock the boat, even backing repressive measures when threatened with instability from below. But their support for specific rulers was increasingly based on performance legitimacy—primarily the continuation of economic prosperity—rather than deeper loyalty. And when that legitimacy collapsed, as in the Philippines after 1982 or Indonesia after 1997, the elite made it clear, whether through the vote, rallies, public statements, or the withdrawal of their investments, that they wanted change.

Trenchant critiques of ruling regimes were not new in the contemporary period, of course. In independent Southeast Asia they were often met by brutal repression, just as they had been in the colonial era; sometimes even the same prisons were used. For many years ruling elites, who monopolized most channels of information, had not only been able to harass such critics but to suppress their memory. In Thailand, for example, the writings of generations of dissidents, from Tienwan, Phraya Suriyawat, and Nai Pridi Phanomyong to Jit Pumisak ("How many people reap luxury from our toil! / We ride on the buffalo, but they ride on us"), had to be rediscovered by the student radicals of the 1970s. Even in the Philippines, with the freest press in the region, Andrés Bonifacio was only reanointed as the leader of the "revolt of the masses" half a century after his death in 1896.

Toward the end of the twentieth century, however, it was harder to prevent criticisms from being heard, circulated, and remembered. Except for religion and the monarchy—and even they were not always exempt—no topic was sacred or immune from attack: government, economics, ecology, culture, corruption, sex, minority relations. In some societies, commentary could be open and direct; Renato Constantino built a long journalistic career writing about "Our Captive Minds" (1957), "The Miseducation of the Filipino" (1966), the need for a "Nationalist Alternative" (1979), and the "Synthetic Culture" (1985) produced by globalization. Elsewhere criticisms were often indirect, particularly in authoritarian states like Vietnam, where novels and films were allowed somewhat more license than openly political speech, and Indonesia, where satirical comments occasionally came out of the mouths of *wayang* puppets. And there were always jokes and rumors, hidden narratives created to contest official myths. In Indonesia Suharto's wife Tien was sometimes called "Mrs. Tien Percent," referring to the cut she allegedly extorted from all foreign investors. When relief aid supposedly going to flood victims in Thailand or the Philippines did not get through, it was widely attributed to corruption on no greater authority than "It is said that . . ."

This chorus of voices offered a wide variety of solutions to the problems Southeast Asians faced. Some were piecemeal and specific: remove this corrupt official, stop building that dam. Some were nostalgic and vague: restore traditional values—or even royalty—and all our problems will disappear. (The philosophical articulation of "Asian values" was often associated with defenders of authoritarianism, who feared "liberal democracy" above all.) Some were doctrinaire: join the revolutionary vanguard leading the masses, or lie back and embrace the free market and accept whatever it brings. Some were purely academic, but others were intended to, and did, lead to action.

Coping with Modernity: Action

SOUTHEAST ASIANS who hoped to promote political change often took the conventional route of joining the bureaucracy, the ruling party, or—especially in Myanmar, Indonesia, and Thailand—the military. But even when these organizations recruited widely, the top places often appeared to be reserved for those who had family connections, such as Singapore's deputy prime minister Lee Hsien Loong, son of Lee Kuan Yew, or Philippine president Gloria Macapagal Arroyo, daughter of former president Diosdado Macapagal. Another limitation to this approach was that though it might lead to personal advancement or minor reform, it was unlikely to produce structural change.

"Democracy movements" in Southeast Asia (as in China) represented an alternative approach, which actually succeeded in toppling regimes in Thailand and the Philippines as well as threatening them in Myanmar, Indonesia, and Malaysia. By "democracy" its advocates did not necessarily mean "one person, one vote" but a mix of other ideas: greater human rights (particularly freedom of speech, assembly, and the press), more responsiveness to public opinion, even an end to corruption. These movements took distinctive form in each country, but all tried to tap into the belief that ordinary people had a right to speak out on matters of state and to be heard by those in power.

A third approach was to bypass the government and organize people to struggle for justice directly. Hundreds of NGOs proliferated in the region—as they did all over the world—in the last third of the twentieth century, frequently raising issues that governments had neglected, such as agrarian reform, workers' safety, women's liberation, minority rights, and environmental issues. Women, often marginalized in conventional politics, tended to be relatively overrepresented, which some claimed led to a more people-centered, nurturing approach to social and economic problems than governments offered.

NGOs came in a bewildering variety of shapes and sizes. A few could mobilize tens of thousands of supporters marching for their cause, while others consisted of little more than a few visionaries with typewriters and active imaginations. Some, such as branches of Oxfam, Greenpeace, and Friends of the Earth, were offshoots of global movements, while others were purely local. The NGO Forum on Cambodia was founded overseas in 1986 but relocated to Phnom Penh in 1994; by 2002 their "agenda for advocacy" had shifted from international to national issues: civil society, development, environment, land mines, and women. A wilderness of acronyms sprung up in the region, from ARENA (Asian Regional Exchange for New Alternatives) to ZOTO (Zone One Tondo Organization).

NGOs also differed widely in tactics. Some functioned primarily as political pressure groups, lobbying for legislative change, clamoring for human rights, and protesting against corruption and the excesses of globalization. Usually based in the capital city, they tended to be politically and electronically well-connected, always available for a downtown rally or a media quote. Others largely ignored the capital and focused on change at the village or precinct level: forming agricultural or handicraft cooperatives or religious self-help groups, such as the "Basic Christian Communities" of the Philippines; standing together against the encroachments of landlords, factory owners, or dam builders; teaching each other how to read or loaning out small amounts of money to worthy micro-projects.

Insurrection—direct armed confrontation with governments—was the final recourse of those who sought change in modern Southeast Asia. By the beginning of the twenty-first century, it had largely been abandoned, except in self-defense, by those with specifically economic agendas (aside from what remained of the Communist Party of the Philippines). Not only had industrialization brought prosperity to many Southeast Asians, but developments in China and the former Soviet Union had cut off external support for leftist guerrilla movements and undermined their ideals.

Rebellion remained, however, a live option for separatist movements. Underlying many of their grievances, expressed in a vocabulary of religion and ethnicity, was a sense that the fruits of development had been enjoyed far more by the center and the majority population than by fringe-dwellers and minorities. In Aceh, Maluku, the hills of Myanmar, and the islands of the southern Philippines were peoples who felt that, among other affronts, their livelihood was being siphoned off to Jakarta, Yangon, or Manila.

At the start of the third millennium—in what is now a universally accepted global calendar—it was by no means clear how all these various social and economic conflicts would end, whether regional prosperity would continue to rise and perhaps even be shared more equitably, or whether everything would implode. What seemed certain, however, was that Southeast Asians themselves would have more to say about the outcomes than they had during the previous century and a half of colonialism, neocolonialism, and proxy wars.

Further Readings

Broad, Robin. *Plundering Paradise: The Struggle for the Environment in the Philippines.* Berkeley, 1993.

Hurst, Philip. *Rainforest Politics: Ecological Destruction in South-East Asia.* London, 1990.

Ong, Aihwa. *Spirits of Resistance and Capitalist Discipline: Factory Women in Malaysia.* Albany, 1987.

Oshima, Harry T. *Economic Growth in Monsoon Asia.* Tokyo, 1987.

Pinches, Michael, ed. *Culture and Privilege in Capitalist Asia.* London, 1999.

Robison, Richard, and David S. G. Goodman, eds. *The New Rich in Asia: Mobile Phones, McDonald's and Middle-Class Revolution.* London, 1996.

Rodan, Garry, Kevin Hewison, and Richard Robison, eds. *The Political Economy of South-East Asia: An Introduction.* Melbourne, 1997.

Scott, James C. *Weapons of the Weak: Everyday Forms of Peasant Resistance.* New Haven, 1985.

Stenson, Michael. *Class, Race and Colonialism in West Malaysia.* St. Lucia, Queensland, 1980.

Szanton, Maria Cristina Blanc. *A Right to Survive: Subsistence Marketing in a Lowland Philippine Town.* University Park, Pa., 1972.

Wolf, Diane. *Factory Daughters: Gender, Household Dynamics, and Rural Industrialization in Java.* Berkeley, 1992.

Wu, Yuan-li, and Chun-hsi Wu. *Economic Development in Southeast Asia: The Chinese Dimension.* Stanford, 1980.

which had a frontier with the British protected states), embarked on a policy of armed "confrontation" *(konfrontasi)*. The Philippines, for its part, resurrected long abeyant claims to Sabah, based on treaty concessions entered into by the Sulu sultanate, now part of the Philippines, with Western entrepreneurs a century earlier. Despite this opposition, the new state came into being in September 1963, but minus Brunei, which had opted to stay out.

The internal politics of peninsular Malaysia were affected at once by the new arrangements, for the Singapore PAP decided to participate in the 1964 general elections on the basis of the slogan "a Malaysian Malaysia"—by which was meant a Malaysia in which no one community (the Malays were clearly intended) should have a monopoly on nation-building and its prerogatives. This struck at the heart of the implicit compact between the Malay and Chinese partners in the Alliance and prompted a sharp Malay response. Finally, for fear that Malaya's own delicate communal balance would be irremediably upset if matters continued to deteriorate, Kuala Lumpur in August 1965 asked Singapore to leave the federation, and the island was thereafter an independent city-state.

Singapore's expulsion from Malaysia and its implications for the dominant Malay role in federal politics led to some disquiet in Sarawak and Sabah, the remaining "new members." Both had large and increasingly politically active non-Malay (and non-Muslim) indigenous populations. The Ibans alone in Sarawak and their counterparts the Kadazans in Sabah accounted for some 30 percent of the local population, against much smaller groups of Malays (and considerable numbers of Chinese). Though both states enjoyed a greater degree of autonomy than any of the peninsular states, resentment was felt at what was seen as Kuala Lumpur's insistence on the imposition of the Alliance pattern of politics. The adoption throughout Malaysia of the term *bumiputera* (son of the soil) and the extension thereby to Kadazans, Ibans, and other indigenes of the constitutionally protected privileges secured to Malays did little to lessen this resentment. But the political center of gravity in Malaysia remained in the peninsula and in Kuala Lumpur, as became abundantly clear in 1969.

A New "Emergency" and Its Consequences

AT THE general elections in May of that year, the Alliance, its share of the popular vote falling from 58 percent to 48 percent, lost twenty-three of its parliamentary seats to opposition parties and thereby lost also the two-thirds majority that had in the past enabled it to secure the passage of constitutional amendments. Similar swings took place at the state level. The beneficiaries included PAS, whose demands for an Islamic state played to substantial Malay dissatisfaction with UMNO (United Malays National Organization) and Alliance policies and achievements, but the principal gainers were the DAP and Gerakan parties, as Chinese voters, especially in the cities, deserted the MCA (Malayan

Chinese Association) and elected no fewer than twenty-one of their candidates to parliament and many more to state assemblies. DAP and Gerakan victory processions in Kuala Lumpur the next day, amid reports that at least one and possibly three state governments would end up with non-Malay chief ministers, led to a counterdemonstration by UMNO supporters on 13 May and eventually to four days of communal rioting in the city and environs that left some two hundred dead. The events of "13 May," though local and fairly rapidly contained, deeply shocked most segments of Malaysian society and were perceived by many as a rude questioning of the bases on which political and economic life had been conducted since 1957.

With a state of emergency declared and parliament suspended and replaced by a National Operations Council, which had military and police as well as political and civil service members, the task began of assessing why the social order had started to unravel and what to do about remedying the situation. Diagnoses were numerous but tended to suggest that significant numbers of Malays, especially, had lost faith in the capacity of the preindependence compact and its political managers to deliver what had been promised: the prospect of a greater share in the country's wealth and, less tangibly, in important cultural determinants of the new society, such as language. Considerable numbers of Chinese, for their part, frustrated by constitutionally guaranteed Malay access to certain privileges and opportunities but with new-found strength at the ballot box, had turned to more communalist forms of political expression in search of redress. The solutions proposed by the government and the ad hoc, broadly representative National Consultative Council established in 1970 resulted in the resumption of parliamentary government in February 1971 but on terms and in pursuit of policies in many ways markedly different from what had gone before.

The major changes were constitutional, ideological, economic, and political. Return to parliamentary government was premised on the passage of a Constitution (Amendment) Act that, though complex, had two main ends: to remove from public discussion (including in parliament) certain sensitive issues already entrenched in the constitution (in particular, the special position of the Malays and the status of the rulers) and to increase the numbers of Malays and other *bumiputera* receiving university education. Ideologically, a new Department of National Unity enunciated a set of "Principles of State" (Rukunegara) to which allegiance was to be promoted, consisting of Belief in God, Loyalty to King and Country, Upholding the Constitution, Rule of Law, and Good Behavior and Morality. The similarities of this formula to the Panca Sila ideology of neighboring Indonesia, similarly beset by postcolonial social division, are plain. Efforts were now made through formal and informal institutions to foster a sense of common national identity and purpose. Constitutionally the position of Malay as the sole national language was strengthened, and a new policy to accelerate its adoption as the medium of instruction at all school levels was embarked upon.

Some of the most significant changes lay in the economic realm. Embodied in what became known as the New Economic Policy (NEP) and set out in successive four-year Malaysia Plans were two principal objectives: first, the reduction and eventual eradication of poverty, irrespective of community; and, second, a restructuring of society so that identification of ethnic community with economic function would be progressively reduced until eliminated. The central element in the second objective was a proposed redistribution of owner-ship and control of the Malaysian economy so that by 1990 Malays and other *bumiputera* should own and manage 30 percent of the share capital in commerce and industry, other Malaysians 40 percent, and foreigners 30 percent (contrast-ing with an estimated 1.9 percent, 22.5 percent, and 60.7 percent respectively in 1970). To attain these ends a great variety of stratagems were employed, including creation of a range of state-sponsored statutory authorities to pur-chase and hold shares in public companies, foreign as well as local, on behalf of the *bumiputera*.

Politically, the principal development after the resumption of parliamen-tary government, manifested at general elections in 1974, 1978, 1982, and 1986, was the evolution of the Alliance model of political compromise into a Barisan Nasional (National Front) model. Begun pragmatically as an electoral strategy in the early 1970s by Tun Abdul Razak (Tengku Abdul Rahman's successor as prime minister from 1970 until his death in 1976), somewhat as the Alliance had begun in 1951, the BN was an UMNO-dominated coalition of some ten parties (membership has fluctuated), several previously in opposition but now given an opportunity to share in government. The main advantage of the Barisan coop-tative model for UMNO was that it allowed it to form partnerships with Chinese leadership groups outside the seriously weakened MCA. It also worked, at least for a time, to mute the political effect of increasing differences within the Malay community itself (partly on Islamic and partly on other grounds) by offering the possibility of direct participation in government without belonging to UMNO, though the resulting decline of PAS as a political force in the late 1970s pointed to the perils of this kind of embrace.

Islamic issues came increasingly to the fore from the early 1970s onward. They did so partly in response to Islamic resurgence in the Middle East and the growing ability of Islamist movements to communicate internationally through electronic and other media, partly as a result of social changes in NEP Malaysia: rapid urbanization of previously rural Malay communities and growing intra-Malay disparities of wealth and consumption. The rise of the *dakwah* (Islamic intensification and revival) movement expressed through such groups as ABIM (the Malay Islamic Youth Organization), Dar al-Arqam, and Tabligi Jama'at, posed serious challenges for the UMNO-dominated Barisan government. These were met by the adoption of state Islamization policies that placed new emphasis on Islamic education, by the creation of government *dakwah* and similar agencies, by broadening the writ of Islamic *shari'a* courts for Muslims, and by the passage of statute law (where previously only *shari'a* law had obtained) to provide for the possibility of Islamic banking and insurance. Policies of this kind accelerated after the Barisan government was successful in 1982 in coopting at ministerial level the charismatic ABIM leader Anwar Ibrahim.

The Mahathir Era

THE ACCESSION of Dr. Mahathir Muhammad as prime minister following the general election of 1981 marked the beginning of an era of remarkable economic development accompanied by a growing authoritarianism that was to persist well into the new century. Attempts to diversify Malaysia's long-term (and colonially derived) reliance on the primary production of rubber and tin and a few other commodities had begun as early as the 1960s, with government promotion of small-scale manufacturing industry and import substitution. During the 1970s the emphasis of industrialization strategy shifted to manufacturing for export, with a growing role for heavy industry. By 1990 the combined contribution of rubber and tin to total exports had fallen to less than 5 percent and that of manufactures had risen to 60 percent, largely as a result of direct foreign investment. With an annual increase in GDP averaging 8 percent into the mid-1990s, per capita incomes rose from U.S.$148 a month to U.S.$720, well above any of Malaysia's neighbors except Singapore and oil-rich Brunei. Central to these changes was the pursuit of the goals set out by the NEP: the reduction of poverty irrespective of ethnic group and transfer of a significant proportion of ownership and control of the economy to Malays and other *bumiputera*. By the time the NEP formally ended in 1990, the 49 percent of the peninsular population living below the poverty line in 1970 had been reduced to 15 percent (many of whom were no longer rural Malays but Indian estate labor and poor Chinese in the "new villages"), and the NEP's target for *bumiputera* wealth ownership had been substantially achieved.

The social transformations wrought by the trebling in size of the Malaysian economy in the two decades following 1970 and by state interventions associated with this expansion were considerable. Rapid urbanization meant that whereas in 1970 only 27 percent of the population lived in urban areas, some 51 percent did by 1991. A labor force that had been predominantly male was now 40 percent female, with large numbers of Malay-Muslim women working outside the home for the first time and some 44 percent of all women in gainful employment. Rising wages and standards of living translated into new consumption patterns and consumerist values similar to those of the West. Pursuit of the NEP goal of redistribution by means of government-owned enterprises

Small-town prosperity: street scene, Seremban, Negri Sembilan, Malaysia, 1990.

and subsequent privatization schemes requiring at least 30 percent *bumiputera* participation resulted in a burgeoning Malay middle class, many owing their wealth to links with UMNO, itself a major owner of corporate business as well as a source of patronage and access to resource rents (excessive profits derived from exclusive access to natural resources). Politically, the period was characterized by centralization of executive power and UMNO hegemony within the Barisan Nasional. There was growing encroachment on other branches of government, reduction of the powers of Malaysia's nine constitutional monarchs, and erosion of the independence of the judiciary, together with stifling of open dissent through the Internal Security Act—which permits indefinite detention without trial—and strict control of the press and other media.

Two episodes of political upheaval toward the end of the century reinforced governmental authoritarian tendencies already present. The first was brought about by a threat to Mahathir's leadership and a split within UMNO in 1987–1988, and the second by the financial crisis of 1997. An attempt to unseat Mahathir as party president in the late 1980s by an UMNO faction styling itself Semangat '46 (Spirit of 1946, the year of the party's founding) was narrowly defeated but led to a court case that resulted in UMNO's deregistration and rebirth as UMNO Baru (New UMNO). At the ensuing general election in 1990, the BN faced an opposition coalition of Semangat '46, PAS, and the DAP, the first time disparate opposition parties had successfully followed the Alliance pattern. Though UMNO lost significant Malay support, winning only seventy-one of the eighty-six seats it contested (down from eighty-five at the previous election) the governing group retained its two-thirds parliamentary majority, though with a reduced share (52 percent) of the popular vote. At the ensuing general election of 1995, widely criticized as marred by unfair government constraints but held at a time of high national prosperity, the BN and UMNO more than reversed these losses, and it looked once again as though the Mahathir-led Barisan Nasional was impregnable.

Early in 1998, following a long period of extensive corporate borrowing—with a high current account deficit and major government spending on infrastructure projects, and in the context of the regionwide financial crisis that had started in Thailand and spread to Indonesia—the Malaysian economy went into recession. Existing tensions between Mahathir Muhammad and Anwar Ibrahim, his deputy prime minister, finance minister, and presumed heir, turned to open disagreement over finance policy. On 2 September Mahathir sacked Anwar, amid charges of abuse of office, corruption, and sexual misconduct. Three weeks later Anwar was arrested under the Internal Security Act. In April 1999, after court trials that aroused wide public skepticism in Malaysia and were seen elsewhere to fall short of international standards, he was found guilty and sentenced to six years in prison.

Anwar's arrest and trial occasioned a substantial protest movement under the slogan "Reformasi," following the democratic reform movement of this name that had led to the fall of President Suharto of Indonesia the previous year. The movement brought together a wide spectrum of opposition focused on government "cronyism," the decline of civil liberties, and suppression of dissent, and it led to the founding of a new political party, KeAdilan (National Justice Party). In the general election of November 1999, KeAdilan, PAS, the DAP, and Parti Rakyat (People's Party) formed a Barisan Alternatif (Alternative Front) and made considerable gains in predominantly Malay areas, though the Barisan Nasional was returned to power with its two-thirds majority intact. UMNO, however, with only 72 out of the BN's 148 seats, had for the first time lost its majority within the governing coalition. Following the election, the seventy-seven-year-old Mahathir announced that, after eighteen years in office, this would be his last term.

Further Readings

Gomez, Edmund Terence, and Jomo K. S. *Malaysia's Political Economy: Politics, Patronage and Profits.* 2d ed. Melbourne, 1999.

Jomo K. S., ed. *Malaysia's Eclipse: Economic Crisis and Recovery.* London, 2001.

Lee Kam-hing and Heng Pek-Koon, eds. *The Chinese in the Malaysian Political System.* Kuala Lumpur, 2000.

Milne, R. S., and Diane K. Mauzy. *Malaysian Politics under Mahathir.* London, 1999.

Munro-Kua, Anne. *Authoritarian Populism in Malaysia.* Basingstoke, 1996.

Muzaffar, Chandra. *Islamic Resurgence in Malaysia.* Petaling Jaya, 1987.

Roff, William R. "Patterns of Islamisation in Malaysia, 1890s–1990s." *Journal of Islamic Studies* 9, 2 (1998): 210–218.

Chapter 30

Singapore and Brunei

THE PENINSULAR Malay states, after the effective defeat of the Communist insurgency, had experienced a relatively straightforward passage to independence from colonial rule in 1957. What of the other British possessions and protectorates in the area? The creation in 1963, on the initiative of Malaya's prime minister, of a larger Malaysia that included the Borneo territories of Sarawak and Sabah (and for a time Singapore) seemed to put an end to speculation. Singapore's exit from Malaysia shortly afterward, however, left the final status of the island—and of the sultanate of Brunei, which had declined to join Malaysia—still unresolved.

Singapore: Independence and Innovation

SINGAPORE'S history during the second half of the twentieth century was largely determined by the two features that clearly demarcated it from the rest of the "British Malaya" of which it had been a part—its highly urban character and its predominantly Chinese population. From being a British colonial possession, it moved a good deal more slowly toward independence than peninsular Malaya, principally because of British fears that the overwhelmingly Chinese island and its military base would succumb to communist subversion. Limited representative institutions were introduced in 1951, and a constitutional commission three years later recommended larger measures of participation and self-government. Following elections in 1955, the moderate left-wing Labour Front, led by David Marshall, a Singapore-born Jewish lawyer, was able to form a coalition government with local UMNO (United Malays National Organization) and MCA (Malayan Chinese Association) members. Tengku Abdul Rahman's successful visit to London in early 1956, during which he obtained the assurance of independence for Malaya, prompted Marshall to make a similar trip in December. He was offered, he complained, only "Christmas pudding with arsenic sauce"—limited independence with continued British control of defense and internal security. His case had not been helped by widespread middle school and labor disorders. Marshall resigned and was replaced by the colony's first Chinese chief minister, the trade unionist Lim Yew Hock. In the course of the next year, by pursuing tough policies toward dissidence and reassuring the British, Lim was able to get a firm promise of independence for 1959.

At elections in that year, the Labour Front lost the support of the Chinese-educated segment of the electorate and victory went overwhelmingly to the People's Action Party (PAP). Led by a Cambridge-educated lawyer, Lee Kuan Yew, the PAP, a pragmatic socialist party that in later years was to move markedly to the right, gained wide support from the Chinese proletariat by working closely with more doctrinaire left-wing and communist groups. The uneasy alliance between the right and left wings of the party, however, started to unravel when the leadership found that socialist tenets were ill matched with the state's heavy dependence for its very existence on servicing local and international capital, and it finally came apart in 1961. The divisive issue at that point was the proposal to join Malaysia, strongly favored by Lee Kuan Yew and those closely associated with him but bitterly opposed as a neocolonialist plot by the party's left wing, which seceded and formed a new party, the Barisan Sosialis (Socialist Front).

Though the PAP continued in power, it learned to exercise much tighter control over factions within the party. It also began to establish the grass-roots organization that enabled it to enjoy the remarkable social control that has continued to be its hallmark. Consolidation of PAP authority in the period leading up to merger with Malaysia in August 1963 (and to elections the following month, in which it gained thirty-seven of fifty-one Legislative Assembly seats) was greatly assisted by the arrest and long-term detention early that year of a large part of the Barisan Sosialis leadership on grounds of complicity in the Brunei revolt the preceding December and sympathy toward Indonesia's "confrontation" policies.

Membership in Malaysia, however, was to bring its own problems, and attempts by the PAP to engage in federal politics without due sensitivity to the complexities of peninsular Malaysia's very different ethnic and rural-urban mix earned it increasingly strong animosity from Malaysia. When this culminated in Singapore's ouster from the federation in August 1965, the now wholly independent city-state (population 1.75 million) was faced with a future in which it was at odds with its much larger and more powerful neighbors and had few resources other than its inherited role as a regional entrepôt and the talents and energies of its people. To add to Singapore's difficulties, Britain announced in 1968 that beginning in 1970 it would withdraw from its military role east of Suez and phase out its Singapore military base, a major contributor to the state's economy. The PAP rose to these challenges by embarking on a "politics of survival" and self-discipline for the state's "rugged society," instituting measures directed both toward total social mobilization and social control and toward economic growth. The latter was to be based on attracting foreign capital to industrial development, especially in the fields of electronics, shipbuilding and repairing, petroleum processing, and communications.

The two decades from 1965 saw singular success on both political and economic fronts. At four- and five-yearly elections from 1968 through the mid-1980s, the PAP swept the board more and more completely, Singapore becoming in effect a one-party state. Though this process was assisted at the outset by the continuing detention of opposition leaders, a Barisan Sosialis boycott of the electoral system, and some manipulation of constituency boundaries, the party's strength came increasingly to depend on its careful articulation with nominally nonparty Citizens' Consultative Committees and People's Associations at all local levels, on efficient and clean (if increasingly authoritarian) government, and on the provision of a wide range of social services unmatched elsewhere in Southeast Asia. In economic terms the PAP provided Singapore with one of the world's fastest-growing economies, achieving (along with Hong Kong) an overall standard of living second only in Asia to that of Japan and well in excess of anything else in Southeast Asia. The shift from entrepôt to manufacturing and service industries together with extremely stringent controls on labor enabled the state to maintain double-digit rates of growth in gross domestic product throughout much of this period, declining slightly only in the world recession of the mid-1980s. Along with this growth, and made possible by it, came heavy investment by the state in urban renewal, land use planning and reclamation, and infrastructure development in transport, communications, and public utilities.

Singapore's transition from colonial dependency in 1945 to Southeast Asia's most thriving entrepreneurial state and a major regional—and indeed global—communications center by the early 1990s, though made at some cost in personal liberty and self-expression, carried many obvious benefits for its citizens. Per capita income rose from U.S.$1,000 in the early 1960s to U.S.$15,000 in 1995, with little unemployment. Nearly two-thirds of its citizens lived in government-built housing, provided with a wide range of social, cultural, and health-care amenities, and by 1995 infant mortality levels were half those in the United States. Family planning programs moderated population growth so successfully that concern was being expressed by the end of the century at low levels of reproduction, especially among the better off and more highly educated. An integrated national education system, basically English and mother tongue, with special importance given to performance in the upper levels, prepared young people for entry into a technologically demanding work force. There was, however, a long way to go. In 1980, 44 percent of Singaporeans aged twenty-five and over still possessed no formal educational qualifications at all, 38 percent had been educated to primary level, 15 percent to secondary level, and only 3.4 percent to tertiary level. Though these figures improved as younger echelons moved into the work force, the political elite remained relatively small, comprising mainly upper-level civil servants and technocrats, educational and other professionals, business managers, and a number of wealthy Chinese-educated merchants. With a total population by 2000 of four million—77 percent Chinese, 14 percent Malay, and 8 percent Indian—Singapore faced sensitive issues relating to ethnicity, though there was little overt unrest.

As Singapore moved toward the close of the twentieth century, after two decades characterized by effectively unchallenged and increasingly authoritarian PAP rule, three political issues of consequence for the party emerged. The first was how to manage the transition from the Lee Kuan Yew cadre of PAP leaders to a successor generation. The second was how to ensure political legitimacy in a virtually one-party state that emphasized technocratic development and social control over democratic participation. And third, the party sought a way to place the accumulated financial reserves of the state as well as power over senior judicial, civil, and military appointments beyond the reach of any non-PAP elected government, however unlikely such a contingency might seem.

The party machine had from its early years been carefully selective in vetting and approving its parliamentary candidates, who were frequently hand-picked by the prime minister and senior cabinet colleagues. By the 1980s most Singapore members of parliament (MPs) had backgrounds in the state bureaucracy, business management, law, and the universities rather than direct experience of grass-roots politics. Once in parliament they underwent training regimes, mentored by senior colleagues, that laid great emphasis on policy-making skills and the importance of party loyalty and teamwork. Promising members were groomed for junior and, later, higher office. From this process emerged Goh Chok Tong, an English-educated graduate and business manager who had entered parliament in 1976 and held several ministerial appointments before being named in 1985, at age forty-four, as first deputy prime minister and heir apparent to Lee Kuan Yew. It was to be a further five years, however, before he succeeded Lee, who thereafter held the special cabinet post of senior minister. Goh appointed as his deputy prime minister in 1991 Lee's Cambridge- and Harvard-educated son, former brigadier general Lee Hsien Loong, who later also became minister of finance.

The transition to the new generation was marked by a carefully calculated but limited liberalization of political style, thought necessary because of a decline in the PAP's electoral performance during the 1980s. From enjoying a complete sweep of parliamentary seats in the 1976 and 1980 general elections, with 75 percent of the popular vote, the PAP slumped (in its own terms) in 1984 and 1988, losing first one and then three seats in a now eighty-one-member house. At the same time the party's share of the popular vote fell to 63 percent and then 62 percent. Though the international economic downturn of the mid-1980s was recognized as contributing to disillusionment, there was growing evidence that the PAP's autocratic and unforgiving style of government and unremitting insistence on social control had played a major role in alienating voters.

For a small city-state with a population of little more than four million, Singapore has an immensely complex electoral system, the product of repeated amendments to the constitution made possible by the PAP's complete control of the legislature. The party had governed into the early 1980s without a single opposition member in parliament. Though resolute on the necessity of the dominant party model of governance for Singapore and the "Asian values" it was said to embody—in contrast to the adversarial party politics of the West, which were declared dysfunctional and dangerous—the PAP was aware of the deficit in democratic accountability associated with one-party states. Accordingly it went to great lengths to bring about a controlled parliamentary opposition of its own design, while suppressing—through preventive detention, court defamation actions, and control of the press and other forms of speech—all political activism of which it disapproved. Before the 1984 general election, parliament passed a constitutional amendment providing that if no opposition politicians were elected, the top three losers with at least 15 percent of the constituency vote should be offered Nonconstituency MP status, with reduced voting rights. In 1990 a further amendment made provision for the appointment of up to six Nominated MPs, to be chosen by a special Select Committee from distinguished "nonpartisan" citizens. These measures did not prevent the election in 1991 of three members from the opposition Singapore Democratic Party and one from the Workers Party, much the largest opposition component in Singapore's history.

At the constituency level, further complexities in the electoral system were evident. The total number of constituencies rose, as a result of population growth and boundary manipulation, from 69 in 1976 to 84 in 2001. Of these only 9 were single member constituencies, the remaining 75 being Group Representation Constituencies (GRC), introduced in the 1980s, which must be contested by party lists consisting variously of four, five, or six candidates, one of whom must be a Malay or other minority candidate. Though established with the declared purpose of ensuring representation of minority communities, the GRC system has been widely perceived as disadvantaging opposition parties, which have difficulty in assembling and funding the requisite teams. Outside parliament some attempt was made early in the new century to relax tight controls on political activity, with the establishment of a "Speakers' Corner" in September 2000, following the imprisonment of the secretary-general of the Singapore Democratic Party for speaking in a public place without a permit. For the most part, however, Singapore remained one of the most tightly controlled though nominally democratic states in Southeast Asia.

The PAP's third area of political concern related to safeguarding the resources of the state and elements of its own authority in the unlikely event of defeat at the polls. In July 1988, ahead of the general election held later that year, the government published a White Paper titled "Constitutional Amendments to Safeguard Financial Assets and the Integrity of the Public Services." This document proposed the creation by constitutional amendment of a directly elected president (the office had until then been by government nomination), who, holding office for six years, would have veto power over the annual budgets of the government, state boards, and key government companies, and a right to make all senior judicial, military, and civil service appointments. The intention, it was said, was to provide a "two-key" solution (in which the prime minister held one key, the president the other) if a profligate government were to seek to squander the state's accumulated financial reserves (said to be the highest in the world on a per capita basis) or undermine its public authorities.

Courtesy of the Singapore Tourism Board

The modern skyline: twenty-first-century Singapore (with "Merlion," a creature with a lion head and fish body, designed as an emblem for the Singapore Tourism Board in 1964).

427

Suitability of candidates for the office, which would have a six-year term, would be established by a three-member Presidential Election Commission, two members of which would be government appointees. A bill enacting these and a number of additional provisions (among them that the president would have the right to refuse a government recommendation to declare a state of emergency and the final say in the release of political detainees) became law in January 1991, with the first election held in 1993. Though it had been widely expected that the first elected president would be Lee Kuan Yew, who had just relinquished the premiership, he did not in fact run, and the post went to a PAP-supported candidate, Ong Teng Cheong, who had been secretary-general of the National Trades Union Congress. He was succeeded in 1999 by R. S. Nathan, a senior civil servant who had been ambassador to the United States.

Though Singapore was not as adversely affected by the 1997–1998 financial crisis in Southeast Asia as most of its neighbors, growth fell from 8.7 percent per annum in 1997 to 0.4 percent in 1998, and there was a sharp rise in unemployment and a fall in personal income. Despite this, the PAP appeared not to have been held responsible by the electorate, the party taking eighty-two out of eighty-four parliamentary seats (many uncontested) in the general election of 2001, with 75 percent of the popular vote, a return to 1970s levels. Economically, Singapore was quick to embrace the "new economy" of globalization, moving to extend economic liberalization and adopt measures to enhance the financial sector and sign up for greater transactional transparency. Such policies were not much replicated, however, in the civil sphere, where stringent controls continued on information and the media.

Brunei: Oil and Authoritarianism

THE BRITISH administration that returned uncontested to Brunei after the Japanese surrender in 1945 had two main aims: a resumption of colonial protectorate rule in the name of Sultan Omar Ali Saifuddin III and rehabilitation of the Seria oilfields, which were operated by the British Malayan Petroleum Company, a subsidiary of Royal Dutch Shell. Both aims were wholly acceptable to the sultanate establishment, which was not to challenge British control until much later. Five years after reoccupation the Seria wells were producing one hundred thousand barrels a day and some U.S.$7 million in annual revenue, making the state the wealthiest country per capita in Southeast Asia. This disparity in national wealth—which turned Brunei into something more like an Arabian Gulf state than a Southeast Asian one—has continued to grow. Today the territory is the third largest oil producer in Southeast Asia (after Malaysia and Indonesia) and the world's fourth largest producer of natural gas. Despite fluctuating petroleum prices, it has vast overseas financial reserves, estimated by 2000 at close to U.S.$30 billion, with annual investment earnings equivalent to the state's revenue budget—this in a tiny (5,270 sq km) country with just over 300,000 inhabitants, of whom only some 65 percent are citizens. Given the territory's great wealth, it is perhaps not surprising that it has adopted as its formal name Brunei Darussalam—Brunei Abode of Peace. It has been a peace bought at a price, however, for the state's political and social history over the past half century has been characterized by an authoritarian rule that has suppressed dissent and excluded from public affairs all outside the patronage of the royal establishment.

In 1959, two years after the resumption of British protectorate control, Brunei acquired a constitution that, while recognizing the paramount political authority of the sultanate (sometimes claimed to be the oldest in Southeast Asia), made provision for a partially elected legislature. This acted as the stimulus for the emergence of popular political expression, principally through the left-wing Partai Rakyat (People's Party), led by A. M. Azhari, which had links with similar groups in Malaya and Singapore. Though the party won all sixteen elective seats in the August 1962 elections, it soon came into conflict with Sultan Omar (and separately with the government of Malaya) over plans for the future of the territory, preferring a local merger with its Sarawak and Sabah neighbors to absorption in the proposed Malaysia. Thwarted in this aim, the party led an armed revolt in December 1962, which was rapidly put down by British troops from Singapore; its leaders were jailed. Much of the constitution was suspended, and a state of Emergency Rule was declared that is still in effect.

In 1963 Brunei declined to join Malaysia, and in 1967 Sultan Omar abdicated (for reasons that have never been fully explained) in favor of his son Hassanal Bolkiah, though he remained for some years a powerful figure behind the throne. Subsequent constitutional progress was slow, despite Britain's urgings and its desire to reduce territorial and military commitments east of Suez. Sultan Hassanal Bolkiah ruled with a council of appointed ministers, with himself as prime minister and later minister for defense, and a number of other members of the royal family in ministerial posts. In 1983, in preparation for full independence on 1 January 1984, the sultan proclaimed the state a Melayu Islam Beraja, a Malay Islamic Monarchy, later declaring this form of government to represent "God's will."

The ideology of MIB, as it became known, is based on a variety of Bruneian cultural traditions, ranging from sultanate rule to Malay language, dress, and art, and the Islamic religion; it places strong emphasis on behavioral patterns of civic responsibility and social deference. In fact, though some 67 percent of the population of Brunei is Malay (including immigrants from elsewhere), there are substantial numbers of tribal indigenes (6 percent), a large Chinese population—the core of Brunei's commercial life—estimated at over 15 percent of the total, and a large, tightly controlled immigrant labor force. Of the total population of 260,482 enumerated at the 1991 census, only 171,099—mainly Brunei Malays—

were citizens, with 18,857 recorded as permanent residents and 70,526 as temporary residents. Most Chinese, however long they had lived in Brunei, were denied citizenship and, having lost the status of British Protected Persons at independence, were legally stateless.

Following independence a new political party, the Brunei National Democratic Party (BNDP) was launched in May 1985, led by Malay businessmen seeking commercial advancement. Despite an apparent association with a segment of the royal family, government officials and employees were debarred from joining, and membership was small. Party leaders called for "full democracy" in Brunei and an end to emergency rule. Five months after its formation the party split, a more pro-regime faction breaking away to form a separate Brunei National Solidarity Party dedicated to supporting the existing government and the MIB ideology. In January 1988 the BNDP, having persisted in its appeals for radical change, was banned and its leaders jailed.

Though the 1997–1998 financial crisis in Southeast Asia affected Brunei less than most of its neighbors, the state did not emerge entirely unscathed. The crisis gave renewed impetus to attempts to diversify the economy and lessen dependence on petroleum products, which have contributed historically over 60 percent of GDP. Any substantial change, however, whether economic or political, seems likely to be long term. Estimates in the 1990s suggested that even without projected further deep-sea exploration, oil reserves of 1.6 billion barrels would last until 2018 and natural gas reserves of around one trillion cubic meters, until 2025.

Further Readings

Cunha, Derek da, ed. *Singapore in the New Millennium: Challenges Facing the City-State*. Singapore, 1999.

Hill, Michael, and Lian Kwen-Fee. *The Politics of Nation Building and Citizenship in Singapore*. London, 1995.

Lee Kuan Yew. *From Third World to First: The Singapore Story 1965–2000: Singapore and the Asian Economic Boom*. New York, 2000.

Lingle, Christopher. *Singapore's Authoritarian Capitalism: Asian Values, Free Market Illusions, and Political Dependency*. Fairfax, Va., 1996.

Mauzy, Diane K., and R. S. Milne. *Singapore Politics under the People's Action Party*. London, 2002.

Saunders, Graham. *A History of Brunei*. Kuala Lumpur, 1994.

Tan, Kevin, and Lam Peng Er. *Managing Political Change in Singapore: The Elected Presidency*. London, 1997.

Tremewan, Christopher. *The Political Economy of Social Control in Singapore*. New York, 1994; reprint 1996.

Vasil, R. K. *Governing Singapore: A History of National Development and Democracy*. St. Leonards, N.S.W., 2000.

Chapter 31

Indonesia

The First Fifty Years

INDONESIA's first fifty years began with the triumph of decolonization and ended in challenges to the nation-state. By 1959 Indonesia had rid itself of most vestiges of colonialism. It had expelled Dutch citizens, nationalized Dutch businesses, replaced civilian with military rule, and was about to launch Sukarno's conception of an Indonesian form of government in "Guided Democracy." In the early twenty-first century the state was imperiled by two contrary forces: regional movements of Acehnese and Papuans wishing to separate from Indonesia, and Islamic groups aiming to submerge Indonesia in an "Islamic superstate" with Malaysia, Brunei, the southern Philippines, and the Malay Muslim provinces of Thailand. At the beginning of the period, Sukarno was launching himself as "president for life," about to send Indonesian troops into West New Guinea (Irian) and the new Federation of Malaysia. By the end, powerful leadership and strong central government had given way to short-term presidencies and governments unable to stop violence.

Under President Suharto (served 1967–1998) Indonesians became healthier, more literate, and more urbanized. Indonesia's oil and natural gas financed transport, communications, and industry. The heavy hand of government attracted multinational corporations that turned Indonesia into an exporter of manufactured goods. Until the Asian monetary crisis, which began in 1997, millions experienced rising living standards in contrast to the poverty and dramatic inflation of the Sukarno years. A middle class emerged, characterized by conspicuous consumption, foreign degrees, and travel. Throughout this period ordinary Indonesians experienced rising levels of violence at home from the armed forces and private militias. More and more Indonesians were on the move in search of jobs and new lives in distant parts of the archipelago or were displaced by ethnic and religious conflict.

In the 1960s Sukarno had abandoned his independent foreign policy for alignment with Beijing; by 2002 Indonesian territory had become a site for international terrorist organizations. Sukarno's "continuous revolution" and Suharto's "development" were tools to sustain their different visions for Indonesia. Fifty years after independence there were challenges from within and abroad to the idea of Indonesia itself.

Guided Democracy

GUIDED DEMOCRACY, or "democracy à la Indonesia," to use another Sukarno term, gave the government and its partner, the armed forces, the authority to decide what citizens should know and think. People were encouraged to understand themselves as members of groups characterized by a distinctive function such as gender, age, or occupation. The National Council that replaced the elected parliament of 1955 was filled by representatives of women, youth, peasants, workers, and the armed forces. Sukarno's model required the incorporation of all groups within one government. The cabinet expanded to more than three hundred members to accommodate this concept. Reconciliation of the contrary agendas of Islamists, nationalists, communists, and the armed forces necessitated, as Sukarno saw it, rule by presidential decree, censorship of news, banning of parties that refused to join the national family, and martial law.

Under Guided Democracy the armed forces muscled into civilian life. Their ideologues justified a dominant voice in the country's social and economic development by manipulating the history of Indonesia's struggle for independence. Because the armed forces had "saved" the nation from the Dutch, they claimed, they had the duty to assume a police role in preserving it from enemies within as well as defending it against external threat. Sukarno attempted to balance military power through mass organizations that dominated public space and intimidated opponents in universities, art circles, labor unions, and religious schools. Guided Democracy meant promotion of ties with communist countries, rising anti-Western rhetoric, unreflective mass organizations, a nationalism of race, and a commitment to crush colonialism.

In 1960 Sukarno launched the Front for the Liberation of West Irian. The Dutch had not ceded control of this easternmost portion of their colony in 1949 and, following Indonesia's independence, had focused on building up a Papuan identity and the beginnings of modern infrastructure there. West New Guinea resembled many parts of Indonesia with its mountainous, forested landscape, its land-bound population, many languages, and kin organization. It had entered archipelago histories as a source of slaves and forest products and a recipient of goods and technologies brought by Muslim and Christian traders from other parts of Indonesia. The sultans of Tidore and Bacan had ceded their New Guinea territories to the Dutch in the 1890s. From the second decade of the twentieth century, the Dutch had explored the interior and established deep within it prison camps for opponents of colonial power. Sukarno argued that common experience of Dutch rule made it part of Indonesia. He controlled Indonesia's thought-world in the early 1960s and so had the support of many when he sent in the armed forces in 1962 to oust the Dutch and to begin transforming West New Guinea into Irian Jaya (Great Irian).

Fierce opposition to colonialism and former colonial powers prompted Sukarno to "confront" the formation of Malaysia in 1963 and send guerrilla fighters into the former British dependencies on Borneo designated to join Malaysia instead of Indonesia. He broke off diplomatic relations with Britain and Malaysia, and withdrew Indonesia from the United Nations. By contrast, Sukarno appeared unperturbed by colonialism in East Timor. On a state visit to Portugal in 1960, he declared that East Timor did not belong to Indonesia, because it had remained outside the Dutch colonial state.

The international context of Sukarno's presidency was the Cold War. The domestic context was one of rapid population growth and economic crisis, as the government nationalized Western-owned businesses and restricted the activities of Chinese Indonesians, who made the economy work through their dominance in the professions and manufacturing, control of wholesale and retail trade, and near monopoly of capital and moneylending. Severing political and economic ties with the West cut Indonesia off from Western investment and technology, and made it reliant on the Soviet Union and China for aid. As Indonesians became poorer, Sukarno found enemies within (the Chinese) and abroad (Western capitalists and neocolonialists). Thousands of Chinese left Indonesia in the 1950s and 1960s, some fleeing anti-Chinese measures that excluded them from universities and jobs, others excited by the new China being built by Mao.

Sukarno maintained rage against the Dutch, reminding new generations of Dutch racism and demanding that Indonesia should matter on the world stage. The republic's first ministry had been the Ministry of Religion, established to attract support from Islamic countries and to inaugurate an era in which Muslim rights would predominate and Christian rights shrink. Sukarno sensed organized Islam as a threat to national unity, however. He forced the ministry to recognize Bali's Hinduism as an approved religion and thus offer full admission to Balinese within the Indonesian state. He moved "belief in God" up from its fifth ranking to number one in the state ideology of Panca Sila, determined that Indonesia would be a religious state (all citizens would be obliged to believe in

God) rather than have a state religion (Islam). Under Guided Democracy, the Ministry of Information surpassed the Ministry of Religion in importance. Sukarno used it to promote himself and his vision of Indonesia. He took the titles "Mouthpiece of the Revolution" and "Bearer of the People's Message." He glorified a national spirit that was always burning and declared 1965 a "year for living dangerously."

Living Dangerously

IN HIS Independence Day address for 1965, Sukarno proclaimed the Jakarta-Beijing axis. He allowed the Communist Party to begin giving military training to members of its affiliated organizations, who would form a "fifth force" to keep revolution boiling and to eradicate enemies. Government control of the press, the noise of demonstrations, and the monopoly of the streets by the Communist Party, which claimed in 1965 a membership of 3 million (with 30,000 trained cadres), concealed opposition to Sukarno and his allies, most notably from people with Islamist agendas.

In the histories of Indonesian communities, opposition to governments headed by sultans and governors-general had often been led by religious leaders whose claims to authority were based on the Qur'an or prophetic visions. They preached a simple message: eliminate foes because they are not Muslim or do not uphold Muslim principles. The Dutch were gone by the 1960s. The intent to eliminate enemies in the name of Islam was now directed against Indonesia's communists, seen as the heirs of Stalin and Mao. The communists' ideology also entailed elimination of an enemy, one who was depicted in class terms. Landowner and tenant had fought each other in east Java's villages in 1948. The 1955 elections showed that villages there remained deeply divided, with landowners most likely to vote for Nahdlatul Ulama, the party of Islamic leaders, and most tenants likely to vote for the Communist Party. Sukarno supported reapportionment of landholdings as an answer to rural poverty. In 1963 the Communist Party launched "unilateral actions" in east Java, land grabs intended to take rice fields from their owners for allocation to their tenant neighbors.

The frenzy of killing that engulfed Java and Bali in 1966 and 1967 was kindled by a coup launched on 30 September 1965 by Sukarno's palace guard in the name of clean government and putting the revolution back on track. A "Revolutionary Council" led by Lieutenant Colonel Untung denounced corruption of the armed forces; officers who controlled nationalized businesses were accused of diverting funds from the state to family and associates. The army's top leaders were seized and murdered, their bodies dumped at the training base for the nation's "fifth force."

General Suharto crushed the coup. He identified the Communist Party as the perpetrators, implicated Sukarno in the plot, and placed him under house arrest until his death in 1970. Through control of media and disposition of army units, Suharto promoted an atmosphere in which army and civilians murdered Indonesians identified as communists and their sympathizers. Village headmen felt pressured to draw up lists of enemies; Muslim and Catholic youth groups felt entitled to kill them. The years of Sukarno's rule, with its suppression of opposition, roiling of the public for big causes, and identifying enemies, had produced an attitude of "kill first before communists kill you" among certain disaffected people. In Aceh religious leaders issued a *fatwah:* Muslim men were obligated to rid their region of godless communists.

Through such state-sponsored mass murder, Indonesia became part of the global history of bloodbaths and the involvement of civilians in killing. It sparked little attention in the West, where political activists were focused on the Vietnam War. Suharto's media instincts led him to coin a term sinister to Westerners to describe the coup: Gestapu (an acronym for the "Thirtieth of September Movement"). In recent years claims have been made that Indonesia's Chinese were the main victims. Diplomatic relations with China were broken in 1966, China's embassy was burned, and Chinese language and civilization courses disappeared from the university curriculum, along with the study of Marx, Lenin, and Weber. For many years after, Chinese were discouraged from displaying Chinese characters on shop fronts and celebrating religious festivals outside their temple grounds. But most victims were Javanese. More than five hundred thousand were killed in Java and in transmigration areas around the archipelago. Balinese killed 5 percent of their own community. Village Indonesia has traditions of lynching thieves; the period between the overthrow of Sukarno and the consolidation of power by Suharto seemed like lynching on a national scale.

Sukarno's nationalism and promotion of unity had been failures, but today his era is regarded with nostalgia in many quarters. Sukarno is revered as "proclaimer of independence" and honored for having a deep love of Indonesia and Indonesians. Already under Suharto his rehabilitation had begun. Jakarta's new international airport was named for him, and the state created a grand marble mausoleum, with symbols of Bali, Java, Islam, and the nation, which has become a popular site of pilgrimage. His daughter, Megawati Sukarnoputri, adopted Sukarno's slogan *Merdeka!* (Independence!) in her campaign for the presidency. The press now remembers that he made Indonesia respected abroad.

Order and Development

GENERAL SUHARTO extracted from Sukarno a transfer of presidential powers. A purged national assembly confirmed Suharto as president in 1967. He adapted Sukarno's forms of government to establish his own authority and create a modern economy. He kept Panca Sila as the state's ideology, transforming it from a set of ideals designed for broad appeal into a tool of government control, and inserted it into the school curriculum from kindergarten through university. Aspirants for government jobs and promotions had to enroll in Panca Sila courses. In 1985 Suharto proclaimed it the sole set of principles for every legitimate organization, including political and religious associations. Panca Sila enveloped all lawful Indonesian life within itself. This claim was made transparent in the symbol of the pentagram (representing Panca Sila's five principles) framing the Arabic letters for Allah, which was placed on top of mosques.

Suharto elaborated Sukarno's concept of "functional groups." He transformed Golkar, an army-sponsored federation of anticommunist organizations, into the state's representative, viewing competing parties as divisive and opposition as un-Indonesian. Only Golkar, which was controlled by senior army officers until the 1990s, was allowed to open branches in towns and villages. Suharto required parties with Muslim agendas to group themselves into a federation. This United Development Party, stripped of Muslim labels and symbols, was granted official status outside Golkar; it was paired with the Indonesian Democracy Party, a coalition of parties with nationalist or Christian agendas. Leaders of the two coalitions and their candidates for elections had to be approved by the government. Opponents who refused to join the state political process were jailed.

Like Sukarno, Suharto imposed his power through the armed forces. For the first two decades of his regime, officers from the armed forces headed government ministries, agencies, and major businesses, such as Pertamina, the state oil company. A bureaucracy of military officers was installed parallel to civilian regional administrators down to the village level. Men in uniform guarded entrances to university buildings, were stationed at major transport intersections, and sat in offices where the public went to do business, whether to register for residence permits or purchase tickets to a tourist venue. Under the "Army in Villages" (Tentara Masuk Desa) program, platoons of soldiers were assigned to help village men who had been drafted to build roads and clear ditches, while their officers exhorted village headmen to implement government goals.

Officers of the armed forces were expected, as under Sukarno, to supply the deficiencies in their budget allocations by expanding into businesses such as logging, transport, and security services. Many sought business partners from Indonesia's Chinese communities. Military men had access to state licenses to set up a firm or import specific goods; Chinese entrepreneurs had business expertise but were shut out of commercial opportunities by laws designed to foster indigenous (pribumi) businessmen—meaning Muslims—unless they had a military patron. Relatives and close supporters of the president secured for their own companies monopoly rights to build cars, operate tollbooths, control the textile and packaged food industries, and run radio and television. Connection to the first family conferred privileges at banks, in land deals, and in labor contracts; some called it "crony capitalism."

Alternate sources of power—labor unions, churches, Islamic charity groups, nongovernmental organizations—were monitored or silenced by bans, imprisonment, and physical menace, including "mysterious killings" by government agents—which Suharto in his autobiography termed "shock therapy" for Indonesians. The noisy public life favored by Sukarno was replaced by the quiet uniformity of national life. Villages were expected to compete for cleanliness and order; government staff wore uniforms to designate their rank and branch in the state's service; wives of officials were drafted to bring programs of "uplift" to the urban and rural poor and to encourage lower-class women to limit family size.

Guided democracy was dismissed as the "old order." Suharto's "New Order" government sought Indonesia's readmission to the United Nations and renewed ties with the West. Indonesia's economic planners now established goals for training engineers and computer scientists; they borrowed from Western nations and Japan. They organized investment in regional economies for the benefit of the center. Aceh's oil, for instance, was extracted and processed within industrial enclaves by foreigners and Javanese according to directives established in Jakarta. Acehnese saw profits flowing out of their province to sustain the wealthy lifestyles of a corrupt national elite and to finance programs for Javanese.

Steel, cement, plastics, textile, and food-processing industries opened opportunities for rural Indonesians, who circulated between new industrial zones and home villages, piecing together multiple jobs and varied skills in both manufacturing and agriculture. Greatly increased numbers of motorized pedicabs, buses, and motorbikes sped millions to new work sites and to schools. Thousands of private schools sprang up alongside the government system to cater to the demand for computer skills and English.

Industry, transport, and schools made Indonesians mobile as never before. People moved from village to district town; they also ventured across the archipelago in response to opportunity or as part of government programs to redistribute populations. Madurese, for instance, migrated to Dayak territory in Kalimantan to take up tracts of farmland or work in the logging industries that were wiping out the island's rainforests. Butung Islanders moved to farm in Ambon; Buginese became shopkeepers in Timor; Javanese and Balinese migrated to Sulawesi, Irian, and Timor to grow rice or staff government offices. Batam Island, in the Riau Archipelago, was developed in the hope of becoming a second Singapore and drew unemployed hopefuls from across Indonesia. Many migrated to the capital; by 1990 the greater Jakarta area had a population of 17 million. The armed forces also made Indonesians mobile as units were stationed in regions far from their home base, and a domestic tourist industry targeting the new middle classes circulated Indonesians around the archipelago.

This new mobility changed the character of regions. Areas that formerly had had a Christian majority (Minahasa, Ambon) had majority Muslim populations by the 1990s, while 50 percent of Irian's population has become Muslim through the immigration of Javanese since the 1980s. Some ethnic groups saw immigrant Indonesians as competitors for use of land, water, and minerals that their traditions said were theirs because their ancestors had first discovered and named their territories. One consequence of greater mobility was a struggle between locals and migrants for control of local government and regional economies.

Through its control of media, the school curriculum, and symbols in public space, Suharto's New Order government promoted a new understanding of being Indonesian. Sukarno's nationalism had been based on opposition to colonialism and ongoing revolution; Suharto's was premised on being modern, classified, and orderly. Indonesians could see themselves on display in the Mini Indonesia theme park in Jakarta, where every ethnic group had its quaint distinctive culture, all joined together through the homogenizing experience of a national superculture of modernity. At the same time, Javanese culture was elevated, as Javanese vocabularies permeated Indonesian official-speak. Suharto's government suppressed public debate of religious, ethnic, and class issues, and fashioned a national rhetoric of unity of purpose and spirit. Fundamental problems could not be resolved under these conditions, so the aggrieved tended to be receptive to men who offered violent solutions.

Ending the New Order

SPORADIC VIOLENCE was one response during the Suharto years, as, for example, when Dayaks drove Chinese Indonesians off farms in West Kalimantan through murder and arson. A different path was taken by organizations with Islamic agendas. Denied the right to win power through the ballot box under New Order rules, organizations such as Muhammadiyah and Nahdlatul Ulama turned to transforming Indonesian communities through missionary activity to fellow Muslims. Such activity was called *dakwah,* an Arabic term meaning a summoning to revitalize religious commitment. *Dakwah* also entailed creation of a network of schools, hospitals, and businesses parallel to government institutions where clients could gain modern services while receiving a message fundamentally opposed to Suharto's promotion of secular development toward a consumer society. The message also resonated with Indonesian nationalist pride, for it said that modernization was not the same as Westernization. Indonesians could gain the benefits of modernity—science, technology, mass education, rising incomes—through Islamic forms of government and Islamic morality.

An immediate consequence of turning from politics to social programs was the Islamizing of public space. Indonesia's streets became filled with new and repaired mosques and prayer houses, Islamic schools, and women with a new look: matching headscarves, tunics, trousers, and socks. Public notice boards with Arabic letters multiplied; electric sound equipment amplified prayer calls and dominated the day with Islamic rhythms. Radio and television programs featured Islamic "pop" music, newspapers carried "Ask Uncle Haji" advice columns, and people were busy in their spare hours in new prayer circles and Qur'an study groups. Where revival communities became sufficiently strong, they were able to ban vestiges of pre-Islamic practice, such as village offerings to guardian spirits and ritual communal feasts. Domestic and mosque architects turned to Islamic forms for inspiration. Personal etiquette changed with avoidance of the Western handshake and increased demarcation of men's from women's space at home and in public.

Increasing numbers of young men joined Islamic study groups when they enrolled in Western universities or went to Islamic countries to study, some returning home sporting an Islamic (male) look of Middle Eastern robes, head coverings, and beards. An Islamic "think tank" known as ICMI (Ikatan Cende-kiawan Muslim Indonesia) was established in 1990 with presidential endorsement. It campaigned against Christian and Chinese involvement in public life and championed Islamic causes in Indonesia's foreign policy. In the name of social improvement, Islamic groups successfully pressured the government to set up an Islamic bank, license an Islamic newspaper, close down the state lottery, and increase the expenditure of public funds on Islamic causes.

People with personal Islamic agendas were well placed in senior administrative, educational, and army posts when Suharto's grip on power weakened in 1997. The government's ability to shape public culture had been based on its monopoly of military and economic power. When Indonesia's currency collapsed in 1997 and millions lost their jobs, the government was judged impotent as well as corrupt, the pawn of international money markets and the servant of Western financial institutions. Indonesia's middle classes, created by Suharto's development programs, had been susceptible to his threat that challenge to his New Order would bring back the chaos and bloodshed of 1966 and the loss of everything they had gained since then. They could tolerate outbreaks of arson and looting of Chinese businesses, even attacks on Chinese men and women by hired thugs, but they could not forgive the military for attacks on their own children in universities. In May 1998 Suharto, Indonesia's "father of development," was pressured to resign in favor of Vice President Habibie.

Habibie represented the Islamizing of modernity in Indonesia. He had built up Indonesia's aerospace industry, served as minister for science and technology, and headed ICMI. He was of Buginese-Javanese parentage and a graduate of the German education system; he represented the new Indonesia of independence.

But as a civilian he lacked Suharto's power base in the armed forces, and he had no national reputation to sustain a claim like Sukarno's to be the mouthpiece of all Indonesians. He lifted bans on public expression and freed public life. Groups that during the Suharto years had nursed fears, angers, and hatreds with no legitimate outlet for public debate or practice in political compromise now turned on their enemies. They fought for control of jobs and resources, for turf, to oust rivals from positions of power. They fought to expel migrants or rid their districts of the symbols and representatives of rival religions. Suharto fell as modernizing Indonesia entered the age of electronic communications. Internet cafes in cities across the archipelago brought the web to many young people, and things that could not be said under Suharto now galvanized millions. Explosions of violence in Sulawesi, Ambon, Halmahera, and Kalimantan turned hundreds of thousands of Indonesians into refugees, fleeing to camps to escape mobs and find shelter when homes and jobs were destroyed.

The new openness also reanimated civil rights groups. They organized to assist the poor; they demanded reform of the legal system, prosecution of Suharto, and separation of police and military powers. There was a multiplication of parties wanting reform of the political system, a new constitution, reduction of Golkar's powers, and removal of Habibie from office because of his close association with Suharto. Allegations of abuse of military power could now be leveled against the nation's senior officers, and demands for investigation of the private wealth of the Suharto family and associates were publicized.

Protests for constitutional reform, clean government, and restraints on the armed forces were made in the name of a better Indonesia, which at the beginning of the twenty-first century numbered over 210 million people. There were also groups challenging the nation-state itself in the name of regional homelands, and many argued that a better Indonesia would be an Islamic Indonesia. Under Suharto people were required to suppress difference, to subscribe to a single, acceptable Indonesian type. After Suharto people felt free to express every kind of difference. There was a multiplication of associations for self-help, for reciting the names of God, for winning elections, for democratizing Indonesia, for launching jihad.

Many analysts have noted the impact of Iran's religious revolution to explain the vocal support of Islamic causes in Indonesia since the 1980s and the use of Islamic vocabulary to bring about social change. Yet throughout Indonesian histories Islam has always been an enemy of government. Prophets would emerge to denounce sultans and the Dutch and promise a new way through inauguration of Islamic rule. By the 1990s modern communications and propaganda techniques brought such prophets archipelago-wide audiences and followings that reached as far as Malaysia. Arab Indonesians, descendants of Hadrami traders and Javanese mothers, who had been encouraged, during the Suharto years, to stress their Indonesian heritage, now emerged to promote the

Arabizing of Indonesian Islam. They called for the reduction of Christian rights and Christian space in Indonesia. Many Islamic groups opposed the presidency of Nahdlatul Ulama's Abdurrachman Wahid (1999–2001), who defended Indonesia's folk Islams, and of Sukarno's daughter, who succeeded him.

A Nation under Challenge

FOR NEARLY a century the Indonesia that people visualized stretched from Sabang Island in its western extremity to Merauke town on the border that divides West New Guinea from the territories east of it—which today form the independent country of Papua New Guinea (PNG). Ideologues and scholars justified insistence on colonial borders by identifying unifying cultural content: historical links forged between societies by the ancient kingdoms of Srivijaya and Majapahit, common customs and artistic motifs, Malay language, and Islamic religion. The nationalist rhetoric of 350 years of resistance to Dutch rule also justified a single Indonesian state. But this conception of diverse communities united in a single past is today being contested at both ends of the archipelago.

Hasan di Tiro of the Free Aceh Movement countered this unitary reading of history in the 1980s, arguing that Aceh had never been a vassal state to Srivijaya or Majapahit. It had developed, he claimed, from a harbor polity on Sumatra's northern tip into a sultanate whose political reach had extended south through military conquests, marriage alliances, and conversion of Sumatran communities to Islam. The state of Aceh-Sumatra had been subdued and its sultanate abolished through a long war fought by Dutch and Javanese troops. Aceh had entered the colonial state only in 1903. It had sustained its difference from the rest of Indonesia during the revolution, for Dutch troops had not attempted to reoccupy Aceh. Opposition to Christian rule over Muslims had made Acehnese willing to export fighters and funds to oppose Dutch forces elsewhere in the archipelago, but Aceh had achieved its independence following the collapse of Japanese power. The Dutch should therefore have transferred independence to Aceh-Sumatra in 1949 as a state separate from the Republic of Indonesia. Instead, di Tiro argued, the Dutch had delivered Aceh to rule by the Javanese and a new form of imperialism.

Di Tiro's reading of history was rejected by Jakarta, but the Acehnese succeeded in cementing their reputation as Indonesia's most committed Muslims. Because of their support of the revolution in 1959 Sukarno had conferred special status on Aceh. While its unique customs were recognized by Jakarta governments, neither Sukarno nor Suharto was willing to allow an autonomous region to develop far from the capital or to see an independent state control Indonesia's water highways, take over its huge oil and gas reserves, and present itself alongside Malaysia as an economic and ideological competitor with the Indonesian state. Outbreaks in Aceh in the 1950s in the name of the Islamic

State of Indonesia were put down, and rebellions in the late 1980s were again crushed by the national army.

Suharto's mode of dealing with Aceh combined three broad approaches. He kept potential opposition under surveillance by requiring *ulama* to join a state-sponsored religious council, and he coopted their support by opening up prestigious educations and jobs for their sons. He made Aceh a site of transmigration for Javanese farmers so that pockets of immigrants were interspersed among locals. And he sent in Indonesia's armed forces to suppress opposition. Indonesia's national army had been born of the revolution. It was made up of professional soldiers under central command and private militias of civilians committed to local leaders and specific causes. The strategy of involving civilians in killing was seen as acceptable when the enemy was Dutch, but in the 1990s the use of civilians to kill their compatriots in Aceh came to be viewed differently. Indonesian troops were accused in the newly freed media of kidnapping, torture, rape, and forced relocation of Acehnese, and of fomenting divisions among them.

Aceh's independence movement (called "Movement of Disturbers of the Peace" by the Indonesian military) had no single agenda. Supporters opposed Jakarta's rule for many reasons: to win regional autonomy, to control the gas and oil, to inaugurate rule of Islamic law, to become an independent country. The enduring opposition and shock at revelations of Indonesian army abuses led Indonesia's constituent assembly to grant full autonomy to Aceh in 2000 and to permit Islamic law to supersede Indonesian law there. A religious police force was recruited, and a compulsory new dress code for men and women was introduced as the first aspects of an Islamic state that politicians and *ulama* could agree on. By 2003 Indonesia's president and national army had resolved to crush Aceh's separatists through military force. Acehnese civil servants were ordered to take loyalty tests, and Acehnese living throughout the archipelago were required to register with the police.

Through Islam Aceh is knit into the histories of societies across Indonesia. Acehnese *ulama* became part of the Islamic intellectual tradition in the seventeenth century. They developed Malay into a language of Islamic scholarship, preaching, and translation of Arabic and Persian texts. Acehnese missionaries traveled the archipelago's sea highways, while students of Islam came from neighboring and distant lands to Aceh's schools to study. Thus Aceh had contributed to the creation of Indonesia. At the other end of the archipelago, in the twentieth century, Indonesia had contributed to creation of the idea of Papua.

Sukarno set in motion the military and political strategies for wresting control of West New Guinea from the Dutch, but Suharto transformed it into Irian, Indonesia's twenty-sixth province. The symbols of the national state—red and white flag, portraits of president and vice president, public monuments, street names—gave the territory the look of Indonesian towns, while the development of a school system teaching the nationally mandated curriculum, which included Indonesian history and Panca Sila, gave the province's youth a common language and a shared set of concepts. Irian was officially integrated into the Indonesian state in 1969, as Suharto launched his program of development. Western investment in the extraction of Irian's minerals brought in men with managerial and technical skills, a modern infrastructure, and units of the national army to protect the mines and many related businesses established by Indonesians from across the archipelago. New job opportunities and "empty" land brought massive migration from Indonesia's other provinces.

High school graduates from Irian's many speech groups and tribes now had a common language in Indonesian in which to process their reactions to the rapid transformation of their home territory. For many, being part of Indonesia offered opportunity. Indonesia's armed forces supported traditional chiefs in power; Indonesia was a source of university education for their sons; Indonesia's national constituent assembly offered a new arena for their politicking. For others, the incorporation of Irian into Indonesia was experienced as colonialism. Javanese and Buginese monopolized jobs in government and business, as they had the connections necessary under Suharto's economic system of patronage to gain licenses and monopolies. The region's wealth was ripped out of jungles by Western and Indonesian partners with no local voice on investment of profits. Indonesian laws controlled the press and suppressed dissent.

Those who had studied Indonesian history in school could equate Indonesian policies in New Guinea with colonial rule. They formed the Organization for Papuan Independence (OPM), using Indonesian as their language, and took *Merdeka* (freedom), a word emotively bound up in Indonesia's history of nationalism, as their goal. When a group raised OPM's Morning Star flag in Biak in 1998 to signal their aspirations for Irian control of Irian destinies, Indonesian troops tore it down and fired on protesters.

The fall of Suharto brought louder demands for freedom from Indonesian rule. A meeting in 1999 demanded the renaming of Irian as Papua, an end to Indonesia's annexation of the territory, and an interim local administration under United Nations supervision. Jakarta's ruling elite, committed to the idea of Indonesia, opposed the name Papua, which suggested that Irian's youth were looking east across another colonial era border to PNG and visualizing a Papuan-Melanesian identity. In order to preempt the movement, the nation's policy-making body authorized display of Papuan symbols alongside Indonesian, offered more autonomy, and, in a move interpreted by many Papuans as "divide and rule," proposed division of the province into three.

Indonesians widely shared the view that incorporation of Irian into the state brought "uplift" and modernity to Irianese. Indonesians clothed naked Irianese bodies, codified Irianese customs, and preserved their traditional arts through festivals in Jakarta. Indonesia brought electricity, modern medicine, rice agriculture, a single currency, and a national culture to backward tribespeople. Many Indonesians also saw their role as bringing the advantages of twentieth-century living to East Timor and emphasized that the territory received the highest per capita expenditure of development funds from the national budget during its nearly twenty-five years as Indonesia's twenty-seventh province.

Southeast Asia's newest state differs from its fellows, because it gained its independent status (in May 2000) not as the product of revolt against European rule, but through rejection of Asian rule. The Democratic Republic of East Timor consists of the east half of the island of Timor and a small territory around the port city of Oecusse inside Indonesian West Timor. Histories written during East Timor's quarter century under Indonesian rule begin their narrative with the Portuguese, who conquered the territory back in the sixteenth century, and stress the region's complete separation from Indonesian histories. Historians today are engaged in constructing a history of unique identity within a single East Timorese past. But Timor can also be linked into Indonesian histories. The island lies within the eastern archipelago where Malay and Papuan languages meet. It shares with many of Indonesia's communities kin systems, tribal political organization, artistic motifs, and symbols. While surrounded by water, Timor's peoples have a land-bound culture. Their relationships with the outside world were mediated through sea peoples who exported Timor's forest produce and introduced crops, technologies, and knowledge systems of other civilizations.

Timor communities lay at the far end of long trade routes and were made known through the observations of outsiders. Javanese called them "easterners" and tribute-paying vassals. Timor was the last port of call for Portuguese and the farthest backwater of a Portuguese string of settlements linked through Goa to Lisbon. Treaties negotiated by Portuguese and Dutch colonial governments established the border dividing West from East Timor in 1914, but long before that the policies of the two European powers had produced differing paths of development. West Timor was knit into the Netherlands Indies, where Malay was the lingua franca, Islam the religion of the majority, and colonial policy aimed at transforming people into wage earners and consumers. East Timor was knit into Portugal's empire, which included Brazil (until 1822), Angola, Mozambique, Macau, and Goa. Its language of elite schooling was Portuguese and the religion of its missionary enterprise, Roman Catholicism. Being small and distant, East Timor did not attract much Western investment, and Timorese remained subsistence producers rather than wage laborers until 1974, when Portugal announced its decision to end colonial rule.

Portuguese rule had generated a Catholic, Portuguese-speaking, urban elite, whose members organized themselves into three parties in 1974 to compete for control of the state. The Timor Democratic Union and the Revolutionary Front for the Liberation of East Timor (Fretilin) opted for Portuguese as the new state's language; the Democratic Union wanted continuing ties with Portugal, while Fretilin looked to Portugal's African territories for models. The Timor Popular Democratic Association, in contrast, looked west to Indonesia, the territory's largest and most important neighbor, with whom Timorese shared many cultural traits. Indonesia, as a rapidly modernizing country and member of the Organization of Petroleum Exporting Countries, had a wealth of human and natural resources; it represented enormous opportunity for a territory of around seven hundred thousand people with low literacy rates and an economy based on subsistence agriculture. The Popular Democratic Association advocated Indonesian as the language of the future; its leaders expected jobs because of their support for integration with Indonesia. They "invited" Indonesian army units to depose Fretilin, which had defeated its rivals and seized control of the administration in August 1975.

East Timor rejected incorporation into Indonesia because of its different colonial heritage and because of the brutal nature of Indonesian rule, which began with troops crossing the border in December 1975. The Indonesian army and associated militias of pro-Indonesian Timorese fought resisters in difficult mountain and forest terrain. They patrolled the few metaled roads in convoy and took over towns. A population in poor health quickly succumbed to the loss of food supplies and lack of medical care. One hundred thousand died in the first years of Indonesian rule through war and war-related starvation and illnesses. By 1979 Fretilin-led resistance seemed over, its leaders dead or captured, and Suharto's government launched its program of integration and development. Indonesian became the national language, a school system teaching the Indonesian national curriculum replaced that of Portugal, Panca Sila became the province's ideology, and Indonesian symbols proliferated. When East Timor was "opened" to Indonesia, investment and Indonesians flowed in.

Although Indonesia's development program appeared to be integrating Timorese into the republic, East Timorese resisters had what the Acehnese did not: the support of an international lobby. When Portugal withdrew its administration, its officials estimated 30 percent of Timorese were Catholics and 70 percent were followers of local spirit systems. Indonesia's ideology of Panca Sila required everyone to register as a believer in one of the state-approved religions. By the end of Indonesian rule, most Timorese had converted to Catholicism. Indonesian rule had produced a Christian East Timor, and East Timor's Christian representatives built up an international Catholic lobby in support of independence.

The overthrow of Suharto and the eruption of public conflict across the archipelago opened the way for East Timorese to press their demands for independence. President Habibie, confronted by problems of every kind, bought time in 1999 by offering East Timorese a referendum on whether to remain within Indonesia or withdraw from it. In the vote, conducted by a United

Nations team, 78.5 percent of East Timorese opted to exit Indonesia, a result most Indonesians perceived as creating a precedent for other breakaway movements and as weakening the nation. The Indonesian army and militias made revenge attacks against the new state as they withdrew.

For almost all Indonesians, incorporation of East Timor had signified a commitment to defeat European colonialism. For Christian Indonesians, East Timor had expanded the number of Christians in the nation. The loss of East Timor damaged national pride. It shrank Christian space at a time of heightened tensions between Christians and Muslims, sharpened anti-Western sentiments, and brought foreign troops under United Nations command to the borders of the state.

For the new country of East Timor, independence called for the creation of unity among the different speech and generation groups, a gathering in of its people scattered in refugee camps across Indonesia, and the resolution of grievances that had resulted in civil war. The new state had to build an economy, find accommodation with Indonesia, and determine if its political models lay in Melanesia, in former Portuguese colonies, or in Indonesia.

The career of Megawati Sukarnoputri also challenged the idea of Indonesia. Aisyah, Indonesia's largest organization for women, sought a ruling from Indonesia's leading Islamic experts in 1999 on whether it was lawful for Muslims to vote for a female president, as the constitution of 1945 had no gender qualification for president. Some religious leaders questioned the sincerity of Megawati's personal dedication to Islam; others demanded that she declare an agenda committing Indonesia's government to Islamic goals. Some politicians attributed her following in the Indonesian Democracy Party of Struggle to kinship politics rather than an enlarged political sphere for women.

As a presidential campaigner, Megawati stressed loyalty to the nation-state. As president (since 2001), Megawati signaled acceptance of East Timor's exit from Indonesia by attending its independence ceremonies. Her strategy for preserving Sukarno's state "from Sabang to Merauke" was legislative recognition of "special characteristics" of each region and the transfer to provincial administrations of many of the powers absorbed by central government under Suharto. She argued that tolerance was the quintessential Indonesian characteristic and that it represented the ideal of most of Indonesia's Muslims.

Megawati's Indonesia allowed Chinese Indonesians to celebrate Chinese festivals and Hindu Indonesians to be equal members of the nation. The weakness of her government prevented it from ending violent contests for land, jobs, and religious freedom in many regions of the archipelago state. In 2002 Megawati attended religious ceremonies at the Borobudur temple to mark the birthday of the Buddha. Indonesia's vice president, Hamzah Haz of the (Islamic) United Development Party, absented himself from the Buddhist ceremonies, though he joined dignitaries at an official reception that followed. These decisions marked two different visions for Indonesia as it entered the twenty-first century.

Further Readings

Cribb, Robert, ed. *The Indonesian Killings of 1965–1966: Studies from Java and Bali.* Clayton, Victoria, Australia, 1990.

Elson, R. E. *Suharto: A Political Biography.* Cambridge, U.K., 2001.

Hooker, Virginia Matheson, ed. *Culture and Society in New Order Indonesia.* Kuala Lumpur, 1993.

Riddell, Peter G. *Islam and the Malay-Indonesian World: Transmission and Responses.* London, 2001.

Sukarno. *Sukarno: An Autobiography as told to Cindy Adams.* New York, 1965.

Taylor, Jean Gelman, ed. *Women Creating Indonesia: The First Fifty Years.* Clayton, Victoria, 1997.

Toer, Pramoedya Ananta. *The Mute's Soliloquy: A Memoir.* Translated by Willem Samuels. New York, 1999.

Wessel, Ingrid, and Georgia Wimhofer, eds. *Violence in Indonesia.* Hamburg, 2001.

Woodward, Mark. *Islam in Java: Normative Piety and Mysticism in the Sultanate of Yogyakarta.* Tucson, 1989.

Chapter 32

The Kingdom of Thailand

THE DRAMATIC political changes that swept Thailand in the early 1970s could hardly have come at a worse time for the kingdom. International events over which the Thai had no control inflamed the situation. The world petroleum crisis of 1973–1974 curtailed economic growth and fueled general inflation, while global commodity prices, on which Thailand depended for exports, also slumped. Early in 1975 the long Indochina War finally reached its climax, as communists took full power in Vietnam, Cambodia, and Laos. In withdrawing from the region, the United States closed its bases and pulled the plug on most of the economic and military assistance it had been providing to Thailand over the previous two decades. In this tumultuous period Kukrit and Seni Pramoj, two brothers who led contending political parties, each tried without success to forge coalitions that could govern and manage Thailand's multiplying problems. The task was more than they, or anyone, could have been expected to handle.

From Crisis to Crisis

ON 6 OCTOBER 1976 demonstrations that had begun weeks earlier on the untimely return of General Thanom to Thailand exploded into a riot at Thammasat University in Bangkok. Rightist elements, abetted by the police and some military factions, embarked on an orgy of violence, lynching, beating, burning, and killing demonstrating students. The military establishment interceded and imposed a regime even more authoritarian than the one that had governed Thailand before 1973. The new regime, ironically, was presided over by a civilian law professor, Thanin Kraivichien, whom the military selected as prime minister. In the widespread and brutal suppression of the left that followed, thousands of young men and women fled the city for the forests to join guerrilla movements dominated by the Communist Party of Thailand.

Before this political polarization reached its extreme, however, the army intervened again and in October 1977 replaced Thanin with General Kriangsak Chomanand, a relatively moderate figure. For most of the next decade, there was only one prime minister, General Prem Tinsulanonda (1980–1988). The Thai military, less unified than it had been when Phibun, Sarit, and Thanom acted as military strongmen, proved now to be more accommodating of various interests within the society and more moderate in its treatment of dissent. The insurgents in the countryside dwindled, and a modestly lively—if less exuberant—political life resumed.

Equal opportunity resistance: female communist guerrillas, Thailand, 1970s.

Through the 1980s and 1990s a succession of crises served to emphasize the limits against which Thai society and the various political actors would repeatedly test themselves. The first was the fallout from the political chaos of the mid-1970s. Thousands of young Thai had left their schools and universities in 1976 and fled the cities to join the communist-led insurgency in the countryside. Rural fighting between Thai military forces and the insurgents went on for several years. By the early 1980s, however, at the initiative of General Saiyud Kerdphol, the government developed the fruitful strategy of welcoming young dissidents back to the cities and expressing an understanding of their distress. Stubborn party leaders, mainly Maoists, sparked internal battles within the communist movement and thereby encouraged many young people to desert the party in the early 1980s.

A second major crisis blew up in the late 1980s and early 1990s. This one sprang from the economic successes of prime ministers Prem and General Chatichai Choonhavan (1988–1991). Under their leadership the economy boomed with the easing of internal conflict and the growth of energy self-sufficiency. Unfortunately, economic advances went along with the increasing

449

appetite (or greed) of the military and the impatience of many high-ranking officers with what they saw as civilian inefficiencies.

The slide back into overt military rule accelerated with a bloodless coup in February 1991. Once again the military ended up dominating Thailand's political institutions. Military leaders felt compelled to make a move in the direction of parliamentary government with elections in March 1992, but the premiership was taken by a military man, General Suchinda Kraprayoon, who did not run for the office. Massive demonstrations soon ensued, centered particularly in the middle stretch of Rajadamnoen Avenue near the Grand Palace in mid-Bangkok. Suchinda's following was weak, and the best he could do was to bring into the city old colleagues from the air force, army anti-aircraft regiments, and the like, who are thought to have been responsible for several hundred student deaths. The navy refused to get involved. One of their ships sailed up and down the river behind the Grand Palace and Thammasat University displaying banners that pointedly read, "The navy does not kill people."

Late in May 1992, as public awareness of the bloodshed and the barbarism of Suchinda's repressive policies became known, public support rallied to support the students and others demonstrating against the regime. Street battles had spread over the city, and the expensive automobiles of business people ferried the wounded to hospitals. One articulate businesswoman, interviewed on ABC Television news, said, in perfect English, "I am so ashamed of our country." The bloody crisis was cut short when King Bhumibol called in Suchinda and the leader of the civilian demonstrators, a retired general, and lectured them both—in front of television cameras—on proper political and moral behavior. Suchinda was clearly uncomfortable and resigned soon afterwards; the king appointed Anand Panyarachun as interim prime minister until new elections could be held in September.

In the months leading up to new elections, the political factions fell, perhaps a little too neatly, into two groups, referred to as those "on the side of the angels *(phak thep),*" meaning primarily reform-minded civilians, and those "aligned with the forces of evil *(phak Mara),*" referring to the military and their civilian allies. While Anand's technocrats got government back into order, a public investigation was mounted into the hundreds still missing from the ranks of the demonstrators. The investigation, however, never revealed its findings. The election was very close, and it was not certain who would win until, while the votes were still being counted, certain moneyed interests persuaded one fence-sitter who controlled a block of votes to join with the "party of the angels." The Democrat Party came to power controlling 185 out of 360 parliamentary seats, and the new civilian prime minister was Chuan Leekpai, a politician from Trang, in the south.

In the aftermath of this political chaos, all seemed well on the surface, but there were disturbing developments below. The economy sputtered and slowed, though both the largest cities and the nearby countryside seemed still to be prospering. Thailand's AIDS rate flirted with dangerous levels, as the sex trade bloated unsavory parts of the cities. The money that was flowing into the kingdom helped expand the overheated economy and contributed to the quiet subvention (and subversion) of the military while the political parties, although popular, especially in the growing cities and towns, grew disgusted at public corruption and rampant government and underworld brutality.

One might have expected such abuses to be reined in by civilian parliamentary politics, but instead they seemed to accelerate. It became increasingly clear that the analytical categories once used to examine Thai society and politics were no longer adequate to the task. Only a generation before, Thai people and the scholars who studied them spoke in terms of a few monolithic, hierarchical structures in Thai society, the interplay among which shaped politics, economics, and intellectual life. As late as the time of Sarit, in the early 1960s, we could speak of the army, the monarchy, the Buddhist monkhood, the bureaucracy, the Chinese business community, and the peasantry, and conclude that we had covered all the elements of Thai society that "mattered." We could explain continuing military dominance by referring to the unity of the army in the face of a disunited and even fractious urban population (meaning the bureaucracy and the Chinese, as far as politics was concerned) and an amorphous, subsistence-oriented peasantry. All these elements were held to be rigidly structured in an authoritarian fashion, with those wearing uniforms lording it over those without, those with more stripes on their shoulders ordering around those with fewer, and the king and Buddhist monks serving as the upholders of eternal values while everyone else attended to more immediate material concerns.

All such interpretations were seen to be invalid as Thailand changed. A generation before Thailand had been a relatively small society with a minuscule elite and an invisible middle class of obedient bureaucrats and Chinese. By 2000 it had doubled in size to a country of more than 60 million persons. The percentage of Thai who lived in cities rose to 20 percent. Where 85 percent of the population once were rice farmers, now fewer than half the households in the kingdom gained their livelihood from agriculture. And where there were just 10,000 university graduates in all of Thailand in 1947, there were now several million. The society was now too large, too diverse, too well educated, too cosmopolitan to be neatly boxed into a few clear-cut hierarchical, vertical structures—or, for that matter, into horizontal "class" structures.

The Thai experience of the mid-1970s may someday be viewed in retrospect as cathartic, but for most of those who lived through it, it was a period of intense pain and shock. People awakened to a Thailand that they did not realize was there: a nation of conflict, contention, incivility, outrage, and injustice, whether viewed from the left or from the right. The task of the next generation of Thai to wield political power would be to determine, by the exercise of their wisdom and humanity, whether the wounds from that experience would fester or heal.

A positive note for many Thai toward the end of the century was the series of commemorations of the long rule of King Bhumibol Adulyadej, who had acceded to the throne as a boy in 1946 and been crowned in 1950. Military rulers from Sarit onward had promoted the monarchy as one of the cornerstones of Thai national identity, and most of the people felt that the king had fulfilled his role well, crediting him with much of the putative "stability" the country claimed. When he became the longest-ruling monarch in Thai history and then when he celebrated his fiftieth year as king, it was a time for national rejoicing. The same occasions, however, automatically gave rise to some apprehension: having prospered so under King Bhumibol, what would the country do when he was gone?

Toward a New Millennium

IN A WAY, the nastiness of the 1970s foreshadowed the conflict and disorientation of the 1990s. With increasing prosperity (and the distractions of much more accessible sex and drugs), there was even more for politicians to fight over. Chuan's government, for example, could not surmount the political infighting of the early 1990s and was replaced in mid-1995 by a new government headed by Banharn Silapa-Archa. While the Chuan administration had been relatively clean and honest, Banharn's was marked by the politicization of many institutions, especially the Bank of Thailand, which for so long had successfully managed Thailand's economy.

Few observers were surprised that new elections at the end of 1996 ousted Banharn and replaced him with General Chavalit Yongchaiyudh. It was too late for Chavalit to repair years of severe damage to the economy, which collapsed in July 1997. The baht fell from around 25 to the dollar, a level it had retained for decades, to 56 to the dollar by the following year. Many banks, industries, and property companies failed. The ensuing political chaos finally concluded with new elections that resulted in Chavalit's replacement by the durable Chuan Leekpai as prime minister in November 1997.

Chuan and his new government had to face two major innovations. They had to deal, first of all, with the economic collapse. They chose to negotiate with the International Monetary Fund, but these agreements brought new, and to some quite unpalatable, economic reforms. The end result was a stabilization of the economy, though hardly a return to earlier prosperity. By 2000 the exchange rate hovered around 40 baht to the dollar. Economically, two developments helped save Thailand. One was the development of indigenous energy resources (mainly gas), especially from drilling in the Gulf of Thailand. The other was the cumulative effect of population control. In the mid-1960s population growth was outpacing economic growth, forcing the government to build thousands of new schools and train thousands of new teachers just to maintain compulsory education for the first four years. The military governments of the period refused to promote population control out of fear that, while poor Thai would limit their population expansion, the Chinese minority would not be so obedient and would continue to consume government resources and further tip the social balance of the kingdom in their favor.

In silent tribute to the determination of the rural (and urban) poor (and more prosperous) men and women to limit their population growth, a popular movement brought rapid decreases in population growth in the 1960s and 1970s, to the point where the growth of Thailand's population barely exceeded replacement level, falling to a rate lower than any other country in Southeast Asia except Singapore. This meant that government expenditures formerly allocated to primary education could now be used for secondary schooling.

Diversification was another key to Thailand's economic success. Visitors who once had observed seemingly endless rice fields now saw a much greater variety of crops (like marigold flowers, which could be fed to chickens to make their flesh more yellow), while supermarket shoppers in the United States might note that almost all the shrimp and pineapples were imported from Thailand. Equally important was the expansion of tourism, which now became the largest single component of the economy, exceeding not only the old staples (rice, teak, tin) but also the newer manufactures (computer components, automobiles and parts, textiles and clothing). Tourism included a very large labor ingredient, and much of that labor had to be well trained.

For all the economic bustle and corruption, what preoccupied many people in the 1990s was political change, focusing on the most important constitutional innovations since the 1970s (or in some cases since the 1930s). Now both houses of parliament were fully elected and held to supposedly high moral and educational standards. Prime ministers were required to be elected members of the lower house. Elected members were required to file public statements of their financial involvements, and some were now dismissed from office, forcing new elections (repeatedly in the upper house toward the end of the century).

Despite all this, political power could still be bought and sold, and major government contracts were similarly influenced. A great deal of money continued to be used to sway elections even to relatively low offices, and very large sums were injected into the system from nominally illegal activities. There was even a major intrusion of cash into the foreign relations of Thailand. Some argued that drug money was involved in the military clash between Thailand and Laos in 1987–1988, just as lumber money heated up relations with Myanmar and Cambodia in the following decade. These neighbors might justifiably complain of Thai economic hegemony, though some such complaints were mixed with considerable jealousy, as evidenced by the anti-Thai riots that broke out in Phnom Penh in January 2003.

After several years of discussion and argument, Thailand finally adopted a new constitution in 1997. The welcome document featured a new openness of government, and increased environmental protection and enhanced social welfare. The bicameral legislature now centered on an elected house of representatives of five hundred members, most of whom represented single-seat constituencies, while the remainder were elected at large. The two-hundred-member senate, also elected, was to play a secondary role. Suffrage was extended universally, but all candidates for election to either house were required to hold at least a bachelor's degree. Implementation of the new constitution was delayed while candidates were held to supposedly rigorous tests that attempted to screen out ties to financial interests.

It was in this context that the telecommunications tycoon Taksin Shinawatra became prime minister in March 2000, after an election in which more than 70 percent of the electorate participated. Taksin's position was clouded by claims that much of his considerable wealth had been hidden in the accounts of his family and friends, and that a great deal of money had found its way into the hands of impecunious voters. In a split decision, the courts ruled otherwise, and Taksin became premier. Early issues that challenged the government were the ongoing role of financial interests in politics, the continuing fragility of many financial institutions, and the draconian concessions the country had been compelled to make to the International Monetary Fund. The government also showed increasing sensitivity to foreign press criticism and banned a number of periodicals (such as the *Far Eastern Economic Review* and *The Economist*) and publications from sale and distribution in Thailand.

At the beginning of the new millennium, Thailand's economy had stabilized, as formerly impoverished parts of the country (like the northeast) had improved their economic status. Thais could still complain of continuing uneven distribution of wealth, but now there was a great deal more wealth to fight over than there had been thirty years earlier.

Further Readings

Knodel, John, Aphichat Chamratrithirong, and Nibhon Debavalya. *Thailand's Reproductive Revolution: Rapid Fertility Decline in a Third-World Setting.* Madison, 1997.
Pasuk Phongpaichit and Chris Baker. *Thailand: Economy and Politics.* Kuala Lumpur, 1995.
———. *Thailand's Boom and Bust.* Chiang Mai, 1998.
Saiyud Kerdphol. *The Struggle for Thailand: Counter-Insurgency, 1965–1985.* Bangkok, 1986.
Suehiro, Akira. *Capital Accumulation in Thailand, 1855–1985.* 1989; reprint Chiang Mai, 1996.
Wyatt, David K. *Siam in Mind.* Chiang Mai, 2002.
———. *Thailand: A Short History.* 2d ed. New Haven, 2003.

Chapter 33

❀

The Philippines since 1972

WHAT IS the consequence for a nation if its most successful and brilliant politician turns out to be corrupt and evil? What is the impact on a society if the man sworn to defend its values openly flaunts them, corrupting both the institutions of society and its underlying values? What does it do to an economy if its chief executive plunders in excess of 10 billion dollars, creating a "kleptocracy"? What happens to the notion of a constitution as the supreme law of the land if statutes are flaunted and whims of an individual become law?

Ferdinand Marcos was demonic. A political genius, a self-promoter, and a confidence man, he fabricated his own identity, believing his own mythology. He dominated his nation, diminishing its destiny. The brazenness of his many lies quite staggers a historian's imagination, but for far too long far too many people accepted this fraud with a willing suspension of disbelief. While Ferdinand and Imelda pretended to be John and Jackie Kennedy, they behaved like Lord and Lady Macbeth, establishing a conjugal dictatorship.

Martial Law

MARTIAL LAW shattered Philippine democracy and challenged, at least temporarily, the *ilustrado* monopoly of power. This century-old oligarchy had long confused class interest with national priorities. The "old order" was characterized by inequalities and inequities. Migrant rural laborers and peasant tenants rarely got a just share of the harvest. The urban proletariat lacked a fair wage or the protection of effective unions. Many smart, ambitious students were denied upward mobility. An underemployed intelligentsia, unable to find adequate opportunity at home, emigrated, often never returning. To some who stayed, communism offered an ideological rationale to explain the contradictions of Philippine society.

Marcos justified his declaration of martial law in the context of the Cold War by claiming Philippine society was at risk because of these contradictions. A few at home and some abroad initially accepted his assertion that "constitutional authoritarianism" was a bulwark against chaos, embracing the political right out of fear of the radical left. Richard Nixon, for example, reflexively endorsed martial law rather than lamenting the abolition of constitutional freedoms and democracy. It became fashionable to compare Marcos to Lee Kuan Yew of Singapore, since both justified the surrender of personal freedom as a necessary concomitant to economic progress, anticommunism, and nation building. In contradistinction to Lee, however, Marcos used martial law for personal aggrandizement. "Crony capitalism" mocked economic development and distorted the economy. Imelda became a symbol of conspicuous consumption, compulsively buying shoes, properties, and friends.

One significant historical discontinuity was Marcos' empowerment of the military. Martial law catapulted military officers, often from humble circumstances, into power. The chain of command stretched into every province and hamlet. Marcos used it to impose control and quash what he defined as threats to the nation—a communist insurgency and an Islamic war of liberation in the south. The officer cadre drew its cohesion from the democratic centralism of every military, where promotion is often based on ability, not birth. Marcos rewarded his loyal troops with upward mobility comparable to that afforded officers in Indonesia, Thailand, Myanmar, and Vietnam. But he also corrupted and politicized them, shattering their American-inspired respect for civilian control. Generals grew rich, and officers were rewarded for stifling dissent. Using the Philippine Military Academy as its training ground, the new military elite challenged the oligarchy, suggesting that the Philippines had become more like its sister nations all across Southeast Asia.

Resistance

IRONICALLY, Marcos also empowered dissident elements in society. His actions prompted some Filipinos to react violently, while others responded silently. Key *ilustrado* families, suddenly cut off from wealth and power, went abroad. Some, years before, had transferred wealth out of the archipelago; others just fled incarceration. The Marcos government was delighted to see such oligarchic clans go, often only permitting their exits in exchange for their businesses or land. Upper-middle-class professionals, doctors, lawyers, and civil engineers also fled, taking precious skills abroad. Marcos tolerated this brain drain as well as an exodus of unemployed laborers who went on contract to the Middle East, the United States, or wherever a visa could be secured. Migration lowered domestic unemployment, while greatly increasing the flow of foreign exchange back to the archipelago.

In Mindanao and Sulu, violence erupted when Marcos moved to disarm Muslims. Chronic underinvestment, timber and copra concessions to Marcos cronies, and Christian migration south fused with a global reawakening of Islamic identity to mobilize indigenous Muslims. Four centuries of hostility and distrust exacerbated this anger. An Islamic identity reshaped by mullahs gave ideological justification for geopolitical anger. The Moro National Liberation Front (MNLF), founded in 1968, had demanded full independence, although this really just meant increased regional autonomy. But after martial law, when Marcos moved to suppress the MNLF by military means, the rebellion claimed fifty thousand "freedom fighters." Marcos, cynically, gave the Philippine military an enemy—the Muslims—to justify army growth.

Martial law exacerbated socioeconomic tensions generally; the "have-nots" lost ground, and some reacted violently as standards of living deteriorated. The percentage of families below the poverty line increased dramatically. Squatters lived on garbage heaps, while children begged along the boulevards. Farmers lost their land, degenerating into an agricultural proletariat, while rural schooling and health care delivery deteriorated. The favored few, especially Marcos' cronies, formed private armies to protect their homes and economic interests.

The New People's Army (NPA), the military arm of a resurgent Communist Party of the Philippines (CPP)—a very different party from its earlier namesake—gained support from human distress. Marcos, who had cited a communist menace to legitimize martial law, became its best recruiter. The party enlisted students and intellectuals who despaired of gaining opportunity. Over thirteen years, approximately twelve to fifteen thousand guerrillas were recruited, prompting both American and Filipino military observers to anticipate large scale NPA attacks.

U.S. bases at Subic Bay and Clark seemingly encapsulated the nefarious reality of neo-imperialism. Moreover, the collaboration of American corporations and global banks with Marcos suggested to many that America was the "Great Satan." The United States equipped Marcos' army, helped to train his new officers, and embraced his corrupt generals. But Marcos' real genius was his capacity to manipulate the Americans while sounding anti-American. The Pentagon readily supplied weapons to an increasingly bloated Philippine military —the army tripled in size—even though some of those weapons wound up being used against it. Army units, operating in the Muslim areas of Mindanao and elsewhere across the archipelago, often degenerated into marauding gangs, robbing, raping, brutally torturing, and plundering. Extralegal execution was so common that a special euphemism for it was coined: "salvaging."

Benigno Aquino: Hints of Mortality

MOST traditional politicians ("trapos"—the acronym also means "dish rag" in Tagalog), judges, and journalists accepted martial law or went into exile. Marcos shrewdly calibrated his brutality to sustain authority. Benigno Aquino was a unique case. He was arrested within the first hours of martial law, charged with murder, tried by Marcos in a military court, and sentenced to death. The cover of the last pre–martial law press run of the weekly news magazine *The Philippine Free Press* pictured Aquino targeted through the crosshairs of a rifle with the caption, "Senator Benigno S. Aquino: Target?" Never distributed, that issue was dated 30 September 1972. For the next seven years Aquino was held, often in solitary confinement, too popular to be executed but too dangerous to be freed.

Born in 1932, Aquino was the son of a mainline prewar politician who collaborated with the Japanese and was facing a treason charge when he died in 1947. Benigno, universally called by his nickname, Ninoy, was, like Marcos, a graduate of the University of the Philippines; both pledged the same fraternity. He married Maria Corazon (Cory) Cojuangco, a daughter of one of the wealthiest mestizos in the Philippines; the couple lived in Hacienda Luisita in Tarlac, one of the biggest private estates in the archipelago. (Corazon's first cousin Eduardo Cojuangco would later become one of Marcos' closest cronies, as the family split irrevocably during martial law.) Greatly influenced by Ramon Magsaysay, Ninoy entered politics at an early age. At twenty-two he was elected the country's youngest mayor; later he was its youngest vice governor, and at the age of thirty-five he became the youngest senator.

Marcos tried to break Aquino's will during his confinement, but Aquino, refusing to accept a pardon that required acknowledging his "crimes," stayed in jail long after his political allies were released. Some people who face adversity are broken by it; many more remain more or less unchanged; Aquino seems to have been one of those rare individuals who grew. After Marcos relaxed the severity of martial law, Aquino became politically active from prison. When his doctors reported that he needed a coronary bypass operation—a diagnosis that has never been independently corroborated—Marcos agreed to allow him to leave for the United States, hoping to rid himself of his undaunted rival.

The only thing Marcos could not control was his own health. He suffered from a degenerative illness, lupus erythematosus, which attacked his kidneys. As his illness progressed, the rivalries within the small clique around the president increased. The minister of defense, Juan Ponce Enrile, lost out to Marcos' cousin and most faithful supporter, General Fabian Ver. Central to these court intrigues was Imelda, who clearly hoped to inherit her husband's job. By the early 1980s, the body politic was sick like the president. Endemic army abuse, a new proliferation of warlordism, rampant corruption, and the collapse of the Philippine economy had given both the NPA and the Muslim resistance succor. The oil shocks of 1973 and 1979 had raised import prices dramatically and destabilized export prices. Between 1979 and 1983 the nation's foreign debt doubled. Inflation was rampant. The frail president no longer controlled events.

When Aquino heard the false rumor that Marcos was dying, he returned to the archipelago, anticipating imprisonment on his return. Philippine security forces boarded his plane to "escort" him. Despite wearing a bulletproof vest, he was shot in the back of the head within seconds of leaving the plane. His assassination on 21 August 1983 altered his nation's history; it galvanized Filipinos and dominated the world's news. The Philippine government maintained that Aquino had been assassinated by a lone radical, but for most people the real question was whether Marcos himself ordered Aquino's death. More probably, Imelda and General Ver, who had the most to lose by Aquino's return, organized the assassination.

The following day, Corazon, Aquino's widow, flew home from Boston, instructing that Ninoy's open coffin be transported around the country, displaying his body to challenge Marcos and rally the people. Millions of ordinary Filipinos paid their respects. Yellow ribbons appeared everywhere, confetti from telephone directory yellow pages fluttered from high-rise offices. Ninoy joined the pantheon of national martyrs with José Rizal and fathers Gómez, Burgos, and Zamora.

EDSA *and Corazon Aquino*

MARCOS did not die, surviving until 1989, long after he was forced from power. The two and a half years after Ninoy's assassination were an era of political turmoil and economic catastrophe, of corrupt courts of inquiry and sham elections. Although Ronald Reagan remained Marcos' friend, other American leaders demanded a new approach to the Philippines. Even the Pentagon came to see Marcos' unpopularity as a threat to American retention of Subic and Clark. Marcos called what the press referred to as a "snap election" for 7 February 1986. Believing that the opposition would not rally to any one candidate and seeking to restore his mandate, he was sure he could rig the outcome, however vocal his critics.

Dramatically, the Roman Catholic archbishop of Manila, Jaime Cardinal Sin, intervened openly, demanding a fusion ticket with Aquino running for president and one of her key challengers, Salvador (Doy) Laurel, for vice president. Sin issued a series of pastoral letters, and thousands of priests, nuns, and lay leaders mobilized to wage a struggle for "good over evil," for Aquino over

Marcos. The CPP, deeply divided about how to react to these sudden events, made a serious tactical error in deciding to sit out the election, assuming that Marcos would win through corruption and anticipating that the resultant cynicism would help it gain power. The NPA suspended military activity, leaving a nonviolent opportunity to the moderate democratic opposition. A watchdog group, NAMFREL (the National Movement for Free Elections), mobilized tens of thousands of men and women to defend the ballots.

The level of corruption that election day was stupendous. Ballot boxes were stuffed, fraudulent tally sheets were inserted, and voting rolls reflected both those alive and those dead. Millions of people's names were removed from voting rolls, deregistering them. Meanwhile, poll watchers from NAMFREL chained themselves to the ballot boxes. Hundreds of millions of pesos, many with identical serial numbers, flooded the countryside as traditional vote buying took place. Marcos claimed victory, debasing the electoral process further.

In this chaotic environment Minister of Defense Enrile and General Fidel Ramos seized two important military installations on Epifanio de los Santos Avenue (EDSA) in Quezon City—technically the national capital but part of

"People Power": nun and marines, Quezon City, 23 February 1986.

Photo by Tom Gralish/*Philadelphia Inquirer*, courtesy of D. J. Steinberg

Metropolitan Manila—in an open attempt at a preemptive coup against Marcos. Sin appealed by radio for citizens to gather there, turning the conspirators into patriotic defenders of Cory and democracy. Tens of thousands of civilians responded in what became known as "People Power," filling the space between the rebel soldiers loyal to Enrile and Ramos and those supporting Marcos.

Ver wanted to fire on the civilians to make them scatter, but Marcos, tired, ill, and beaten, understood that to slaughter innocent citizens would doom him even if he could suppress this rebellion. Nuns and seminarians knelt before tanks to pray; citizens put flowers in the muzzles of guns. The rebellion succeeded. Enrile declared a provisional government with Aquino as president. Marcos, his family, and other key loyalists, including Ver, fled to Clark Air Base and then to Hawai'i, where the United States granted him asylum. To the world press, the story seemed part television sitcom and part modern-day passion play.

Aquino was inaugurated on 25 February 1986, thanks to the abortive coup and "People Power." If this tale were myth, it would conclude, "And they all lived happily ever after." But this is history, where "ever after" never happens. Poverty, hunger, social polarization, and a staggering national debt were Marcos' legacy. Filipinos basked briefly in the world's adulation. "People Power" had toppled a dictator; the Philippines had shown the world a new way to democracy when marking a ballot was no longer sufficient. But EDSA did not address the deep structural problems in Philippine society. Was EDSA a "revolution," a "restoration," or a "reformation?" Was a new age dawning or an old age returning?

Democracy and the electoral process were soon restored. Habeas corpus and an independent judiciary, free speech, and free press returned. But Corazon Aquino, despite her moral decency, never resolved other issues, in part because of a series of attempted military coups against her government. Young, dissident middle-rank officers, loyal to Enrile, had earlier founded a Reform the Army Movement (RAM). Now they plotted to seize power, withholding that vital allegiance required of armed services in any democratic state. To them Aquino exemplified the failed leadership of the "old order"; they objected less to martial law than to Marcos' failure to use it to restructure Philippine society.

The first coup attempt was on 6 July 1986, the last on 6 October 1990. In between several were farcical, but on 1 December 1989 some three thousand troops, many from the best-paid elite units, rebelled. Before that coup was suppressed, 95 people were killed and 580 wounded, two television stations had been seized, the commercial airport closed, and there was an aerial attack on the presidential palace. Jets from Clark patrolled the skies over Manila, a not-too-subtle reminder that toppling Aquino was unacceptable to Washington.

Further complicating her presidency were the ongoing Islamic rebellion, increasingly funded from abroad, and a renewed challenge from the CPP, which, understanding its error in standing aside during EDSA, sought to overthrow both *ilustrado* resurgence and the capitalist economy that empowered it. They tried unsuccessfully to discredit Aquino, seeking to sully her near mythic bond to the masses. At its zenith, the party claimed to be on the verge of early victory, but deep schisms and an internal rectification debate fragmented its leadership. The politburo imploded.

Such dynamic instabilities defined the parameters of Aquino's presidency. She came to power with a vice president, Laurel, who was never loyal, often flirting with the military. Her cabinet included both her late husband's supporters and those like Enrile (her minister of defense) and Ramos who had served Marcos. Early on she proclaimed that her government's legitimacy was based on EDSA, not the election, an awkward truth. Then she promulgated an interim "freedom constitution" until a new constitution could be drafted and ratified. She had to abrogate the 1972 Marcos constitution to restore constitutional protections and decide how to dispose of laws, contracts, and deals generated by twenty years of cronyism and corruption.

She established a Constitutional Commission and appointed delegates strikingly similar to those who had gathered at Malolos almost a century before. They were educated, wealthy, and predominantly lawyers; many were close to the church hierarchy. Their final document of over one hundred pages reaffirmed established verities, protecting private property, confirming a highly centralized government in Manila, defining an evolutionary trickle-down vision of social justice, and stressing education and a bill of rights—rather than serious land reform—as bulwarks for the poor and disenfranchised. The fifteen new justices of the Supreme Court were, similarly, men and women committed to "old order" values. Under Aquino there were efforts to promote good government, curb corruption, increase tax compliance, end tax evasion, cleanse the bureaucracy, and restore the rule of law. Committed to universal education, improvements in national health (but not birth control), and a higher standard of living for all Filipinos, Cory understood what the average Filipino needed. But her sincerity was not enough to solve the problems her country faced.

During Marcos' last years there had been a precipitous fall in the per capita gross national product, and prices doubled between 1983 and 1985. The Aquino administration was reformist, market-focused, internationally oriented, and technocratic. The sugar and coconut monopolies created for Marcos' cronies were abolished. The government ceased operating state-subsidized corporations, selling many cheaply either to the old establishment or to new Chinese entrepreneurs, and pursued the stolen billions Marcos had transferred out of the archipelago. While some funds were repatriated, especially by Marcos' cronies who wanted to come home, most of these efforts failed.

Aquino also had to renegotiate the external debt left by Marcos. In 1986 the debt service repayment requirement was U.S.$3.2 billion, equal to 34 percent of the exports of the nation. Nearly 40 percent of the national budget was committed to service those obligations. The country was so deeply in debt to other governments, to foreign banks and creditors, and to itself that it could not fulfill its international obligations and still generate sufficient revenue to jumpstart the economy. Southeast Asia was moving toward globalization, and the Philippines needed to participate in that global economy. The coup attempts weakened the peso, prompting foreign investors to turn elsewhere for new investment opportunities. Unrest in Mindanao and military action by the NPA also chilled the economic climate.

The End of Neocolonialism

MANY FILIPINOS wanted to end American neocolonialism. Both Ronald Reagan and George Bush had supported Marcos. In 1986 Reagan had snubbed Aquino, even after Marcos had fled, choosing neither to congratulate her by phone nor to visit the Philippines during a trip from Indonesia to Japan. As vice president, George Bush had hosted Marcos in 1981, soon after a rigged election, and said, "We love your adherence to democratic principles—and the democratic processes." Such disdain for genuine Philippine democracy angered Filipinos, especially since the American government remained parsimonious. Speaking before the U.S. Congress in September 1986, Aquino said: "You have spent many lives and much treasure to bring freedom to many lands that were reluctant to receive it. And here you have a people who want it by themselves and need only help to preserve it."

Twenty thousand American military personnel and twenty-five thousand dependents were still stationed at Clark and Subic. Sixty-eight thousand Filipinos worked there, making the United States the second biggest employer in the country. The bases injected over one billion dollars a year into the economy, including half a billion for supplies and services. That very economic reality was galling to many Filipinos, since it seemingly induced them to sell their birthright for material gain.

Under the terms of the lease agreements, any renewal needed to be negotiated by September 1991. The Filipinos wanted to call payments "rent," while the United States refused, speaking instead of economic, military, and development assistance. In June 1991, Mount Pinatubo, dormant for over six hundred years, erupted in central Luzon with a violence that staggers the imagination. Clark was rendered virtually useless, prompting the United States to announce that it would abandon that base, while also lowering the amount offered for compensation. Almost simultaneously, the collapse of the Soviet Union eliminated the major justification for the naval base at Subic. America lost interest just as the Philippines was demanding either enormous sums of additional money or complete withdrawal.

The Aquino government needed money and military supplies to fight the Muslim insurgents and the NPA, but Aquino herself spoke of the bases as "a lingering vestige of our colonial past." In July 1991 U.S. and Philippine negotiators finally reached an agreement to extend the lease at Subic for ten years in exchange for approximately U.S.$200 million a year and other multilateral aid programs. The Aquino government needed sixteen votes in the Philippine Senate to ratify this treaty; it fell short. That rejection altered the Philippine-American relationship and the geopolitical military realities of Southeast Asia. The U.S. navy withdrew within a year, and a major symbol of neocolonial asymmetry ended.

Fidel V. Ramos

ON 11 May 1992 every political office in the land—president and vice president (elected separately), all 24 senators, 200 members of congress, 73 governors, 1,543 municipal mayors, and thousands of other local officials—was contested. For the two dozen senatorial seats there were 265 candidates. In all, 82,450 people competed for 17,205 elected positions. This unique election was the result of Marcos' long rule and the new constitution, which mandated a completely new electoral slate.

It was a fair and open election. Power was peacefully transferred. Nearly 80 percent of the 32 million eligible voters participated. Cardinal Sin supported a losing candidate. Few cared about Washington's priorities. Traditional party structure no longer guaranteed electoral success. There were seven candidates for president, including Eduardo Cojuangco. Imelda Marcos flamboyantly returned in a chartered 747 to campaign. Both the senate president and the speaker of the house sought the presidency, as did General Fidel Ramos, Aquino's loyal chief of staff during those several coup attempts, but approximately a third of the nation voted for Imelda, Cojuangco, or Salvador Laurel, all of whom, like Ramos, had been closely linked to Ferdinand Marcos. A Protestant in an overwhelmingly Catholic country, Ramos won. Joseph Estrada, a former senator and popular grade "B" movie actor, was elected vice president on Cojuangco's ticket.

Ramos, nicknamed "Steady Eddie" by the press, provided sustaining leadership over his six-year term. At his inauguration he bluntly noted that the nation was in trouble, but he had the good fortune to be president during an era of global prosperity. He focused on public works, while accepting a regimen of fiscal discipline demanded by the International Monetary Fund. He restructured much of the Marcos debt overhang and emphasized "the four D's": devolution, decentralization, deregulation, and democratization. Decision making was theoretically pushed down to local and provincial levels. The economy was freed from excessive government regulation; local entrepreneurs and foreign corporations were allowed to compete in the marketplace without restrictions.

The Ramos administration sought to end corporate and individual tax evasion, as the expatriation of funds to Hong Kong, Macau, and the Bahamas siphoned money away. It won international approval and foreign investment by abolishing foreign currency controls; the peso was floated, allowing Philippine goods to compete successfully on a global market, though at the cost of on-going devaluation. "Trade, not aid" became government policy. Banking reform, including a willingness to let foreign banks compete with local ones, broke the monopoly of certain families and made the economy more transparent.

During the Aquino years, the power utilities had rarely been able to meet demand. "Brownouts" had been endemic, and economic progress was hamstrung by shortfalls in electricity, water pressure, and telecommunications. Ramos got the traffic lights and the computer screens to stay on. He also transformed Subic Bay into a civilian facility, granting it duty-free status and taking advantage of some of the fixed assets left behind by the U.S. navy, including 1,800 bungalows, a 9,000-foot runway, an independent electrical power plant, a country club and golf course, as well as a highly skilled local work force.

The administration also faced threats of violence on various fronts, though a rising tide of economic prosperity and good police work reduced the risks somewhat. Ramos lifted the thirty-five-year ban on the CPP; his goal, to let the party function openly, was part of a larger strategy of reconciliation. In the military, rebellious colonels and majors once again became loyal officers. Gregorio Honasan, former idol of the RAM movement, signed a cease-fire with the government and returned to mainstream politics, ultimately winning for himself a senate seat in 1995.

Muslim provinces had the highest infant mortality and illiteracy rates in the archipelago and desperately needed substantial infrastructure investment, although they accounted for 60 percent of Philippine exports of raw material, including prawns, pineapples, timber, bananas, and copra. The rise of a global fundamentalist Islamic network transformed their struggle. President Qaddafi of Libya and others in Saudi Arabia supplied Nur Misuari of the MNLF and other local Muslim leaders with money, weapons, and a militant ideology. As part of the overseas Filipino diaspora, hundreds of thousands of men and women went off to work in the Middle East as domestics, construction workers, or professionals. The Philippines became a portal linking radical Islam to globalization.

But in many respects it was politics as usual. Imelda Marcos was elected a congresswoman from Leyte, her native island, and her son, Ferdinand Jr. ("Bong Bong"), won his father's old congressional seat from Ilocos Norte. To peruse the winning list of governors, congressmen and women, and senators was to be reintroduced to the great families. Ramos himself, Marcos' second cousin, was just such a child of an *ilustrado* family. His father, Congressman Narciso Ramos, had been foreign minister; his sister, Leticia Ramos Shahani, with degrees from

Wellesley and the Sorbonne, was a senator and chair of the Foreign Affairs Committee.

Among the legacies of President Ramos was his decision not to amend the Aquino constitution in order to permit himself to serve a second term. Ramos was interested but ultimately accepted the constitutional prohibition. Cardinal Sin and Mrs. Aquino had to organize mass protests to remind Ramos not to be tempted, but it worked. In sharp contradistinction to other countries across Southeast Asia, where the economic had been defined as more important than the political, in the Philippines, the obverse was true.

Joseph Ejercito Estrada and Gloria Macapagal Arroyo

THE 1998 presidential election was a further endorsement of democracy. Initially there were eighty-three candidates for president. One fringe candidate organized a party called the Civilian Independent Candidates against Traitors and Satanic Agents in the Philippines. Another delighted the press by announcing that he had returned from heaven specifically to run for president. But once the lunatic fringe was winnowed out, there were several perennials seeking the job, including Imelda Marcos and a grandson of Sergio Osmeña.

The victorious candidate was Vice President Estrada. Nicknamed "Erap"— a spelling reversal of the Tagalog word *pare*, meaning "buddy"—he was an aging Don Juan. In mediocre films of high romance and low art, he always played the good guy, the hero who challenged wicked hacienda owners or wealthy Chinese merchants, inevitably triumphing against overwhelming odds. Estrada's appeal to common folk appeared to challenge the *ilustrado* monopoly of power. In his inaugural address, he claimed, "Now power is with the people, one of their own has made it."

Reality was more complicated. The people around Estrada had in fact been power brokers under Marcos. Eduardo Cojuangco, Marcos' crony of cronies, and billionaire Lucio Tan, who owned Philippine Airlines, made key economic decisions. At first the Filipino public enjoyed the fact that their president was "so human." Estrada had a potbelly and wore his hair like Elvis Presley. He smoked, drank heavily, and was a self-proclaimed womanizer. He spoke of his ten children and of his wife as the mother of three of them. He held cabinet meetings in a nightclub that he owned, often making decisions in the wee hours of the morning in a haze of tobacco and alcohol.

But a scandal involving kickbacks from *jueteng*, an illegal numbers game widely played by many poor Filipinos, toppled Estrada, who had used a fake name to transfer millions of dollars to his own account. On the day he was impeached, the Manila Stock Exchange rose by 16 percent, though his allies blocked his trial in the Senate. Forty thousand citizens rallied against him, marching on the presidential residence. In January 2001 the Philippine Supreme

Court, insisting that the "welfare of the people is the supreme law," ruled unanimously that the presidency was vacant and stripped Estrada of his office, though he continued to maintain his innocence.

There was talk of "People Power II," of a greedy and corrupt president overthrown in a new type of national plebiscite, but there were also serious questions about the constitutionality of Estrada's removal. Was this a "soft coup"? Was popular recall a legitimate way to remove a duly elected president? But the military did not protect Estrada, while Sin, Aquino, and others—including many foreign observers and investors—celebrated his fall. Estrada was jailed on corruption charges, accused of "economic plunder," while the Supreme Court swore in his estranged vice president, Gloria Macapagal Arroyo, as president.

President Arroyo was a trained economist, the daughter of a former president, a member of the Philippine establishment, a scion of *ilustrado* culture. Sophisticated, modern, international in outlook, she reconfirmed that women are politically empowered, a reality that Filipinos have taken for granted. When she became president, *ilustrado* hegemony was also reconfirmed; she seemed to be a restoration leader for the new millennium. Yet just three years later she—and the class she represented—would again be challenged by a movie actor (Fernando Poe, Jr., a close friend of Estrada) whose career was built on playing a hero of "the masses." Clearly the struggle for the right to rule and represent the Philippines was far from over.

Further Readings

Aquino, Belinda A. *Politics of Plunder: The Philippines under Marcos.* 2d ed. Quezon City, 1999.

Bonner, Raymond. *Waltzing with a Dictator: The Marcoses and the Making of American Policy.* New York, 1987.

Hawes, Gary. *The Philippine State and the Marcos Regime: The Politics of Export.* Ithaca, 1987.

Hedman, Eva-Lotta E., and John T. Sidel. *Philippine Politics and Society in the Twentieth Century: Colonial Legacies, Post-Colonial Trajectories.* New York, 2000.

Hutchcroft, Paul D. *Booty Capitalism: The Politics of Banking in the Philippines.* Ithaca, 1998.

Kessler, Richard J. *Rebellion and Repression in the Philippines.* New Haven, 1989.

McCoy, Alfred W. *Closer than Brothers: Manhood at the Philippine Military Academy.* New Haven, 1999.

———, ed. *An Anarchy of Families: State and Family in the Philippines.* Madison, Wisc., 1993.

Riedinger, Jeffrey M. *Agrarian Reform in the Philippines: Democratic Transitions and Redistributive Reform.* Stanford, 1995.

Sidel, John T. *Capital, Coercion, and Crime: Bossism in the Philippines.* Stanford, 1999.

Chapter 34

✾

Vietnam after 1975

From Collectivism to Market Leninism

AT FIRST GLANCE the regime that the Vietnamese communists created at Hanoi, in the image of the far bigger Soviet Union of Lenin and Stalin, represented more of a break with its national past than that of any other major postcolonial Southeast Asian state. Thailand kept its monarchy and Malaysia its sultans, and even Cambodia retrieved its kingship in the 1990s. Modern Indonesia's continuities with its old Dutch colonial bureaucratic traditions have been frequently noted, and the Philippines has preserved political and judicial institutions bequeathed it by the Americans. Even the Myanmar military dictatorship of the 1990s used a body of binding laws a significant (if minor) percentage of which were inherited from the British colonial administration. No such continuities were evident in the regime created incrementally at Hanoi from 1945 on.

The Crisis of the Party State at the Century's End

AS IN other communist party states, the Vietnamese party resembled a paramilitary formation, with a general staff and mass organizations (youth leagues, labor unions, women's federations, professional associations) through which it attempted to dominate its society. The party's own central committee (with 150 members in 2001) supposedly mobilized members, through periodic meetings and congresses, to discuss party policies. But discussion had to be coupled with obedience to party leaders' decisions, following a pseudodemocratic formula known as "democratic centralism" that Lenin had first used in 1906. In reality the party and the country were ruled by a tiny "standing committee" of the party central committee's own smaller political bureau (or, in Leninist short-hand, "politburo"). This oligarchy of party leaders, headed by the party's general secretary, then tried to command the separate but subordinate hierarchy of the government, headed by a premier or council of ministers. The effectiveness of this command was qualified by the fact that the government apparatus, reflecting its original total planning responsibility for the country's economy, became increasingly bloated. North Vietnam, in 1960, had thirty-one government ministries or similar bodies; by 1986 the communist government of all Vietnam had doubled this number to sixty. The government was supposedly accountable to an elected National Assembly; party liberals hoped that in time this assembly might become an outpost of real democracy in Vietnam. The formerly Maoist party elder Truong Chinh published a large book on the "problems of the Vietnamese socialist state" in 1985 in which he complained that the party had never been able to "systematize" its own political structures.

Because of its lack of "systematization," the real political life of the Vietnamese party state after 1975 was often at considerable variance with its forms. Patron-client ties between senior and junior leaders—sometimes formalized in Western social science jargon as "symbiotic clientelism" or "Leninist patrimonialism"—pervaded the policy-making environment. These ties mediated the tensions within the oligarchy about just how much the party state should interfere in Vietnamese economic life. Under the long and stagnant reign of party general secretary Le Duan (from 1956 to 1986), the politburo was a theater of nepotism. Le Duan's reign also saw the marginalization of some of the creative people the aging party elite still possessed, most notably Vo Nguyen Giap, the party's military hero, evicted from the politburo in 1982. (The victor of Dienbienphu was sidelined as head of the state family planning commission, prompting jokes in Hanoi streets about "field marshals who fit IUDs.")

With the introduction of the reforms in the 1980s known as "renovation" *(doi moi)*, the party state tried to save itself by shifting to a less centrally planned, more market-based economy, seeking increased involvement with the procedures and institutions of global capitalism. In this era a series of party general secretaries came and went: Nguyen Van Linh in 1986, Do Muoi in 1991, General Le Kha Phieu in 1997, and Nong Duc Manh (the reputed unacknowledged son of Ho Chi Minh) in 2001. But none of these leaders would tolerate the emergence of competitive rival political parties. Opposition groups within the communist party itself, such as the Club of Former Resistance Fighters in 1987 (veterans of the National Liberation Front, or NLF, based in Ho Chi Minh City, who wanted Vietnamese government leaders to be chosen by secret ballot), were suppressed.

That opposition groups could germinate at all inside such a small and socially unrepresentative communist party showed how serious Vietnam's economic and political crisis was. In 1997, more than two decades after the war with the Americans ended, the party's total membership (2.1 million) amounted to slightly less than 3 percent of Vietnam's population. This contrasted with the 5 percent of the Chinese people who were members of the Chinese Communist Party and the even higher percentages of the population enrolled in some Eastern European communist parties before their regimes foundered in 1989. The average age of Vietnamese party members had actually increased between 1976 (38.6 years) and 1995 (43.6 years) despite the overall youth of Vietnam's population. Over one-quarter of the party's members were retired officials or cadres; fewer than one-tenth of its members were workers, mocking its Leninist claims to be the vanguard of the working class. The party also remained stronger in the north than in the south.

The party's lack of representativeness, vividly exposed in the gap between its patriarchal managerialism (in 1995 only 16.9 percent of its members were female) and Vietnam's considerable female work force, aroused complaints within the party establishment itself. In 1969, during the American war, 32 percent of the members of north Vietnam's village and ward people's committees had been women; by 1982 this statistic (for the whole of Vietnam) had shrunk to less than 6 percent. The party's difficulties in attracting members among Vietnam's ethnic minorities were even worse. Among some important minorities in the northern hill country, like the Hmong (whose numbers more than doubled between 1960 and 1989), party membership was less than 1 percent of the population in 1990. The party's lack of appeal among the minorities was underlined by the conversion—by clandestine missionaries and short-wave radio broadcasts from the Philippines—of tens of thousands of minority villagers in northern provinces like Lao Cai to Protestant Christianity. This trend could only remind historically conscious communist leaders of the way Catholic missionaries in the early 1800s had lured large numbers of poor people away from allegiance to Vietnam's equally elitist Confucian bureaucracy.

Corruption inside the party reinforced the decline of its political magnetism. Duong Thu Huong, herself the daughter of a party cadre, published a 1988 novel *Paradise of the Blind,* which recounted the degeneration of an incorruptible party executive into the agent of a black market network among Vietnamese expatriates in the Soviet Union. Her novel sold tens of thousands of copies before it was suppressed and she was expelled from the party. Higher up in the party, in the politburo itself, the liberal Tran Xuan Bach suggested to a Hanoi congress of Soviet bloc social scientists in 1988 that the social sciences had the tasks in Vietnam of creating full consciousness of the power of democratic freedom in each individual and of destroying the "bureaucratism" that had robbed socialism of its "prestige." Shortly after Bach expressed this mandarin-like hope that the intellectual elite's social sciences could substitute for democratic elections as a force for making party rule more accountable, he too was expelled from both the politburo and the central committee.

The Vietnamese party state nonetheless survived the meltdown of Marxist-Leninist regimes in Europe, because, unlike them (but like its Chinese counterpart), it was not facing strong ethnic nationalism or a large, highly educated, critical white-collar class. But its survival still raised big questions. Was it true (as some scholars argued) that the peculiar political structures generated by Marxism-Leninism unintentionally reinforced traditional elements in the political culture such as clientelism in response to pressures created by such regimes? And if it was true that the voluntary "detotalization" of a Leninist state like Vietnam had no successful historical precedents, were Vietnam's post-1986 reforms to be caught in a standstill? The purpose of the reforms was to restrict arbitrary state power over the economy. Yet the necessary agent of the reforms was the state itself. The postwar world's two successful examples of sudden transitions from planned to less planned economies, West Germany and Japan, had required foreign military occupations to make them work.

The Postwar Collapse of the Collectivist Dream

IN 1975 Vietnam's communist oligarchs, giving themselves high marks for their victory over the Americans, resolved to create a full communist order in Vietnam as quickly as possible. That meant a totally planned ideal polity in which nature, history, geography, and human psychology would all be remade in the spirit of a military campaign. The publication of a new Vietnamese translation of Goethe's *Faust* in Hanoi in 1977 might have been an omen. The oligarchs were not impressed by the increasingly successful capitalism of Japan and of their Southeast Asian neighbors. They studied Southeast Asia's ethnic Chinese business people aloofly, reading polemical Russian interpretations of them as the "tools" of China.

By 1976 the oligarchs had renamed their state the Socialist Republic of Vietnam. They centralized power over the south from Hanoi rather than considering any kind of federalism, and they even changed the name of Saigon to Ho Chi Minh City. In September 1975 money-changing tables, protected by soldiers, had been set up in the south's cities and villages to impose socialist currency; the more than 3 million people of Saigon were given a mere three days to dispose of their old piasters. Armed with fresh Vietnamese translations of Lenin's 1918 tract about "the immediate tasks of the Soviet government," which called for the use of mass organizations and consumers' cooperatives to wrest control of the distribution of goods away from counterrevolutionaries in the aftermath of a revolution, Vietnamese party cadres directed peasant associations and women's associations to take over Saigon's retail trade. They also sponsored noisy street demonstrations against the south's biggest ethnic Chinese traders, vilifying them individually as "the cigarette king" or "the farm tools king."

But the economic results of this frenzy were frustrating. By 1978 the south's more than forty state trading companies in farm products could get their hands on no more than about 20 percent of the south's foodstuffs. This exposed both their own weaknesses and the hostility of southern farmers to communist economic visions. Smuggling and speculation spread, in both north and south, in response to the collectivized economy's inefficiencies. In 1965 the black market had accounted for only about 13 percent of the general circulation of retail goods in the north; by 1980 it accounted for almost 38 percent and far more than that in food services.

Meanwhile the communist state, connecting salvation to spatial engineering, also tried to reconfigure the boundaries of Vietnamese provinces. The country's seventy-two provinces in 1975 were reduced and merged into a mere thirty-eight hybrid provinces by 1978. Such large amalgamated provinces, produced by manipulations at odds with Vietnamese administrative traditions, were designed to convert Vietnam into a single integrated economic machine, in line with Lenin's view that regions could be defined "scientifically" rather than historically in order to further such projects as national electrification. But spatial engineering from above generated enormous costs, ranging from postal address changes to quarrels about the locations of government offices. As the utopian values of the revolution waned, old provinces that had been abolished in 1978, such as Nghe An and Vinh Long, slowly reappeared. By the end of the twentieth century, history had almost triumphed over revolutionary science: Vietnam had sixty-one provinces and centrally attached cities, nearly as many as in 1975.

Farm collectivization was another form of administrative space management. Planned agricultural cooperatives, by eliminating private ownership of the land and thus the oppression of landlords, were supposed to end the alleged isolation of peasants, their reputed lack of specialization, and their presumed inability to rise above the level of self-sufficiency. After 1975 Hanoi attempted to extend its agricultural cooperatives to south Vietnam. This ambition collided with the fact that the war with the Americans and the CIA's campaign of terror (Operation Phoenix) had killed the thousands of locally born party organizers who best understood southern villages and were indispensable to the success of even a moderate rural revolution there. Even worse, the old-fashioned southern landlord class, whose depredations might have made the introduction of cooperatives more popular, had been driven from the countryside by 1975. They had not been able to survive the fighting, a southern land reform law of 1970 (in which American funds supplied their compensation), and the rise of an entrepreneurial group of capitalist farmers ("middle peasants" in communist terms), helped by U.S. aid and investment, who relished marketing their produce on free markets and had little desire for communist-style collectivization.

The regime's relentless pursuit of a single form of economic rationality encountered equally instructive challenges in the mountainous and midlands regions of Vietnam, where 250 of the country's 400 counties were located. This was where Vietnam's ethnic minorities lived. More than half of north Vietnam's increasingly impoverished farm cooperatives in the early 1980s could be found in its eight mountain provinces, the homeland of the Hmong, Yao-Mien, Nung, and Tai minorities, among others. Here Hanoi government planners, introducing cooperatives, abused the minorities' notions of what a natural community was. The minorities were compelled to conform to the sizes of lowland Vietnamese villages, even though their own traditional mountain hamlets had been smaller. This type of spatial engineering made it difficult to find minority leaders who could understand the cooperatives' administrative procedures.

Vietnam's shocking, if brief, border war with China in 1979 was simply the international relations version of the widening gulf between ideology and reality that afflicted domestic policy-making. Marxists claim that socialism, having triumphed over monopoly capitalism and imperialism, guarantees peace; this was the first wholly undisguised war in history between major communist states. The war had a variety of immediate causes. China and Vietnam had competed with each other for the right to be the chief foreign patron of the revolutions in Laos and Cambodia. But after 1975 the Pol Pot regime in Cambodia had showed intense enmity to Vietnam and assaulted the borders of southern Vietnam. Vietnam thereupon invaded Cambodia and installed a more manageable government in Phnom Penh (January 1979), reminding the world as it did so of imperial Vietnam's recurrent colonial manipulations of Khmer politics and greatly embarrassing Pol Pot's Chinese patrons. China responded with an invasion of Vietnam's northern border provinces (February 1979). This was halted after failing to end the Vietnamese military occupation of Cambodia, which continued to 1990. Truong Chinh, once the preeminent apostle of Maoist thought among the Vietnamese communist leaders, revealed the fantastic fears that lay behind this war in December 1979, when he accused China of wishing to "occupy Southeast Asia" in order to "conquer the world." He went on to argue that Beijing's two-pronged attack on Vietnam in the north and by its Khmer Rouge "servants" in the southwest repeated the tactics of the Chinese "feudal" court in the eleventh century, when it had allied itself with the Chams against Ly dynasty Vietnam.

Apart from Cambodia, Sino-Vietnamese relations foundered upon the two governments' increasingly contradictory involvements in the Cold War duel between the American and Soviet superpowers. China feared the Soviet Union and sought greater intimacy with the United States even before the Vietnamese communists' war with the Americans had ended. Vietnam allied itself with the Soviet Union, alarming China. There were also border disputes and a tragic controversy over the nature and behavior of the overseas Chinese people of Vietnam, who had enjoyed dual citizenship privileges there until 1978.

Overseas Chinese merchants had by then become the scapegoats for Hanoi's inability to impose its revolutionary blueprints readily on the conquered south after 1975. As Sino-Vietnamese tensions mounted, ethnic Chinese refugees, including veterans of the Vietnamese army and communist party, fled from Vietnam. They went either to southwest China or by sea to Hong Kong and noncommunist Southeast Asia as part of a disheveled stream of "boat people" that eventually resulted in more than a million refugees. Hoang Van Hoan, a longtime associate of Ho Chi Minh and a member of the Hanoi polit-buro itself until 1976, also fled to China in 1979, becoming one of the most senior defectors in history from an established communist government. Other unhappy Vietnamese, such as the hundred thousand or so political prisoners who had served southern governments before 1975, could not escape. They were detained in Stalinist-style camps and in many instances died in them.

This extraordinary accumulation of self-inflicted disasters and assaults from outside threatened the Vietnamese communist state with system breakdown. The price of hostility to China was a claustrophobic dependency on the Soviet bloc at the worst possible time, when the bloc itself was about to collapse (as it did between 1989 and 1991). The dependency did have a benign side; the Soviet Union, one of the world's leading scientific powers, had as of 1987 trained almost half of the Vietnamese communist cadres with university-level educations, while Soviet aerial photography, space satellite surveys, and geo-physical probes gave Vietnam its first truly modern maps of its own national territory. Economic dependency, in contrast, was catastrophic. Billions of rubles in Soviet aid created the illusion of a domestic economic surplus that Vietnam did not really have, generated consumer demands that the country could not afford, and overwhelmed and distorted the management capacities of the Viet-namese state, detaching it from local realities.

In 1978 Vietnam joined the Council for Mutual Economic Assistance (COMECON), the Soviet-run trading bloc created at the height of the Cold War in 1949. By the time Vietnam joined it, COMECON's international trade had dropped to less than 10 percent of world trade as a whole. COMECON assigned arbitrary production tasks to its different members. It compelled Vietnam to orient its foreign trade to distant, uneconomical markets in Siberia and East-ern Europe. In one characteristic incident, in 1987, Vietnam signed a COMECON agreement to export millions of pieces of clothing, at state-rigged prices, to the Soviet Union and Eastern Europe in return for raw materials and button-sewing machines. As the Soviet bloc fell apart and its deliveries failed, Vietnam was left with hundreds of thousands of unsold buttonless garments.

By this time, the weaknesses of Vietnam's collectivized agriculture had be-come a nightmare. Official calculations themselves suggested that the average yearly productivity of one Vietnamese farmer in 1985 was less than half that of a Thai farmer. Meanwhile the beleaguered Vietnamese government, which had forced the northern hill country minorities' cooperatives to pursue grain production at the expense of their more varied and familiar traditional agriculture of soybeans, oranges, peanuts, and opium, had to come to their rescue with imported rice. Collectivization's attempt to make farmers into the rural facsimiles of paid factory workers did not suit the seasonal and dispersed nature of farm production. The Soviet-style collective mode of farming, introduced into a tropical Asian society with a dense population and a shortage of land, could not achieve the economies of scale and specialized divisions of labor that Leninist propagandists had once celebrated in the Soviet Union. And the egalitarianism of the cooperatives' "work points" pay system, combined with the Vietnamese state's intensifying demands for rice with which to feed its swelling numbers of salaried functionaries, destroyed farm workers' incentives. By one inside estimate, Vietnamese farmers at the end of the Le Duan era (1986) were being allowed to keep no more than twenty kilograms of unhusked rice out of every hundred kilograms they harvested.

So much for the failed hopes of another twentieth-century experiment in political utopianism. The Vietnamese experiment attracted less attention than the communist millenarianisms of Cambodia or China. But it was not significantly more modest in its aims. Even before it eroded, the experiment's ideology was remarkably eclectic. It combined a Marxist faith in the global achievement of a universal civilization in which pure rational enlightenment could overcome all cultural and historical differences with a Leninist political siege mentality and a Maoist determination to make collectivized labor substitute for the industrial infrastructure that poor countries lacked. The experiment probably also gained legitimacy in Vietnam from its limited affinity with earlier Vietnamese rulers' dreams of legislated agrarian equality, such as the "well-field" and "equal field" ideals of the Tonkinese lord Trinh Doanh (r. 1740–1767). During the experiment, Vietnam related itself to the Soviet Union and Eastern Europe not by geographical proximity or culture (as it had with China in the precolonial period) but by a shared creed of imagined developmental time.

Vietnamese communism also had similarities with the global neoliberal economics that was to replace it; 1986 would not be a complete break. The practical subordination of all human activities to the primacy of economic growth and the pretense that state policies were the nonpolitical fulfillment of universal laws of development were just two such continuities. But in the villages, the interaction of the values and practices of different periods took its own forms. The revolutionary state, between the 1950s and 1980s, had created new types of political power in order to manage the assets confiscated from private landlords: the political power represented by party committees, people's councils, and even the administrative boards of the cooperatives themselves. In many villages this power fell into the hands of cadres and officials whom one Hanoi insider derided as the "new strongmen" *(cuong hao moi)* or "new bullies." The new bullies were a neotraditional social formation, not a complete return to tyrannical village elders of the old days. Like them, the new strongmen relied on family and lineage connections that the revolution could not extinguish, but unlike the old village elites, they could defend and augment their power by the use of political resources and police sanctions from outside the village, accusing villagers who resisted them of being antiparty as well as antigovernment. Here the expanded use of the "primordial" family ties that held this "new caste structure" of cadres together was reinforced by the collectivized villages' greater dependency on the state. It was only in the late 1990s that retired party cadres living in political "hot spot" villages (as they were now anxiously called in Hanoi) began to lead their abused neighbors in violent protests against corrupt currently serving cadres, reenacting as they did so the part played by retired scholar-gentry in precolonial villages in the ancient struggle for the human rights of rural underdogs in Vietnam. Underdog-defending NGOs like the Assembly of the Poor in Thailand had yet to develop.

Vietnamese Leninism's Partial Shift to Market Economics

THE PARTY STATE was forced to redefine itself by changing from a planned economy to a more market-directed, export-promoting economy anxious for outside capital investment, similar to those elsewhere in Southeast Asia. The sixth party congress' formal ratification of the *doi moi* reform program occurred in 1986, but some reforms had begun before then. The party central committee's Directive No. 100 (1981) had already contracted farming responsibilities to village households, away from the cooperatives, and had allowed farmers greater freedom to market their crops. The politburo's Resolution No. 10 (1988) finally renounced collectivism. The resolution recognized village households as "autonomous economic units," though not as independent family farmers, and transferred land use rights and with them decision-making power directly to such households. Cooperatives no longer had a managerial function, surviving merely as a purveyor of services.

The party state stopped short of conceding outright private property ownership, however. Land still belonged to the state, even if a new Land Law of 1993 desperately tried to create "peace of mind" in the villages with land use tenures of as long as fifty years (compared to thirty years in China's equivalent reforms). Vietnam's millions of newly entitled state tenants were allowed to mimic private ownership, receiving the rights to rent their land tenures, mortgage them, exchange them, transfer them, and even inherit them. The National Assembly debate over the Land Law demonstrated how diverse even officially sanctioned opinion about the land could be in Vietnam. Southern delegates complained that even the fifty-year tenures were not long enough, demanded that inheritance rights be extended to relatives beyond immediate households, and lamented that the maximum size of the land use tenures (three hectares) was too small to facilitate agricultural business enterprises. But the reforms were a big short-term success. Vietnam, which had had to import rice in the 1980s, became one of the three biggest exporters of rice in the world (with Thailand and the United States) by the end of the 1990s and also became a major exporter of coffee for the first time.

Farming reforms were only part of the drive to help Vietnam achieve a more rapid convergence with the economic productivity of regional and global capitalism. There was also a state-directed legal revolution. In the decade after 1986, a blizzard of new laws tried to remake the Vietnamese socialist republic in the image of its investment-seeking neighbors. Laws to protect foreign investment, private business enterprise laws, corporation laws, export and import tax laws, bankruptcy laws, state enterprise laws, laws encouraging domestic investors, and even a state budget law, as well as land laws, were introduced, based on theoretical appreciation of equivalent laws elsewhere. To help train managers, specialists, and advisers for a new effort at state formation, Vietnam even legitimized the formerly disdained "capitalist" subject of political science in 1991, becoming one of the last of the old Soviet bloc countries to do so.

Photo by N. G. Owen

Enjoying life under *doi moi:* Tay Ninh, 1994.

The immediate result of all the new laws was that typical symptom of legal globalization: a gap between the legal state and the real society, perhaps more extreme than any previous such gap in Vietnam's history. Vietnamese party cadres, skilled at orchestrating mass movements in wartime, had little experience in managing society by law and legal norms. Moreover, most of the new laws were "framing" laws, concerned with regulating very broad problems. Characteristically, they had to be applied in combination with a host of shadowy administrative guidelines, issued in delayed and uncoordinated ways by a multitude of state agencies. The reflexes of legal obedience of the population for which they were designed were weak: in the late 1990s about one-third of the officially assessed taxes on households and businesses were never collected. Then there was Vietnam's cultural diversity. The new civil law code of 1995, with its passion for standardization, could not cope with such diversity, one insider warned: how would its categories, borrowed from Roman law, address such phenomena as the "Malayo-Polynesian" matrilineal definitions of legal authority over household property found in Vietnam's central highlands?

The new laws, like the old Soviet-style cooperatives, were intended to accelerate history and create mass habits that did not yet exist; they were not rules for coordinating an industrial society whose values were already formed. The globalization of capitalist institutions could become a state-directed cultural borrowing process that, if successful, might be used to redeem the image of the old managerial state. Vietnam's first stock exchange, which opened in Ho Chi Minh City in 2000 (one of about fifty new such national stock markets that appeared in Asia, Africa, Latin America, and Eastern Europe in the decade or so after 1985) was a potential example. Its purpose, banking and finance ministry cadres explained, was to cure Vietnamese of their traditional disorderly, low-volume approach to markets. It was also to function as a laboratory for the stimulation of modern "risk-taking" economic behavior in Vietnam and as a tool for increasing the state's economic power.

After Vietnamese relations with China were normalized again in 1991, the Chinese leaders who visited Hanoi celebrated the similarities of the reform processes in the two Asian Leninist states. The general pattern in both was that economic reform preceded political reform, and there was little Russian-style "shock therapy" from above. In addition, the Vietnamese state followed the Chinese state's formula of attempting to transform itself from a revolutionary charismatic community to an agency for celebrating ethnic pride. The 1991 party congress proposed to harness the power of the world's estimated three hundred thousand overseas Vietnamese "intellectuals" in order to help develop Vietnamese science and industry, even if some of these intellectuals, ranging from mathematicians to some remarkably talented film makers, also threatened to import subversive ideas from the outside. In the 1990s Vietnam's new (1988) Nationality Law came under savage attack, even by Foreign Ministry cadres, for failing to recognize the dual citizenship of Vietnamese people living abroad (which could limit Hanoi's power over them when they visited Vietnam), thereby violating the "inner feelings" of solidarity of the Vietnamese people.

But the ways in which the Vietnamese reforms differed from the Chinese ones were at least as important. First, Vietnam was a poorer country than China: Vietnamese economists themselves calculated that Vietnam's industrialization was one or even two decades behind China's. Second, Vietnam lacked China's huge domestic market, meaning that while individual incomes remained low, it was more difficult for Vietnamese reformers to attract foreign investment or develop economies of scale. Third, before the reforms Vietnam had been more isolated from the global capitalist economy, not sharing Maoist China's anomaly of having the bulk of its external trade with capitalist countries that did not recognize it diplomatically. The crisis of Vietnam's sudden loss of Soviet and Eastern European aid combined with the costs of its military occupation of Cambodia meant that the Vietnamese reforms began in an atmosphere of economic disintegration, not just of stagnation as in China. Fourth, despite remittances from overseas Vietnamese, Vietnam lacked a Hong Kong: an offshore stronghold of capitalism, populated by an ethnically alike people, which allowed it quick access to business know-how and investment capital. This pointed to a more general historical difference between the two Leninist regimes. Business values are harder to imagine positively in countries that have never had their own successful merchant classes. Unlike China, precolonial Vietnam had lacked formidable indigenous merchants, relying like much of the rest of Southeast Asia on Chinese and Indian merchant diasporas. The Vietnamese collectivist state, with its state-owned enterprises, had to start from scratch, substituting for such merchants rather than expropriating and replacing them, as China was able to do.

Such differences between the Vietnamese and Chinese reform environments help to explain Vietnam's remarkable reinvention of itself in the 1990s as an officially "Southeast Asian" country, seeing itself this way for the first time in its history. The countries of the Association of Southeast Asian Nations (ASEAN) began to absorb up to 40 percent of Vietnam's exports, replacing the lost markets of the vanished Soviet bloc. Vietnam joined ASEAN in 1995; eminent Vietnamese writers like Dinh Gia Khanh had already begun to publish books with titles like *Vietnamese Popular Culture in Its Southeast Asian Setting* (1993). ASEAN and its prospective ASEAN Free Trade Area (AFTA) quickly acquired multiple functions in the Vietnamese imagination. On the one hand, they were seen as supplying the necessary external stimuli for a domestic "renovation" project whose internal stimuli were feared to be not strong enough: ASEAN free trade would force Vietnamese businesses to improve their competitiveness by reforming their technology and organization. On the other hand, membership in a large ASEAN common market area would compensate for Vietnam's small

domestic market and allow Vietnam to compete for foreign investment funds on more equal terms with south China. Here Vietnam's discovery of its "Southeast Asian" identity could serve as a new weapon in the very old struggle against Chinese domination.

For such reasons, Vietnamese propagandists, in 1995, celebrated the virtues of what they called "the great ASEAN family" as robustly as they had once celebrated those of the Soviet trading bloc. Entering ASEAN was a gamble. Vietnam's legal system was still underdeveloped, compared to its neighbors, and the country lacked a body of English-speaking business managers of the sort found in Bangkok or Manila. The Vietnamese revolution's whirlwind changes in its chosen geographic allegiances showed how modern doctrines of progress could reduce notions of space and region to contingent categories. But Vietnamese leaders had finally and apparently unconditionally embraced the promising postcolonial vision of "Southeast Asia," which had gone unrecognized for so many years right under their noses.

Further Readings

Beresford, Melanie. *National Unification and Economic Development in Vietnam.* London, 1989.

Bui Tin. *Following Ho Chi Minh: The Memoirs of a North Vietnamese Colonel.* Translated by Judy Stowe and Do Van. Honolulu, 1995.

Chan, Anita, Benedict J. Tria Kerkvliet, and Jonathan Unger, eds. *Transforming Asian Socialism: China and Vietnam Compared.* Canberra, 1999.

Fforde, Adam, and Stefan de Vylder. *From Plan to Market: The Economic Transition in Vietnam.* Boulder, 1996.

Kleinen, John. *Facing the Future, Reviving the Past: Social Change in a Northern Vietnamese Village.* Singapore, 1999.

Kolko, Gabriel. *Vietnam: Anatomy of a Peace.* London, 1997.

Pelley, Patricia M. *Postcolonial Vietnam: New Histories of the National Past.* Durham, N.C., 2002.

Tai, Hue-Tam Ho, ed. *The Country of Memory: Rethinking the Past in Late Socialist Vietnam.* Berkeley, 2001.

Templer, Robert. *Shadows and Wind: A View of Modern Vietnam.* New York, 1999.

Werner, Jayne, and Danièle Bélanger, eds. *Gender, Household, State: Doi Moi in Vietnam.* Ithaca, 2001.

Chapter 35

Cambodia since 1975

CAMBODIA, which as late as the 1960s was still characterized by some observers as a "sleepy" country of "peaceful" people, had by the mid-1970s shown itself capable of as much radicalism and violence as any other society in the world. In Phnom Penh in early 1975 the ineptitude of the Lon Nol regime and the disintegrating military situation were exacerbated by the influx of perhaps two million refugees from rural areas who had poured into Phnom Penh and Battambang since 1972. By March 1975 most public services in both cities had broken down. Food was running low. Khmer Republican forces, despite massive infusions of U.S. aid, were unable to loosen the grip of Khmer Rouge units encircling the towns. On 17 April, soon after Lon Nol and the staff of the U.S. embassy had flown out to safety, the communists seized control of Phnom Penh. Battambang fell a day later.

Democratic Kampuchea

THE APPEARANCE of the victorious troops was disturbing to urban dwellers, who welcomed an end to the fighting. The newcomers were silent, unfriendly, and dressed in peasant black. They were also heavily armed and in many cases very young. Within twenty-four hours in Phnom Penh and a week in Battambang, the Khmer Rouge ordered all the inhabitants of these cities—close to three million people in all—to walk away from their homes and take up agricultural work in accordance with a doctrine, derived from Maoist China, that poor peasants and unskilled manual workers were the only worthwhile members of society. Swift and total ruralization fit closely with the utopian ideas that Saloth Sar and his colleagues had developed in their years in hiding and at war. For the time being, perhaps because he feared a renewal of the fighting, Sar kept the existence of the Communist Party and his own role secret from outsiders.

Thousands of Cambodians died in the exodus and thousands of others, particularly former soldiers, were executed at this time en masse. As millions of people criss-crossed the country, they soon discovered that money, markets, private property, schools, and organized religion had ceased to exist. They were told that a faceless "higher organization" *(angkar loeu),* probably a pseudonym for the Communist Party's central committee, was in command of Cambodian life. Children old enough to work were often separated from their parents for weeks or months at a time. Supposedly peasant-based reforms in linguistics, clothing, female hair styles, adornment, and courtship, to name a few, also came into effect in 1975, and in early 1976 a party spokesman proudly declared that "two thousand years" of Cambodian history had ended. By "history" he probably meant the lopsided, exploitative relationships that had characterized Cambodian society for millennia. Official broadcasts promised a society in which there would be "no exploiters and no exploited," but these relations persisted, with new victims and beneficiaries, in the top-down style favored by the regime.

Amid all this turmoil the leaders of the revolution were happy to remain concealed. As "new people" (evacuees) were absorbed, often painfully, into populations of "base people" loyal to the regime and as the nation took up unpaid agricultural work, Saloth Sar and his colleagues took up residence stealthily, under heavy guard, in the abandoned capital.

Cambodia's third constitution was promulgated in early 1976, naming the country Democratic Kampuchea (DK). DK's flag, like all others in independent Cambodia, bore a stylized image of Angkor Wat. Soon afterward, following elections for a rubber-stamp National Assembly—undoubtedly carried out for overseas consumption—an unknown figure named Pol Pot was "chosen" as DK's prime minister; only a year later would he be identified by outsiders as Saloth Sar. Prince Sihanouk, hitherto the nominal chief of state, was pushed aside into nearly three years of house arrest. Democratic Kampuchea had some of the trappings of a socialist state and received warm recognition from many communist countries, but the local Communist Party kept its existence a secret until October 1977 and also concealed its fruitful alliances with China and North Korea. The party's leaders relished working in secret, and by not calling themselves communist, they were able to pretend, in public, that the revolution had no precedents in history and was a purely Cambodian affair.

The party's four-year plan, scheduled to begin in September 1976, was shelved, but the 110-page text provides interesting insights into the utopian thinking of the regime. The document called for a "super great leap forward," a phrase borrowed from China, and promised that within the lifetime of the plan, DK, by mastering the laws of history, would leapfrog several phases of social evolution and arrive at the supposed pinnacle of socialism. The goal could be achieved, the plan suggested, by increasing agricultural production to the point where export earnings from crops, especially rice, could pay for imports of farm machinery and for a long-term program of industrialization. The plan called for yields and exportable surpluses more than twice as high as any in prerevolutionary times. The text ignored the facts that Cambodia was emerging from a devastating war, that the expansion would have to rely on an inexperienced, poorly motivated work force (for the brunt of rice cultivation fell on "new people" evacuated from the towns), and that the country faced severe shortages of livestock, seed, herbicides, and tools. To override these difficulties, which it failed to mention, the plan called on the liberating energies of the people's collective, revolutionary will.

Farmers were enjoined throughout the DK era to harvest "three tons [of rice] per hectare," another slogan borrowed without attribution from China. The goal was nearly three times higher than average yields in earlier times and proved impossible to attain, except in a few districts that had good soil, a well-fed labor force, and sufficient water. In order to provide water on a national basis for year-round rice cultivation, huge reservoirs and dams were constructed throughout the country without heavy machinery or engineering expertise. People worked on them and on cultivating rice for as much as fourteen hours a day, twenty-seven days a month. Years later, asked about the DK era, the first thing that many Cambodians recalled, besides inadequate food, was having been made to "dig earth and raise embankments." Between 1975 and 1979 tens of thousands of men and women, especially former urban dwellers, died of undernourishment and exhaustion. Few people except soldiers and party cadres ever got enough to eat. The high quotas for rice production could rarely if ever be met, and serious malnutrition occurred in much of DK, where cadres cut people's rations, but seldom their own, to obtain the "surpluses" demanded by the state. Cambodia also spurned Western medical practices (except for high-ranking cadres), with the result that tens of thousands of people also died from untended or misdiagnosed diseases.

At least two hundred thousand others, and probably more, were executed by DK as enemies of the state. At first victims were drawn from the ranks of Lon Nol's army and from the so-called exploiting classes of prerevolutionary Cambodia. By mid-1976, however, the party leaders began to suspect that plots were being hatched against them in the army and in the eastern part of the country, with Vietnamese connivance. Pol Pot and his colleagues began to purge suspected military units and party members on a massive scale. To receive many of the suspects, a secret interrogation facility known by its code name S-21 was established in May 1976 on the grounds of a former high school in Phnom Penh. By January 1979, when a Vietnamese invasion drove the Khmer Rouge from power, over fourteen thousand men, women, and children, including many high-ranking party cadres, had passed through S-21. Almost all of them were interrogated and tortured. All but half a dozen were put to death. Some four thousand of their so-called confessions, along with masses of documentation from the prison, have survived. In the confessions some prisoners admitted to working simultaneously for the CIA, the Vietnamese communists, and the Soviet secret service. Others confessed to hiding Vietnamese in tunnels dug inside Phnom Penh, though no such tunnels were ever found. High-ranking cadres confessed to having betrayed the party from the day they had joined it. Elsewhere in the country, tens of thousands of men and women were held in "education halls," or prisons, where conditions were harsh and most died of mistreatment or execution.

Pol Pot and his colleagues believed that enemies surrounded them. What mattered most to them was that all of these people, whether they were innocent or guilty, admitted their guilt before being put to death. The number of people targeted and the obvious horrors of the regime meant that at least some of those locked into S-21 and other prisons had indeed plotted against DK. However, most of the charges were spurious. Thousands of people were put to death because they were named by other people, rather than because they had done anything themselves. The purges tore apart the administration and placed new burdens on an exhausted, sick, and terrified population.

The exact number of regime-related deaths in the DK era will never be known, but informed estimates suggest that nearly two million people, or a quarter of the population, died in less than four years from malnutrition, overwork, untreated diseases, or execution. Since most of the victims were ethnic Khmer, the French writer Jean Lacouture coined the term "autogenocide" to describe what had taken place. There is no evidence that Pol Pot and his colleagues set out to preside over so many deaths, but when the regime collapsed, none of them expressed sustained regret, and all of them were quick to blame traitors and Vietnamese for everything that had gone wrong. DK delivered few benefits to its supporters, many of whom were purged. Its dogmatic and heartless policies bore little relation to Cambodian reality; they made no sense to most Khmer. The traumas that survivors suffered later on and the long-term effects of so much violence, distrust, and fantasy on the population as a whole are impossible to calculate.

Cambodian communists had been hostile toward Vietnam since 1973, when Vietnamese troops withdrew from Cambodia, under the terms of a cease-fire arranged with the United States, leaving the Khmer Rouge forces on their own.

After 1975, DK had sought the patronage of Maoist China, already at odds with Vietnam, because Vietnam was allied with the USSR. The Chinese provided military equipment to DK for defensive purposes, but Pol Pot and his colleagues assumed that China would support them if they made war against Vietnam. This miscalculation led them onto an intrinsically suicidal policy of extended confrontation.

Until the end of 1976, relations with Vietnam were chilly but correct. Skirmishes along the land and sea frontiers soon broke out, however, provoking brutal incursions by Khmer units into Vietnam. By mid-1977 Vietnam had become Cambodia's "enemy number one." Following Pol Pot's state visit to China in October of that year, Vietnamese forces invaded eastern Cambodia. They remained there for several months before withdrawing in an orderly fashion. The campaign led Pol Pot to declare victory in public and then secretly purge thousands of cadres, soldiers, and military leaders from the affected region. In 1978, as these purges intensified, several hundred Khmer, to save their lives, sought asylum in Vietnam, where the Vietnamese quickly formed them into a government in exile. Throughout 1978 DK's leaders tried desperately to open up their country to outside recognition while continuing both their war with Vietnam and the purges that swept through the party.

On Christmas Eve 1978 Vietnam, using more than one hundred thousand troops, launched a massive invasion of Cambodia. To the outside world, they claimed that the fighting was being carried out by a Cambodian liberation front. Despite fierce resistance by DK troops, the country cracked open like an egg. Phnom Penh was occupied on 7 January 1979—Pol Pot had fled the day before to Thailand on a helicopter—and the DK regime disappeared almost overnight. In its place the Vietnamese swiftly installed a sympathetic cabinet composed of Khmer Rouge defectors, like Cambodia's future prime minister, Hun Sen, then only twenty-seven years old, and Cambodian communists who had been living in Vietnam for many years. Soon afterward, Vietnam's prime minister, Pham Van Dong, flew into Phnom Penh and signed a treaty of friendship with the newly installed regime, which called itself the People's Republic of Kampuchea (PRK). Its new flag bore an altered image of Angkor Wat.

Recovery and Repression

THE LEADERS of the PRK and their Vietnamese advisers moved quickly to restore institutions destroyed or abandoned under the Khmer Rouge, including cities, money, schools, markets, and freedom of movement. Political controls remained severe, however, and it soon became clear that some form of top-down socialism would be imposed on the bone-tired population. Many Cambodians came to believe that Vietnam's supposedly temporary occupation fit into a long-term strategic plan to join the components of Indochina into a Vietnam-dominated federation.

Famine conditions and uncertainty about Vietnamese intentions pushed hundreds of thousands of Cambodians into Thailand, where refugee camps opened up in 1979 and 1980. Tens of thousands more wandered around the country, looking for work or relatives and trying to reoccupy their former homes and plots of land. In the ensuing chaos, few crops were planted, and tens of thousands of people starved. By 1981 over three hundred thousand refugees, passing through the Thai camps, had found new homes in France, Australia, the United States, and elsewhere. A similar number remained in the camps, often for longer than ten years, fed and housed under the auspices of the United Nations. Many were unwilling to go home. The PRK, in any case, considered the refugees unreliable and did not welcome any of them back.

In the meantime, remnants of the Khmer Rouge army that had stumbled across the border were welcomed, fed, and refitted by Thai military authorities fearing a Vietnamese invasion. Pol Pot also received continuing support from China and indirectly from the United States, which was eager to punish Vietnam both for its invasion of Cambodia and for defeating the United States. With such powerful allies, DK forces were able to pursue their fight against the Phnom Penh government, and throughout the 1980s DK held onto Cambodia's seat at the United Nations, the only government in exile able to do so.

As news about the DK era reached the outside world via refugees and the PRK, the United States and its allies sought to save face by backing the formation of a "coalition" government on the Thai border. The coalition consisted of the Khmer Rouge and factions made up of refugees who were loyal to Prince Sihanouk (who in 1979 had returned to live in Beijing) and others loyal to a former prime minister, Son Sann, who had at one time sided with the Khmer Republic. The factions represented successive phases in Cambodian political history. Each of them hated the other two, and all three, united in their hatred for Vietnam, were despised by the PRK.

Throughout the 1980s fighting continued between the Khmer Rouge forces and their relatively inactive allies, on the one hand, and the Vietnamese army and their Cambodian protégés on the other. In the course of the war, Vietnam lost over twenty thousand men, and casualties on the Khmer Rouge side were also high. In the 1980s and early 1990s, hundreds of thousands of antipersonnel mines were planted along the Thai-Cambodian border and around army units, which then moved on without leaving maps of the minefields. For over a decade, thousands of Cambodian civilians have been maimed or killed as they stepped on mines while going about their daily lives,

The international stalemate in Cambodia began to alter in the late 1980s, following the loosening of Soviet power in the communist bloc. One effect of the process was to deprive Vietnam and Cambodia of substantial Soviet aid. Vietnam could no longer sustain its army in Cambodia. The last units were withdrawn in September 1989. Shortly before their departure the PRK introduced a series of popular reforms. These included legalizing private property, altering the flag, changing the country's name to the State of Cambodia (SOC), and amending the constitution to restore Buddhism as Cambodia's state religion. The death penalty was also abolished.

Although the regime now claimed to be a "liberal democracy," its unelected leaders, under Prime Minister Hun Sen, remained in place; there were few laws on the books; party members were favored above other citizens; and opposition parties were banned. Economically, Cambodia opened up in the early 1990s to foreign exploitation. Hundreds of thousands of tons of timber and millions of dollars worth of gemstones were exported, without any controls, to Thailand and Vietnam. The exports enriched entrepreneurs and officials on both sides of each border as well as Khmer Rouge forces, who had seeped into the gem fields of northwestern Cambodia after the Vietnamese withdrawal. The benefits to the population as a whole were nil.

In Phnom Penh lifting restrictions on real estate led to a boom in speculation and construction. A more permissive atmosphere now allowed government officials to pocket large sums of money from informally levied charges for service, verdicts, contracts, or favors. The safety net provided by Vietnamese-style socialism was abandoned. The boom produced a "black economy" in much of the country. Rampant official corruption, which had been absent from the country since 1975, reemerged.

Because of the ongoing fighting, military expenditures had dominated the PRK budget, and no national tax system was in place to provide revenue for basic services. There was also little incentive to punish corruption by high officials. This woeful situation continued into the twenty-first century, when the gap between Cambodia's small elite and the masses of rural poor became much wider than it had been in the 1960s.

Outside Phnom Penh the population was generally poorer, less healthy, and worse served than at any time since the 1920s. The rate of infant mortality was one of the highest in the world; so was the birthrate. Malaria and other fevers were endemic in some parts of the country, as was malnutrition. By the late 1990s the incidence of HIV-AIDS in Cambodia was the highest in Southeast Asia. The frequency of mental illness, traceable to the traumas of the 1970s and the absence of medication, was also high. Schools and hospitals were poorly equipped, poorly financed, and poorly staffed. The judicial system was poorly trained and its employees so poorly paid that most judges were susceptible to bribes.

Compromises

AFTER A DECADE of confronting economic, military, and political problems, the leaders of the SOC had failed to solve most of them. To some extent, the ruling party and its Vietnamese mentors were to blame, but many of Cambodia's problems in this period were imposed from outside the country. Perhaps this has always been the case. By 1990, as the Cold War drew to a close, it became clear that without drastic changes in the foreign support that the SOC and the government in exile were receiving, Cambodia's problems would remain unsolved. After a series of complex diplomatic moves by the United States and other interested parties, many hoped for the massive intervention of the United Nations, which would preside over a caretaker regime pending national elections.

An international conference convened in Paris in October 1991 to formalize these arrangements. Under the terms of the agreement, a temporary government was established in Phnom Penh made up of representatives of the incumbent SOC and the three components of the government in exile. The factions formed a Supreme National Council (SNC) under Prince Sihanouk, who returned home briefly in November 1991 after twelve years in exile. The SNC's decisions were monitored by U.N. officials on the spot.

In effect the agreements withdrew the patronage of larger powers from the contending Cambodian factions before reinserting the factions (in theory) into a nonaligned Cambodia, where they would be free to compete for political advantage. Vietnam, to be sure, had all but ended its patronage of the SOC. In Paris the United States and its allies formally ended their support for the so-called noncommunist resistance, while China withdrew its patronage of the Khmer Rouge. Pol Pot's faction reentered Cambodian politics not as a component of a government in exile, but as an indigenous, fearful, and discredited faction. Many observers inside the country and overseas were dismayed by what they saw as granting legitimacy to a group considered to be guilty of genocide or crimes against humanity. However, the change in status for the Khmer Rouge as well as their squalid history ultimately proved fatal to the movement, which was unable to function in the open.

The arrangements made in Paris called for the four factions to disarm and to assemble in collection points known as cantons. They also envisaged the repatriation of some three hundred thousand Khmer in refugee camps in Thailand and national elections for a constituent assembly that would be charged with drafting a new constitution. While all this was taking place, the day-to-day functions of government were to be monitored by the United Nations. To achieve these goals, the United Nations established a short-term, multinational protectorate over Cambodia known as the United Nations Transitional Authority in Cambodia, or UNTAC.

UNTAC arrived too late and moved too cautiously to gain the respect it needed from the Cambodian factions. In May 1992 the DK faction expanded the territory under its control and refused to disarm, asserting that the Hun Sen regime and its armed forces were still controlled, from hiding, by the Vietnamese. The DK faction also refused to be monitored by UNTAC. For these actions, they were neither punished nor chastised. The SOC also refused to disarm or to allow UNTAC officials to oversee the daily operations of most of its ministries or the national police, as envisaged by the Paris agreements.

UNTAC embarked on its unprecedented, utopian, and multifaceted mission sluggishly and with foreboding. Its mandate was ambiguous, its time was limited, and most UNTAC personnel knew nothing about Cambodia. All were conscious that the civil war might resume at any time. By the time the mission ended in October 1993, it had cost over U.S.$2 billion, making it the most costly operation to date in U.N. history. Much of the money went into inflated U.N. salaries. The extravagance and insensitivity of many UNTAC personnel were widely criticized. Phnom Penh became more crowded and more prosperous in these years, but the rural economy stagnated, the country's infrastructure remained abysmal, and security was marred by over two hundred politically motivated killings. Khmer Rouge forces, claiming that Vietnam remained secretly in control of Cambodia, massacred more than a hundred Vietnamese civilians in 1992–1993. The SOC's police, for its part, targeted activists from other political groups. None of the offenders was arrested or brought to trial.

More positively, the Cambodian media in 1992–1993 enjoyed unaccustomed freedom that outlasted the UNTAC era. Local human rights organizations, unthinkable in any previous regime, also flourished and remained a powerful force in Cambodia in the early twenty-first century. Other positive developments included the peaceful repatriation of over three hundred thousand refugees from Thailand and the national elections themselves, which took place in July 1993, following a massive voter registration campaign conducted by UNTAC staff. Although the DK faction refused to take part, the elections were freer and fairer than any in Cambodia's history. At least four million men and women—over 90 percent of registered voters—went peacefully to the polls. The message they delivered was ambiguous. A royalist party, under the French acronym FUNCINPEC, won seven more seats for the constituent assembly than did the government's Cambodian People's Party (CPP). An anticommunist, anti-Vietnamese party won ten of the remaining eleven seats. For the first time in their history, a majority of Cambodians had voted against an armed, incumbent regime. They had courageously rejected the status quo. What they were voting for, besides peace (which remained elusive), was less clear.

The SOC refused to accept the election results and by the end of the year had imposed a fragile compromise on FUNCINPEC whereby Cambodia would have two prime ministers: Prince Norodom Rannaridh, FUNCINPEC's leader, and the CPP's Hun Sen, who had held office since 1984. Over the next few years, thanks to Rannaridh's indecisiveness and several shrewd moves by Hun Sen, the royalist party was marginalized and lost its voice in decision making. The 1993 constitution restored the monarchy and placed Sihanouk on the throne he had abandoned in 1955. Becoming a king again pleased the seventy-one-year-old monarch, but without access to funding or weapons, he was unable to influence events. Throughout the 1990s, pleading poor health, he spent long periods of each year outside the country.

The losers in 1993, aside from those who had voted against the government, were the Khmer Rouge. The movement was outlawed in 1994, and thousands of its followers soon defected to the government. Efforts to dislodge the remaining military units were unsuccessful, but as Thai government support for the Khmer Rouge faded and defection from the movement increased, the Khmer Rouge leadership split between those looking for a modus vivendi with Phnom Penh and those wanting to rekindle the revolutionary conflict. In August 1996 Ieng Sary, DK's former foreign minister, defected to Phnom Penh. He received a royal pardon and was allowed to establish a base, with several thousand followers, in the relatively prosperous enclave of Pailin in Cambodia's northwest. Over the next few months, the remnants of the Khmer Rouge came apart. Pol Pot, in ill health, was sidelined by a brutal military commander named Ta Mok, and in June 1997 he was put on trial by the new ruling faction of the Khmer Rouge for trying to restart the civil war. Subjected to the same kind of winners' justice that had sent hundreds of thousands of Cambodians to their deaths in DK, Pol Pot was condemned to life imprisonment in his two-room house. Ten months later he died in bed, an apparent suicide.

In Phnom Penh the coalition was under strain. FUNCINPEC efforts to recruit Khmer Rouge defectors to protect the party's leaders angered Hun Sen, who had recruited thousands of them into the national army. In July 1997 he launched a preemptive coup against his partners. In the surprise attack, over a hundred FUNCINPEC officials and security personnel were killed. CPP casualties were minimal. Widespread looting accompanied the coup. Several donor nations, appalled by these events, suspended aid, and Cambodia's entry into ASEAN was postponed. After he had consolidated power in his own way, Hun Sen found himself and Cambodia treated as pariahs. Donor nations and U.N. officials urged him to sponsor honest elections in 1998, as scheduled, for the National Assembly.

Despite some violence against opposition party workers before the elections, the elections themselves were relatively free and fair. Parties opposed to the CPP gained 60 percent of the vote but were unwilling to form an alliance, so a neutralized FUNCINPEC and the CPP agreed to form another coalition, with Hun Sen as the sole prime minister. By the end of 1998, Cambodia was at peace for the first time since 1970. For the first time in decades, the government was not the subject of foreign concern nor dependent on a single foreign patron. Instead, generous aid poured into Cambodia from over twenty countries, and the kingdom, via its membership in ASEAN, was participating as fully as it could in the affairs of Southeast Asia.

The 1998 elections revealed the sophistication and enthusiasm of the voting public. As Cambodia's bloated, underpaid army slowly demobilized and as opposition pressures against the CPP became less worrisome to Hun Sen, there were encouraging signs that the government might begin to direct some of its attention and more of its revenues to the social sector neglected for so long. Whether the endemic corruption among high officials could be curbed remained doubtful, given that Hun Sen seemed to feel that the continuing support coming from these figures and their followers was more important than their unethical behavior. In the 1990s Hun Sen, for his part, abjured his socialist past, was proud of his modernity, and was eager to learn more. He relished the title "strongman" and spent much of his time, as Sihanouk had done, outmaneuvering and neutralizing opposition, occasionally resorting to force.

In January 2003 anti-Thai riots broke out in Phnom Penh, sparked by a line of dialogue in a Thai TV drama suggesting that Angkor Wat should revert to Thai control. As police and foremen stood by, mobs burned down the Thai embassy and a Thai-owned hotel before being brought under control. The riots revealed the deep resentment felt by many Khmer toward Thai domination of Cambodia's economy and also drew on convenient readings or misreadings of the Cambodian past. In the wake of the riots, there were perhaps as many grounds for optimism of a cautious kind about Cambodia as there were for pessimism. The grounds for pessimism, unfortunately, seemed more persuasive, given that Cambodia has so many people, so few resources, and such a self-confident, self-serving ruling party. The prospects for responsive, transparent governance, given the low priority placed on the concept by those in power, were still dim. In facing the future, however, Cambodia no longer suffered from its perennial concerns, including interference by its neighbors, the patronizing disdain of international backers, and its partly self-imposed isolation from the outside world.

Further Readings

Becker, Elizabeth. *When the War Was Over: Cambodia and the Khmer Rouge Revolution.* Rev. ed. New York, 1998.

Brown, Frederick Z., and David Timberman, eds. *Cambodia and the International Community: The Quest for Peace, Development, and Democracy.* Singapore, 1998.

Chandler, David. *Brother Number One: A Political Biography of Pol Pot.* 2d ed. Boulder, 1999.
———. *Voices from S-21: Terror and History in Pol Pot's Secret Prison.* Berkeley, 1999.

Chandler, David, Ben Kiernan, and Chanthou Boua, trans. and eds. *Pol Pot Plans the Future: Confidential Leadership Documents from Democratic Kampuchea, 1976–1977.* New Haven, 1988.

Gottesman, Evan. *Cambodia after the Khmer Rouge: Inside the Politics of Nation Building.* New Haven, 2002.

Hinton, Alexander Laban. *Why Did They Kill? Cambodia under the Shadow of the Khmer Rouge.* Berkeley, 2004.

Jackson, Karl D., ed. *Cambodia, 1975–1978.* Princeton, 1989.

Ponchaud, Francois. *Cambodia Year Zero.* 1977 (in French); trans. Nancy Amphoux. New York, 1978.

Vickery, Michael. *Cambodia, 1975–1982.* Boston, 1984; reprint Chiang Mai, 1999.

Chapter 36

❋

Laos since 1975

For nearly thirty years the Lao People's Democratic Republic (LPDR) has been governed by the Lao People's Revolutionary Party (LPRP), an offshoot of the Indochina Communist Party founded by the Vietnamese during the First Indochina War. The party came into the open after the communist victory in 1975, abandoning the pretense of their previous "united front," the Pathet Lao. It was deeply unpopular among most educated Lao and among the Hmong minority, and numbered only twenty-five thousand members in 1982, but it displayed extraordinary survival skills, rarely resorting to high levels of popular repression.

Vietnamese Patronage

The LPRP was less harsh and inflexible than its counterparts in Vietnam or Cambodia. Indeed, what Grant Evans has called Laos' "peripheral socialism," which hints at this flexibility, was one reason for the party's remaining in power for so long. Another was the exhaustion that the Lao people felt at the end of the Second Indochina War and the failure of any group opposed to the LPRP to make headway against the Lao police or among the population. A more decisive reason, however, was the party's long-standing and fruitful reliance on Vietnamese assistance and advice. This relationship, which had deep roots, contrasted sharply with the antagonism between the Cambodian and Vietnamese communist parties before 1979. The leaders of the LPRP all enjoyed close ties with Vietnam, and several, including Prince Souphanuvong and the party secretary, Kaison Phomvihan, who became prime minister after 1975, were married to Vietnamese. A twenty-five-year treaty of friendship was signed with Vietnam in July 1977 (when Cambodia and Vietnam were at war with each other) and subsequently augmented by dozens of bilateral agreements, which bound Laos more closely to Vietnam than it had ever been bound to Siam in the precolonial era or to the other components of French Indochina. Throughout the period, Vietnam also guaranteed Lao security (thus protecting itself from capitalist Thailand) by stationing some forty-thousand troops in Laos.

The LPRP's leaders construed this subordinate relationship as crucial to their survival as a ruling party and also to the survival of Laos as an independent state. They welcomed Vietnamese guidance on education, fiscal policies, and agricultural collectivization—which soon failed. They also followed Hanoi's initiatives in foreign policy. These included Vietnam's estrangement from China in the late 1970s (as well as its rapprochement with China later on) and the arrangements put in place by Vietnam after 1979 that sought to bind the constituent parts of Indochina even more closely to each other. Ironically, by 1979 Vietnam, despite its anti-imperialist rhetoric, had effectively replaced France in its eagerness to "protect" Cambodia and Laos not only from outsiders, but also from their own worst instincts, exemplified for Hanoi by the excesses of the Khmer Rouge in Cambodia. There are many resemblances, in fact, between Vietnam's policies toward its neighbors and France's lofty notion of its own "civilizing mission."

From 1975 to the early 1990s, Laos continued to be a theater of the gradually deescalating Cold War. In this context continuing Vietnamese patronage was seen by the Vietnamese and probably by many Lao as well as a high but perhaps acceptable price to pay to retain Laos' independence vis-à-vis its other hereditary protector, Thailand. Vietnamese assistance to Laos was supplemented by generous infusions of funds and technical assistance from the Soviet bloc. Because the LPDR retained Laos' seat at the United Nations continuously after 1975, Laos also received assistance from the United Nations and other donors who were prevented from assisting Cambodia in the 1980s by its effective exclusion from that organization.

The Lao communists had come to power via a bloodless coup; after the late 1970s they were never seriously challenged. Nonetheless, the first years of communist control were grim for many noncommunist Lao, as well as frustrating for the communists, who assumed that prosperity would follow from their coming to power. In the late 1970s thousands of former government workers, members of the elite, and Lao army veterans fled the country to avoid the "reeducation" camps, which were scarcely distinguishable from prisons. The

Hmong minority, most of whom had taken up arms against the communists all through the 1960s and 1970s, was especially targeted for punishment, and tens of thousands of them fled the country. So did many Sino-Lao shopkeepers and entrepreneurs in Vientiane as well as noncommunist Vietnamese whose families had lived in Laos for generations.

These were losses in skilled labor that the new government could ill afford. The LPRP in these years set in motion some poorly thought out, utopian programs, spearheaded by agricultural collectivization, from its new headquarters in what had been until 1975 a capacious U.S. embassy housing compound. Many socialist policies were adopted without considering their applicability in the Lao context or their cost. Nonsocialist conduct and "decadent" Western culture were condemned, and the activities of the Buddhist sangha were sharply curtailed; ordinary Lao were expected to assume new, revolutionary personalities. A five-year plan, launched in 1981, set unachievable targets, relied heavily on foreign capital, and achieved few of its goals.

At the LPRP's third congress in 1982, the party's leader, Prime Minister Kaison, blamed the nation's shortcomings on "subjectivism and oversimplification." A more pressing problem, mentioned obliquely at the time, was the resurgence of corruption and patronage networks at all levels of the regime. Problems that Kaison failed to mention included the dead hand of single-party rule and the suppression of dissent. Despite the LPRP's dogmatism, however, it was surprisingly flexible when compared to its counterpart in neighboring Democratic Kampuchea. The agricultural cooperatives established in 1978, for example, were unsuccessful and widely resented but were drastically modified after less than a year in operation. By the mid-1980s, it was estimated that 90 percent of Lao farmers worked their own land.

In 1985 the LPRP celebrated its first ten years in power. Its leaders were justifiably proud to have maintained Lao independence and something resembling socialism in the face of continuing pressures from Bangkok and the West. At the anniversary celebrations, Kaison and his colleagues predictably praised Indochinese solidarity, the empowerment of the people, and the country's economic advances. For the first time in its recent history, Laos was self-sufficient in rice and some other commodities, though its rice yields were still among the lowest in the world. Behind the façade, Laos was desperately poor, deeply dependent on foreign aid, and unable to finance even the most basic social services on its own. Educational statistics were particularly disheartening: in the mid-1980s, 80 percent of Lao primary students in 1985 failed to complete the fifth grade, and national literacy hovered around 50 percent. Outside the capital and a few larger towns, health services were almost nonexistent. Most statistics classified Laos as one of the ten poorest countries in the world. These conditions continued to apply in the early 2000s, despite a range of reforms. The price for Lao independence and the costs inflicted on the people by one-party rule were high.

Global Connections

BY THE late 1980s, as the Cold War drew to a close, the top-down economic guidance by the LPRP gradually relaxed, and more pragmatic policies were put in place. Kaison was the moving force behind these changes, battling more conservative factions in the party. Market forces were tentatively allowed to reemerge, and relations with Thailand and other ASEAN states improved. During these years the withdrawal of Soviet bloc aid, Vietnam's decision to put less emphasis on Indochina, and a perceived need on the part of the aging Lao leadership for the country to join a wider, more integrated world led to a flurry of liberalizing activity that would have been impossible to predict a decade before. Vietnamese troops withdrew in 1989. In rapid succession elections, a new constitution, and legal reforms laid some of the foundations for a modern state. Kaison died in 1992, and leadership was passed, successively, to other elderly members of the party. The 1992 constitution made no mention of socialism, but the LPRP kept its name and remained firmly in power. In elections for the National Assembly in 2002, all the candidates but one were party members. Newly negotiated bilateral agreements with countries like Japan and Australia as well as less formal openings to China and Thailand signaled a new flexibility in Lao foreign relations. Laos became a member of ASEAN in 1997.

In April 1994 the first bridge across the Mekong, connecting Laos to Thailand, was inaugurated. The bridge symbolically opened a new era in Lao history, as globalization and the market forces that came with it replaced Cold War animosities in the politics of the region. The LPRP sought to slow the pace of change, and in this respect differed from the formerly communist Cambodian People's Party to the south, but its leaders were only partly successful. Tourism boomed, and Thai popular culture spread rapidly in urban areas. The depletion of Lao forest resources continued at an alarming rate. In the 1980s, policy-makers in Beijing and entrepreneurs in southern China came to perceive Laos as one of several gateways for Chinese trade goods, and perhaps settlers as well, to enter Southeast Asia. Chinese aid financed the construction of a network of highways in northern Laos, linking southern China with the region. The long-term consequences of these linkages are difficult to predict, although it is clear that Laos has no real bargaining power in its evolving relations with China.

None of these connections could have been foreseen in 1975, when Laos was deeply entangled in the Cold War and the rivalry between Thailand and Vietnam, with Laos as the bone of contention, resembled the rivalry between these countries in precolonial times. The end of the Cold War had far-reaching, unpredictable effects on the way Laos related to the outside world. Globalization in Southeast Asia tended to defuse antagonisms—often funded from abroad—that had characterized relations between nation-states and, ironically, had played a major role in the French creation of "Laos" at the end of the nineteenth century.

With its political independence no longer under threat, Laos found itself for the first time in its history as a small but permanent entity within an increasingly integrated region. Although the LPRP remained in power, traditional politics was losing command. To oversimplify the issue, Laos had exchanged the contentious patronage of Vietnam and Thailand for the corporate protection of ASEAN and the benefits, such as they were, of globalization. Whether ASEAN or any other body could keep Laos, in the longer term, from becoming an informal annex of southern China or a disempowered extension of Thailand remained to be seen. The resilience and creativity of the Lao people and the political skills of some Lao leaders provided limited grounds for optimism, but available statistics and precedents from elsewhere suggested, as they had for many years, a crowded, gloomy, and impoverished future.

Further Readings

Brown, MacAlister, and Joseph J. Zasloff. *Apprentice Revolutionaries: The Communist Movement in Laos, 1930–1985.* Stanford, 1986.

Evans, Grant. *Lao Peasants under Socialism and Post-Socialism.* Chiang Mai, 1995.

———. *A Short History of Laos: The Land In Between.* Chiang Mai, 2002.

Evans, Grant, and Kelvin Rowley. *Red Brotherhood at War: Vietnam, Cambodia and Laos since 1975.* 2d ed. London, 1990.

Chapter 37

Burma Becomes Myanmar

THE MILITARY COUP of March 1962 that ended the civilian government of U Nu took place during an era of strident nationalism and fears of neocolonialism in much of Asia and Africa. Far from immune to this atmosphere, Burma was driven in on itself; most of the international linkages that had brought it into the global economy during the previous hundred years were cut off. The army began by dismantling the political structures that had arisen in the first fourteen years of independence and replacing them with others that the Revolutionary Council, as the coup group named themselves, could supervise. The two chambers of the legislature were dissolved, the president was removed, the separate state governments were abolished, and the courts were centralized under a new supreme court. More gradually, many of the administrative arrangements first introduced in the colonial period were also removed or modified along lines advocated by radical nationalists in the 1930s. The chairman of the Revolutionary Council, General Ne Win, was given full executive, legislative, and judicial powers. At the state or divisional and local level, control of the implementation of government policies was unified under Security and Administration Committees, usually led by a military commander, which supervised the activities of the civil bureaucracy and political life as well.

The Burmese Road to Socialism

INITIALLY the Revolutionary Council attempted to form a national unity party with the leaders of the political parties that had been active in the 1950s. However, except for one left-wing group, they all refused, apparently believing that the military eventually would hand power back to them as it had done in 1960. Such a belief proved to be illusory. None of the leading politicians of the 1950s ever returned to power, and most were soon forgotten. The Revolutionary Council subsequently established its own political party, the Burma Socialist Programme Party (BSPP) in order to mobilize support for the government and dominate rival political forces. The BSPP, founded on 4 July 1962 and made the sole legal party in 1964, remained a "cadre" party until the early 1970s, when it was declared a mass party. Until then its membership remained essentially synonymous with the membership of the Revolutionary Council. By 1972 there were still only 79,459 full members, 58 percent of whom came from the army. Membership expanded rapidly after that, and in 1981 there were a million and a half members, about 5 percent of the population. Advancement in government employment and privileges such as scholarships and paid holidays were increasingly linked with party membership. The party, however, generated little genuine enthusiasm among its members.

The Revolutionary Council implemented even more nationalistic economic policies than those of the 1950s. All foreign and larger domestic businesses were nationalized, and several thousand Indians and Pakistanis returned to South Asia when their means of livelihood was taken from them in 1963–1964. All internal trade in essential commodities such as rice and other grains was declared a government monopoly, and both internal and external trade came officially under government control. Though many of the Revolutionary Council's economic policies were unpopular—especially among the urban middle class, which lost the most in terms of wealth and security—peasants initially benefited when the government declared all their debts forgiven in 1963 and then abolished land rents in 1965. However, as all ownership of land was formally held by the state, the peasants came increasingly under government control, and as government rice purchase prices declined, so did production; soon Burma lost its position as one of the preeminent rice-exporting countries of the world. Foreign exchange revenues also declined, and throughout the 1960s economic growth was minimal. Corruption became widespread, and the people came to rely on the black market to make up for the inadequacies of the government distribution system.

The rationale for the Revolutionary Council's economic polices was published in 1962 in a statement known as "The Burmese Way to Socialism." This was explained further in 1964 in a major ideological document called *The Correlation of Man and His Environment*. It combined some of the analytical categories of Marxism-Leninism with the basic philosophical ideas of Theravada Buddhism, including impermanence and the concept that evil in this life is caused by humanity's inherent greed, which only a strong state can control in the name of higher spiritual needs. As the party handbook declared, "Human beings can be corrupted. Therefore it is necessary to establish a socialist democratic living relations society [sic] that is able to analyze and control constantly the misconduct that causes corruption by humans." Thus, the outwardly radical socialist economic and political doctrines of the Revolutionary Council came to be explained to the people of Burma in terms of the conservation of historically received moral and religious principles.

In 1974 a constitution was introduced establishing a socialist one-party state similar to its counterparts in Eastern Europe and China. However, there were significant differences. The bulk of economic activity, particularly agriculture, remained in private hands, and the country remained nonaligned in the Cold War. The BSPP remained the sole governing body until 1988, and its subordinate organizations for peasants, workers, youth, women, and veterans were intended to serve as the means through which the people's will was expressed. The local Security and Administration Committees were replaced by elected councils, which had a large role in carrying out central government policies. The party's chairman, former general Ne Win, remained until the end of his reign in 1988 the leading figure in politics, but much of his power was by then wielded by subordinates, most recruited from the army. While the party never developed an institutional life for itself, widespread corruption made control of the party worthwhile in an economy of increasing privation.

The creation of a one-party socialist state did not come about without conflict. Students, who had played a large role in anti-British demonstrations in the colonial period and who provided a constant critique from the left of the government in the 1950s, demonstrated in July 1962 against the Revolutionary Council's policies, including the abolition of the independence of Rangoon University. The army responded with a prompt and oppressive display of power, arresting student leaders and blowing up the student union, a center of political activism for several generations. Students again demonstrated in 1974, when they used the occasion of the funeral of former United Nations secretary-general U Thant to express not only their dissatisfaction with the fact that the world leader (who had been a close associate of former prime minister U Nu) was not given state honors, but also their sense of isolation and lack of opportunities. After 1962 university education was no longer a key to success, and unemployment among the educated began to rise to high levels, as the economy had not expanded sufficiently to absorb all the new graduates. Moreover, the standard of education declined following the decision in the mid-1960s to require that all education be in Burmese, and the universities were cut off from foreign contacts. Adequate textbooks were no longer available, and a sense of gloom had settled around the university, previously one of the most politically and intellectually lively institutions of higher learning in Southeast Asia.

Others echoed the students' complaints. Workers demonstrated for higher wages at about the same time as the U Thant protests, and for a period in early

1975 Rangoon was under martial law. Discontent also developed within the ranks of the armed forces, and plots against Ne Win were reported. These and subsequent attempts to change the nature of the leadership failed, however, because of the fundamental loyalty of most of the officers toward the last surviving leader of the independence generation. Ne Win became increasingly isolated and out of touch with conditions in the country, and finally his decisions appeared to be driven as much by superstition as by reality.

The Army, Civil War, and Economic Collapse

IN ADDITION to attempting to carry out a major restructuring of wealth and power in Burmese society, throughout the period after 1962 the army carried on a continuing war against the insurgent forces, ethnic and communist, that they had been fighting since 1948. By the government's own account, it faced four major and eleven minor armed opposition groups in 1981. Its strategy combined continued armed pressure as well as political attempts to undercut the opposition's appeal. By the mid-1980s, several of these groups, including the Karen (Kayin) National Liberation Army (KNLA) and the Burma Communist

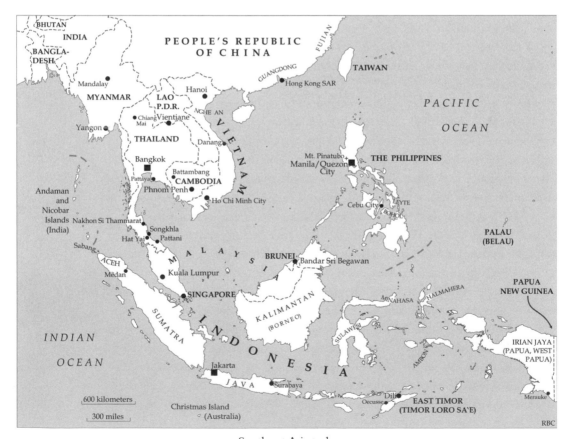

Southeast Asia today

Party (BCP), were being severely tested. External contacts provided the support
to continue fighting. The KNLA, the armed force of the KNU (Karen National
Union), had survived for many years through its control of the smuggling
"gates" with Thailand, where it extracted a 10 percent levy on all goods smuggled into Burma—largely consumer goods—and out—largely cattle, timber,
and gemstones. By 1985, however, because of Burma's improved cooperation
with the government of Thailand and the army's greater control of border areas,
the KNLA had lost many of its financial resources and was apparently atrophying.

Burma's communist movement suffered a major defeat in 1967, when the
army drove it out of the Bago Yomas (mountains), where it had established a
redoubt. Forced to retreat to the Chinese border, the aging party leadership surrounded itself with troops from the ethnic minorities in the region, especially
Shan and Wa. The party was further weakened by changes in the attitude of the
Chinese Communist Party toward antigovernment communists in Southeast
Asia. The BCP, like their allied ethnic insurgent force, the Kachin Independence
Army, had been strongly backed by China during the Cultural Revolution of
the mid-1960s, when China called the Ne Win BSPP government a reactionary
force like the Guomindang in Taiwan. However, as China's relations with
Burma improved from the early 1970s, external support for the communists and
the Kachin Independence Army waned, and the government was able to reassert
its control over much of the north. By the mid-1980s China was once again,
as in the 1950s, providing economic assistance to the government and cooper-
ating in redemarcating China's long border with Burma, first negotiated in 1960.

Burma's foreign policy from a year or so after independence was marked
by a consistent policy of neutrality. The government never entered into military alliances. Aid was accepted only when there were no political conditions
attached, and the government was willing to forgo aid when it appeared to compromise Burma's international position. Except for the communists and several
of the ethnic insurgent groups, all shades of political opinion in the country
endorsed this policy. The Revolutionary Council's first statement after taking
power in 1962 was to reaffirm its commitment to nonalignment. A glance at
the map and a quick review of the foreign policy orientations of Burma's many
neighbors demonstrates the logic of such a policy.

Burma is located at the point where East, South, and Southeast Asia meet.
It is bordered by several larger powers, particularly India and China, who were
at war in the 1960s and who subsequently developed close relations with
opposing superpowers, the Soviet Union and the United States respectively. If
Burma had chosen to ally itself with either of its bigger neighbors or with
either of the superpowers during the Cold War, the effect would have been, at
a minimum, to create a powerful potential opponent along one of its borders.
It is located along major "fault lines" of Asian international politics and has managed to avoid being dragged into one or another of the continent's wars since

1945 by making clear that it will assist no state with designs against any of its neighbors.

The depth of the government's belief in the efficacy of nonalignment was demonstrated most clearly in 1979, when it withdrew from the Non-Aligned Movement itself at the Havana summit, because too many of the movement's members, such as Cuba and the Philippines, were too obviously aligned. Similarly, Burma remained outside of ASEAN until 1997, by which time it was clear that membership was no longer perceived as necessarily implying an anti-Chinese or pro-American foreign policy orientation. Burma throughout has been a member of the United Nations, however.

While pursuing a foreign policy designed to reassure its neighbors that the country posed no threat to them, the BSPP and the army developed a defense strategy predicated on a doctrine of total people's war: guerrilla warfare for defense against foreign invasion and antiguerrilla warfare for counterinsurgency. The former was based on the militarization of the whole society, not just the army itself. The BSPP and its auxiliary youth, women's, workers' and peasants' organizations as well as the Red Cross were all cast in a military guise as a potential ready reserve to be called on in the event of an invasion. Such a policy allowed the army to remain relatively small and ill-equipped in comparison to its neighbors or even some of its domestic armed opponents. Given the parlous condition of the economy, however, the country could afford little else.

In terms of their goal of turning Burma into a developed, equitable society, the socialist policies pursued by all governments since 1948, but most especially the autarkic version of independent socialism pursued since 1962, were failures. By the middle of the 1980s the economy was nearing a major crisis. Agricultural productivity had reached the limits of available technology, while the population was continuing to grow. A brief spurt of economic growth stimulated in the late 1970s by foreign loans and assistance had passed, leaving only debt in its wake. The state-run industries were failing to produce the goods demanded by the population. Even the government had become dependent on black market goods from Thailand for basic supplies.

In August 1987 BSPP chairman Ne Win secretly announced at a meeting of senior members of the army, the party, and the government that the socialist experiment had been a failure. He ordered the leadership of the country to come back with ideas about how to abandon the one-party system and change economic policies. News of this announcement was soon available via the rumor mill, the only source of information in the country. What little prestige the government retained was undermined further when Burma was declared a "least developed nation" by the United Nations.

Soon after Ne Win sprang even bigger surprises. First, on 1 September 1987, the government announced that the strict regulation and control of the rice market and the markets for eight other basic agricultural commodities would

be ended, presenting the possibility of a return to free market conditions. What
appeared to be a step toward much welcome reform was then dashed five days
later, when Ne Win announced, to the surprise of even his most trusted associates, the demonetization of large denomination bank notes and their replacement with new 45 and 90 *kyat* denominations. Effectively at the wave of a hand,
60 percent of the currency in people's pockets was made worthless. Though
most people thought the move was directed against black marketers who held
large quantities of *kyat,* it could also be seen as an effort to control inflation by
soaking up liquidity in an economy with no effective banking system.

The Struggle for Democracy

WITH confidence in the rationality of the government now completely sapped,
inflation soared. Food security was threatened, but the population appeared
resigned to their plight. Then in March 1988 what started as a brawl among
students at a Rangoon teashop soon spread into nationwide demonstrations
against Ne Win and the BSPP. In town after town, underlying resentment began
to rise up, and soon the authorities appeared to be losing control. Ne Win summoned an extraordinary meeting of the BSPP in July, announced his resignation,
and called for a referendum on the formation of a multiparty political system
in the country.

Ne Win's surprise resignation, made without identifying his successor,
shocked the delegates at the party conference. Rejecting his call for a national
referendum on forming a multiparty system, they chose former general Sein
Lwin to succeed him as president and chairman of the party. Unrest continued, and seventeen days later Sein Lwin resigned, to be succeeded by a leading
civilian figure in the regime, Dr. Maung Maung, who immediately began
liberalizing political conditions and promised to move quickly to a multiparty
democratic constitution. This did not halt the demonstrations, however, and one
month later, on 17 September 1988, an army government calling itself the State
Law and Order Restoration Council (SLORC) was installed. Imposing martial law,
the army set out to stop the antigovernment demonstrations. Officially 451 persons were said to have been killed, but other sources claimed that more than a
thousand were shot on that day. Others had died earlier. Burma, which had been
largely ignored by the world for the previous twenty-six years, was now held
up in the media as a pariah state, roundly condemned for the poverty and
violence that were the result of the autarkic policies of a formerly revolutionary generation.

The SLORC maintained the policies that Maung Maung had established and
promised that multiparty elections would be held as soon as stability was
restored. A procedure for political parties to register their existence was soon
established, and by the end of the year 174 had registered. Students, politicians

from the 1950s, opportunists, and professionals were all caught up in the apparent new political freedoms available. By far the largest of the parties was the National League for Democracy (NLD), headed by former brigadier Aung Gyi, Ne Win's deputy at the time of the 1962 coup; General Tin Oo, Ne Win's deputy in the 1970s; and Daw ("Aunt") Aung San Suu Kyi, the daughter of General Aung San. Aung San Suu Kyi was instantly popular with the crowds. Having lived all of her adult life in England until she returned to Burma earlier in the year, she represented both continuity with her martyred father and something new, not connected with the politically murky pasts of all the old men who were seeking power in the name of the people. Her speeches and writings attempted to explain democracy in Buddhist idioms, just as U Nu had done in the 1950s.

The elections promised in September 1988 did not take place until May 1990, by which time Aung San Suu Kyi had been barred from running because of her marriage to a foreigner and had been placed under house arrest for inciting antigovernment demonstrations. In the event, the election for 485 seats in the People's Assembly took place peacefully under very constrained campaigning conditions. The NLD won 60 percent of the vote and 392 seats. In the euphoria of victory, and naively unaware of the realities of power, one of the NLD leaders threatened legal action against senior army officers for their actions before the election. The army, however, made it clear that they would not hand over power to civilian successors until a new constitution was drawn up and a government formed. While the NLD held the moral high ground in the eyes of democrats, the army had might and, equally important, self-confidence on its side. A standoff ensued as the army effectively ignored the result of the election and set out to restructure the political and economic institutions of the country to their liking.

Between the 1988 uprising and the 1990 elections, another unexpected event had occurred that was as dramatic and important for Myanmar—as the country was officially relabeled in English in 1989—as the fall of the BSPP. Early in 1989, following a decision by the Chinese Communist Party to end its support for the Burmese Communist Party, the ethnic minority troops that formed the overwhelming majority of the local communist forces revolted against their aging ethnic Burman leaders. The troops then entered into cease-fire agreements with the Myanmar army. These allowed the former insurgents to keep their weapons and administer their territories with a good deal of autonomy. In exchange, the government agreed to assist in the economic development of their regions. As opium poppy was the largest cash crop in a region of widespread poverty, the government was quickly accused of consorting with drug producers. The government soon established a crop substitution program to wean the farmers off the drug trade and promised that production would end by 2005. As the amount of land under poppy cultivation began to decline after 1995, the manufacture of synthetic drugs in the Golden Triangle began to grow.

The human cost of the interminable civil war was recounted by the first chairman of the SLORC, Senior General Saw Maung, in a speech in January 1990. Noting that 28,000 Myanmar soldiers had died fighting the insurgents between 1953 and 1989, and more than 40,000 were receiving disability pensions, he estimated the total lives lost, including civilians and insurgents, to be over a million. He concluded, "Indeed, this is really no good. How nice it would be if all work together for the country."

A new strategy was then sought to end ethnic insurgencies, which still raged. By the middle of the 1990s, seventeen former insurgent forces had entered into cease-fire agreements. Of the major insurgent groups, only the KNU failed to reach a modus vivendi with the government. The peace allowed for extensive programs of road and bridge construction, as the antiquated infrastructure, largely developed before World War II, proved wholly inadequate for the expanding trade that emerged. Road transport to China was opened, and a legal border trade replaced the rampant smuggling of the 1980s to supply the consumer demands of Myanmar. Nongovernmental organizations (NGOs) were for the first time given permission to work with communities in Myanmar to raise educational and health standards.

The newfound economic freedom heralded by the events of 1988 and the subsequent cease-fires was not, however, without a cost. Myanmar remained one of the poorest countries of the world, and the booming Thai economy attracted nearly half a million illegal immigrants from Myanmar in the 1990s. The drug trade combined with the sex trade led to a growth of the incidence of HIV/AIDS, which was largely unknown before economic liberalization. Nor did insurgency end entirely, as the KNU and two or three other smaller insurgent forces refused to agree to a cease-fire. The continuing warfare along the border resulted in more than one hundred thousand refugees living in camps in Thailand. Allegations that Myanmar citizens were being forced to work for the army in and out of combat situations led to an investigation by the International Labor Organization and prompted calls for Myanmar goods to be banned in Western markets.

The failure of the army to hand over power to civilians and the issues of the drug trade and forced labor became intertwined in a complex international set of issues unlike any Myanmar had experienced before. A country that had been isolated from the trends of globalization for more than a generation was now expected to meet the developed world's definitions of universal standards of political, social, and economic rights. But as the economy of Myanmar failed to grow significantly because of the international boycotts and sanctions imposed on it by Western governments as well as inept economic management, the ability of the government to generate the resources to fund rapid change was greatly constrained.

Since 1988 Myanmar has become more involved in the Southeast Asian region and has joined a number of international organizations, most importantly ASEAN. Trade and investment from neighboring countries, particularly before the 1997 Asian economic crisis, gave manufacturing and tourism an unprecedented boost. Agricultural productivity has grown, and Myanmar has rejoined the world of rice-exporting countries and has begun to export other crops, such as coffee and buckwheat, as well as old staples such as beans and pulses.

At the turn of the millennium, none of the major issues that led to the army taking over the government in 1988 had been resolved. A stalemate existed between the military government and the badly battered democratic forces led by Aung San Suu Kyi, who was awarded the Nobel Peace Prize in 1991 for her nonviolent efforts to establish a democratic regime in Yangon but remained under house arrest for most of the next decade. Similarly, while the cease-fires that most of the ethnic insurgents had entered into with the army continued to be observed, no political resolution of the grievances of the minorities had been achieved. The process of drawing up a new constitution ended in 1996 when the NLD walked out of a constitutional convention established by the government, stating that the process itself was undemocratic. The State Peace and Development Council (SPDC), as the SLORC was renamed in 1997, and its chairman, Senior General Than Shwe, presided over the nation much in the style of the old regime of General Ne Win.

Further Readings

Aung San Suu Kyi. *Freedom from Fear and Other Writings.* London, 1991.

Maung Maung. *The 1988 Uprising in Burma.* New Haven, 1999.

Mya Than and Joseph L. H. Tan, eds. *Myanmar Dilemmas and Options: The Challenge of Economic Transition in the 1990s.* Singapore, 1990.

Pedersen, Morten B., Emily Rudland, and R. J. May, eds. *Burma/Myanmar: Strong Regime/Weak State.* Adelaide, 2000.

Rotberg, Robert I., ed. *Burma: Prospects for a Democratic Future.* Washington, D.C., 1998.

Selth, Andrew. *Burma's Armed Forces: Power without Glory.* Norwalk, Conn., 2002.

Silverstein, Josef. *Burma: Military Rule and the Politics of Stagnation.* Ithaca, 1977.

Steinberg, David I. *Burma: The State of Myanmar.* Washington, D.C., 2001.

———. *Burma's Road toward Development: Growth and Ideology under Military Rule.* Boulder, Colo., 1981.

Taylor, Robert H., ed. *Burma: Political Economy under Military Rule.* London, 2001.

Afterword

❀

THIS BOOK has addressed a number of themes and raised many questions. Some
have to do with changes and continuities in modes or sources of authority: who
got to rule, through what sorts of institutions, supported in what ways? Others
focus on economic resources: what were they, who controlled and benefited
from them, and how did the resources themselves and the patterns of their
ownership and distribution change over time? The social dimension of history
has also been considered: how did people live together in the past, and how were
these arrangements and relationships changed by new forms of authority and
new modes of production? Finally, we have looked at what French historians
call "mentalities": what (and how) did Southeast Asians know and think in the
past, and how does that compare with what they know and think today?

A few broad answers to these questions are clear, though many more are
not. Over the past three centuries most Southeast Asians were governed by local
rulers, then by foreigners, and finally by Southeast Asians again. In the course
of time, the state has generally grown larger and stronger, under both foreign
and local rule. Meanwhile, the economy has become more varied and complicated, with a much higher proportion of production intended for the market—
national or international—than for domestic consumption and with large-scale
enterprise playing a more dominant role in the organization of production. The
material wealth of Southeast Asia has clearly grown, but its distribution has
remained badly skewed; there is still some doubt as to whether the poor

Courtesy of R. H. Taylor

"Lean against the pillar and listen." Children in upland Myanmar.

majority are much better off than they were before, although they certainly live longer on the average. Technological advances are apparent everywhere, but not all of them have been beneficial, and the environment of Southeast Asia is in a precarious state in the first decade of the twenty-first century.

There are also many more people in Southeast Asia today than there were in the eighteenth century, and a much higher proportion of them live in cities, where they can affiliate not just with their own kinfolk and neighbors but with others who share common interests in politics, religion, culture, or business. Many people now identify with the "nation" (and the state that purports to represent it) more than with their tribe or local community, though identification with religion also remains strong. At the same time, more Southeast Asians today receive formal education in secular (nonreligious) subjects and so are at least exposed to modes of discourse associated with globalization and the modern West. Beyond this, however, the complexities of the processes of change in the different nations and localities of Southeast Asia are so formidable that it would be foolhardy to attempt any final summing up.

What of Southeast Asia's future? Historians are understandably cautious about prediction. But we know that the past and our understanding of the past play important roles in shaping the future and coming to terms with it. Part of our intention in this book has been to contribute to this process of understanding. If questions remain, we would remind our readers (and ourselves) of the Vietnamese proverb "If you know something, speak, but if you don't know, lean against the pillar and listen."

Notes

PAGE   *Introduction*

12   "The White Man's Burden" was first published in *McClure's Magazine* 12
         (Feb. 1899).

         Part 1: The Dynamics of the Eighteenth Century

41   Nguyen Du's poem appears in Pham Van Dieu, *Viet Nam Van Hoc Giang Binh*
         (An exposition of Vietnamese literature) (Saigon, 1961), pp. 46–78.

52   Iskander Thani ("the king of the whole world") is quoted in Anthony Reid,
         ed., *The Making of an Islamic Political Discourse in Southeast Asia* (Clayton, Vic-
         toria, Australia, 1993), pp. 18, 103.

53   On the king of Myanmar as a "despot," see Vincentius Sangermano, *A Descrip-
         tion of the Burmese Empire,* trans. William Tandy (London, 1966), p. 73.

54   "Academic democracy" and "hereditary Caesars" are quoted in Nguyen Van
         Phong, *La société vietnamienne de 1882 à 1902* (Paris, 1971), p. 109.

55   "Vietnamese, pirates, or enemies" is from Akin Rabibhadana, *The Organi-
         zation of Thai Society in the Early Bangkok Period, 1782–1873* (Ithaca, 1969),
         pp. 16–17, 73.

56   The Javanese royal chronicle comparing Amangkurat III with a "Chinaman"
         is quoted in Soemarsaid Moertono, *State and Statecraft in Old Java* (Ithaca,
         1968), pp. 85–86, 39–40.

61   On the definition of a Confucian "gentleman," see Le Quy Don, *Van Dai Loai
         Ngu* (Classified discourse from the library) (Hanoi, 1961), 1:235–237.

PAGE

64   Hatta's ideas about "indigenous democracy" can be found in Herbert Feith and Lance Castles, eds., *Indonesian Political Thinking, 1945–1965* (Ithaca, 1970), pp. 32–40, 37.

69   Thieu's poem is translated in Huynh Sanh Thong, *The Heritage of Vietnamese Poetry* (New Haven, 1975), pp. 105–115.

70   Yasadipura is quoted and analyzed in Ann Kumar, "Java: A Self-Critical Examination of the Nation and Its History," in Anthony Reid, ed., *The Last Stand of Asian Autonomies* (New York, 1997), pp. 321–343.

Part 2: New Choices and Constraints

78   Benedict Anderson, *Imagined Communities*, rev. ed. (London, 1991), p. 169.

89   Dalhousie's apprehension about being "shown the door" is quoted in Dorothy Woodman, *The Making of Modern Burma* (London, 1962), p. 139.

89   Mindon's "cautious" remarks are quoted in Henry Yule, *A Narrative of the Mission Sent by the Governor-General of India to the Court of Ava in 1855* (1858; reprint Kuala Lumpur, 1968), p. 109.

99   Mongkut's "total revolution" is from Sir John Bowring, *The Kingdom and People of Siam* (London, 1857), 1:226.

110   Phan Huy Chu's observations are found in his *Lich Trieu Hien Chuong Loai Chi* (A classified survey of the institutions of successive courts) (Hanoi, 1962), part 3, vol. 29, pp. 47–48.

110   Le Quy Don's definition of a Confucian "gentleman" is from his *Van Dai Loai Ngu* (Classified discourse from the library) (Hanoi, 1961), 1:235–237.

111   Ho's attack on concubinage is found in Huynh Sanh Thong, *The Heritage of Vietnamese Poetry* (New Haven, 1979), pp. 99–100.

113   Quang-trung's edict was drafted by Ngo Thi Nham; see Cao Xuan Huy and Thach Can, comps., *Tuyen Tap Tho Van Ngo Thi Nham* (Selected works of prose and poetry of Ngo Thi Nham) (Hanoi, 1978), 2:103–109.

114   "Confucian of Chinese culture" is from Christophe Bataille, *Annam* (Paris, 1993), p. 91.

115   The poems of Nguyen Dinh Chieu and Phan Van Tri are found in Huynh Sanh Thong, *Heritage of Vietnamese Poetry*, pp. 199–200, 202–208.

118   Gia-long's imagery of Cambodia as a "child" is recorded in a manuscript chronicle from Wat Srolauv (1858) at the Buddhist Institute, Phnom Penh, p. 23.

119   "We have tried to punish and reward" is from *Dai Nam Thuc Luc Chinh Bien* (Primary compilation of the veritable records of imperial Vietnam) (Hanoi, 1962–1973), vol. 15, p. 113.

121   Duang's "What do you want me to do?" is quoted in Charles Meyniard, *Le second empire en Indochine* (Paris, 1891), p. 403.

122   For the full text of the 1884 treaty, see Georges Taboulet, *La geste française en Indochine* (Paris, 1955), 2:67–72.

127   The lines from the "Babad Dipanagara" are translated in Ann Kumar, "Dipanagara (1787?–1855)," *Indonesia* 13 (April 1972): 103. "Ngabdulkamit" was the title previously bestowed on Diponegoro by the "Ratu Adil."

139   "Communication with the native princes" is from an 1817 state paper, "Our Interests in the Eastern Archipelago," quoted in Demetrius Charles Boulger, *The Life of Sir Stamford Raffles* (London, 1897), p. 270.

PAGE

144   The provision that the Resident's advice "must be asked and acted upon" is from the sixth clause of the Pangkor Engagement, 20 January 1874, reprinted in C. Northcote Parkinson, *British Intervention in Malaya 1867–1877* (Kuala Lumpur, 1964), pp. 322–323, among other sources.

149   Basco's "first task" is quoted in María Lourdes Díaz-Trechuelo, "The Economic Development of the Philippines in the Second Half of the Eighteenth Century," *Philippine Studies* 11 (April 1963): 228.

151   "A caricature of the *Indio*" is typical of the anti-Filipino rhetoric of Francisco Cañamaque, quoted in H. de la Costa, "Development of the Native Clergy in the Philippines," in *Studies in Philippine Church History,* ed. Gerald H. Anderson (Ithaca, 1969), pp. 99–100.

151   "Suspicious and unenlightened" are the words of Sinibaldo de Mas, *Report on the Condition of the Philippines in 1842* (Manila, 1963), pp. 64, 169; emphasis in original.

152   "An Anglo-Chinese colony" is from Carlos Recur, quoted in Edgar Wickberg, *The Chinese in Philippine Life: 1850–1898* (New Haven, 1965), p. 72.

153   Ileto's discourse on "hidden and inarticulate features" in Tagalog society is from his *Pasyon and Revolution: Popular Movements in the Philippines* (Quezon City, 1979), pp. 13, 15.

153   The decree giving the Chinese "complete liberty" is quoted in Wickberg, *Philippine Life,* p. 52.

154   The fear that mestizos would become "lords of the entire archiplego" was expressed by Joaquín Martínez de Zuñiga (ca.1805), quoted in Wickberg, *Philippine Life,* p. 142.

154   "The work-hand, the goatherd" is again Sinibaldo de Mas, *Report,* pp. 27, 133.

154   Izquierdo's "a cross and . . . a sword" was quoted by Edmund Plauchut (1877) in *Documentary Sources of Philippine History,* comp. Gregorio F. Zaide (Metro Manila, 1990), 7:258–259.

155   Burgos' cry is also quoted by Plauchut in Zaide, *Documentary Sources,* 7:267.

156   Rizal's "farewell, Spanish Government" is from a letter to Mariano Ponce, April 1889, quoted in John N. Schumacher, *The Propaganda Movement: 1880–1895* (Manila, 1973), p. 228.

156   Rizal's comments on "a numerous educated class" is from his famous essay "The Philippines within a Hundred Years" (1890), quoted in Horacio de la Costa, *Readings in Philippine History* (Manila, 1965), p. 229.

156   Rizal's final insistence on reforms "from *above*" (emphasis in original) is recorded in W. E. Retana's transcription of *The Trial of Rizal,* trans. and ed. H. de la Costa, 2d printing (Quezon City, 1996), pp. 118–119, 172–173.

Part 3: Economic, Political, and Social Transformations

168   "If I could ride those trains" is from Luis Taruc's first autobiography, *Born of the People* (New York, 1953), p. 16.

174   The future Sultan Idris is quoted in J. M. Gullick, *Malay Society in the Late Nineteenth Century* (Singapore, 1987), p. 167.

175   "Men of *Nanyang*" is from N[giong] I[ng] Low, *Chinese Jetsam on a Tropic Shore* (Singapore, 1974), p. 115.

177   The Chinese lack of "polite manners" is referred to in an early-nineteenth-

PAGE

century Javanese text, summarized in Ann Kumar, "Java: A Self-Critical Examination of the Nation and Its History," in Anthony Reid, ed., *The Last Stand of Asian Autonomies* (New York, 1997), p. 324.

177 "If the Thai work 50 per cent" is quoted from the Chinese protagonist of *Letters from Thailand,* by "Botan" [Supha Lusiri], trans. Susan Fulop (Bangkok, 1982), p. 58.

184 "Hell on Earth" is from Tran Tu Binh, *The Red Earth: A Vietnamese Memoir of Life on a Colonial Rubber Plantation,* trans. John Spragens, Jr. (Athens, Ohio, 1985), pp. 23, 33, 26.

186 "A land of gold" is from Tan Malaka, *From Jail to Jail,* trans. Helen Jarvis (Athens, Ohio, 1991), 1:43.

189 That Filipinos would not work "unless paid" is from Forbes, *The Philippine Islands* (1928; rev. ed., Cambridge, Mass., 1945), p. 235.

189 "A Javanese without an advance" is from G. L. Gonggrip, quoted in *Indonesian Economics* (The Hague, 1961), p. 31.

197 The Javanese noblewoman quoted is Raden Ajoe Mangkoedimedjo in "Les progrès de la gent feminine" (1909), trans. Claudine Salmon, *Archipel* 13 (1977): 125.

198 The visitor to the Binondo cigar factory was Francisco Mosquera y García (1880), quoted in Ed. C. de Jesus, *The Tobacco Monopoly in the Philippines* (Quezon City, 1980), p. 40.

218 "Caviling little lawyers" were decried by José Ma. Peñaranda, 1834, quoted in Norman G. Owen, *The Bikol Blend* (Quezon City, 1999), p. 51.

219 Orwell's remarks on being hated as a police officer are from his essay "Shooting an Elephant" (1936), in *Inside the Whale and Other Essays* (London, 1962), p. 91.

223 Kartini's reflections on the Dutch are from a letter of 23 August 1900, as translated by Joost Coté in *On Feminism and Nationalism: Kartini's Letters to Stella Zeehandelaar 1899–1903* (Clayton, Victoria, Australia, 1995), pp. 49–50.

224 "Accept their fate" is from Truong Chinh and Vo Nguyen Giap, *The Peasant Question (1937–1938),* trans. Christine Pelzer White (Ithaca, 1974), pp. 7–8.

228 Sisuriyawong is quoted in Sir John Bowring, *The Kingdom and People of Siam* (1857; reprint Kuala Lumpur, 1969), 1:465–466.

233 "At the tax farmer's shed" is a poem by Maharik, quoted in 1957 by Jit Poumisak, in Craig Reynolds, *Thai Radical Discourse: The Real Face of Thai Feudalism Today* (Ithaca, 1987), p. 141.

236 The plantation recruiters' song is from Diep Lien Anh, *Mau Trang—Mau Dau* (1965), quoted and translated in Ngo Vinh Long, *Before the Revolution* (Cambridge, Mass., 1973), p. 107.

243 "Straitjacket by choice" is from Renato Constantino, *Neocolonial Identity and Counter-Consciousness* (London, 1978), p. 252.

245 Pinpin's views on "Castilian" as a "cure" for Filipinos are analyzed in Vicente Rafael, *Contracting Colonialism* (Durham, N.C., 1993), pp. 55–83.

245 On spelling "Thai" with an "h," see Thamsook Numnonda, "Pibulsongkram's Thai Nation-Building Programme during the Japanese Military Presence, 1941–1945," *Journal of Southeast Asian Studies* 9, 2 (September 1978): 234–247.

246 For Soeriokoesomo's argument, see Herbert Feith and Lance Castles, eds., *Indonesian Political Thinking, 1945–1965* (Ithaca, 1970), pp. 183–188.

PAGE

246 Kartini's letter of 25 May 1899 is translated in Joost Coté, *On Feminism and Nationalism,* p. 1.

248 On "French skin" see Alexander Woodside, *Community and Revolution in Modern Vietnam* (Boston, 1976), p. 22.

250 Nhat Lin is quoted in Woodside, *Community and Revolution in Modern Vietnam,* p. 4.

257 The British merchant in Bangkok was Charles Stuart Leckie, quoted in Chatthip Nartsupha and Suthy Prasartset, eds., *The Political Economy of Siam, 1851–1910* (Bangkok, 1981), p. 144.

260 "Dragons out of worms" is quoted by R. J. Wilkinson, "The Education of Asiatics," in Cd. 835, Great Britain Parliamentary Papers, 1902, 687.

260 "Teach them to lick the soles" is from Tengku Abdullah Ahmad, "Apa-Kah Faeda Merdeka?" *Seruan Azhar* (Cairo), 3 (October 1927): 492–493.

261 "Half devil and half child" is from Rudyard Kipling, "The White Man's Burden," first published in *McClure's Magazine* 12 (February 1899).

262 The British lack of desire "to give the children" even "a smattering" of useless knowledge is from Frank Swettenham, *British Malaya* (London, 1907), p. 248.

262 The "vast mass of ignorant people" are referred to in the *Report of the Philippine Commission* 1903, 1:59.

263 Syahrir's views on Indonesia's lack of "spiritual and cultural life" can be found in Soetan Sjahrir, *Out of Exile,* trans. Charles Wolf, Jr. (New York, 1949; reprint 1969), pp. 66–67.

267 The virtues of newspapers are recounted in *Al-Imam* (Singapore), 1:6 (November 1906).

270 Prajadhipok's lament is quoted in Benjamin A. Batson, *The End of the Absolute Monarchy in Siam* (Singapore, 1984), 187.

275 "Filipino agent" Torres is quoted in Elmer Lear, *The Japanese Occupation of the Philippines, Leyte, 1941–1945* (Ithaca, 1961), 228–229.

276 Confesor's "more precious than life itself" is from Courtney Whitney, *MacArthur: His Rendezvous with History* (New York, 1956), 136–138.

Part 4: Passages Out of the Colonial Era

284 Hofstadter talks of Roosevelt's "carnal larynx" in his "Manifest Destiny in the Philippines" (1952), reprinted in *American Imperialism in 1898,* ed. T. P. Greene (Lexington, Mass., 1955), p. 66.

284 "Islands or canned goods" comes from Finley Peter Dunne, *Mr. Dooley at His Best* (New York, 1938).

284 McKinley's intention to "educate the Filipinos ... and Christianize them" was stated to a group of Protestant ministers in 1899, first reported in *The Christian Advocate* (22 January 1903); the statement can be found in D. B. Schirmer and S. R. Shalom, *The Philippines Reader* (Quezon City, 1987), pp. 22–23, among other sources.

285 Mabini attacked Aguinaldo in his *La revolución filipina* (1903), as translated in Austin Craig, *The Filipinos' Fight for Freedom* (Manila, 1933), p. 340.

285 "This unique system of war" is from *Literary Digest* (1900), quoted in Stuart Creighton Miller, *"Benevolent Assimilation"* (New Haven, 1982), p. 150.

PAGE

285   "The happiness, peace, and prosperity" is from McKinley's letter of instructions to the Taft Commission, 7 April 1900, in U.S. War Department, *Annual Report 1900,* I-1, p. 74.

286   "Charmed the rifle" is from a letter by Governor-General James F. Smith to Taft, 7 October 1907, quoted in Bonifacio Salamanca, *The Filipino Reaction to American Rule, 1901–1913* (Quezon City, 1984), p. 37.

287   Taft's concern about "a Philippine oligarchy or aristocracy" is from *Special Report of Wm. H. Taft to the President on the Philippines* (Washington, D.C., 1908).

287   "The feudal relationship of dependence" is from *Report of the Philippine Commission,* 1902, 1:4.

289   "Our heel of Achilles" is quoted in Oscar M. Alfonso, *Theodore Roosevelt and the Philippines, 1897–1909* (Quezon City, 1970), p. 74.

291   "Inextricably linked" is from Pio Duran, *Philippine Independence and the Far Eastern Question* (Manila, 1935), p. 191.

291   Homma's "the leopard cannot change its spots" is quoted in David Joel Steinberg, *Philippine Collaboration in World War II* (Ann Arbor, 1967), p. 49.

323   The Sawbwa's "if there be a suzerain" is quoted in Ni Ni Myint, *Burma's Struggle against British Imperialism (1885–1895)* (Rangoon, 1983), p. 107.

336   The view that imperial order is based on "fear of superiors … terror of one's master" is quoted in Nguyen Van Phong, *La société vietnamienne de 1882 à 1902* (Paris, 1971), p. 308.

338   Phan Chu Trinh's speech is found in Thai Bach, *Thi Van Quoc Cam Thoi Thuoc Phap* (Forbidden literature in the French period) (Saigon, 1968), pp. 456–482.

343   On Ho as an "awfully sweet guy," see Robert Shaplen, *The Lost Revolution: The U.S. in Vietnam, 1946–1966* (New York, 1966), p. 29.

346   The first sighting of "light at the end of [the] tunnel" in Vietnam has been traced back to General Henri Navarre, shortly before the French defeat at Dienbienphu in 1954; Stanley Karnow, *Vietnam: A History* (New York, 1983), p. 189. The phrase was popularized in a U.S. presidential public relations offensive in late 1967.

347   Johnson's harangue of South Vietnamese leaders is found in Neil Sheehan et al., *The Pentagon Papers as Published by the New York Times* (New York, 1971), pp. 495–496.

347   It was Samuel P. Huntington who complained of the lack of an organized political system in South Vietnam in Richard M. Pfeffer, ed., *No More Vietnams?* (New York, 1968), p. 245.

348   The term "nervous society" comes from Kim N. B. Ninh, *A World Transformed* (Ann Arbor, 2002), p. 146.

355   The British demand for "a special measure of reconcilement" is from British Embassy to the Department of State (Washington), 13 November 1945, reprinted in *Foreign Relations of the United States 1945* (Washington, D.C., 1969), 6:1368.

362   The "unvarying calm" of the Khmer is remarked on in France, Archives d'outre-mer (Aix en Provence), Cambodia 3E 7(6), annual report from Kratie, 1925–1926.

367   "The aspirations of the Little People" is from the Sangkum statutes, as recorded in Great Britain, Public Records Office, FO 371 1012/55G, British Legation Phnom Penh, letter of Littlejohn-Cook, 27 March 1955.

PAGE

369   Swank's comment that the war "was losing more and more of its point" is found in United States, State Department, U.S. Embassy Phnom Penh's 2806, 31 August 1973.

Part 5: Coping with Independence and Interdependence

379   J. H. Boeke's views on dualism are most fully articulated in his *Economics and Economic Policy of Dual Societies as Exemplified by Indonesia* (New York, 1953).

385   Sukarno's remarks on "bald-headed professors from Oxford or Cornell" are quoted in Herbert Feith and Lance Castles, eds., *Indonesian Political Thinking, 1945–1965* (Ithaca, 1970), p. 119.

387   On Mahathir's "Look East" program, see D. K. Mauzy and R. S. Milne, "The Mahathir Administration in Malaysia," *Pacific Affairs* 56, 4 (Winter 1983–84): 617–648.

387   Soehoed's interpretation of the disadvantages of following Japan is found in his "Reflections on Industrialisation and Industrial Policy in Indonesia," *Bulletin of Indonesian Economic Studies* 24, 2 (August 1988): 43–57.

389   The Widjojo-Wilopo debate is found in Feith and Castles, *Indonesian Political Thinking,* pp. 379–385.

395   On "Asia that can say 'No!' " see Mahathir Mohamad and Shintaro Ishihara, *The Voice of Asia,* trans. F. Baldwin (Tokyo, 1995), originally published in Japanese as *"No" to ieru Ajia* (1994).

400   "The thrill of living in the city" is from Win Pe, "Rangoon the Capital City" (1961), in Helen G. Trager, ed., *We the Burmese* (New York, 1969), p. 91.

403   "Slums of hope" and "slums of despair" were terms coined by Charles Stokes in 1962 and applied to Asia by Laquian in "The Asian City and the Political Process," in D. J. Dwyer, ed., *The City as a Centre of Change in Asia* (Hong Kong, 1972), pp. 41–55.

403   Mahathir's "We no longer have the right to blame others" is quoted in "Restructuring Society and Poverty Eradication: The Road Ahead," in V. Kanapathy et al., *The Mahathir Era* (Petaling Jaya, 1989), p. 90.

403   The necessity for "pain and force" was asserted by V. Kanapathy in "The Mahathir Era: A Brief Overview," in Kanapathy et al., *The Mahathir Era,* p. 26.

410   Jit's "We ride on the buffalo" is quoted in Yuangrat Wedel with Paul Wedel, *Radical Thought, Thai Mind* (Bangkok, 1987), p. 121.

410   Constantino's 1957 and 1966 essays are both reprinted in *The Filipinos in the Philippines and Other Essays* (Quezon City, 1966); *The Nationalist Alternative* (Quezon City, 1979) and *Synthetic Culture and Development* (Quezon City, 1985) were published separately.

463   Bush's praise of Marcos' "adherence to democratic principles" is from the United States, *Department of State Bulletin* 81, 2053 (August 1981): 30.

463   Aquino's speech to the U.S. Congress is reported in *Time,* 29 September 1986.

470   Tran Xuan Bach's speech attacking "bureaucratism" was printed in the party newspaper *Nhan Dan,* 27 October 1988.

473   The accusation that China wanted to "conquer the world" is from Truong Chinh, "Ve Van De Cam-pu-chia" (On the question of Kampuchea), *Tap Chi Cong San* (The Communist journal) 1979, 12:1–21.

476   On the "strongmen" and "primordial" ties, see Dinh Thu Cuc, "Nong Dan Va Nong Thon Viet Nam Hien Nay" (Vietnamese peasants and villages at present), *Tap Chi Cong San* 1988, 5:43–46.

498   "Human beings can be corrupted" is from *Myanma Hsoshelit Lansin Pattiwinmya Letwe* (Burma Socialist Programme Party members' handbook) (Rangoon, 1978), p. 20.

505   "Indeed, this is really no good" is from State Law and Order Restoration Council, *Chairman Commander-in-Chief of the Defence Services General Saw Maung's Addresses* (Yangon, 1990), 1:328.

About the Authors

DAVID CHANDLER holds degrees from Harvard College, Yale University, and the University of Michigan. He taught at Monash University from 1972 to 1997 and from 1979 onward served as research director of its Centre of Southeast Asian Studies. In 1998–2003 he held successive visiting appointments at the University of Wisconsin, Cornell University, the University of Michigan, and Georgetown University. His books include *A History of Cambodia* (3d edition, 2000), *The Tragedy of Cambodian History: Politics, War and Revolution since 1945* (1991), *Brother Number One: A Political Biography of Pol Pot* (2d edition, 1999), *Facing the Cambodian Past: Selected Essays* (1996), and *Voices from S-21: Terror and History in Pol Pot's Secret Prison* (1999). He lives in Melbourne, Australia.

NORMAN G. OWEN went to Occidental College, Los Angeles, then received a Marshall Scholarship to study Southeast Asian history at the School of Oriental and African Studies, University of London. He returned to the United States to take his master's and doctorate degrees at the University of Michigan and taught for many years there, at Australian National University, and finally at the University of Hong Kong, from which he recently retired as Professor of History. His publications include *Prosperity without Progress* (1984), *The Bikol Blend* (1999), and, as editor and coauthor, *Compadre Colonialism* (1971), *The Philippine Economy and the United States* (1983), and *Death and Disease in Southeast Asia* (1987). He also wrote the chapter "Economic and Social Change" in *The Cambridge History of Southeast Asia* (1992).

WILLIAM R. ROFF, a Scot, received his bachelor's and master's degrees from the University of New Zealand and his Ph.D. from Australian National University. He is Emeritus Professor of History at Columbia University and Honorary Fellow in the Department of Islamic and Middle Eastern Studies at the University of Edinburgh. He taught Southeast Asian and Islamic history at Monash University and the University of Malaya and for twenty-one years at Columbia. His publications include *The Origins of Malay Nationalism* (1965; 2d ed. 1994) and, as editor, *Kelantan: Religion, Society and Politics in a Malay State* (1973) and *Islam and the Political Economy of Meaning* (1987).

DAVID JOEL STEINBERG fell in love with the Philippines and its history when he first visited the archipelago in the mid-1950s. He graduated from Harvard University, and after a Fulbright year researching in the Philippines and a Woodrow Wilson Fellowship to Columbia University, he returned to Harvard for a masters in East Asian Studies and a Ph.D. in history. He spent ten years teaching at the University of Michigan; during those years *In Search of Southeast Asia* was conceived and written, and his monograph *Philippine Collaboration in World War II* (1967) won the University of Michigan Press Award. After ten years as vice president at Brandeis University, Dr. Steinberg became president of Long Island University in 1985. He is also the author of *The Philippines: A Singular and a Plural Place* (1982; 4th ed. 2000).

JEAN GELMAN TAYLOR holds degrees from the University of Melbourne and the University of Wisconsin–Madison. Her research interests are in Indonesia and the general history of Southeast Asia. She has administered an international fellowship program for university staff from Indonesian universities through the University of Wisconsin–Madison as well as teaching Southeast Asian civilization. She now teaches in the School of History at the University of New South Wales. She is the author of *The Social World of Batavia: European and Eurasian in Dutch Asia* (1983) and editor of *Women Creating Indonesia: The First Fifty Years* (1997). Her most recent publication is *Indonesia: Peoples and Histories* (2003).

ROBERT H. TAYLOR earned degrees at Ohio University, Antioch College, and Cornell University. He has taught in the Washington, D.C., public schools and at Wilberforce University, the University of Sydney, and the School of Oriental and African Studies (SOAS), London. While at SOAS he was head of the South East Asian Studies Programme and the Department of Political Studies before becoming pro-director of the school and professor of politics in the University of London. Subsequently he was vice chancellor of the University of Buckingham. Currently he is an independent consultant on Myanmar and Southeast Asia. His publications include *Marxism and Resistance in Burma, 1941–1945: Thein Pe Myint's "Wartime Traveller"* (1984) and *The State in Burma*

(1987). He has edited *Handbooks of the Modern World: Asia and the Pacific* (1991), *The Politics of Elections in Southeast Asia* (1996), *Burma: Political Economy under Military Rule* (2001), and *The Idea of Freedom in Asia and Africa* (2002), as well as coediting *ASEAN-EC Economic and Political Relations* (1986) and *Context, Meaning, and Power in Southeast Asia* (1986).

ALEXANDER WOODSIDE received a B.A. in modern history from the University of Toronto in 1960 and a Ph.D. in history and Far Eastern languages from Harvard University in 1968. He taught history at Harvard between 1968 and 1975, serving as the first Young Professor of Sino-Vietnamese Studies at that university. Since 1975 he has taught Southeast Asian and Chinese history at the University of British Columbia. He is the author of *Vietnam and the Chinese Model* (1971) and *Community and Revolution in Modern Vietnam* (1976), and coeditor, with David Wyatt, of *Moral Order and the Question of Change: Essays on Southeast Asian Thought* (1982).

DAVID K. WYATT studied philosophy at Harvard College and Southeast Asian history at Cornell University. He taught at the School of Oriental and African Studies, University of London, and at the University of Michigan before returning to Cornell in 1969, where he served as director of the Southeast Asia Program and chairman of the Department of History, and where he was the John Stambaugh Professor of History before retiring in 2002. He has traveled extensively in Thailand and Laos. His publications include many translations of Thai chronicles as well as *The Politics of Reform in Thailand* (1969), *Thailand: A Short History* (1984; 2d ed. 2003), *The Chiang Mai Chronicle* (with Aroonrut Wichienkeeo) (1996), *The Royal Chronicles of the Kingdom of Ayutthaya* (editor; translation by Richard D. Cushman) (2000), *Siam in Mind* (2002), and *Reading Thai Murals* (2003).

Index

Nguyen Van Thieu, 347–348
Nhat Linh, 250
Nienhuys, Jacobus, 184, 186
nirvana (state of being transcending life and death), 37
NLD. *See* National League for Democracy
nom (Vietnamese script), 111, 113
Non-Aligned Movement, 502
Nong Duc Manh, 469
Nongkhai, 167
nongovernmental organizations. *See* NGOS
Norodom Rannaridh, Prince, 489
Norodom Sihanouk, King and Prince, 365–368, 482, 488–489
Norodom Suramarit, King, 367
Norodom, King, 121, 361, 363
North Korea, 482
NPA. *See* New People's Army
NTUC. *See* National Trades Union Congress
Nu, Thakin, U, 329–330, 333–334, 497, 499, 504
NUF. *See* National Unity Front
Nur Misuari, 465
Nusatenggara (the Lesser Sundas), 6, 165

Oecusse, 444
Office of Strategic Services (OSS), U.S., 343
oil: in Brunei, 428, 430; in Indonesia, 431
Omar Ali Saifuddin III, Sultan, 428–429
Ong Ten Cheong, 428
Ong, Aihwa, 405–406
Onn b. Jaafar, 318
OPEC. *See* Organization of Oil Exporting Countries
Opium War, 97
opium, 404–405, 504–505
orang asli (minorities in Malaysia), 235
orang Melaka (people of Melaka), 252
orang Melayu (Malay people), 252
Organization for Papuan Independence (OPM), 443
Organization of Oil Exporting Countries (OPEC), 269, 382, 445

oriental despotism, 53–54, 63, 70
Orientalism, 345
Orwell, George, 213–214, 219, 246–247, 259–260
Osmena, Sergio, **286,** 288–290, 292
OSS. *See* Office of Strategic Services
Ottoman empire, 55

Pacific Rim of Fire, 10
Padang, **44**
Padri Wars, 46, 131–132
Pagan Min (King), 88
Pahang, 139
Pak Nam, 103
Paknampho, 257
Pakubuwono, Sultan, 299
Palaung, 83
Palembang, 31
palm oil, 382, 414
Panay, 188
Panca Sila, 306, 417, 433, 435–436, 443, 445
Pangkor Engagement, 144–146
Pan-Malayan Islamic Party (PAS), 415–416, 418, 421
pan-Thai movement, 354, 357, 373
PAP. *See* People's Action Party
Papua New Guinea (PNG), 441, 443
Parian (Chinese ghetto in Manila), 148
Paris agreement, 1991, 488
Paris peace talks, 346
Partai Indonesia Raya (PKI), 298
Partai Komunis Indonesia (PKI), 434
Partai Nasional Indonesia (PNI, Nationalist Party of Indonesia), 298, 309
Partai Sarekat Islam Indonesia (Sarekat Islam), 339
Partai Rakyat (People's Party), 421
party state, Vietnam, 468–469, 471
PAS. *See* Pan-Malayan Islamic Party
Patani, 36, 43, 69
Pathein, 25, 33, 167
Pathet Lao (Lao Nation), 374–375, 492
patron-client relationship, 26–27, 67, 469, 471
Pavie, Auguste, 206, 373
Payson, 49, 155
Pearl Harbor, 274

Production Notes for Owen, *The Emergence of Modern Southeast Asia*

Book design and composition by Diane Gleba Hall
Typeset in Monotype Bembo
Printing and binding by Thomson-Shore, Inc.
Printed on 60 lb. Finch Opaque, 500 ppi